DATE DUE

APR 29 2010	

GAYLORD

PRINTED IN U.S.A.

D1443151

Japan's rapid industrial development and economic growth in the decades after World War II brought dramatic environmental damage. Japan diverges from the typical story of industrial democracies, however, in the scale and speed with which it was able to reduce air and water pollution, despite the absence of national environmental lobbying groups. As local protest movements grew more vocal in the early 1970s (though they failed to coalesce into effective national lobbying organizations), the Japanese government moved, after some resistance, to regulate industrial pollution.

In *Environmental Politics in Japan,* Jeffrey Broadbent shows, through a detailed examination of the Japanese political process and its environmental policy outcomes, how social, cultural, and political-economic factors interacted to bring about environmental degradation and eventual partial restoration. Broadbent's case study of heavy-industry growth and environmental protest in rural Japan illustrates how pro-growth and pro-environment coalitions mobilized and struggled to affect government policy at all levels in Japan. His analysis explains why, in the face of that pressure, the Japanese government succeeded in reducing pollution, but failed at solving other important environmental problems, such as dense urbanization and industrial concentration. Drawing on his study, Broadbent presents the first integrated, empirical critique and reconstruction of leading theories on the state, protest movements, the political process, and environmental problems. In so doing, he reforms our understanding of Japanese society and the general relationship between society and the natural environment.

Advance praise for *Environmental Politics in Japan*

"Bringing to bear an impressive array of social science theories, Jeffrey Broadbent gives us the most comprehensive work to date on how Japan, a densely populated country that was a 'polluter's paradise' until the 1960s, achieved one of the world's most dramatic environmental turnarounds. Political scientists, sociologists, and students of Japan will find a wealth of material here for puzzling over solutions to a central policy challenge at all levels of development in nations today: how to find the right mix between economic growth and environmental protection. The author shows how culture, protest, and elite politics intermeshed in Japan's quest for its own answer."
– Susan J. Pharr, *Harvard University*

"This is a first-class book that sets aright the misperception that Japanese politics and social protest cannot be understood from a synthesized class and political process viewpoint. It shows how class theory and resource mobilization arguments can be synthesized and that protest is an important source of political change in comparative context."
– J. Craig Jenkins, *The Ohio State University*

"By bringing his own intense involvement in Japanese culture to bear skillfully and reflectively on issues of great general importance, Jeffrey Broadbent has served everyone who wants to know about environmental politics, the shaping of popular struggles by state structure, and the character of Japanese local life. He writes with analytical passion."
– Charles Tilly, *Columbia University*

"Through his superb Japanese language ability and detailed field work, Jeffrey Broadbent has achieved the highest level of Japanese studies, on a par with Western sociologists such as Ronald P. Dore and Ezra Vogel. This book offers a stimulating comparative and theoretical analysis of political power in ACID (advanced, capitalist, industrialized democratic) societies including Japan."
– Joji Watanuki, *Sofia University*

Environmental Politics in Japan

Environmental Politics in Japan

Networks of Power and Protest

JEFFREY BROADBENT
University of Minnesota

CAMBRIDGE
UNIVERSITY PRESS

PUBLISHED BY THE PRESS SYNDICATE OF THE UNIVERSITY OF CAMBRIDGE
The Pitt Building, Trumpington Street, Cambridge CB2 1RP, United Kingdom

CAMBRIDGE UNIVERSITY PRESS
The Edinburgh Building, Cambridge CB2 2RU, United Kingdom
40 West 20th Street, New York, NY 10011-4211, USA
10 Stamford Road, Oakleigh, Melbourne 3166, Australia

First published 1998

Printed in the United States of America

Typeset in Caledonia

Library of Congress Cataloging-in-Publication Data
Broadbent, Jeffrey.
Environmental politics in Japan : networks of power and protest /
Jeffrey Broadbent.
p. cm.
Includes bibliographical references (p.) and index.
ISBN 0-521-56424-7 (hb)
1. Environmentalism—Japan. 2. Environmental policy—Japan.
3. Human ecology—Political aspects—Japan. I. Title.
GE199.J3B76—1997
363.7′00952—dc21   97-24297
                                                          CIP

A *catalog record for this book is available from*
the British Library.

ISBN 0 521 56424 7 hardback

To my son and daughter, Eben and Leafye,
and to all the other children
and young people of the world,
that they may teach us how to
tread lightly on Mother Earth.

Contents

Figures and tables

Tables

Preface

All societies confront a mounting dilemma: how to continue economic growth or some other way of improving the quality of life, and yet minimize or reverse its negative effects on an already severely deteriorating environment. We depend on and aspire to the benefits of economic growth. And yet in pursuit of growth, we extract and exhaust resources and damage our natural environment. This damage extends to other species, and eventually to humans, as well as to the integrity of the global ecological system as a whole. Many natural scientific studies indicate that increasing environmental degradation is an objective fact; no amount of human denial can make it go away. This situation presents humanity with the Growth/Environment (GE) dilemma: If we grow jobs and profits, it seems, we further destroy the environment. But if we protect the environment, we slow down the economic growth that makes increasing profits and jobs possible, thereby threatening both. A middle way between these two extremes may exist, but it is proving hard to find.

The GE dilemma plagues most societies – highly industrialized or just developing. We are all caught on the horns of this dilemma, as time will make increasingly apparent. How can we resolve it? How can we garner the benefits of growth without paying its environmental costs? Technological optimists think new technology will fix it for us. But if not, we need to find some way to fine tune our global societal productive and eliminative systems to fit within the limits of "Spaceship Earth," while still providing for the crew members. The solution to this problem may require new arrangements and agreements among all concerned, and draw on the work of social scientists.

The GE dilemma promises no simple solution. It is an issue fraught with tension, passion, and conflict, a human product, to be sure, but a very complex one, not easily changed in direction and effect. To understand the forces in society that have created, and can therefore change, this dilemma, we have to study closely how it has come about. We need to consider both its genesis and its exodus, the conditions of its appearance and its transformation. To do this, we need to use detailed studies of cases of pollution reduction and other environmental successes to improve our general understanding and our ability to model and theorize the subject. Even very limited success stories may help us learn how to better coexist with our planetary ecology.

With this aim in mind, I chose to study Japan. Japan promised to be a particularly useful case for addressing all of these questions because of the intensity of its GE dilemma. Within one small and – from the natural resource point of view – unlikely country in the decades after World War Two, Japan produced an unexpected series of so-called "miracles" and debacles: the economic miracle, the pollution debacle, the pollution miracle, and the urban debacle. Suffice it to note here that in both directions – miraculous and tragic – Japan far outperformed its U.S. and European counterparts. The miracles were not the product of saintly visitation, nor were the debacles attributable to the devil. They resulted from a great deal of hard work and disciplined social organization that sometimes sacrificed too much.

While modern Japan's political and economic institutions closely resemble (and often came from) Western models, its culture and social relations have deep East Asian roots. It would be reasonable to suppose, therefore, that the sociocultural differences between Japan and the other advanced capitalist industrial democratic (ACID) societies, which all have Anglo-European roots, may have had a great deal to do with the unexpected rapid-fire sequence of Japan's miracles and debacles. Some scholars readily resort to sociocultural explanations, while others reject them vigorously. Perhaps the better task is to see how, to arrive at a satisfactory explanation of these issues, we have to mix and merge sociocultural and political-economic factors.

Questions such as these set the stage for my research project. In the late 1970s, I was reading about these issues behind the white marble facade of William James Hall at Harvard University. To me, as a graduate student in sociology, Japan's miracles and debacles posed many puzzling questions about conventional explanations of macro-societal behavior. Had some cultural ethic or belief, I wondered, first propelled the national government or business elites into environmentally destructive forms of growth, and then led them to graciously bequeath the pollution miracle to the people? Marx would not have agreed with such an explanation, but Weber or Durkheim might have. Or had it been a contest of opposed material interests, the government or business elites pursuing glory or wealth, and the victimized citizens finally forcing the elites into redressing the accumulated pollution problems – through elections or the pressure of protest movements? What did Japan's pollution debacles and miracles imply about how policies change, about the relationship between state and society, in the ACID societies? So ran my thesis-seeking cogitations while in the ivory tower of academia.

My own driving interests in this topic started much earlier, though. Having come from a working-class and Quaker background, I participated vigorously in the events and movements of the 1960s. Bemused by these conflicts, in the late 1960s, I sought the contemplative retreat of a Buddhist monastery. In the middle of California's Ventana Primitive Area at Tassajara Zen Mountain Center, I practiced *zazen* (sitting meditation) under the guidance of Zen Master Suzuki Shunryu. Without realizing it, I also imbibed values central to Japanese culture. After a year or so of meditating, building rock walls, and hiking the wilderness, I emerged with a new sense of direction – pursuit of an undergraduate major in Buddhist Studies at the University of California, Berkeley. This program led to the study of Japanese at the International Christian University in Tokyo, Japan (1971–1972). Upon my return to UC, Robert Bellah showed me an intellectual discipline able to explain how culture and political-economy interact – the Weberian project within the discipline of sociology. My curiosity piqued, I used an M.A. degree in Regional Studies-East Asia at Harvard University to segue into Harvard's Ph.D. program in sociology. The subject of environmental movements and politics in Japan posed interesting questions about the interaction of culture and political-economy, eventuating in my research and this book.

As my activist background betrays, I approach the subject with deep concerns about environmental deterioration. But I also want a middle-class standard of living. In other words, I embody the GE dilemma. I am therefore sympathetic to both sides of it – pro-growth and pro-environment. Furthermore, I am a social scientist, which means I try to keep my personal values from biasing my analysis. In this book, I pursue an objective understanding of causality based on the analysis of accurate information. I hope that this research can contribute to our collective consideration of these important issues, whatever our individual interests.

To reduce bias, I have adopted a narrative style of presentation, punctuated by occasional interpretation. The narrative relies on quotations from actors on all sides of the issues as well as on statistical and other data. My own gloss and interpretation come mainly in the conclusion section of each chapter. I hope that this level of detail and the distinction between actors' and author's voices will lead readers to form their own conclusions, and to argue with mine if they wish.

I was fortunate to secure funding for the project with a Fulbright Fellowship. Taking my family with me to the field, I moved to the neighborhood of Takeshita in Oita prefecture, Japan, about five miles downwind from a big new industrial complex, and on the coast slated for another industrial complex. Oita prefecture was a good place to study the GE dilemma and Japan's response to it. In the post-war years, Oita had grown in tandem with Japan, and had suffered much of the same joyful prosperity and sorrowful pollution. After about fifteen months in Takeshita, we moved to the mountain farming village of Obasama, a few miles inland from Oita City, for another fifteen months.

In 1978, when I moved to Oita, an active struggle between the pro-growth and the pro-environment forces was still underway. I had hoped to finish my research in Oita and move on to another, contrasting site for the second half of our stay. Instead, we ended up staying in Oita for a total of two and a half years (1978–1981). The complexity and subtlety of life and politics there drew me in deeper and deeper. Even two and a half years proved too short a time. On my return to Cambridge, I hoped to finish the thesis in six months, but it took an extra year. Soon after graduation, I received a three-year post-doctoral fellowship at the University of Michigan, and confidently predicted the book would be finished by the end of the first year. Here I am, however, fourteen years later, typing the final version. Reality is messy.

I have designed the book in a narrative but modular fashion. The reader interested in a particular theoretical issue can turn directly to the relevant chapter. Chapter 1 sets up the basic questions of the study, the reasons for the mini-"pollution miracle" that took place inside Japan's more well-known economic miracles and pollution debacles. Chapter 2 reviews rural Oita prefecture's chase for prosperity through industrialization and its somewhat disappointing outcomes, within the theory of regional industrial growth. Chapter 3 analyzes the effect of Japan's wave of pollution protest, which peaked in the early 1970s, on the 1970 "Pollution Diet" and the fourteen strict pollution control laws it passed. Chapters 4 and 5 delve into the mobilization of protests against pollution in Oita prefecture – a local example of this national wave of protest – and uses these cases to think about the general theory of movement mobilization. Chapter 6 turns to the issue of local social control and patron-client political machines, a widespread phenomenon strongly evident in Japan. Chapter 7 examines questions about the dynamics of struggle between protest movements and the local authorities. In this case, the movements exacted a significant compromise, that the local government would meet Three Conditions – consensus, harmony, and an environmental impact assessment – before building more industry. Chapters 8 and 9 trace the problem of implementation – how local government met these conditions in letter but not in spirit. Chapter 9 also puts Japan's environmental politics in international perspective. The concluding Chapter 10 summarizes the findings and discusses their significance for broader theoretical questions about the causes and cures of environmental problems.

My research efforts were only possible through gracious and patient help and guidance from many teachers, mentors, citizens of Japan, and financial and educational institutions. Robert Bellah, Theda Skocpol, George Homans, Schmuel Eisenstadt, Jeffrey Paige, and Charles Tilly provided me with basic, if divergent, theoretical coordinates. Ezra Vogel, the chair of my Ph.D. thesis committee, as well as Robert Bellah, George DeVos, Tsurumi Kazuko, John Pelzel, Watanuki Joji, John Campbell, Ejima Shusaku, and Robert Cole guided me in East Asian studies. Colleagues such as Kabashima Ikuo, Michael Reich, David Riesman, and Edwin O. Reischauer provided important introductions to key people in Japan. The late Professor Matsubara Haruo generously hosted my affiliation with Tokyo University and provided much valuable guidance. The following people provided very helpful comments on parts or the whole of drafts of the book or related papers: Charles Tilly, Martin King Whyte, Jeffrey Paige, Michael Schwartz, Jeylan Mortimer, Ron Aminzade, Ezra Vogel, Robert Bellah, Margaret McKean, Allan Schnaiberg, Riley Dunlap, Doug McAdam, Sidney Tarrow, David Knoke, Joe Galasckiewicz, Harvey Molotch, Karen Feinberg, Gretchen Priest, David Hall, Uygar Ozesmi. I deeply thank them all for their generous instruction, advice, help, and encouragement. The remaining flaws in the work are entirely of my own making.

In addition, I owe profound gratitude to the many residents of Japan – in Oita, Tokyo, and other places – who let me into their lives, educated me about their values, society, and politics, and enlightened me on its hopes and struggles over growth and the environment. Chief among them are Governor Hiramatsu Morihiko, Mayor Sato Masumi, Fujii Norihisa, Inao Toru, Rep. Sato Bunsei, Hoshino Shinyasu, and the Nakaya Kentaro family. Many others in Oita and throughout Japan contributed in innumerable ways. I apologize to them for the time I took from their busy lives, and thank them profoundly for their many kindnesses.

Also, I wish to thank my (then) wife Gretchen Priest and our two children, Eben and Leafye, for their part in the field work. Gretchen and the kids opened my eyes to aspects of Japan that I never would have seen otherwise. Gretchen made friends with local people and joined in their activities in ways I never would have. For instance, she borrowed empty rice fields and planted rice the old way, by hand, growing and harvesting enough rice to feed our family. She also studied the traditional Shinto festival dances performed in our village, and joined in cultural activities and environmental activism at a local Buddhist temple. These activities opened opportunities for participation in community life.

Eben and Leafye sat on the laps of our neighbors and landlords, the Iizukas and later the Abes, watching television and eating snacks. The kids were aged one and three when we arrived in Japan. They were blond moptops whom the neighbors in Takeshita and Obasama treasured, with their typical affection for children. Within a year, they came to consider Japanese their native language. We entered them into the Hibari kindergarten, where they became increasingly fluent. Even when home from kindergarten, they played and conversed with each other in Japanese, not English. On our return to the United States after those years, when Gretchen ushered Leafye into the crowded Los Angeles airport, five-year old Leafye exclaimed in surprise, "Mama, they're all foreigners (*gaijin bakkashi desu*)!"

I also wish to thank my present wife, Jeylan Mortimer, for the steady emotional support and help in so many other ways that really made the completion of this book possible. Several times, over my recent years with Jeylan, I despaired of ever telling a coherent story and drawing a reasonable theoretical conclusion out of my mass of field experiences and notes. She stood by me with great patience and firm encouragement, and really was the spiritual midwife of this book's birth.

This research would have been impossible without the generous financial support of the Fulbright Predoctoral Fellowship (1978–80) and the Japan Institute of Harvard University (1980–81). I completed follow-up interviews while on another research project in Japan from 1988 to 1990, supported by the JUSEC (Japan-U.S. Exchange Commission) Fulbright, the Fulbright-Hays Fellowship, and the National Science Foundation. To all these sources of institutional support and their officers and staff, I extend my heartfelt gratitude and my hope that the product proves worthy of the investment.

1

Growth versus the environment in Japan

A "navel" engagement

The December wind blew cold over the choppy waters of Beppu Bay in southern Japan. Fighting the blast and cutting through the waves, 200 boats proceeded along the coast, each flying a red flag. Their length and shape marked them as fishing craft: 20 to 30 feet long with a tall cabin near the bow. Normally their owners spent their days far apart on the shallow waters of the bay, fishing for the prized *tai* red snapper. Today they sailed in a grim convoy toward the shipping port of Oita City. Each vessel carried several fishers, their faces tanned by sun, wind, and salt. The boats were dwarfed by the towering candy-striped smokestacks of steel and oil refineries along the shore.

On the other side of the smokestacks, a convoy of buses and cars rolled along the main road. It headed toward the same destination as the fishing boats: the office of the governor. About 250 villagers filled the vehicles: old women with scarves covering their heads, teenage girls dressed in high school uniforms, farmers with hands gnarled from years of wielding the hoe, and several high school teachers, some silver-haired and others young. They joked noisily, but the nervousness in their laughter betrayed their anxiety about their undertaking.

The fishers and the other villagers opposed Governor Taki's plans for further industrial development. The second phase of the New Industrial City (NIC) would cover their beaches with concrete and fill in their shallow offshore waters with mud to make an industrial site. They feared that the factories would pollute their air. In 1971, the year before, the previous governor, Kinoshita Kaoru, had held a meeting in Kozaki Village to explain his policies.[1] He had assured the villagers that the proposed factories would not produce much pollution. But they had already witnessed how much the first phase of the project had disrupted the fishing villages of Nakajima, Misa, and Iejima. The paper mill had

---

1. All names are in Japanese name order, with family name first and given name second.

pushed Nakajima aside. Misa and Iejima now huddled in the shadow of gigantic smokestacks. The villagers had come to distrust Kinoshita's reassurances and felt demeaned by his refusal to take their concerns seriously. His successor, Governor Taki, apparently intended to treat them in the same way.

Even so, they were afraid to confront the governor directly. After all, he had graduated from Tokyo University, the seat of academic authority and the in-cubator of central government officials. He now held the most prestigious job in the prefecture.[2] Only a few decades ago, until the end of the Second World War, such officials had handed down directives from the Emperor. Even now, some people thought of officials as above them in social status, and bowed uncritically to their will.

Beneath their outward confidence, the citizen protesters struggled with these doubts. As farmers, fishers, and schoolteachers from quiet villages, who were they to question the governor's judgment? Could they understand the experts' larger plans and purposes? Could they, should they, did they dare intrude their little demands on such plans? Though nervous and uncertain, their anger and worry impelled them forward.

The fishers moored their boats and marched to the prefectural government office building. There they converged with the rest of the villagers, who were emerging from the buses and cars. The buildings, constructed in the squarish 1950s "bureaucratic modern" style, projected an air of impersonal authority. Not by accident, the office building stood across the street from the green moat and sheer white walls of Oita's old feudal castle.

During the feudal period, from the sixteenth to the nineteenth centuries, the local lord had little fear of invading armies. Rather, the castle walls protected him from local peasants who rose in protest in times of famine. On those occasions, the peasants smashed the sake brewers' warehouses and redis-tributed the rice hoarded within. Then they appealed to the feudal lord for help. They were never admitted to the castle; at best, the lord gave temporary help in feeding the villagers. To discourage such audacity in the future, however, he often executed the peasant leaders and displayed their heads on spikes (Broad-bent, 1975).

Times had changed. The castle now housed a Hall of Culture for community events and performances. On Respect for the Aged Day (*keiro no hi*) the elderly met there and received the mayor's congratulations. Sometimes, women staged flower-arranging exhibits and traditional dance performances. Popular musi-cians and Kabuki troupes stopped there on their national tours. On May Day,

2. Japan is divided into 47 prefectures (*todofuken*), each with a prefectural government (*jichitai*). The country as a whole is slightly smaller than California. The average size of a prefecture is 3100 square miles (8000 square kilometers).

even the red banners of the socialist labor unions massed in the castle yard before moving out onto the city streets in orderly parade.

The new seat of authority, the prefectural office building, lacked the forbidding walls of the old Oita castle. A receptionist in a glass cage on the first floor was the only barrier. She stared in shock at the throng of villagers trooping up the stairs toward the governor's office.

The protestors filled the dimly lit hall outside the governor's office; thirty or forty made their way inside. At the far end of the room, behind a broad polished desk, sat the distinguished-looking, white-haired Governor Taki. The vice-governor and several other officials flanked him on either side. The governor looked upon the villagers calmly but gravely, like a father about to chastise errant children. They fell silent (Nishio, 1979).

A retired high-school teacher, the person of highest social status among the villagers, slowly stepped forward. He handed the governor a document stating the villagers' two central concerns: first, that the smoke from the proposed factories would be trapped over their village by the mountains just behind, and second, that the landfill would destroy the coastal spawning beds for the red snapper, ruining the fishers' livelihoods.

Governor Taki read the note carefully and then spoke. He understood their position well, he said. He promised to fairly represent their opinions in prefectural policy. Then he stood up in a gesture of dismissal. To his surprise, the assembled protestors did not respond with the expected humility.

Fishers have an independent streak bred by constantly risking their lives against the sea and can react fast in emergencies. They had braved heavy seas to sail in from Saganoseki; their tempers were short. One young fisherman, Nishio, could not restrain his anger. As he recalled later:

When I saw that (the governor was leaving), I got mad and said, "Just wait a minute" and made him sit. At that time I wasn't an official negotiator and hadn't made any preparations for a statement. Anyhow, I was mad and just let him have it.

"Hey, buster," I told him, "do you have a belly button?"

. . . As might be expected, the governor looked insulted and scowled back at me. But he answered, "yes."

Then I said, "Well, to tell you the truth, I got a belly button too; so if you got a belly button also, we got the same value as human beings."

He answered "Yes, that's right."

Then I shot back, "If that's so, how come you have the right to kill me?"

A photograph of the confrontation showed an unshaven Nishio scowling at the governor. Nishio continued,

That was the spark, and then everybody let loose at him. From that point the real talk with the governor began. During it, everyone got to say everything they wanted to.

After that, we pulled out and went home in high spirits. For a while after that, the prefecture stopped its (development) activities (Nishio, 1979, p. 10–13).

Such effrontery from a poor fisherman, a junior high-school dropout, was rare and shocking in Japan. Japanese society, particularly in the traditional Oita Prefecture, exalts both officialdom and education. Many older citizens became deferential in the presence of either. Yet a tradition of protest coexisted with this tendency to deference. In feudal times, as mentioned earlier, peasants had marched against merchants and corrupt officials when confronted by famine or crisis (Bix, 1986). Now, under the growing threat of pollution, the villagers' concern had reached a peak. In the hearts of some, they had come to the governor as supplicants, begging him to consider their plight. The dignity of the governor's attempted exit had almost ended the audience. Nishio, however, cleared the air with a caustic frankness that opened the way for complaints.

A framework for understanding

Governor Taki and fisherman Nishio, and the groups behind them, expressed and embodied the two sides of a social dilemma – the contested choice between economic growth and environmental protection.[3] The dilemma they faced – the growth/environment or GE dilemma – appears in many guises. This dilemma confronts authorities, entrepreneurs, activists and the general population in industrial and industrializing societies alike. Increasingly, it is at the root of many conflicts around the planet.[4] As the effects of pollution and subsequent ecological disruption intensify, environmental protection may become less of a dilemma and more of an imperative. But it will always be contested. Each environmental solution will always have its pros and cons, its defenders and detractors.

The GE dilemma has gradually ripened since the mid-1960s, as many nations grew in population and prosperity. Most people want to enjoy the fruits of material progress. Widespread popular hopes, as well as demands from those who profit most, have exerted a strong push for continued economic growth.[5]

---

3. "Social dilemma" is a formal sociological term, defined as a situation in which a group holds two competing goals which are mutually contradictory (Messick & Brewer 1983; Yamagishi 1995). It is related to the larger class of events known as dilemmas of collective action (Ostrom, 1990).
   4. Even recent ethnic conflicts in Africa have been traced to the dilemma of a growing population and scarce resources (Homer-Dixon, 1993).
   5. Growth has been seen as desirable by liberal economists and Marxists (Baran, 1957) alike, albeit seen as working best under different institutional circumstances. Economic growth is usually defined as the increase in a nation's average per capita goods, services and income (Teune, 1988, p. 14). If the size of a nation's population increases at the same rate as its economic expansion (or

With growth, societies discarded greater amounts of waste, some of it toxic, into their surrounding air, water, and soil.[6] Overwhelming the absorptive capacity of the natural environment, this waste turned to pollution – substances which damage the health and functioning of nature and its inhabitants, including human beings (Franck & Brownstone, 1992, p. 246).[7] As the damage intensified, so too have the complaints of its victims and their supporters.

To resolve the GE dilemma, we will have to find a way to define and satisfy needs and wants that does not destroy the environment. Some commentators call this ideal state a sustainable society or steady-state economy – one that keeps its consumption and waste at levels that will enable long-term survival.[8] The attainment of such a society, though, seems blocked by more than technical difficulties. Conflicting interests and beliefs have littered the politics of the environment with broken promises.

A sustainable society seems unlikely unless we better understand the processes and policy decisions that have created the GE dilemma in the first place. We also need to study the successful steps toward sustainability that some societies have already taken. The case study method allows us to investigate thoroughly the *how* and *why* of such policy decisions and processes.

This book looks at how and why the GE dilemma arose, and was partly

greater), however, growth by this definition will not occur. Nonetheless, even under such conditions, the society's total output of waste, and hence pollution, will increase. Accordingly, the GE dilemma will still arise. At some point, the pollution will overwhelm the region's or planet's carrying capacity, disrupting the necessary conditions for various species, including the human (Arrow, Bolin, Costanza, Dasgupta, Folke, et al., 1995; Catton, 1980; Gore, 1993). This point has come to be termed a "limit" to growth (Hirsch, 1976; Meadows & Meadows, 1971). As a result, wealthy nations have already started to "export" their pollution. A globally sustainable solution, however, might require a steady-state economy that does not grow (Daly, 1980). At the same time, some forms of growth, such as those which emphasize services, by not increasing the sum total of pollution, may be sustainable (Brown, 1991; Commoner, 1990; Daly & Cobb, 1989, p. 147).

6. "The environment," in this usage, consists of the natural ecological processes necessary to sustain the present forms of animal and plant life. These processes are in dynamic and delicate equilibrium, forming an ecosystem with a limited carrying capacity (Harper, 1996, p. 12–22). This definition would include, for instance, the necessary balance of chemicals in the atmosphere to prevent cosmic radiation and the "greenhouse effect" of global temperature rise, within the natural ecosystem (Harper, 1996, p. 110–31).

7. In nature, when organisms expand their numbers beyond the carrying capacity of their environment, they tend to suffer sudden and catastrophic decline. The use of stored energy, mainly from oil, has given humanity the ability to overshoot its normal carrying capacity in terms of numbers and living standards. However, the capacity limits are now starting to reassert themselves in the form of declining fisheries, desertification and degradation of soil, changes in air chemistry leading to acid rain and global warming, and a host of other problems (Catton, 1980; Harper, 1996).

8. The quest for a sustainable economy and society received increasing attention in the late twentieth century (Daly & Cobb, 1989; Gore, 1993; MacNeill, 1990; World Commission on Environment and Development, 1987).

resolved, in Japan during the decades from the 1950s to the 1990s. Within Japan, the story of the GE dilemma in the southern prefecture of Oita, where the "navel" engagement happened, represents Japan's broader dynamics in a nutshell. Japan and Oita represent good sites for several reasons.[9] Western-born theories about those causes and cures, and about politics and protest more generally, require testing in non-Western societies to determine their scope (McAdam et al., 1996, p. 29). With its Western institutions but Eastern cultural background, Japan represents the perfect case of "experimental" variation for this task. If Western theories hold in Japan, they should hold anywhere.

Moreover, Japan's unusual performance in both economic and environmental matters adds to its significance, making it a critical test case for theories of the GE dilemma. In the 1960s, Japan produced an "economic miracle" – the fastest economic growth then known in the capitalist world (Johnson, 1982). Along with the miracle, unfortunately, came an environmental debacle, the world's worst pollution. Despite its pro-growth momentum, though, in the 1970s, Japan reduced its sulfur dioxide air pollution much more quickly and thoroughly than other advanced, capitalist, industrialized democratic (ACID) societies (Table 1.4). Japan's pollution improvements left many environmental problems untouched, as discussed below. For a crowded and resource-poor country like Japan, though, its speedy reduction in air and water pollution, compared to its wealthier ACID counterparts such as the United States or Germany, indeed has some miraculous qualities. Oita Prefecture mirrored and embodied these dramatic changes.

Japan's mini-pollution "miracle," so contrary to the theory that taking care of pollution is a luxury, may shed light on how to solve the GE dilemma as well as the pitfalls of such attempts.[10] By the same token, Japan's environmental politics present an opportunity for inquiry into the politics of ACID societies. The scope of our theories about the state, political power, democracy and the role of social protest movements can be tested and expanded through the study of Japan. Its pollution-related miracles and debacles, by their very unusualness, prompt one to ask *why* – what political processes and larger social structures brought about Japan's reduction in air pollution, unmatched in the West, yet in so many other environmental issues, led to default? Japan's urban debacle – its inability to redistribute industry to the hinterlands despite trying – constitutes a

---

9. I use the term "societal," rather than "social," to emphasize that my analysis includes all relevant dimensions of society: culture, social relations, and social institutions, as well as politics and economics in the more "realist" sense.

10. A critical case is one that seems to run contrary to the predictions of a theory. It is therefore a good choice for study because it has the strongest possibility of either confirming or disconfirming the theory (Lijphart, 1971; Walton, 1992).

representative case of the politics of default. Do Western ideas about the state and politics, such as pluralist democracy, class domination, state autonomy, corporatism, and party-centric models, adequately explain such outcomes? Or do these policy outputs require a home-grown theory, like the "network state" described below? Likewise, do social movements operate by the same principles as in the United States or Europe, and to similar effect? Are new resources and new ways of framing problems as important to their mobilization? Japan's environmental miracles and debacles, then, promise to reveal especially telling lessons about a number of subjects: the GE dilemma, politics, social movements, and the nature of Japanese society.

We want to ask both *how* and *why* Japan's miracles and debacles came about. The *how* question concerns the pattern of power and influence – who did what when, with what effect on policies and outcomes?[11] The *why* question, in contrast, concerns the reasons that such a pattern of power and outcomes exists – an explanation in terms of general societal theories. *How* did organizations, groups and individuals in Japan – social actors – create and then partially solve the GE dilemma? But also, *why* did they do so – what personal, organizational and societal motivations and conditions drove their decisions and actions? And especially, a crucial question to environmental sociology, how and why did the "voice of nature" finally achieve voice, if it did, within the political process?[12]

These questions all contribute to answering our central problem – what determines a society's response to rising levels of pollution? Does the *natural intensity* of pollution (for example, the concentration of sulfur dioxide in the air) determine the intensity of a society's attempt to fix the problem? Or does the *social intensity* – the sheer numbers of people affected – determine its response? Japan's pollution miracle, the social intensity view implies, may have come about simply because the victims of pollution outnumbered those benefitted by growth. Americans tend to see the world in those kind of terms – majority

---

11. At this point, it would help to define terms more closely. Agency, as a term in sociological theory, refers not to a bureaucratic organization, but to the creative attempt by any social actor, individual or organizational, to bring about change. Agency is the opposite of structure – a predefined set of roles that force actors into forms of behavior. Power, as I use the term, is the ability of an actor or a structure to control other actors and outcomes fully. Influence is partial power – the ability to affect or contribute to an outcome. This definition expands beyond the classic Weberian definition of power, which stressed the ability to dominate others and achieve ends, despite resistance (Weber, 1978). It includes the Parsonsian notion of power as the ability to produce effects, through not only domination, but cooperation as well (Parsons, 1960). It differs from Wrong's definitions of power as intentional and influence as unintended (1979).

12. By "voice" I refer to Hirschman's use of that term to signify political participation (Hirschman, 1970).

rule and the clash of interest groups, each pursuing its own benefits. The pluralist view assumes that all such groups can achieve voice in politics. Other political models, though, argue that great imbalances in resources and power give effective voice to some and not to others. The natural and social intensity of pollution provide realist lenses to investigate a society's reaction to pollution.

More than such realist principles may have been at work, though. Japan's culture and social institutions may have profoundly affected its responses to pollution. Perhaps Japan's East Asian cultural roots – maybe its Shintoist respect for nature or its Confucian respect for authority – hastened response to its air and water pollution. Or perhaps its social institutions, such as the informal patron and client relationships that organize politics at all levels, channeled the society's response to rising pollution in the most effective ways.

Hunches and hypotheses such as these, rampant among social scientists and journalists alike, fall into three large theoretical camps: political-economic, social institutional and cultural. These three camps pitch their tents on very different "home domains" (Alford & Friedland, 1985). They adopt very different assumptions, that is, about the mainsprings that drive the interaction among politics, society and nature.

To illustrate their differences, for instance, the three camps would give us very different explanations of Taki and Nishio's "navel" engagement. The political-economic camp would point to differences in material interests – struggle over who should get the objective costs and benefits of growth had driven Taki and Nishio into confrontation. The social institutional camp would argue that the formal rules governing voting and parties, as well as the social status differences between the two parties, had kept the protestors from getting proper political representation, thereby driving them into unruly protest. The cultural camp would point to the dominant politicians' values of conquering nature in order to foster growth and national pride, versus the villagers' values of treasuring the natural sea and mountains that cradled their daily lives.

Even this cursory analysis, though, shows that no single viewpoint is sufficient, and perhaps all are necessary, to construct an adequate explanation. Larger political-economic structures, expressed as government and business demands, had forced Governor Taki to support a form of industrial growth that had serious drawbacks. When the protestors invaded his office to complain about these policies, institutional norms at first held them silent in awe of the governor. In pulling the belly-button metaphor out of his rough fisherman's background and applying it in those august premises, Nishio exercised creative agency with shocking effect. Nishio won the "navel" engagement by suddenly breaking the expected norms of proper behavior for an illiterate fisherman toward a prefectural governor in rural, early 1970s Japan.[13] Likewise, Nishio won by bringing the issues into the open, overcoming the governor's tactic of trying to avoid open discussion. In this incident, structural forces and creative agency interacted in a plastic malleability that shifted the course of events ever so slightly.[14]

As in this example, so do many incidents exhibit a complex mixture of causal factors. Moreover, the incidents multiply as politics pushes toward conclusions. To understand politics, I argue, we have to examine strings of incidents that lead up to specific, concrete and important shifts in governmental policies. In the case at hand, a number of explicit policy shifts produced, or rather embodied, Japan's pollution miracles and debacles. The strings of incidents leading up to these shifts appeared as encounters, conflicts and alliances, among movements, organizations, government ministries, businesses, political parties and others. As one incident sparked off the next, they traced networks of power and protest, constructing society and history in the process. These networks embody the "on-going accomplishment of collective action" (McAdam, McCarthy & Zald, 1988) at all levels of society (Knoke, 1990). Our lack of knowledge about the dynamics of this unfolding process remains the most "glaring deficiency" in the field (McAdam et al., 1988, p. 728).[15] Therefore, the study of numerous incidents provides evidence toward answering the big questions about the political process raised by the three theoretical camps. After discussing the GE dilemma and Japan's response at greater length in the next sections, I will probe deeper into these three camps and the questions they raise.

Concretely, this study investigates five major shifts in government policy that materially affected Japan's and Oita's GE dilemmas. These five policy shifts serve as the object of explanation or, in the language of statistics, the "dependent variable." The first two and the fifth policy shifts reflect the dominance of pro-growth interests, and therefore illustrate the politics of *causing* the GE dilemma. The third and fourth policy shifts resulted from the dominance of the

13. Sewell refers to this as the "transposition" of a sanction from one structural context to another (Sewell, 1992).

14. Here I draw on a social psychology of power and influence. French and Raven identified five types of exchange media through which actor A could influence B to comply with a request: coercion, (economic) inducement, provision of vital information, embodiment of a collectively motivating cultural symbol (such as a national office representing the nation and the flag), or presentation of an emotionally important reference (such as a photo of a starving child) (French & Raven, 1959). To this I added a sixth medium of influence, evocation of a collectively-accepted social norm defining proper behavior (Broadbent, 1989a).

15. See also Burstein et al., 1995, p. 276; Knoke, 1990; Tarrow, 1988, p. 435; Tuma, 1992, p. 1828.

pro-environmental coalition, and therefore illustrate the politics of *curing* the GE dilemma.

The first policy shift concerned the contents of the NIC Law passed in 1962 (Chapter 2). The second, at the prefectural level, determined the type of industry brought to Oita in the early 1960s (Chapter 2). The third policy shift, back at the national level, consisted of the 1970 "Pollution Diet" and its fourteen strict regulatory laws (Chapter 3).[16] The fourth shift, at the prefectural level, concerned Governor Taki's 1973 concession to meet three conditions before resuming landfill No. 8: consensus, harmony and assessment (Chapters 4 through 7). The fifth was Governor Hiramatsu's 1980 announcement that the government had met and fulfilled the three conditions, and was legally free to resume landfill No. 8 (Chapters 8 and 9). These policy shifts, resulting from strings of political incidents at national, prefectural and local levels, both exemplified and embodied Japan's responses to the GE dilemma. Understanding their *how* and *why* carries us a long way toward explaining the GE dilemma, the relationship between state and society in Japan, and the entrance of the voice of nature into politics.

To foreshadow my conclusions, I find that Japan's relatively rapid response to its GE dilemma, in comparison to other ACID societies, was initiated by its relatively high *social intensity* of pollution – the sheer numbers of people polluted. Class structures, a capital-centrist labor coalition, provided a similar energizing dynamic to the creation of pollution-victim strata in all ACID societies. Therefore, they could not explain Japan's particular rapidity of response. Formal and informal social institutions – in particular the articulation of interest groups through horizontal and vertical social networks and the activism of high school teachers and their unions – channeled the material interests so engendered to produce Japan's miracles and debacles. Cultural categories, values and beliefs peculiar to Japan, on the other hand, were so diverse as to provide all protagonists with ready rationalizations, and therefore had only a minor causal role.

The growth/environment dilemma

The GE dilemma calls into question the well-known motto of a certain manufacturing company, symbolic of the industrial age, that "progress is our most important product." The dilemma forces us to question the assumption of this motto. It forces us to ask, is progress dependent upon increased industrial

---

16. The Diet is Japan's national legislative body, consisting of an Upper and Lower House, or House of Councilors (*Sangiin*) and House of Representatives (*Shugiin*).

manufacturing? Can we find a "technological fix" through making our productive processes less environmentally harmful, perhaps by using microelectronics (Hannigan 1994, p. 183)? Or must we ultimately just "reduce, recycle and reuse?"

The GE dilemma comes about when society's economic expansion exceeds nature's ability to absorb society's waste products. The dilemma represents "the inescapable conflict between two socially desirable goals: economic productivity and environmental quality" (Commoner, 1990, p. 82). It appears most acutely in the abuse of common pool resources like air and water, which ownership does not protect (Ostrom, 1990, p. 30). Those for whom the costs of pollution and other disruptions exceed the benefits of industrial growth are directly afflicted with the GE dilemma. Those who sympathize with them may also be impelled to act upon the GE dilemma.

In the Oita case, the GE dilemma arose because factories and refineries had polluted the air and water, increasing the social costs of growth to the surrounding communities. In this respect, Oita's dilemma was typical and representative of those around the industrialized and industrializing world. By the 1960s, many local cases of severe pollution damage had appeared. By the 1970s, the damage was appearing on a global scale. Other negative results of growth included acid rain, smog, toxic waste, extinction of species, destruction of the ozone layer, possibly even a warming of the global temperature with attendant potentially devastating ecological changes. These problems could spur famine, war and global insecurity (Homer-Dixon, 1993). The intensification of environmental destruction, in other words, revealed limits to growth. Critics asked: If growth fouled its own nest, could it long continue (Gore, 1993; Meadows & Meadows, 1971)?

The intensifying GE dilemma gave birth to environmental conflict, especially in the ACID societies. The GE dilemma quickly became a hotly contested political issue. It gave birth to protest movements and new political parties. Whether or not people agreed that the natural ecology was in serious crisis, few would deny the issue's political importance. In response, the study of environmental politics burgeoned internationally.[17] The existence of the GE dilemma has forced many people to fundamentally rethink the relationship between society and nature, question why human society overshoots its environmental limits and damages its environment (Catton, 1980), incorporate the effects of the natural ecology into the study of human society (Kroll-Smith & Laska,

---

17. See, for instance, Gorz, 1980; Landy, Roberts, & Thomas, 1990; Lash, Gillman & Sheridan, 1984; Reich, 1991; Switzer, 1994; Smith, 1992.

1994), and found new fields such as environmental sociology and political ecology.[18]

Japan's miracles and debacles

Japan's response to the GE dilemma differed from those of the other ACID societies in crucial ways. After the end of the Second World War, Japan generated an unlikely set of "miracles" and "debacles." Observers marveled at its economic miracle – the world's most rapid industrial growth. This growth soon brought levels of prosperity previously unknown in Japan's history. In the 1960s, however, after growth and prosperity came the world's worst industrial pollution – an "environmental debacle." Miracle and debacle each attracted worldwide attention. Scholars have documented both, but have yet to fully explore their relationship (McKean, 1993).

Japan's drive to conquer postwar poverty and devastation propelled it to amazing economic feats. From the 1950s to the mid-1970s, the annual rate of economic growth in Japan far outstripped that of the other ACID societies (Figure 1.1). By 1976, the Japanese economy had grown to fifty-five times its size in 1946, far outpacing its European counterparts (Figure 1.2). Japan had only 0.3 percent of the world's surface area and 3 percent of the world's population. Despite its diminutive size, by the mid-1970s, Japan accounted for about 10 percent of the world's economic product (Johnson, 1982, p. 6). Growth brought great improvements in the standard of living for the entire Japanese population. As mentioned earlier, some observers termed this an "economic miracle," a phoenix reborn from the ashes of war (Johnson, 1982). (For the stages of postwar Japanese economic growth, see Table 1.1 later in this chapter.) During the 1950s and 1960s, few were aware of the dangers of pollution. A textbook proudly proclaimed Osaka the "capital of smoke" (*kemuri no miyako*) (Kawana, 1987, p. 132).

Tragically, Japan's economic miracle produced a pollution debacle. Atmospheric concentrations of sulfur dioxide (SO_2) rose from .015 parts per million (ppm) in the atmosphere in 1960 to .060 ppm in 1965 (Figure 1.3). This intense pollution caused asthma and other respiratory diseases. Nitrogen oxide (NO_2, NO_x) air pollution stood at .005 ppm in 1960 and rose slowly but steadily to .03 ppm in 1980, with no sign of decline; automobiles, a major source of NO_x, had become increasingly numerous. In the Inland Sea, red tides, a

---

18. For environmental sociology, see Buttel, 1987; Catton, 1980; Catton & Dunlap, 1978; Dunlap & Catton, 1994; Humphrey & Buttel, 1980; Schnaiberg, 1980; Schnaiberg & Gould, 1994. For political ecology, see Roussopoulos, 1993.

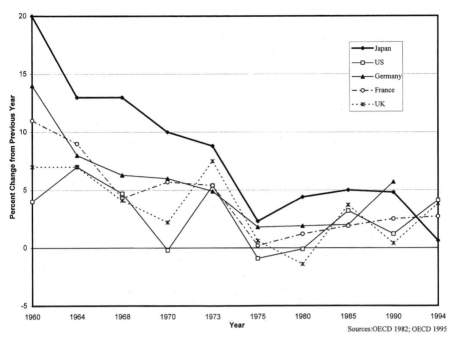

Figure 1.1: Comparative annual percentage change in GPD (ACID societies 1960–1994)

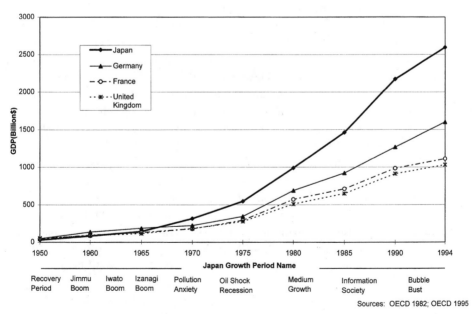

Figure 1.2: Comparative annual change in gross GDP (ACID societies 1950–1994) with Japan growth period names

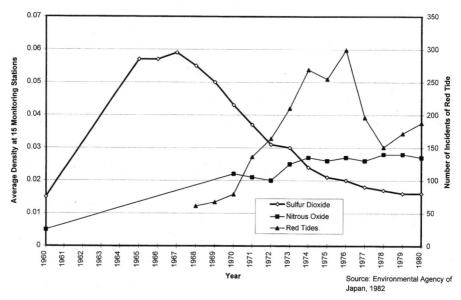

Figure 1.3: Air and water pollution intensity in Japan (selected indicators)

growth of algae destructive to fish, resulted from chemical water pollutants from factories and farms. Cases of red tide rose from 60 in 1968 to 300 in 1977, and since then have varied in intensity with no general decline. Japan produced the world's worst health damage from industrial pollution (before the Chernobyl nuclear plant accident). These included deformities in the infants and adults of Minamata and Niigata due to mercury (Ishimure, 1990), skin lesions due to cadmium, and respiratory problems caused by the choking smog of Yokkaichi (McKean, 1981; Huddle, Reich, & Stiskin, 1975; Uchino, 1983, p. 169; Kelley, 1976). During this period, ecologist Paul Ehrlich likened Japan to a "miner's canary." The canary died when poisonous gases were present in mines, signaling the miners to leave. In the same way, Japan warned other nations of the dangers of industrial pollution (McKean, 1981, p. 204; Ui, 1992).

Japan, however, proved to be a clever canary. Due at first to MITI's informal guidance of industry, after the mid-1960s, the concentration of SO_2 began a long decline, until it reached .015 in 1980 (Figure 1.3). In the early 1970s, the Japanese government passed strict anti-pollution laws and established an environmental agency to enforce them. At the 1972 United Nations Conference on the Human Environment (UNCHE) held in Stockholm, all the ACID nations pledged to reduce their sulfur dioxide air pollution. Japan was the only

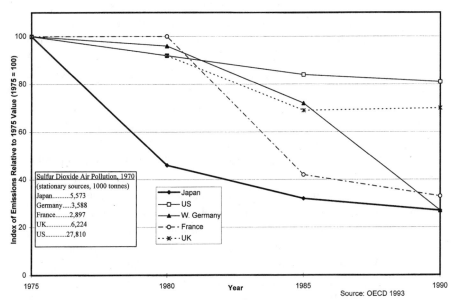

Figure 1.4: Comparative reduction in total sulfur dioxide air pollution, ACID societies

nation that did so. During the 1970s, Japan's investment in pollution control equipment increased sharply (Organization of Economic Cooperation and Development, 1993). Within a few years, these measures attracted international recognition. The percentage of gross national product (GNP) invested by private enterprises in anti-pollution equipment was three times higher in Japan than in other ACID societies (OECD, 1977, p. 71). By the 1980s, Japan boasted 80 to 90 percent of the world's "smoke-scrubbing" facilities for cleaning sulfur dioxide, one of the worst air pollutants, from smokestack gases. As a result of such measures, air pollution due to sulfur dioxide declined much more rapidly in Japan than in other ACID countries (Figure 1.4). Japan also reduced pollution in other ways: increased efficiency in energy use, moving noisy factories out of Tokyo, and recycling programs. In view of what had gone before, this turnabout was as miraculous as Japan's economic achievements (Tsuru & Weidner, 1989).

This pollution miracle left a great deal undone, however. Despite numerous public policy attempts, the Japanese government could not stop the relentless surge of big-city growth – its urban debacle. This led to the overcrowding of Tokyo and the depopulation of the countryside today. The Japanese government ignored many types of pollution, responded inadequately to others, and allowed producers to "export" pollution by moving polluting factories to Third World countries. In the 1990s, air pollution-related respiratory diseases, due to nitrous oxides and other air pollutants, were still a widespread problem. In 1990, almost twenty years after their major court victory, many victims of the infamous Minamata and Niigata mercury poisoning cases still suffered in silence without government help or support. The Bullet Express train still shakes the walls and the rattles windows of the countless city apartment buildings it passes (Funabashi, Hasegawa, Hatanaka, & Kajita, 1988). Diesel trucks and buses shower pedestrians and drivers with thick black soot. Developers turn forests and beaches into ski and golf resorts and yacht clubs with little restriction (Miller, 1989, p. 2). Big companies obtained government funds to dam the Nagara River, even though damming it will do more harm than good. Farmers in Japan use more pesticides per hectare than any other nation (Vig & Kraft, 1990).

Escaping from their own national laws through an "export of pollution," Japan's heavily polluting oil, aluminum, and other refineries have set up shop in Indonesia, Venezuela, and Brazil – the Showa Denko aluminum refinery, for example, rejected by Oita Prefecture, moved to Venezuela. Japanese trading companies systematically strip Southeast Asia's rain forests of their wood. They use the exotic hardwood to make cardboard boxes and concrete forms in Tokyo because it is so cheap. As a result, some observers have called Japan the world's "eco-outlaw" (Begley & Takayama, 1989, p. 70).

Furthermore, the Japanese government proved utterly incapable of controlling the crowding of people into urban environments – one of the greatest causes of pollution and other social problems. By the 1970s, as a result, Japan had the highest density (per square kilometer) of industry, energy use, and population of any nation (Figure 1.5) (Richardson & Flanagan, 1984, p. 410).

When Japan's postwar industrial surge began, factories sprang up mostly in the big cities such as Tokyo and Osaka, along the Pacific Coast. As a result, wages in rural communities such as Oita averaged about 60 percent of those in Tokyo and Osaka. At first unaware of the pollution, young people flocked to the big cities in search of jobs. Between 1960 and 1980, 18 million people migrated from the country to the city. During that period, the proportion of the total population of Japan living in cities over 100,000 increased from 40 percent to 56 percent (Fukutake, 1989, p. 102). The proportion living in the three major metropolitan areas (Tokyo, Osaka, Nagoya) rose from 36.9 percent (1955) to 48.2 percent (1985) (Fukutake, 1989, p. 100–101). Cities could not build enough roads, sewers, and schools to keep pace with the human flood. Land prices skyrocketed, so that urban workers found it ever harder to buy homes. At the same time, rural villages declined, their schools and fields went unused, and

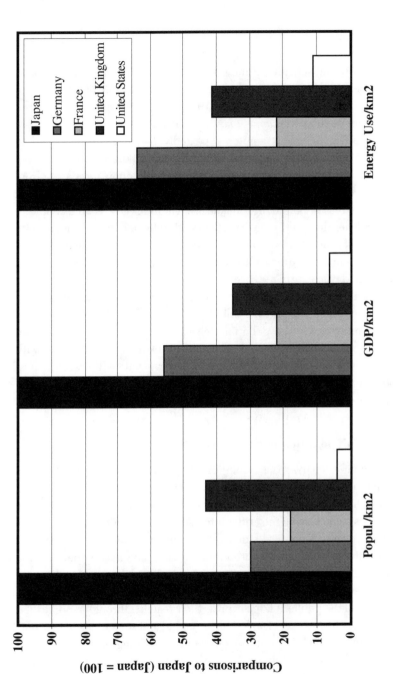

Figure 1.5: Comparative population and industrial density, ACID societies, 1970

Source: OECD 1993

their social groups and activities disintegrated (Adachi, 1973). The proportion of full-time farmers in the work force declined precipitously, from 50.5 percent in 1950 to 14.3 percent in 1985 (Fukutake, 1989, p. 94). Officials called this the overcrowding/depopulation (*kamitsu kaso*) problem.[19]

Policy measures, though attempted repeatedly, had little effect on urban crowding. The New Industrial Cities (NIC) Law of 1962, intended to help hinterland areas grow, failed to draw much industry or population away from the big cities. Where it succeeded, the law sometimes helped bring in heavy industry that increased pollution dramatically. The NIC Law is an example of the growth policies that set the stage for Oita's GE dilemma. In the end, despite such policy efforts, big city crowding continued unabated, producing the stuffed subways and cramped quarters of today's Tokyo. The result, in contrast to the pollution miracle, is an "urban debacle."

Because of these miracles and debacles, Japan presents a "paradigm of inquiry" about pollution policies and politics (Gresser et al., 1981, p. 27). Given Japan's economic miracle and pollution debacles, its pollution miracle was an unlikely outcome. How could this island society – lacking resources, dense with people, and obsessed with growth – have resolved even one of the world's most severe pollution problems? Examination of the political process leading up to our five policy shifts should shed light on this question.

How *did Japan's pollution miracle come about?*

Democratic politics enables the resolution of oppositions by peacefully negotiated means such as elections. Certain coalitions may dominate the political system, though, biasing it toward their favored policy-stances, weakening the voices of critics, even forcing the critics into taking unruly action to get heard.[20] In the formal terms of political studies, the dominant coalition constitutes a *polity* – a combination of official authorities with decision-making powers and, if there are such, the interest groups in society who have their ear on the most regular and easy basis (Tilly, 1968). Against this dominant coalition, other organized groups and the public at large express their reaction through more distant means – regular institutional means such as voting, and sometimes means outside the institutions, such as protests or disruptions. Through their interaction, the dominant polity and the subordinate challengers generate an ever-unfolding political dynamic that continually transforms contemporary societies. Within

---

19. For an examination of this problem, see Fukutake, 1989, p. 104; Masumi, 1995, p. 270–280; National Land Agency of Japan, 1979.

20. As the insightful maxim that politics is the "mobilization of bias" suggests (Schattschneider, 1975).

this broad similarity of process, ACID societies show great variation in specifics, with potential impact on the kinds of policies they make and implement.

Political contention over pollution unfolded in Japan as it did in many other ACID societies, but it differed in its details and outcomes in significant ways. From the end of the Second World War, the dominant polity, a "Ruling Triad" composed of government ministries, the Liberal Democratic party which controlled the national legislature (the "Diet"), and a highly organized big business community, worked together to create very rapid economic growth. As a by-product, this growth produced a great deal of noxious air, soil and water chemical wastes which polluted surrounding communities and the natural environment. The industrializing elites were very unwilling to recognize and deal with the seriousness of this pollution for public welfare. In reaction, during the 1960s, as in other ACID societies, a wave of environmental movements erupted in towns and villages throughout Japan. After a few years, the dominant elite compromised and adopted strict regulations which dramatically reduced the most obvious forms of air and water pollution.

In broad outline, the same course of events happened in other ACID societies as well. The United States, Germany, France and England all experienced a similar political process (see below). The details of political interaction and specific outcomes differed, though, in ways that may be important for understanding how to solve the GE dilemma. For one thing, the similar waves of environmental protest left a residue of national interest groups, such as the Sierra Club and the National Wildlife Federation in the United States and the Green party in Germany (Griffith, 1990). In Japan, however, the pollution protest wave left little in the way of a national political presence. Although vigorous in the late 1960s and early 1970s, in Japan the wave of environmental protest mysteriously faded away leaving only a few, relatively weak national public interest groups that could claim grassroots origins. If movements cause political change, as some argue, and if Japanese environmental movements were relatively weak, little policy change should have occurred in Japan.

Yet, despite the absence of national environmental lobbying groups, the Japanese Diet passed the world's strictest set of anti-pollution laws, which I call a "pollution miracle." Asking why the Diet did so forces us to cast a searching light into the heart of the Japanese polity, the Ruling Triad, to seek out its operating principles. It may be that the Ruling Triad passed these laws to preempt the issue and deflate the movements. But if so, such an act required more collective forethought and coordination than evident among political elites in the United States, at least. In any case, the Pollution Diet raises many questions about the operating principles of Japanese politics, its pattern and distribution of power.

Some observers believe that Japanese protest movements, despite apparent weakness, were the crucial factor in causing Japan's pollution miracle.[21] Others, however, argue that movements were not important in causing this change – that it was initiated by the state:

The pollution cleanup in the early 1970s . . . may have been spurred as much by Western media attention to the plight of Japanese pollution disease victims and Western criticism of Japan as a "polluter's paradise" as by citizens' protests (Pharr, 1990, p. 231).

Not protest movements, Pharr argues, but a "prevailing climate of feeling" (a cultural structural change) swept the bureaucrats into favoring pollution control (Pharr & Badaracio, 1986, p. 246–47). Pressure from the United States, the United Nations, and Western media was the primary cause of this shift. Before the shift, Japan was a "polluter's paradise." The change, Pharr believes, ushered in an era of confrontation between state and business that made Japan a polluter's hell. After a few years this situation mellowed into a more amicable, but still strict, anti-pollution regime.

The Japanese process of pollution politics may indicate basic institutional or cultural differences from the West. These differences may appear within the national elite power structure itself, as well as in the community power structure and its relation with the national power structure, and in the mobilization and subsequent trajectory of protest. Institutional differences may have constituted a distinct "political opportunity structure" that shaped and channeled the process of political contention and its outcomes (Kitschelt, 1986; Tarrow, 1994).

U.S. and European-based models of the relationship between state and society include the pluralist, elite, class, corporatist, state-autonomy, and party-centric principal-agent models. Scholars of Japan have begun to advocate distinctive models of the East Asian state – the "network state" and the "bureaucratic paternalist" state. As a distinctive institutional form, the network state model may help explain Japan's anomalous series of miracles and debacles and the mysterious disappearance of its once vigorous surge of environmental movements. The next section discusses the various models of power at the state and community levels, and how social movements unfold within these contexts. The discussion situates these models within the three theoretical camps.

Why *the GE dilemma and Japan's response?*

People are frustrated by the seemingly inexorable quality of the dilemma. To quote oceanographer Jacques-Yves Costeau:

---

21. See Funabashi, 1992; Ishida & Krauss, 1989, p. 334; Masumi, 1995, p. 7; Matsubara, 1971.

We are prisoners of a system that uses more resources per capita every year. Whichever way we count, the balance between resources and waste is growing more and more negative (*New York Times,* Jan. 30, 1994, p. 4).

Why are we faced with this dilemma? Why have society and the environment interacted in such potentially disastrous ways? Why do people ignore the environmental consequences of their actions? What changes are likely to cure this state of affairs?

The social sciences have been slow to recognize the GE dilemma. For the most part, they assume that our technical skills have made us exempt from the laws of natural ecology (Dunlap & Catton, 1994; Dunlap & Catton, 1994b). The presence of the GE dilemma, though, indicates that we are not exempt. To do research on the GE dilemma, we need to create a truly environmental social science – one that recognizes the importance of interaction between society and the natural environment (Dunlap & Catton, 1994b; Stern, 1993). This effort has started within a number of disciplines. In the 1960s, environmental sociology started with a very generalized juxtaposition of population size, the organization of society, the environment and technology (Duncan, 1961). It has gradually become more sophisticated in tracing and describing the intricate pathways of interaction between the environment, politics, the economy, social institutions and culture.

Each of the three theoretical camps explains our issues of concern in its own way. Commentators in the *political-economic* home domain tend to explain politics and social movements by reference to the material interests and material means held by various groups. In the environmental domain, the traditional definition of opposed classes by their ability to exploit the benefits of production shifts to include classes defined by their evasion of or subjugation to the mounting environmental risks from new technologies of production (such as nuclear energy or pesticides) (Beck, 1992; Douglas & Wildavsky, 1982).

Political-economists often attribute environmental destruction to businesses, which act from the pressures of the capitalist marketplace. Faced by aggressive competition, businesses often choose to make pollution and other negative consequences of growth into an "externality" – something outside their sphere of responsibility (Cable & Cable, 1995, p. xi; Daly, 1980). By dumping their massive waste heedlessly into the common air, water and soil, they save money. Business managers choose technologies of production, including resource extraction techniques and processing chemicals, that are efficient, even if they destroy the environment (Commoner, 1972; Commoner, 1990). Local real estate speculators, similarly, invite rampant growth in order to raise the value of their land holdings, thereby producing a "growth machine" (Molotch, 1975).

In the political-economic view, protest movements too are practical, rational and seeking self-advantage. In one view, movements arise when the members of an aggrieved group think they have a good chance to gain something from using unruly methods.[22] They often draw this conclusion, some theorists argue, when they happen to have acquired resources that empower them: money, time, knowledge, facilities (McCarthy & Zald, 1977; Zald, 1991). In their decision to protest, they may also weigh the political opportunities and threats they face – whether the authorities are likely to forcibly suppress, ignore or welcome their complaints (Tarrow, 1994; Tilly, 1978).

As a capitalist class, businesses exercise profound control over state policy (Block, 1977), either by direct, instrumental means (Miliband, 1969), or by structural means – because a healthy capitalist class produces jobs for society and vital revenues for the state (Poulantzas, 1973). In pursuit of their interests, capitalists as a class pressure the government to not pass or to relax pollution regulation (O'Connor, 1973). Such policies may deny popular demands, causing the state to lose popular legitimacy (O'Connor, 1973; Offe, 1984).

Many Japanese, and some Western, scholars find the class model accurate for Japan, so certainly it is one to consider.[23] Japanese pollution critic Ui Jun, for instance, argued that pollution was an inherent product of the Japanese capitalist economy:

> Japanese economists have pointed out a number of factors in the success of Japan's capitalist economy. The things most stressed have been low wages and trade protection. Now I am adding a third factor: the neglect of pollution . . . permitting the economy to dirty its own clothes. The problem of pollution is an essential part of the capitalist economy of Japan . . .

In the mid-1960s, Ui concluded that "the present technological system itself is necessarily producing pollution and cannot be separated from pollution" (Ui, nd, pp. 9–10). Only a few years later, however, Japan carried out its "pollution miracle," casting doubt on Ui's thesis. Pollution may not be such an "essential part" of capitalism. At the very least, we must consider the degree to which cultural and social institutional contexts modify the political effects of the capitalist class.

To the extent that "the state" with its ministries and agencies is an independent actor (Skocpol, 1985), though, it might push destructive growth for its own reasons. The revenues derived from a healthy economy enhance the power and prestige of the state. Officials might want these revenues, even if not following

---

22. This position, if strictly adhered to, gives birth to the free rider paradox: why would a self-interested person expend effort for a social movement fighting for a good, like clean air, that would benefit everyone, not just movement members (Olson, 1975)? To solve this paradox, theorists have increasingly referred to social institutional and cultural factors, as reviewed in following paragraphs.
23. See, for example, Halliday, 1975: 271–272; Furuki, 1978; Matsushita, 1980; Yanaga, 1968.

the dictates of business leaders, and so allow severe pollution to mount. Competition among states (Skocpol, 1985) may generate its own logic of growth and environmental destruction, as radioactive waste around nuclear weapons sites in the U.S. and former USSR testifies. "The government," therefore, may be neither a tool of capitalists nor a neutral actor responding to interest groups throughout society (Ostrom, 1990, p. 216). Rather, it may be a direct source of the GE dilemma. The thesis of Ministry of International Trade and Industry (MITI) guidance of the Japanese economy would support such a view (Fukui, 1992; Johnson, 1982, p. 17, 44; Vogel, 1979).

Kitschelt found that states that were more receptive to public concerns reacted more quickly, and managed to defuse and prevent large-scale protest mobilization. States that rejected public concerns, though, amplified protest. At the same time, states that had a strong capacity to make and implement new policy became the targets of protest, while states perpetually mired in gridlock did not (Kitschelt, 1986). Since the subjects of his study were all ACID societies, the causes of these intersocietal differences must have been more institutional and cultural than political-economic. Complementing these conclusions, another research team found that states which allowed the unimpeded formation of public opinion generated strong protest movements, while states which attempted to contain public opinion defused protest (Kriesi et al. 1995). These studies indicate that states which preemptively respond to public concerns and dampen public debate have lower levels of protest.

Other theories in the political-economy camp widen the societal basis of economic demand. Treadmill theory sees the GE dilemma as rooted in a class coalition between capital and labor – both classes profit from a more productive, and hence more environmentally destructive, economy (Schnaiberg, 1980; Schnaiberg and Gould, 1994). Both classes use their economic resources, extracted ultimately from the environment, to fund political parties, attain political power and control the state, using it to perpetuate the destructive system (Gould, 1993, p. 231). This point of view parallels the *elite* and *corporatist* models. In elite models, the leaders of major institutions (Dahrendorf, 1959; Mills, 1956). In corporatist models, the peak associations of tightly organized capitalist and working classes work with state ministries to create an "orderly, stable and effective" pro-growth policy-making process that occurs largely outside the parliament (Schmitter, 1981, p. 293). Many studies of Japan identify a "Ruling Triad" of dominant elites: the Liberal Democratic party, the bureaucratic ministries, and the big business interest groups. They disagree about which if any of these three dominate the Triad, or how power shifts among them (Fukui, 1977; van Wolferen, 1989, p. 109).

The Ehrlichs attribute the problem to an even broader group – the growing population and their collective consumption and waste (Ehrlich & Ehrlich, 1990). These theories "democratize" the economic interest-based growth impulse beyond the capitalist class to wider populations. It implies that the basic cause of the GE dilemma lies in demands for growth arising from mass society, not from elites or the state. If so, this situation would put protest movements as a minority, representing, not an inarticulate public as they so often portray themselves, but rather a severely victimized minority, if not just a "grumpy" or NIMBY one.[24]

Social institutionalists, on the other hand, hold that the home domain of politics, social movements, and other aspects of society, lies in institutionalized social roles and patterns, the "rules of the game." They see power as distributed by historically constituted political institutions that embody and reproduce these rules (Moe, 1984; Reed, 1993: 50; Skocpol & Campbell, 1995; Steinmo, Thelen & Longstreth, 1992). Derived from this position, principal-agent theory holds that the legally constituted authority, in a democratic system the elected representatives, is the "principle" or controlling power, while the governmental bureaucracy is its agent. One set of scholars has applied this viewpoint to the study of Japanese politics, arguing that the LDP controls the policy outputs of the government, not the state ministries as others argue (Ramseyer & Rosenbluth, 1993).

The institutional viewpoint has many variations. Ostrom points out that any solutions to environmental problems are choices and games that only operate within specific institutional conditions (Ostrom, 1990, p. 215). New ideas get clipped to fit the paths described by existing institutions (Weir, 1992, p. 192). Political norms may affect pollution politics (Powell & DiMaggio, 1991; Reed, 1993). Existing stratification systems, as institutional structures, attributing high and low status to classes, genders, racial and ethnic groups, drive people into conspicuous consumption or expose them to extreme environmental hazards.[25] Actors tend to adapt to the rules, stay within them routinely and ritualistically, and use the existing opportunities, at least until severely disrupted. In this view, the rules involve the commitment of all involved, rather than the cynical manipulation of the powerful. Protest movements appear when leaders violate expected norms (Scott, 1976). They attract members through friendship and kinship networks within local social institutions (McAdam et al., 1988).

---

24. This acronym refers to "Not-In-My-Back-Yard," the cry of protest movements that just want to move pollution out of their neighborhoods, not reduce or end it entirely (Freudenberg & Steinsapir, 1992).

25. For perspectives on status competition and consumption, see Hirsch, 1976; Veblen, 1992. For environmental racism, see Bullard, 1990; Taylor, 1989. I discuss ecofeminism under culture rather than social institutions.

The pluralist model falls into this camp. Closest to the popular conception of democracy, it argues that the state is the neutral representative of majority opinion. Almost any earnest group, pluralism argues, can achieve a significant voice in policy making through the existing institutions (Dahl, 1961; Polsby, 1995). Traditional pluralism finds few adherents among students of Japanese politics.[26] One study argues that the mass media have increased the amount of effective pluralism in Japan (Kabashima & Broadbent, 1986). Comparative work on this model reveals a degree of central coordination in Japan that renders pluralism dubious (Knoke, Pappi, Broadbent & Tsujinaka, 1996).

Some institutionalists stress the formal side of the rules, embodied in legitimate institutions, especially the state, with its constitutional rules regulating voting, political parties and the powers of ministries and governments (Cowhey & McCubbins, 1995; Skocpol & Campbell, 1995). Others say the rules can also be very informal, appearing, for example, in the norms of everyday behavior and the backstage channels of access to decision-makers by special interest groups (Jepperson, 1991). In either case, institutionalists argue that political outcomes, including presumably growth and environmental policies, are strongly shaped by these formal or informal patterns of rules and roles, which arise over historical time and change only slowly.

Recent work explains US-Japan policy-making differences in terms of formal institutional rules (Cowhey & McCubbins, 1995). These rules distribute power to the ruling political party, in the Japanese case the Liberal Democratic party (Cohen, McCubbins & Rosenbluth, 1995, p. 178). This party is the "principle" and the administrative bureaucracy is its "agent" (Ramseyer & Rosenbluth, 1993, p. 4). The LDP, they say, gets the "best information," which enables it to control the bureaucrats "cheaply" (Ramseyer & Rosenbluth, 1993, pp. 3–5). One study attributed the decline of the nuclear power industry in the U.S. versus its flourishing in Japan to political choices made within "different institutional environments." The U.S. constitution allows a number of veto gates, slowing down the licensing process, while in Japan, the majority party controlled all nuclear power licenses, streamlining the approval process (Cohen, McCubbis & Rosenbluth, 1995, p. 201–202).

Social anthropologist Chie Nakane argues that all of Japan's institutions, political and otherwise, conform to an institutionalized social pattern – an "inverted V" or a structure built of vertical norms of loyalty. These norms are not dependent upon belief, but upon acceptance of propriety – a set of proper ways

---

26. Watanuki, for instance, explicitly notes that pluralist democracy has not yet reached sufficient development in Japan (Crozier, Huntington & Watanuki, 1975).

of doing things. In politics, for instance, once a group has accepted state guidance,

> . . . the state's administrative authority . . . can be transmitted without obstruction down the vertical line of a group's internal organization (Nakane, 1970, p. 102).

If citizens defer to leaders in matters of economic growth and pollution, they would not protest very much even when environmental disasters occurred. Their acquiescence would be the result, not of internalized values, but of embedded norms: habits, rules, rituals and social networks.

The network state model depends upon the existence of such normative, informal networks. Okimoto argues that, by this means, the Japan state enjoys an informal business-corporatism. The Japanese state works not by formal authority, he says, but through its "network of [cooperative] ties to the private sector" and the "structure of LDP-[state] bureaucracy-interest group alignments" (1989, p. 226). These informal personal ties allow MITI to make national economic policy cooperatively with businesses and then persuade them to follow it (Evans, 1995, p. 59). As close analogy, though, the "bureaucratic-inclusionary state" model, extends the idea of informal network corporatism to labor and other interest groups throughout the population (Inoguchi, 1983). Likewise, others noted a "flexible and responsive . . . patterned pluralism" in which groups negotiated with the bureaucracy over policy (Krauss & Muramatsu, 1988).[27] Some speculate that the effective pluralism of this model amounts to a "Japanese style democracy."

Those in the *cultural* camp, however, represent a third distinct viewpoint on these issues. They claim that a society's implicit categories – its dominant morality and values – shape the motives, perception and political choices of power-holders as well as protestors, and thereby affect or determine a society's macro-behavior.[28] In the "politics of ideas" (Quirk, 1995) and "epistemic communities" (Haas, 1990; Haas, 1992), reigning ideologies and dominant values shape the climate of opinion and bring about the major policy trends. The silent revolution thesis and related ideas, for instance, argue that environmental movements are driven by a new cognitive framework (Eyerman & Jamison 1991), perhaps

---

27. Cited in Okimoto & Rohlen, 1988, p. 209.

28. The term "culture" is used in many different senses (Berger, 1995, p. 14). Here I am referring to the sociological usage of the term which defines culture as implicit categories: "abstract ideas (norms, values, style, strategies, repertoires, etc.) and the symbols that imply or represent them" (Berger, 1995, p. 19), and distinguishes culture from social structure, the roles, relations and larger patterns engaged in by social actors (Berger, 1995, p. 62). In making a distinction between social institutions and culture, I further distinguish norms – collectively agreed upon, expected patterns of behavior – as the formative elements of social institutions, from culture – personal values and beliefs derived from other sources than immediate social expectations (Jenks, 1993).

on the basis of the "post-material" values of a new middle class.[29] In a similar vein, some theorists argue that the popular adoption of values justifying the exploitation of nature drives the destruction of nature.[30] Ecofeminists charge that values of patriarchy justify not only male domination and exploitation of women but of nature as well.[31] Some scholars argue that these destructive values must be, and gradually are being displaced by more environmentally benign ones (Dunlap, 1992; Nash, 1989).[32]

In this vein, some theorists argue that, before they join and create social protest movements, actors must adopt new ways of framing or interpreting a circumstance. They have to move from seeing something as benign to seeing it as unjust (Gamson, 1992, p. 68), and from resigned acceptance to a sense of violated rights and moral outrage (McAdam, 1982). Likewise, in order to create shifts in state policies, actors must persuade authorities to accept new "definitions of environmental problems" (Hannigan, 1994, p. 185). Values, beliefs and interpretations, in this camp, drive politics, so therefore must be changed before policies can change. Through this process, they hope, societies will "learn" better environmental manners (Milbrath, 1989).

Many scholars have discerned distinct cultural values behind Japan's economic and political performance. One scholar found an analogue of the Protestant ethic in Japan – a set of Buddhist values driving merchants to accumulate and invest (Bellah, 1957). However, extending that logic to explain Japan's GE dilemma meets some obstacles. The major Japanese religious traditions, Shinto and Buddhism, advocate harmony with nature, not domination over it (Suzuki, 1973). Hence, they seem unlikely sources of environmentally destructive values.

Japan's Confucian heritage, on the other hand, may be indirectly responsible for its GE dilemma. Confucian moral teachings probably encourage Japanese people to give credence and trust to their leaders more readily and less critically than in the Western societies.[33] Sexism, the subordination of women, is an

29. Dalton, Kuechler & Burklin, 1990; Inglehart, 1977; Klandermans, 1991; Offe, 1985a.

30. Dunlap & Catton, 1994; Nash, 1989; White, 1967.

31. A large ecofeminist literature has appeared, including Gaard, 1993; Merchant, 1990; Mies & Shiva, 1993; Nelson, 1990; Shiva, 1990; Steger & Witt, 1988; Warren, 1990.

32. The new environmental paradigm represents the ethical viewpoint on nature expressed by such well-known works as *Silent Spring* (Carson, 1962), Aldo Leopold's Land Ethic in *A Sand Country Almanac* (1949), the philosophy of deep ecology (DeVall & Sessions, 1985) and *The Rights of Nature* (Nash, 1989).

33. For instance, see Benedict, 1946; DeVos, 1973, Chs. 7 and 14; Doi, 1973; Dore, 1987, Chp. 5; Fukui, 1992; Hamaguchi, 1985; Kamishima, 1983; Kyogoku, 1987; Lebra, 1976; Markus & Kitayama, 1991; Nakane, 1970, p. 22; Okimoto, 1989, p. 170; Pye, 1985; Smith, 1983. Such attitudes have historical roots. From the Meiji Restoration (1868) to the end of the Second World War, the Japanese state tried to make people believe in the idea of a "family state" (*kokutai*). This idea fused

integral part of this paternalistic ideological paradigm (So & Chiu, 1995). Pye claims the Japanese

have learned how to master dependency and to use paternalism to inspire collective efforts which are hard to achieve in more individualistic, ego-centered cultures (1985, p. 181)

Deferential values may strongly support vertical political institutions, especially in a tightly bounded, relatively homogeneous society such as Japan (Lamont, 1989, p. 141). Scholars in other camps, however, express great skepticism about cultural explanations of Japanese society.[34]

The network state model, while operating through informally institutionalized social networks, also partakes of cultural factors. In the network state model, the members of the ruling triad – ministries, LDP and big business – accept common implicit categories, in this case an overarching national purpose, very strongly. Therefore, the network state represents a social structure infused with an ideological cultural structure.[35] This implies a different form of power. Western models assume that power is a quality of the actor, and that political actors are atomized and disparate, coming together only to serve instrumental purposes (Skocpol & Campbell, 1995; Wrong 1979). The Japanese state's use of personal ties implies the use of cooperative or paternalistic power, though, rather than conflictual power.[36] In Western political-economic theory, this kind of network relationship should render a state very vulnerable to corruption – the use of high office to collect rents. How much that happens in Japan remains an open question.

Many observers of Japan do not agree with the state-centralized image of the network state model. Johnson stated that "Japan persisted with high-speed growth long after the evidence of very serious environmental damage had become common knowledge" (Johnson, 1982, p. 284). This treatment indicates something less than a state's network paternalism toward environmental protesters. To the contrary, for decades, pollution victims met with corporate denials and government collusion (Upham, 1987). In keeping with this reality, some people charge that the Japanese state practices an undemocratic, bureaucratic arrogance toward weaker groups, not a solicitous paternalism (Steinhoff, 1992, p. 194). Some argue that the Liberal Democratic party (LDP), not

identity, kinship, and government, and added a Confucian "sense of responsibility" (Smith, 1973, pp. 125–136).

34. See, for instance, Dale, 1986; Johnson, 1982; Mouer & Sugimoto, 1979; Mouer & Sugimoto, 1986; Reed, 1993.

35. See Evans, 1995; Kumon, 1992, p. 129; Okimoto, 1989, p. 145.

36. On this point see Mann, 1986; Parsons, 1960, pp. 199–225; Weber, 1968, p. I, 53; Wrong, 1979.

the state ministries, has been the center of policy formulation (Calder, 1988), because of its control over the Diet (Ike, 1980, p. 40; Thayer, 1969). Prefectural governments too have been noted to possess considerable policy-forming initiative.[37] Also, the mass media may have a powerful agenda-setting effect on politics (Kabashima & Broadbent, 1986). In addition, opposition parties, unions, and citizens' movements may exert a measure of influence.[38] We must examine their connections within the active network of power.

The three camps – political-economy, social institutional and cultural – encompass an enormous diversity of ideas, even when focused on this fairly delimited problem. Even in their diversity, the three camps do not encompass all the relevant aspects. In particular, theorists within each camp differ on whether human behavior is more "agentic" – creatively and voluntarily embarked upon by a social actor as an "agent" of their own fate, or more structural – predetermined by a higher-order patterning of roles. To simplify the differences among the points of view, their essential postulates may be arrayed on a two-dimensional table, as discussed in Chapter 10 (Table 10.1). Even this table, though, does not encompass all the relevant aspects. The literature identifies three "faces" of power, for instance – three basic tactics used to reach decisions and exert influence within mass political systems. These three faces are: open discussion, hidden and manipulative setting of the agenda for discussion by interested parties, and persuasive manipulation of the desires and beliefs of the other party (Lukes, 1974). Crenson termed the second type "non-decisions" because they are de facto decisions made without the full knowledge of all interested parties (Crenson, 1971). Gramsci referred to the third type as "ideological hegemony" (as cited in Lukes, 1974). The three camps, then, give us a common ground on which to begin our discussion, but not on which to conclude it.

We need not, in any case, try to reduce our explanation to a single theory. Elements from all three camps might well contribute to the complex chain of causation leading up to a major policy shift (Craiger, Goodman, Weiss & Butler, 1996).[39] Many social scientists now reject reductionist explanations. They agree that social reality represents an intricate web of interactions between economic,

---

37. Among those who have noted this: Broadbent, 1988; Reed, 1986, p. 170; Samuels, 1983.

38. An enormous literature has grown up documenting the activities and impacts of peripheral groups in Japanese politics. For instance: Apter & Sawa, 1984; Iijima, 1984; Ishida & Krauss, 1989; Kano, Kinbara & Matsunaga, 1977; Lewis, 1980; Masaki et al., 1976; Matsubara & Nitagai, 1976; McKean, 1981; Miyamoto, 1970; Steiner, Krauss & Flanagan, 1980; Tsujinaka, 1993; Ui, 1979.

39. Others who have tried to trace the interaction of movements and power structures have resorted to similar methodological tactics. One author describes his approach as "a nondogmatic, eclectic attitude toward theory, a willingness to bring to bear whatever proved helpful for reconstructing the full history and for analyzing and interpreting its meanings" (Szasz, 1994, p. 163).

political, social, and cultural dimensions (Adam, 1993; Broadbent, 1989; Stern, 1993, p. 1897). Some Marxist political-economists, for instance, have rejected the idea of a determining economic "base" to society (Burawoy, 1985, p. 225). At the same time, though, earlier attempts at holistic systems theory are in general disrepute. We have no generally accepted understanding, therefore, of how that multidimensional interaction works.[40] Social reality is likely to be a complex amalgam of structural factors and antagonistic, agentic tactics in dynamic tension with each other (Foucault, 1983, p. 211). To grasp this dynamic bundle, we must perform the synthetic task of seeing how the various factors, cognized above as discrete entities, exist and combine in "messy" reality.[41]

Accordingly, rather than applying any particular theory too hastily and risking a conceptual truncation, we must first "map the broad terrain" of interaction (Ostrom, 1990, p. 214). When we try to do so, it is true, this terrain quickly turns into a bewildering labyrinth, and our theoretical map into a Minotaur of ambiguity. To make our way through the terrain, then, the safer way is to go step by step. That is, to trace the genetic chain of influence relations as they unfold between social actors, in the alliances and their conflicts. This genetic chain will be our multicolored thread – leading us through the labyrinth as it weaves our goal, the larger-patterned cloth of power.

My main body of analytical concepts comes from social movement theory, and will be used as needed. In the last quarter of the twentieth century, social movement theory experienced a tremendous and vital flowering, providing a host of new concepts for the analysis of dynamic collective action. These concepts express the essential theoretical tensions between the three theoretical camps discussed above, so they are handy tools. I apply these concepts – resources, social solidarities, interpretive frames and political opportunity structures – throughout the book. I use them for the analysis and understanding not only of the mobilization and conflict trajectory of social movements, but also of all other social actors.

The general perspective I use combines these elements into a synthetic framework (Figure 1.6) that posits a zone of plasticity between structure and agency. This plasticity zone applies to interactions using any of the three forms of interaction: political-economic, social institutional and cultural dimensions,

---

40. It may not have a unified logic. Society may be "sutured" into spaces operating under different logics. Indeed, in that sense, a theory of society may be "impossible" and "infinite" (Laclau & Mouffe, 1985, p. 152–9).

41. Science can be characterized by two main approaches. One thinks in terms of holistic systems, the other in terms of discrete variables (Craiger et al., 1996). Synthesis, as I use it here, takes the former approach.

as well as across them. The established structural complex of a society at any given time, in its politics, economics, religions, and other spheres, is a dense and often self-contradictory amalgam of values, norms and institutions. When problems arise, actors work within a field of agency to find new solutions, and then attempt to impress them upon the existing structural complex. The resulting clashes engender a process of conflict that results in either stabilization or change in the status quo.[42]

The existing patterns of power, through their regular operation, contain the seeds of their own transformation. The political process produces a new distribution of rewards and sanctions which gives rise to new groups, or activates old ones, pursuing new (ideal, normative and materially defined) interests. New groups or activated old ones put existing patterns of power under pressure and even change them. At the same time, though, the existing structures provide the ground on which new interest groups get started, and may also act to constrain them. Figure 1.6 presents a schematic diagram of this dynamic process of structure-agency interaction and feedback.

This feedback process finds concrete expression in the political pressuring among actors that connect genetically through time and have an impact upon the outcomes of issues. Each exercise of pressure between two actors (individual, organizational or diffuse) inspires the next in a number of parallel and intersecting chains around a given issue. The concessions made by the governor in the "navel" engagement, for example, brought about pressure from the business community that forced him to renege. Looked at longitudinally, the series of pressures describes a "spiral of conflict" that unfolds over time (Heirich, 1968). Looked at cross-sectionally, the pressures describe a policy or political network. Combined, the unfolding spiral and the cross-sectional network deepen our understanding of the political process that produced the five policy shifts.[43]

---

42. Those interested in a more extensive discussion of this approach should consult Chapter 10 (Table 10.1) and Appendix 1.

43. Many scholars have commented upon a like conception of this process (Burstein, Einwhoner & Hollander, 1995, p. 277; Knoke, 1990; Mann, 1986, p. 27; Steinmo et al., 1992). Their presence reflects not only material exchange, but mutual cognizance of general symbolic and normative contexts and the already existing broad pattern of power (Giddens, 1984). Given the variations possible in their components, political networks too can have widely varying qualities in "rich, organic mixtures" (Homans, 1974; Emirbayer & Goodwin , 1994; Etzioni, 1968; French & Raven, 1959; Broadbent, 1989a). Mann identifies four types of power networks: ideological, economic, political, and military (in sometimes "promiscuous" combinations) (Mann, 1986, p. 2, 17). He neglects another important type, social institutional (normatively relational) networks (Granovetter, 1985). We will need to consider all these, as they condition the effective channels through which active power flows.

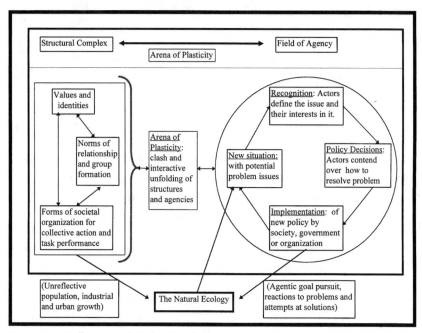

Figure 1.6: Collective political action: between structure, agency, and nature

Within the unfolding spiral of pressures, single relationships have the potential, albeit rarely, to switch the course of change onto very different tracks (Abbott, 1992; Aminzade, 1992; Griffin, 1992). In Weber's "switchman" metaphor, for example, ideal interests had the capacity to shunt the juggernaut of economic growth onto a different track (Weber, 1947). At the same time, social or political-economic interests might also lead to an important switch in the direction of change. In any case, politics and history unfolds as a problem-impelled, path-dependent, interactive process between structures and agencies, along the three dimensions of exchange and expressed in many different tactical modes.

Research site and methods

Within Japan, Oita Prefecture proved to be an excellent vantage point for addressing the research questions posed here. As a small prefecture on an island in southern Japan, Oita may seem rather geographically and culturally limited. However, the prefecture tied directly into national growth plans and reflected all the problems, benefits, and responses to growth, including pollution in good

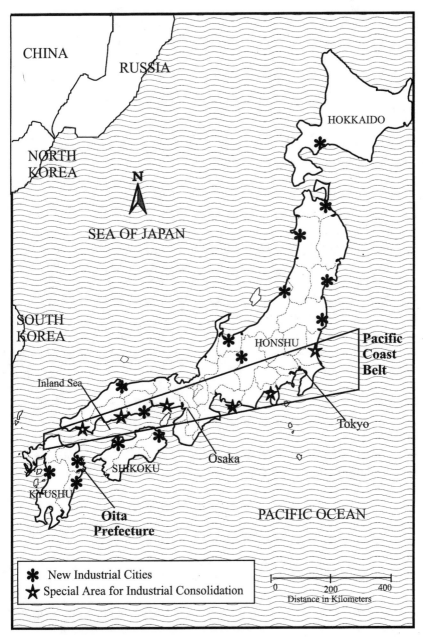

Figure 1.7: Map of Japan with Pacific Coast Belt, NIC, and SAIC sites

measure. It also reflected the influence of international aspects of this global problem. Therefore, as a piece of the national and global fabric, Oita has the capacity to reveal much about the balance of local, national and universal forces at work producing the GE dilemma (Tilly, 1984b).

In the decades after the Second World War, Oita tried to emulate the rapid industrialization of central Japan, and as a result also suffered from intense industrial pollution. The little prefecture exhibited societal dynamics similar to those happening on the national scale, being an inseparable part of the national whole. Oita demonstrated these dynamics on a smaller scale, thus making them more comprehensible. Oita Prefecture is on the southern island of Kyushu, at the western end of the Inland Sea. This location placed the prefecture outside the Pacific Coast Belt where most heavy industrial growth had occurred (see Figure 1.7). When I entered the field in 1978, the prefecture still boiled with conflict over growth and environmental issues.

For most of its history, Oita had served as the agricultural hinterland to the national urban centers. It had a large, pre-First World War copper refinery and an agricultural chemical plant predating the Second World War, but was famous mostly for its mushrooms, hot springs, and white sand beaches. Oita's main cities, Oita (pop. 341,307 in 1980) and Beppu (pop. 133,786 in 1980) – respectively the industrial Pittsburgh and the tourist Miami of the prefecture – lay on the shores of Beppu Bay (Figure 1.8). To the north, small fishing villages dotted the coast up to Nakatsu City. East of Oita City, in the township of Saganoseki, the hamlets of Baba and Kozaki and the town of Saganoseki (Seki Town) became the sites of dramatic environmental conflict. South of Seki Town, along the jagged coast, the small port towns of Usuki and Saeki also gave birth to environmental movements. Behind Oita City, the Oita and the Ono Rivers had created flat deltas suitable for farming and building. Other coastal places did not enjoy such deltas. In Kozaki, for instance, back a few hundred feet from the shore, steep hills quickly became green, sharp volcanic ridges. Behind the ridges lay jagged mountainous terrain interspersed with narrow valleys and some highland plains. Japan has nothing resembling the vast, fertile agricultural heartland of the United States; for centuries, Oita's people had carved their fields out of the mountain slopes.

In the late 1950s, Oita Prefecture, eager to lift itself out of rural poverty, embarked on an ambitious industrialization program. This program placed the tall, candy-striped smokestacks along the shore and brought some jobs and prosperity. By the late 1960s, however, severe air and water pollution plagued Oita. In the worst areas, respiratory disease increased. Red tides disturbed the coastal waters more frequently.

As air and water pollution intensified, so did grassroots protest. In 1973,

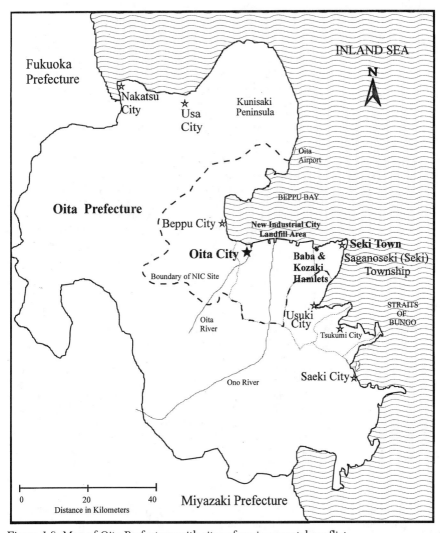

Figure 1.8: Map of Oita Prefecture with sites of environmental conflict

protest movements pressured Governor Taki into suspending the plans for Industrial Landfill No. 8. The governor agreed not to lift the suspension until meeting three conditions: local citizens' consensus, an end to fighting in the fishing union, and an environmental impact assessment.

Table 1.1 summarizes Japan's and Oita's post-war growth and environmental and social problems. It divides the postwar years into eight stages extending

Table 1.1. *Japan and Oita: Stages of post-war growth and problems*

Period: Years	Events in Japan	Events in Oita
Recovery (1945–55)	Rebuilding of basic economy from war devastation. Beginning of light export industry. In 1955, economy surpasses prewar peak. First outbreak of Minamata mercury poisoning in 1953.	Slow rebuilding of Oita City, 1945–55. Many youths leave for big-city jobs. Pulp plant locates in Nakaiima area; residents protest.
Jimmu Boom (1955–58)	Average GNP growth 7 percent per year. Prosperity "unequaled since time of Emperor Jimmu" (660 BC). Huge increase in consumer economy led by advertising to overcome old austerity ethic. Factories are built near central cities and switch to cheap imported oil for fuel. This causes air pollution in Yokkaichi.	Governor Kinoshita announces Oita-Tsurusaki Seaside Industrial Park. Plans call for Landfills No. 1–5 on Oita City shore, 6 and 7 on Tsurusaki shore, and 8 across Beppu Bay. Misa/Iejima villages resist.
Iwato Boom (1959–64)	Average GNP growth 12 percent per year. Ikeda Cabinet 1960 "Income Doubling Plan" urges industry to go to crowded Pacific Coast Belt. Rural complaints lead to New Industrial Cities (NIC) Law to spread industry to hinterland. First successful citizen protest. First local government pollution prevention agreement with business.	Oita Prefecture supporters in Tokyo form the Kyushu Oil Company to industrialize Oita. Oita builds Landfill No. 1 and the Kyushu oil refinery on it. Tsurusaki Fishing Union protests. Oita is designated an NIC and finished landfills for a planned oil complex. Landfills No. 2, 3, and 4 on the coast of Oita City.
Izanagi Boom (1965–69)	Average GNP growth 12 percent per year. Japan changes to export promotion policy. Second largest GNP in non-Communist world. Growing pollution problems and protests. Diet passes ineffective 1967 Basic Law on Environmental Pollution. First large antipollution movement.	New Japan Steel (NJS) builds blast furnace steel refinery on Landfills No. 3 and 4. Showa Denko builds petrochemical refinery on No. 2. Ministry of Construction designates Oita one of seventeen most polluted cities in Japan. Showa Aluminum wants to build refinery on No. 8

Table 1.1. *Continued*

Period: Years	Events in Japan	Events in Oita
Pollution Anxiety (1970–72)	Many horrific pollution incidents stir popular concern. Environmental movements help elect wave of left-wing mayors and governors. Diet passes comprehensive, strict set of pollution laws and sets up the Environmental Agency. Business and government invest heavily in pollution control equipment.	Governor announces Landfill No. 8 will be on Kozaki/Baba shore in Saganoseki (Seki) Township. Kozaki village and Seki Fishing Union protest: petitions to mayor, governor, and Environmental Agency in Tokyo; bellybutton confrontation. Showa Petroleum withdraws; Teijin Rayon and Showa Oil will come instead. Mitsui signs contact for No. 7.
Oil Shock (1973–77)	OPEC raises oil prices, causing severe recession in oil-dependent Japan. Average GNP growth 3 percent. Business and government less willing to invest in pollution control equipment. Government relaxes some pollution standards.	Kozaki and Seki send delegation to Environmental Agency, threaten to riot there. Governor Taki concedes suspension of No. 8 until Three Conditions are met. Oita starts No. 7 Landfill. Movement leader elected to Seki Town Council, but Council approves No. 8.
Medium Growth (1978–1982)	Second OPEC oil price hike. GNP growth at 3 percent. Domestic refinery complexes cancelled. Environmental laws weakened further.	Governor Hiramatsu announces Three Conditions met, end of No. 8 suspension, but does not start construction. No. 7 Landfill finished, No. 6 begun.
Information Society (1983–91)	Growth policy changes from heavy manufacturing to information technology. MITI sponsors Technopolis Plan to build mini "Silicon Valleys" around Japan.	Oita designated as a Technopolis site, builds consumer electronics complex across Beppu Bay. Governor Hiramatsu initiates other growth schemes: "One Village-One Product Movement."
Bubble Bust (1991–95)	Land prices collapse. Deep recession. Ruling party (LDP) loses control of Diet.	Landfills No. 6 and 7 still unoccupied (except minor buildings). No prospect of making No. 8.

from 1945 to 1995.[44] These stages trace Japan's recovery from wartime devastation through successive expansions to the mid-1990s (also see Figure 1.1). The stages also trace the appearance of pollution and other attendant social problems and the politics thereof. Rapid economic growth brought prosperity but also caused urban sprawl, rural depopulation, and environmental pollution. In the early 1990s, Japan's seemingly unstoppable economic expansion suffered a setback. The economic bubble burst and led to a recession. The post-war political dominance of the ruling party broke asunder. Our story, however, starts with earlier events.

From 1978 to 1981, the initial and residential research period, I lived with my family in two neighborhoods. Takeshita, on the coast, lay within Oita City near the industrial complex that caused the pollution and behind new coastal landfill slated for more industry. Eventually the pollution made my children sick, so we moved to Obasama, a farming village about 10 miles behind Oita City, for a healthier environment. At each site, we found friendly neighbors and learned many lessons. Oita provided a window on the political dynamics of growth and pollution in Japan and, through that, on a broader picture – the GE dilemma in ACID societies.

When I began my field research, I viewed myself as a white-coated researcher in a social laboratory, an invisible, moving eye, seeing but unseen. Gradually, however, the reality of my presence in the community forced me into the position of neighbor and participant. I realized that understanding the situation was not a matter of "gathering data." It required sensitivity to nuances of thought, language, and activity that could only come with vulnerability. Fluent in Japanese, I talked, participated, enjoyed acceptance, and at times suffered rejection. I became more open and vulnerable to local people's reactions (Pollner & Emerson, 1983; Thorne, 1988). Originally, I had intended to compare two cases of regional industrial growth and pollution controversy in Japan. Instead, my involvement in untangling the complexity and subtlety of the reality of one caused me to stay in Oita for the full research period. The longer I stayed, the more the social reality seemed like a chaotic stew, and the further it diverged from the simple theoretical frameworks I had brought with me. The fieldwork

---

44. Scholars divide post-war Japan into periods in different ways. The recent history of Japanese industrial policy produced by MITI reports the following stages of economic growth: post-war recovery period (1945–1955), technical innovation introductory period (1955–1965), high economic growth period (1965–1975), stable economic growth period (1975–1985), and industrial structural adjustment period (1985–1990) (interview with Hashimoto Michio, April 3, 1990). Consideration of social, political, cultural, and environmental changes, however, yields the eight-stage model used here. Other periodizations, which contribute to the eight-stage model, include Matsubara, 1977, and Iijima, 1994.

experience, far from the ivory tower of academia, awakened me to the complexity and messiness of society (Mann, 1986).

I used many methods of gathering information about events. These included active approaches such as in-depth interviews, observation of bureaucratic activities and participation in village life and movement meetings. They also included passive tactics. I accumulated piles of clippings from newspapers, movement magazines, prefectural statistics, and many other sources. For interviewing, I used a snowball sample technique appropriate for network research. My initial respondents introduced me to others involved in growth and environment politics. In all, I conducted about 500 interviews in Japanese with the decision-makers and participants in growth politics. My respondents came from all levels of society: village, town, city, prefectural, and national. In interviews ranging from a few minutes to many hours, sometimes in multiple conversations, they told me about their motivations, their use of sanctions and tactics, and their roles in the political process. My approach carries the ethnographic fieldwork method further into the study of elites and power structures (Hunter, 1995).

Upon returning to the United States, I categorized this mountain of material, creating an index of more than 800 response categories. I sifted through the information, searching for important events and seeking to decipher the motives, sanctions, and tactics that influence events. I tried to grasp the situation from the standpoint of the participants. Taking clues from grounded theory (Glaser & Strauss, 1967), I built a pragmatic narrative description of the events, based on how the participants construed and constructed them (Griswold, 1994; Sayer, 1993; Weinberg, 1994). From this, I extracted simplified models of events and the political process.

The Japanese tale of Rashomon is an ancient expression of the post-modern feminist insight that no single viewpoint is necessarily "right."[45] In Rashomon, observers provide completely divergent accounts of a murder. The stories about events related in this book draw from the divergent viewpoints of their participants. They have the Rashomon-like quality of a "reality" seen from many viewpoints. Winners and losers are not always clear. The same person could harbor deeply mixed feelings about an issue. Groups changed sides over time. People gave different accounts of the same "reality." As I absorbed more of the local culture, though, I began to understand events from the residents' point of view. I began to see how their points of view contributed to the construction of those events (Agar, 1983; Geertz, 1973; Giddens, 1993).

---

45. See, for instance Collins, 1991; Kaplan & Grewal, 1994; Smith, 1987.

The main body of most chapters in this book consists of narrative stories about political relationships and events. The conclusion section of each chapter, however, usually switches to a more theory-driven, analytical style. At that point, I hold the narrative up against the various received theories – of politics, social movements and the environment – to see if it bears any resemblance. Sometimes they do, and I exclaim, "Aha!" Just as often, however, they do not, and force me to build a new theory or revise the old.

Most sociological studies analyze many cases to derive general principles from them. This generalizing approach suffers reliability problems because it assumes a high degree of comparability among cases. Furthermore, the generalizing approach usually takes data from only one level of each case – macro, meso, micro, or individual. I reverse this approach. I study one case in depth and consider the interaction among its levels over time. I then draw from a wide range of theory to explain the perceived reality and to reformulate the theories (Ragin & Becker, 1992; Szasz, 1994). This method resembles the extended case-study approach (Burawoy, Burton & Ferguson, 1992). Yet it differs in that I juxtapose, refine and synthesize a wide range of existing theories against the narrative story.

Summary

Japan's miracles and debacles, combined with its historical background and current social structure and culture, make it an ideal setting for investigating the societal causes of the GE dilemma. Japan's pollution miracle was most unexpected, according to our theories of power in ACID societies. For that very reason, the case of Japan may offer some clues as to how a society may resolve its GE dilemmas, even under adverse conditions.

Chapters 2 through 9 present a historical narrative of Japan and Oita's political response to growth and environmental problems. Each chapter addresses a phase or level of that process and explores related theoretical questions. This organization bridges the gap between narrative and theory. It keeps events in chronological order. The process of unfolding is crucial to the theoretical explanations. Social process and structure, like the wave and particle states of the electron, coexist.

Chapter 2 addresses Oita's initial industrial take-off and its subsequent relations with national elites that created its GE dilemma, using this story to assess theories of regional development. Chapter 3 focuses on national pollution politics and the Pollution Diet, including the national cycle of pollution protest, using the story to assess models of the power structure and the impact of social movements on policy change. Chapters 4 and 5 explore the mobilization and early trajectory of pollution protest in villages and towns along the Oita coast, applying social movement theory. Chapter 6 traces the reaction of Oita's elites to this protest, thinking about theories of social control. Chapter 7 traces the struggle between movements and elites up to the Three Conditions policy shift. Chapters 8 and 9 describe elite tactics to nullify this movement victory. Chapter 9 assesses the effects of pollution protest on national politics and public opinion, bringing the story up to the 1990s. Chapter 10 uses data from the entire study to (re)construct theories and models of politics, social movements, Japanese society, and the causes and cures of the GE dilemma.

2

Visions and realities of growth

Growth startup

A *hunger for growth in Oita*

The farming village of Obasama, where we lived for 15 months, consisted of thirty-two wooden farm houses spread out on the mountainsides among terraced rice paddies. The houses had straw tatami-mat floors in the living areas and wooden floors in the dining and new kitchen areas, but still retained their old dirt floor kitchens with wood-fired stoves (*kamado*). Their white walls and gray tile roofs were scattered among the terraced rice paddies. Mossy gray lines of stone walls terraced the oblong rice paddies that climbed the mountain slopes. The paddies were emerald green in spring and summer, straw brown in fall and winter.

Before the Second World War, village life had been very humble. Villagers lived on what they grew – barley, rice, bean curd (*tofu*), vegetables. Only the rich peasants could afford to eat rice. Most ate barley, and gave the rice they grew to their landlord. Villagers got fresh fish only occasionally. A traveling merchant, usually a retired sumo wrestler, occasionally walked over the mountains from Beppu carrying 130 pounds of it on his back. More distant villages could only get salted fish. Back then, the farmers thatched their roofs with straw. Only the village headman, a large landowner, had a bath. This bath was a gigantic iron pot (*goeimon buro*) heated from below by a fire. After the headman's family finished bathing, the other villagers filed in to bathe with the same hot water.

After the Second World War, mechanization and agricultural chemicals had eased their work and improved their harvests. By the time I arrived in 1979, the farmers boasted that they lived a "cultured life" (*bunka seikatsu*). This meant many things. They had secured the basics: good food, good shelter, good health. They had roofed their houses with blue tiles and gotten their own bathtubs.

Tractors and other machines, chemical fertilizers, and pesticides had relieved their backbreaking work in the rice paddies and given them time to work in the new factories.

Beyond that, they enjoyed undreamed-of consumer luxuries: televisions, refrigerators, cars, and a wide variety of foods. Thanks to radio, TV, telephone, and transportation, they felt integrated into the nation. With their new salaries, they were even able to take trips abroad. This new lifestyle signified their passage from isolated pre-war peasants to full participants in the new, booming Japan.

Prosperity had its price. All the fireflies and dragonflies, once the joy of children and the subject of song, had been killed off by pesticides. Abe-san, our landlord and a farmer from a farming household of many generations, explained the situation:

> The pesticide stays on the rice and causes sickness and birth deformities in people. In the old days, there was a good balance between good bugs and bad bugs. They did not do too much harm to the harvest. The grasshoppers ate the rice bugs (*unga*). But the good bugs are weaker to the pesticides and die first, so once you put on pesticides, you have to put on more and more.

Abe-san regretted the loss of the fireflies, but felt the exchange worth it:

> If we didn't use chemical sprays, we couldn't work out the factories or on construction projects . . . and then we couldn't live a cultured life (Abe Genshi, 1980, interview).

Abe-san was living the GE dilemma. Despite his ready acceptance of the trade-off, however, Abe-san was none too sure it would continue long. For centuries, the lot of the average Japanese peasant had been to eke out a marginal existence. Abe-san felt a nagging suspicion that the modern prosperity would soon evaporate.

Many people in Japan held similar suspicions. Despite modern affluence, they still worried the economic miracle would collapse, dumping them once again into poverty and scarcity. This fear of scarcity beset even Japanese elites. A middle manager for the Mitsubishi Trading Company told me, "We have to invest abroad because we need it for insurance. One day the big earthquake will devastate everything in Tokyo." This kind of anxiety pervaded economic activity. The Japanese likened their economy to a bicycle – if it did not keep going fast, it would fall over. Japan's hunger for growth and its response to the GE dilemma must be seen against this backdrop of national anxiety.

Growth for what?

When people use available money (capital) to build factories that produce and sell (or distribute) increasing quantities of goods, they cause growth (Teune, 1988, pp. 60–61). Economists tend to see growth as an unalloyed good. The "invisible hand" of market competition will lead to prosperity for all. Critics question this assumption (Daly & Cobb, 1989; Ophuls, 1977; Teune, 1988). They say the market also has "invisible feet," pollution, rampant urbanization, and others, which kick society.

Growth may raise the general level of prosperity, and enrich some greatly, but it also produces zones of the victimized (Funabashi, 1995). The victimized are so not only due to environmental degradation. The "growth machine" model, for instance, argues that the local real estate owners (*rentiers*) stimulate local growth to raise the value of their own land holdings, causing environmental degradation, urban sprawl, and other problems (Molotch, 1975; Logan & Molotch, 1987). Similarly, the dependency school argues that growth caused by external investment (from the metropolitan or central capitalist countries) exploits the lesser developed countries, causing distorted development.[1] As noted in Chapter 1, the Treadmill of Production model argues that an implicit class compromise between big capital and big labor for more profits and wages speeds up the growth dynamic in environmentally destructive ways. These arguments reveal a basic similarity in all critiques of economic growth: severe inequities in the distribution of its benefits and costs. All these inequities may stem from similar root causes – the nature of which is the basic question of this book.

Growth and its effects depend on a variety of actors and background structural complexes – economic, governmental, social and cultural (Figure 1.6) – the exact mixture of which remains highly debated. Economic arguments point to the need for a skilled and disciplined labor and management force, a market for the goods, means of transportation, a responsible financial system, and a policy of turning profits back into productive investment (within the nation) rather than siphoning it off for personal gain. Economists stress the role of the market, propelled by the business entrepreneur following the profit motive to service or create a demand (Rostow, 1960). In addition, much research has pointed to the helpful role of government in propelling growth (Smith, 1984; Evans, 1995). Governmental actors include the federal or national government (Tarrow, 1991), local government (Goodman, 1979; Haupt, 1980; Zukin, 1985, p. 358), or political coalitions linking national and local levels (Fleischmann & Feagin, 1987; Molotch & Vicari, 1988). Sociologists, on the other hand, stress the social networks among business people and other forms of social capital (Granovetter, 1985). Cultural values that promote individualism, savings, and investment may also be very basic to growth (Weber, 1958; Inkeles, 1974).

1. For an entry into the voluminous work in this field, see Baran, 1957; Wallerstein, 1983; So, 1990; Cardoso & Faletto, 1979; Evans, 1971.

This chapter will probe the sources of economic growth in Oita that set the stage for the ensuing "navel" engagement and other pollution conflicts. Much of Oita's growth impulse, I found, originated in the hunger for a better life held by masses of ordinary people, exemplified by our landlord, Abe-san. But after government and business elites seized upon this hunger, they used it to justify very different goals and outcomes (Scott, 1995, p. 29).

Local roots of growth

In the 1950s, Oita Prefecture was agricultural and poor. It lay off the beaten track of commerce, tucked away on the southern island of Kyushu. Oita's mushrooms, hot springs, and white sand beaches attracted tourists. They kept some farmers, merchants, and hotel keepers employed. But they offered little to Oita's restless youth, who hungered for modern jobs. In Oita, only the Nikko copper refinery and the Sumitomo agricultural chemical company offered such jobs.

By then, Japan had already started rebuilding its big cities. Many cities had been bombed and reduced to charred rubble. The rebuilding created jobs in Tokyo, Osaka and Nagoya. Ironically, the migration of rural youth to fill the jobs made rural conditions even worse. Every year, 5,000 to 10,000 of Oita's middle-school graduates could not find work in Oita. At that time – the 1950s – few students went on to high school. Seeking to escape their poverty, many left to seek their fortunes in Osaka or Tokyo. At Oita's train stations and ports, in an annual ritual of parting, sobbing parents waved goodbye to their fifteen-year-old boys and girls. The parents worried because they knew the kids faced danger in the big cities. Some of their daughters would be seduced away from the hard regimens of the Osaka factories into the night world, lost forever. Farmers feared their eldest sons would not return to take over the farm and carry on the family name. They complained, "No one has pride in farming anymore" (Interview, Oita LDP politician, 1989). Emigration left the countryside depopulated and devitalized.

Japanese culture stresses identity with family, village, and prefecture. This cultural orientation intensified the pain of separation (Fukutake, 1989). After many generations of settled residence, Oitans felt deeply connected to their home town and prefecture (Markus & Kitayama, 1991). These values made Oitans very critical of the local lack of jobs. They talked wistfully about "catching up" to Tokyo. Throughout the 1950s, the Oita Godo Newspaper complained bitterly about the prefecture's "1 percent economy." Despite having 2 percent of Japan's population, the prefecture produced only 1 percent of its economic product. The prefecture had far more farmers in its work force (50.2 percent) than did Japan as a whole (32.6 percent). It had a corresponding lack of manufacturing workers (9.2 percent) compared with the nation (21.9 percent) [Nomura (Sogo Kenkyujo) Nomura Research Institute, 1979, p. 48]. The low income of farmers dragged Oita's average income down to 67 percent of the national average (in 1960).

Under these circumstances, the idea of progress acquired an irresistibly rosy hue. If they could get big business to locate in Oita, people thought, their problems would be solved. Big business would bring a cornucopia of benefits: local jobs for youth, general prosperity, a "cultured life" (bunmeiteki seikatsu). The media fed this ground swell of popular hope. Governor Hosoda fielded the idea of making a small coastal industrial park. It became a hot political issue in the 1955 gubernatorial election.

Elections were something new for Oitans. The Occupation authorities had pried open the political system, giving new power to subordinate groups. The Occupation had reduced the state's symbolic and legal powers and weakened the dominant economic classes. In their place, the Occupation set up democratic institutions and stimulated the teaching of democratic values. The new Constitution allowed basic freedoms, political party formation, local and national elections, and universal voting rights. These new freedoms greatly improved opportunities for informed popular participation in politics (Richardson & Flanagan, 1984, Ch. 2)

Newly released from jail, union leaders and opposition politicians quickly formed unions and parties that soon attracted massive memberships (Fukutake, 1989). Many Japanese people had become thoroughly disillusioned with the old authoritarian state. They were hungry for new ideas and directions. The old ruling elites and groups, disoriented and partially dismantled, were hard pressed to stay in power. Stained by wartime fascism, distrusted by large segments of the public, they had lost legitimacy.[2]

The Japan Socialist party (JSP) quickly grew to rival the Liberal and the Democratic parties in size. In the 1947 national elections, the JSP garnered about 26 per cent of the popular vote and won 143 seats in the House of Representatives (Richardson and Flanagan, 1984, pp. 76–78). At that time,

---

2. Weber defines three types of legitimacy: traditional, legal-rational and charismatic (Weber, 1947). The wartime Japanese state capitalized on all three to convince the public of its rectitude. When the loss of the war revealed the enemy to be a benefactor to many, that rhetoric quickly lost believability. The national government thus lost much of its traditional and charismatic legitimacy. The dominant political party, the LDP, subject to increasingly frequent and severe scandals, gradually weakened the legal-rational legitimacy of the Diet in the public eye (Richardson & Flanagan, 1984). Based on the widespread impression that officials worked faithfully for the benefit of the nation, though, the state ministries retained great legal-rational legitimacy until the 1990s.

each conservative party also received about 26 per cent of the vote. The Communist party received less than 4 per cent.

In the 1955 elections, Oita's two conservative parties, the Liberals and the Democrats, supported the coastal industrial park idea (Interview, LDP politician, 1989). At the national level, the two parties merged that year to form the Liberal Democratic party (LDP). Locally, though, they fielded separate candidates for governor in that election. They faced the JSP's charismatic candidate, Kinoshita Kaoru. In his 1955 gubernatorial campaign speeches, Kinoshita also supported the coastal industrial park idea. He envisioned the industrial park bringing in plentiful jobs and revitalizing local businesses (Kinoshita, 1973). On this basis, Kinoshita won the 1955 election and three more, continuing in office until 1971.

Despite his party affiliation, Kinoshita was no socialist. He had joined the Socialist party as a "marriage of convenience" so that he could enter the race for governor. Kinoshita had been a pillar of the wartime government: representative to the national legislature (the Diet), lawyer, and mayor of Oita City. The Occupation purged him from politics in 1946. As soon as the purge was lifted, he returned to politics. By affiliating with the JSP, he removed his wartime stigma (Kinoshita, 1973). In a personal interview, he expressed his frustration with JSP socialist rhetoric:

I wasn't a socialist, I was a rationalist. [Like the JSP,] I opposed the Emperor system. I recognized that England and America, both capitalist countries, were the most advanced. The Japan Socialist party has to face this fact, but it won't (Interview, Kinoshita Kaoru, January 1979).

Kinoshita saw industrial growth as the key to progress:

In order to exist, Japan has to master scientific knowledge and produce manufactured goods. Agriculture is no good. I knew this. At the time I became governor, I thought, Oita has to become an industrial prefecture.[3]

As revealed here, Governor Kinoshita seemed more concerned with national progress than prefectural progress. Kinoshita's nationalism contrasts with the attitudes of U.S. governors, who see growth strictly in terms of local progress (Haupt, 1980; Goodman, 1979). With the ripening of Oita's GE dilemma, these two goals came increasingly into conflict. This sorely vexed the governor.

The governor was the central figure in prefectural policy-making (Muramatsu, 1986; Steiner et al., 1980, pp. 318–19). He did not have to seek legisla-

3. To nail home his divergence from the Socialist party, the ex-governor added that he liked many of General MacArthur's reforms, but he felt that Article Nine of the new Constitution, which prohibited Japan's possession of military forces, was wrong. Not only should Japan have its own military, he said, it should have nuclear weapons, "because they are the cheapest weapon for a good self-defense."

tive approval for many of his programs (Richardson and Flanagan, 1984, p. 44–45). Under him, the Prefectural Government became the main vehicle for local growth. The governor, in consultation with staff and favored prefectural elites, determined the political agenda (Lukes, 1974; Bachrach and Baratz, 1970). They operated by controlling the legislative and public agenda, much as they had in the past. As the social tensions produced by their growth policies ripened, however, this tactic came increasingly under fire.

Kinoshita recruited Sato Taiichi, a labor union organizer, to head the Prefectural Government's Commerce, Industry, and Labor Section (*Shoko Rodo Bu*). Sato was an unusual and creative activist. He had been imprisoned during the war for trying to unionize soldiers in the Japanese Manchurian army. After the war, he immediately started organizing unions in Oita, and brought their political support to the JSP. According to Sato, the strength of these unions had been crucial in electing Kinoshita (Interview, Sato Taiichi, April 1989). In appointing Sato, then, the governor reassured the unions of their voice in his government. In turn, the political left placed its hopes for a better future in Governor Kinoshita's hands.

Many concerns impelled Kinoshita and Sato to support growth. The governor had promised that during his campaign. Both believed growth would bring local prosperity and provide local jobs, contracts, and customers. At the same time, they had ulterior motives. A big accomplishment would give Kinoshita and Sato a prominent place in prefectural history (Interview, anonymous, 1989). The prefectural JSP hoped that industrial growth would enlarge the working class, strengthening its supporters. The prefectural LDP constantly pressured them for construction contracts for its business supporters. As the idea of growth moved toward reality, these tangential interests and pressures started to shape its content.

Among their concerns, Oita's poverty remained central. Sato and other members of the planning staff had to escort new middle-school graduates to Osaka or Tokyo and find them jobs in small and middle-sized industry. Sato said that

Trouble occurred around job hours, food . . . sleeping conditions were bad . . . Resistance arose among the Oita kids and I had to go solve it (Interview, Sato Taichi, April 1989).

Sato's concern for the prefectural youth, based on his strong identification with the prefecture as a community, spurred his efforts for industrialization. This "thick" identification was to prove an important driving force behind growth in other ways as well.

Seeking a way to bring factories to Oita, Sato studied the Keynesian "full employment plan" used in England. This government-led growth coincided nicely with Japan's statist traditions as well as Sato's socialistic leanings. It gained favor among Japanese local and national government planners (Johnson, 1982). Sato urged government "pump priming" – investment in infrastructure (landfill sites, water systems and roads) – to attract industry. This approach, Sato said, "corrected Marx" by guiding capital to act in socially responsible ways (Interview, Sato Taichi, 1980). It also accorded with revisionist currents in the JSP that favored the gradual, not the revolutionary, path to socialism.[4]

In addition, by industrializing Oita, Kinoshita and Sato hoped to solidify their party's electoral base (OGN, April 25, 1962). They assumed that industrialization would increase Oita's working class, which would vote for the JSP. At the same time, the local LDP also supported industrialization, but for a different reason – providing business for local contractors and merchants. The seeds of conflict already lay dormant within the pro-growth coalition.

During Governor Kinoshita's first term, prefectural finances were so bad that he could not make much headway on the growth plan. But toward the end of the term, national prosperity helped local finances return to even keel. Japanese prefectures receive about 70 percent of their discretionary funds in the form of subsidies, grants-in-aid, and tax rebates from the national government. This leaves them with only "30 percent [financial] local autonomy" (*san wari jichi*) (Steiner et al., 1980, p. 447). (State governments in the United States collect and control about 70 percent of their revenue.) Accordingly, improving national finances provided the prefecture with enough discretionary funds to start looking into the project.

Looking for boosters

Governor Kinoshita and Mr. Sato gravely doubted that big business would invest in Oita Prefecture. Oita lay far from Tokyo, the educational, cultural, commercial, and governmental hub of the nation. It was an obscure hinterland area. Furthermore, they knew big business might be leery of becoming hostage to a socialist party-affiliated local government. Nonetheless, with characteristic energy, Sato went to Tokyo and knocked on corporate doors. By 1956, he had convinced a major paper company to build a branch in Oita.

Paper mills put out a noxious smell and pollute the waters terribly. Because of this, big cities no longer want them around. At the time, though, most Oitans were not concerned about environmental pollution. The rosy vision of growth

---

4. This school of thought is called "Sanogaku" after Mr. Sano, a leader of the labor movement who was arrested during World War Two and forced to change his views. Governor Kinoshita had been his lawyer.

dimmed such fears. In addition, Sato knew that one new major investment in Oita might bring in others.

In 1955, the paper company built its pulp mill on the west bank of the Ono River near the Sumitomo Chemical Plant. To give it a site, the Oita government had to displace the whole village of Nakajima. The Nakajima villagers did not succumb without a long, harsh, and sometimes violent fight. Trying to prevent the pulp plant from acquiring their land, the villagers barricaded the streets and kept outsiders out. In response, the Tokyo-based construction company, notorious for its violence, sent in trucks full of thugs (Interview, Oita construction company official, 1990). However, local elites restrained the company's impulse to use violence and averted bloodshed. Eventually, it acquired the land anyhow. Already, to the Nakajima people, the vision of industrialization looked a bit tarnished. To this day, by the Ono River bridge, the smell of hydrogen sulfide nauseates the new visitor, but local people say they get used to it.

The pulp mill success emboldened Kinoshita and Sato. If one factory would come, why not more? The questions were, how to get them and where to put them? Local businesses had cold feet, and land cost a great deal, on the rare occasions when it was available. Kinoshita and Sato did not relish more protracted fights with displaced villages to secure industrial land. A better way, they decided, was to build more land. They could fill in the shallow waters along the coast of Oita City, as a map of the area shows (Figure 2.1).

Governor Kinoshita tried to convince local businesses to expand and build bigger plants in the proposed seaside zone, but they refused. Local business faced a formidable "economic opportunity structure." Small and medium-sized businesses usually survived as subcontractors to the conglomerates (*keiretsu*). Mitsui, Mitsubishi, and other giants ordered, determined, and marketed their product (Gerlach, 1992, p. 68).[5] Without the giants' approval, banks hesitated to make large loans to local businesses. Many local businesses would not dare expand. Nor could they. Central government laws and directives favored the coordination of regional growth through the national business federations and big companies. Furthermore, the coastal project lacked local incentive. It involved making new land by filling in the sea. Local investors did not already own the industrial land. Fishing families held the rights to use the coastal waters.

Unlike Molotch's landowners in Santa Barbara (Molotch, 1975) who produced the "growth machine," therefore, speculators in Oita had less opportunity to profit from rising land prices. Furthermore, building landfill was an immense task beyond the technical skills of local construction companies. The "big

---

5. This system of controlled marketing also prevents the entry of foreign goods. It was a major point of the U.S. criticism of Japan in the 1989–91 Structural Impediment Initiative talks.

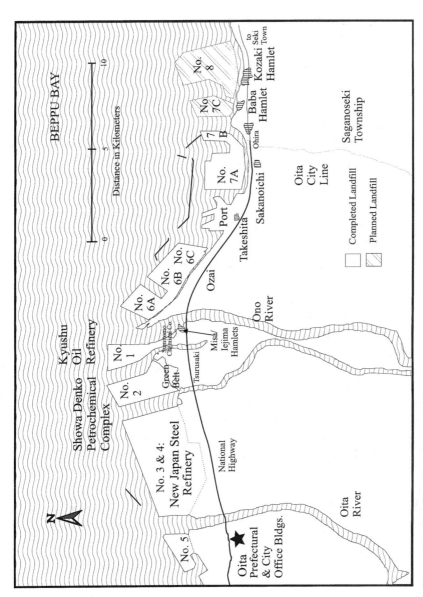

Figure 2.1: The Oita New Industrial City

hands" (*ote*) – the big Tokyo construction companies – would scoop up most of the profit. For these reasons, no local class of growth boosters leapt forth from the Oita business community.

To assemble the requisite technical know-how for the project, Kinoshita and Sato began to build a network of trustworthy experts, academics, and influentials in 1957. They did not reach out blindly; they appealed to fellow Oitans. In Tokyo, virtually every prefecture has its own "home prefecture" club (*kenjinkai*) that keep old-home (*furusato*) nostalgia alive in the hearts of first-generation Tokyoites. Nostalgia burned warmly in their hearts because Tokyo had become urbanized so fast. Even in 1985, one-third of Tokyo residents had been born in rural areas.[6] In 1960, this figure was much higher. Home-prefecture identity drew people together from disparate statuses and professions, illustrating the strength of that identity. (In contrast, New York City or Washington, DC, have no Iowans Club or Floridians Club.)[7]

Sato and Kinoshita asked the Tokyo Oitans Club to form a "booster" circle for home prefecture growth. Through the Club, they recruited a powerful circle: two university professors of industrial location; the president of Hokkaido Electric; Hiramatsu Morihiko, a rising young MITI bureaucrat married to the daughter of the mayor of Oita City; Kuze Kimitaka, an official in the Ministry of Local Autonomy; and Miura Giichi, a right-wing "fixer" (*kuromaku*, lit. "black curtain"). These conservative figures, staunch LDP supporters, were at first a little suspicious of the JSP governor. But their loyalty to Oita Prefecture brought them into cooperation. In Japan, such collective identities create a propensity for networking that can be activated when needed.

From feudal times, Oita (then Bungo) had enjoyed a good network of representatives in Tokyo (Edo). The feudal lords (*daimyo*) had to maintain part-year residences in Edo, at the feet of the Shogun. From all over Kyushu, the lords used Bungo as their port of departure for the boat trip up the Inland Sea to Osaka, and thence to Edo. Oita boatmen visited the big cities and became cosmopolitan, even though loyalty to fief and lord remained paramount. Social change, rather than destroying local loyalties, transformed and used them. People found work in the cities through hometown ties. As a result, Japanese

6. The 1985 population of the Tokyo metropolitan area was over 30 million, one quarter of the entire population of Japan. Of this, about 10 million had come there by migration from other parts of Japan (Kokuseisha, 1988)

7. However, such clubs have been noted in the cities of another rapidly developing society, in Istanbul and Ankara, Turkey (personal communication, Uygur Ozesmi). They are likely the typical result of rapid industrial growth and urbanization, rather than some particular cultural characteristics.

society retained strong collective loyalties and sentiments (Nakane, 1970; Vogel, 1979; Lebra, 1976).

The rosy vision

In 1958, Governor Kinoshita, his officials, and the booster group refined and formalized plans for an Oita-Tsurusaki Seaside Industrial Zone (*Oita Tsurusaki Rinkai Kogyo Chitai*). They envisioned a model industrial park that would entice labor-intensive industry – a shipyard or an auto assembly plant – to Oita. This industry would employ young people and teach them semi-technical skills. The university professors modeled the industrial park on the best Western designs, with a 400-meter-wide green belt between the factories and the city. The initial plan was small, about 52 acres, enough for a few medium-sized factories.

The young MITI bureaucrat Hiramatsu, however, had other ideas. An Oitan described Hiramatsu as "one of the moving figures behind Japan's rapid development, with a lot of personal power" (Interview, anonymous, 1979). Hiramatsu had just returned from a world tour of major industrial complexes. He had been impressed by regional "growth pole" strategies in the United States and France, and wanted something bigger for Oita.

A few major industries started with a little government help, Hiramatsu argued, would send off a wave of economic stimulus (*hakyu koka*). This wave would spread throughout the surrounding area, stimulating local manufacturing and employment. Hiramatsu suggested that Oita start with an integrated oil and steel refining complex that would provide this stimulus. This idea, he said, was not a national government strategy at the time, but his own creative suggestion (Interview, Hiramatsu Morihiko, 1980).

His suggestions ran contrary to Oita's hopes to immediately bring labor-intensive factories, but made sense as a long-term strategy. In any case, the blessing of a strong MITI official made the whole project seem much more feasible to Sato and Kinoshita. At this juncture in Oita's growth-decision process, then, a national government official forcefully inserted a new idea – that of a steel-petrochemical complex. This idea and MITI's support for it changed the trajectory of Oita's growth. Adoption of the refinery complex plan cemented the bond between Oita and Hiramatsu.

In 1958, the Governor announced the Seaside Industrial Zone plan to the public. The official plan aimed to create:

... a base in steel and oil refineries, and about 300 modern machinery, electricity, shipyard, automobile, and chemical factories all situated carefully in a big green belt . . . (which) will provide full employment for the prefecture (OGN, April 25, 1962).

These visionary claims garnered wide public support. The prospect of industrial growth excited prefectural officials and ordinary citizens alike. On the horizon, it seemed, they could see the treasure ship of Japanese mythology coming into port. Few worried about pollution. Stories of London's sparrows turned black from smoke only excited admiration (Interview, anonymous, 1989).

Within the JSP, however, some critics voiced doubts. They feared that cooperation with "monopoly capital" could bring no good. The big conglomerates would exploit the prefecture and hurt its citizens. Sato, the enthusiastic booster within the JSP, disagreed. Big industry, he argued, would pay high wages and increase union membership. This would both help the prefectural economy and increase the number of JSP supporters. These two points of view reflected two approaches to capitalism within the socialist camp: rejection versus accommodation. As events unfolded, neither proved very realistic.

Recruiting big business

By the time of his second election campaign (1959), Governor Kinoshita had launched a campaign to bring Tokyo businesses to the Seaside project. This pleased both the moderate wing of the JSP and the LDP, each for their own reasons. From that election on, both the JSP and the LDP supported Kinoshita. He became a multi-party candidate, something fairly common in Japan, where prefectural loyalties often loom larger than ideological differences.

By then, the circle of boosters included Oita's two representatives to the lower house of the national Diet. Ichimanda had been Chairman of the Board (*sosai*) of the Bank of Japan and several times Minister of Finance. Nishimura had been the vice president of the LDP. The circle also included Mayor Ueda of Oita City and Kato Tadashi, a local businessman and politician who was Ichimanda's chief supporter. These boosters pushed other LDP officials into support of Oita's growth efforts.[8] LDP support could cut red tape and break down bureaucratic barriers. But it could not force businesses to build plants in Oita.

Accordingly, the Governor and Sato went "hat in hand" from door to door of the big Tokyo companies. To their dismay, they met only cold rebuff. Big business had no interest in moving to Oita. A move to the hinterland would raise shipping costs and complicate communications. Business leaders liked Tokyo for status reasons too. Since 1603, Tokyo had been Japan's combined Washington, Boston, New York, and Pittsburgh – simultaneously the center of government, culture, commerce and industry. Living there meant one had "made it." One company manager, Sato said, even pronounced Oita's name "Daibun" (a

---

8. Such as Iwasaki Mitsugu, the LDP treasurer (*kanjicho*).

possible reading of the Chinese characters, but one displaying shocking ignorance). This mistake made Kinoshita and Sato even more ashamed of their prefecture's backward status and fueled their determination to "catch up." But they were losing confidence. Getting the pulp factory began to seem like a fluke. Within the centralized Japanese system, they had few levers left to pull.

The growth fellowship

Frustrated but not yet crushed, the Governor returned to the Tokyo Oitans Club. Once again, hometown solidarity rescued the cause. More influential Oitans joined the booster circle: industrial leader Nakane Sadahiko, Diet representative Goto Fumio, even the famous underworld fixer Miura Giichi. Each member of the circle contributed a special kind of influence.

Nakane Sadahiko mobilized support within the Tokyo business community (Interview, anonymous, 1988). Nakane, former high official in the wartime Bank of Japan (*Nihon Ginko*), had suffered MacArthur's purge. Afterward, like so many others, he quickly rebounded, taking the post of president of the Sanwa Bank. Nakane's talent for writing *waka* poetry had solidified his prestige in elite circles.

To build big business support for Oita, Nakane turned to his friends Hoshino Yasunosuke and Ando Toyoroku. Not by accident, both were presidents of companies in the Mitsui group (*keiretsu*), which already had close, almost paternal interests in Oita. Hoshino led the mammoth Mitsui Bussan trading firm, which conducted most of the conglomerate's trade. Ando presided over the Onoda Cement Company, a Mitsui Group member. Onoda Cement used about a third of the Nikko refinery's copper from Oita's Seki peninsula. Strengthening ties with Oita could benefit both company and prefecture. Accordingly, Hoshino and Ando worked hard to generate wider business interest in Oita (Interview, anonymous, 1988). This chain of influence indicates that rather than operating through often-used social networks, project entrepreneurs such as Hoshino picked from among their potential social networks to find people with a potential interest in the project, activated those relations, and used what collective identities they could refer to, to solidify them.

Once you secure corporate willingness, Sato explained, if you want to build a large-scale landfill project, you have to get your paperwork right. Representative Goto Fumio ushered the project smoothly through government bureaucracies and permits. Goto was a very powerful political figure. A Tokyo University graduate, he had been in charge of the Bureau of Internal Security (*Keihokyoku*) during the war under the Ministry of Home Affairs. He had been Minister of Home Affairs during the 2–2-6 Incident in 1931 when right-wing militarists assassinated the Prime Minister. Then he had been Minister of Agriculture and General Director (Somu Chokan) of the colony of Taiwan. After the purge, he too rebounded quickly. In Sato's words, the fixer Miura Giichi said "make him a Diet representative," and it was done (Interview, Taiichi Sato, April 1989). After the war, as a Diet representative, Goto had uncommon influence with all the Cabinet ministers.

Perhaps Miura Giichi brought the most power to the Oita Growth fellowship. Miura was a very influential right-wing fixer in post-war Japanese politics. A prominent Oita LDP politician said that Miura and another fixer (Mitarai Tatsuo) played crucial roles in Oita's growth project. Miura Giichi, nicknamed the "Muromachi Shogun," led the Japan National Essence Society (*Nihon Kokusuikai*). His offices occupied the entire fourth floor of the Mitsui Building in downtown Tokyo. LDP politicians, business leaders, and bureaucrats such as Goto and Nakane, who had been members of the wartime government, resonated deeply with his fierce traditional patriotism.[9]

Five or ten fixers exercised great political power. One LDP politician told me fixers could dictate the decisions of powerful ministers of state (Interview, anonymous, April 1989). Fixers, he explained, got their power from "black money" and connections to extreme right-wing political groups and criminal syndicates (*yakuza*). Sometimes, they backed up their demands with violence.[10] In their public persona, though, fixers presented themselves as patriots, as "fighters for the nation" (*kokushi*) defending the restoration of the Emperor. From this point of view, industrial growth augmented national glory.

Sato Taiichi visited Miura to ask for his help on the Oita project (Interview, Taiichi Sato, April 1989). Socialist versus reactionary, they stood at opposite political poles. But Miura liked the younger Sato. Besides coming from the same prefecture, Sato's mother led the Oita branch of the Japan National Essence party. During Sato's visit, Miura, to show his cooperation with the Oita growth cause, called the Prime Minister and told him to appoint Ayabe Kentaro as Minister of Transportation. The PM replied, "That's difficult." In Japanese, that usually signifies total refusal. Shortly thereafter, Ayabe became Minster of

9. An incident just after World War Two made him famous. A candy store near the Imperial palace planned to build a three-story building. From the top, common people could have looked down upon the Imperial palace for the first time in Japanese history. Such effrontery infuriated Miura. He mobilized a group of followers and staged a riot in the partially constructed building. The riot stopped the building at two stories. This incident certified Miura's purity as a right-wing nationalist.

10. Though their influence has declined somewhat, fixers still exercise considerable influence. Kodama Yoshio, a "disciple" of Miura Giichi, famous for his role in facilitating the Lockheed bribery of Prime Minister Tanaka, provides a more recent example. See Kaplan & Dubro, 1986, Chp. 4.

Transportation. This post gave Ayabe convenient influence over road and harbor permits, just when Oita needed them.

This diverse group of boosters, motivated by a common allegiance to their home prefecture, applied insistent pressure on big business and the national government. President Ando of Onoda Cement spearheaded the effort within the Mitsui Group. He and his colleagues decided to found the Kyushu Oil Co.(*Kyuseki*) and build its refinery in Oita. In 1960, the Yahata Steel Company, also affiliated with Mitsui, agreed to back Kyuseki. Yahata Steel had wanted to build an oil refinery somewhere in Kyushu anyhow, and responded to the boosters arguments about the attractiveness of Oita.

Ando identified *deep trust* among the Oita boosters, based on their common prefectural origins, as the most important ingredient in making the Kyushu Oil Company (Interview, Ando Toyoroku, 1980). This deep trust, and the group solidarity it engendered, crucially facilitated Oita's growth. The integrating force of collective identity and social networks among the members of the Oita Growth Fellowship supports the network state concept (Chapter 1). The personal relations among MITI official Hiramatsu, business, and political leaders and local government officials illustrates its basic tenets – that the Japanese state guides the society through a dense network of personal ties.

In order to make growth happen in Oita, the actors creatively used existing symbolic and normative forms (deep trust and groupism) to build the necessary social networks and operating organizations. Existing institutional structures posed certain barriers to Oita's growth, which the actors had to overcome creatively. Conversely, this also means that existing structures did not dictate that growth should take place in Oita and not elsewhere. Rather, actors drew on symbolic and normative elements in creative ways to make something new happen, for their own instrumental purposes. By these acts, the Oita boosters switched the juggernaut of national growth onto a slightly divergent track, sending it to Oita instead of some other prefecture. But as they did so, ironically, they also changed the meaning and effects of growth for Oita.

Power to the periphery?

In Japan, the task of preparing "infrastructure" is more extensive than in the United States, where flat land is plentiful. If the purpose is lucrative enough, Japanese developers often construct land afresh by filling in shallow coastal waters. In 1959, using Yahata Steel's promises as collateral, the Oita Government borrowed money and let out contracts for Landfill No. 1. A Tokyo construction firm started work, employing local subcontractors for parts of the job.

They built a concrete wall out from the shore, down several kilometers, and back in again. The rectangle enclosed a space of 1,229,000 square meters. Barges with huge hoses sucked up mud from the floor of Beppu Bay and filled in the rectangle, creating Landfill No. 1 (see Figure 2.1).

An oil refinery – distillation towers spread over acres laced together by an undergrowth of pipes – resembles a metallic jungle. Crude oil percolates through the pipes and down the towers under central, computerized guidance. Finished in 1968, the Kyushu Oil refinery symbolized the modernity of Oita Prefecture. But even while it was under construction, Kinoshita and Sato knew it would not help their social goals very much. Running the plant did not require many workers, and half of those would be specialists with lots of training. As a result, the refinery would not provide many jobs for locals. Governor Kinoshita and the other growth boosters knew this from the start. The refinery was only the first step. It was a signal of Oita's potential for industrial growth that would attract other industries. Next, Governor Kinoshita planned to bring in more labor-intensive industries such as auto manufacturing. Such industries would provide the high paying, semi-skilled jobs that local people wanted, and train them for the jobs too.

National elites had other ideas. In 1960, to satisfy its business supporters and urban voters, the LDP Ikeda Cabinet advocated the "Income Doubling Plan" (*Baizoron*). This famous plan predicted a growth rate of 9 percent per year. The Economic Planning Agency (EPA) decried this estimate as too optimistic, but it turned out too modest. Between 1961 and 1965, the economy grew at an average rate of 10.4 percent. The Income Doubling Plan targeted growth a little outside the crowded cities, in the already heavily industrialized Pacific Coast Belt (see Figure 1.7). To provide industrial labor, the Ikeda Cabinet wanted to move excess agricultural population and new industrial investment to this area (Interview, MITI official, July 1979). The thrust of growth, in other words, did not extend to Oita.

Oita had not been alone in its desire to industrialize. Many hinterland prefectures faced similar problems. Mizushima, just across the Inland Sea from Oita, was no exception. Oita and Mizushima joined forces and jointly petitioned the national government for help. Local government finances remained under tight national supervision, even after the liberalizing reforms of the Occupation. Along with grants, they wanted central government permission to sell bonds. Grants and bonds would pay for the initial investment in industrial infrastructure: the landfill, roads, and water mains that would attract companies.

Their petition set an example that spread with contagious rapidity. It mobilized a social movement for growth, with local governments as recruits. Soon, the cry for growth came from all rural quarters. In all, thirty-nine prefectures, including almost every rural one, as well as forty-four municipalities, joined the chorus. Dozens of petition delegations headed for the national government.

The drafters of the Income Doubling Plan, high-placed members of the Ruling Triad, had not expected this hinterland reaction. Despite being caught off guard, in short order the LDP called for a program of aid to industrialize the hinterland. With typical efficiency, the government appeared to be well on its way to solving the problem.

To design the law, the LDP requested a number of government ministries and agencies to submit competitive drafts. They put a great deal of effort into these drafts. Administration of the flow of resources would enhance the winning ministry's prestige. In addition, ministries or agencies mandated for social welfare goals hoped-for improvements in rural quality of life.

To provide an overall framework for this effort, the National Land Agency (NLA, *Kokudocho*) completed its First National Comprehensive Development Plan in 1961 (National Land Agency, 1961). This plan envisioned growth poles (*kyoten kaihatsu*) in rural areas to pull industry and population away from the cities. Its stated purpose was alleviation of the poor living conditions caused by the overcrowding/underpopulation problem. The same theme was to characterize all subsequent national land use plans.

MITI official Hiramatsu had brought the growth pole idea back from a study tour in Europe, where it was popular. Hiramatsu also admired the gigantic oil and steel refinery complexes in the Soviet Union. In theory, the economic stimulus (*hakyu koka*) from a large oil and steel refinery core would stimulate medium and small satellite industries all around it. This would produce local jobs, raise income levels, keep local youth in the region, and reduce the overcrowding of the cities (*Shukan Daiyamondo*, 1975, p. 78).[11] Betraying their lineage, the MITI planners called these refinery cores by their Russian term, *kombinat*. Japan was not a socialist command economy, however. Ministries could not *order* industries to the hinterland. At best, they could only induce them with incentives: tax holidays, good port facilities, land to build on, and a good water and highway system.

Three ministries submitted drafts of the NIC Law: MITI, the Ministry of Home Affairs (MOHA), and the Ministry of Construction (MOC). They fought jealous turf wars over whose draft law would be accepted, each pursuing its own mandate and prerogative. Some ministries approached the task with a genuine zeal for public service; others saw it as a chance for doling out patronage. MITI wanted to foster national economic growth. MOHA wanted to solve social

11. Special issue on regional economy.

problems by moving jobs to the hinterland areas. MOC worked with giant real estate companies to expand the building of public works projects, from which the companies profited handsomely. Another four ministries added amendments to their drafts (Interview, former MITI official, July 1990). Among these competing drafts, MITI's draft seemed most economically feasible.[12] MITI argued reasonably that given budget constraints, government growth subsidies should focus on just one or two growth poles. Otherwise, MITI bureaucrats argued, the policy would not work – it would be unable to stimulate a strong wave of rural industrialization and jobs. Furthermore, MITI argued, if confined to a few sites, the NIC Law would not harm the Pacific Coast Belt focus of the Income Doubling Plan.

Comments from a young official from the Ministry of Construction, who had just finished a two-year assignment with the National Land Agency (in 1980), illuminated their difference in mandates. He had enjoyed working at the National Land Agency, he said, because the job had been creating ideal development plans for the nation. He felt depressed about returning to the Ministry of Construction. In the MOC, he said, "politics" would distort fair and rational plans (Interview, MOC official, 1979).

By this comment, the official was referring to the constant, often successful pressure from construction companies and their cooperating LDP politicians for government contracts for public works. In what one Japanese political scientist called a "pork barrel network" (Masumi, 1995, p. 11), Japanese construction companies colluded in the well-known *dango* system to raise the level of their bids, thus forcing the government to pay exorbitant rates for public projects. Some of this excess profit went to the top LDP Diet politicians who had represented their interests to the MOC. These LDP politicians then used the money to fund their group of supporting LDP Diet members (*habatsu*), who in turn used the money to fund their local electoral activities (as described in Chapter 6).

As a result of this system, Japan is littered with expensive public works projects – roads, dams, railroad stations, landfill, seawalls – of dubious or no utility.[13] This system of public works largess not only unnecessarily damaged much of the Japanese natural landscape. It also contributed to the huge government budget deficits that led to Japan's 1991 "bubble bust" and subsequent recession.[14] Each year in Japan, public works projects cost about US$300 bil-

---

12. In 1960, MITI had already drafted a "National Plan for the Adequate Distribution of Industry."

13. For evidence and research on the influence of the construction industry in politics, see Masumi, 1995, p. 244.

14. For information on this causal connection, see Masumi, 1995, p. 11; Pollack, 1997.

lion, more than the U.S. military budget (Pollack, 1997). This was a "growth machine" on a gigantic scale, a "construction state" (*doken kokka*) as critics called it (McCormack, 1996).

The Ministry of Home Affairs, as well as its later, like-minded National Land Agency, though, were not party to this growth machine, nor were they concerned solely about national economic growth. Their mandate was to help local government finances, and to plan for a national use of land and distribution of industry that would help solve social problems, such as rural depopulation and urban overcrowding. A former director of the National Land Agency revealed the tension between his agency and the growth plans of the LDP:

The Ikeda Cabinet pushed for growth in the Pacific Coast Belt area. But we [bureaucrats at the National Land Agency] . . . pushed for the New Industrial Cities law to reduce regional differences in income and stop the over-concentration of population (Interview, NLA official, 1979).

The Ikeda Cabinet's support for growth in the already-developed Pacific Coast Belt area undercut any attempt to spread growth to genuinely underdeveloped hinterland areas in Kyushu, along the Japan Sea, and in Northeastern Japan. In the ministries and agencies, officials charged with designing the NIC Law drafts began to feel frustrated and manipulated.

The Ikeda Cabinet initially approved of the NIC Law drafted by MITI, perhaps as the plan which forced the least industry outside the Pacific Coast Belt. MITI's rationality, however, did not square with political realities. To make MITI's draft into law, the Diet had to pass it. If the LDP voted as a bloc, as it usually did, it could pass any normal law. Party unity, though, broke down over the MITI bill. Rural Diet representatives argued that aid to just one or two sites would not appease the widespread rural demands. Provision of such poor patronage, they cautioned, might endanger the LDP's rural support.

Faced with this dilemma, Miyazawa Kiichi, a Lower House representative and Cabinet Minister of the Economic Planning Agency, took action. He called together a group of eight other powerful LDP politicians. The group included Kono Ichiro, Ohira Masayoshi and Sato Eisaku (both future prime ministers). The group demanded more sites (Interview, MITI official then affiliated with NIC project, 1990). As a result, the LDP Policy Affairs Committee (*Seichokai*) changed the MITI draft from asking for one or two sites to proposing growth subsidies for fifteen sites. Economic Planning Agency officials criticized this change. They argued that having so many sites would greatly dilute the aid to each one, rendering the NIC policy meaningless. Nonetheless, the Diet passed the bill into law in 1962.

In its new form, the NIC Law satisfied both rural LDP politicians and the construction companies and their LDP supporters.[15] With so many sites, many rural LDP politicians would be able to get their home prefecture designated. This would bring them political capital – legitimacy in the eyes of voters. At the same time, the large Tokyo-based construction companies would become the main contractors for the many public works projects in the hinterland that the NIC law would stimulate. This would bring in large profits, with some of it skimmed off to their LDP friends. Even if having so many sites did seriously weaken the social impact of the policy and ultimately run the Prefectural Governments into useless debt, the symbolic attractiveness of the NIC Law to growth-hungry rural areas served elite purposes well.

The NIC Law presented its social objectives in clear terms. The first paragraph of the Law stated:

> The purpose of this law is to stop the over-concentration of population and industries in the big cities, to correct regional imbalances and to stabilize employment. By providing locational conditions and city facilities for industry, it will foster the growth of New Industrial Cities that will become centers of growth and progress in the hinterland. This will contribute to a balanced form of national growth and popular economy (Japanese Government, nd, p. 1801).

The new growth poles, the law stated, would stimulate related industries in the area, spreading employment and skills outward in concentric waves (*hakyu koka*). As a result, the law predicted, by 1970 each designated site would grow to 4,900 acres of new industrial land, an industrial output value of $2 billion, and a population of 300,000. However, as we shall see, while landfill and output grew, the local employment and skills training effects lagged far behind.

Making the New Industrial City

Defining "progress"

Once the NIC Law passed, prefectures in good faith competed for designation as one of the fifteen sites. They hoped the law's provisions would help them industrialize, despite shrunken subsidies. They developed and submitted a proposal for NIC growth, with details of harbors, roads, and other infrastructure. This process wended through a labyrinth of regional councils, review boards, and government ministries and agencies. At every juncture, informal negotiations lay beneath the formal surface. Securing designations required mobilizing great political pressure, thoroughly mixing the formal and informal.

---

15. Extensively reported on in national newspapers in the 1963–4 period.

In Oita, the governor and prefectural bureaucrats produced a draft NIC plan. The prefectural legislature played little role here, as Japanese law does not require local legislative approval for such plans. The governor secured LDP approval by prior informal "root-binding" (*nemawashi*) consultation. The NIC draft first went to the prefectural NIC Advisory Council for citizen review. NIC Law required a local advisory council (*shingikai*) to provide "citizen participation" (*jumin sanka*) in the planning process. Its forty members were local scholars, businessmen, and "authorities" hand-picked by the governor (who also served as Council chairman), plus a few representatives from MITI and other national ministries. One prominent LDP Diet representative commented:

The Planning Office selected people for (advisory council) membership who reflected the prefecture's thinking . . . They didn't select anyone in the opposition, because they'd upset things . . . (Interview, Oita University professor, October 1978).

The Council approved the draft plan largely as received. A conservative professor of economics, business community advisor and frequent member of such councils, commented:

All the members agree with the Prefecture's plans, so there is no serious discussion. At one meeting after thirty minutes of discussion, the official asked for approval . . . the Prefecture only wants approval of what they've already prepared (Interview, Oita University professor, April 1979).

Local critics called the Council another "invisibility cloak" (*kakuremino*) strengthening bureaucratic real power.

After securing local approval, the Prefectural Government consulted extensively with regional and national elites. Oita's Diet representative took the plan to the Kyushu LDP for review by its Development Council. This Council integrated all the plans into a "vision" of Kyushu's growth (Interview, Tokyo LDP official, April 1979). The Kyushu LDP presented this "vision" to the Kyushu Industrial Structure Advisory Council. Operating under MITI, this Council worked at both regional and national levels to integrate economic functions and growth. MITI published the results of the Council as an "Industrial Structure Vision" for the Kyushu Region. The 1978 edition, 474 pages long, provided a comprehensive analysis of the Kyushu economy, sector by sector, and its future growth. Beyond this, the vision represented the ideological consensus of major regional conservative elites.

The Diet representatives then took their adjusted plans back to their home prefectures. The governor changed the content to follow the LDP's and MITI's guidelines. At this time, MITI wanted to expand Japan's oil and steel refinery capacity. It needed new areas for the construction of ultra-modernized refineries. As Okimoto notes, the relationship between MITI and big business was one of cooperation, not control (Okimoto, 1989). This advice ran counter to Oita's original hope to provide many local jobs. But MITI persuaded Oita officials that the complex would stimulate local growth based on the growth pole approach.

Following MITI's guidance, Oita's plan abandoned labor-intensive industries. Oita gave up on auto manufacturing and accepted a refinery complex instead. The new draft took an upbeat note, arguing that such a complex would strongly stimulate economic growth throughout the prefecture.[16] Under this rationale, Oita's proposed NIC site expanded from the immediate landfill areas to a much wider surrounding area. This new area covered 1,155 km² (9.2 percent of the entire prefectural area), including three cities and seven towns (see Figure 1.8). The refineries, the planners argued, would provide raw materials to local manufacturers. In turn, the local factories would hire and train the local farming youth. This would increase skill levels, pay and standard of living, consumer demand, and the local business economy.

When Oita finally submitted the plan to the national government, a number of ministries tugged at different parts of it. The Ministry of Transportation controlled harbor construction; MITI determined the type of industry and its productive capacity; the Council of Bureaucratic Vice-Ministers (*Jimujikan Kaigi*) coordinated ministerial demands for the plan. Then the plan went to the Regional Industrial Development Advisory Council and the NIC Deliberation Council for review and comment. The powerful big business leaders and top academics on these Councils made them more than mere rubber stamps for the bureaucracy. The supposed "citizen-representation" function of the councils worked in this case, largely because the "citizens" were mainly representatives from big business.

Petition politics

During this review process, Oita conducted an informal but intense campaign to secure designation. The campaign followed the traditional form of "petition politics" – local notables trying to persuade, cajole, and pressure the ministries into designation. In some ways, the repertoire of informal pressure norms had changed little from the late nineteenth century. Officials accepted and expected petition groups. Officials and petitioners alike accepted and expected this form of pressure, with its nuances of deference and paternal responsibility. It formed an institution, with roots in the identities, beliefs, norms, and practices of the actors.

---

16. For the importance of linkages, see Hirschman, 1981.

These informal hierarchical institutions continued despite the Occupation's democratization of the formal political institutions. The Occupation's changes had weakened the state and given more formal power to the voter. From a strictly rational point of view, then, it would have made more sense for the petition groups to address only Diet members. They had the formal power to make decisions. The real practices of power, however, did not entirely follow the new formal institutions. The LDP did not dominate politics as the principal actor, nor did the ministerial bureaucracy act only as its "agent" (Ramseyer & Rosenbluth, 1993). To the contrary, power grew from a complex set of institutionalized relationships among these and other elites. The practices of petition politics recognized and honored these institutions.

In this campaign, the governor carefully gathered and placed his "chess pieces" – Diet members, Tokyo elites, prefectural officials, and local citizens' groups. Despite varying motives, the several types of supporters joined forces under the common banner of prefectural growth. The collective symbol of growth for their home prefecture became their collective motivation – a moral rationale lubricating smooth cooperation. Oita's LDP Diet members led the groups and opened ministerial doors. The groups approached the ministries with the posture of earnest supplicants, appealing to paternalistic mercy and concern. Often, like protest movements, they sat in the ministerial halls all day. Unlike protest movements, they did not use anti-institutional methods. They sat there to demonstrate, not their opposition to the government, but their "sincerity" – their readiness and eagerness to comply with government policies (Lebra, 1976). They wanted to show the officials that if designated as an NIC, industrial growth would go smoothly in Oita. They left the halls promptly and politely at 5 pm.

In the midst of Oita's stampede toward industrial growth, a few doubters held back. Some Socialist party members voiced concern about cooperating with monopoly capital. Even some conservative politicians saw danger in an NIC designation. At one meeting in 1962, an LDP Diet member cautioned the governor:

You should realize that the government only cares about building industry. Designation as an NIC could delay the building of public facilities in the prefecture (Interview, anonymous, 1979).

By public facilities, he meant schools, sewers and other socially needed projects. Putting the project under national government direction, he implied, would exacerbate, not solve social problems. Surprisingly, other conservative observers were equally hesitant. Okita Saburo, the dean of pro-government economists in Japan, commented publicly in 1963:

. . . judging from government policies up to now, I fear that the NIC projects will emphasize production first and neglect the people's life and culture . . . (OGN, July 13, 1963).

These doubts did not dissuade Oita's officials from their vision of growth.

The Tokyo Oitans club created the "New Industrial City Construction Promotion Alliance," with Mr. Nakane of the Kyushu Oil Company as its head. Ten top members of the Tokyo business and financial elite, along with Goto Fumio, Oita's powerful Diet representative, joined the Alliance (Interview, Sato Taiichi, 1989).

Petition politics wove its own web of entanglements. Oita's Diet representatives did not work free – they demanded favors in return. If a community wanted to get local projects funded, they had to show high voter turnout for the politician. The quid pro quo went high into the LDP. Ono Bamboku, one of the most powerful LDP leaders (Thayer, 1969), reportedly demanded a one million yen political donation from Governor Kinoshita in return for securing the NIC designation (Interview, Oita official affiliated with the process, 1979). The governor angrily refused. Shortly thereafter, Minister of Construction Kono Ichiro, evidently cooperating with Ono, said that Oita would not get the NIC designation. Clearly, the LDP was not a monolithic entity working under a unified policy. Numerous factions competed for advantage and resources; the members of a different faction were fair game.

However, Governor Kinoshita and Sato believed that Ono and Kono were bluffing in order to get political donations. They did not believe that Ono and Kono had such total power over NIC designations. Concerned, though, the Governor met with the officials in charge of the Economic Planning Agency. They reassured him that politics would not intervene, that Oita Prefecture would receive designation as an NIC site.

In 1964, the Prime Minister approved Oita as one of the fifteen New Industrial Cities. Many local citizens rejoiced and looked forward to a cornucopia of benefits from modernization. The local newspaper ran a series of articles entitled, "The Dawn of Hope – Oita's NIC" (OGN, January 1964). Few people worried about the rider on the designation that urged caution about pollution.

Oita's LDP Representative Murakami, a member of the Ono faction, claimed credit for the NIC designation. Governor Kinoshita denied that. An Oita official told me that, actually, the LDP had played an insignificant role in Oita's NIC designation. Ultimately, he said, Oita got the designation because of its good harbor facilities and location within the Inland Sea. To business interests, these provided good conditions for a major new refinery complex. Despite this, the LDP clearly fought for the *image* or reputation of providing public works – one of its best political resources.

Oita's NIC plan

Oita's NIC plan confidently expressed its vision of growth:

The Role of the New Industrial City

The New Industrial City on Oita's shore will develop large scale industry at its core. It will urbanize the area . . . [in order] to stop the over-concentration of population and industry in the big central cities. Also, as a growing point of Kyushu's development, it is planned to correct regional (economic and population) imbalances and stabilize local employment. In that way, it will help balance national development and improve the public economy (National Land Agency, nd, pp. 33–34).

The plan specified an oil and steel refinery complex as the core of the project. Given the scarcity of land, Japanese developers often fill in shallow coastal waters to provide space for such a project. Oita's original plans had called for a small landfill area, about 10 to 20 hectares (28 to 56 acres). During the NIC planning process, however, the area ballooned to 1,066 hectares (2,633 acres, about 1 mile wide and 2 miles long in total area) (Oita Prefectural Government, 1983). The plan envisioned Landfills No. 1 through 5 stretching from the Oita River on the west to the Ono River on the east, a distance of about 8 kilometers (see Figure 2.1). This area later became known as Phase One of the NIC. Later, Phase Two (announced in 1970) added another 1,100 hectares to the total. This made Oita's NIC area arguably the world's largest landfill project.

The plan envisioned small and medium-sized businesses nurtured by the core complex. The core refineries would improve their management skills, upgrade their technology, modernize their facilities, and stabilize their labor force. Chemical, ceramic, and machinery fabricators would come to use the flow of raw materials from the refineries. The Prefectural Government would construct the necessary land for factories, housing, industrial and residential water and sewage systems, roads, railroads, and harbor. The influx of new workers would double the population in the NIC site. At the same time, the plan vowed to:

take all due precautions so that industrial pollution will not interfere with the residential environment, farming, forestry or fishing industries, or tourism.

It would separate residential land from industrial sites by a green belt to prevent pollution. It would also:

prevent problems due to sudden rises in land prices resulting from industrial and residential development.

At this time, the NIC plan did not mention Phase Two, which so stirred later controversy.

The governor worked hard to whip up enthusiasm for this daunting growth plan. He dangled the marvels of modernization before the public's hungry eyes. He claimed that the NIC stimulus would raise the productive output of the Oita

City area eight-fold, from 218 million yen (1960) to 1,672 million by 1970. Industrial production would rise from 60 percent to 81 percent of the GPP (gross prefectural product), sharply increasing industrial jobs and tripling average income (Mainichi Newspaper, October 22, 1961). He predicted that the population of Oita City would swell from 461,732 (1961) to 700,000 (1971), and total prefectural population from 1,187,000 (1965) to 1,300,000 (1980). These visions of prosperity heartened the prefectural folks who wanted jobs for their kids. MITI's growth pole idea carried the day.

How much and to whom?

Political pressures continued to shape the NIC Law during its implementation. As usual with Japanese law, the NIC Law was very vague. It did not specify how much aid it would give to each site. Ministries continued to feud and argue over this question, each citing their own statistics, projections, and rationales. MITI still wanted large and effective grants to one or two sites (Interview, MITI official then affiliated with the NIC project, July 1990). The Ministry of Home Affairs (MOHA) pushed for medium-sized subsidies to many sites. The Ministry of Finance, trying to tighten the purse strings, advocated a bare minimum of total aid (OGN, December 6, 1963).

Ultimately, the budget-cutting Ministry of Finance won. It limited NIC grants to help for infrastructure: roads, water, and sewage pipes. Otherwise, the NIC sites would have to finance the projects through bonds. The NIC Law gave the sites permission to increase local indebtedness by selling bonds. The bond money would pay for the landfills and infrastructure, until recompensed by sale to companies. The law also compensated the NIC sites for some revenue lost by tax write-offs to incoming companies.

Although the NIC Law was becoming increasingly symbolic in content, big business still opposed it. The central headquarters of big business – the Federation of Economic Organizations (*Keidanren*) – did not want any incentives doled out to promote such inefficient industrial locations. The business community worked to sabotage the NIC Law. Within a year, the Federation of Economic Organizations demanded additional NIC-type sites, all within the Pacific Coast Belt (as the Income Doubling Plan had advocated). LDP faction leaders took up these demands within the top party council, the Policy Affairs Committee.[17] Miyazawa, the LDP Cabinet Minister of the Economic Planning

17. One source of business influence came from its ability to fund LDP campaigns. Successful LDP Diet candidates used an average of about $2 million in a single election campaign (Asahi newspaper, survey of Diet Representative finance sources, April 10, 1989) (Richardson and Flanagan, 1984, p. 186). The organization of the business community also supported the LDP's

Agency, pressured the EPA bureaucracy to approve aid for the new sites – even though the sites directly contradicted the stated redistributive intent of the NIC Law. In March 1963, the LDP passed a rider that added six "Special Area for Industrial Consolidation" (SAIC) sites to the NIC Law. All were to receive the same benefits as the first fifteen. In the Cabinet meeting of July 9, 1963, EPA Minister Miyazawa announced his success, stating,

I have consulted with the various ministers and their opinions concur. After final negotiations in the LDP, I will designate the [NIC and SAIC] sites in the Cabinet on July 12 (Iijima, 1990).

The fifteen approved NIC sites lay in the hinterland, well outside the industrial areas. The six SAIC sites all lay within the Pacific Coast Belt. They were close to the big urban markets where growth would have occurred anyhow (see Figure 1.7).[18] In combined area, the fifteen NIC and six SAIC sites covered about 20 percent of Japan's land area.

As a result of such political maneuverings, the NIC Law lost much of its ability to attract industry to the hinterland. The number of sites went up and the aid to each went down. Their number and expansive area made a mockery of the NIC plan's original social goals. The NLA official quoted earlier summed up the results:

In actuality, most of the growth did take place in that [Belt] area . . . MITI had guidance power, but did not use it (Interview, NLA official, 1979).

In the face of pressure from big business interests, MITI caved in. It did not exercise the strong leadership of some depictions (Johnson, 1982).

When the new NIC sites learned how small the grants would be, they became upset. They quickly formed an alliance. They managed to get a "Special Bill for

dominance. The Japanese economy was highly centralized. The Mitsubishi Group alone accounted for 3 percent of the total Japanese GNP. If one counts the extensive subcontracting networks, large conglomerates (*keiretsu*) controlled more than 90 percent of Japanese mining and manufacturing (Halliday, 1975, p. 275; Caves & Uekusa, 1976, pp. 499–500). Within a conglomerate, many of the stocks of each member company were exchanged and held in common (*kabu mochiai*), and directors served on each other's boards (Clark, 1988). Business and industrial associations (*gyokai*) clustered under class representative organizations such as the Federation of Economic Organizations (Keidanren), the "Foreign Ministry of Japanese Business," and the Federation of Employers' Organizations (Nikkeiren) (Vogel, 1979, p. 113). Keidanren coordinated opinions, collected political contributions, and appointed business representatives to government advisory councils. Big businesses also accepted many retired ministerial officials into their top positions. This concentration, sharp organizational focus, and interlock with government helped big business as a whole exert effective political influence.

18. As the final step in the process, in November 1963, the Advisory Council on Regional Industrial Development – attached to the Prime Minister's Cabinet and headed by Mr. Kojima, a prominent businessman and leader of the Federation of Business Organizations – approved all the NIC and SAIC sites.

Increased National Aid [to the NIC Sites]" passed in 1964. This bill marginally improved their lot (OGN, April 29, 1964, and December 26, 1964).

"Marriage with industry"

After designation as an NIC, Oita raised funds by selling bonds and from loans and local budget. Soon barges and derricks sailed into Beppu Bay with Mitsui Real Estate Construction Company as general contractor. They dropped ten-foot diameter concrete "jacks" into the water along the perimeter of the landfill area. Thousands of these jacks piled up to form the landfill walls. Enormous pumps on the barges sucked up mud from the exterior seabed and piped it into the enclosure. After some months, the mud filled up the concrete-walled rectangle and dried out. The Prefectural Government built roads, water mains, and green belts.

NIC construction put Oita's finances into a precarious situation. To recoup this investment, the prefecture had to sell the landfill to a wealthy company. Noting this distress, a prominent national businessman comforted Oita:

Making an NIC . . . is like marriage. To get a high status bride, one must naturally change the tatami (straw mats) and replace the paper screens. Similarly, in making the NIC, the citizens' burden will increase and local government will feel financial pressure.

The businessman added that the cost of "redecoration" would be worth it in the long run:

To set up a house is quite an ordeal. But there is a pleasurable future waiting (OGN, March 16, 1964).

Professor Okita and other early doubters would not have been impressed. Nonetheless, Oita plunged forward in hot pursuit of industrial "matrimony." To entice industry, the Oita government lowered the locational tax rate and the infrastructure repayment conditions. Then the governor and officials knocked on many business doors in Osaka, seeking an industrial "bride."

With MITI's help, things went smoothly. By then, Yahata Steel, the backer of Kyushu Oil Company, had merged with Fuji Steel to become the New Japan Steel Company.[19] The governor went to New Japan Steel again, and secured an agreement for a major steel refinery in Oita. In 1964, Showa Denko followed suit with a major petrochemical refinery for Oita (see Figure 2.1).

The inaugural ceremonies for the new steel refinery's first blast furnace took

---

19. The merger was no surprise. Before the Second World War, the two companies had originally been part of the same company, Japan Steel. Occupation authorities had broken them up under the new anti-monopoly law.

place in April of 1966. A runner brought a blazing torch from the ancient Shinto shrine of Usa, about 55 kilometers to the north. He ran up to the base of the blast furnace, a towering cylindrical behemoth adorned with a baroque tracery of pipes, dials and wheels. With gestures steeped in antiquity, a Shinto priest, clad in traditional white robes and a lacquered black hat, waved a branch of green leaves over the mouth of the furnace, blessing it. The runner inserted his torch. With a great roar the interior burst into brilliant red flame. A shrine of new Japan, built by modern technology but imbued with the old gods, sprang to life.

The blast furnace soon began smelting ingots. Red-hot slabs of steel rolled down its long automated conveyors. Presses stamped them into blocks and sheets to feed the factories of Asia's new giant. These events make clear the driving symbolic force of industrial growth. The capitalist's search for profit was hardly the sole social force driving Oita and Japan's race for growth. At a deeper level, industrial growth represented a symbolic vindication of Japan's ethnic worth and status in a national and global race for collective prestige – for making one's reference group recognized and esteemed by outsiders, by the larger global society.

In August of 1968, the Oita Showa Denko Petrochemical Complex started operations. At that time, residents of Niigata Prefecture were suing the Showa Denko company over the "Second Minamata" mercury disease it had caused there. To improve its public image, the company made great efforts to develop a "clean" petrochemical plant on Landfill No. 2 in Oita. Though still publicly unrepentant for its mercury pollution, the company did not want to give unnecessary ammunition to its critics. It installed tall smokestacks, oxygenating baths for effluents, and a wide green belt, almost a forest, between the refinery and Oita City. The green belt's width came close to the ideal one called for in Oita's original seaside development plan. It succeeded much better than the single file of wilting trees planted in front of the New Japan Steel refinery. Despite Showa Denko's efforts, though, the petrochemical refinery's cracking towers and tall smokestacks rose high above the trees, very visible from the nearby city.

Three refineries formed the core of Oita's NIC, Phase One: Kyushu Oil, New Japan Steel, and Showa Denko Petrochemicals. The pulp plant and subsidiary industries operated nearby. Phase One had transformed Oita City's coast from white beaches to gray industrial zone, punctuated by tall candy-striped smokestacks. The former fishing villages of Misa and Iejima lay in the middle of this zone. Enveloped in smoke and noise, their residents had quickly developed doubts about the benefits of progress. For most Oitans, though, the smokestacks remained icons of modernity until the end of the decade. Then, public realization of the extent of pollution and resulting conflicts gradually tarnished their gleaming symbolism. After setting up the NIC core in the mid-1960s, though, most Oitans waited expectantly for the wider economic stimulus effect.

Polarization over progress

Local boosters profiteer

The construction of the NIC refineries redefined the economic institutions of the prefecture. It started a host of changes to the distribution of profits, wages, and health. These in turn produced new interest groups and movements and new political conflicts.

When the construction of the NIC core picked up, local businesses at last jumped on the bandwagon. Government contracts to build the NIC infrastructure brought great profits to local construction companies, such as that owned by Kato Tadashi. The professional associations of manufacturing, commercial, real estate, and construction sectors prepared for growth. Merchants enlarged or built new stores to handle the expected flood of new workers (Nishi Nihon Newspaper, November 3, 1961).

Ironically, their very boosterism set in motion two local social forces that further knocked Oita's NIC plans off course: real estate speculators and community improvement demands (Interview, Tokyo City Government official, 1979). Local investors bought up land in the path of growth or on the edges of the landfill areas. Town and prefectural legislators pressured the Prefectural Government to provide that private land with infrastructure (roads, water mains) at inflated prices. Petitioning through the same town politicians, neighborhoods near the planned site demanded new roads, sewers, and other facilities too. Sometimes, Diet politicians knew where the Prefectural Government would build new roads. They bought up land in that area and then sold it back to the government at inflated prices (Interview, Oita news reporter, January 1980). Under the symbolic umbrella of collective growth, certain well-placed actors angled for selfish advantage. A functional collective effort generated structures and opportunities they could exploit.

At first, Mitsui Real Estate Construction Company played general contractor for Oita's NIC complex. As construction proceeded, however, local contractors demanded more direct contracts, not subcontracts through Mitsui (Interview, Mitsui official, 1980). These locals became a potent group of growth boosters for their own profit. They created a local "growth machine" (Molotch, 1975).

Kato Tadashi (a fictitious name) played a central role among these boosters and deserves detailed consideration. The leader of the Kozaki environmental movement identified Kato as its "chief enemy." He resembled the U.S. style local "booster" motivated by real estate speculation. Kato had a colorful history. Soon after the Second World War, he gained notoriety as a competition boxer under the name "Young Kato." In a meteoric rise, he carried his fight into the business and political worlds.

Of all the people I interviewed in Oita, he was the only one routinely described with fear. During the 1950s, Kato owned a gravel trucking business. As with many construction firms at the time, he grew wealthy from the post-war reconstruction boom. In Oita, this included helping build the NIC landfill. On separate occasions, three respondents repeated the same gruesome story. Kato, they charged, had ordered his gravel truck drivers, if they hit and seriously harmed a pedestrian, to back up and kill them with the wheels of the truck. That would reduce the insurance payments (Interviews, Oita newspaper reporters, 1979 & 1980). True or not, the story illustrates how people perceived Kato.

His ruthless reputation did not stop his social ascent, though. Kato parlayed his business success into ownership of a golf course, a bank, and a television station. He won election to the Oita prefectural legislature, attaining high office there. His children married the children of Oita's top officials. As one respondent said, "He dropped his past and became a gentleman." During an interview, Kato proudly showed me pictures of the Crown Prince and his wife visiting his golf course. Not the money, but the social status it could buy, seemed to be his motive. His example supports the status-attainment theory of the GE dilemma – that driven individuals exploit the environment to attain the material symbols of social status (noted in Chapter 1; see Hirsch, 1976).

Kato never lost his fearsome aura. He did not play by the usual group consensus rules. He did not join the faction of a Diet representative. Other local LDP politicians described him as a "lone wolf." They feared Kato's potential for violence if opposed. They described incidents where Kato faced down other LDP politicians by projecting this implied threat, saying "dare you oppose *me?*" (Interview, Oita news reporter, 1980).

Local profiteers in Oita bore a strong resemblance to their counterparts in Santa Barbara (Molotch, 1975). The Japanese speculators, however, were less dependent on outside private investment to jack up their profits. They used local government projects for that purpose. Without government NIC contracts, the local land market would have been inactive.

Kato exemplifies the "rational actor" (*homo economicus*) of economic theory who seizes on local opportunities to pursue his personal material profits with great cleverness. Kato and local boosters continued to push Oita into more landfill and industrial growth long after growth had lost its economic or environmental benefits for the prefecture as a whole. In other words, the rational pursuit of monetary self-interest by a few actors reduced the collective benefits of a public policy – the NIC project. This is a typical example of the "tragedy of the commons" in which individual overuse damages public goods (Hardin, 1980; Ostrom, 1990).

Although Kato was probably extreme in this regard, such actors are frequent in the business sector of any capitalist economy. Despite its reputation for "groupism," Japan has many such individualists. They tend to pursue individual interest to the detriment of collective welfare, if they can profit from producing urban sprawl and environmental pollution.

Rational choice theory assumes that most actors in all societies are so motivated (Hechter, 1983). The findings here, to the contrary, indicate that only a select subset of actors – often businesses – may be consistently so motivated. These few, though, may contribute strongly to producing social problems such as the GE dilemma. They are not the sole cause, though. The massive, centralized bureaucracies of Japanese government also helped transform, distort, and exploit local citizen initiatives (Scott, 1995). This transformation occurred through not one but a mosaic of causal factors.

Economic dilemmas

The NIC project distributed new costs and benefits, both material and symbolic. These sparked the formation of new interest groups, each aiming to further their gains or halt their losses. The NIC's costs and benefits, however, were not always self-evident. Leaders and concerned citizens socially constructed their response. In so doing, they used more than the new material costs and benefits. They mixed in ideologies, identities, relational practices, and institutions. All these swayed citizens' interpretations of their new situation. The relative role of material, institutional and symbolic forces in defining and settling Oita's GE dilemma remains the core of the analysis. Hence, we need to appraise the NIC's material effects.

Booming output

Local critics charged the Oita NIC with many faults. The refinery complex, they argued, had failed to stimulate the local economy and had imposed severe pollution on the area. Instead, they contended, investment should have directly fostered local industries. These critiques echoed and presaged many made at the national level (Miyamoto, 1973). One book called the NIC program "illusory prosperity" [Kita Nihon Shimbun (Northern Japan Newspaper), 1984]. These critics maintained that big business had exploited the rural areas with little

Table 2.1. *Growth in output value for Oita Prefecture by sector, 1960–1975*

Sector	Year			Increase 1960–75 (%)
	1960	1971	1975	
Textiles	25	65	NA	NA
Chemicals	39	444	1029	2,500
Steel	1	21	1395	120,000
Petroleum	0	407	1625	280,000
Non-ferrous metals	235	868	162	(−69)
Fabricated metals	3	88	182	50
Machinery	6	70	NA	NA

Source: Nomura, 1979.

concern for their effect on local residents. Defenders, on the other hand, said the NIC Law had succeeded (Nakamura, 1978).

In sheer volume and value, Oita's economic expansion more than kept pace with the national "miracle." In the critical years 1960 to 1975, Oita's gross prefectural product (GPP) expanded dramatically. Between 1965 and 1974 alone, Oita's GPP expanded from 86.6 trillion yen (at 250 yen to the dollar, about $346 million) to 697.5 trillion yen (about $2.8 billion). This eight-fold expansion outstripped the three-fold expansion of the national economic miracle, as well as the other NICs, during this period. For this reason, Oita's officials called their prefecture the "best student" (*yutosei*) among the NIC sites.

Between 1960 and 1975, Oita's GPP changed dramatically from mainly agricultural to an emphasis on industrial raw materials. Steel went from 0.1 to 27.1 percent of its GPP (a 1200-fold expansion in output value), with other raw materials following suit (Table 2.1). Even so, by 1975, the massive NIC steel, oil, and petrochemical refineries had achieved only 66 percent of their original goals (Oita NHK television broadcast, 1979, comments by Prof. Kigasawa). By 1980, industrial raw materials output equaled 49.4 percent of Oita's GPP: steel 22.1, oil and coal 16.3, chemicals 11.0. Along with raw materials, the core refineries brought in about fifty affiliated businesses. Together, this group of new companies produced about 68 percent of the GPP in 1977.

Modern production technology made the refineries relatively immune from recession. In 1989, with older Japanese steel plants shutting down, Oita's steel refinery ran at 85 percent of capacity and produced 13 percent of the nation's domestic steel. Taxes and wages from the refineries helped Oita stay prosperous while older plants and their towns fell on hard times. Prefectural officials took great pride in Oita's industrial accomplishments.

Table 2.2. *Resource effects of the Oita NIC complex*

	Industrial land	Employees	Industrial water	Electricity use	Output	Value added	Sulfur dioxide
Core industrial area (A)	988	5,300	45	294	5,400	12.4	2,950
Surrounding area (B)	1,437	174,000	56.4	336	8,000	23.4	4,500
A/B	.69	.03	.80	.85	.68		.65

Source: Kigasawa, 1978.

Comparison of the core and surrounding areas within the expanded NIC site (see Figure 1.8), however, brings problems to light (Table 2.2). The businesses in the core area (the refineries and their related firms) occupied 70 percent of the industrial land in the NIC site and used 80 percent of the water and 85 percent of the electricity. But they employed only 3 percent of the workers and spewed forth 65 percent of the sulfur dioxides. In addition, the core businesses added only half as much value to their products (because they produced cheap raw materials) as (mostly preexisting) businesses in the surrounding area. The more value a business adds to its product, the more profits, wages, and taxes it can provide the locale.

Furthermore, the refineries imported their raw materials and shipped out their product, so they did not stimulate many local production linkages. Local metal fabricators had little access to the fine new steel from the refinery. Plastics makers could not use the naphtha from the Showa Petrochemical refinery. These materials were promised to conglomerate (*keiretsu*) partners in other areas.[20] Small and medium businesses (capitalized at over 5 million yen) with headquarters in Oita got only 6–7 percent of their orders from NIC-related companies (Kigasawa, 1978, p. 30). This contrasts oddly with the 68 percent of GPP produced by the NIC companies. The refineries even subcontracted their maintenance and transportation jobs to affiliated national companies, not locals. As a result of this selective contracting, the numbers of businesses in Oita with outside headquarters increased dramatically. Clearly, most NIC expenditures and profits went to headquarters and banks in Tokyo, not to locals.

---

20. In Japan, much of the economy is controlled by or through six large *keiretsu*. These *keiretsu* are composed of affiliated firms that produce and handle every conceivable service and product. Their ethic is to keep their business within the *keiretsu* if possible (Gerlach, 1992).

Only local businesses that directly serviced consumer demand performed very well. Food products industries quadrupled and light industry tripled in output. Much of this increase came about as a result of the diffusion of prosperity through the nation. This would have happened in Oita without the NIC presence, as comparison with non-industrializing prefectures (like neighboring Miyazaki) shows.

Nationwide, by 1973 the NIC sites had achieved 81 percent and SAIC sites 68 percent of their 1975 growth goals (*Shukan Daiyamondo*, 1975).[21] Looking more closely, they met 92 percent (NIC) and 89 percent (SAIC) of their industrial growth goals. They completed goals for industrial roads and water systems (74 percent) much better than for schools and sewers (46 percent). Labor-intensive, job-producing industries (machine tools, automobiles) did poorly in all the NIC sites. But

dirty industries like steel, oil refineries, and petrochemicals grew extremely fast. [For these industries, by 1973] the [NIC and SAIC] sites produced . . . one-third of the national total (*Shukan Daiyamondo*, 1975, pp. 79–80).

The refineries had to go to more rural areas, contended the article, because they were "hated in the big cities" (*Shukan Daiyamondo*, 1975, pp. 79–80).

A critical economist from Oita University said that if Oita had invested in local furniture making, for instance, every yen of investment would have employed six times as many workers and generated over twice the total wages (assuming a market for the goods). Contradicting the critics, the Nomura Research Institute contended that without the NIC project, Oita would not have had these investment funds. Therefore, it could not have supported indigenous industry.

Few skilled jobs

During the years 1960 to 1975, Oita Prefecture's workforce changed, but not as the officials had predicted and hoped. The NIC project did not draw much population from the big cities, nor did it strongly industrialize the local work force. The size of the prefectural workforce actually declined slightly, from 569,000 (1960) to 562,000 (1975). Thereafter it increased, reaching 580,588 by 1980. Overall, the total population living in the NIC and SAIC areas, as a percentage of the nation, stayed around 10.8 percent. Because of the automated nature of their industries, they slowed down the rural population drain, but did not reverse it (*Shukan Daiyamondo*, 1975, p. 80).

21. Special issue on regional economy.

The number of workers in Oita's primary sector (farming, fishing, forestry, mining) declined from 50 percent to 25 percent of the total. Secondary sector (manufacturing, construction) workers increased from 16 percent to 24 percent, with most of this due to a rise in construction jobs. Tertiary sector (services) workers, however, increased from 34 percent to 51 percent (Oita NHK television broadcast data, March 1980). In other words, most of the new jobs were for waiters, barbers, sales clerks, bar hostesses, janitors, tellers, and government officials.

These workers were non-unionized and had centrist voting habits. This change confounded Kinoshita and Sato's hopes for expanded Socialist party support. The trend also held at the national level. Japan was becoming a "post-industrial" society (Fukutake, 1989, p. 108). With this change, unionization rates declined from a high of 56 percent in 1949 to 31 percent in 1980 (Fukutake, 1989, p. 112).

The three core refineries added about 5,500 jobs in total. With 3,700 workers, the Oita steel refinery could produce as much as the old North Kyushu City steel refinery had with 12,000. Requiring advanced skills, the refineries often brought in technicians from their other factories. Locals, if employed by the complex, usually ended up in menial jobs. Still, for Oita, this counted as progress. The number of high school graduates finding jobs within the prefecture went from 46 percent in 1972 to 60 percent in 1977 (Oita NHK television broadcast data, March 1980).

During this period, living standards in Oita improved. New roads, buildings, and shops went up all over. The city reorganized neighborhoods (*kukaku seiri*), driving straight paved streets through the old crooked villages. People bought new consumer items: cars, coolers (air conditioners), and color TVs. But this happened in all of Japan, rural and urban. Oita did not "catch up" with Tokyo. In average wages, it ranked forty-first in 1960, and thirty-ninth in 1980 (among the 47 prefectures and municipalities). According to a local survey, Oitans attributed their new affluence to the general growth of the Japanese economy, not to the New Industrial City (NHK data, survey conducted in 1980).

Prefectural debt

The construction of landfill and infrastructure used up 66 percent of Oita's scarce NIC investment funds. The remaining 34 percent went for houses, parks, and public use water (Okuda, 1978, p. 25). Under other circumstances, the local parts of these funds would have gone for schools and public facilities.

Since the NIC law did not disburse large grants to finance local growth, the main burden fell on prefectural shoulders. Between 1964 and 1974, Oita Prefecture invested about $330 million (72.5 billion yen) of public bond money to construct NIC landfill, roads, and other industrial infrastructure. By 1974, the prefecture had recouped about $266 million: $226 million from sales of the landfill and $40 million from the new tax revenues. This left a prefectural debt of $63 million for the construction of roads and other non-landfill infrastructure.

Many voices rose in criticism of this debt. In 1967, the Economic Planning Agency criticized the NICs for the strain they put on local finances, as well as their pollution and lack of fit with changing national economic needs. A history of Oita Prefecture states:

> The Prefectural Government paid twenty-five percent of the gigantic funds invested to build the NIC. This led to many sacrifices. As a result, when compared to other prefectures, Oita lags in cultural development (Watanabe, 1975, p. 266).

Here, "cultural" refers to public amenities: roads, schools, libraries, sewers. This large debt became a structural force impelling the prefecture to continue its quest for growth, long after it seemed reasonable to many observers. An official of the Environmental Agency (EA, *Kankyocho*) told me that by the late 1970s, recouping this debt was the main impetus driving the prefecture's continued quest for NIC-style growth (Interview, EA official, 1980). In this view, the Oita government acted like a compulsive gambler, hoping to recoup past losses on the next big win.

Economic disillusionment

The NIC's ambiguous economic results put the local business community under great tension. Some local companies profited from Oita's NIC project and became boosters. Others felt little benefit or outright harm, and lost faith. Machinations by self-interested actors inflated the project's cost and made public facilities like parks less feasible. Sometimes, they even hindered the completion of the basic landfill and infrastructure.

By the late 1960s, local businesses became increasingly aware that the NIC refineries were not producing a wave of economic stimulus. They had eagerly anticipated new contracts, but were bitterly disappointed. Nor did the expected flood of new customers come. On the contrary – national chain stores set up local branches and reduced the clientele of the local stores.

This caused a split in the business sector between those who profited and those who did not. Some merchants, the banks, and the construction company trade associations continued as vocal boosters. They even organized public opinion to support growth, an unusual activity for a sedate group. In 1978, for instance (to jump ahead), the Oita Chamber of Commerce held a big public meeting to show support for Phase Two of the complex. The meeting roster lists seventy-two support groups, mostly trade associations in retail, wholesale, construction, and food manufacture. Together, they encompassed the industrial sectors that profited, or hoped to profit, from continued NIC-style growth.

Other merchants and small manufacturers felt bitterly disappointed, and withdrew from actively boosting the project. As early as 1967, some of them demanded that the prefecture build labor-intensive industry that would help the local economy – machinery factories or shipyards, not oil and steel refineries. They opposed Mitsubishi's plans for an iron ore storage area, or the expansion of the Showa Denko petrochemical plant onto new landfill area. Summing up this attitude, one official of the Oita Chamber of Small and Medium Size Firms confessed to me in 1978,

for small and medium businesses, the [industrialization project] has not been a big plus . . . (Interview, Oita Chamber official, November 1978).

Officials of the Association of Small and Medium Businesses (ASMB) complained that the project produced few subcontracts for local businesses and did not train local manufacturers to use new skills. The ASMB officials told me that the NIC had ended up being little more than an "export platform" for making and shipping steel and petrochemicals to the big cities (Interview, ASMB officials, 1980). In their eyes, the Oita local government had, as had other local governments, become a kind of real estate agent for Tokyo corporations (Masumi, 1995, p. 272). This conclusion aligns closely with what theories of internal colonialism and dependent development would have predicted (So, 1990).

Even Sato Taiichi, the former "growth czar" under Governor Kinoshita, completely lost his earlier idealistic faith in growth. By 1970, speculators had led Sato to reflect bitterly:

In no time at all, my hopes have been crushed . . . the secret maneuvers (*anyaku*) of [real estate] brokers have caused disorderly growth . . . (OGN, 1970).

He began to criticize heavy industrialization as a way of making local jobs. Instead, he urged the revitalization of agriculture (OGN, Sept. 20, 1967). With Sato, words and ideas always led to action. When I met Sato in 1980, he had retired from government and become president of a dairy company, bottling and selling milk products from Oita farms.

The Prefectural Government tried to prop up the flagging spirits of the business community. The governor urged local businesses to work harder to adjust to the needs of the big businesses, and to think of serving national industrial priorities (OGN, Dec. 5, 1967). During the Second World War, the government had constantly exhorted people to sacrifice for the greater good. After the war, however, people realized that this Imperial exhortation had been ill-founded. People became quite cynical about exhortations to blind obedience and sacrifice. Ideological exhortation had lost its effectiveness.

In Oita, debate over NIC effects polarized sharply. The Oita Prefectural Government unflaggingly touted the NIC's virtues. It argued that the NIC had already brought prosperity to Oita and would bring more in the future. The business community split over the issue. Branches of the big Tokyo companies and local companies that had profited supported it. Local businesses that had not profited became quite cynical. Opposition political parties and Sohyo-affiliated unions turned increasingly critical. Environmental movements sprang up. Public opinion gradually soured on the NIC project and distrusted government "experts." In a referendum, citizens indicated future priorities should be for social infrastructure: schools, roads, and parks, not more industrial infrastructure.

Articles in the local magazine *Advance Oita* expressed trenchant criticism. Between 1972 and 1977, articles asked "For whose sake (was this industrialization occurring)." In a May 1978 article, Prof. Okuda (Department of Economics, Oita University) contended, "The (NIC) Phase One has hurt Oita Prefecture's Finances." In a July-August 1978 article, Professor Kigasawa (same affiliation) contended, "Phase One has hurt Oita Prefecture's Economy."[22] An article decorated with rotten tomatoes compared the Oita government to the wartime Japanese government: both fanatically stuck to rotten policies – the war, and for Oita, Phase Two of the NIC.

Critics agreed that the NIC project had not succeeded as a growth pole. It had not stimulated local businesses. It had not provided many jobs or helped local agriculture. Rather, they charged, it had exploited Oita for its resources (harbor, labor) and had caused many problems: prefectural indebtedness, environmental pollution, urban sprawl, lifestyle/job disruption. Investment in local producers, they argued, would have produced better results.

The Prefectural Government, on the other hand, never wavered in its praise and support of the NIC project. In response to the critics, the government hired the prestigious Nomura Research Institute to analyze the NIC's effects. The results showed a net positive effect on the prefectural economy. In 1983, Oita issued a pamphlet in honor of the thirtieth anniversary of the Oita Seaside Industrial Zone. Oita's Governor Hiramatsu wrote with pride:

---

22. Throughout Japan, the NIC program gave rise to considerable debate and criticism. The intellectual parentage of Kigasawa's critique lay in Miyamoto Kenichi's book, *Is This Kind of Regional Development OK?* (Miyamoto, 1973). Miyamoto also charged that NIC-style growth used a lot of resources and produced much pollution, but had little benefit for local economies. Miyamoto also suggested "city-scale industry" as an alternative.

The New Industrial City Plan has blossomed and come to fruit as one link in making our prefecture prosper (*chiiki zukuri*). This result is due to the Oita Seaside Industrial Zone (Oita Prefectural Government, 1983).

The Governor claimed he had accomplished this by consensus, ". . . with the understanding and cooperation of the prefectural residents . . ." This glowing assessment hardly squares with the critics' charges.

Anti-NIC resentment continued to simmer in the Oita business community. However, this resentment led to little active opposition. Local businesses lacked the organizational resources to mount an effective opposition to NIC-style growth. In the United States, local small and medium businesses organize themselves through a local Chamber of Commerce and fraternal organizations that coalesce, define, and represent their interests. In Japan, the local business community has the same set of formal organizations (modeled on the U.S. example). Again, the informal institutions of power make them less politically independent.

Local business organizations operate under their national headquarters, which big business dominates. Furthermore, as Oita's NIC grew, the proportion of firms started by non-Oita firms gradually increased. Their managers came to dominate Oita's Chamber of Commerce. A local businessman, active for a conservative LDP Diet member, complained about this. Big business had come to control Oita's Chamber of Commerce, he said, and expected local small business people to meekly follow their policies.[23]

These two factions – local and national business – saw the Prefectural Government in entirely different lights. Local businesses and citizens harmed by the NIC tended to see the Prefectural Government as favoring big business. National business managers, however, saw the Prefectural Government as defending local interests. One Mitsui manager complained that the Prefectural Government did not defend business interests of any sort. Rather, he said,

the Prefectural Government's basic interest is residents' welfare. They must listen to the residents. If [resident opposition] gets strong, the legislature will say 'no' to the company.

In one case, a manager explained, his company tried to get the Oita government to raise the level of permitted pollution a little. This was necessary so the company could build a new petrochemical refinery on Landfill No. 7. The Prefectural Government refused to comply (Interview, Mitsui official, December 1978). In another incident, the Prefectural Government refused to allow the Showa Denko petrochemical complex to expand inland because of preexisting residences.

---

23. Large oligopolies control more than 90 percent of Japanese mining and manufacturing (Halliday, 1975, p. 275; Fukutake, 1989, p. 84; Caves and Uekusa, 1976, p. 499–500).

Obviously, each side's interests color its perceptions. This should be a caution for sociologists who only investigate the state from the standpoint of local, ordinary residents. From that viewpoint, the state will always look like the handmaiden of capital. From the viewpoint of capital, however, the state may seem like the defender of "the people." The defining power that social location has over perception of "reality" produces the "Rashomon effect" of conflicting interpretations found repeatedly in this book. This tendency may also contribute to common biases in social scientific research.[24] The lesson here is that each actor is caught in the grip of multiple dilemmas.

Despite growing criticism, resistance, and a shifting base of supporters, the governor determined to push ahead with the NIC project. In 1970, he announced plans to build Phase Two. This would add more gigantic landfills a little further east on the coast (see Figure 2.1). Phase Two, he argued, would at last bring in plentiful semi-skilled jobs and contracts for small businesses. The plan called for shipbuilding and machinery factories. This was odd. In the late 1960s, the Japanese shipbuilding industry had already started a long decline as a result of world recession and competition from South Korea and Taiwan. MITI had halted new shipyard construction. Five years earlier, in 1965, MITI had already cautioned Oita to give up its plans for manufacturing industry and settle for a second oil refinery (OGN, March 24). Oita's NIC plans were becoming more farfetched and fanciful.

Oita's environmental dilemma

Along with its economic effects, Oita's NIC produced a more subtle and insidious problem: environmental degradation. Old steel mills like the ones in Kita Kyushu City belched smoke unblushingly. In comparison, the steel mills in Oita's NIC project worked more efficiently and therefore put out less pollution. Furthermore, the tall smokestacks spread the smoke far and wide, diluting how much fell on any given area. In addition, the refineries built green belts, strips of tree-lined park land between their sites and Oita City. These varied in width and effectiveness. The green belt in front of the steel refinery was only a few meters wide. It did little to hide the immense refinery and smokestacks behind it, nor to keep its dust and smoke from the city. The green belt in front of the Showa Denko petrochemical refinery was much wider, however, and provided some measure of visual relief for local residents.

---

24. A similar effect has often been noted by social scientists. For instance, W. Lloyd Warner's work notes that perceptions of the class structure change by class location of the respondent (Warner, 1963).

Despite these improvements, the NIC refineries added a great deal of air and water pollution to the area. They wrought environmental havoc in Misa and Iejima. The Kyushu Oil and Showa Denko Petrochemical plants destroyed the villages' beach front, blocking their access to Beppu Bay. When New Japan Steel's first blast furnace started operations, pollution worsened in the area (Fujii & Takaura, 1974, pp. 14–21). The tall candy-striped smokestacks belched gasses day and night. Increasingly, the Misa-Iejima residents suffered coughing, bronchitis, and other respiratory diseases.

In 1972, the Environmental Agency designated Oita City as one of Japan's fourteen most heavily polluted cities. Oita's Otozu River had become famous in the Environmental Agency as one of the ten most polluted rivers in Japan, because of pollution from the Sumitomo Chemical plant (Interview, EA official Tomisaki, April, 1979). A high-ranking prefectural official (retired) told me that he had toured all the polluted areas of Japan in the early 1970s and concluded that

. . . next to Muroran, Oita was the worst . . . the river was yellow, and the air was ten times worse than now . . . (Interview, former Oita prefectural official, September 1979).

The same degree of pollution was true of NIC and SAIC sites nationwide. The 1967 Basic Law against Pollution designated fifty places that required pollution prevention plans. These places included all but one of the NIC and SAIC sites (not designating only Nakaumi). As one review concludes, "The NIC and SAIC sites were built at the sacrifice of the environment" (*Shukan Daiyamondo,* 1975, p. 81).

In 1970, the Oita Doctor's Association analyzed health statistics in the Misa-Iejima area. It found that air-pollution related diseases had greatly increased (from 32 to 55 percent of complaints among new patients) since the NIC plants arrived (Fujii and Takaura, 1974, p. 19 and graph 12). In addition, a local high-school teacher and his students carried out a house-to-house health survey. They found that 35 percent of Misa residents and 45 percent of Iejima residents suffered from air-pollution related diseases. Sixty percent of Misa's elementary school children reported throat inflammation (Fujii and Takaura, 1974).

The mounting evidence of pollution illness shocked the prefecture. The discovery of malformed fish in Beppu Bay, attributed to water pollution, exacerbated public worries about pollution in Oita. These findings marked powerful steps toward public awareness of the GE dilemma.

Before the end of the Second World War

Oita's pollution was only one example among many in Japan of that era. The intense pollution of the 1960s represented the culmination of a long history of industrial pollution in Japan. Many excellent works have reviewed the history of Japan's pollution.[25] Here, a brief review will suffice to set the stage for the emergent national cycle of environmental protest.

Severe pollution was first seen in Japan during the Tokugawa Period (1603–1868) with the tailing piles of iron and copper mines. Runoff from these piles poisoned farmer's fields and caused disease. Often, the state forced the mine owners to pay compensation, a principle that resurfaced in the 1970s (Iijima, 1994, pp. 12–14).

In the Meiji Period (1869–1912), the state initiated a headlong rush to achieve a "rich country and strong military" (*fukoku kyohei*). This meant rapid industrialization, a stance that continued into the post-Second World War period. New coal-burning power plants, textile mills, steel refineries, and chemical plants polluted the air and water of the cities. Given its policies, the state became less willing to respond to citizen protest (Iijima, 1994, pp. 14–18).

Postwar pollution

The rapid growth of Japan's post-war economy depended in part upon a careless disposal of toxic waste into the "commons"–public air, water, and soil. The feverish pace of building also encased vast stretches of Japan's natural coastline and waterways in concrete for easier industrial use. As Ui Jun charged, pollution (*kogai*) was an integral part of Japan's growth at that time.

In the late 1950s and early 1960s, the first pollution illness victims, suffering from mercury and cadmium poisoning, attained media and public recognition. Subsequently, the wider public began to complain about pollution from metal and oil refineries, mines, and chemical plants. The rise in sulfur oxide and nitrous oxide air pollution and red tides in the coastal waters (Figure 1.3) indicated the general decline of the environment. By the mid-1960s, Japan had achieved an international reputation as the most polluted country in the world, a veritable "Pollution Kingdom" (*Kogai Okoku*). Innumerable reports of pollution damage to schoolchildren, workers, families, and communities shocked the public (Upham, 1987; Gresser et al., 1981).

Societal causes of "illusory prosperity"

On its surface, as intended, the NIC Law looked like a major concession to popular demand. Calder accepts it as such, citing it as one example of Japan's "periodic power to the periphery." The LDP, he claims, maintained its post-war

25. See, for instance, Huddle et al., 1975; Upham, 1987; Ui, 1979; Miyamoto & Shoji, 1972.

rule by granting "compensation" to injured parties (Calder, 1988, pp. 283–4, 306). A pro-periphery bias in Japanese politics, he claimed, spurred

strong economic development in the national periphery . . . by developing local infrastructure around as well as in, regional centers (Calder, 1988, pp. 280–281).

In Japan, as in many ACID societies, politicians bring lots of pork to the periphery, mainly government-funded construction projects like bridges and tunnels. But the NIC Law did not push heavy manufacturing industry and related jobs to the periphery as promised. The political-economic pressures propping up LDP rule – its role as patron funneling the largess of corporate coffers to dependent rural clients – made self-interested politicians produce the NIC Law as an exercise in symbolic politics. These political-economic pressures were, in other words, the "structural" conditions behind the weak effects of NIC projects on local economies.

The NIC Law ended up more dramatic fiction than effective policy. What social forces drove the polity members, ministries, and party alike to enact such a policy charade? The Law's history indicates they did so to escape the social dilemma posed by growth – to maximize capital accumulation and still minimize public complaint about its side-effects. Without such a measure, the Japanese Ruling Triad would have faced an increasing loss of legitimacy, and a quicker electoral threat.[26]

By the early 1960s, business and government recognized the need for expansion. The huge oil tanks, piles of ore and slag, and fleets of giant tankers of refineries took up large areas of land and sea. By the 1960s, they no longer fit into the crowded big cities and main ports. Big business already wanted new harbors, preferably on the mild waterways of the Inland Sea. Neither LDP nor business leadership, however, wanted to move factories and refineries to remote hinterlands in Kyushu, Northeast Japan, or on the western, Japan Sea side of the nation. The Income Doubling Plan that preceded the NIC Law envisioned new industrial and port investment along the Inland Sea near medium-sized cities like Hiroshima. Big business did not want to go to the real hinterland areas, though. Staying close to the major urban markets minimized transportation costs and maximized profits.

This form of growth pitted two massive pressure groups against each other: big business pursuing their economic interests and the rural hinterland population seeking jobs and progress. Ministries within the state took sides and formed opposed factions. A senior official of the National Land Agency, intimately involved with these events, described this opposition:

---

26. This point parallels that made in O'Connor (1973).

There were two opposing [forces], economic efficiency and regional [decentralized] growth, two different opinions. All the rural Diet representatives totally opposed [further concentration on the Pacific Coast Belt]. The big business leaders (*zaikai*) [wanted it] . . .

These contradictory demands put the LDP in a bind. As an organization, the LDP had no intrinsic reason to oppose rural demands for industry and jobs. The party did not like post-war urbanization either. In the city, people often drifted away from the LDP (Richardson et al., 1984). The LDP had an easier time retaining rural voters than urban ones.

However, the LDP could not afford to ignore either side of the issue. Big business poured money into the party's coffers at the top of the party organization. The local voters poured votes in at the bottom. If business and local voters wanted contradictory things, this put the LDP into a dilemma. Some local voters received LDP patronage, and voted accordingly. But some scrutinized the larger issues and might become critical of the LDP. Therefore, the LDP could not afford to appear to ignore rural demands for growth. Yet, to go against business preferences, thereby possibly reducing the inflow of money from big business, would have greatly weakened the LDP.

The patronage system partly smoothed over this division of interest. Many rural voters judged the worth of LDP politicians by the amount of community and personal patronage they brought, not by their national policies. Voters expected politicians to bring subsidized construction projects to the community (Dore, 1978). They also expected personal patronage: monetary gifts, sake parties, trips to hot springs resorts, introductions to important people, and so forth. In campaign speeches, LDP politicians often boasted about their "pipeline" to the central government, the source of subsidies for community projects. At the same time, the LDP depended upon business contributions to keep personal patronage flowing in local communities.

When rural problems became very acute, though, more local voters became critical of the LDP and started to vote for other parties. The LDP only ruled the Diet by a thin margin, so this prospect scared LDP leaders. Accordingly, the LDP needed a way to placate both interest groups.

The NIC law nicely rescued the LDP from this bind. Symbolically, as noted above, the law addressed rural concerns for industrial growth. Substantively, though, it did not help much in spreading growth beyond the Pacific Coast Belt and Inland Sea.

This outcome of the Law was not simply the product of watered-down compromise. It was a conscious strategy of social control by the dominant polity members. A senior official of the National Land Agency, involved in the NIC politics, described the political process:

Big business leaders need the [political] support of all the [LDP] Diet representatives, so they let them ask (for the NIC law).

The official charged that big business orchestrated ministries to submit NIC drafts as an exercise in pretense (*tatemae*):

(The big business leaders) asked the ministerial officials to put on a good act [that investment was going to the outlying regions], but to put all the real investment into the Pacific Coast Belt area . . . (Interview, NLA official, 1979).

Big business leaders understood the situation. They wanted the LDP in power, not some leftist coalition that would tax and control them.

The NIC Law was therefore, in theoretical terms, a type of *non-decision* – a manipulated political deal that placated local concerns by seeming to serve them, thereby reducing debate on the issue.[27] Japanese critics term this kind of policy a "fairy cloak" (*kakuremino*) because it rendered invisible the underlying social welfare problems caused by the existing style of rapid, centralized growth.

Ordinary Japanese citizens would, with great irony, call this political charade another instance of *tatemae*. Japanese think of *tatemae* as their own peculiar cultural characteristic. It is not. The NIC Law exemplifies the universal principle of "symbolic politics" – politicians commonly twisting the facts to manipulate public opinion (Edelman, 1977). Compared with the United States, however, the Japanese public has less gumption and opportunity to scrutinize and criticize the claims of politicians. As a result, its ironic laughter includes more resignation.

In summary, we can say that the "switchman" that brought about the NIC Law as a solution to the social dilemma of growth was not cultural, as Weber might have predicted (Chapter 1). It was, to the contrary, political-economic. The political-economic agency of business actors and their state allies pushed the LDP into policies that profoundly affected the social effects of Oita's, and the nation's, industrial growth. This pattern of agentic pressures not only intensified the social harm from growth, it also set the stage for the environmental dilemmas that would later come to the fore.

Conclusions

What kinds of causal pressures put Oita on a track of growth that led to these outcomes? The outcomes – refineries instead of manufacturing plants, few local jobs, pollution, destruction of the natural coastline – did not fulfill the hopes of local people. Perhaps this should not raise alarm. Few projects ever attain their ideal outcomes. Was Oita's NIC just another example of the perennial imperfec-

---

27. A term used by Crenson (1971) for hidden agenda-setting – an instance, in other words, of Lukes's second face of power. See Bachrach and Baratz, 1970; Lukes, 1974; O'Connor, 1973.

tion of all human projects? Or can we find real decision-points that, if they had allocated resources differently, might have led to more benefits and fewer harms to the local community? Or is this the wrong standard – should we be measuring the outcomes by what central government or big business wanted? Who really won?

In the Oita case, judging from the evidence presented above, the demand for growth first welled up from the ordinary people. They wanted local jobs for their children. They also hungered to be "civilized," equal in status to Tokyo. The new governor, educated in modernist ideals at Tokyo University, feeling a paternalistic responsibility towards his citizens, and hoping to strengthen electoral support for his political party, responded to that demand. The original impulse toward growth, in other words, was not imposed. It welled up from popular demand.

Governor Kinoshita and his staff, finding themselves rebuffed by Tokyo big business, engaged in some creative "agency" on their own part. They approached influential Oitans living in Tokyo. By appealing to their collective identities as prefectural "expatriates," the governor recruited supporters for Oita's industrial growth project. This group, as related above, brought about the formation of the Kyushu Oil Company, which built Oita's first oil refinery. This success set the process of industrialization in motion, attracting more large-scale refineries to Oita. Once again, we find a demand welling up from lower status actors, this time using channels of identity and social ties to attract the resources of industrial investment. Scholars have noted the creative role in policy formation played by prefectural governments in Japan (Samuels, 1983; Reed, 1986). This was especially the case for local policies started by opposition-party local governments, such as Governor Kinoshita (Steiner et al., 1980, p. 329; Reed, 1986b). In the Oita case, though, the nominally Socialist party-affiliated governor quickly lost control of the project.

Oita's NIC project depended upon central elites for subsidies and investment. The more Oita became dependent, the more its plans suffered conversion to central purposes. As a result, the hoped-for benefits of the NIC project ran into difficulty – the project produced few skilled jobs for locals but abundant pollution. This untoward outcome posed new problems and tensions for the community.

This outcome did not come about primarily because of demands for speculative profits from *local* real estate speculators, as the growth machine model would predict (Molotch, 1975; Molotch & Logan 1987).[28] Rather, it came about

---

28. Later versions of the growth machine thesis, based in part on my case study of Oita, recognized the great variability in causes of distorted growth induced by different structural contexts (Molotch and Vicari, 1988).

largely because national elites, mainly those in the Ruling Triad, used Oita's growth impulse for their own ends. The members of the Ruling Triad were not of one mind about how they should use Oita. But in the process, the ends drifted far from Oita's original hopes.

Which Triad member really won – the state, the LDP or big business? *Why* did they win?

The state: The Japanese state had pursued the goal of rapid national economic growth consistently since the Meiji Restoration in 1868. To some degree, the Meiji Government even created the industrial capitalist class (Reischauer & Craig, 1978). After the end of the Second World War, economic ministries such as MITI pushed for rapid growth to increase national pride and strength, not just to serve business interests. In their essential intent, at least, ministries exhibited considerable autonomy from interest groups (Skocpol, 1985).

However, numerous ministries disagreed on how many NIC sites there should be. MITI wanted only 2 sites, in order to invest heavily in each, making them prosperous, efficient and a strong local economic stimulus. Other ministries wanted more sites, each according to their mandate. To wit, the Japanese ministerial state exhibited little internal consensus. To the contrary, the Japanese state splintered into contending factions: sub-governments, ministries, and agencies, each with its own, often conflicting agenda (Campbell, 1984). Hence, we cannot attribute a unified "will" to the Japanese bureaucratic state as an entity.

In this form of relative state autonomy, each faction within the state *reflected*, but did not *represent*, the interests of a different constituency in civil society: MITI reflected the interests of business, Ministry of Home Affairs (Jichisho) reflected that of prefectural governments, Ministry of Labor that of labor unions, Ministry of Construction that of construction companies. Some state ministries, at least, tried to temper and rationalize the general interests of their constituent sectors in civil society – temper a sector's interests with a dash of national or public interest, as defined by the ministry. And rationalize it by attempting to help the whole sector, not just an individual company. However, this attempt was often subverted by *realpolitik.*

As a result of *realpolitik,* even MITI, a ministry highly driven by a sense of national purpose, was not able to define the effect of the NIC program. At this time, in the early 1960s, MITI was at the peak of its reputed powers to control big business (Johnson, 1982). Yet, as the chapter shows, MITI's authority over the NIC program was quite ineffectual.

The LDP. The ruling political party discarded MITI's rational, achievable NIC plan (two sites) in favor of a plan fated to fail in its social goals (fifteen sites). This scattered distribution of grants reduced the potential effectiveness of each NIC site as a regional growth pole. But it increased their overall effectiveness in getting votes from many hinterland areas. Given its interests in getting votes, the LDP would no doubt have preferred to give even more substantive growth to the hinterland. However, organized big business pressured the LDP into even more concessions – the 6 additional NIC-type sites (the Special Industrial Development Districts, see Figure 1.7). These 6 new sites, all in the Pacific Coast Belt, further reduced the effectiveness of the NIC sites as instruments of moving growth to the hinterlands.

Big business. Business interests did not instrumentally control the state ministries by inserting their own class members into office (Domhoff, 1995; Miliband, 1969). Nor did business exercise a structural dominance, forcing ministerial officials to serve business interests because of their crucial importance for the national economy (Block, 1987, p. 67; Poulantzas, 1973). Accordingly, neither instrumental nor structural theories accurately describe this pattern of power.

Instead, big business exercised considerable direct control over the LDP, given its massive campaign contributions. The LDP in turn controlled the Diet, with its power to approve legislation. The LDP's legislative power forced the ministries to tailor their bills to fit what would pass. They did so through constant informal consultations. Through this mechanism, the outcomes favored business interests.

The results of NIC-style growth – reduced employment effects and increased pollution – most closely served the immediate interests of big business. More investment went to the hinterland than big business wanted. But on the whole, the interests of big business received greater service than those of the LDP or the ministries. By strengthening certain industries, these results also served the immediate economic interests of organized labor. Organized labor, though, had little say in these decisions.

By what mode of power, by what "mutual accommodations" (Samuels, 1987, p. 9), did the Triad reach this outcome? In particular, we need to identify the principles by which members of the Triad negotiated their compromise decisions.

Regarding the public, the Triad operated mainly through the second and third faces of power – secret decisions by elites, and elite hegemony in defining and manipulating public hopes and demands (Lukes, 1974). By dangling the bait of hinterland progress in the face of local desires for the benefits of growth, national elites enlisted the enthusiastic cooperation of regional and local elites and publics. The locals pursued this bait with great vigor, only to be shunted onto contrary tracks that led to disappointment.

Within the Ruling Triad, though, more open modes of decision-making prevailed. Each actor was aware of the genuine interests and actual bargaining terms of the other. This accurate awareness probably characterizes elites in most ACID societies. Unlike in many Western societies, however, the material interests of each elite, although structurally defined as different, did not coalesce into clashing ideological stances. Rather, their mutual influence attempts were couched in more conciliatory terms.

Pressure within the Triad flowed through embedded social networks imbued with "fellow-feeling" – built on long-term contacts, work in the same agencies, friendships and loyalties soaked in sake. The most important networks came about through the top ministerial officials who retired to take top posts in business, the LDP and as prefectural governors. These "old-boy" networks retained much loyalty to central ministerial purposes. This situation reverses the typical Western situation, where politicians insert political appointees into ministries, making them even more subject to politics. The Japanese practice, to the contrary, constructs the core network of the Triad out of highly trained, generally loyal and nationally minded cadres. For this reason, these social networks are better able to serve national, rather then private, purposes, and foster less nepotism and favoritism than Western theory would expect.

These networks transmitted not so much material threat, then, as the cultural agency of new policy proposals and the social agency of persuasion. In an elaborate arena of plasticity, these networks softened the borders of structural contradictions generated by different immediate interests. This softening enabled compromise solutions sufficient to preserve the collective interests of the Ruling Triad.

Each elite and its subdivisions knew fairly well its own interests and the scope of its own powers, the interests and powers of its partners in the Triad, and the systemic conditions under which the balance of these interests and powers waxed and waned. None of them, though, could perfectly predict how societal events would unfold and affect their collective interests in maintaining Triad hegemony. Therefore, through these networks, the elites had to constantly negotiate and adjust their relative influence over policy outcomes and implemented realities. The relative power of each elite depended on the type and degree of threat facing the Ruling Triad as a whole.

When threats to the regime dictated substantive policy concessions, the LDP sought new directions and ideas. If protest from hinterland prefectures threatened the stability of the regime, for instance, the LDP requested policy proposals from ministries and agencies, initiating a "paper war" among them. During this process, the LDP negotiated the developing proposals with the peak associations of big business, and sometimes organized labor as well.

Through this "party-mediated corporatism," ministerial proposals were severely modified.

As a result, the policy process and its outcomes differed from case to case, depending on the degree and kind of threats to the Triad regime. If continued regime dominance required some restraint in the rapidity of industrial growth, the LDP and the state had some power to persuade business accordingly. This process was not fully orchestrated by any single elite or by the Triad collectively. Rather, it was a non-directed series. History happened "behind their backs," continually confronting the elites with new crises and popular opposition (Block, 1987, p. 52). As a result, what theorists call the relative autonomy of the state varied over time and by policy area (Skocpol, 1985).

In general, this shows that the ministerial state took a reactive, not proactive, role within the Ruling Triad. A ministerial official summed up this role as follows:

Industry determines the broad framework of the economy. The bureaucrats adjust industry's desires to avoid severe internal struggle between labor and capital to keep the country peaceful and developing (Interview, anonymous, 1980).

As long as sufficient peace prevailed in civil society, the ministries had the least power, the LDP more, and organized big business the most power to adjust policy in their favor.

These conclusions contradict many theoretical ideas about the Japanese pattern of power that have been advanced in the field. They do not support Johnson's contention that MITI largely orchestrated Japanese economic growth during this period. They contradict Evan's idea that a developmental state such as Japan's needs "corporate coherence" (Evans, 1995, p. 12). They run contrary to Okimoto's contention that

the state . . . harmoniz[es] the collage of interests articulated by corporate and organized lobbyist groups and blend[s] them in the pursuit of broad national interests (Okimoto, 1989).

Clearly the Japanese state was *not,* as some assert, "firmly in the driving seat" (Appelbaum & Henderson, 1992, p. 21). To extend the same metaphor, rather than being like a good car driver, the state behaved more like a "back-seat driver" with a multiple-personality disorder.

Which of the theorized factors best explain this pattern of power? Scott claims that the social institutional logic of a highly centralized bureaucracy produces the divergence of elite and local interests. This logic reduces local interests to abstract indicators, giving local needs reduced priority (Scott, 1995; Weber, 1978, p. 975). The data in the Oita case do not support this thesis. If such a logic had been universally at work, the central state would have been uniformly disparaging of hinterland employment needs. Instead, the ministries and agencies were more protective of local interests in intent than business or the LDP. Furthermore, each ministry took a different stance on the issue, according to their mandate and constituency. These findings indicate no overarching institutional logic forcing central ministries to disparage local interests. Rather, ministerial ineffectiveness came about due to the actual distribution of effective power.

If big business was so influential, then, did the fate of the NIC program follow the structural logic of capitalist growth? Imposition of an exploitative style of growth on the hinterland resembles the thesis of "dependent development" (Amin, 1976; So, 1990, p. 104). In dependent development, multinational corporations enter Third World developing societies to exploit their cheap resources and labor. In like fashion, Japanese corporations went to Oita Prefecture to exploit its resources (good harbor, cheap labor), not improve its standard of living. This is a kind of "internal colonialism" (Hechter, 1975).

However, the situation differed from ordinary colonialism or post-war neo-colonialism in many ways. Foreign aid may be considered a symbolic sop to Third World countries, in return for hosting exploitative foreign companies. Hinterland areas such as Oita, though, existed within the same political system as their metropolitan state and central businesses. Accordingly, the hinterland had a greater degree of political voice at the center. This voice enabled them to extract a larger degree of compensation from the state in return for their troubles – routine grants for building roads, schools, and libraries, for example – than possible for Third World countries and their metropolitan exploiters. But given Japan's system of local finance, Oita could have extracted the same level of support from central government even if it had not industrialized.

Despite some forms of beneficial growth through such grants, though, by the early 1960s the over-centralization of industrial growth and its attendant social problems had started to make people more cynical about the Ruling Triad regime. These problems had started to produce, in other words, a serious national change in the public beliefs – a shift in the structure of culture. This change foretold a potential crisis of legitimacy for the Ruling Triad (O'Connor, 1973). Such a crisis could have led to electoral difficulties for the LDP, even to the collapse of the Ruling Triad structure.

To ward off this crisis, the Ruling Triad responded with a two-pronged strategy. On the one hand, the Triad produced the NIC plan which redistributed some prosperity, largely symbolic but partly real, to hinterland areas. On the other hand, the Triad exercised new forms of soft social control over oppositional politics in the periphery, as later chapters will show. This two-pronged strategy sufficed to reduce discontent over regional economic growth enough to avert any electoral shifts. When the costs of this style of growth mounted still further through industrial pollution-induced illness, the strategy proved insufficient.

So far, this theoretical explanation has focused on material structural factors. Beside these factors, though, less "rational" sanctions and motives helped to bind the Ruling Triad into an effective pattern of collective action. The members of the Triad all internalized an element of collective belief and followed certain normative rituals (Powell and DiMaggio, 1991). The peak elites were few, linked closely, in constant communication, willing to compromise, and in basic ideological agreement on nationalist, ethnic, and racial principles. The collective identities and social relationships (symbolic and normative ties) common to this community lessened the tendency of groups to clash over divergent policy objectives. These identities and connections created a dense (highly networked) and adjustable policy community or network (Heclo, 1978).

As this chapter shows, the result was not necessarily "consensus" over immediate goals, but consensus over rules of the game which facilitated collective adjustment around broader collective goals. This form of consensus reduced the "wasted" effort – inter-organizational friction and political gridlock – so common to more divided polities (Coase, 1988; Granovetter, 1985; Williamson, 1975).

At the prefectural level, though, such relations had different policy implications. In Oita, social networks facilitated local growth and political control, but did not greatly augment prefectural power in relation to the national elites. Governor Kinoshita, not a central ministry retiree and furthermore affiliated with the Socialist party, was not inside the most powerful social networks. He had to work with Oita-based networks. Though useful in attracting big refineries to the prefecture, these networks could do little to overturn national elite priorities about what kind of business should come – refineries, not job-producing manufacturing plants. In other words, the influence of local networks had to fit within, and could not contradict, the overarching Triad principles of capital accumulation and regime stability.

In most instances, regional growth plans in other ACID societies produced similarly ambivalent or dismal results (Isard, 1975; Zukin, 1985). Does this similarity of outcome indicate a similarity of cause? Oita's problems did not derive from something uniquely Japanese, but from the inherent dominance of business interests over state policy-formation in all ACID societies. However, Japan produced some variations on this general structural theme – the centralization of Japanese institutions gave the Ruling Triad elites greater ability to "softly" suppress complaint and resistance from society, compared to other ACID societies.

Pro-business structural bias should not be equated with complete business dominance over other actors, though, not to speak of perfect elite control over the societal ramifications of their decisions. Policy decisions made by Ruling Triad members set in motion societal changes that would slowly undermine the material, social and cultural structural bases of their own domination. Heavy industrialization along the Pacific Coast Belt continued to induce centralized urbanization. With that, farming continued to decline, and the urban work force mushroomed. In the urban areas, family size shrank and community bonds weakened, leading to a decline in traditional forms of local authority. These kinds of changes gave the local public more civic "space" in which to think about political options. Resulting in a widening diversity of party support, as well as increased alienation from politics altogether. In addition, specific problems resulting from this course, such as pollution, disabused people of uncritical beliefs about the benefits of progress. Societal feedback loops such as these set the stage for new political coalitions, new social problems, new ways of framing them, and new forms of political contention – as subsequent chapters show.

3

Protest and Policy Change

Protest and national politics

As the GE dilemma intensified, so did public complaints about the situation. At first, government and corporations made little response to the complaints. Institutional rejection of public complaints stirred up a national wave of environmental protest. The number of anti-pollution protests swelled during the 1960s, cresting in 1970 and 1973 (see Figure 3.1). Protest movements in Oita rose together with this wave. Anti-pollution protests sprang up throughout the prefecture. Grassroots movements struggled with the authorities and pro-growth interest groups. Then countermovements entered the fray in support of growth. After a period of conflict, protests in Oita and the nation gradually cooled down but did not disappear. They continued to sputter through the 1980s and into the 1990s.

The peaks of the protest wave marked a political turning point. The Japanese government radically shifted its handling of the GE dilemma, producing its pollution miracle. Given other ACID societies' sluggish response to their own pollution dilemmas, why did Japan shift so suddenly to an effective pollution regime? As noted in Chapter 1, one of the principal debates in this field is whether or not environmental protest movements played an essential role in causing this shift. As a general principle, some theorists doubt that waves of protest have much effect on government policy (Tarrow, 1993). Other forces, such as international pressures and advancing knowledge, may have played a larger role, as Pharr, 1986 argued (Chapter 1).

To answer this question, we need to look closely at the political process that unfolded between state and society at the national level. One side of this process concerns the policy agenda within the Ruling Triad, which set the framework for the unfolding conflict. At the same time, we need to look at the pressure coming from the protest movement sector in society. This chapter will thus trace these national-level interactions. Subsequent chapters will present a more detailed look at the mobilization and trajectory of movements in Oita Prefecture, especially in the town of Seki. This will help to clarify the micro- and meso-processes and forces beneath the macro-structural alliances, conflicts, cycles and policy changes.

Why waves and cycles of protest?

The term "social movement" (SM) refers to collective action taken by relatively powerless people and groups over a sustained period, in "sustained interaction with elites, opponents and authorities" (Tarrow, 1994, pp. 2–4; Tilly, 1978). But this definition is insufficient, for it could apply to political parties and interest groups as well. Movements also use unorthodox means of collective action, disrupting or changing the normal symbolic or organizational routine (Burstein et al., 1995, p. 277; McAdam, 1982, p. 25). This is the source of their political punch, for authorities fear movements' disruptive potential and may strike deals with them for that reason.

Movements' collective action can take many forms. Tactics can range from spontaneous riots to highly organized demonstrations. Movements can advocate many sorts of changes – in how people think, judge, and relate (cultural and social norms), in the policies of the authorities (government reform) or other elites (business, military), or in the very structure of society, business, and government (revolution). Within a social movement, many different organizations can spring up and represent a variety of opinions and ideologies. These organizations may define distinct goals, tactics, and strategies, producing a variety of encounters and events (collective action) within the broad sweep of the movement. This protean quality makes movements hard to analyze.

A number of studies have shown that movements rise and fall in historical cycles and waves. A cycle of protest occurs when the total number of protest organizations and events increase in number and intensity, spread from one type of movement to another, reach a plateau or peak, and then decline. The cycle spreads by a "rapid diffusion of collective action from more mobilized to less mobilized sectors." Some imply that in a cycle of protest, the first type of movement will spark off other types of movements (Tarrow, 1994, p. 156).[1] For

---

1. The concept "cycle of protest" has received much attention (Kriesi et al., 1995, p. 113; McAdam, 1995; McAdam, Tarrow & Tilly, 1996; Traugott, 1995). Tarrow has been the main developer of this concept, but his definitions left unclear whether such a cycle had to involve multiple movements of different types, or could also be used in reference to the rise and fall of a single movement (Tarrow, 1983; Tarrow, 1989; Tarrow, 1994). This definition bears upon his hypothesis that a sudden opening of the political opportunity structure (POS) stimulates a cycle of protest. In order to clarify this question, I use the term "cycle of protest" to refer to a time when one

instance, the Civil Rights movement in the U.S. stimulated the student and anti-war movements that closely followed it. Accordingly, the CR movement was one wave of protest within the larger cycle. As protest diffuses, more, and more types of people and groups get involved. This widens the circle of debate and action. Protestors develop new theories and ideologies about the causes and cures of their problems (collective action frames). By trial and error, spontaneity and intention, they invent new tactics to express their grievances (protest reper-toires). The growth of the movement intensifies its interaction with elites (au-thorities and well-connected dominant groups). These pressures can lead to repression, reform, or even revolution (Tarrow, 1994, p. 153).

These features show that a movement is fluid and dynamic. Not only do the number of protest organizations and events grow; the kinds of protest tactics and their rationales also change over time. It is easier to study a stable object, but social movements (and their organizations) are not unified objects with a core essence (Melucci, 1995, p. 45). Looking at movements as fluid, in flux within a larger cycle, requires a more dynamic, processual view of them. Many prominent students of social movements call studying the dynamics of move-ments the most knotty problem and most "glaring deficiency" in the field (Tarrow, 1988, p. 435; McAdam et al., 1988, p. 728).[2]

The dynamics of social movements occur on the three societal levels noted in Chapter 1: interpersonal (micro-level: neighborhood), interorganizational (meso-level: community and society), and whole societal (macro-level: national or international). Substantively, as applied to movements, the micro-level refers to the mobilization of members and resources within the local neighborhood to start a movement organization. The meso-level refers to the unfolding of en-counters between movement organizations and the dominant elites and au-thorities (as well as other societal actors). Finally, the macro-level refers to the rise and fall of the entire movement (environmental, peace, labor, and so on) over a long sweep of time (years or decades). Each conditions and contributes to each other.

Micro-level mobilization processes have been most studied. The macro-cycle of protest is a rapidly growing field of study. Thus far, the meso-level remains uncharted territory for social movement research. The micro- and meso-levels

---

type of movement (i.e., labor) intensifies and then stimulates other types of protest, such as student and environmental, causing an increase in the general level of protest. In contrast, I refer to the rise and fall of a single type of protest movement as a "wave" of protest. Obviously, a number of distinct waves of protest could rise and fall within a single cycle of protest. One theoretical question then becomes, how does the sudden opening of the POS variously affect the start of a cycle of protest, and of different waves of protest?

2. See also Koopmans, 1993; McAdam, 1983, p. 735; Rucht, 1990, p. 168.

will be dealt with in later chapters (4 through 8), when we examine the Oita movements. This chapter will examine the long-run, post-Second World War macro-cycle, the wave of environmental protest within it, and the structural forces of its rise, impact and fall. It brackets the micro- and meso-levels for now.

Clearly, for a cycle of protest to start, movements have to mobilize: recruit members, gather resources, set up an organization, launch initial activities, have some enduring presence. Why do people start doing this? There is no necessary link between suffering and protest. People suffer great injustices for long periods of time without erupting in protest. At certain times, however, massive upheaval does occur, and may lead to momentous changes. Why do movements erupt at certain times and not at others? This addresses the central question of Chapter 1: the degree of realist, materiality versus social-constructedness of the factors spurring environmental politics into activity.

Tarrow takes a state-institutional and political-economic structural view. He maintains that social movement cycles are "triggered by quite short-term changes in political opportunity" (Tarrow, 1994, p. 65). In this, he goes beyond Kitschelt's argument that political context channels the target and outcome of protest (1995). By political opportunity, Tarrow refers to the response of the dominant political institutions to protest activity. Specifically, he argues that shifts in ruling alignments, the new presence of powerful allies, and internal cleavages within the dominant elites provide the favorable response that trigger cycles of protest (Tarrow, 1994, p. 18). In the end, states often close in on and finish off cycles of protest. Other scholars say that not external opportunities but new tangible resources such as time, money, and good organization, enable and spur the eruption of movements – a different sort of realist structural explanation (McCarthy & Zald, 1977; Tilly, 1978).

Other schools of movements take a more cultural position. A cultural agency view argues that an increase of grievances, often irrational and misguided ones, ignites wide-scale protest (Smelser, 1963). The political process model also recognized cultural agency, arguing that in order to act on pollution, people first needed to think of it as a "problem," not just an inevitable fact of life. They needed, in other words, to cognitively and morally "reframe" the problem: cognitively by understanding the connection between pollution and ill-health; morally by judging the situation to be "unjust."[3] Such reframing was deemed necessary before a cycle of protest could start (McAdam, 1982; Snow & Benford, 1992).

A realist view forces us to ask, though, can a new frame adopt any interpreta-

---

3. The distinction between cognitive (knowledge) and moral (ethical, emotional) aspects of reframing has so far been largely overlooked in the social movement literature (Snow & Oliver, 1995).

tion, or must it be closely tied to the material reality to stimulate protest? Gamson threw this challenge to the proponents of the frame view (Gamson, 1992). Some studies imply the connection is quite loose. One study, however, found a very close linkage: Radioactive gas leakage from a nuclear reactor stirred up feelings of "suddenly imposed grievances" that sparked the Three Mile Island protest movement (Walsh, 1981). Contrary to a radical social-constructionist view, then, grievances may have a very close relation to the intensity of imposed material harm. If so, this might mean that an objective increase in harms, rather than changes in frames, political opportunities or resources, crucially determines the cycle of protest. To evaluate the validity of these explanations, we have to look closely at Japan's wave of environmental protest, and the degree to which it was stimulated by other protest movements that preceded it.

Protest and response

Chapter 1 explained how pollution intensified as the first decades of Japan's economic miracle progressed. If protest is closely tied to the objective, physical intensity of pollution, one would expect to see a close relationship between the rise of pollution and the rise of complaints (expressed grievances). The rapidity with which complaints translated into protest would depend upon how effectively the government responded to the new problem. To the degree to which the response is socially constructed, however, the relationship between objective levels of pollution and complaint would weaken and become arbitrary. What this way of posing the question fails to consider, though, is that the government might find ways to suppress the expression of complain and its outbreak into active protest. This alternative would be a product of the political opportunity structure.

In Japan, levels of pollution started to rise as the nation industrialized through the 1950s. As measured by the concentration of sulfur dioxide in the air, one of the most obvious forms of urban industrial pollution, pollution was at its peak in 1965. Despite this, rates of complaint to local governments about pollution did not start to rise until the late 1960s (Figure 3.1).[4] Then, complainants sought public recognition of the pollution problem, financial compensation, medical

---

4. Data on the wave of environmental protest in Figures 3.1, 3.2, and 3.3 come from the tabulation of Asahi newspaper mentions of such events, collected as part of my research. Other data in these figures come from published sources as noted. Newspaper reporting of waves of protest often lags behind the reality until a threshold is reached, after which the events make the front page in profusion. Accordingly, the real curve of events from 1960 to 1970 is probably a more gradual ascent, rather than the sharp ascent shown in Figure 3.1.

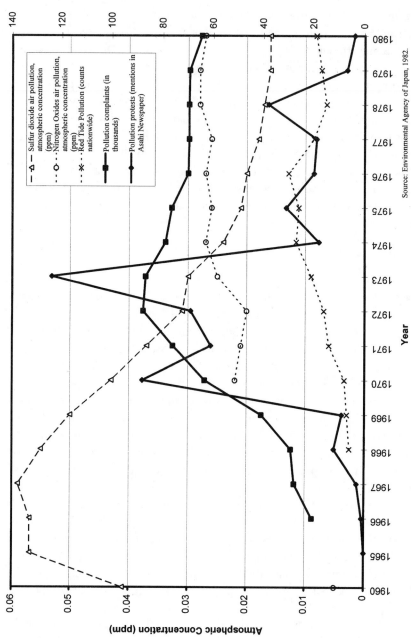

Figure 3.1 The rise of pollution, complaint, and social protest in Japan, 1960–1980

Source: Environmental Agency of Japan, 1982.

treatment, and tighter regulations. The timing of this "complaint curve" indicates a loose relationship with the level of pollution. This indicates that, in the Japanese case, the expression of grievances was not a direct function of the intensity of pollution. Rather, it must have been affected either by (or both) a framing process that took time, or by some exercise of social control over the expression of complaint (or some other non-theorized factor).

There is considerable evidence of elite refusal to recognize the problem, and of social control that hampered the expression of complaint. During this period, though, four terrible incidents of industrial pollution-caused community illnesses occurred: Minamata mercury poisoning, Niigata mercury poisoning, Yokkaichi asthma, and the Itai Itai cadmium poisoning. These four cases turned into core symbolic icons (Szasz, 1994, p. 84) of industrial pollution, widely reported in the mass media. They have been thoroughly studied and reported (Gresser et al., 1981; Huddle et al., 1975; McKean, 1981). The four incidents crystallized the pollution problem in the public mind and galvanized protests about other pollution around the country. The mayor of Yokkaichi, for instance, coined the term "pollution illness" (*kogaibyo*) to express his recognition that industrial air pollution had caused a citywide plague of severe asthma.

The four incidents evolved through similar stages. When the pollution illnesses initially appeared in the 1950s, the victims were rebuffed by the companies, the authorities, and even their own communities (Upham, 1987). In almost every case, pollution victims "encountered corporate denials (and) collusion of government and industry," which publicly denied the existence of serious illness from industrial pollution (Upham, 1987).

If the victims continued to complain, the polluting company offered them small traditional condolence payments (*mimaikin*). This symbolized corporate sympathy for the sick, but was not an admission of causal responsibility (Upham, 1987). Usually, the companies kept right on polluting, and the pollution got worse.

Until the mid-1960s, most prefectural and national government effectively ignored pollution complaints.[5] The Ministry of Health and Welfare (MHW) acknowledged the existence of pollution-related illness, but it was powerless to affect legislation for decades (Johnson, 1982, p. 284; McKean, 1981). Members of the pro-growth Ruling Triad were well aware that pollution was wreaking havoc with public health. But publicly acknowledging this would have hampered its principal goal of national capital accumulation. For decades, it tried to hold the nation steady on the course of rapid growth. This meant directing all

---

5. Government avoidance of pollution problems was hardly unique to Japan. During this period, it was common practice in other ACID societies (Brown & Mikkelsen, 1990; Landy et al., 1990).

investment into new factories and supporting infrastructure, not pollution control equipment. In this, it was very successful. During this period, Japan achieved one of the highest investment-to-consumption ratios in history (McKean, 1981).

However, this level of productive growth depended in part on the neglect of social welfare problems such as industrial redistribution or pollution prevention. The Ministry of Health and Welfare made several studies showing a connection between industrial pollution and the severe cases of illness, only to be ignored. Sympathetic academics with impressive credentials conducted further studies, issued reports favorable to the victims, and stirred public concern for their plight. But MITI and the corporations did their best to discourage, discredit, and demoralize the victims. They resisted all victim complaints for recognition, not to speak of compensation. They even cut off funds for university pollution research projects (Upham, 1987). At this point, in other words, elite growth strategies supported the Japanese critic's argument that pollution was an inherent part of capitalist growth (Ui, nd).

The national Ministry of Health and Welfare had tried to inject concern for pollution and other problems into Japan's industrial growth policies of the 1950s and 1960s, but with little effect – as the NIC Law outcome showed. Undaunted, determined to work for its mandate of public health, in 1953 the Ministry of Health and Welfare conducted the nation's first national survey of pollution and drafted a bill to protect the living environment. The Ruling Triad opposed this bill, and at that early time no strong public concern supported it, so it died (McKean, 1981, p. 215). The Diet passed some anti-pollution laws in 1958 and 1962, but they were quite weak and given to MITI for enforcement, so they had little effect (McKean, 1981, p. 216). So these early elite allies of environmentalism had little success.

At the same time, the environmental wave of protest did not take off from barren ground. As theory would predict, it inherited the impulses of a broader cycle of protest (Figure 3.2). Environmental activists learned much from the well-known protests against the United States-Japan Security Treaty. Student and opposition party protests against the treaty peaked at the two main dates of its renewal, 1960 and 1970. In between, a national student movement arose to oppose Japan's support for the U.S. military in the Vietnam War (Apter & Sawa, 1984). Within this movement, a number of student organizations became more radical, and developed strong anti-state and anti-capitalist explanations for the Vietnam War and Japan's complicity. A few extremely radical sects engaged in violent revolutionary tactics, sometimes against each other or their own members (Steinhoff, 1992). Others tried to diffuse protest tactics by cooperating with citizens' movements. The farmer-student protest movement against Narita Air-

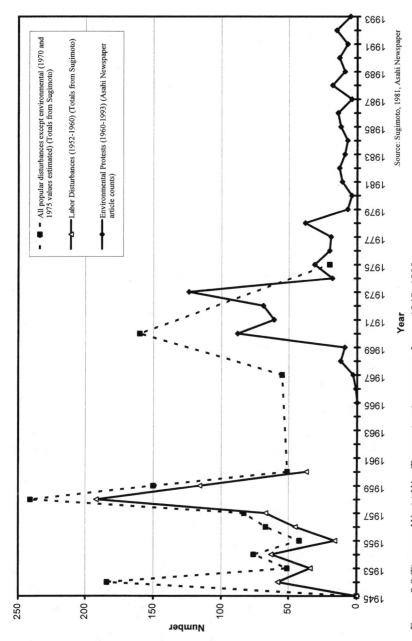

Figure 3.2 The post-World War Two cycle of protest in Japan, 1945–1993

Source: Sugimoto, 1981, Asahi Newspaper

Legend:

- - ■ - All popular disturbances except environmental (1970 and 1975 values estimated) (Totals from Sugimoto)

─△─ Labor Disturbances (1952-1960) (Totals from Sugimoto)

─◆─ Environmental Protests (1960-1993) (Asahi Newspaper article counts)

Year

Number

port is the most well-known example (Apter & Sawa, 1984). Student veterans of these movements helped seed communities that wished to protest pollution with leaders having a good knowledge of organizing and tactics.

A gradual process of reframing took place that made environmental protest more feasible nationwide. During the 1960s, the mass media published more and more reports of pollution around the nation, as these years proceeded, which helped set the tone of public opinion. These reports reached a crescendo in 1970. In addition, citizens' willingness to express their grievances, as we will see later, signaled a growing belief in the democratic rights of the individual and the community, including the right to a healthy living environment. Unexpectedly enough, though, encouragement to protest even came from factions of the Japanese state. In order to spur public awareness of the seriousness of the pollution threat to their health, the Ministry of Health and Welfare installed pollution metering stations at busy points in the major cities. These stations continually flashed the concentration of air pollutants at that site onto illuminated signs for all the passersby to read. MHW officials, frustrated by their inability to pass pollution control policy, hoped that by setting up these stations, they would stimulate popular outrage over the severe levels of urban pollution and cause a wave of demand for environmental protection (Kawana, 1988). This effort also contributed to the popular reframing of the problem which occurred in the late 1960s.

Japanese people on the whole, having only recently emerged from the horror and privation of the Second World War, had become quite wary of their government and state. With the problem ignored by authorities and corporations, the growing pollution around the nation only heightened the frustration felt by ordinary people with politics-as-usual. The normal channels of complaint – talking with elected officials and bureaucrats – did not bring relief. In the mid-1960s, when the news media began to publicize the four big pollution-poisoning cases, and the MHW began flashing up-to-the-minute reports of sulfur dioxide and nitrous oxide concentrations on the street corner, this underlying wariness began to coalesce into something stronger. Continuing government and corporate denial fanned the flames of resentment.

At first, public protest movements appeared in areas already subject to severe pollution, and the government reacted sporadically. By the late 1950s, industrial pollution damaged the fishing catch in Tokyo Bay. Local fishing people broke into and rioted inside a polluting factory. Shortly thereafter, in 1958, the national government passed two laws to protect water quality in Tokyo Bay [Asahi Newspaper, August 1, 1970, cited in (Matsubara, 1971, p. 156). See also (Iijima, 1994, p. 20). When air pollution in Yokkaichi caused severe asthma, the government passed a law controlling particulates. Japan's anti-pollution movements of this era have been reviewed elsewhere (Huddle et al., 1975).

By the mid-1960s, a new type of movement appeared that aimed at stopping a potentially polluting project, rather than complaining after it had been built. The success of the first of these movements signaled a new era of citizen empowerment. In 1964, the government announced plans to build an oil refinery complex in Mishima-Numazu. Local residents feared its pollution and organized a strong grassroots movement to oppose and stop the plan (Lewis, 1980). The government again reacted in a conciliatory manner. MITI and the MHW jointly carried out an environmental impact assessment in Mishima-Numazu, Japan's first (Hashimoto, 1988, p. 68). The results indicated that there would be no harm to health from the complex.

This did not convince the residents. They organized local protest movements, which grew and applied pressure on the Numazu town council. Finally, the council voted to reject the proposed complex, which effectively stopped it. Mishima-Numazu and several other towns (with movements) in that era stopped factories dead.

This would not have been so unusual in the United States, which grants a great deal of autonomy to municipalities. But it was new to the staid bureaucrats of the national ministries and industrial leaders. An official in the Ministry of Health and Welfare commented,

MITI and the Economic Planning Agency were shocked when in September the residents stopped the Mishima-Numazu *kombinat* plan (Hashimoto, 1988, p. 76).

Government officials had not expected grassroots movements to take over local governments and determine growth policy for their area. Another bureaucrat commented,

[this incident] forced us to see that if the majority of citizens, who hold the vote, oppose [a project], both conservative and opposition politicians in the legislature will oppose development (Hashimoto, 1988, p. 70).

The same official commented on the elite's dawning realization of the new importance of politics and movements:

Even though we say the national ministries have the right to implement laws, their effectiveness depends upon how much backup they have in politics and public opinion (Hashimoto, 1988, p. 68).

The new strength of civil society was in fact merely the actualization of democratic rights found in the post-war Constitution. But these rights and their practice were still very foreign to Japanese bureaucrats, many of whom had served under wartime and pre-war authoritarian governments. To everyone's surprise, the new grievances imposed by Japan's GE dilemma spurred local citizens to make use of the new rights and formal institutions (Steiner et al., 1980, p. 448).

The Mishima-Numazu protest and others like it, argued an Asahi Newspaper article, made the government and big business (*zaikai*) worried that soon, if things went on this way, they would not be able to build factories anywhere. As a result, the national government passed its first comprehensive anti-pollution law, the Basic Law against Pollution (Asahi Newspaper, August 1, 1970, cited in (Matsubara, 1971, p. 156). This new law did not placate the citizens, however. Scholarly critics charged that the anti-pollution laws of the time did not adequately control or prevent pollution (Matsubara, 1971, p. 157).

The Mishima-Numazu incident was just the opening shot. A surge of environmental protest movements and progressive local governments followed. Among them, victims of the "big four" pollution cases filed court suits and initiated research to support them (Gresser et al., 1981, p. 29–30, 41). This growing wave of opposition through the courts dismayed the establishment. Since democratic rights and institutions were so new, they had not yet devised effective informal social control strategies to counter them. Before and during the war, the government had readily called out the police and military to suppress such protest. But now it was hesitant to do so. In the face of rising protest, the establishment had to devise new, informal social control strategies to try to accomplish the same ends. But for the first few years of this cycle of protest, such means did not work effectively, leaving the field open to social movements.

Throughout the 1960s, the number and intensity of environmental protests continued to mount (Figure 3.1).[6] Protest escalated through the 1960s and reached a peak in 1970. Protest boiled over in a variety of forms, new and traditional.[7] Movements prayed at local shrines, galvanized village government, gathered in angry crowds, and blockaded their villages as they had done in feudal times. But they also drew on the modern worldwide repertoire of protest, spread through the labor and student movements that preceded them, and contemporary environmental movements in other ACID societies. They staged sit-ins and demonstrations on land and sea, picketed factories and shut them down, and held public discussion forums. Movement organizations and protest events in Oita during this period exemplify these types of protest (see Chapter 4).

---

6. This data comes from two sources: (1) a count of environmental protest events in the Asahi newspaper; (2) a count of protest events reported in a year-by-year compendium of Japanese environmental incidents that ends in 1975 (Iijima, 1979).

7. Appendix 2 contains a chronology of post-war movement mobilization.

Soon after the wave of complaint to local government began its rapid climb, the number of public protests also started to climb. This parallelism shows that, once people had formed enough of an injustice frame to propel them to complain to the authorities, it did not take much more to bring them out onto the streets. People did not require a long period of suppressed frustration while they tried appealing through the orthodox channels of complaint. They did not need many years to wake up from a deferential political morality to one which justified protest, which some theories of protest (McAdam, 1982) or of Japanese culture (Ch. 1) might imply. Villages harbored their own traditions of resistance to the state, often nurtured over numerous instances from Tokugawa times a hundred years previous. In addition, the debacle of the Second World War had highly disabused many people of the claims of the state. Accordingly, frustration with official response to this problem mounted quickly. In a few years, people all over Japan went from grievance to protest. They needed very little learning or reframing to realize that the only effective political means they had available, given government and business intransigence, were unorthodox ones.

Did popular grievances accurately reflect objective conditions, or were they a form of collective delusion or panic spread by contagion, as collective behavior theory suggests (Smelser, 1963)? Did inflammatory but misleading information, or irresponsible agitators, whip up mass hysteria? Studies do report that the mass media can instigate waves of public concern over issues, despite no real change in the incidence of the problem (Fishman, 1978). To the contrary, the data indicate that a very rational, albeit lagged, process was at work. People were initially resistant to recognize the dangers of pollution, and felt hesitant to complain about it. When the media, public intellectuals and the government started to make it acceptable to complain, though, a wave of pent-up worry quickly burst forth as formal complaint, and then as overt protest. The next chapters will explore in detail how the threat of pollution illness translated into complaint and protest at the local level. For establishing the contributory causes of the wave of environmental protest, though, it is sufficient to show that the lagged relationship between the rise of pollution and the rise of complaint and protest (Figure 3.1).

After its peak in the early 1970s, the wave of environmental protest declined rapidly, as did all other forms of protest. However, environmental protest did not die out altogether. Rather, it continued on at a moderate level, paralleling the continuing existence of other forms of pollution like nitrous oxides and red tides.[8] This continuance indicates that once the progress frame had gotten

---

8. Red tides result from the explosion in a population of red algae that gives off a poisonous

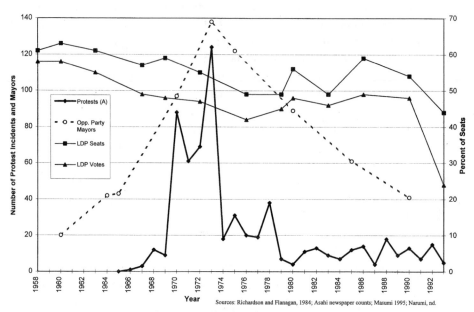

Figure 3.3: Environmental protest and political context, 1958–1993

tarnished, and the pollution frame had become widely recognized, environmentalism became a permanent part of the popular subculture. The new environmental paradigm noted in Chapter 1, in other words, had taken root in the popular mind. This new paradigm remained ready, should the objective need arise, to give moral support to the new repertoire of protest techniques – lessons from experiences of barging into the governor's office in the "navel" engagement and other unruly means – possessed by the subcultures of communities.

What then of theories about the importance of the political opportunity structure? Did some change or opening take place – some realignment of elites or institutional change that gave grassroots protest a better chance for success? The evidence indicates not. No real change occurred in the political opportunity structure, either just before the upsurge of environmental protest or during its initial rise (1955–1969) (Figure 3.3). During the late 1960s, members of the Ruling Triad were closely allied and powerful. MITI was at the height of its ability to guide the economy and business investment (Johnson, 1982). Busi-

substance toxic to fish and other organisms. The red algae blooms in the sea due to the presence of chemicals in the water from agricultural fertilizers, industrial effluents, and household sewage. For current information on this problem in Japan, see the web site: http://seminar1.cc.it-hiroshima.ac.jp/seminar/ibatetsu/waterpollution.html.

nesses had recovered from wartime devastation and were expanding rapidly. The LDP suffered a decline in popular vote (from 58 percent in 1960 to 48 percent in 1969 elections), but retained a comfortable majority of Diet seats (63 percent of the seats in 1960, 57 percent in 1967). The ruling alignment, in other words, did not shift, suffer internal cleavages, or spin off powerful new allies for the movements. On the contrary, the political left, which was the natural ally of the environmental protest movements, grew progressively more fragmented and weak (Richardson and Flanagan, 1984, p. 77). In sum, changes in the political opportunity structure did not provide the incentives that initiated the wave of environmental protest.

However, if we look at the environmental movements as part of a longer cycle of general protest, the theory gains in validity (Figure 3.2). The labor movements that arose in the 1940s and tried to stage a general strike in 1949 were definitely freed and initially encouraged by the liberal regime installed by the Occupation. In a few years in the late 1940s, labor union membership shot up from very little to almost 50 percent of the working population. Strikes were frequent as workers exercised their new rights to improve working conditions.

After the Occupation suppressed the general strike, though, the labor movement began to have doubts about the liberality of the occupiers. Movements began to turn against the Americans as well as against employers and the Japanese government. The Allies relinquished political control of Japan in 1952. Soon thereafter, the two conservative political parties combined to form the LDP, establishing the "1955 system," which lasted until the LDP lost power in the Lower House in 1993. During this period, the LDP exercised hegemony over Diet politics, putting union representation through the Socialist, Communist, and centrist parties permanently on the sidelines. Frustrated by this single-party dominance, the union movement joined with university students and the leftist parties to oppose the US-Japan Security Treaty. This movement peaked first in 1960, at the first signing of the treaty, and then again in 1970, at its second signing (during the Vietnam War). The anti-Security Treaty and anti-Vietnam War movements in Japan produced cadres of dedicated protest leaders, many of whom became high school teachers.

During this tumultuous era, the conservative LDP-dominated government, along with signing the Security Treaties, also made attempts to revise the Constitution, centralize power, and reduce the Occupation-inspired educational curriculum's stress on democratic values. The Japan Teachers' Union stood at the forefront of opposition to these moves (Duke, 1973; Thurston, 1973). Based on this experience, many of the teachers and their students joined and led the anti-pollution movements in villages and towns throughout Japan. This training and influx of anti-government cadre, already primed with a frame justifying protest against an arbitrary government, was a major social mechanism in the diffusion of protest in the larger cycle of protest.

What combination of factors did initiate the cycle, then? Tarrow assumes that favorable changes in the political opportunity structure will lower the costs of protest (arrests, loss of jobs, social sanction) so much that citizens will not hesitate to protest. Resource mobilization theorists, on the contrary, assume that the acquisition of new resources will add enough to citizen power to enable it to readily bear the external costs of protest. Both of these approaches assume a constant preference for protest on the part of citizens. The change-in-grievance approaches, on the other hand, argue that a change in preferences (grievances) prompts mobilization and cycles of protest.

A good explanation of the Japanese wave of environmental protest combines all these viewpoints. The physical harm imposed by pollution established a mobilization potential (Klandermans, 1993). Given stable preferences for a good and healthy life, people disliked this new harm, but were not always sure where it came from – so insidious is the effect of pollution. Once the source of their declining health had been identified by mass media and local activists, they were able to activate existing traditions of protest and cynicism toward elites. With these values, most people required little reframing or cognitive liberation to justify unruly protest.

When they became agitated enough to complain, to their surprise, people discovered their new political opportunity structure – one that had already existed for several decades under the post-war Constitution, but one which most people (beyond unionists and university students) had not had occasion to use. This situation initially gave social movements an open field for expansion, which they rapidly took advantage of. In other words, it was not a sudden opening of the political opportunity structure that sparked protest, but rather a sudden imposition of grievances that gradually dawned on people, as they reframed it, that pushed people to discover and use a political openness they already had without knowing it. Protestors created their own political opportunity structure by electing mayors and governors from the opposition parties, frightening the LDP with the possibility of loss at the national level too. This pressure helped push the LDP into compromise (Figure 3.3).

National and prefectural response

Why policy change?

Social movements can engender many types of outcomes. Considering political movements, such as Japan's environmental movements, research identifies four main types of outcome: full success (reform or revolution); co-optation (symbolic participation in the elite polity but not substantive policy reforms); preemption (authorities grant real reforms in order to take away the movement's rationale and weaken it); and failure (rejection and demise) (Gamson, 1990; Kriesi et al., 1995, p. 212; Kitschelt, 1986). A movement's policy success can be reactive, stopping a harmful policy, and proactive, bringing about a new beneficial policy. A proactive impact requires having a genuine voice in the policymaking process. Beside policy changes, movements can also produce structural impacts. They can change important alliances and they can change societal institutions (Kriesi et al., 1995, p. 210). Reform movements can change institutions. The U.S. civil rights movement, for instance, engendered new government laws and government agencies and electoral realignments (decline in the popularity of the Democratic party among white southerners) (McAdam, 1982; Morris, 1984).

The exact degree of changes in policies and structures a movement causes is very hard to pin down. Along with movements, many other forces impinge on dominant elites. It is hard to be sure movements are the sole or main cause of any change (Kriesi et al., 1995, p. 208). Furthermore, a movement's impact is mediated by both its internal resources as well as its external context. Internally, a movement organization's degree of bureaucratization and centralization, as well as its strategies, can affect its success (Gamson, 1990). Externally, an elite's and a state's receptivity to grassroots challengers, and their effectiveness in carrying out policy, also affect a movement's success (Goldstone, 1980; Kitschelt, 1986). Effective response can preempt movements and deflate them (Gamson, 1990).

As noted in Chapter 1, many scholars argue that protest movements played an important role in pushing governments to pass environmental legislation in the United States and Europe. However, research on the effect of environmental movements on government pollution policy in Japan has been less in agreement. Some scholars give very little weight to environmental movements, attributing the 1970 Pollution Diet policy changes instead to international pressure or to the proactive role of the state seeking to maintain social control through compromise (Pharr et al., 1986). Pharr further argues that the Japanese ministry-business relationship in pollution politics went through three phases: (1) until the mid-1960s, government and business were tacitly collusive in avoiding and denying the problem; (2) from the mid-1960s to the mid-1970s, they were adversarial and regulatory; (3) from the mid-1970s until the mid-1980s, they were cooperative in reaching solutions (Pharr et al., 1986, pp. 236–237).

This three-stage model sets up a paradox. During the first period, government and business colluded to push for rapid growth and capital accumulation.

Pollution control, as had industrial redistribution (during the NIC issue), threatened to hamper these goals. Pollution control contravened the basic principle of the first stage. How then could the state suddenly turn on business, demand pollution control, and aggressively regulate it? That seems more like the (idealized) U.S. model of state-business relations. Where could the Japanese state, if truly enmeshed in a collusive relationship with business (which implies a good deal of business control over the supposedly regulatory agencies), have found the political will and wherewithal to make such a sudden (and brief) change of posture? The rapidity and thoroughness of pollution reduction suggests a great deal of collusion in that phase too, rather than arms-length regulation. Perhaps the network, corporatist state allows for a different form of policy coordination among the members of the Ruling Triad than that found within U.S. issue networks and iron triangles.

Other scholars of Japan (both Japanese and Western) argue that social movements, not the proactive state, were the prime movers in bringing about the Japanese pollution miracle (see Chapter 1):

. . . the residents' movement played a decisive role . . . in pushing the government to change its environmental policy in the early 1970s (Funabashi, 1992, p. 15).

And:

Due to pressure from anti-pollution public opinion, movements and progressive local governments, the national government completely revised the Basic Pollution Law in 1970 (Miyamoto, 1978, p. 158).

If social movements were such a big factor, the Ruling Triad must have made the pollution miracle, not really proactively, but preemptively – forced to concede a little so as not to lose a lot. If so, the mechanism of response among the Ruling Triad members may have been somewhat different than the proactive state model. In order to weigh these theories, we need to trace the response of the Ruling Triad to movements and external pressures.

A symbolic shift

Even before environmental protest surged in Japan, officials in the Ministry of Health and Welfare were concerned about the public health effects of severe smog pollution in the big cities. The MHW officials, chief among them Hashimoto, knew that other ministries as well as the LDP and big business had little interest in pollution control at that time. Therefore, the MHW officials devised a proactive tactic to raise public concern, that they hoped in turn would apply pressure upon the dominant members of the Ruling Triad (Kawana, 1988, pp. 23–24). The MHW managed to get a "Particulate Smoke Regulation Law" passed, which defined better air quality standards without provision for enforcement. Then the MHW set up electronic bulletin boards on major urban intersections that flashed the concentrations of various air pollutants to the public. As Hashimoto said of that tactic,

We were in the minority without power or money. In order to push forward pollution prevention administration, we had no other way but to inform the public (cited in Kawana, 1988, p. 24).

Publicly, the LDP and the economic ministries made no response to (or even denied) the growing wave of environmental complaints and protests. But privately, they worried about the political implications. In 1964 and 1965, in order to better watch over the situation, MITI and the Ministry of Health and Welfare (MHW) both created pollution bureaus. These two ministries represented the two poles of government opinion on the GE dilemma. MITI wanted to continue rapid growth whatever the social cost; the MHW wanted to give priority to cleaning up and preventing pollution and protecting public health.

In 1964, in an "epoch-making" event, the MHW proposed forming an Advisory Commission on Pollution (Hashimoto, 1988, p. 71). Hashimoto, the middle-ranking official in the MHW behind these ideas, set out to build a consensus among other elites that pollution prevention was necessary and good. At the time, the economic ministries, development banks, and big business regarded pollution control as a waste of money. They disdained the MHW as poor and weak (Hashimoto, 1988, p. 71). To provide business with pollution-equipment subsidies, Hashimoto got the MHW to borrow from national social security funds (with approval from the Ministry of Finance and MITI). Then he approached Hiramatsu, the head of MITI's new pollution bureau (and by coincidence, Oita's later governor), and convinced him to support the scheme too. Together, Hashimoto writes,

we went around to persuade the industrial and economic groups. The two of us went to the Federation of Economic Organizations, the Keizaidoyukai, the Japan Chamber of Commerce, and the Tokyo-Chiba Improvement Organization. The Ministry of Health and Welfare approached the National Governors' Association, the National Mayors' Association, and related prefectures and municipalities. With this push, the National Mayors' Association established a Pollution-Countermeasures Conference and backed us up (Hashimoto, 1988, p. 72).

The cooperative relationship between these two officials from opposing ministries illustrates a community-like ethos among elite policymakers. All the elites have a strong sense of national identification. This permits an easy "we-feeling" and cooperation through informal channels.

As an issue-entrepreneur, trying to exercise a form of creative, cultural agency, Hashimoto worried that he could not convince the LDP. In 1964, however, the LDP had just created its Pollution Committee. Under its leader, a "warm, enthusiastic" Diet politician from Osaka, this committee had already visited severely polluted sites and had talked with top LDP leaders about them. Some LDP members fought for pollution control. During a visit to a big pulp plant that was polluting Tokyo's Sumida River, Hashimoto related, the plant manager strongly criticized the LDP Pollution Committee. The LDP politician replied that

pollution is the distortion of economic progress. We absolutely must correct it. The LDP intends to firmly do this (Hashimoto, 1988, p. 72).

In this way, Hashimoto built wider consensus for better pollution control. The fragmented nature of the LDP allowed some members to respond positively.

Hashimoto's efforts bore fruit. In February 1964, Finance Minister Tanaka Kakuei created the Pollution Prevention Service Corporation (*Kogai Boshi Jigyodan*). This unit took over the MHW's efforts to subsidize pollution equipment investment by industry.[9] In 1965, the Diet approved this corporation as well as an Advisory Commission on Pollution (another MHW proposal). This advisory body was not a mere rubber stamp, as prefectural bodies had been. It served as a forum for officials, business leaders, and academics to discuss pollution issues. It "played a critical role in determining many of the important policies embodied in the Basic Law" (Nishimura, 1989, p. 18). The Diet also created national legislative pollution committees, perhaps the first in the world (McKean, 1981, p. 216). Thereafter, the Economic Planning Agency changed the name of its five-year economic growth plans to socioeconomic growth plans, and incorporated more social indicators.

Hashimoto's story illustrates how environmentalist ideas entered into and spread through the inner circle of policymakers. Having created a new policy idea, Hashimoto and Hiramatsu jointly used their social networks among the LDP and big business headquarters to persuade the other elites to accept the idea. The community quality of the Japanese polity (inner circle of top elites) facilitated the spread of ideas and new policies. To outsiders, of course, this incremental process of change is invisible and out of reach. This contrasts with the U.S. situation, in which government bureaucrats are bound by strict rules not to lobby Congress or interest groups (Interview, official of U.S. Department of Commerce, 1995).

The growing concern about pollution also affected local governments. In 1965, under Ministry of Health and Welfare (MHW) guidance, Oita Prefecture

---

9. In 1965, investment in pollution equipment was extremely low, only 0.3 percent of total industrial investment in Japan.

began surveys of the NIC factories' potential air and water pollution. On its own, the Oita government set up a Pollution Countermeasures Advisory Council (April, 1966). It also concluded pollution "memorandums" (*oboegaki*) with a number of the companies: Kyushu Electric (November 1965), Showa Denko petrochemical (May 1965), Kyushu Oil refinery (March 1969), New Japan Steel (December 1969), Tsurusaki Pulp (February 1970), Nikko Copper Refinery (May 1970), and others. However, these memorandums were "gentlemen's agreements." The company agreed to minimize pollution, but the agreements lacked regulatory standards or enforcement provisions. As a result, the agreements had little effect on pollution output, as Oita's growing air and water pollution testified.

At the MHW's insistence, the Pollution Advisory Council's August 1966 report urged some revolutionary reforms: human health should have priority over economic growth; industries should be held "strictly liable" for pollution damage, even when they had not been legally negligent (no-fault liability); industries should pay for pollution prevention measures (McKean, 1981, p. 217).

This went too far for some members of the Ruling Triad. Despite Hashimoto and Hiramatsu's attempts at consensus-building, the economic costs such restrictions would impose caused strong differences of opinion. Economic interests broke asunder the ideological consensus Hashimoto had sought to foster. The economic ministries (MITI and the Ministry of Construction) and business organizations (Federation of Economic Organizations and others) flatly rejected this report (Nishimura, 1989, p. 19). They advocated the exact opposite: Economic growth would continue to get top priority, because it would produce higher living standards and health; pollution standards would not be fixed by law; any polluter who observed legal standards would not be liable for damages; and the government had to help pay for pollution cleanup (McKean, 1981, p. 218). The MITI-LDP-Federation triad blocked any immediate legislative action on the report (McKean, 1981).

At this juncture, however, the LDP had to contend with more than business interests. The party's proportion of the total popular vote and its seats in the Diet had slipped greatly. In 1958, the LDP received a comfortable 57.8 percent of the popular vote and 61 percent of the seats in the Lower House. By 1967, buffeted by urban opposition parties, it garnered only 48.8 percent of the popular vote. With the help of conservative independents, the LDP still secured 57 percent of Diet seats, retaining its rule.

The party worried that mounting environmental protest might further reduce its share of the popular vote and eventually end its majority in the Diet. LDP party leaders began to think that some sort of response to the protestors was necessary. The MHW kept up its pressure for a law on responsibilities for pollution damages. Finally, in 1966, the Prime Minister's Office directed the MHW to draft a basic law for Pollution Control (hereafter, the Basic Law).

The MHW's draft supported the Council's reform recommendations. The draft said that "the protection of the people's health and welfare takes precedence over the pursuit of corporate and economic profit." It advocated strict industrial liability and the establishment of an administrative compensation fund and an Environmental Agency.

This draft sparked fierce dispute. MITI and the Economic Planning Agency attacked the MHW's emphasis on public health and the environment (McKean, 1981, p. 19; Hashimoto, 1988, p. 112). The business community also severely criticized the MHW's draft. The Federation of Economic Organizations said, "The industrial community has a great deal of unease about this draft of the Basic Law" (Hashimoto, 1988, p. 112).

Under fire, the Prime Minister removed all of the MHW's strong regulatory and "health-first" provisions from the draft. For the "health takes precedence" phrase, the Prime Minister's draft substituted the infamous "harmony clause" – "Protecting the people's health from pollution shall be carried out in harmony with healthy economic progress" (Hashimoto, 1988, p. 112; Gresser et al., 1981, p. 24). The public and mass media interpreted this phrase as indicating that the government had succumbed to business and economic ministry priorities (McKean, 1981, p. 219).

In August 1967, this weakened bill passed the Diet as the Basic Law for Pollution Control. The Basic Law did little to regulate or sanction industrial pollution (McKean, 1981, p. 220). Resulting pollution standards went largely unenforced. As a result, the Basic Law became another example of "symbolic politics," like the NIC Law. It provided a symbolic response to a complaining sector of the public, but did little to remedy the real problem. But this time, unlike the NIC case, symbolic rewards did not quiet down public demand.

The first concrete product of the Basic Law was the 1968 Air Pollution Control Law. Following the recommendations of a scientific committee, this set strict emission standards for sulfur dioxide. The petrochemical, power, and other industries fiercely opposed the standards. They said it was unwarranted scientifically, was too costly to achieve, and would handicap Japanese business in the world market. As a result, the government relaxed the resulting air pollution standards, and largely neglected to enforce them (McKean, 1981, p. 221).

Curiously, however, the actual atmospheric levels of sulfur dioxide pollution started to plummet at the same time (see Figure 3.1). MITI had begun an initiative to guide power plants to build tall smokestacks to scatter the pollution over a wider area, thus reducing its density at urban monitoring stations. MITI also urged the plants to buy low-sulfur crude oil, even though it cost more, because burning it would cause less sulfur dioxide air pollution. At the same time, MITI bureaucrats worked on lowering the cost of desulfurization technology. They calculated that the adoption cost would not raise production costs more than 1 percent in most cases, not a significant burden to industry (Nishimura, 1989, p. 22). This indicates the immediate success of informal guidance by MITI, which had jurisdiction over the power sector, in getting power plants to cut their emissions without legal regulation.

At the same time, a number of ministries introduced new environmental initiatives. The MHW created the Environmental Pollution Control Service Corporation, a quasi-governmental special corporation (*tokushu hojin*) that installed pollution equipment in businesses and lent them money to pay for it, made available from the national pension fund at a low interest rate.[10] The MHW also created "industrial apartment buildings" (*kogyo danchi*) in non-residential areas of Tokyo (such as on the way to Haneda airport) and moved the most polluting small- and medium-sized factories there.

MITI adopted some new anti-pollution policies, such as the requirement that any new industrial complex devote one-quarter of its land area to a green belt buffer zone along any residential areas, and urged the use of low-sulfur fuels.

Given the ineffectiveness of the Basic Law, other sorts of pollution, public protest, and international criticism continued to mount. In 1967 and 1968, pollution victims from the big four incidents filed suit against the companies responsible for their illnesses (the Minamata and Niigata mercury poisonings, Toyama cadmium poisoning, and Yokkaichi asthma cases). In 1970, a national survey showed that there was mercury and cadmium pollution in many waterways. Photochemical smog hospitalized school children in Tokyo. In 1970, 71 percent of big city residents said they were suffering from pollution (48 percent in other cities, 32 percent in towns and villages).[11] In addition, President Nixon targeted Japan's lack of pollution control as an unfair trade advantage, a hidden subsidy to its industry (Nishimura, 1989, p. 261). The United States passed the National Environmental Protection Act (NEPA) in 1969 and established the U.S. Environmental Protection Agency. But at that same time, Japan was still acquiring its reputation as the "archipelago of pollution" (Matsubara, 1971, p. 158).

Given the lack of comprehensive government response, environmental movements turned to opposition parties for support. Movements supported Socialist party candidates who promised to address the pollution issue. With

10. Interview data, Hashimoto Michio, April 3, 1990. See also Nishimura, 1989, p. 18.

11. Yomiuri newspaper, "Kogai Mondai" (pollution problems), Gekkan, Yoron Chosa 2 [August 1970], 55. Cited in McKean, 1977, p. 225.

movement help, many of them won the office of mayor and even governor. This led to a rising tide of opposition party (progressive) mayors and governors (see Figure 3.2) (McKean, 1981, p. 22–25; Steiner et al., 1980). The number of progressive mayors went from only 20 in 1947 to 138 in 1973 (out of 643). By 1970, their areas included Tokyo, Osaka, Kyoto, other big cities, and over one-third (38 percent) of the entire Japanese population (Steiner et al., 1980, p. 326). These progressive local politicians passed many innovative local pollution laws (McKean, 1981, p. 221–224; Reed, 1986). They also invented many new forms of grassroots political participation that gave greater voice to ordinary citizens (Broadbent, 1988).

The Pollution Diet

In polluted areas, the LDP had lost much of its former support (McKean, 1981, p. 227). It saw that the weak symbolic measures of the 1967 Basic Law had not satisfied public demand. The national wave of protest movements presented the LDP with a crisis (Interview, Hashimoto Michio, April 3, 1990). Party leaders worried that this trend might lead to a serious loss of votes and Diet seats in the next general election.

In response, in July 1970, Prime Minister Sato Eisaku created a new Cabinet-level group, the Central Pollution Countermeasures Headquarters, with himself as chairman. He brought in fifteen middle ranking officers from concerned ministries (MITI, Welfare, Transportation) and nineteen junior officers to help them out, all on full-time assignment (Kato, 1989, p. 3). The Headquarters group had to do something concrete – symbolic measures would no longer suffice. The group's vice-chairman told the Diet that the Basic Law's "harmony" clause had become:

an inflamed appendix and had to be surgically removed. The MITI Minister (Miyazawa) agreed with this. Removal would not hurt the business community. If it was not removed, the public would question the connection between the LDP and the business community (Asahi Newspaper, August 10, 1970).[12]

The group's substantive purpose was to amend and improve the 1967 Basic Law. To do so, it had to reconcile the opposition of MITI ("growth first") and the MHW ("health first"). It also wanted to prevent the government's internal dissension from becoming public (Asahi Newspaper, November 10, 1970, as cited in Matsubara, 1971, p. 160). To the public, the Ruling Triad wanted to represent government as one smoothly functioning unit, unaffected by public

12. All Asahi newspaper citations in this section are from Matsubara, 1971, p. 156–166.

pressure, unassailable from outside. Cracks in this facade could weaken the Ruling Triad's grip on symbolic legitimacy, an essential ingredient of rule.

The Headquarters group met often and took policy proposals from many sources, even from the opposition parties. The ministries fought for influence over the draft. As had happened with the Basic law, the group's draft proposals turned toward punishing and fining the direct source of the pollution, industrial companies. At the same time, the group proposed giving the prefectures greater power to set their own, stricter regulatory standards.

In August of 1970, Sato convened the Cabinet Ministers' Pollution Counter-measures Conference. The ministers made hurried decisions, without taking much time for broad consultation (*nemawashi*) with ministries and business. Even the responsible offices of the related ministries had little idea how the ministers would change the bills (*Energii to Kogai,* 140. December 3, 1970: 1129).

Following the recommendations of the Headquarters group, the Cabinet Ministers had agreed within two months to a number of important revisions to the Basic Law. They agreed to remove the "harmony" clause, designate the financial responsibilities for pollution cleanup, clarify national and prefectural division of regulatory powers over pollution, and greatly strengthen measures against air and water pollution (Kato, 1989, p. 3). In their draft, the ministers eliminated the "harmony" clause and inserted one that read, "More than economic growth, we must first give priority to the people's health and life environment" (Matsubara, 1971, p. 163). Prime Minister Sato himself decided to create the Environmental Agency to manage these new laws (Kato, 1989, p. 3).

During this process, big business resistance resurfaced, but not as sharply. The Federation of Economic Organizations (FEO) again voiced opposition, but only to a few of the more objectionable demands (McKean, 1981, p. 235). The FEO opposed both punitive civil (criminal) laws against industrial polluters and greater prefectural regulatory powers.[13]

To further calm the business community, Sato publicly reaffirmed that pollution control must not slow down rapid economic growth (cited in Matsubara, 1971, p. 158). He argued that all parties, national and local government, and business and the citizens must share responsibility for ending pollution (Asahi Newspaper, August 4, 1970). The vice-chairman of the group also made similar pronouncements, telling the Diet that "we won't just adopt the MHW's 'health protection first' attitude" (Matsubara, 1971, p. 159). Under business pressure, the ministers removed all clauses enforcing preventative measures (regulations that would apply to plans for an industrial plant) from the draft. As a result, the

---

13. Matsubara, 1971, p. 161; *Energii to Kogai,* 139 (November 26, 1970): 1124.

new legal measures would only apply to proven, existing polluters. Business's lack of total opposition indicated a change of attitude from self-righteous defiance to acquiescence (McKean, 1981, p. 235).

Why did big business – the third powerful member of the Ruling Triad – soften its resistance? Top business leaders worried that widespread environmental protests (such as labor protests) could disrupt productivity. In Mishima-Numazu, protest movements had already stopped a big project. "If the worsening environment and pollution illness is not attended to," they thought, "further growth may become impossible" (Uchiyama, 1978, p. 271). In short, the disruptive potential of social protest loomed large in the minds of business leaders (Piven & Cloward, 1971; Schwartz, 1976). This realist structural pressure was a crucial causal link in the political process.

Lowered business resistance let the LDP take a tougher stance in favor of pollution control (compared with the way it handled the NIC issue). It had many reasons to do so. The number of pollution incidents and protests continued to increase, and the United States had just created its own new environmental laws and agency (Kato, 1989, p. 3). The LDP regime itself may have been at stake. Even MITI Minister Miyazawa (an LDP faction leader) argued in 1970 that the level of social concern had "changed completely" since 1967 (when the Basic Law was passed). Partial amendments, he said, would no longer suffice. Miyazawa's support proved to be a turning point for Japan's formal pollution policy.

During the framing process, the MHW continued to debate MITI over how much of the pollution cleanup costs business should have to pay. Their arguments reflected typical and universal disagreements over how to solve the GE dilemma in capitalist society. In terms of social rationales regarding this issue, the pro-business side usually argues that the demand for production and consumption arises ultimately from society, and therefore society should pay the cleanup costs through taxes. The environmentalist side replies that, if they do not bear direct responsibility, the makers of industrial pollution, refining and manufacturing businesses, will have little incentive to clean up their production processes. From a third point of view, social rationales aside, it may be that the state or business elite are quite willing to sacrifice social welfare for the attainment of other goals, such as state power or business profits. The MHW's draft of the new laws argued that polluting industries should bear between one-third and all of the cost. The MITI draft left that point vague (as the Basic Law had, which in that case led to inaction). Prime Minister Sato had argued that everyone bore the responsibility for pollution. What he meant, it turned out, was that everyone should take a loss for cleaning it up: lower industrial profits, lower wages for labor, higher consumer prices (Matsubara, 1971, p. 165). In line with

MITI's stance, ultimately, business was not held responsible for the major portion of cleanup costs.

Along with a substantive response, the LDP tried new methods to reduce public anger at polluting companies. The LDP put great energy into a "national people's movement to drive out pollution." The theme of this movement was that trying to fix responsibility for pollution and the costs of its cleanup was ideological and political, by which it meant leftist or Communist. In its draft planning document for this "movement," the LDP stated its purpose clearly:

We must oppose the radicals who want to blame pollution on the [LDP] government and decrease public political trust (Matsubara, 1971, p. 166).

Such attempts indicate that the LDP and other members of the Ruling Triad were alarmed by the wave of public protest. The party's attempts at turning the public finger of blame away from big business and the LDP did not succeed. In contrast to the polite petition delegations from Oita seeking aid for regional industrial growth, environmental protest movements were quite willing to disrupt the social order. To defuse the electoral and economic threat posed by these protest movements, the Triad had to respond with substantive, effective, and public changes.

In November 1970, the Cabinet Ministers Conference presented its fourteen anti-pollution bills to the Diet. The Diet passed them all. This earned that legislative session the name "Pollution Diet" (Nishimura, 1989, p. 27). The fourteen new laws established a strict set of pollution regulations, including the Polluter Financial Responsibility Law and Pollution Crime Punishment Law, revisions of the 1967 Basic Law, Air and Water Pollution Prevention Laws, Natural Park Laws, Poisonous Material and Agricultural Chemical Control Laws, Waste Disposal Law, and others. Their statement of purpose of these laws gave great weight to environmental protection:

By making clear the obligation of corporations, the national government and local government to prevent pollution, as well as by establishing the legislation that will be the basis for pollution prevention regulations, we prepare for the general advance of anti-pollution policy. With this, we intend to protect the health of the citizens and preserve the life environment (cited in Iijima, 1994, p. 23).

However, one should note certain gaps. The statement of purpose eliminated the words in the ministers' draft that had given health and the life environment "greater" priority than the economy. Furthermore, the new laws did not set specific pollution emission standards or limits. They left enforcement entirely up to national and prefectural government bureaucracies, which were supposed to pass and enforce specific regulations. The laws did not provide any funding for regulatory enforcement (Matsubara, 1971, p. 167). Government agencies decided on emission standards for sulfur oxides, carbon monoxide, water quality, and noise in 1971, but critics judged them insufficient. An Asahi editorial commented, "I don't think this level of regulation will remove pollution from our country" (June 16, 1971). In contrast to the 1969 U.S. National Environmental Protection Act (NEPA), the fourteen Japanese Diet laws had no requirements for environmental impact assessments of government-funded industrial projects, nor any mention of citizen participation.

The lack of specific provisions was typical of Japanese law. All Japanese laws are written in vague terms, so as to require interpretation by a government ministry. Upham concludes that

(the laws) remain legally informal – legal non-events that do not increase the possibility of judicial intervention or ministerial loss of control (Upham, 1987).

In the United States, laws state clear and specific performance standards. That way, individual citizens can defend their rights, sue corporations and governments, even be their own lawyers. U.S. style puts great power into citizen hands. Many consider this vital to democracy. In Japan, elites purposely avoid such a devolution of power by making laws as vague as possible and not stating any specific standards. This leaves much greater power in ministerial hands, as later events in Oita demonstrated. In particular, economic bureaucrats feared that environmental impact assessments with public participation would create many stumbling blocks to carrying out growth plans.

To coordinate the implementation of the new laws, Prime Minister Sato proposed (and the Diet established) the Environmental Agency (EA) on May 24, 1971. Its Director General received a seat in the Prime Minister's Cabinet. The Agency's mandate was to promote pollution control, nature conservation, and related issues. Its activities included making and implementing key environmental laws, establishing environmental quality standards, conducting research, and coordinating environmental administration (which is diffused among many ministries). On a brighter note, though, the Asahi admitted that the new EA provided a place for centralized control of all the scattered pollution regulations (January 26, 1971).

The EA suffered from numerous problems. Since it was an agency, not a ministry, however, it did not have its own permanent management cadre. Officers came on loan from the MHW, MITI, and other ministries (Organization of Economic Cooperation and Development, nd, p. 24). Also, its budget was much smaller than fully fledged ministries (by as much as 95 percent) and it had less authority (Interview, Hashimoto Michio, February 23, 1990).[14] Further-

14. The budget of the Environmental Agency started at 8 billion yen in 1972, but rose quickly to 45 billion in 1980, remaining stable thereafter.

more, it got very few of the existing environmental regulatory powers held by other ministries. MITI, for instance, kept the power to regulate pollution from power plants, which had become such a large source of air pollution. The EA got only the power to regulate automobile exhaust, a serious but consumer-based source of pollution.

To show seriousness of intent, however, Prime Minister Sato appointed a dedicated figure as the Environmental Agency's first Director General. Oishi Buichi, a former medical doctor and public health advocate, took his mandate seriously. He enacted a number of important symbolic measures that made him very popular among average citizens, if not among business leaders. The first Environmental White Paper described Japan as a "melting pot" (*rutsubo*) of pollution. Oishi took the unusual step of visiting the victims of the Minamata disease and apologizing to them.

The EA set about its task with zeal. Its Pollution Advisory Council rapidly reduced the allowable levels for sulfur dioxide, one of the most obvious air pollutants. The Council also relaxed the burden of causal proof, making it easier for citizens to win suits against polluting companies. The EA created the famous "polluter pays principle" following a European example (Nishimura, 1989, p. 29; Organization of Economic Cooperation and Development, nd, p. 29). This forced companies to pay compensation to victims out of fees paid to local government, assessed according to their emissions of sulfur dioxide. The extent of the required changes shocked some of the polluting industries. In the words of one bureaucrat, the new regime converted a "polluter's heaven" into a "polluter's hell" (Nishimura, 1989, pp. 261–265).

Director Oishi, Hashimoto, and other EA officials attended the 1972 United Nations Conference on the Environment in Stockholm. Conference resolutions roundly criticized Japan's severe pollution, but also recognized that its condition was only the most severe symptom of a worldwide illness. Director Oishi made a famous speech pledging that Japan would greatly improve its pollution situation. All the attending nations signed a pledge to reduce atmospheric SO_2 pollution levels. The ideas Oishi brought back from the conference included the Environmental Impact Assessment (EIA) with local resident participation.

Hashimoto said he came away impressed with the world SO_2 agreement, and worked hard to achieve it: "We took the call seriously and by the 1980s had reduced SO_2 emissions by 85 percent." But as time passed, Hashimoto was disillusioned to see that no other nation made much progress. Levels in United States and England, for instance, showing virtually no decline even up to 1989 (Figure 1.4) (Organization of Economic Cooperation and Development, 1993, p. 17). Hashimoto commented ruefully, "Now, in 1989, they have called for a 30 percent reduction by 1992" (Interview, February 1990).

Unprecedented Japanese court decisions between 1971 and 1973 gave victory to the Minamata and other major pollution victims' suits. The judgments imposed stiff punishments and fines on the polluting industries (Gresser et al., 1981). Traditionally, Japanese courts almost never championed popular rights against the establishment (Upham, 1987). The movement victories signaled a new era and spurred citizen movements throughout the country, including Oita, to use the courts (Gresser et al., 1981, p. 44). This new legal threat put more pressure on bureaucrats to interpret the new anti-pollution laws strictly.

The new pollution regime had effects on local pollution politics as well. The EA's initial zeal played a crucial role in Oita's GE dilemma. In 1972, the EA urged Oita's Governor Taki to conduct an impact assessment on the potential environmental effects of its NIC's Phase Two plan (see Chapter 5). The new laws also empowered prefectures to set their own standards for air, water and noise pollution appropriate to local conditions (Gresser et al., 1981, p. 25). As a result, after 1970, the number and quality of prefectural pollution laws suddenly jumped. The adoption of tougher pollution regulations and supportive procedures such as citizen referendums at the prefectural level depended on the political orientation of the dominant coalition (see Chapter 8).

Later in 1972, the Sato cabinet fell. Tanaka Kakuei became Prime Minister and avidly proposed plans to "rebuild" the Japanese islands. The owner of real estate companies, Tanaka was like Molotch's Santa Barbara "rentiers" on a colossal scale. He had plans for ambitious construction projects all over Japan. This quickly brought him into conflict with EA Director General and activist Oishi. Tanaka replaced Oishi with an inactive Director General (Koyama Nagemori).

Prime Minister Tanaka's growth-first orientation could have spelled the end of Japan's pollution miracle. But certain powerful politicians within the LDP demanded that the government continue to give serious attention to pollution. After a short interval, one of these figures emerged. The Prime Minister appointed Miki Takeo, a powerful LDP faction leader, as the third EA Director General. Miki resumed the activist stance of the Agency. He established strict standards for auto exhaust.

The outspoken Miki did not last long in this position. He publicly criticized the corruption of the Tanaka cabinet and was forced to resign in July of 1974. In December of that year, however, the Tanaka cabinet fell in a corruption scandal. In an ironic turnabout, Miki became Prime Minister (Kawana, 1988, pp. 568–610). During his era, Miki continued a fairly vigorous anti-pollution regime despite the Oil Shock and a recession.

Miki is an example of the "anti-mainstream conservatives" who played a swing role within the LDP. These figures forced the LDP to respond to social crises when they reached a certain threshold (Calder, 1988, p. 444). Their power derived from the factionalized organizational structure of the LDP. At times, power bargaining among the factions allowed some voices of conscience to successfully leverage for welfare or pollution control-oriented policies. This kind of swing role within the conservative party proved important in some of Oita's pollution issues as well.

With LDP support, sporadic though it was, the EA vigorously implemented pollution control laws for its first few years. The EA and the courts interpreted the fourteen pollution laws strictly. After 1973, they forced a number of polluting companies to pay large fines, pay for medical costs of victims, and build pollution-prevention facilities. In addition, the growing activism of the high courts helped the EA.

As a result, Japan's international reputation changed within a few years from "islands of pollution" to pollution-control model. The international community came to rate Japan's pollution regulatory system very favorably. A 1977 OECD report concluded that Japanese "trends in environmental quality . . . are on the whole . . . more favorable than in other countries" (Organization of Economic Cooperation and Development, 1977, p. 67). Even environmentalists praised its policies as the most thorough and effective in the world (Huddle et al., 1975).

So made and implemented, the new laws effectively spurred industry to control some of the more noxious and obvious sources of air and water pollution. Once agreed on, industry worked hard to meet the standards. The 1971 court verdicts in favor of pollution victims added the fear of restitution payments and punitive fines to business's earnestness at this task (McKean, 1981, p. 235).

Regarding air pollution, the government gradually strengthened industrial requirements for desulfurization technology and subsidized it. By 1990, Japan possessed about 90 percent of the modern stack gas desulfurization equipment in use throughout the world (Interview, Tokyo Electric Company, 1990).[15]

As a result, environmental conditions improved dramatically. Acute heavy metal mercury poisoning did not break out again. Asthma cases and photochemical smog incidents decreased. After a few years, Tokyoites could once again see Mount Fuji on good days. Inland Sea "red tide" outbreaks came less frequently. However, the 1970 laws had clear limits; they reduced damage to human beings but did not help other life forms – the fish in the Inland Sea or the wildlife in national parks (Gresser et al., 1981, p. 25 and fn. 119, p. 423). The

---

15. The terrible atmospheric pollution produced without such equipment is illustrated by U.S.-owned copper refineries in Peru. These produce a sulfurous air-pollution smog in surrounding communities so thick that cars need to turn on their headlights during the day (*New York Times*, Dec. 13, 1995).

new laws neglected to create a broad national environmental protection plan. Also, they did not urge an environmental impact assessment with local citizen participation, the way NEPA had. This became a hotly contested issue in Oita.

Forces of change

Japan's sudden passage and implementation of effective anti-pollution legislation, compared with the other ACID societies, may have been a "pollution miracle." What set of social forces shaped and created it? We started with several theories: the responsible ministerial state, foreign criticism, and environmental movement pressure. How do they rate?

Clearly, a proactive state did play an important role. Without the continued efforts of the MHW, the requisite pollution-control policy ideas would not have been waiting in convenient form. Without MITI's administrative guidance to power plants, the sulfur dioxide levels would not have started to plummet before effective laws were passed. However, was the proactive state a sufficient condition to make the pollution miracle happen? That is dubious.

MITI's guidance, directing electrical power plants to reduce the intensity of emissions by scattering them more widely (perhaps because of Hashimoto and Hiramatsu's efforts at consensus-building), exemplify a proactive state. But these efforts were quite limited. In other areas of pollution control, little appears to have been accomplished by informal guidance before 1970. Beyond that, the state strongly resisted making formal laws that would make standards public and incite popular demand to enforce them. Until 1970, the MHW found its "radical" proposals continually rebuffed or removed from drafts by the LDP, because of business objections. As a result of this constellation of forces, the first formal policy response to the wave of protest, the 1967 Basic Law, turned out to be largely symbolic in content.

Only when the electoral threat to the LDP and the productivity threat to big business (from protests and from court fines) both increased sharply did the LDP pass substantive formal legislation. Both of these threats came from the rising wave of protest. In other words, the wave of protest changed the Ruling Triad's political opportunity structure for the worse. In general theoretical terms, popular agency created an unfavorable structure of threatening political-economic sanctions for the Ruling Triad. This popular agency emerged from the plastic situation of two contradictory political-economic structures: increasing pollution in the natural environment on the one hand, and a Triad goal of rapid capital accumulation that long rejected compromise despite the mounting harm. The subsequent rapid shift in policy shows that this policy goal was not generated by institutional structures such as decision rules. Rather, the goal of accumulation grew from the combined, structurally defined material interests of big business and the ministerial state.

The new post-war constitution, though, had imported latent institutional arrangements less favorable to the dominance of this Triad than in pre-war times. The institutional structure of democracy allowed popular movements to defeat the LDP at the polls in many municipalities, and threatened such at the national level. Unable to change these institutions, all members of the Triad perceived a threat to their continued collective hegemony. With years of ministerial retirees entering the command posts of LDP politics and business, the Triad had indeed become something of a community of interest and identity.

Under this new electoral threat to regime stability, business leaders became more agreeable to take more substantive measures against pollution. Accordingly, the Pollution Diet and its immediate aftermath did not really mark an "era of confrontation" (Pharr et al., 1986). Rather, the comparative rapidity and effectiveness of the Japanese pollution miracle (Figure 1.4) indicates business's willing, if grudging, compliance with the new pollution control goals. Without such compliance from business, Japan would have suffered the policy-grid-locked fate of the other ACID countries.

Foreign criticism sharply increased at the same time. Was it more important than movement pressure? To be sure, Japanese bureaucrats often eagerly adopted foreign policy ideas, as with the growth pole idea in the early 1960s. The 1969 U.S. National Environmental Protection Act (NEPA), passed shortly before the Pollution Diet, may have provided a cognitive model for policy reform in Japan. However, the biggest international influence on the environment – the U.N. Conference on the Environment, which denounced Japan's pollution – happened a year *after* the Pollution Diet. Intellectually, Oishi joined this new "epistemic community" of global environmentalists. He said he picked up his environmental assessment and citizen participation ideas at the U.N. conference (rather than from similar U.S. NEPA provisions). But back home inside the Triad, Oishi found few receptive minds. The statements of LDP and business leaders revealed great concern about the effects of protest movements, but none about foreign criticism. Internationally minded ministerial officials may have been very concerned about foreign criticism. But, as our case studies have shown, such officials had little effect on policy content unless other circumstances made the LDP and business concerned. Accordingly, I conclude that neither foreign criticism, new ideas, nor a proactive, autonomous state were central causes of Japan's pollution miracle. Rather, we have to ascribe that policy shift to political pressures generated by the wave of environmental protest within Japan.

This success happened "behind the backs" of the protestors, though. Most of them did not have national policy change aspirations. Neither did Japanese environmental protest movements establish a strong national presence (as they have in the United States and Europe). They did not elect their own representatives to the national Diet and cause policy change that way, as the pluralist model predicts. Rather, they achieved a measure of national policy influence because they forced the Ruling Triad to preempt the pollution issue in order to maintain its political hegemony. Getting preemptive policy concessions is a recognized form of movement success (Gamson, 1990), so I conclude that the environmental movement played *the* crucial role in ushering in Japan's pollution miracle.

However, given the Ruling Triad's strategy of strengthening its domination by fostering an impression of untouchable omnipotence, it did not publicly acknowledge the effect of movement pressure. More importantly, preemptive anti-pollution laws were not the only elite response. Along with reducing the pollution, the elites planned to undercut and defuse the opposition by discrediting the model of citizen social activism and by rectifying the moral debts to the public accrued by the (polluting) actions of business and government (Upham, 1987, p. 56). Chapters 4 though 8 show how these social control ploys played out at the local level.

Conclusions

The Japanese case does bear out the hypothesis that a sudden opening in the political opportunity structure initiated a broad cycle of protest over diverse and changing issues – started by labor, continued by students and diffusing to local communities. However, after the early changes introduced by the Occupation in the 1940s, the political situation remained essentially stable. If anything, it grew more centralized and conservative, and less receptive to protest. Despite that, from the 1960s, a wave of environmental movements welled up, peaked, and declined. Where this picture differs from the POS-stimulated hypothesis, though, is that protest was not mainly transferred to succeeding constituencies – labor to students to polluted communities – mainly by packets of emotional excitement or tactical repertoires. These played their role, to be sure. Rather, the sudden heavy imposition of heavy pollution costs established the basic mobilization potential for environmental protest. Without this basic incentive, little mobilization occurred. Once present, though, the added factors of leaders affected by earlier waves of protest helped the nascent grievances coalesce into protest activity.

According to Figure 3.1, it took some years for local people to frame pollution as a justifiable grievance. Once so framed, though, the grievances quickly led to a wave of complaints to local government. Finding no effective response, frustrated by government, party, and business, locals quickly turned to unruly public protest.[16] The rapidity of local mobilization indicates that, contrary to some theory, people did not need extensive cognitive liberation from deferential political beliefs. Rather they applied already existing subcultural codes that justified protest behavior. The next chapter will show in detail the different processes by which cognitive framing and the application of these codes transpired.

The fact that increased harm from pollution could lead to reframing and protest indicates that the Ruling Triad elites did not exercise very effective ideological hegemony over the public mind. The Triad had tried to convince the public to give blind and uncritical approval to industrial growth, but in the face of pollution and other problems, had failed. In addition, the rapidity of translation from frustrated grievance into protest indicates an absence of coercive repression. If the police had jailed or shot the early environmental protestors, as they do in some countries, the wave would not have had the political effect it did in Japan. Movements mobilized relatively free of coercive repression. They enjoyed the freedoms of assembly, speech, and media that their newly open political institutions provided. This openness, though, had not just come upon them – it had been that way for two decades. Therefore it cannot be counted as the cause of the mobilization. Rather, until the start of the wave of protest, most citizens had not felt impelled to draw on their new political freedoms. The imposition of new grievances had pushed them into making use of these freedoms, as well as of the available resources (time, facilities, education) and protest ideologies latently present within their communities. People activated these latent resources when they needed them. Later chapters will examine this mobilization process in greater detail, but it is worth noting at this point that these movements did not, contrary to theory, mainly draw their membership from the new middle class (professionals).

Once mobilized, environmental protest movements used the new political institutions (elections and courts) to push for better pollution control. The Japanese polity produced an effective response to some movement demands, weakening their rationale for existence. Japanese government response to air pollution proved better than that of other ACID societies. In turn, this broad, popular mobilization awakened the dominant Triad from its general acquies-

---

16. The rapidity of massive protest mobilization also runs contrary to expectations by resource-mobilization theory that grievances are constant. The facts also cast doubt on predictions by reframing theory that an extensive process of cognitive liberation would be necessary before mobilization could occur (both noted at the beginning of this chapter).

cence with the political status quo, and forced it to invent new, more subtle means of social control.

This pattern of government response resembles Calder's model of "crisis and compensation" – the LDP, he argues, maintained its dominance by compromising at the right time and in the right way (Calder, 1988). As with the case of the NIC law (Ch. 2), though, the LDP's response was not as ready to strike a deal, or as proactive, as that model implies. The LDP response evolved through a gradual political process. The LDP did not start with a substantive policy response to popular demands. Instead, it first tried symbolic politics – words without substance. The NIC Law turned out to be mostly symbolic (Ch. 2). Similarly, the 1967 Basic Law on pollution was symbolic. Only insistent public pressure forced the LDP to concede a more substantive policy response – the fourteen laws of the Pollution Diet.

The grudging attitudes with which the Ruling Triad embarked upon the making of Japan's pollution miracle shows, also, that they had not gone through a paradigm-shift in values. The new environmental paradigm had not penetrated and transformed their values, as it had begun to in activist segments of the public. The ideas and values of the movements, by themselves, did not have much effect on the LDP, the state, or its policies. The Ruling Triad was not ignorant of these ideas. The MHW had been advocating them for a long time. They spread through the Ruling Triad by the efforts of a few idealists such as Hashimoto. They may have had some informal effect on Hiramatsu and a few other middle-ranking MITI officials. But, even if most Triad members had no developed philosophy in either direction, their policy stances and actions paralleled those predicted by the nature conquest-oriented human exemptionalism paradigm.

In conclusion, at the national level, among the groups struggling over opposed political-economic goals – growth versus environmental protection – the relative possession and use of political-economic sanctions largely determined which side would win. When the wave of environmental protest imposed or threatened political-economic sanctions (through elections, courts, factory stoppages), the Ruling Triad made substantive concessions. By the mid-1970s, though, when protest movements lost their sanctioning potential, the effectiveness of environmental policy declined.

Among the allies on each side of this issue, arrangements were less dependent upon the possession of realist sanctions. Within groups or alliances holding like motivations and pursuing like goals, collective organization depended on a dense network of personal ties. These ties facilitated the flow of communication, personal believability, and trust among them (Okimoto, 1989). Within the Ruling Triad, on the one hand, this sense of community overcame the mutual estrangement that stalemated the elites of some Western ACID societies (Crozier, 1973; Crozier, Huntington & Watanuki, 1975). It produced greater inter-elite consensus on the necessity of the policy innovations, and hence a more effective implementation. Afterward, individual companies still sought to dump waste illegally. On the whole, however, local governments implemented the new regulations faithfully, and the mainline industrial conglomerates tried to abide by them. Likewise, as the following chapters will show, the protest movements also depended heavily upon existing social institutions for mobilization and survival.

This essential cooperativeness at the core of the power structure helped produce Japan's striking efficiency in reducing air pollution. Toward outsiders, though, the networked community at any level was, as Pharr says, "inherently exclusionary" (Pharr, 1990, p. 208). The networked community intensified elite tendencies to avoid revealing their decision-making processes to the public. It led them to govern by the second, third, and fourth modes of power as much as possible. When public protest mounted, the elites gave gradual concessions – symbolic at first and only substantive when necessary, but presented these to the public as paternalistic, autonomously generated policy changes. Along with those concessions, as the following chapters show, the elites made new efforts to exercise soft social control that would dampen the protest movements.

4

Movement startups

The mobilization process

Oita Prefecture contributed its share of movements to Japan's rising tide of environmental protest. None of Oita's movements became as famous or as epoch-making as Mishima-Numazu or the four big pollution cases. But in their way, they typified the era. They faced situations similar to those faced by other movements around the country. Oita's New Industrial City factories were not the only cause for protest. In the 1950s and 1960s, many factories and power plants set up shop around the prefecture, mostly in easily accessible coastal towns such as Saeki, Usuki, and Nakatsu. Unhindered by pollution regulations, these factories and power plants threatened to or did pollute their surroundings. They provided the physical, environmental conditions that might generate a movement. This caused a mobilization potential. Actualizing that potential required group recruitment, discussion, organizing, and strategizing (Klandermans & Tarrow, 1988).

This chapter and the next look at eight communities along the shore of Oita's industrial projects. Some mobilized and fielded fierce resistance, while others did not. One produced a countermovement that tried to nullify the staunch antipollution movement in the neighboring hamlet. How to account for the difference? Why did some of the Oita communities suffering from pollution (or its imminent threat) produce a protest movement and others not? An existing physical threat or deprivation alone is not enough to spur protest (Tarrow, 1994, p. 51). Pollution or other harm may cause unhappiness or bitterness in many individuals, but this may result only in a mobilization potential, not mobilization itself. Environmental devastation afflicted a number of Oita communities without setting off protest.

To mobilize – to move from individual complaint to collective protest – is often an arduous and chancey process. Mobilization consists of five phases: talking, leadership, recruitment, organizing, and strategizing, as discussed be-

134

low. In the talking phase, people come to realize that they face a common problem and reach some agreement on its cause. At that point, someone may emerge as a leader. The coalescing group will often attract or try to recruit more adherents. When enough new members join the group, it may generate a (formal or informal) organizational structure. In the process, the leaders will choose certain sanctions and tactics for attaining their goals and, under certain circumstances, launch into collective action. For action to occur, each phase requires appropriate institutional conditions.[1] Observers debate the relative importance of changes in local material resources, social organization, values and beliefs, and the structure of opportunities and threats, in ushering the process along. Some communities negotiate this birth process and produce fledgling movements. Others smother the impulse at one stage or another.

Early theorists stressed the role of new grievances in setting off the mobilization process. Some argued that these grievances came from new irrational beliefs "akin to magic" (Smelser, 1963). Others said they came from unrealistic "rising expectations" created by sudden social change (Davies, 1962). Later theorists rejected this emphasis on irrational grievances. They stressed the importance of protest as a purposeful, rational political tactic and resource (Lipsky, 1968). People always have grievances, they argued. They only mobilized, though, when they suddenly got new resources (time, money, facilities, knowledge, social organization), enough to give them a chance of success (Jenkins, 1983; McCarthy & Zald, 1977; Tilly, 1978). In addition, the leader would be an "issue entrepreneur" who helped create the necessary organization (Jenkins, 1983). The weakening of the dominant political elites and institutions (the political opportunity structure) also added to the resources of an aggrieved group (Kitschelt, 1986; Tarrow, 1994; Tilly, 1978).

Reflecting on this resource opportunity approach, however, other scholars returned to the idea of grievances. Some argued that the sudden imposition of new objective costs set the spark of mobilization (Szasz, 1994, p. 84; Walsh, 1981). Others stressed the importance of subjective changes, or "reframing," in the meaning people gave to issues and behavior (Dalton, 1995, pp. 316–317; Eyerman & Jamison, 1991; Snow & Benford, 1992; Snow & Oliver, 1995). This included the "cognitive liberation" from a defeatist or deferential political culture (McAdam, 1982, p. 48–51) and the production of a new collective protest identity (Melucci, 1995). In this school, a new frame will succeed in drawing members to a movement to the degree it "rings true with extant beliefs, myths" (Snow et al., 1992, p. 141). Meanings may be embedded in normative social

---

1. Smelser proposes a "value-added" process for the appearance of social movements (Smelser, 1963). The process proposed here builds on that and many other studies, but allows for a wider variance of potential causal conditions at each phase.

networks that help their spread (Broadbent, 1986; Emirbayer et al., 1994, p. 1439; Friedman & McAdam, 1992, p. 170; Powell & DiMaggio, 1991; Snow, Zurcher, & Ekland-Olson, 1980). Collective meanings that constitute the culture of a local community – its "life-world" – may provide the basis for mobilization against the intruding policy machinations of an impersonal bureaucratic state (Inglehart, 1977; Offe, 1985b). Critics charge, in essence, that the subjective emphasis of the reframing view too readily returns social movement analysis to the irrational motivations stressed by earlier approaches (Gamson, 1992). Some have attempted to synthesize the range of dimensions noted here (Broadbent, 1989; Emirbayer & Goodwin, 1994, p. 1442; Friedman & McAdam, 1992; Knoke, Pappi, Broadbent & Tsujinaka, 1996, p. 223; Morris, 1992).

These debates about the mobilization process address the crucial problem of change in political institutions. The forces they address govern the appearance of new political groups. The debates concern the degree of "subjectiveness" and "objectiveness" in motivations, sanctions, and tactics. They concern the relative degree of symbolic construction and material production as the basis of social structure and action (the analytical questions raised in Chapter 1). These questions apply not only to mobilization within less privileged strata, but also among the elites. Chapter 2 approached Governor Kinoshita's mobilization of support for Oita's industrial growth from this perspective. The debates express the broader framework sketched in Chapter 1.

Japan provides a good setting for studying questions about the relative weight of these factors in the mobilization process. Japan has a strongly embedded and relatively homogeneous culture. Permanent resident non-Japanese ethnic groups [mostly of Korean descent] constitute less than 1 percent of the population. If a collective culture channels action anywhere, it should do so quite noticeably in Japan. One scholar argues that Japan's "cultural values of self-denial, aversion to conflict, and the primacy of welfare of the group or community over that of the individual" hampered protest mobilization (Pharr et al., 1986, p. 241). Accordingly, if reframing is a necessary part of the mobilization process, it should show up strongly in Japan. Movement participants should have to struggle to reinterpret their senses of injustice, efficacy, and identity. Another scholar suggests that the reframing for Japan's environmental movements came about as a result of the spread of a Marxist symbolic framework. This framework interpreted pollution as an issue of "big business versus the person in the street." The spread of the framework, he argued, sparked protest mobilization (Reed, 1986, p. 48). This, too, if present, should be observable in our case study.

This chapter and the next provide sketches of the initial mobilization process (and some of later stages) of pollution protest groups. These occurred in eight communities in Oita in the 1960s. The chapter also sketches in some earlier movements for historical background. The sketches are of varying length and depth. They indicate the important factors in their mobilization. Chapters 6 and on follow through a subset of these movements – those of the Seki communities (Kozaki, Baba, and the Seki Fishing Union) and Misa-Iejima.

That all these mobilizations occurred in roughly the same time period and area, in response to similar problems, reduces many sources of variation. It holds constant the general patterns of culture and social relations, the overarching political framework and economic conditions, and the type of problem that confronted them. Holding these constant allows us to compare the eight communities for more subtle differences: framing, resources, very local political opportunities, economic and social class composition. These differences might explain why some communities fielded protests while others did not.

Early mobilization in Oita

Feudal times

Protest movements have a long history in Oita Prefecture. Even the peasants of the Tokugawa Era (1603–1868) erupted in uprisings (*hyakkusho ikki*) against rice-hoarding sake-brewers and incompetent samurai administrators (Broadbent, 1975; Bix, 1986). During the Tokugawa Era, Oita Prefecture was the feudal domain of Bungo. On several occasions, in times of famine, starving peasants mobilized into protest movements against their condition. Similar events occurred after the end of the feudal period, during the early Meiji Period (1867–1913). Such peasant revolts established the basic "repertoire" of social forms of protest, the prototypes, for later movements in the prefecture. Tilly talks about a repertoire of protest in which ordinary folk convert traditional rituals or festivals into vehicles for protest (Tilly, 1978). These movements left behind in the villages a latent subculture of opposition to authority.[2]

2. According to feudal custom, the feudal lord had the duty of establishing emergency granaries to provide for the peasants in times of famine. But these were sometimes neglected, and merchants hoarded stores of grain for profit instead. In times of poor harvest, this neglect became painfully apparent to the peasant villagers. When pushed to the extreme, they sometimes reacted in collective upheaval. They coalesced in marches and riots, venting their anger at local businesses and culminating in a presentation of grievances to the government authorities. First, an angry crowd of famished peasants would march forth from their isolated villages and converge upon the town. There, they would smash into the warehouses of the local rice and sake merchants and distribute their hoarded stores of rice. In their rage, the peasants would often destroy the merchants' houses as well. Then they would march to the feudal castle. Their leader would try to gain an audience and beseech the feudal lord (*daimyo*) for redress of their ills. If he were rebuffed by the feudal lord, the peasant

Early Seki movements

When the Nikko company built its copper refinery on the tip of the Saganoseki peninsula in 1917 (Figure 2.1), local farmers objected strenuously. They feared that the acrid smoke from the refinery would blight the mountains and ruin the mulberry trees, on which their silk industry depended. Ignoring them, the town officials agreed to the refinery. The farmers felt betrayed. The angry farmers swarmed into town and cut through the village leader's house pillars, a tactic (*uchikowashi*) drawn straight from the Tokugawa period (Broadbent, 1975). The police brutally suppressed this protest, beating and arresting 100 participants. Nikko built the mill, and it operates there to this day.

A few years later, the railroad planned to extend its tracks out the narrow coast of the Seki peninsula to Seki town and the copper mill. The farmers and local villagers rose in protest again. They complained that the smoky, coal-fired locomotive would have showered their hamlets and fields with soot and disrupted their lives with noise. Unexpectedly, they succeeded this time. They forced the railway to turn south at the start of the peninsula, at the hamlet of Kozaki.

In analytical terms, the (threatened) sudden imposition of pollution impelled the local farmers into collective action. The farmers did not leap into action without social reference points, though. They drew on their history of peasant movements, which gave them a culture of resistance and a repertoire of protest actions. They mobilized despite a very threatening political context.

During World War Two, the government assumed partial ownership of the Nikko refinery and increased production. Enough of the refinery's sulfur dioxide-laden smoke fell on local fields to kill off trees and silk worms, destroying local sericulture and orange (*mikan*) groves. The company paid for the dead mulberry and mikan trees, but the money only amounted to about two years' profit from silk-making. At that time, if anyone complained about the pollution, the police would come around and investigate him. This frightened protestors into silence (Interview).

The early Seki movements mobilized despite a very repressive, unreceptive structure of political opportunities. The repressiveness of the system did not

leader would sometimes go all the way to the national capital of Edo. Picking an appropriate opportunity, he would run up to the Shogun's palanquin, and on bended knee hold out a petition on the end of a stick. Sometimes the Shogun would take it, and even send a committee of inquiry to the prefecture. If it was found that through mismanagement, the feudal lord had caused the famine or had not properly provided for reserves in storage granaries, he could be reprimanded or even removed from office. But the peasant leader always paid the supreme sacrifice for his audacity, as often did his entire family. As a stern warning to other peasants, the peasant leader's head often appeared on the end of a pike outside the castle walls.

eliminate protest mobilization, however. So political opportunities must be far from the only factor involved. The costs of inaction and loss of livelihood and health for self and family outweighed the costs of police beatings. A tradition of protest justified and characterized sudden bursts of mobilization, without the need for much moral reframing of the issues.

State repression left a legacy of bitterness and fear in village memory. It did not make people inwardly deferential to elites. Rather, it made them outwardly acquiescent and fearful of protesting. After the war, the copper refinery remained in operation and spewed out clouds of sulfurous smoke. Gradually, despite the harsh memories, signs of protest emerged again.

The swelling wave

Protest against industrial pollution erupted in the mid- to late 1960s in Oita. Along with the NIC, many other industrial projects threatened the health, livelihood, and lifestyle of local residents in towns throughout the prefecture. These included the hamlets of Misa and Iejima next to the NIC refineries as well as other coastal towns such as Saeki, Usuki, and Nakatsu. When the Prefectural Government announced its intentions to build more NIC landfills and factories, protest erupted in the communities of Ozai, Baba, Kozaki, and Seki, which would suffer the effects. These protest movements adopted different goals and achieved different outcomes. They also felt the effects of different combinations of (the theorized) social forces upon their mobilization process.

Recognizing Seki pollution.

As a candidate for the newly legal Japan Communist party, Himeno won election to the Seki town council (legislature) in the 1960s. All the other councillors belonged to the LDP. Himeno knew the dangers of air pollution. He had suffered from tuberculosis for five years, and suspected the Nikko smoke had caused it. His father, a farmer, had participated in the 1917 anti-copper refinery movement and been beaten by police. Until 1935, his father had made silk, but then the Nikko pollution had ruined it. Himeno thought that the Nikko smoke had probably harmed other residents' health too (Interview 126, Oct. 16, 1979).

Respiratory illness is less visible than denuded hillsides. In 1967, Himeno conducted an air pollution study and a resident health survey. He found a sulfur dioxide concentration of 0.8 ppm in the town's air. In 1979, the legally permissible maximum was 0.04 ppm (Interview 126, Oct. 16, 1979). In addition, Himeno found very high rates of asthma, bronchitis, and other respiratory diseases. Nikko refinery workers were the sickest. Eighty percent of retired

Nikko workers had severe asthma; five had died from lung cancer. In residential areas near the refinery, one in seven households had a tuberculosis patient. Tuberculosis and bronchitis rates for Saganoseki City and township far exceeded the national rates. Subsequently, a Kyoto University health survey of Saganoseki City found liver and lung cancer rates to be 2.6 times the national average (Oita Godo newspaper, March 28, 1972).[3]

After Himeno announced his findings in 1967, the copper refinery made belated efforts to atone. It planted trees, and sent nurses around to inquire about health problems at all local homes. Severe pollution, Himeno said, had sensitized Seki residents to pollution issues. This sensitivity added impetus to later environmental mobilization. Himeno's survey inspired a cognitive reframing of pollution, and planted the seeds of focused grievance in the heart of the people of Seki.

Unrest in Misa and Iejima

For centuries, the villages of Misa, Iejima, and Nakajima had clustered together among the pine groves of Oita City's white sand beaches next to the Ono River (Figure 2.1). By the standards of the time, they had been able to make a good living from fishing.

Gradually, industrial plants encroached on their area. In 1936, just before World War Two, the Sumitomo Chemical Company built an agricultural pesticide plant on the eastern side of the villages. Local people felt it posed some hazards, but during those years of increasingly authoritarian government, had little recourse but to accept it. Over the ensuing two decades, effluent from the plant flowed into the river. It caused the cultivated *nori* seaweed along the coast to turn red and die. The plant's smokestacks were only about 100 feet in height (unlike the later tall, candy-striped ones), so their smoke fell heavily on the local neighborhood. Despite this, the government had taken no interest in the plant's effects on local health.

In 1955, the Oita government initiated its Seaside Industrial Zone plan. As its first move, the administration of Sato Taiichi succeeded in recruiting the Tsurusaki Pulp Company. Land was scarce. The Oita government planned to move aside homes in the hamlet of Nakajima to make space for the pulp plant. The fishing people of the hamlets, not wanting to move and afraid the pulp plant would pollute their fishing waters, resisted it fiercely. The city and the prefecture sent officials to persuade them. When an Oita City politician came to the hamlet for that purpose, the fishermen threw him into the sea. Then the Prefec-

3. Specific rates available.

tural Government sent an official who showed the fishing people a jar of perfectly clear water. He said it was a sample of the pulp plant's effluent, showing its harmlessness. The pulp plant, he asserted, would not pollute local waters at all. A Misa resident said that the politicians and government officials refused to listen to the fishing people's reasons for opposition. Finally, the fishers barricaded their hamlet for a while, refusing to talk with any of the officials.

Their resistance did not last long, however. In the 1950s, there was no general awareness about pollution. This issue did not much concern other Misa residents and the neighborhood council (*jichikai*). Nor were people accustomed to using the neighborhood council democratically to represent their opinions. Rather, it had always conveyed collective duties to them. During that era, the Misa resident explained, most people implicitly trusted the prefectural officials. People would blindly follow the officials' lead. Also, back then, he said, people did not have much education. This meant they could not think of good reasons to refute the politicians' persuasive arguments (Interview 271, Nov. 1978). The Prefectural Government mobilized city and prefectural legislators from the Misa-Iejima area to persuade the more recalcitrant fishing people to go along. Without wider support, organized resistance to the pulp plant collapsed.

Next, the Oita government wanted to start building Landfill No. 1 in front of Misa and Iejima. This time the plants would sit right on top of their traditional fishing grounds. The Prefectural Government could not simply take away these pieces of the bay, however. The fishing families had a legal right to the fishing grounds. To fill them in, the Prefectural Government had to persuade the fishing families to sign away their rights in return for financial compensation.

The fishing people in Misa and Iejima also objected to this plan. Again, however, their protests did not spread to other residents of the village. Some residents worked for the Sumitomo Chemical Company, which discouraged participation in such protests. Furthermore, the Prefectural Government offered the fishing families what seemed like good compensation (at the time) and promised that the new factories would hire them. As a result, the fishing families ultimately surrendered their fishing grounds. In doing so, they sacrificed many time-honored values. They could no longer fish those waters. Nor could they take fish or shellfish anywhere locally, because of their fears of mercury pollution. Their bucolic hamlets became filled with industrial noises, bad air, and the noise of traffic. They could no longer relax on the beaches and coastal pine groves.

In return, the fishing people received compensation payments of about $38,000[4] (equivalent to about two years' income). All had to find new employ-

4. 3.8 million yen (100 yen = $1).

ment. A few used the money to start new businesses or invest in land, and they prospered from the change. Others used it to rebuild their homes or wasted it. A few found jobs in the new factories, mostly as laborers (Interview 113, 1979, with local fisherman). The landfill went ahead.

In quick succession, the government added Landfills Nos. 2 through 5 just to the west of Landfill No. 1. The fishing people of Tsurusaki City held a sit-in against Landfills Nos. 3 and 4 in 1961. However, they also soon changed to "conditional opposition," the condition being a better compensation payment offer. The landfills proceeded.

By the mid-1960s, the oil and steel refineries belched forth huge quantities of air- and water-polluting effluents. Shortly thereafter, Misa and Iejima residents noticed an increase in respiratory illnesses in the villages, and suspected it came from air pollution. The Prefectural Government ignored their complaints. Since the fishing people had sold their rights to the sea, they felt they had to acquiesce in the government's plans.

In 1970, Fujii Norihisa, a civics teacher in a high school near Misa and Iejima, became concerned about local air pollution and respiratory illness. Fujii was an unusual person. Besides being a high school teacher, he was also a Zen Buddhist priest with a deep love of nature and a great compassion for the less fortunate. Like Christianity, Buddhism teaches universal compassion. In contrast to Christianity, it also teaches that human beings have a very diminutive stature within nature and the cosmos (Nash, 1989, p. 113). From these roots, a Buddhist perspective can stimulate values of deep ecology (DeVall & Sessions, 1985) and an activism to help the suffering. Fujii was also active in the (Socialist party-affiliated) Japan Teachers' Union, which stood in constant opposition to the authoritarian impulses of the central government (Cummings, 1980). He was very much the critic of blind deference to the government and the dominant business elites. Other unionists in Oita referred to him as a "samurai for the environment." Fujii was an energetic spark plug of an organizer, earnestly and constantly helping and coordinating fledgling environmental movements around the prefecture.

Fujii had the students in his civics class conduct a house-to-house health survey in Misa and Iejima. They found the rates of bronchitis and asthma were higher than national averages. High school teachers have higher credibility and status in Japan than in the United States, so Fujii's results made a great impact on the local communities. The survey results confirmed residents' suspicions that their plague of respiratory diseases came from industrial air pollution. They compared themselves to famous cases like Yokkaichi. The survey results made them realize that the Prefectural Government, with its pronouncements that no pollution existed, had lied to them.

Fujii's survey results helped the villagers see the deterioration of their collective health as a problem with a cause. The information strengthened existing grievances. In a word, it helped the villagers *reframe* their ill-health, from "personal troubles" to a "common cause" – the factories – and a "common cure" – better regulation by the Prefectural Government. This particular act of reframing depended more upon new information than on liberation from a deferential culture. The new facts fit within an already existing "injustice frame" of distrust of the state and the big businesses (Gamson, 1988). Fujii's survey strengthened the "mobilization potential" of Misa and Iejima. Afterward, when asked by movement leaders from Seki, Misa and Iejima readily erupted in protest (Chapter 7).

Throughout the nation, the sorry spectacle of "dirtied hamlets" such as Misa helped fuel growing doubts about industrial growth throughout the prefecture. In 1970, stronger pollution protests erupted in the prefecture and throughout the nation. Emboldened by that wave of protest, the Misa fishing people once again voiced their grievances.

Saeki City

Saeki City, another of Oita's coastal small port towns, lies over the mountains and down the coast a short way from Seki. During the early 1960s, a plywood factory polluted the surrounding neighborhood (called Hinode) with smoke and black ash. The ash soiled laundry hung out to dry. Local residents worried about its effects on their health. Many of them complained to Katayama, the seventy-year-old head of the Hinode neighborhood (*ku*) council.

Katayama was both head of the ku and local "boss" for the LDP. He had served as an officer of the prefectural LDP and treasurer of the Saeki LDP branch organization. He always passed on requests to LDP leaders in Oita City, who had been ever-responsive to loyal clients. To Katayama, the LDP had always been helpful. So, in 1965, he asked the Oita LDP bosses to tell the plywood factory to stop polluting the air. He expected the party would take care of the problem. To his shock, this time the LDP did nothing (Interview 146, 1979).

Katayama genuinely cared about his neighborhood. Lack of LDP response upset him. Frustrated, he circulated a petition among *ku*-residents against the plywood company's pollution. After getting almost everyone to sign, he took the petition to the company and asked them to reduce their pollution. The company refused. To his dismay, the LDP leaders criticized him harshly for the petition. They told him to endure (*gaman*) the pollution. Both LDP and the company rebuffed and ignored his ensuing entreaties.

This shocking turn of events forced the elderly man to reconsider his up-to-then happy dependence on the LDP. Katayama asked a prefectural LDP politician to come and inspect the pollution. The politician replied "I can't come, my elders (*senpai*) would criticize me." Frustrated by LDP unwillingness to deal with pollution, Katayama turned elsewhere. He asked Socialist party politicians to come and inspect the pollution. They responded a number of times. He began to talk about switching his support to the JSP. His increasing alienation worried LDP leaders in Oita City.

One day, an LDP representative came to Katayama's house and offered him a large sum of money. This money, the man said, was to "pacify" his neighbors. Katayama should give them presents and some fancy dinner parties. This would compensate them for the pollution and weaken their desire to complain it. The LDP habitually used money in this way to defuse issues, buy votes and support candidates. It was the basis of the LDP political machine.

The pollution issue put the LDP in a bind. The party collected campaign funds from local and national businesses on a regular basis. No doubt the plywood factory was a contributor. The LDP could not ask its owner to lose money by investing in pollution control equipment. By not asking, however, the LDP alienated the pollution victims. It tried to bridge this gap with increased patronage money to provide symbolic compensation (parties, presents). Given the pervasive Japanese deference toward leaders, such gifts carried the persuasive imprimatur of a higher-status person.

Surprisingly, however, Katayama did not loyally accept the money and carry out the pacification. On the contrary, the money offer incensed him and he refused it. Why did he not behave like a typical LDP "local boss" and follow orders? For Katayama, it was a moral issue. Katayama explained that for a long time, he had been unhappy with the LDP because it had a "high-handed tyrannical" attitude toward the common people (Interview 146, 1979). The pollution issue brought his unhappiness to a head. He felt that going along with the pacification scheme would have made him responsible for the pollution too.

Instead, Katayama intensified his protest activities. He criticized neighboring *ku*-heads who had complied and accepted the money. His group repeatedly petitioned the mayor, who rebuffed them. Then Katayama got the signatures of all the *ku*-residents on an agreement to sue the plywood plant over its pollution. With this threat, in 1969 the mayor interceded and asked the factory owner to install pollution prevention equipment. The new, expensive equipment, while not perfect and not used consistently by the plant, did reduce the pollution. When in operation, the equipment daily filled a dump truck with ash that had formerly been showering the neighborhood.

In 1970, Katayama tackled another pollution problem. Waste from the Kojin

Company's pulp plant had turned Saeki Bay into a coffee-colored lagoon. By this time, anti-pollution movements had risen around the nation. Riding this wave of concern, Katayama formed a "Citizen's Forum" citywide coalition to pressure the Kojin Company to clean up the bay. By then, he had quit the LDP and become a supporter of the JSP. He recruited help from the party and affiliated unions.

This time, Katayama had a lever – evidence of collusion. An engineer working for Kojin had leaked information to a JSP politician about political corruption. The Oita pollution bureau official was supposed to make unannounced spot checks on Kojin's water pollution output. Actually, the bureau informed Kojin bosses when they were coming. On that day only, Kojin would divert its fluid wastes to a holding lake (Asahi Newspaper, Oita edition, Oct. 2, 1971). Katayama threatened to make this evidence public and embarrass or even sue the Prefectural Government (Interview 249, 1979). To avoid this, the Prefectural Government forced Kojin Company to reduce its operations in order to meet the effluent standards of the time (OGN September 29, 1971). In 1973, when the EA passed tougher water quality standards, Kojin had to clean up even further. The company could not meet these standards, so it went out of business. As a result, after some years, Saeki Bay returned to its original blue color.

When I asked Katayama why he had rejected the LDP money and embarked on anti-pollution activism, he replied:

I was born in the Meiji Era. People of that time are stubborn (*ganko*). . . . If you want to organize a movement, you need a strong sense of purpose (*shin'nen*) and desire to work for the common good. . . .

Katayama expressed a clear and strong sense of moral purpose and a good knowledge of the issue. He also wanted to spread this to others:

Japanese have a very narrow way of thinking. They are used to high-handed tyranny from elites. This affects the movement. We must change this.

In other words, Katayama saw a need to reframe popular attitudes toward authority – to change Japanese political culture. In social movement theory terms, he wanted a widespread "cognitive liberation" from uncritical deference to elites. Presumably, such a fundamental change did not happen in Saeki. Nonetheless, he organized a protest movement and cleaned up several environmental messes. How was that possible?

People with strong internal morality like Katayama are perhaps more unusual in Japan than in the United States. Typically, social scientists characterize the Japanese sense of morality as "situational" – going along with the group and the powerful leader (Markus et al., 1991; Nakane, 1970; Lebra, 1976). Katayama was not like this at all. Katayama's rugged inner-directed personality gave him an independence of judgment. This independence enabled him to withdraw from his role as a small boss tied to the prefectural LDP organization.

From that point on, the Japanese group orientation worked for, not against, his movement. Nakane argues that the strongest feature of Japanese social structure is the strong personal loyalty between leaders and subordinates. Personal loyalty to the next highest leader, not the whole abstract group, motivates people (Nakane, 1970, p. 64). If a middle-level boss defects from this vertical structure, he can take his subordinates along too. Ironically, then, vertical deference, rather than liberation from it, helped give Katayama's protest movement a solid membership. This characteristic Japanese-style organizational dynamic appeared in other mobilization cases as well.

The neighborhood people had no trouble understanding that pollution from the plywood plant dirtied their laundry and posed a health threat. Their sense of grievance, in other words, quickly and accurately mirrored the physical reality. Pervasive government denial of pollution barely touched their accurate perception of the reality. From ancient times, furthermore, it had been the custom to take such problems to the hamlet or neighborhood leader, in this case Katayama. Abiding by the leader's response, as long as it did not involve violence, also fit within ancient custom. If Katayama argued that petitions and legal action were necessary, many would follow. In other words, to engage in collective action, the average residents did not require an external intellectual impulse to jog them into reframing – either of their perception of the problem or, in this case, of their relation to authority.

The movement leader, however, had to be a trusted leader. Only such a person had the bonds of trust necessary to readily mobilize a group. Without such a leader, a sufficient critical mass of protestors could not be assembled. Local social structure, in other words, mediated individual rationality. The strong collective identity of the *ku*-residents, when organized through a traditional leader, made them more readily identify a collective benefit as a personal benefit. Unlike Western assumptions, this indicates that when viewed cross-culturally, the boundaries of the "self" are expandable. They need not only outline the biological organism, as we are socialized to accept in the West, but under some circumstances, they may encompass a group of people.

Usuki City

In 1970, the Osaka Cement Company suddenly announced its intention to landfill a section of Usuki Bay and build a cement plant. The Prefectural Government announced its support for the plan. The section of Usuki Bay lay in front of Kazanashi, a fishing village within the boundaries of Usuki City (see

Figure 1.8). People in Usuki were already aware of the pollution a cement plant could produce. One such plant had already been in operation in the neighboring town of Tsukumi for some years. The plant had dusted the town with its chalky air pollution. The stuff solidified in gutters. Residents complained of respiratory problems, and suspected pollution as the cause. Later surveys proved them right: Tsukumi had even higher asthma rates than the infamous Yokkaichi City. Doctors said the chalky particles solidified in people's lungs.

News about the Osaka Cement Company's plan made the Kazanashi villagers afraid for their health and livelihood. Not only would it dust them with chalk, the plant would also occupy their fishing grounds without offering any compensation to the fishing families. The villagers had heard of Mishima-Numazu and other successful protests. The women of Kazanashi village started a dogged resistance campaign and kept it going (Matsushita, 1978).[5] Braving the winter cold, the women floated a large raft on the waters planned for the landfill and fearlessly conducted a waterborne "sit-in." This prevented surveying and other initial landfill construction activities. Finally, the mayor called the police to haul the women off.

In an unusual turn of events, Usuki's top business leaders declared their support for the Kazanashi protest. The three leading families of the town owned medium-sized (but very large for the town) businesses making soy sauce, miso (soybean paste), and medicine. Making those products required clean air. The cement factory threatened to put them out of business. These local elites provided crucial resources to the protest movement: legitimacy that aroused very strong community support and the funds to fight a long court battle.

The three elite families had effectively "appointed" the mayor, and thought they controlled him (Interview, Usuki, 1979). They expected him to oppose the cement company plans too. To their complete surprise, the mayor issued a statement of support for the plant! They found out that the cement company and prefectural officials had put enormous pressure on the mayor and coopted his support.

Rejected by the government, the elite-villager movement members adopted unusual tactics. They continued with dramatic demonstrations and sit-ins. At the same time, they sued the Prefectural Government in local court. The suit

---

5. When a Japanese rural village decides on a policy, as the ideology of *wa* indicates, all the villagers are expected to go along. In the traditional practice of "shunning" (*mura hachibu*), the ostracized villagers were excluded from eight of the ten important collective functions, including collective planting and harvesting of rice fields, marriage ceremonies, festival participation, and attendance at the village government meetings. They retained rights to help from the community only in the case of fire and for attendance at their funeral. In Kazanashi, the minority of villagers who supported the landfill plan were ostracized by the rest of the village for years afterward.

contested the landfill permits given by the Prefectural Government. Lawyer Yoshida, affiliated with the Japan Communist party, represented the movement gratis. In this case, capitalists, humble fisherfolk, and communist politicians cooperated against outside business interests. As with the Oita's NIC growth fellowship, common material interests and a sense of community overrode ideological and status differences.

The Usuki case received good coverage from sympathetic reporters. It made the court suit nationally well-known as a tactic for stopping harmful growth plans. National attention made the local case very visible. The local movement kept up pressure too. The Usuki movement won its suit in 1973 and stopped the cement plant. Two business leaders told me that constant local movement pressure was crucial to this legal victory.

In this case, the sudden threat of new grievances spurred protest. By 1970, the necessary cognitive and moral reframing had already occurred in the example of the neighboring town and through the national news media. The traditional collective identity of the villagers strengthened their solidarity in struggle. Sheer economic self-interest, not networks, ideology, or collective identity, brought the town business leaders into coalition with the villagers. As a result, the movement had excellent resources available: status, money, connections, and facilities.

Still, it was the fiery dedication of the Kazanashi women that spearheaded the movement. That came not from money or status, but from their love of their village and families. And lawyer Yoshida worked free. So new resources did not spark mobilization or really determine its outcome. Certainly, the formal freedoms of the new political institutions and the courts allowed the movement to expand and succeed. In general, though, the Usuki case does not fit any one mobilization theory very well. Rather, an amalgam of contingent factors made it happen.

Nakatsu City

Matsushita Ryuichi made tofu in the town of Nakatsu. He liked the rural atmosphere of his coastal town (pop. 60,000) in northern Oita Prefecture. Many young people went off to the big city, he admitted, but he did not find the urban bright lights attractive. As a young man, he decided to make his life in Nakatsu. At the same time, he developed a strong philosophy that argued that rural life was preferable to urban life, and began to write books about it.

In the late 1960s, the national government put forth the Suonada Development Plan. This called for landfill along most of the western Inland Sea. In

1971, the plan selected Buzen, the neighboring town to Nakatsu, as the site for a giant landfill and electric power plant. This would also affect Nakatsu's coast. Matsushita Ryuichi felt that government and popular fascination with "progress" was quite misplaced. Rather, the real quality of life was to be found in a settled community doing traditional sorts of work. These feelings, coupled with the wider national outrage conveyed in the media and various movement conventions, led Matsushita to organize a movement against the Suonada Plan. The movement was not organized so much in opposition to material threats to health or livelihood but in opposition to the lifestyle consequences of industrial growth.

At its greatest strength, the movement drew 500 people to a protest meeting. Progressive unions and political parties supported Matsushita's efforts. However, Matsushita disparaged their motives. The unions and parties sent their members to movement rallies. But when Matsushita asked a unionist why he came to the meeting, the unionist replied, ". . . I don't know what's going on here. I just came because I was told to come."

This kind of support frustrated the philosophical Matsushita. He was not interested in numbers of attendees, he wanted people to learn to appreciate nature and the bucolic community more. He concluded that union and opposition party support just came from their need for a political posture, not from any real commitment to his way of framing the problem. Union and party leaders, who had allocated scarce resources to the Nakatsu movement, might have disagreed.

In 1972, the movement secured promises from twenty-one out of thirty City Council members in Nakatsu to oppose the electric plant. But when the matter came to an actual vote, almost every council member voted in support of the plant (Interview 243, May 10, 1979). The movement failed and the electric plant was constructed. Since it was built in neighboring Buzen, the threat to health and livelihood from pollution was relatively little. This made it hard to activate a wider range of Nakatsu residents, who were not of a philosophical bent. As a result, in the face of an LDP and business dominated City Council, the surge of mobilization petered out. The LDP controlled the council – and the outcome.

The tofu maker's movement failed. But he continued on to develop his philosophy of the simple life in a number of novels. He became a nationally famous author. One of his books, *The Women of Kazanashi* (*Kazanashi no Onnatachi*), presented a sympathetic history of the fight against the Usuki cement plant (Matsushita, 1984). Matsushita's books contributed to a growing local culture of environmentalism in Oita Prefecture and in the nation.

Reactions to Phase Two

Non-mobilization

In 1965, the Oita government publicly announced its plans to build NIC Phase Two. Though not yet approved by the central government, the plans represented the governor's hopes. Landfills No. 6 and 7 and the port were to extend five kilometers up the coast from Phase One to the border of Saganoseki township (see Figure 2.1). Landfill No. 8 was to go to the other side of Beppu Bay, invisible across the blue water and no threat to Saganoseki.

Landfills No. 6 and 7 would devour the beaches and coastal waters of Hoso, Shiomi, and Takeshita hamlets (all in Ozai township), and Sakanoichi town. This would destroy the lucrative shallow water areas where nori seaweed cultivators had set up their frames and where fish spawned and regenerated the wider commercial fisheries. Furthermore, the factories would urbanize the area, turning bucolic hamlets into busy byways filled with strangers. People grumbled about these changes. Hoso and other hamlets called meetings to discuss the issue and organize protest demonstrations. A woman in our neighborhood said,

People resisted the landfill plan and went on demonstrations. We did a demonstration on the day they began the actual landfill construction (Interview 70, 1978).

The main participants in the protests were from opposition unions, such as the Teachers' Union (the neighbor woman) and the Communist party. Fishing and seaweeding families did not put up strong resistance because their harvests had already long been devastated by the Sumitomo plant. On the contrary, Landfill No. 6 finally gave them a chance to get compensation for their loss. One local seaweed cultivator said he had received compensation equivalent to about $200,000 (five times what the Misa fishing families had gotten and thirteen times his annual seaweed income). But still, he confessed, he had no good way to use the money (Interview 113, 1979). Except for a few people from the Socialist or Communist parties, most people in the area, he said, wanted the landfill and growth.

The sporadic protest never jelled into a popular movement. As one local environmental lawyer put it,

A Hoso movement arose in response to Kozaki's call. But in 1972 it changed to a conditional struggle and then disappeared (Interview 145, November, 1979).

One Ozai fisherman said that he came from one of the four original "netlord" (*amimoto*) families of the area. These families were all main-houses and controlled the surrounding branch-houses. When the netlord families decided to accept compensation payments, this effectively snuffed out most of the resistance in Ozai (Interview 255, December 1979). Taking a personal solution to the pollution problem, the Ozai fisherman had moved to another town to get his children out of the polluted Ozai air.

A neighborhood businessman criticized the mild Hoso opposition movement as resisting "only for the sake of increased compensation payments." Most people in the area, he said,

> did not have an opinion. Small and medium business owners were 98 percent for the landfill. They would get contracts and profits . . . Japanese people give up easily . . . (Interview).

The change of goals from absolute to conditional opposition signaled the death of protest. Why did protest die out so easily here, but grow so strong in the not-so-different hamlet of Kozaki, just a few kilometers to the east?

For the study of social movements, non-mobilization is as important a question as mobilization [Gamson, 1990 (second edition), p. 138]. How does one study a "non-event?" Actually, non-mobilization is not a "non-event." Unless it springs from total ignorance, not caring about an impending threat is an act. It is the decision that the threat is not "worth" doing something about. The mobilization potential never moves into recruitment, organization, and action. This "failure" occurs as a result of social forces, which must be examined.

Living behind Landfill No. 7 taught me something about how people think about pollution. My family and I moved into a house in Takeshita in October 1978, and stayed until January 1980 (see Figure 2.1). My then wife, Gretchen, and our two young children, Eben (one) and Leafye (three), came with me to Oita. Takeshita lay near the shore, a few kilometers east of Oita City and the Phase One refinery complex. We rented a traditional wooden house, with straw mat (*tatami*) floors, gray tile roof, and ancestral Buddhist altar. The mother of our landlord, a school teacher, had lived there until her recent death.

When we arrived, Landfill No. 7 and the port facilities had already been constructed. Modernization was rapidly encroaching on the hamlet. The muddy flats of the landfill areas stretched half a kilometer out from the old shoreline. The flats ended at the concrete retaining wall that held in the mud. Beyond that lay a channel for ships and a breakwater to keep out the waves.

Along the shore, a 40-meter-wide coastal industrial highway already cut between the village and its former beach. Another broad new highway ran along the hill behind Takeshita. Its off-ramp descended past the hamlet down to the muddy landfill on the shore. In coastal hamlets nearer to Oita City, new urban planning had already straightened the narrow, crooked streets of the old hamlets. Houses had been rearranged into straight rows with easily passable roads between them.

Standing on the concrete retaining wall, looking westward up the coast, one could see the smokestacks of the Phase One complex etched clearly against the sky and distant mountains. To the east, on the far tip of the Saganoseki peninsula, the twin smokestacks of the Nikko Copper Refinery stood tall and black against the sky. Being so near the refineries, I worried about air pollution. But the neighbors reassured me that they suffered no ill effects from air pollution. During the day, none of the industrial smokestacks emitted much visible smoke; the sky was blue and the air did not smell polluted. So I believed them.

After we had been in Takeshita about six months, my kids and wife started to cough severely throughout the night. I took my family to a clinic in Oita City. The doctor diagnosed their coughs as bronchitis. It was caused, he said, by air pollution. I replied, "Hum, that's very interesting to me, because I'm studying pollution in Oita." As soon as I said that, the doctor changed his diagnosis: "No," he said, "really the bronchitis had not been caused by air pollution" but by something else, perhaps the weather. The doctor did not want me to attribute my family's illness to air pollution. Our little tiff over how to "frame" the bronchitis shocked me. It started to make me aware of just how salient this issue really was in Oita, even though no one ever talked about it.

Before moving to Oita, my family had lived in the pristine and unpolluted environment of rural Vermont. This made them, it turned out, especially sensitive "litmus papers" for the presence of pollution. Upon further questioning, a neighbor reluctantly admitted,

Well, it's true that colds never seem to go away once you get one. They call it, what's that word, um, 'pollution disease' (*kogaibyo*) or something.

People who see no way of changing a bad situation often try to forget about it or even deny it. My neighbors had lived in Takeshita for decades; in some cases, for many generations. They did not want to wake up every day thinking how terrible it was. Once a change is made and fixed, people tend to give up. They were rooted there.

We were not. Finally, in October 1979, seeing no other way to regain health, we left Takeshita and moved to the small farming village of Obasama. Located in the mountains 15 kilometers behind and to the west of Oita City, this village did not suffer from industrial air pollution. After just a few weeks in Obasama, the terrible night coughs disappeared, never to return.

The immediacy of the GE dilemma for the people of Takeshita awakened me to the ambiguities of "modernization" and the subtleties of pollution-induced illness. To a greater degree than earlier social problems, the GE dilemma makes everyone into both a perpetuator and a victim – both benefited and harmed by the problem. Most of us want the benefits of growth, and have a hard time curbing our appetites. Our consumerism makes us all to some degree complicit in the GE dilemma. In addition, pollution-caused illness is insidious and hard to distinguish from "normal" illness for a long time. Complicity and insidiousness encourage denial. People may prefer to deny a pollution-illness rather than demand a solution that might halt economic progress. Or after unsuccessful attempts at change, people may feel forced to acquiesce in a bad situation, and prefer denial to living with constant worry. The general lack of neighborhood concern, even among the very "victims" themselves, opened my eyes to these questions.

To understand the general principles of why, despite this tendency toward denial, some communities successfully mobilized protest, we have to consider a few more cases. These we now turn to in the next chapter.

5

Protest against Landfill No. 8

A shocking announcement

While Landfills No. 6 and 7 and the harbor aroused only sporadic protest, Landfill No. 8 led to a big fight. In September 1969, the Showa Denko Company, owner of the Showa Denko petrochemical plant on Landfill No. 2, announced its desire to build the world's largest aluminum smelter on Landfill No. 8. People in Oita knew that aluminum smelters make much pollution. Since Landfill No. 8 was to go across Beppu Bay, however, people in Seki did not worry too much about it.

In January 1970, however, the Oita government suddenly announced a change of plans. The sea floor in the old place was not good for landfill. It now planned to build No. 8 on the coast of Saganoseki, in front of the hamlets of Kozaki and Baba (see Figure 2.1). No. 8 would be huge: a total of 4 square kilometers.[1] Governor Kinoshita again painted a glowing picture of the social benefits of growth. In 1970, the Japanese economy was booming. This time, he said, high-employment companies would come for sure. By then, though, not all residents believed him so readily. The bloom had already fallen from the rose of industrial modernity.

The announcement shocked many Seki people. Not only would No. 8 come to their doorstep, it might bring an aluminum refinery too! Aluminum refineries dump vast quantities of red sludge waste into waters, and use copious amounts of (oil-generated) electricity. Showa Denko representatives tried to dispel local fears by stressing the positive effects of the plant. It would produce 300,000 tons of aluminum per year, they said, and employ 3,000 workers. Its economic effects would spread out and invigorate small industry in the prefecture. While the

---

1. This was two-thirds the size of the huge Landfill No. 3–4, which held New Japan Steel in Phase One of Oita's NIC (6.9 square kilometers), and much larger than any of the other landfill areas.

Prefectural Government indicated interest in Showa Denko's proposal, it also publicly admitted ambivalence about the potential pollution.

The announcement on Landfill No. 8 set in motion a decade of mobilization and conflict. On the one hand, the project promised intense pollution and disruption to the Kozaki area of Seki. This made many people detest the project. On the other hand, local political and economic leaders promised the project would bring prosperity and pushed for it. They offered incentives and applied pressure to get locals to agree with it. A series of movements and countermovements erupted. Did people participate in these movements because they wanted to prevent the losses to personal health and livelihood that pollution threatened? Or did some change of awareness about pollution, some new framing of the situation, sweep over them first, rather independent of the objective threat posed by pollution? Or could some other factor, such as new resources or a suddenly weakened political authority, account for their mobilization? Some scholars state categorically that "frame alignment . . . is a necessary condition for participation" in a social movement (Snow et al., 1986, p. 464; Klandermans, 1992, p. 80). From that viewpoint, recruitment of members to a movement requires the alignment "of individual and SMO interpretive frameworks" (Snow, Rochford, Worden & Benford, 1986, p. 467). It may be, though, that grievances and frames of resistance had been present all along, and were just triggered by these new threats.

One way to investigate such questions is to compare contrasting cases. Within Kozaki (administrative) village, the two hamlets of Kozaki and Baba each gave birth to a movement, but they were movements of diametrically opposite stances. The Kozaki movement vehemently opposed No. 8. The Baba movement just as vehemently supported it. Within each hamlet, submerged voices for the contrary point of view grumbled in the background. Turmoil over No. 8 also erupted in Seki City. The Seki Fishing Union split into two factions and bloody fistfights over the issue. The Seki Chamber of Commerce sponsored a pro-8 campaign as well. The dynamic interaction of these movements among themselves and with outside parties provides useful material bearing upon our theoretical questions. We examine their initial mobilization here. Their ensuing trajectory will unfold in the following chapters.

The Seki setting

The physical setting and social structure of the Seki communities added to the conflict. Saganoseki township occupies a peninsula jutting eastward into the Bungo Straits (Figure 2.1). Through the Straits, the Pacific Ocean enters the Inland Sea, bearing tankers, freighters, and fishing boats. A steep mountain backbone runs the length of the narrow peninsula. Hamlets and the single town cluster along the narrow strip of land between the mountains and the sea.

Landfill No. 7 ended at the border of Saganoseki township. On the other side of the border lay the coastal hamlets of Baba, Kozaki, Nakanohara, and Ohira, with Kisagami located a little back from the coast behind Kozaki hamlet. For centuries, they had been separate hamlets. After the war, the national government combined these villages into a single administrative "village" (*mura*) called Kozaki. Then it combined Kozaki village with Saganoseki Town into a single township called Saganoseki. Despite this administrative interference, the original hamlets still remained as distinct social units, with their own social networks, hierarchies, occupational characteristics, and internal governance. This distinctiveness was the basis for their diverse reactions to the NIC Phase Two plan.

Each hamlet held several sub-units known as *ku* (about forty-five households). Each *ku* held several *han* (about fifteen households). Each *ku* and *han* had its elected head, who made sure local minor administrative duties (garbage collection, festival contributions, and so on) went well. The larger hamlets had a *ku*-chair to represent all the *ku*-heads to the mayor. Kozaki hamlet (a subdivision within Kozaki village) had eight *ku*; Baba, Ohira, and Kisagami had about three each. The *ku* and *han* in Kozaki hamlet reacted somewhat differently to the threat of Landfill No. 8, some playing important roles in the mobilization and continuance of protest. The head of each *ku* was the official link to the mayor. That link gave the *ku*-head the power to affect some resource allocation within the *ku*, such as tax assessments of homes and land.

One important social structural difference between the hamlets was in the proportion of full-time fishing families. Baba was the most active fishing village, with 33 full-time fishing families out of a total population of 667. In addition, another 35 or so Baba families drew some of their income from part-time fishing. Kozaki hamlet had only 6 full-time fishing families, and an equal number of part-time fishing families, out of a much larger population of about 1,471. Nakanohara had 5 full-time fishing families and Ohira 11 (population about 300). These full- and part-time fishing families had fished the coastal waters off their hamlets for generations. Landfills No. 7C and 8 would bury these waters. In return for giving up their rights to fish these waters, the families were eligible for large compensation payments from the Prefectural Government. The higher proportion of such fishing families in Baba provided the financial basis for the formation of a pro-landfill political stance by the hamlet. Conversely, the very low proportion of compensable families in Kozaki hamlet made resistance to the landfill more reasonable. However, these financial matters were only one component of the mobilization and organization of collective action for or against the landfill. Separate narratives will explore that process for each Kozaki and Baba.

In these hamlets, hedges, yards, and houses stood in crooked confusion along the border lines of ancient fields. Narrow roadways lined with flowering bushes wound among them. In the foothills of the mountains behind Kozaki, a Shinto shrine housed the god (*ujigami*) of the hamlet. Farther up the mountain trail, another shrine housed the remains of Sekkan-sama, an ancient warrior and guardian spirit of the hamlet. The bamboo grove along the top of the sea wall usually muted the sound of the waves. When the sea was up, though, the booming voice of the waves echoed through the hamlet. On the other side of the sea wall, on good days, a 30-meter-wide beach provided a pleasant place to picnic and swim.

Down the picturesque coast about 6 kilometers, along the sometimes precipitous highway, lay the town of Saganoseki. The winding coastal road revealed scene after scene reminiscent of traditional ink-brush paintings: curved stony beaches ending in rocky escarpments, a lonely pine clinging to a jagged rock in the midst of the surging sea, a sacred Shinto straw rope strung between two jutting shards of rock in the sea. These scenes embodied the Japanese love of nature. They made manifest the Buddhist and Shinto aesthetic of nature's mystery and grandeur.

But modernity intruded. On the beach, mixed with the black stones, lay shards of blue plastic buckets, bottles, and polystyrene. The trash floated in from coastal villages and boats. The villagers had always used the sea as a garbage can. In the past, it cheerfully digested their fish bones, vegetable scraps, wood, straw, and nails. Now they threw in plastics and vinyls, and the sea tossed them back. The villagers did not seem to notice, and continued their habits unchanged.

At the tip of the peninsula, Saganoseki town and the Nikko copper refinery clung to the last scrap of level land. The gray tile roofs of closely packed houses flowed like a wavy seascape over the town. Two small harbors full of fishing boats dug into both sides of the town. On the northern side, the fishing boats shared their port with giant ore ships and freighters feeding the copper refineries.

Despite its rurality, people packed densely together in Saganoseki. In 1980, the township's 49.5 square kilometers of land housed 19,000 residents, averaging about 385 inhabitants per square kilometer (much higher than the national average of 307). Moreover, steep mountains covered most of the peninsula, crowding people even more densely onto the few flat areas. This resulted in an average density for level land of about 3,000 people per square kilometer (approaching Tokyo with it's 5,404 per km). At the western end of the township, closest to Oita City, Kozaki Village had 3,834 inhabitants in 1980 (down from about 5,000 in 1955) from four original hamlets: Kozaki (pop. 1,471), Baba (pop. 667), Ohira (population about 300), and Kisagami (population about 500) (see Figure 2.1).

From 1955 on, Saganoseki's population steadily declined (like most rural towns in Japan). Young people complained about the general lack of jobs, layoffs at the Nikko copper refinery, and the high price of land for housing. They left to seek work in Osaka and Tokyo. Despite that outflow, the population density kept land prices very high.[2] Many residents grew unhappy with the population decline. Merchant and service businesses wanted more customers. To them, the prospect of industrial growth with its accompanying workers seemed very attractive.

Kozaki's reaction

The Governor's January 1970 announcement that Landfill No. 8 would come to Kozaki shocked people there. They were already well aware of the dangers of pollution. The copper refinery started polluting the area in 1917, and had continued ceaselessly since then. One young man from Kozaki testified,

> . . . pollution from Nikko was very terrible . . . in 1969 it blighted and blackened several hundred hectares of orange (*mikan*) groves. . . . Many people (were found to be) dying of tuberculosis . . . So for Saganoseki, pollution was a very acute problem (Hearings, No. 34).

The pollution from Phase One had also become notorious throughout the prefecture:

> . . . gas . . . had leaked out, fish . . . had suddenly died, people found malformed fish in Beppu Bay . . . Black oil . . . flowed into seaweed cultivation areas . . . causing hundreds of thousands of dollars of damage (Hearings, No. 34).

Knowing about severe pollution a few kilometers up and down the coast from their hamlet, people in the Kozaki village area felt they had a right to worry. In addition, mountains taller than any smokestack stood behind their hamlet. If a smelter or other factory came to Landfill No. 8, the youth feared the strong east winds would blow the smoke against the mountains. From there, gradually cooling, it would settle thickly on the hamlet.

Members of the Kozaki Young People's Group (*Seinendan*), mostly young women, talked over the issue. The Seinendan consisted of young adults ages

---

2. In the town proper, residential land sold for at least 150,000 yen ($1500) per *tsubo* (3.9 square yards). In comparison, the same area sold in neighboring Sakanoichi for only 30,000 yen ($300).

eighteen to the upper twenties. It was a feature of all Japanese villages, supported by the village council and helping with festivals and activities. The young women converted this innocuous group into a forum for discussing the pollution issue. They mobilized an existing organizational resource and used it for new ends.

The young people had been reading news about pollution problems in other parts of the country. Furthermore, whenever they went shopping in Oita City, they drove past the new NIC refinery complex and saw what had happened to Misa and Iejima. Misa and Iejima provided visible evidence of what Kozaki might become. As they talked, a consensus emerged among them that they ought to find out more. They decided to investigate how bad the pollution might get. Several members went to inspect Showa Denko's aluminum smelters in Niigata and Mizushima. What they discovered they did not like. The smelters polluted the surrounding sea with red mud, fluoric acid, and ore tailings. Their power plants burned great quantities of heavy fuel oil, spewing out massive amounts of sulfur-dioxide laden smoke. The youth also found out that Showa Denko had wanted to build its proposed smelter near Hiroshima, but had been refused permission because of its pollutants. The Seinendan's research confirmed its worst fears. Landfill No. 8 looked as if it would ruin their village.

With this knowledge in hand, the members had to convince their parents and other elders. Kai Yoshimaru, an old Kozaki farmer who was also a retired school teacher and a small boss, described the mobilization process this way:

. . . these young people . . . taught us older ones . . . They formed a research group at the temple (Kyosonji), to study how bad the pollution would be (Interview 261, 1979).

"We talked a lot when farming was slack," he told me. The youth got the elders to talk over their worries about pollution. Local farmers feared that the smoke and wastes would ruin their oranges (*mikan*) and other crops. Fishing people did not want to lose their hereditary coastal fisheries. Retirees did not want to live with bad air and clamor. Mothers feared for their children's health.

Along with warnings about the dangers of pollution, the young activists also conveyed their new sense of rights to their elders. The new democracy allowed protest. The riot police would not beat them. This new political framing was not the key that unleashed protest, however. The Seki farmers had boiled over in protest against the copper refinery in 1917, as had starving peasant villages for centuries before them. They had done so within the framework of existing political institutions, justified by the expectation of Confucian benevolence from the ruler. They had been trying to set the system right (Broadbent, 1975). Under the influence of the Kozaki youth, however, the elders gained exposure to a new vision of citizen political participation. This new vision more strongly justified the defense of individual and community rights (McKean, 1981). Unlike pre-war times, furthermore, the police did not crack down on their mobilization efforts, which further assuaged their fears (Interview 153, August 7, 1979).

Many of the elders who joined the movement were the parents, grandparents, or more distant relatives of activist youth. Two retired and highly respected school teachers, Yuki Tsutomu and Inao Kiyohide, served as informal leader and second-in-command. One participant commented, "Yuki was a great leader and drew big crowds" (Interview 89B, 1979). Kinship networks partly defined the spread, intensity, and tenacity of movement support. This became more apparent as the movement developed. Recruitment of elders was doubly important because they held effective power in the community council. The (usually male) elders occupied the posts of *ku* and *han* head. In that position, they spoke not only for themselves but for their entire three-generational families.

The recruitment of respected, high-status elders was crucial for the success of the movement. The youth alone could not have been effective leaders in village society. The elders' support was not inevitable. Some of the elderly still held firmly to older customs of deference to elites. A middle-aged woman activist said, "It is the special characteristic of the Japanese. They need a leader" (Interview 88, 1979). In this situation, high-status local elders had the capacity, like Katayama in Saeki, to give the stamp of propriety to the mobilization process. In this social context, activists could recruit adults by using their deference for movement purposes. Activists could bend habits more easily than break them.

In February 1970, all the neighborhood (*ku*) heads of Kozaki signed a petition against Landfill No. 8 and presented it to the governor. On February 22, they organized a rally against No. 8 in Seki City, attended by local fishing people. The newspaper reported widespread concern and fear in Seki over the No. 8 plan (Interview 261, 1979). The movement was spreading.

To head off the mounting resistance in Kozaki, Governor Kinoshita decided to hold an "explanation meeting" about No. 8 at the Kozaki elementary school. On July 26, 1970, 600 local residents gathered there to listen to his explanation. Officials showed the villagers a map that showed the landfill extending for 2.5 kilometers along their coastline and 2.5 kilometers out into the bay. The scale of the landfill dwarfed the village and shocked the residents. The Governor refused to reveal his exact choice of industry for the landfill. He emphasized that the prefecture's purpose was not just to bring in factories, but to improve prefectural welfare. The head of the Prefectural Government planning office promised to request the highest standards of pollution control from the incoming factories. On that point, the governor admitted that the villagers

. . . must expect some pollution. But if it seems dangerous to health or life, it's important for you to use political means to get the factories to stop polluting (OGN, July 28, 1970).

By "political means," the governor meant that the villagers should notify the Prefectural Government.

The governor and staff felt that, by holding an explanatory meeting, they had made a big concession to post-war democracy. In their understanding, the new democracy meant they owed the people some explanation of their plans. It did not mean that they should solicit public criticism or respond to the public will (as it often does in the United States). On the contrary, the officials hoped their prestige would awe local people into acceptance of No. 8 and quiet down the protestors.

The activist youth of Kozaki took exception to this dismissive treatment. One of them complained that "suddenly the plan was put before us and we were told the sea was going to be filled in" (Hearings, 1978). At the meeting, the officials ignored hostile questioners. They tried to orchestrate an appearance of village support. Another movement activist said:

Those who would ask questions were already designated, and even the contents of their questions were checked beforehand . . . one (undesignated) person who raised his hand to ask a question was ignored. There were no free questions and answers (Interview)

A high-school teacher from Kozaki corroborated this:

. . . in the explanatory meeting . . . the prefecture did not respect the opinions of questioners . . . the prefecture decided the time and questioners ahead of time, through the mayor and the neighborhood residents' association. [The Prefectural Government did this] because there was already a resistance movement (Interview 249, 1979).

According to a Kozaki young person, when the citizens tried to object, the governor belittled their fears:

It's now an era when men can go to the moon, so we will solve such trifling problems as pollution. There is nothing to worry about . . . (Hearings, May 15, 1978).

These quotations reveal a large gap between the officials' and the youths' ways of framing the situation. To the officials, the explanatory meeting was a special "ritual of audience" with a person of exalted status. The officials had expected that their solicitous attention to local concerns would pacify local resistance. In pre-war times, a governor's personal attention had often been enough to quiet disgruntled residents. Furthermore, local officials believed, the leader's decision should set the moral consensus (*matomari*) and the lesser community members should follow it.

The activist Kozaki youth, however, had quite the opposite idea. They no longer believed in deference to elites, if many ever had in the village. The officials' values found little positive resonance among them. On the contrary, they judged such government paternalism as "feudal," as reeking of old, pre-democratic habits. Nonetheless, as noted earlier, they were willing to mobilize local people through their loyalties to traditional hamlet status relations, as long as the local boss broke with the prefectural LDP and other elites.

In June 1970, a second industrial proposal for Landfill No. 8 appeared. The Imperial Rayon Company (*Teikoku Reiyon*) and Showa Oil Company announced their joint plan for the world's largest chemical fiber complex. This complex included an oil refinery, petrochemical cracking plant, and synthetic fiber factory. The complex would process 500,000 barrels of oil per day, turning it into 500 tons of tetron and 100 tons of nylon. This was two and one-half times the capacity of refineries in Phase One.

Again, the Kozaki youth group investigated. They visited the infamous Yokkaichi oil complex and listened to residents complain about pollution-induced asthma. They calculated that No. 8's power plants would burn much more heavy fuel oil than those in Yokkaichi. They had observed how the Oita NIC refineries, under cover of darkness, released heavier volumes of smoke than during the daytime. They knew that the residents of the villages near those refineries, Misa and Iejima, were coughing and in ill health. They feared, reasonably, that their hamlet would become an even worse "valley of pollution."

Through its research and discussions, the Kozaki Seinendan came to feel that the benefits of No. 8 would be outweighed by its costs. As a result, they began to feel justified in opposing it. Slowly, their discussions turned to tactics – how to oppose the landfill. In thinking about this, they could hark back to Kozaki's traditions of sporadic local protest. They had heard about protests in Saeki and Nakatsu. At the same time, they had only to read the papers to notice the rising national cycle of environmental protest.

During the 1970s, it seemed that every day the national press trumpeted new pollution incidents, protest movements, and court suits. The media generated a collective awareness of the problem throughout the nation. It helped local groups know they were not alone in their concerns. The Kozaki Seinendan avidly devoured this current of national concern.

After convincing a core of close elders, the members of the youth group began to organize wider resistance and formalize their plans. Led by the young women of the group, the members put up posters around the hamlet warning of the dangers of pollution from the aluminum smelter, the power plant, and the petrochemical-rayon complex. They talked with many residents and tried to convince people of the importance of making their opinions heard. The activist youth enthusiastically recruited allies and members. As an elderly farmer explained, the youth "handed out leaflets, put up wall posters and built up public opinion until the whole hamlet was against it" (Interview 261, 1979). The initial mobilization of anti-Landfill No. 8 consensus took place through the activists' personal networks, which spread widely throughout the village. Women played an especially important role in the mobilization effort. As one leader, a woman, explained,

Women are the base of the movement. They want to protect life and health. They are the mothers of kids and do it for them. Men have jobs so they can't participate. Women are at home (Interview 88, 1979).

The dominant structure of gender roles in Japanese society defined women as outside the realm of politics and power (Bestor, 1989, p. 235). Ironically, this freed them from a degree of social control, giving them greater freedom to mobilize. The gender aspect of mobilization and struggle comes out in many ways as the Seki story unfolds.

To recruit supporters, the activists appealed to people's sense of solidarity and identity with the traditional community. In rural Oita, this was a powerful incentive, stronger than in the more recent urban neighborhoods of Tokyo (Bestor, 1989) and the more transient U.S. community.

A traditional Japanese hamlet is much more ingrown and parochial than any Midwestern small town. The core families have been there for hundreds of years. Their backgrounds are intertwined with other core hamlet families and many families bear the same surname (Beardsley, Hall, & Ward, 1959). In Kozaki's Koneko ku, Inao was the prevalent family name. Families only there for a generation or two were still newcomers, and of lesser status.[3] In addition, the collective work required by rice agriculture had deepened the sense of solidarity and social ties. Villagers felt they belonged to a "community of fate."

Since antiquity, the hamlet god (*ujigami*) symbolized this feeling of communal solidarity. Most hamlets and urban neighborhoods have their ujigami shrine (Bestor, 1989, p. 18). The ujigami shrine did not function like a church in a U.S. community, gathering the believers. Rather, the shrine stood for the implicit unity and identity of resident and community. Shintoism has innumerable gods (*yaoyorozu no kami*), spiritual essences that when prayed to, can enter natural objects such as mountains, big rocks, big trees, or sacred shrine objects. These shrines usually molder away in the background, with no live-in priests and only

---

3. Until recent decades, newer families were not allowed to carry the main portable shrine in hamlet festivals.

occasional rituals. Rather than being an object of conscious religious choice, the ujigami is the recipient of most residents' unquestioned identity.[4] This closed corporate identity of the hamlet had both good and bad consequences for the activists. As their support broadened, the activists could claim to represent that corporate identity, and hence the will of the ujigami. The more they did so, the less they could appeal to those in other hamlets in Seki. On the seventeenth day of each month, a group of Kozaki women held a prayer meeting (*kigansai*) at the hamlet's Shinto shrine. During the strongest years of the movement, forty to fifty women would attend. They asked the ujigami to prevent the construction of Landfill No. 8 and protect the village. A leader of the women's group said they also prayed to "strengthen their group unity and to keep themselves from compromising" (Interview 88, 1979). In other words, they were quite aware of the social functions of religion.

Higher up the hill stood a Shinto shrine to Sekkan-sama. Sekkan-sama was an ancient samurai with quasi-divine status. Movement leaders refurbished this small shrine and erected a plaque explaining it. Several women claimed to receive psychic messages from Sekkan-sama on how to help the movement. Sometimes their messages conflicted, however, leading to some friction.

Every New Year, the young men of the hamlet, drunk on rice wine, lifted the hamlet god onto their shoulders in a portable shrine. They staggered from door to door, presenting every home with the god's New Year's blessings. As the environmental struggle unfolded, it built on this ritual. The movement festooned the route of the portable shrine with flags proclaiming absolute, uncompromising opposition to No. 8.[5]

Some movement leaders felt the unity of hamlet and nature quite deeply. A poem by one of them, published anonymously in the movement newsletter, eloquently expressed this sense of sacred unity as a reason to oppose No. 8:

In the breeze which bears the fragrance of the tides,
    the tall canna plant crisply shakes its red flowers.
Starting from the sea and weaving through the green trees
    the white road returns to the sea.
The shrill voice of the cicada
    circles in a vortex up to the sky.
From afar, the voices of children call to each other;
    the temporary stillness of a summer's noon.
Even within that, spreading out like the knots of a net,
    indomitable spirits strongly tied together.
Let us leave this healthy nature to our children.

4. Traditional European villages organized around a single church probably also experienced a similar merger of religion and collective identity (Banfield, 1958), as have most traditional peoples.
5. Village folk religions and practices formed the basis of many rural anti-pollution movements in Japan (Tsurumi, 1977, as cited in Gresser et al., 1981, p. 426fn).

Let us not become the fodder of the polluting industry.
If we bury this sacred land, our ancestors will weep.

The sentiments of this poem merge Kozaki hamlet, as a historical community, with its natural surroundings. Together they become a unified sacred entity. The poem fuses individual, community, and nature.

To the extent that the poem reflects the lived identity of Kozaki residents, it indicates the lack of a strong line between self and community. Such an identity, if salient, could overcome the "free rider" problem by motivating residents to defend collective interests (Ferree, 1992, p. 38). Movement leaders gave this feeling historical depth. They likened Kozaki to a "struggle village" of ancient peasants rebelling against an oppressive feudal regime.

As part of this collective identity, some leaders defended the personal intimacy of the rural lifestyle, in contrast to the anonymity of the modern city. One leader said,

Real human lifestyle is to live traditionally. That is the plea of the movement, not just [protest against] pollution. It's also about losing land, livelihood (Interview 144, 1979).

In this light, the leader criticized the authoritarian impersonality of bureaucracy.

In human relations, you have to respect the other person's way of thinking and reply to it. But the bureaucracy only wants to push things onto the people.

This plea merged New Left politics with a vision of traditional village intimacy. It ignored the severe status inequalities of the traditional village, but reflected a deeply felt closeness of the villagers.

Through this many-faceted mobilization process, Kozaki hamlet reached broad consensus to oppose Landfill No. 8. On September 6, 1970, as a result of the Youth Group's continued organizing activities, Yuki, the Kozaki hamlet *ku*-chair, called a big hamlet meeting to discuss the No. 8 problem. He invited all eight *ku*-heads, plus the *han*-leaders within each *ku*, as well as the leaders of the young people's group, women's group, volunteer fire department, and others. The *ku*-heads elected the *ku*-chair to represent them to the mayor. Usually, the *ku* chair and heads decided *ku* matters among themselves. With the surge of spontaneous activism and widespread fear of pollution and devastation from No. 8, however, they felt the need for wider consensus.

The meeting overwhelmingly opposed the landfill project. The meeting decided to give hamlet support to the investigation efforts: Each *han*-leader would collect 800 yen (about $5) from each house for a donation. There would also be a fee of 300 yen at gatherings such as traditional cherry blossom viewing.

The group leaped into energetic activity. The movement initiated a signature-collection drive for a petition that read:

Whatever industry comes, it will inevitably cause pollution. Rather than dangerous industrialization, we hope for progress that will protect homes and fresh food. We want to protect the beauty of nature we have inherited from our ancestors (Hearings, Nos. 46–51).

This petition gives voice to a deep popular feeling. People cherished the unity, in their collective identity as a hamlet, of natural place and deep community. The petition based its total opposition to No. 8 on that moral basis. This gives a new meaning to the defense of "lifestyle" thought to be characteristic of new environmental movements (Offe, 1985b). The moral claim contrasts sharply with that of environmental petitions in Japanese cities or anywhere in the West, which stress instead the infringement of individual and societal rights to good health.

The Kozaki group invited *ku*-chairs from neighboring hamlets to a meeting to generate wider support for the signature drive. Afterwards, movement members went from house to house to collect signatures on the petition. Within a few days, they got the signatures of 1,010 residents of Kozaki and 210 residents of Ohira, virtually all the registered voters in the two villages. On September 15, 1970, the *ku*-chair of Kozaki and the three *ku*-heads of neighboring Ohira hamlet (which was too small to have its own *ku*-chair) presented the petition and signatures to the head of the Saganoseki town legislature. Soon thereafter, they also presented it to the prefectural legislature.

In response, the Seki town legislature immediately created an "NIC Phase Two Plan Pollution Counter-Measures Special Committee" to consider the petition. As the name of the committee indicates, however, even at that early juncture, the politicians did not intend to stop No. 8. They only agreed to minimize pollution from its industries. Except for JCP member Himeno, the legislators were almost entirely within the LDP fold.

On the following day, the Kozaki movement convened a big "General Mobilization Meeting for Residents Against the Landfill" in Kozaki hamlet. Yuki Tsutomu, the Kozaki *ku*-chair, headed this meeting. Regular community organizations such as the Young People's Group, the Ladies' Group, and the Volunteer Fire Department joined the meeting. According to a newspaper account, 500 people attended. They included white-collar workers, farmers, shopkeepers, and homemakers. Women constituted over half of the group. At this meeting, the movement activists founded the "NIC Phase Two Landfill 8 Absolute Resistance League" (hereafter, the Kozaki League). The elderly high-school teacher Yuki Tsutomu became its first chair.

At the meeting, a Kozaki woman, the mother of several activist youths, eloquently stated its theme:

We've been told to sacrifice ourselves, during the war for the sake of the nation, and since the war for the sake of the economy. But in Kozaki, which has no flat land behind it, (the landfill project) would be equivalent (for us) to living inside a factory (OGN, September 17, 1970).

This woman was a widow and an employee at the local post office, hence a member of the postal workers' union (Zentei, a Sohyo and JSP affiliate). Sohyo-affiliated unions had already for decades been fighting the national government's attempts to centralize power and gut the democratic Constitution. Her statement reflected the union's profound doubts about the state. Likewise, a number of Kozaki residents had become less willing to sacrifice themselves blindly for the plans of the state. The aftermath of the war, plus the growth of democracy and the stress of pollution, had forced local people to rethink and question not only government policies, but their role as citizens. Mrs. Inao also had a strong faith in Buddhism, which provided a certain moral basis for her criticism of No. 8.

The Kozaki League immediately embarked on a wide range of educational and political efforts. It announced its existence by presenting formal greetings to the mayor and other politicians. It gave out literature stating the reasons for its formation. Over the next few months, the League carried out more petition signature campaigns. It also invited academic lecturers to Kozaki to explain the dangers of pollution, and held demonstrations at the prefectural and town offices (OGN, September 19, 1970).[6] The only road from Oita City to Seki Town ran through the center of Kozaki hamlet. Over this road, the League stretched banners with bold characters proclaiming "Protect Nature," "Protect our Hometown," "Don't destroy the sea and mountains," and "Those who conquer nature will be conquered by nature."

The Youth Group's role was crucial. Traditional social norms espoused deference, not criticism, toward political leaders and their decisions. Why did these young people become so critical of and active against the Prefectural Government's Landfill No. 8 plan? A number of social forces converged to make this possible: cultural, educational, and organizational. As cases noted earlier have demonstrated, the culture of deference was really not very deep in Japan. People were quick to note their losses (due to pollution) and were critical of government decisions that caused them. However, the older generation did not have the social structure to support the talking stage. Their reliance on vertical ties to local bosses as the accepted complaint mechanism reduced their ability to discuss matters with other community members outside their family.

6. Many details of Kozaki movement history are taken from a chronology of its activities, *Ashiato* (Footprints), Kozaki, May 1973.

In contrast, the Kozaki youth represented the first generation raised and educated to believe in horizontal (democratic) rather than vertical ("feudalistic," as they called it) political relations. The Japan Teachers' Union had staunchly supported and defended the new democratic curriculum for elementary and secondary schooling (Cummings, 1980).[7] The thirteenth article of the new Constitution promised the people "life, liberty and the pursuit of happiness." To many, this implied a right to a healthy environment (Hanayama, 1980, p. 194). The more adventurous among the youth felt encouraged by the democratic values taught in their education, enough to want to try out the new rights in practice.

In addition, some of the youth came from family backgrounds that encouraged resistance to the state and elites. Some of their parents were members of left-wing (Socialist and Communist party-oriented) unions, such as those for high-school teachers, post office workers, and national railway employees. These unions, newly liberated or starting up in the post-war period, were very wary of the authoritarian tendencies of the Japanese state. Also, some of the youth had been in college or had siblings in college, where they joined student movements. Japanese student movements bloomed during the 1960s, just as they had in all ACID societies. The movements adhered to a variety of New Left ideologies, all of which supported greater democracy and opposed the state and business elites.

One of the Kozaki activist youth explained the effect of the new educational values on movements in Japan:

Environmental movements were new in 1970. They did not come out of the old labor movements. The movements came out of the democratic education in elementary schools . . . We were taught to value each individual very highly (Interview 125, 1979).

The Kozaki youth felt liberated. Older elites in Oita City (company owners, and conservative politicians), though, were horrified by the new values. They saw the post-war focus on individual rights to be horrible and destructive of Japan's real virtues. The elderly president of a real estate company in Oita explained:

7. Secondary school teachers in the Teachers' Union, disillusioned with wartime authoritarianism and fearful of the state's attempts to return to it, strongly conveyed these new values to students. "New Left" student movements at the universities honed and fine-tuned these values into a political strategy. They rejected revolutionary (Communist party) top-down authoritarianism as much as they rejected Imperial authoritarianism. Instead, they devised a strategy of helping local popular discontent as a vehicle for strengthening opposition to the state. The alliance of student movement and farmers in opposition to the Narita airport expansion grew from this strategy (Apter & Sawa, 1984). Inao Toru's return to his home village of Kozaki to help with the anti-Landfill No. 8 movement was another example.

The United States put too much individualism into the Japanese, who didn't know democracy. Therefore, it became easy to stir up movements. That is no good. Their pursuit of personal benefits harms the progress of the prefecture and the nation. . . .

The Occupation, they thought, had destroyed traditional Japanese virtues and unleashed a wave of selfishness and egotism:

Due to American influence, the heart of our people has been lost – our way of thinking that, if it's for the progress of the whole, it's good to sacrifice yourself. . . . The Japanese strength from group unity has been lost.

Oita officials and elites attributed the Kozaki movement's willingness to upset the social order to an excess of "citizen ego." By this they meant hamlet collective identity. The Kozaki movement was hardly a grouping of American-style individual egotists. Accusation of irresponsible "egotism" has long been a favorite tactic of the Japanese elite. They use it to undercut and delegitimize the opposition parties and popular movements (Aiba, Iyasu, & Takashima, 1987, p. 4). Despite their profound difference in values, however, the real estate company president did agree with the movement activists on one thing, that education had caused this new libertarianism:

. . . Because of post-war democratic education . . . the people no longer abide by the larger social cohesion (*matomari*) (Interview).

A leader of Oita's Democratic Socialist party (the conservative split-off from the JSP) echoed this sentiment:

Japan is narrow and densely populated, so we need close cooperation. . . . Buddhism teaches us to forget our desires and serve others. . . . Freedom has to connect to the overall social coherence (*matomari*). The United States broke the unity and coherence of the Japanese spirit (*yamato damashi*) under the Emperor and introduced liberalism (Interview).

This idea of social coherence reflected and adhered to the traditional vertical form of Japanese social structure. Traditionally, this vertical social structure ran from the ordinary citizen up through a hierarchy of bosses and leaders to the Imperial State, which spoke in the name of a quasi-divine Emperor (Ishida, 1984). In the post-war era, elites thought fondly of this all-embracing traditional social order. With its demise, they had lost status and social control.

The DSP politician referred to the Buddhism ethic to justify deference to *his* preferred leader, the prefectural pro-growth politician. In his mind, Buddhism implied that people should not protest against leaders. His use of Buddhism stood in ironic contrast to Fujii and Inao's use of it to justify protest. Clearly, general value schemas have a great deal of flexibility. People apply them in ways that fit their immediate situational need (Schuman, 1995).

Sparked by pollution, these opposed frames played out in hamlets and neighborhoods around the nation. As heirs to generations of state ideology, some ordinary elder citizens still adhered to the spirit of deference. They referred to political elites as "those above" (*okami*). Sometimes, movement activists challenged their traditional values to win them over to the movement. However, this was not always necessary. As noted, many even among the older generation were skeptical of elites.

In sum, the new democrats and the old conservatives held opposite values about the proper political role a citizen should play. To both groups, environmental movements represented more than just complaints about pollution. They represented a challenge to the old ideology of vertical social order and the interest groups that benefited from it. Enlivened by their sense of rights, the youth felt free to consider and discuss what personal injuries pollution would cause them and their village. Because of their own prior liberation from traditional "sacrifice for the state" mentality, they were readily able to reframe pollution – from a duty they should suffer, to an infringement they should oppose.

The Seki Union

Within the Seki Fishing Union, fishing folk began to discuss Landfill No. 8. Most union members feared its effects, especially those who derived their entire livelihood from fishing. The *tai* (red snapper) fish, their most valuable catch, laid its eggs in the shallow waters along the Kozaki and Baba coast. If No. 8 were built, it would destroy this hatchery and seriously reduce the volume of their catch. Despite this negative effect on their livelihood, the Seki fishing people would get no compensation payments. They did not own use-rights to the waters that No. 8 would cover. In partial compensation, the Prefectural Government offered to construct some artificial fish-breeding grounds. The fishing folk knew this would not fully replace the looming loss.

On the other hand, Kawamura, the union president, led a group, including the Baba fishing folk, that supported No. 8. The union president tried to suppress the opposition group, but it continued strongly. A survey by the board of directors revealed that 70 percent of the Fishing Union members opposed No. 8. In the fall of 1970, the Seki Fishing Union voted to oppose No. 8 and the whole Phase Two plan as well (OGN, September 9, 1970). This vote was very damaging to the Prefectural Government's case for No. 8 because it demonstrated formal opposition by a duly constituted organization. Given the emphasis on form and formality in Japanese culture, this kind of opposition stood as a genuine roadblock to the necessary public process of gaining approval for No. 8. The vote touched off a long series of struggles behind-the-scenes for control over the Seki Union.

The Baba countermovement

The hamlet of Baba held the key to resolving the Seki Union roadblock for the Prefectural Government. The little hamlet of Baba (population 667) lay just west of Kozaki hamlet. The fishers of Baba and Kozaki belonged then to the township-wide Seki Fishing Union. The people who actually fished the waters slated for Landfill No. 8 mostly lived in Baba hamlet. Only a few lived in Kozaki. The fishers from Seki Town did not venture there, but went out around the tip of the peninsula and into the Bungo Straits.

Until 1962, the Baba and Kozaki fishing people had their own separate small fishing union, the Kozaki Fishing Union (named for its larger administrative village). Its leaders and most of its members lived in Baba, so I call it the Baba Union. Until 1962, the Baba Union had held the rights to the No. 8 waters.

In the early 1960s, however, the national government embarked on a campaign to combine local administrative districts for easier administration. As part of this, in 1962, under guidance from the Ministry of Agriculture, Forestry and Fisheries (*Norinsho*), the Oita Prefectural Government forced the Baba Union into the larger Seki Union. That merger gave the Seki Union, as a corporate body, control over the fishing rights for the total township, including the Baba/Kozaki coastal area. The Baba Union could no longer relinquish them without the approval of the whole Seki Union.

Originally, the fishing people of Baba had opposed the whole NIC project. As one of them, who lived in a small, ramshackle house in evident poverty, told me:

Around 1958, at the very beginning of the Phase One plan, we opposed it. We were afraid it would destroy our fishing. We were afraid our jobs would disappear. You couldn't say we were happily in favor of it (Interview, Oita City, January, 1981).

The Baba fishers didn't want to lose their livelihood, as the fisherman explained:

Our fishing area will completely disappear under the landfill. We're not happy about that. We don't like losing the fishing grounds . . .

But, he added, they had no choice. They knew their days of fishing the shallow coastal waters were numbered.

. . . each year the catch goes down . . . due to over-fishing and pollution and house waste water. The sea is dirtied.

By 1970, pollution from the Phase One refineries and pulp plant, though ten kilometers up the coast, had washed down and killed off much of the Baba catch.

Furthermore, if No. 8 were built, the Baba fishing families stood to get substantial compensation (about $100,000 apiece) for the loss of their fishing grounds and livelihood. Some fishing families lived in neighboring Kozaki too.

They no longer engaged in fishing as a livelihood, but retained some traditional rights to the coastal waters. They stood to get compensation payments too.

The sale price for the landfill (when the Prefectural Government sold it to a big company) included the cost of these compensation payments. As the No. 8 issue heated up with Kozaki opposition, the Prefectural Government wanted to assure the cooperation of Baba. As an incentive to cooperate, it gave the numerous fishing families in Baba (and the few in Kozaki) a portion of the compensation money in advance.

The Baba fishers felt they had no choice but to accept. They feared the pollution and disruption. If they wanted a livelihood for themselves and their children in the future, they would have to take the compensation payments.

. . . now that [Landfill] No. 7 has come so close and fishing has gotten worse, we had no choice. So we gave in . . . Since the prefecture is doing it, we will go along . . . We hate pollution, but [the pollution in] Tokyo is worse.

The Baba fishers tried to see the bright side. With their compensation money, they would modernize. They could buy larger boats and go fishing in the deep sea. They could set up a business. Maybe, they hoped, the new factories on No. 8 would hire both them and their children. The government had promised as much. Then they would be working for one of Japan's top companies. In addition, company land taxes would pay for new public services. It might not be so bad. The fisherman continued:

We will become 'cultured' (*bunmeiteki*) here. There will be a little pollution, but according to the company, if they regulate it, [it won't be bad] . . . We expect employment for local youth, so they won't have to go all the way to Tokyo. Also, there will be more schools and other facilities around here . . .

In short, the Baba fishing people hoped to attain their vision of modern "culture": good housing, roads, schools, jobs, and a better consumer lifestyle. For the most part, their children no longer wanted to be fishers. The children wanted the high status of work in modern factories, if they could get it.

Their aspirations built on their history. Before the war, most fishing people had lived in poverty, eking out a living under a fishing boss (*amimoto*) who owned the boat and nets. Fishing had been a low-status job. Having lived so long on the geographical and social periphery, they hoped now, at last, to join the "mainstream." They hoped that jobs in modern industries would give them better security and status, as well as a modern lifestyle. These symbolic and material aspirations inclined the fishing people of Baba toward support for No. 8. Launching them into movement action required an organized push from their union leaders.

The Baba Union had its offices in a ramshackle hut on the Baba beach, among the fishermen's little storehouses and boats. The bosses of the Baba Union had a close connection with prefectural elites. Takashima, office manager for the Baba Union, had been a military police officer during World War Two; after that had worked for a big chemical company for nineteen years. On retirement, he returned to his home village of Baba and took up his job in the Baba Fishing Union. As one would expect from his background, Takashima believed strongly in loyalty to authority, which in this case meant the Prefectural Government. His views were typical conservative Japanese values, with their stress on deference to authority and disparagement of grassroots complaints. In Takashima's words, the pollution protestors were

. . . getting too neurotic (over pollution). Just because they're coughing or there's a lot of bronchitis . . . those diseases appear in places where there aren't any factories at all. If this area's going to progress, we have to have a little (pollution). I don't think it will be bad . . .

Takashima felt that the benefits of progress would outweigh any costs from environmental damage:

As for the loss of the natural environment, there's no help for it. If we worry about it, we can't eat. If we work hard at fishing, its not that we can't eat, but . . . my parents died as fishers. My children are going to school and don't want to go into offshore fishing (Interview, Baba, March 1979).

Progress, he believed, required the destruction of nature and the building of industry:

. . . it's the flow of the times. Industrialization is necessary of course. So it's all right, even if we lose the sea. We need to landfill the sea and grow, to help the village, town, prefecture, and country (Interview, Baba, March 1979).

Takashima trusted prefectural assurances about pollution and jobs. "We are not afraid of not getting jobs," he said. "We will demand conditions, and believe the prefecture and companies will follow those conditions . . ." (Interview, Baba, May 1979). In this light, Takashima saw protest not as reasonable objection but as irrational subversion. He characterized the Kozaki League as radical and irresponsible:

. . . [their leader], isn't he left-wing? Since his student days. Isn't he a communist? It would be OK if they put forward some plan on how to make Saganoseki prosper. But they are against everything. They only say, don't wreck nature.

Another Baba Union official echoed Takashima's convictions. This boss told me that the Baba Union approved the Landfill No. 8 plan uncritically, and implied this was the proper way a union should behave:

. . . the (Baba fisher's) union cooperates with the prefecture's policies . . . Without understanding the contents (of the Landfill No. 8 plan), we approved it. As far as the union goes, that's good enough, isn't it? . . . We didn't think about pollution.

The Baba Union's deference to the Prefectural Government, he explained, grew out of personal connections with officials:

We had a connection with Governor Kinoshita. Mr. Tanabe, the general manager of the Prefectural Government, was from Ozai (a neighboring village). So, as a union, we had a personally close connection to the governor. Governor Kinoshita came to explain things to us.

Here, as in all Japanese politics, people used personal connections selectively. They connected with those who would be useful. As in previous examples, ordinary people felt greatly honored that a high-status person should give them personal attention. This was reward in itself. As before, the connections were also the conduits for material patronage – presented as part of the ritual bond between the paternalistic caring "parent figure" (*oyabun*) and the supplicant, trusting "child figure" (*kobun*) (Nakane, 1970). The official continued:

When we go to the prefecture with a request, we ask him (Tanabe). It's a contact we know. We had him make us a fishing port (here). He acts as one of the closest associates (*sokkin*) of the governor. Or for various funding or aid to the union. For instance, we had him make us a big road from the national route 197 to the seashore here. We make these kinds of requests.

In return, the Baba fishers reciprocated with symbolic gifts to the officials: " . . when we catch *tai* (a prized fish) we call the prefectural officials to come and visit [and give them some] . . ." This ritual solidified their patron-client relationship. Because of this close relationship, the official said, the Baba Union had approved the aluminum refinery. Even though it would be located in front of their hamlet, no union member voiced criticism. The Baba official, echoing the words of the LDP, criticized Governor Taki for having been too "passive and weak" on environmental issues. Clearly, this official believed in stern compliance with authority.

The views of these two Baba Union officials illustrate the complex mixture of culture and material exchange that produced the political attitudes and behavior of the Baba Union. They held strongly to a political culture of loyal paternalism. In their minds, this justified the material benefits they and their fellow hamlet residents received from the prefectural officials. The material benefits, in turn, solidified their feelings of loyalty to the elites.

In contrast to the ramshackle house of the ambivalent fisherman quoted earlier, the two officials lived in large, new houses, filled with expensive furniture and bric-a-brac. It looked as though they had profited from their status as gatekeepers between prefectural officials and the Baba Union. This made them all the more loyal.

These two officials repeatedly insisted that the Baba Union and Baba hamlet as a whole stood solidly in support of Landfill No. 8. Similarly, a Baba fisherman said that at first there had been objections to Landfill No. 8, but they had quieted down. Now, he said, all was "round" (*maruku*) and harmonious (*wa*), as a hamlet should be. The pro-8 forces did control hamlet policy. As I later found out, though, plenty of dissent lay just below the surface.

In sum, a number of social forces converged to turn the Baba Union toward support of Landfill No. 8. NIC Phase One had largely destroyed its fishing livelihood already, making the old ways impossible. Large compensation payments promised to help the transition to a different livelihood. This new livelihood seemed more modern, more in tune with the times. Working in a factory for a big firm or shopkeeping would bring better income and status. Union bosses stirred the members up against the Kozaki "radicals" who would deny them these benefits (if Landfill No. 8 did not materialize). Behind the bosses stood the prefectural officials, invisibly guiding the process.

In like manner, prefectural elites created a number of countermovements in the mirror image of the protest movements that so bedeviled them. In Seki town, these movement-like groups publicly demonstrated in support of No. 8. One Saganoseki merchant explained:

The construction companies are openly pushing for Landfill No. 8 . . . The Prefectural Government helps the construction companies, when they want to organize a pro-8 rally. The Prefectural Government sent people from Oita City by bus to increase the numbers (at the rally) . . . (Interview, Saganoseki, 1979).

The appearance of grassroots movements in favor of No. 8 bolstered the impression of local support. Despite all these efforts, Seki public opinion remained staunchly against No. 8.

Soon after the Seki Union's 1971 vote against No. 8, the Baba Union began a vigorous campaign for separation. It wanted to return to its pre-1962 independent status. This campaign escalated tensions within the Seki Union and led to brawls and fistfights. All the Seki Union members knew the purpose of the Baba campaign; separation would allow the Baba Union to sell its fishing rights to the coastal waters for No. 8. Seki Union members knew that allowing the separation of the Baba Union meant allowing the construction of No. 8. The Seki Union members would no longer have a say in the matter. Separation required approval of two-thirds of Seki union members, so it seemed unlikely.

Analysis

Why, in the face of a common pollution threat, did some communities protest and others collapse into acquiescence? How, in particular, could the two tiny hamlets of Baba and Kozaki, nestled next to each other in an ancient backwater, produce such radically different movements? Can differences in material costs

Table 5.1. Factors of mobilization in eight Japanese communities

COMMUNITY FACTOR	Saeki City	Usuki City	Kozaki hamlet	Seki town	Misa-Iejima	Nakatsu City	Ozai City	Baba hamlet
Material structures: Distribution of objective political-economic benefits/harms sets role parameters of action								
Sudden new pollution or its threat that will harm income		•		•			•	
Sudden new pollution or its threat that will harm health			•	•			•	
Pre-existing pollution that had harmed livelihood/health	•			•	•		•	
Opportunity to profit or gain from polluting		•		•			•	•
Sudden material resources provide new means of protest								
Material "plastic": Contradictory material structures encourage material agency								
Divergent maximization	N/A	•	•	•	N/A	N/A	•	N/A
Material agency: Actors voluntarily generate material goals and construct material exchange structures								
Social structures: Existing social organizational patterns set the role parameters of action								
Kinship hierarchy pattern	•		•					•
Social "plastic": Contradictory social structures encourage social agency								
Kinship hierarchy pattern	•		•					•
Boss-led political machine	•		•					
Community government	N/A		•					
Gendered roles	•		•		N/A	N/A	N/A	•
New middle class	•		•			N/A		•
Trust networks	•		•	•	•	N/A		•
Social agency: Actors voluntarily pursue social relations goals and construct social exchange structures								
Breakaway bosses	•		•					

Table 5.1. *Continued*

COMMUNITY FACTOR	Saeki City	Usuki City	Kozaki hamlet	Seki town	Misa-Iejima	Nakatsu City	Ozai City	Baba hamlet
Cultural structures: Existing cultural codes (collective moralities, identities, ideologies) set role parameters								
Uncritical deference to leader			•					
Cultural "plastic": Contradictory cultural structures encourage cultural agency								
Value of traditional community lifestyle	•	•	•		•	•	•	•
Popular identification with community as religious icon		•	•					
Popular identification with community as social group	•	•	•		•	N/A		
Community-service ethic	•		•					
Environmentalist aesthetic					•	•		
Prior anti-authority values	N/A	N/A	•	•	•	•	•	•
Adoption of a new frame of pollution as bad, undesirable					•			
Attainment of cognitive liberation from deference			•					
Cultural agency: Actors voluntarily make cultural goals and construct new collective cultural codes								
Local actors make new collective identity	•	•	•	•	•	•		
OUTCOMES								
Emergence of an informal protest organization	•	•	•	•	•			•
Long-term survival of the protest organization	•	•	•	•				•
Attainment of a major goal	•	•	•	•				

• = Strong effect. N/A = not available (missing data)
Note: text specifies *which actors are affected by the factor.*

and benefits fully explain their divergent responses, or must we also consider differences in their resources, grievances, or opportunity structures?

Table 5.1 lists the relevant societal factors, as identified in the preceding narrative analysis, that impinged on each community and affected its reaction to pollution or its threat. What the table reveals is an extremely variegated pattern of causality, even among these few, similarly situated cases. This indicates, first of all, that human social behavior is moved by an extremely complex and very local set of factors. Action is affected by a multitude of nuanced factors that impinge upon a specific situation. In addition, collective action, the table indicates, is not mostly attributable to just "structure" or "agency," but usually occurs in the plastic zone between those two extremes.[8] That said, what generalized patterns of causality, if any, may we discern in the table?

Table 5.1 shows that all of the protest movements had their inception in the presence or threat of sufficient pollution to cause material harm, either to livelihood or to health. The intensity of this pollution threat varied somewhat by community. The hamlets of Misa/Iejima, Kozaki, and Baba stood to suffer (or suffered) the most severe health problems from pollution. In Usuki City, Seki City, and Baba, pollution posed a threat to livelihood. The Ozai hamlets and Nakatsu City were less threatened by the health effects of air pollution because, given their locations on flat river deltas, the pollution would blow inland and disperse better. Along with physical and economic costs, industrialization would disrupt the traditional pattern close-knit community lifestyles of Saeki City as well as the hamlets of Misa/Iejima, Ozai, Kozaki, and Baba.

In the Oita movements, activists and regular citizens in all the communities (except perhaps Nakatsu) experienced pollution or its threat and recognized it as a danger. Their framing of pollution, in other words, quickly and closely fit the objective reality. Individuals and families quickly became aware of pollution, its source, and the harm it was causing. Certainly, cognition of one's surroundings is a *sine qua non* for action. The debate, though, is over the degree to which cognitions inherently mirror a reality or are colored by subjective beliefs and hopes. The findings indicate either a profoundly accurate grasp of reality, or else that preexisting myths and ideologies in the local community already supported the idea that pollution was harmful.

If the communities had required liberation from a culture of deference to elites (Pharr & Badaracio, 1986, p. 241), presumably their residents would not have been harboring "myths" about the harmfulness of pollution either. The rapidity of mobilization in Kozaki and other communities indicated the widespread presence of opposition frames and "myths" already in place, underneath

---

8. See Chapter 1 and Appendix 1 for explanations of these sociological terms.

a superficial veneer of deference to elites. Such deference, this finding indicates, rather than being based on a morality of gratitude for benevolence, had been based on fear. Postures of deference had been a necessary pretense (*tatemae*), adopted over centuries by the villagers, to ward off attack by predatory elites and governments.

In any case, negative collective framing of an objective harm was not, by itself, sufficient to spark mobilization. The hamlets of Ozai adopted this frame, but mobilization failed in them. Obviously, other factors were also necessary. An objective threat and its negative framing establishes only a mobilization potential, not mobilization itself (Klandermans, 1993). A community had to have several other factors at work as well, if it was to actualize its mobilization potential.

If we look at Table 5.1, we find that those communities that proceeded along the mobilization path to the point of attaining outcome number 1, the emergence of a protest organization, did not have any common combination of factors. Nothing collectively distinguished them from the Ozai communities, which did not produce a protest organization. However, if we look at the communities, Saeki, Usuki and Kozaki, which attained all three of the outcomes, including longer term survival of the protest organization and the attainment of a major strategic goal, a clearer pattern emerges. These three communities had in common the following factors: a kinship hierarchy pattern and trust networks, breakaway bosses who exercised social agency, and common appreciation for the traditional lifestyle.

Why should this particular set of factors have been so important to successful mobilization? In these three cases, evidently, collection action was impelled and facilitated by the retention of tradition, not its breakdown. Some scholars associate popular democracy and grassroots political activism with "modernity" (Inkeles, 1974), but we find the opposite here. Some social movement theorists have advanced the insight, supported by the findings here, that perhaps "new" social movements like environmentalism are not really so new, but have earlier analogues (Calhoun, 1995). Some theorists, in a similar vein, see environmental movements as defenders of traditional lifestyles, ones close to nature and protective of the organically developed community (Habermas, 1981) – a cultural value very much in evidence in Oita's movements – against the intrusions of an impersonal bureaucratic state (Offe, 1985b; Habermas, 1981).[9] Many movement leaders and members in Oita, partaking of this sentiment, mourned the loss of the traditional hamlet community.

In the three most successful mobilizations, people who were invested with

---

9. Max Weber referred to this as the "iron cage" of bureaucratization (Weber, 1958).

community leadership roles by virtue of traditional status – leadership of old-line main families of landlord heritage, *ku*-leaders, owners of the major local businesses – became radicalized into opposing the Triple Control Machine. Their radicalization happened for very different personal moral reasons, but the social structural outcome was the same – block recruitment of ordinary citizens into mobilization and protest (Pinard, 1971, p. 187; Oberschall, 1973, p. 125). The collective identity of these ordinary citizens with their traditional community, sometimes as overtly symbolized by the religious icon of the community god (*ujigami*), reinforced their bonds to the protest movement as an entity, because it was struggling to defend the social organizational basis of such collective identities. Accordingly, I reach the somewhat ironic (from the standpoint of modernization theory) conclusion that traditional values and structures were crucial components of resistance to elite-inspired industrial growth.

The leader so constituted, though radicalized for different personal moral reasons, still had to have *moral* reasons, and tough ones, rather than economic ones of personal gain. Long-term environmental movement leaders in other countries have a similar deep ethical motivation (Reich, 1984; Reich, 1991). Or if motivated by reasons of personal gain, the dimensions of personal gain had to outweigh what the Triple Control Machine could offer as an inducement to capitulation. In either case, some personal, internal motivation had to stabilize the leader's desire to stay the course of protest.[10] Without that consistent motivation, the leader would be likely to succumb to the blandishments of the machine, capitulate, and drag the movement down in the process. The case of Nishio's fall seems to support that generalization. Among the consistent leaders, Inao and Katayama followed strong personal moral principles – those of the humanist New Left and of the old Meiji righteousness, respectively – while the economic elites of Usuki were motivated to save their very successful and lucrative businesses.

Sometimes, breaking with the LDP machine forced movement leaders to reframe their image of politics and their role within it. They realized how traditional norms of deference had discouraged political activism, and argued against such norms. This reframing, though, was not a cause of mobilization. It was a consequence.

When the bosses stayed loyal to the LDP machine, on the other hand, as they did in Baba and in the Seki Union, they made protest very difficult if not impossible. Conservative bosses became the social conduit through which the prefectural officials organized countermovements. Elite support for counter-

---

10. This resembles what sociologists call "value-rationality" (Weber, 1978) and the "inner-directed" character (Riesman, 1950).

movements is a common social control tactic in other ACID countries (Lo, 1982). In the United States, for instance, elites constructed the "Wise Use Movement" against environmental regulation as if it were a grassroots movement (Mitchell, Mertig, & Dunlap, 1992). In Japan, such tactics were essential to the elite strategy of soft social control through the Triple Control Machine.

When mobilization occurred in a more urbanized area, however, it had to use more material interest-based incentives (Broadbent, 1986). In Usuki City, for instance, objective economic interests, not existing social ties, brought business elites to join the village protest movement. In Nakatsu, opposition parties and unions, not informal social networks, provided the bulk of movement participants.

This empirical array of essential factors grants little support to a number of other, received theories of mobilization. Chapter 3 rejected the idea that the wave of environmental protest was stimulated by any sudden opening in the political opportunity structure, or that it was the product of a diffusion of a "madness" of protest enthusiasm. Chapters 4 and 5, as summarized in Table 5.1, show that the diffusion of new ideology thesis does not hold either. New "irrational" beliefs, such as the sudden diffusion of a new anti-business ideology (Reed, 1986) or a hysteria about pollution, did not inspire the mobilization process in Oita.

Contrary to resource mobilization theory, also, new material resources did not play an important role in sparking protest mobilization. The mobilizing communities did not enjoy outside philanthropic donors. If the hamlet residents had better wealth, facilities, and other resources than previous generations, those had already been present since the late 1950s and were on a continual upward course. Indeed, the town of Seki had even produced protest before the Second World War, when resources were much more tight. The sudden presence of new resources, then, could not have been the immediate stimulus to the mobilization of the Oita movements.

Rather, social networks of trust played the greatest role in mobilization. In Saeki, local residents joined Katayama in protest because they trusted him as the traditional *ku* leader. Similarly, in Kozaki, residents joined the protest in part due to their preexisting trust in Yuki or Inao. In Kozaki and Saeki, in other words, activist leaders ripped their subordinate networks away from the vertical social fabric and used them to mobilize insurgency. In Saeki, residents had already been complaining to Katayama about the soot from the plywood factory. The *ku*-head was supposed to receive such complaints. When failure to get redress from the authorities frustrated Katayama, he led his *ku*-members into protest.

In this process, the movement and the new recruits did not need to "align" their interpretive frames very much. Nor did the residents need to form a new collective identity – "we, the pollution victims of Hinode *ku*" – as some theorists assert (Melucci, 1995). Rather, the necessary frames and identities were already present, latent within the local repertoire of political culture and behavior (Tilly, 1978). As community concern over pollution mounted through observation and talking, the residents picked and used frames and identities from that existing repertoire just as a carpenter might pick the right tool for a job. The findings support the tool kit view of rational individuals as culture-users rather than culture-dupes (Swidler, 1986; Swidler, 1995).

Opposition-justifying frames within the community subculture came from many sources. Most Japanese rural areas carried forward an oral tradition about previous protest attempts, often stretching back to peasant rebellions in the Tokugawa era. Since the beginning of the twentieth century, up to the present, some communities (Misa/Iejima, Seki) had continually suffered severe pollution and its health effects. This situation had also stimulated previous, though usually failed, attempts at protest. Furthermore, the horrors of World War Two had deeply imbued the Japanese public with a mistrust of nationalistic elites.

In addition, the Occupation reforms had introduced a host of changes with ramifications for protest. After these reforms liberalized the political system, opposition parties and unions seeded the working class with anti-state and anti-big business values and ideas. In school, contrary to traditional teachings of loyalty to the Emperor and the state, civics classes taught ideas of democracy and personal rights to the post-war generation of youth. By the mid-1960s, this post-war generation was just reaching maturity and political awareness. Their teachers during this era were often members of the Japan Teachers' Union, which fought against the conservative elite for a number of causes. When the objective costs of pollution threatened their communities, these teachers and their former students often provided the initial leadership and activist cadre for the start of mobilization.

Western theories noted here tend to assume that action arises from individual agency within the context of a relatively liberal, pluralistic political institution. Given that starting point, for collective action to occur, the atomized individuals have to come together and build a protest organization. In the process, they need to adopt new collective frames and identities in order to engage in collective action. In Japan, however, despite the socially disintegrative effects of capitalist growth, social atomization has not gone so far, even in the big cities. In Oita's small towns, the old forms of collective organization still persisted strongly, making the process of mobilization quite different. In other words, existing *social* and *cultural structures* awaited the external trigger of sudden new costs imposed by pollution. This material trigger stimulated local leaders into creative agency and use of existing material, political, social and cultural resources to justify and support initial mobilization.

New social-movement (NSM) theory sees environmental movements as arising from the new middle class (middle managers and educated professionals). They attribute environmental activism to the post-material, lifestyle-oriented values of this class (Inglehart, 1977). In Oita, the leadership seems to fit this thesis better than the mass participants. Some movement leaders, as predicted, came from Japan's version of the new middle class. Many were high-school teachers; Katayama was a court reporter . They enjoyed the new middle-class attributes of high prestige, good income, and college education – predicted to produce a concern for environmental issues. Other leaders, though, came from the small business class (a tofu-maker, fishing people) and the medium-sized business class (soy sauce and pharmaceutical factory owners). These leaders seemed to adopt environmentalism as a way to salvage their businesses, rather than as an ideological or moral passion.

Ordinary participants came mostly from the working and lower middle classes: laborers, fishers, and shopkeepers. They were more concerned with issues of livelihood and health than with preserving the environment per se. Hamlets with high proportions of fishing folk, who stood to gain monetary compensation from the landfill, more readily quieted down than communities whose residents were mostly in other lines of work. Material concerns, including both health and livelihood, therefore, were important personal motivators for mass participation in the movement. The centrality of material issues to protest mobilization makes it reasonable to think of the protestors as an "exploited class." If we do so, their protests fit well within a Marxist model of capitalist politics that stresses the importance of class struggle (Block, 1977; Skocpol, 1995).

The potential a movement has for mobilization and success depends in part on the goals it seeks. Reform movements more often attain success than movements with elite-displacing (revolutionary) goals (Gamson, 1990). Among environmental movements, radical structuralists advocate collective action to change the capitalist treadmill of production itself – retreatists want to change production processes with appropriate technology, reformists want to modify existing production processes to clean up pollution, meliorists advocate green consumerism to change production output, cosmetologists try to change public behavior such as littering, social equitists reject the discriminatory aspects of pollution (environmental racism), anti-environmentalists see environmentalists as mere alarmists (Gould, 1993, p. 227). In addition, the NIMBY (not-in-my-back-yard)-style movement wants to prevent pollution in its own community, but is not concerned with changing production processes and consumer or public behavior. A NIMBY movement usually dies down once it meets that goal.

The Oita movements were largely of the NIMBY variety. Except for a few leaders, participants showed little desire to continue with environmental activism once they had staved off the threat to their community. A few leaders – notably Inao, Katayama and Fujii – continued to work for environmental causes throughout the prefecture. None of them became involved with national level efforts, which were extremely weak in any case.

The larger political opportunity structures helped defined this NIMBY-quality of local protest movements. In the West, under a relatively open ruling elite and pluralistic regime, a broad range of environmental movements, from spontaneous grassroots groups (Gedicks, 1994; Bullard, 1993; Freudenberg & Steinsapir, 1992) to highly organized professional lobbying groups (Mitchell, 1979; McCloskey, 1992), were able to establish themselves. In Japan, though, the prefectural and national institutions of power militated against the emergence of a strong environmental public interest group sector at the national level (see Chapter 9). Accordingly, the informal political institutions in Japan encouraged local protest movements to stay local, rather than joining hands and maturing into a powerful national interest group presence.

This complex logic of mobilization contrasts strikingly with the typical Western pattern of rationally driven individuals joining in contractual relations with others to accomplish mutually accepted goals. Clearly, protest in Japan arose on the basis of a very different set of embedded social institutions than common in the United States. Japanese people were rational, but were not atomized individuals. They were bound into community. Therefore, their rationality had to take account of and strategize within a very different social institutional and collective cultural context. The results therefore confirm Nakane's argument that the essential organizational form in Japanese society is the inverted V structure of local deference and loyalty to personal bosses (Nakane, 1970).

The threat to vital interests posed by the protest movements set off a strong elite-led countermobilization, which the next chapters trace.

6

Under the machine

Political dynamics

Once people with grievances have formed a group and reached some consensus about a problem, they may launch into some sort of action. Taking action ushers the group into the public spotlight, and may stir up contention from those threatened by the social changes. Defenders of the status quo, if they have the power, may try to control and suppress the protest group. The opposition of competing interests sets in motion the dynamics of politics. This type of social control from the state and elites sets the conditions for protest movement response.

Dominant elites, such as state officials, top politicians, and business leaders, may have various means of social control available to them (Oberschall, 1978; Marx & Wood, 1975). Often, in less democratic societies, they use the military or police to coerce movements into silence. Business owners may withdraw necessary material goods, such as pay from labor movements. At the same time, elites may attempt to use softer means of social control, such as a barrage of public statements or indoctrination through the educational curriculum (Lukes, 1986; Broadbent, 1983; Pharr, 1990).

In post-war years, the Japanese state has favored soft means of social control. Japanese elites, some argue, exercise control over movements by cutting them off from broader public support – by isolation, marginalization, and containment. In one tactic, elites try to "bait" movements into committing radical acts that will alienate the public (Pharr, 1990, p. 166–167).[1] The elites also used social connections as a means of social control. The last chapter showed how Katayama and other radicalized bosses used their social status and local networks to mobilize protest. Elites, in the same way, as they developed their

---

1. State provocation of protestors into violence is a common tactic of social control in many countries.

response, used similar social networks to reach down into the hamlets and muffle protest. The existence of local conservative political support "machines" has often been noted for Japan (Fukutake, 1989, p. 163; Curtis, 1971), as well as in other countries (Eisenstadt & Roniger, 1984). How these operate in a conflictual political process has been less explored.

As the conflict over Oita's growth problems proceeded, elites mobilized these vertical networks of control. They appealed to potential supporters who were also members of social networks (such as friends, aunts, cousins, and so on) of movement members. This tactic put movements on the defensive even within their own hamlets and neighborhoods. As a result, movements increasingly had to fight for control of local personal networks and hamlet organizations. They could no longer count on them, as they had at first within Kozaki.

Of course, to speak generically, social networks are just one sort of political network. They operate as just one component within the complex structures of power present in any society. The structures include binding ideologies, emotions, categories of thought, and other culturally affected forms of consciousness, as well as economic inducements and threats of physical coercion. The combination of these positive and negative sanctions in any given society or social location may vary widely, affecting the precise process of structural and output transformation.

The first steps of conflict in Kozaki

Differing frames

Governor Kinoshita felt personally affronted by the protests in Seki. He framed the dilemmas of growth entirely differently than the protestors. His purpose in industrializing Oita, along with bolstering the Socialist party, had been to give jobs, customers, and business contracts to Oita. How could these protestors be so concerned with their personal benefits as to hamper the larger good? When I interviewed the retired governor, he lived in a very large home (by Japanese standards) bordered with beautiful, manicured gardens. Looking back on the events, he denied that the NIC project had ever created pollution:

There was no real trouble with pollution . . . The water was not at all dirtied, except by farmers' chemical fertilizers . . . It was nothing at all like Minamata. Cars are a much worse killer.

The governor knew that some health dangers from pollution existed (Kinoshita, 1973). But compared with the benefits of industrial growth for the whole prefecture, pollution costs were minor and only affected a few people. Protest, in that light, was highly misguided. It had to be inspired by some ulterior or irrational motive. The trouble came, he said, not from pollution, but from agitators who stirred up the people:

Lawyers made all the trouble . . . and the people held meetings and made trouble. They should not (have tried to) throw away the diamond of Oita's development potential (Interview 55, 1979).

In particular, no doubt, he was referring to the law firm of lawyer Yoshida, affiliated with the Communist party. This group had been donating its services to environmental movements around the prefecture. Kinoshita thought the JCP was trying to pick up votes by fanning the flames of discontent. He concluded that all the anti-NIC protest movements were "communist inspired" (Interview 55, 1979).

Whatever their motives, the Governor knew, the protestors could jeopardize Oita's whole Phase Two program. The Regional Development Advisory Council and related ministries had to approve the Phase Two plans before construction could begin. Approval was not certain. By 1970, with the NIC program almost ten years old, many national ministry officials thought the program had outlived its purposes (however conceived). They no longer had much enthusiasm for giving out permits for new NIC harbors and landfills. Since the Mishima/ Numazu protests, national officials knew how much local protest could hamper a project. Protest in Seki, the Governor knew, might add enough doubts to make them give up on Oita's Phase Two project.

A reliable governor, furthermore, should be able to quiet down dissent before it erupted. That expectation, drawn from traditional elite political culture, remained embedded in the (conservative) governor-ministry relationship. An impression of smooth paternalistic control raised a governor's status with central bureaucrats. This gave the governor easier access to central resources, like permits for harbor construction. In those circles, Governor Kinoshita had already been stigmatized for his Socialist party background. He didn't want to be labeled inept as well.

Despite these pressures, the Governor knew the situation did not warrant the use of force, nor would that have been electorally defensible. Persuasion, prefectural officials thought, was now the only feasible way to quiet down the protestors. A former chief of the Oita Government's Industrial Bureau explained:

In doing a job . . . the problem is how to convince the opposition. After the war, Japan became a democracy so individual rights were respected. So we listened to the opposition voices and tried to convince and persuade them, and then do our job. It's not like the old feudal times using force. Rather, we have to persuade . . . So we have to convince individuals . . . The job of the official is to get consent.

The official went on to add that in its post-war weakened condition, local government did not really have much alternative to active persuasion:

> If (we don't persuade the residents), they will take us to court. Local government is losing most of (these suits) now . . . The local government doesn't have the legal power to force through its plans without resident consent. The Usuki case is the best example.

Given this new balance of power, he explained, persuasion was not always so easy:

> The special characteristic of Japan is in how we carry out negotiations. The Japanese easily get very emotional. If you make one mistake, . . . no matter how much money in compensation payments you offer them (residents) won't agree (to a policy).

The biggest mistake, in this age of democracy, the official explained, was to slight the residents by implementing plans involving their residential area without informing them beforehand:

> (This occurs when) you don't explain things beforehand to the local people. If you just tell them, "the prefectural or national plan has already been decided, so cooperate," things get difficult (Interview 82, undated, 1978–1980).

Pluralist political theory holds the view that the administrative arm of the democratic state is neutral. The official clearly believed the state should take a proactive, not neutral, role in public affairs. That viewpoint had deep roots in the previous Imperial state, which ruled in the name of a semi-divine Emperor. In those days, the Diet and a restricted electorate had exercised a weak check at most.[2] Many of the personnel from that era still staffed the post-war state.

But in fact, state officials in all ACID societies try to persuade the public of the virtues of their favored policies. Typically, we associate persuasion with officials on television or in the news, arguing their case. But to the Oita Prefectural Government, persuasion involved much more than that. The official justified a paternalistic, "we know what is best" role for the state. Only the means of persuasion, not its intent, had changed. The new situation meant imposing state preferences on the populace by softer sanctions and tactics.

Turncoat ku-chairs

The Kozaki League circulated a petition directed specifically against the Showa Denko aluminum plant. It quickly collected the signatures of 1,010 villagers

---

2. During the Taisho democracy period (1912 to 1926), Japanese democracy reached its pre-war height. Still, suffrage was not universal. In 1925, the passage of a universal manhood suffrage bill granted voting rights to all men over 25 years of age, increasing the electorate from 3 million men to 12.4 million men. But this democratization was soon destroyed by the rise of militarism (Reischauer & Craig, 1978, p. 241).

(about 95 percent of eligible voters). Yuki, the *ku*-chair, presented this petition on September 8, 1970, to the mayor of Saganoseki. While doing so, however, he told the mayor that if a different sort of plant came, the Kozaki people would accept Landfill No. 8 (Interview, 1981). This was contrary to the spirit, if not the letter, of the petition.

When movement leaders heard of Yuki's statement, they were shocked and disappointed. Up to then, all the *ku*-heads and Yuki had voted in staunch opposition to No. 8 (Chapter 4). They wondered how Yuki could have said that. To counter the impression he had made, the League quickly circulated another petition. This one stated explicit resistance to No. 8 no matter what the factory, and received just as many signatures.

Within Kozaki hamlet, however, the activists started to encounter further unforeseen setbacks. In October 1970, Yuki the *ku*-chair convened another residents' meeting to discuss No. 8. At the meeting, three of the eight Kozaki *ku*-heads, one of them the *ku*-chair himself, suddenly expressed support for landfill. This shocked the rest of the *ku*-heads and the movement activists. They had expected that the hamlet would maintain its internal solidarity and consensus against the outside threat. This event shocked movement activists into the realization that their struggle had to be internal, within their own hamlet, as well as external.

Undaunted, the majority of *ku*-heads voted once again to oppose No. 8. They circulated a recall petition through the hamlet, and removed the recalcitrant *ku*-chair from office. Instead, the League pushed for and elected elderly Inao Kiyohide as the *ku*-chair. He had always expressed solid opposition to No. 8. After assuming office, however, a strange thing happened. Inao Kiyohide too began to express support for No. 8. In response, the movement forced him out of office too. Next, the *ku*-heads elected elderly Inao Chitoshi, likewise a movement participant. But, once in office, Inao Chitoshi too "got strange" and began to support No. 8. Once again, the movement forced him to quit the office.

Slowly, the movement activists realized that the repeated switch in *ku*-chair stance was not just due to personal change of heart. Some sort of systematic pressure behind the scenes was pushing the *ku*-chairs to change their stance. The activists slowly discovered that the mayor and other elites had been putting pressure on the elderly *ku*-chairs. Post-war democracy was somehow not working the way the young activists had been taught in school.

The *ku*-chair, once elected, joined the regular meetings of all Seki *ku*-chairs under the mayor. The mayor held sake parties for them, which strengthened their male camaraderie and bonding. The mayor sometimes invited regular *ku*-heads to these parties too, if they needed convincing on some issue. As this relationship deepened, the mayor pressured them to change sides and support

No. 8. Elderly people, explained one Kozaki resident (whose wife was the only female *ku*-head), lacked the moral fiber to resist the mayor:

When a person becomes a *ku*-head, he gradually becomes pro-No. 8 because of contact with the mayor or other bosses . . . Older people have little strength of character. They feel they must obey the words of the superiors (*okami*)

The mayor pursued this tactic, the villager explained, at the behest of the Prefectural Government:

The prefecture knows that if it can control the *ku*-chair, it can control the *ku* residents.

The reason the elderly *ku*-chairs were so vulnerable to the mayor's persuasion was, another villager commented,

in order to get a little status . . . it is so important to get a little praise from or to have lunch with the mayor. For this, they will approve No. 8 (Interview 257, 1979).

That this "status seduction" should occur so readily confirms Nakane's model of Japan as a vertical society. She argues that "the relationship between two individuals of upper and lower status is the basis of the structural principle of Japanese society" (Nakane, 1970, p. 42). The social norm of rank is the basis for Japanese social life (Nakane, 1970, p. 31). In Japan, rank takes on its greatest normative force when both people belong to the same organization and when the ranks are contiguous (one level above or below each other). The elderly people may not have had a direct, long-standing relationship with the mayor. But once they occupied a status and rank within the formal *ku*-government organization, they felt quite compelled to adhere to his wishes. Would this have happened anywhere? Certainly, rank is a powerful norm in all societies. But these incidents indicate that it may be stronger in Japan than in other ACID societies. This may result from the relatively weak development of the self-concept, and hence a weak ability to distinguish self and social status (Markus & Kitayama, 1991).

Some scholars argue that Japanese are "embedded" in and define themselves by their long-term interpersonal relations (Hamaguchi, 1985). At first glance, this argument seems to fit with the norm of loyalty to immediate hierarchy. However, the ease with which the elders switched from loyalty to the movement leader to loyalty to the mayor indicates, to the contrary, a very instrumental, non-embedded quality. If not, how could the elders have allied themselves with the mayor so quickly?

Status seduction had limitations. It had a gender-specific quality. Women, who could not attend the mayor's sake parties, were relatively immune from status seduction. One respondent noted: "My wife is a *ku*-head, but doesn't feel that pressure." She was one of the few *ku*-heads who did not waver in opposition to No. 8.

In addition, status seduction did not come about entirely by normative pressures. It had a decidedly material aspect. Katayama, the leader of the Saeki movement (see Chapter 4), had described how the LDP had offered him large amounts of money not to protest. Katayama assured me that the turncoat *ku*-chairs and heads of Kozaki had succumbed to similar pressures. They

. . . get money and profit (from the LDP). . . . Because of that . . . they keep that position (supporting Landfill No. 8) . . .

Also, business quickly got involved in bribing the ku-heads to accept No. 8. One villager said this always happens in Japan:

When a company decides to locate in an area, they always buy off the main people in the village, like the *ku*-head or *ku*-chair.

For example, he said,

The first [Kozaki] *ku*-chair, who [the movement] forced out of office, had gotten a lot of money. Around 1970, he bought a mansion in Kobe. He was a small druggist not doing too well in Kozaki, so he could never have done that on his own money (Interview).

The pro-No. 8 *ku*-heads, in turn, tried to persuade locals to sell their land to developers:

The current *ku*-head of Koneko helps land sales. He asks people, or rather tells them, to sell their land. If the *ku*-chair asks a person to sell his land, he will do it. People want to go along with what the *ku*-chair says. It's an old custom. It's something to do with personal connections, I think. If they're told something clever, about how they'll profit if they sell their land, they'll go along with it.

Later evidence supports and elaborates this League contention. At the same time, several of the *ku*-heads, including that of Koneko *ku* (where Inao Toru and his family lived) allied themselves with the fishing families of Kozaki, who wanted more compensation money from the prefecture. Some fishing folk in the Kozaki League refused the compensation offer. But once a fishing person had accepted the initial payment, he often felt morally indebted to support No. 8 after that.

The League was frustrated by the repeated seduction of its elected representatives and the gnawing-away of its members. The League asked Okamoto, a young man from Koneko ku, to take on the *ku*-chair position. League leaders thought that Okamoto, as a member of the post-war generation, would be less vulnerable to status seduction by the mayor. And it seemed he would win the election for *ku*-chair. Okamoto himself realized this quite well:

The bosses feared my winning. It would be terrible for them. They feared I might stir up the whole *ku*.

If Okamoto won, he would give voice to the League's stance within the mayor's *ku*-chair group. This would make it harder, Okamoto said, for the mayor to marginalize the Kozaki movement:

Up to now, they have been able to say, 'the anti-8 group is just one part of Kozaki.' But if I became *ku*-chair, anti-8 talk would be brought up at *ku*-chair meetings. This would be more powerful than just among the anti-No.8 Kozaki *ku*-heads by themselves (Interview 257, 1979).

To counter this move, a local conservative boss dissolved the ku-chair system in Kozaki, making the election impossible. Strictly speaking, this was not legal. The movement leaders might have rectified it, if they had complained loudly enough. But they did not. Kozaki's *ku*-council had proved little help to them.

Local bosses

Who were these local "bosses," I wondered, who could cancel Kozaki's *ku*-chair election system? When I first heard the term boss, I imagined gangsters lurking in the shadows. I started to fear for my own safety. I found out that to the ordinary resident, a boss did not carry this fearsome connotation. On the contrary, a boss was someone able to help you solve problems of everyday life – getting a road fixed or finding a job.

A neighbor of mine was a neighborhood boss for a conservative LDP Diet representative. We became good friends, and he told me frankly about his activities. "Bosses," he told me, "are proud of their status. Many people want to become one." Another boss who earned his livelihood as a traditional artist, smiled broadly and boasted that he commanded seventy votes. Politicians came to court his favor. He helped the governor get elected. In return, he told me, the governor had hosted a fancy lunch for himself and a hundred other local bosses. This boss lived right near the most polluted area of Oita. He ignored the stench, and professed being happy about the factories. A boss, I found out to my surprise, saw himself as a local "Santa Claus" (*Daikokusan*), giving out presents and guiding the flock.

Bosses liked the feeling of working for a powerful protecting leader. One boss described the relationship between the higher politicians and the local bosses in traditional fictive kinship terms:

At election time, [town and prefectural politicians] bring money they've gotten from their 'parent' [*oyabun*] Diet politician and give it to their 'child' [*kobun*, referring to local boss]. Through this, the oyabun-kobun relationship gets cemented. This is not something accomplished in a brief time. Over time the relationship becomes very intimate . . .

Some local citizens enjoyed the role so much they spent their own savings to do it.

People told me that bosses often came from the pre-war landlord or net-owner (*amimoto*) class. The Occupation had distributed the land to the tillers, destroying the landlord system. This had been a harsh and stigmatizing system built on the unequal ownership and command of scarce goods. The typical landlord sat on a raised wooden floor and ate white rice; his visiting tenants sat on the lower dirt floor and ate barley. Their bathing methods also demonstrated the same hierarchy. In Obasama, our landlord had a gigantic iron pot (one meter wide, and one meter deep) in an outside hut. That was the family bath, one of the few in the village and a luxury. Just like a soup pot, it was heated with a wood fire underneath. People scooped out the hot water and washed off, then entered clean to soak. While the landlord's family members finished their bath, ten or more tenants lined up outside to take their bath afterward.

Why, I wondered, would the old landlords still enjoy a degree of status and loyalty from their former tenants? This did not make sense to me. Had the old situation been a "moral economy," in which the tenants were grateful for being taken care of by their masters (Scott, 1976; Popkin, 1979, p. 5–8)? One former tenant farmer attributed the old system to sheer economic inequality, not moral values:

In the past, money controlled people. The tenant or poor fisherman was indebted to the landowner or "fish net-owner" (*amimoto*), who would lend him money and take care of him in times of trouble. So, in turn the poor tenant, etc., would go along with the "boss's" wishes at election time and so forth.

But now, a man from Baba who supported No. 8 explained, the relationship had changed:

Bosses are not frightening. They are a place's leaders. It is not like the old tenant/owner relationship, when there was a big difference in wealth between classes. Now, there is not much difference between rich and poor. In the old times, the tenant was on the verge of starving. He couldn't even send his kids to school.

Accordingly, I concluded, villagers must defer to the new bosses, not because of some sentimental residue of deference, but because they provided new kinds of benefits. I was unclear why the new boss status, in that case, had ended up in the hands of the descendants of the old landlord class.

Economic growth, the Baba man explained, had rescued the villagers from their previous poverty, and brought many blessings. Most people had acquired not only their own bathtubs, but also a blue-tile roofed house, a car, television set, washing machine, and air conditioner. They could dine on white rice, sake, and a wide variety of meat, fish, and other "luxury" foods. The most obvious lifestyle-related status differences had largely disappeared. Therefore, people felt grateful to the LDP, the party that had brought this new prosperity.

Most people feel very blessed now. Most people feel the LDP has created this good situation and they're happy and thankful.

Bosses were more than mere symbols of prosperity, however. They were conduits for much personal and community (public works) patronage and services. Speaking of the early postwar years, one villager said:

. . . the boss would call together his 'children' (*kobu* – meaning the villages who accepted his patronage), wine and dine them, and let them know whom he was pushing for election . . .

With resources and connections from the LDP, local bosses could provide loans, job contacts, marriage go-between services, parties, funding for ceremonies and festivals, and many other services. They basked in the glory of their Diet politician's pipeline to the center. As one villager said:

Bosses are those who can be trusted, who help others a lot, or who lead well. We ask the politician for jobs, marriage contacts, and so forth. He has high credibility and can handle the world better than we can.

An experienced local boss fully concurred. For bribery and patronage, he said, he handed out

various complicated things. Overall, it's what the residents want. Give sake (rice wine) to those who want it. Give a person whatever would actually benefit them.

Good election bribery required a great deal of finesse. A skilled "boss" had to know how to dispense patronage personally, appropriately and discretely. The real point was to build up a feeling of loyalty in the recipient. Direct monetary bribes were not large, only ten or fifteen dollars per vote. Their strength lay more in their symbolic content. The bribe that came first most strongly swayed the voter because it symbolized the importance the boss placed on you as an individual. Being bribed made the recipient feel important. It was another form of status seduction.

The boss-run machine still dominated voting behavior. Starting with relatives, friends, and neighbors, and drawing others in, local bosses built up and ran support groups (*koenkai*) for LDP Diet politicians.[3] Bosses built *koenkai* by accumulating personal indebtedness for small favors. They also brought in

---

3. Despite urbanization, the political machines continue to operate, albeit with less efficiency and totalism, in the cities. In a 1989 interview, for instance, a Tokyo ward politician for the Socialist party explained how her LDP opponent treated members of his *koenkai* to a three-day vacation at a hot springs resort at minimal cost.

existing organizations, from judo clubs to tea ceremony societies. Their LDP patron would make occasional ceremonial visits to the meetings of these groups. A *koenkai* served only one Diet representative and the prefectural and town politicians within his faction. The group encouraged residents to trust the politician uncritically, as they would a parent (Thayer, 1969). In return for the constant flow of patronage, villagers were expected to surrender any critical political thoughts. The result was that, as one villager said, most "people don't really care who gets elected; they just follow the bosses' requests." He commented:

Most people still vote by influence of the boss, if he's taking care of their lives for them. The base of the society is still poor, so people respond to the boss system. It's the same in all the rural areas of Japan . . .

An Oita merchant and novice politician who tried to run a more rational, issue-based campaign (on an anti-pollution theme) learned the power of ritual patronage structures the hard way. He reflected somewhat bitterly on the causes of his electoral failure:

The real source of power at elections has nothing to do with policies, ideas, programs, and so on.

Rather, he said, it was prestige of a personal appeal that moved people to vote for you:

It is connections, and who asked a person first, even more than the money. That is the key. It means to the individual that he is treated as important by the candidate.

The key to getting a voter, he said, was to approach him through their close social ties:

The person who can really move votes is the real local yokel (*dochaku*). He can figure out, 'well, if I go through this guy, I can influence this other guy, who has a connection with that woman and can get her to vote for my candidate. But to get her husband's vote, I have to go by another channel.' Knowing these connections is the name of the game.

At the same time, the boss had to give out bribes and other patronage through those channels:

The person with ideals but no money ends up having not much influence on elections and people.

Ideals and issues had nothing to do with votes, he said:

In elections, I would go to ask for someone's vote for such and such a candidate because he supported a certain cause. And the person would say, 'oh yes. I'm really sorry, but I was asked first by so and so, so I have to vote for him.' Even though we had reached agreement about supporting the cause earlier, and about voting for a certain candidate for the sake of the policy, when it came right down to it, people weren't moved by that.

Political influence, in other words, worked through the social context. Local bosses worked hard all year to build up that context, to strengthen the villagers' dependency on the patron. Favors were targeted to each person's needs to get the maximum political effect.

In order to move votes in rural Japan, material benefits had to arrive regularly through trusted friends and convey the sense of constant benevolent care from a paternalistic caretaker. Obviously, local bosses could not acquire these social contextual resources through money alone. They had to start from their central status in the village social networks. I realized that the residue of old landlord-tenant deference relations had provided a good vehicle for the ritual embodiment of patronage. That was why the inheritors of landlord boss status had continued to play the new boss role. In sociological terms, building political obedience required giving out both normative and material sanctions, if not symbolic ones.

None of this patronage was legal. Japanese election laws are even stricter than in the United States. They forbid the use of bribes or other incentives for votes, and also forbid the use of television and radio campaign ads. Officially, candidates are restricted to touring around in loudspeaker cars, making speeches on street corners, and putting up a regulated number of posters. The vast bribery and patronage network therefore works informally and covertly. Every election, the police arrested a number of local bosses for passing out bribes, but never arrested the middle or top politicians who financed and ordered the activity. Local bosses think proudly of these brief arrests as badges of honor awarded for serving their "parent."

Some scholars argue that political behavior is the product of an internalized political culture (Almond et al., 1963). Rather than being the product of an internalized traditional "culture of political deference," however, the preceding information indicates a different analysis. Japanese political indifference could be better described as the product of a purposefully created, machine-based, "soft" political opportunity structure. Certainly, the machine built on and tried to maintain a traditional indifference. But this in turn had been built by past machines and structural conditions.

In its results – the control of popular political preferences – the situation conformed closely to what Gramsci described as ideological hegemony (Lukes, 1986). But in its causation, the situation differed from Gramsci's understanding. The political indifference was not caused by symbolic sanctions through the media and education coloring public awareness. Rather, it was the product of machine-organized social networks of bosses using personal persuasion and status seduction.

Turning up the heat

The prefectural pro-growth elite resorted to several other avenues of persuasion as well – through material and status incentives to individuals and through the manipulation of institutions.

Some of the Kozaki villagers, though not active fishers, had inherited fishing rights in the local waters. Many of these former fishers lived in Koneko ku, the heart of the protest movement. Their individual compensation, if Landfill No. 8 were built, would have been over $100,000. Since their own livelihoods were not at stake, this was an attractive prospect. In order to whet their appetites and weaken their resistance, the Prefectural Government gave them a partial payment, the balance to be paid if No. 8 were actually built. Dedicated anti-No. 8 activists in Kozaki refused this offer, but some took the money. This prefectural tactic increased friction over the issue within Kozaki. Each *ku*-head election became more of a struggle, especially in Koneko-*ku*, where both fishers and the main movement leaders lived.

The prefecture devised additional status seduction tactics to use against the Kozaki League. The prefectural officials were convinced they held high, paternalistic status in the eyes of ordinary villagers. By doing the villagers the honor of a personal home visit, the officials thought they could change villagers' minds. In June 1971, junior prefectural officials walked around Kozaki hamlet on "door-to-door visits." They intended to personally persuade the villagers of the merits of No. 8 landfill, and confidently expected to be meekly received. The attempt turned into a Chaplinesque comedy.

The junior officials expected to be invited in for a pleasant chat over tea. Instead, they found signs on many doors stating bluntly, "we refuse the visit of the prefectural officials." Even more unnerving to them, movement activists dogged their every step. The activists carried walkie-talkies and reported the officials' position and direction. Others then alerted the next likely household not to answer the door. These guerrilla tactics totally frustrated the officials' efforts, leaving them disconcerted and confused. They could not persuade anyone, yet were ashamed to return early in defeat. In the end, the young officials walked disconsolately down to Kozaki beach and spent their assigned days fishing. Considering the distant Phase One smokestacks visible from that beach, they must have felt a certain irony about their stolen recreation.

This clash of expectations exposed deep differences in the two sides' interpretations of prefectural welfare and of proper political behavior. The prefectural officials expected deference. They found defiance. The two sides also commanded vastly different pools of manpower and financial resources. Under different circumstances, as before the war when the military police could strike down protestors with impunity, these might have rolled over the movement. But under the new, post-war democratic rules of the game, the weaker side had enough protection and basic rights to form, develop and express a contrary set of beliefs about Landfill No. 8.

Helping a split

After the Seki Union had voted to oppose No. 8 in 1970 (Chapter 4), prefectural officials realized they would probably not be able to get the Seki Union to hand over its rights to the No. 8 site. The prefecture wished it had never merged the two unions. The Baba Union was by then eager to hand over the rights for compensation, but did not have the authority to do so. By its own hand, ironically, the Prefectural Government had set up a serious stumbling block. It had to solve this problem.

The Oita Prefectural Government wanted the Saganoseki and Baba unions to separate. If that happened, the Baba Union could turn over its rights to the coastal waters in return for compensation. But the Prefectural Government could not publicly support such a split. It had ordered the merger of the unions only a few years earlier, under guidance from the Ministry of Agriculture, Forestries and Fisheries (MAFF). Now, to suddenly advocate their separation would look erratic. It would invite criticism from the MAFF. Local lawyers working with the Seki movement would loudly echo such criticism. So, on the surface, to both the MAFF and the public, the Prefectural Government had to pretend to oppose the separation. Once again, the politics of pretense took center stage.

One prefectural fisheries official, who carried out this maneuver, explained the Prefectural Government's tactics in detail. The Prefectural Government, he said, publicly displayed strong disapproval of Baba's attempt to separate from the Seki Union. To accomplish this,

. . . the chief of the Prefectural Government Local Fisheries Bureau made a (public) trip to Baba to (officially) request that it quit its campaign to split off from the Seki union. . . .

But in fact, he confessed, this trip was only a charade:

This request. . . . was not in earnest (*honne*). It was . . . administrative guidance for appearance's sake only (*tatemae no gyosei shido*). . . . .The fishermen recognized this.

The Baba Union leaders knew the score. The prefectural official said,

. . . I think he informed (the fishermen) secretly that this was not in earnest . . . (Interview, Oita City, October, 1979).

The Prefectural Government told the Ministry of Forestry and Fisheries another story. It explained the matter with these words:

We tried to persuade (the Baba Union,) but it wouldn't obey, so there's no way to stop (the split) (Interview, Oita City, October, 1979).

Public censure of Baba let the Prefectural Government evade blame for the Baba Union's campaign for a split. At the same time, the official explained, the Prefectural Government made its support for the split obvious to the Baba Union. This political double-entendre encouraged the Baba Union to go ahead – it made the Baba fishers feel more certain of Prefectural Government intentions to build Landfill No. 8. It made the Baba fishers ". . . more interested in selling their fishing rights."

The charade was not the rogue action of an overly zealous official. It was officially approved. The Prefectural Government official explained:

The other section heads and the governor knew of this 'persuasion' (*settoku*) (of the Baba fishermen) by 'root-binding' (*nemawashi*); they didn't criticize it (Interview, Oita City, October, 1979).

The government's ready use and acceptance of charade indicates the tactic's normality as an elite social control device. The official referred to it as root-binding – the common Japanese practice of building consensus informally before going public with an idea (Lebra, 1976). Root-binding has often been noted as a means of building consensus within Japanese organizations. But I have not seen it used as a tactic of social control in community politics. Its use indicates an intimate corporate relationship between the Prefectural Government and the Baba Union, as its leaders described (Chapter 4).

Coordination of the parties took place by nuanced signals. With a few oblique comments, in the style of belly-craft (*haragei*), the official conveyed his real intent. The old-line Baba Union leaders knew what he meant. In effect, the hamlet of Baba had become the political puppet (*ayatsuri ningyo*) of the prefectural elites.

By these subtle tactics, the Prefectural Government wriggled out of its bind and maximized its political latitude. Within the confines of its island culture, Japan has practiced the arts of political subterfuge for a millennium. Machiavelli could have learned much here. As in the NIC Law case, structural contradictions led to pretense politics (*tatemae*). The Prefectural Government was pressured by national ministries from above and protest movements from below. With a slick political charade, the Prefectural Government popped out of this bind and preserved its legitimacy.

Machine politics

Mayoral election

Despite the continual defection of *ku*-chairs and growing pressure from conservative bosses, anti-Landfill No. 8 public sentiment in Seki continued to mount. In the late fall of 1970, the Seki mayoral campaign was getting under way. The two candidates, both elected members of the Seki Town Council and both affiliated with the LDP, took diametrically opposed positions on the No. 8 issue. Watanabe, the heir apparent of incumbent mayor Sugino, supported the No. 8 landfill plan. Furuta, the challenger, however, sensing a new political opportunity, sharply opposed the plan. To understand their opposite stances and its outcomes, we must delve into the structural divisions in Seki society.

Out of the tiny electorate of 16,300 eligible voters in Seki, between 417 and 726 votes were needed to win one of the twenty-two Council seats. Being a Council member was not especially rewarding or powerful. It was a part-time job with a very meager salary. All Council members had to have another source of income to survive. This made the role difficult for small business owners, who work long hours, and virtually impossible for ordinary workers and farmers.

In the early 1970s, only three of the twenty-two Council members officially belonged to the LDP. Another seventeen had a strong affiliation with the LDP, but preferred to retain an independent image. They generally followed the LDP policy line, modifying it slightly to fit their factional camp.

These twenty conservative legislators divided into two main camps, the "locals" and the "nationals." The locals contained the Furuta group and the "Research" group (Table 6.1). They saw themselves as defenders of local business interests. The nationals contained the Sugino group and the Nikko Copper Refinery group. They wanted to bring more outside big businesses into town. The local camp thought the national camp was willing to sell out the interests of local businesses.

The remaining two non-LDP councillors at that time belonged to the Japan Communist party. In the late 1960s, Himeno had pioneered research on Nikko pollution-related health damage among the residents of Seki. These two were elected by a faction of the fishing folk.

The elder Sugino had served as Seki mayor for three terms. A graduate of prestigious Kyushu University, he had chaired the National Conference of Town Mayors and Chief Legislators, and held a special award from the Emperor. I interviewed him in his small home in a crowded neighborhood of Seki. His home was connected to his family business, a small rice and sake store. He

Table 6.1. *Seki council groups*

Group name	Number of members	Type of members
Sugino group	6	Two small business owners from Seki Chamber of Commerce, one member of Fishing Union, one Nikko worker (Watanuki). Two LDP members.
Nikko group	5	Three Nikko managers, two Nikko subcontractor managers. All received full backing from Nikko company and Nikko union.
Furuta group	6	Four from Seki Chamber of Commerce. One Fishing Union official, one farmer.
"Research" group	3	All from Seki Chamber of Commerce.
Opposition group	2	Both affiliated with Communist party. Supported by Fishing Union dissident group.

proudly pulled his Imperial award out of a cabinet and showed it to me. His son served as the current town legislator.

The Sugino group cooperated closely with the Nikko group, bringing the faction to eleven members. While serving as legislators, Nikko managers still received their full company salaries, and the company paid for the costs of their election campaigns. Several Council members who owned small businesses that got most of their orders from Nikko also owned the company their main allegiance. In total, this put the Nikko-loyal count at ten out of twenty-two Council members.

Business and labor

Several business organizations exerted political influence in Saganoseki – the Nikko Copper Company, the Chamber of Commerce, and the Fishermen's Union. Their relative political power reflected not only the size of their membership or workforce, but also the autonomy of their leadership and the economic benefits they could distribute. At the top stood Nikko, with solid organization backed by powerful financial resources, and as a major polluter, with a strong interest in keeping pollution protest at a minimum. Next in rank stood the Chamber of Commerce, a loose organization of small- and medium-sized local business owners who influenced their own workers and wanted local profits and prosperity. These two organizations commandeered the two main political factions in the Town Council. The remaining organization – the Fishing Union – more controlled its members than represented them. Its president courted favor with LDP Diet politicians and other prefectural elites. As a consequence, the fishing people, unlike the Nikko and Chamber of Commerce groups, did not vote as a bloc, and had no strong political voice in the Town Council.

For decades, only a dissident faction of fishing people, who had rejected the leadership of the Union president, had any independent political voice. That was expressed through a politician from the Japan Communist party. For years, Himeno's was the only voice that complained about the pollution from Nikko. The only shift in this hegemonic conservative, if internally slightly fractured, domination of the electorate and legislature came when the anti-Landfill No. 8 movement generated enough concern to elect Inao Toru to the Town Council in 1980, where he stayed.

The Nikko Company controlled the strongest political bloc in Saganoseki. It employed 1,000 workers, who belonged to an "enterprise union" that complied with management wishes. Through its Subcontractors Cooperative Group and affiliated construction companies, Nikko controlled the votes of another 2,500 workers. Nikko wielded its 3,500 votes with an eye to maintaining its power in the town. Because of its power, people compared Nikko to a feudal lord. They thought of Seki as a modern day "industrial castle town" (*kigyo jokamachi*) under its domination.

Besides Nikko, outside businesses with interests in Landfill No. 8 also influenced town politics. An LDP-affiliated Seki Town Council member commented:

For the pro-No. 8 group, the Oita (branch of the) Japan Committee for Economic Development (JCED or Keizai Doyu Kai) becomes the window for passing out funds. For example, Showa Oil can't give money directly to the pro-8 group. So, instead, that company gives the money to the Oita JCED and then it helps (by passing the money out locally). One group is Future Saganoseki. The JCED provided its activities fund . . . (Interview 314, 1979)

Future Saganoseki was a group of local young Seki business people that supported the No. 8 project. A fisherman noted how big business ruled local politics:

. . . A lot of wheeling and dealing happens behind the scenes. Only the pretty things come out into the open. Therefore, you can't believe what people tell you. The town is led around by Nikko . . . Nikko gives financial aid to the farmers and Fishing Union.

Other towns are the same. For example, New Japan Steel has a lot of influence in Oita City. You can't resist or fight back against Nikko over the long range. Nikko has resources.

Such backstage control also typifies U.S. "company towns." In the United States, big business often exercised such tactics against environmental movements (Gedicks, 1994; Brown & Mikkelsen, 1990; Schnaiberg & Gould, 1994; Gould, 1993). However, in Japan, business works more closely with the ruling party to exercise soft social control.

The nine members of the Furuta-Research faction clustered around Takashima Goro, local LDP head and political boss. Takashima and most of the other members of this faction were local merchants. Seven belonged to the Chamber of Commerce (four on its council). One owned a local sawmill but was not a Chamber of Commerce member. One was an official of the Fishing Union. This group represented "main street." They described their members as "people of the town, who have no connection with the copper refinery." They displayed a sense of pride in Seki, and disliked the town's subjugation to the Nikko industrial empire. This split between local and national business factions mirrored the split at the prefectural level.[4] In both cases, the local faction usually lost battles for political power, leaving the community more vulnerable to outside interests.

The Seki Chamber of Commerce had 420 member businesses – most of them family shops and small companies with only one or two employees. A few employed as many as 100. They were extremely alert to their economic interests, and organized quickly to defend them. Their workers did not join unions, but depended rather on employer paternalism. This helped business owners control their workers' votes, allowing Chamber of Commerce candidates to collect more than 4,000 votes and seven Council seats. The Furuta-Research faction united in favor of local economic growth, which they hoped would bring prosperity to their small shops and stores. The Junior Chamber of Commerce had 30 young businessmen very active in promoting local economic growth.

In sharp contrast, the Fishing Union, despite its 1,060 members (710 full-time), and the 1,501 farmers (majority part-time), could only manage to elect one Council member apiece. Many fishers and farmers voted for Nikko or business candidates. The leaders of the Fishing Union and the Agricultural Cooperative worked with the LDP machine to swing their vote in that direction.

Undaunted in the face of such countervailing power, the Seki movements persevered. By then, concern over Landfill No. 8 had spread throughout Seki township (Interview 261, 1979). On November 22, 1970, the Kozaki League

---

4. Community research in the United States has often found a similar split between locals and nationals, who differ in their political orientations (Merton, 1968, p. 447).

held a "Saganoseki Townspeople's Big Meeting Against Phase Two Landfill Areas No. 7 and 8" at the Seki elementary school – 1,500 people attended. Kawamura, president of the Seki Fishing Union, and Watanabe, head of the Seki Town youth group, made speeches against No. 8. Both candidates for mayor – Furuta and Watanabe – and a majority of the town legislators also attended. The meeting issued the following statement:

> In order to protect our lives and health, we have repeatedly opposed the landfill plan and petitioned the governor to stop it. Nevertheless, the governor hasn't shown the slightest intention of listening to us. Rather, saying that the plans are already made, he is asking us to sacrifice ourselves (OGN, December 13, 1970).

The League demanded that the Prefectural Government first analyze the pollution caused by Phase One, before going on to build Phase Two (Hearings, Statements No. 90–99).

Shortly thereafter, the League circulated a petition against No. 8 throughout the entire township, and collected 12,300 signatures (75 percent of the 16,300 voters).[5] Of the twenty-two Seki Town Council members, sixteen signed the petition (OGN, October 1, 1970). In December 1970, the League presented this petition to the governor (OGN, August 24, 1971).

Seki town politicians and organizational leaders realized that the cresting wave of protest could easily target them for criticism, or even cause their electoral defeat. They knew that in other communities around Japan (Mishima/ Numazu and many others), environmental movements had elected progressive mayors who had stopped polluting industrial growth. So they attended the protest meetings.

Up to this point, Sugino had been mayor for three terms. The Nikko faction had dominated Seki politics. Sugino's protégé, Watanabe, seemed likely to win the election and continue that pattern. Candidate Furuta sensed, however, that if he appealed to the popular discontent over No. 8, he might pull in enough extra votes to win. A political pronouncement by Governor Kinoshita had the unintended effect of further bolstering his campaign.

During this period, the Prefectural Government had continued its pursuit of business for Landfill No. 8. Showa Aluminum had submitted a formal bid to build its huge aluminum smelter on No. 8. The Governor had also received a bid from Showa Oil and Teikoku Rayon Company for the oil refinery and synthetic fiber complex (mentioned in Chapter 4). This had put Governor Kinoshita in something of a bind. The synthetic fiber complex seemed more likely to produce local jobs. Furthermore, accepting the aluminum smelter seemed likely to

---

5. Social movements often engage in petition signature campaigns, but rarely get more than 10 percent of the population they target (Oliver, 1993).

stir up the worst opposition in Seki. The governor was inclined to accept the rayon and oil refinery complex, rather than the aluminum smelter.

But this was not so simple. Showa Denko, the parent company of Showa Aluminum, had built the petrochemical plant in the NIC First Phase. Governor Kinoshita considered the prefecture lucky to get the petrochemical plant, and felt he owed Showa Denko a favor. Therefore, he did not want to insult Showa Aluminum by publicly rejecting its bid. A clever use of pretense (*tatemae*) gave the governor a way out.

In December 1970, seemingly unaffected by the growing protest in Seki, the governor made a startling public announcement. He had been in Tokyo, talking over the prospects for locating on Landfill No. 8 with two groups of companies. On his return to Oita, he made a sudden public announcement of his decision, without consulting his chief officials. They were bewildered by it (OGN, Jan. 23, 1971). The governor announced that if both contending company groups, Showa Aluminum and the Showa Oil/Teikoku Rayon complex, would each shrink the scale of their operations a little, they could both build their factories on Landfill No. 8.

The news hit Kozaki like a hammer blow. People there had been wondering which form of pollution they would face – red sludge or asthma-producing air pollution. Suddenly, they faced the prospect of getting both. Kozaki hamlet and Seki Town swiftly mobilized a protest. Activists held rallies and had hundreds of people write postcards to Showa Denko. They expressed determined opposition to both the aluminum refinery and the synthetic fiber complex.

The Governor's announcement came just before the people of Seki were to cast their vote for mayor. In January 1971, Furuta won the Seki mayoral seat (see Table 6.2). Although Furuta was informally affiliated with the LDP, not an opposition party, his victory exemplified the tide of alternative, "progressive" mayors and governors swept in by environmental movement support (Chapter 3). The jubilant movement activists felt Furuta's victory demonstrated the fairness of the new, democratic system. But to the Oita government, Furuta's election represented a serious legitimacy problem. With an anti-No. 8 mayor in Seki, the government could hardly claim to the national ministries that the protestors were just a few radical hotheads.

Persuading the mayor

Early in 1971, the Oita government submitted its plan for NIC Phase Two to the Regional Development Advisory Council of the central government. It needed permission from the Council in order to begin landfill construction. To convince the Council that construction would go smoothly in Oita, the governor inten-

Table 6.2. *Electoral results in Oita prefecture, 1955–1995*

Office	Governor (party support)	Prefectural legislature (seats by party)	Oita City mayor (party support)	Oita City legislature (seats by party)	Seki mayor (party support)
1955	Kinoshita (JSP)	Liberal 16 Democratic 12 JSP 3 Other 18	Ueda (unclear)	Ind. 22 Liberal 5 Democratic 5 JSP 4	Mizaki (und)
1959	Kinoshita (LDP, JSP)	LDP 37; JSP 7 Other 5	Ueda (LDP)	Ind. 20, LDP 10 JSP 5, JCP1	Mizaki (und)
1963	Kinoshita (JSP, DSP)	LDP 39; JSP 8 DSP 1; Others 4	Ando (JSP, DSP)	[1965] Ind. 7 LDP 7, JSP 6 CGP 2, DSP 2 JCP 2	Sugawa (und)
1967	Kinoshita (LDP, JSP, DSP)	LDP 30; JSP 8 DSP 1; CGP 2 Other 7	Ando (und)	[1969] JSP 9 LDP 6, Ind. 5 CGP 3, DSP 3 JCP 2	Sugawa (und)
1971	Taki (LDP, DSP)	LSP 29; JSP 7 DSP 3; CGP 2 JCP 1; Other 6	Ando (und)	[1973] Ind. 13 JSP 11, LDP 6 CGP 4, DSP 3 JCP 3	Furuta (und)
1975	Taki (LDP)	LDP 31; JSP 8 DSP 2; CGP 2 JCP 1; Other 4	Sato (JSP)	[1977] Ind. 16 JSP 12, LDP 6 CGP 4, DSP 3 JCP 3	Furuta (und)
1979	Hiramatsu (LDP, DSP, NLC)	LDP 28; JSP 9 DSP 3; CGP 2 JCP 2; Other 5	Sato (JSP, LDP)	[1981] Ind. 16 JSP 13, LDP 8 CGP 4, DSP 3 JCP 3, Other 1	[1977] Watanabe (und)

Table 6.2. *Continued*

Office	Governor (party support)	Prefectural legislature (seats by party)	Oita City mayor (party support)	Oita City legislature (seats by party)	Seki mayor (party support)
1983	Hiramatsu (LDP, CGP)	LDP 33; JSP 8 DSP 3; CGP 2 JCP 2; Other 3	Sato (JSP, CGP DSP, LDP)	[1985] JSP 14 Ind. 13, LDP 8 CGP 5, DSP 4 JCP 3, Other 1	Watanabe (und)
1987	Hiramatsu (LDP, DSP, CGP, JSP)	LDP 31; JSP 9 DSP 3; JCP 2 CGP 1; Ind. 1	Sato (JSP, CGP DSP, LDP)	[1989] JSP 15 LDP 13, Ind. 7 CGP 5, DSP 4 JCP 4	Watanabe (und)
1991	Hiramatsu (same)	LDP 34; JSP 7 Ind. 4; DSP 1 CGP 1	Kinoshita (LDP, CGP)	[1994] LDP 18 JSP 12, Ind. 7 CGP 5; DSP 4 JCP 2	Akase (und)
1995	Hiramatsu (same)	LDP 27; JSP 12 NFP 4; CGP 1 Ind. 2	Kinoshita (LDP, NFP CGP, JSP)	(no election)	Akase (und)

Note: und = Undeclared

sified his campaign to quiet down protest in Seki. He aimed his persuasion campaign against the main centers of opposition in Seki – the Kozaki movement, and now, it seemed, the mayor.

In February 1971, the governor called on the mayors of Oita and Saganoseki to support Phase Two growth. He held an explanatory meeting in Seki City (after the Kozaki *ku*-heads refused his request for a second explanatory meeting in Kozaki). Outside the Seki meeting, the Kozaki movement and dissident Seki fishermen, in their first joint action, boycotted and picketed. The governor spoke to the 200 local supporters who did attend. The same day, the governor talked with Seki business groups to organize further support. He also talked with Mayor Furuta and Seki Fishing Union President Kawamura, asking them to line up the town council, ku heads, and union behind the project (OGN, May 5, 1971).

A knowledgeable prefectural official identified persuasion of the mayor as a key prefectural tactic:

First, (Prefectural Government officials) convince the mayor. They get him to support Prefectural Government policies by promising a lot of public investment in the area, giving the town priority in (funding for) schools, pools, and so forth. Then they show the mayor how his town's tax income will increase with various construction projects.

Under this pressure, although he had been elected because of his anti-8 stance, Mayor Furuta quickly crumbled. In the early summer of 1971, the mayor announced that he would ask the Town Council to pass a statement in favor of No. 8. He instructed his officials to begin drafting a Saganoseki Long-Range Development Plan that included Landfill No. 8. And he sent a letter to all the *ku*-chairs requesting that they convince their residents to support No. 8 (OGN, June 30, 1971). In response, as promised to the mayor, the Prefectural Government announced $325 million in public works in July 1971 for areas behind the Phase Two landfill, including Seki township (OGN, July 2, 1971). Local legislators and business people saw great possibilities for construction contracts in this, and became all the more determined to bring in No. 8.

Mayor Furuta crumbled so quickly on the No. 8 issue for a number of reasons. First, he had never been a Seki movement activist. He did not have a deep commitment to stopping No. 8 or to environmentalist values. Rather, he was a member of the "home town" faction of the Seki LDP. His identity with Seki, as opposed to an outside cooperation such as Nikko, plus his savvy as a politician, had led him to mouth anti-No. 8 slogans during the election. But once elected, conservative pressures quickly changed his priorities.

For one thing, the role of mayor in Japan has no tradition of independent initiative in growth projects. The prefecture had always set the guidelines for such projects. As Mayor Furuta explained to me,

The town makes long-range plans, but within the limits of central and Prefectural Government approval . . .

When it came to large-scale growth projects, he said, outside control got even stronger:

The plan is made by the prefecture in the General Planning Office. The role of the town, since Landfill No. 8 is within our administrative territory, is to give full cooperation to push it ahead . . .

The power of the prefectural and national governments, he explained, partly came from the financial strings attached to any project:

For any project, we have to go through the prefecture to the national government bureaucracy . . . For a school, we go through the prefectural Education Office to the national ministry . . . Mostly, 90% of financing comes from the national and Prefectural Government. This gives them project control.

Chapter Two examined "petition politics" from the prefectural and national point of view. Mayor Furuta confirmed that from the town viewpoint. Obtaining national government approvals and grants required appeal to Tokyo ministries. In the appeal process, the mayor had to play the role of enthusiastic booster. If the project was for this turf, he had to prove local cooperativeness, consensus, and freedom from complications. Signs of strident opposition could scotch approval. The mayor said,

(I go along) in order to show the national government that the town is full of enthusiasm for the project. As one strategy, the prefecture tells the mayor to go. Japan is 'petition politics,' (*chinjo seiji*) . . . We know all the bureau heads. They listen to us well . . . If it's environmental problems, we go to the Environmental Agency; if it's a development problem, we go to the National Land Agency; if it's for permission for an oil refinery, we go to MITI with our request.

In the case of projects strongly pushed by outside elites, the mayor had little choice but to go along, even if it meant contradicting the wishes of most of his own residents. The web of national and prefectural power bound the mayor tightly.

In certain respects, this situation resembles those of other ACID societies. Politicians often knuckle under to special interests and renege on campaign promises (Weinberg, 1994; Brown & Mikkelsen, 1990). In Japan, however, the system of informal pressures is more tightly structured and offers better control to elites. This means the mayor has much less policy autonomy under the governor, the legislature at both levels has much less authority and is much more under the chief executive's control, policy decisions are less in the public spotlight, and the bulk of citizens are even less engaged in political issues than in the United States.

Control by outside elites extended through the mayor into the community. By winning over the mayor, the Prefecture won control of more than just the formal authority of his office. It won great influence over the politics of Seki Township as a whole. As one prefectural officer explained, prefectural strategists knew this very well:

> Once the mayor agrees, the organizations under him, such as his informal political support groups, will follow suit. Then their related family connections will join in, because they all feel 'if this person asks us, we can't refuse.' They all fall into place. Once a group, such as the 'Ku-Chairs' Association,' decides to support a policy, the individual members can no longer officially oppose it.

The mayor exercised both formal and informal vertical control over the township. The mayor, like the governor at the prefectural level, was not an executive officer. He decided town policy through informal consultation (*nemawashi*) with Prefectural Government officials and LDP political bosses. He then submitted the bills to the appropriate Town Council subcommittee for discussion. From there, the bill went to the full Council for public debate and a vote. Bills usually passed as originally submitted by the mayor.

This system decided the content of bills well before any public debate or vote in the Council – common practice in all legislatures under LDP control (at any level). This governance system helped bureaucratic and party rule by minimizing public awareness, participation, and debate. One well-placed, senior, conservative Town Council politician confessed to me that the Town Council had no substantive role in making policy. Policy debates were conducted, he said, solely to present an appearance of local consensus:

> [In the legislature] there is no real debate. It's all empty talk. Everything that comes out in the open is just pretend debate (*tatemaeron*) (Interview).

Empty legislative debate is not unique to Japan. It is so common among ACID societies, in fact, that it has received a somewhat Alice in Wonderland-like theoretical label – "non-decisions" (as in "unbirthdays") (Lukes, 1986; Crenson, 1971). Governance by non-decisions lets a few elites wield tremendous power over the public agenda. Under the busy surface of everyday events, this arrangement of power built a deep (embedded) and soft (manipulative, not coercive) web of power.

The formal powers of the Town Council were, in any case, very limited. It only had power to alter the budget and to change the number of legislators. Even in its budgetary powers, the Council had jurisdiction only over funds derived from local taxes. This gave the Council little financial power over big, centrally funded public works projects like Landfill No. 8. Forty percent of the Seki Town budget (about $8 million) came from local taxes, the rest from national government grants via the prefecture.[6] Only the resident tax and the fixed property tax went directly to the town government.[7] These local taxes paid for bureaucrats' salaries. The Nikko Copper Refinery paid about 60 percent of the town's fixed property tax revenue. Factories on Landfill No. 8 would provide another good source of tax revenue for Seki Town. The tax situation gives new meaning to Mayor Furuta's insistence that No. 8 would be good for "town welfare." The new revenues would fatten administrative and political salaries.

The mayor also enjoyed great informal influence and control in the township. This came with his status within dense personal, kinship, and familial networks. As one resident explained, these networks consisted of:

. . . familial thinking; the fated relationships of living in the same neighborhood (*chien*) and of blood relations (*ketsuen*). In towns or cities, there aren't such (tight) human connections, so politicians can't use this kind of control.

Once the mayor opted to support the prefecture's policies, his formal and informal power webs worked to enact those policies. The previous mayor had already persuaded several of Kozaki's *ku*-chairs to abandon resistance to No. 8. Sometimes the mayor would personally telephone and pressure people to change their minds. He could make life difficult for small businessmen and local workers. Movement sympathizers in vulnerable jobs had to work discreetly and publish their opinions anonymously.

This subtle barrage made protest increasingly difficult to maintain. As one prefectural official asserted:

If you want to resist (official policy) you have to leave all organizations, especially in the rural areas.

Later events demonstrated the truth of his assertion.

The only significant opposition to No. 8 within the Seki political establishment came from the Government Employees' Union (*Jichiro*). This union included all local government employees up to the level of department head (*kacho*). The union was part of the Sohyo Union Federation, and supported the Japan Socialist party. On the No. 8 issue, the union as a body opposed the mayor and supported the protest movements. Several of its leaders actively participated in the movement. But most of the rank and file confined their support to private thoughts and to electoral voting. If they wished to be promoted someday to department head, they knew they had to minimize overt displays of

---

6. U.S. municipalities fill only about 30 percent of their budgets from local taxes (Reed, 1986).

7. Taxes on income, alcoholic beverages, tobacco, and salt went directly to the national Ministry of Finance; taxes on operations, automobiles, and some other items went directly to the Prefectural Government.

resistance. Sometimes, however, union members slipped important pieces of information to movement leaders.

The LDP machine

In the Seki mayoral election, two LDP-affiliated candidates battled each other. At all levels, national, prefectural and town, the LDP was more a loose collection of factions than a unified party organization (Thayer, 1969; Richardson & Flanagan, 1984). These factions often fielded competing candidates, as they did in Seki.

Both candidates asked the LDP and their personal LDP bosses (prefectural and Diet-level LDP politicians) for campaign support. In return, they had to organize local support when higher-level elections came around. In Seki, as in all towns, villages, and urban neighborhoods around Japan at election time, the LDP factional political machines distributed many bribes to secure votes. In the average electoral campaign, an LDP Diet candidate spent about $2 million (Richardson & Flanagan, 1984, p. 186). With election advertising on TV and radio illegal, much of this money went for personal patronage. Local bosses augmented this with a steady supply of services throughout the year. Other political parties did not have these resources available, and so had to gather voters on the basis of union or religious membership. The content of the issues and ideologies ("isms") usually had little effect on people's votes. In the case of No. 8, however, the threat was immediate and palpable enough to make it into a viable election issue.

Bribery of voters was illegal. It had to be done semi-secretly. One favorite tactic, local people told me, was for the candidate to visit the homes of possible supporters for the ostensible purpose of paying respect to their ancestors. The candidate would kneel in prayer before the Buddhist altar that held the name tablets of the deceased, place an offering envelope on the altar and then depart. The envelope would contain the yen equivalent of ten to twenty dollars – an offering, not to the ancestors, but to the voters of the house.

The flow of money came down the channels of the LDP national organization. One elderly *ku*-head described the structure of the LDP patronage machine from personal knowledge:

. . . The local political power structure is very clearly pyramidal. The LDP has authority and strong financial power. (Money comes down) from the Cabinet Ministers . . . to the Diet legislators, to the prefectural legislators, to the town legislators, to the *ku*-heads . . .

This money, he said, was very important in deciding local elections:

A great many elections are moved by money. . . . If the (*ku*-heads) don't follow the opinions of (the Diet legislators), they themselves will collapse. They are tied with strong

ropes. They get money and power from legislators above them and can't get away from it
. . .

And he emphasized the traditional and secret nature of this operation:

. . . this has continued in Japan since the Edo period. It is not something we can get rid of. But no one will speak truthfully to you about it (Interview 146, June 22, 1979).

Another local villager explained where the money came from:

Connections go up to House of Representatives Diet members and then to the corporations. It's all connected. If you put gas in at the top, it will come out the bottom. This has weakened in Oita over the last ten years, but there is still a lot going on . . .

Of course, as described in the previous section, more than money held the LDP machines together. A thick paste of rituals and symbols cemented the loyalty and pride of the participants. Strong norms of vertical personal loyalty made the LDP machines work more efficiently. Without such norms, more funds from the top would have leaked into politicians' and bosses' pockets on the way down. Less would have arrived at the bottom.[8] The machines' monetary delivery efficiency kept the LDP in continuous power for almost four decades. If it had been less efficient – as in Italy, for example – Japan too would have seen greater voter non-participation and more frequent regime changes. But without the material incentives of bribes and community public works, traditional norms and values of loyalty alone would not have sufficed to keep the machines going.

The LDP machine required constant supervision and purposeful construction at all levels. The prefectural LDP worked very consciously and purposefully to construct power and control at the hamlet level. A ku-head described how the LDP chose local ku-heads:

The prefectural headquarters of the LDP selects the *ku*-heads. They choose people likely to support their politicians and abide by the system. The Liberal Democratic party has its roots in these local relationships. For city or town elections, the LDP assembles the *ku*-heads in a big meeting [to pick candidates], because the *ku*-heads know their people best . . . But the LDP leaders make the final decisions. In some places, they don't ask the *ku*-heads' opinions but just pick (Interview 146, June, 1979).

Despite interference by the LDP, the local boss or *ku*-head had to already have the necessary local social connections to make themselves useful. One important connection, a Kozaki movement leader said, was a personal connection to the mayor:

If a person has a direct line to the mayor, he's a real boss, more than if he's a *ku*-chair. The ideal situation is when the mayor and the *ku*-chair are directly connected.

---

8. This is evident in less efficient forms of patronage machines, such as in some Latin American societies (Eisenstadt & Roniger, 1984)

A connection meant a personal relationship built up over a long period. When the two mayoral candidates, Watanabe and Furuta, contended for the Seki mayoral office, their connected bosses contended too. In a kind of spoils system, the bosses under the winning mayor usually got *ku*-chair positions.

The local boss also helped screen and control aspiring local politicians. One local politician described the power of the bosses:

> When a person wants to get elected, he must ask support from the local bosses. They have a pipeline to a lower house Diet representative, to the mayor, and so forth. The aspiring candidate must agree to follow the bosses' requests if elected. So, Town Council members don't usually take individual stands on issues.

He likened the vertical system to the feudal Edo era, when orders flowed down from the feudal lord to the ministers (*karo*), then to the lower officials (*nanja*), and finally to the local implementers (*bugyoja*). In this system, he said, merchants paid off the officials so that they could engage in illegal deals such as buying up oil. Times, he said, hadn't changed much. Clearly, the LDP machines built on a long tradition of vertically organized social control.

In sum, the villagers described an informal but powerful LDP political machine – or more properly, a number of LDP factional machines – that sent their roots down into the hamlet. The LDP machines went from a few LDP faction leaders at the top, to Diet faction members, prefectural legislators, city and town legislators, and then to local bosses. The bosses built loyal *koenkai* support groups among the ordinary residents of their locality. These huge pyramids worked to exchange a downward flow of patronage for an upward flow of votes and uncritical loyalty.[9] One leading LDP politician in Oita explained that the LDP had adopted the ruling maxim of the Tokugawa Shogunate toward the common people: "Make them depend upon you and don't tell them anything" (Interview, 1990).[10]

When opposition to a fundamental LDP policy appeared in an area, as when anti-pollution protest arose in Saeki, the machine poured extra money into the

---

9. The flow of patronage integrated the entire pyramid, from the Prime Minister's cabinet down to the village voter. The LDP solicited (some say extorted) its funds from major corporate donors in a number of guises: contract kickbacks, sales of expensive "party tickets," and overt and covert direct contributions. The most important qualification for becoming an LDP faction leader, a top boss within the party, was the ability to gather such funds and provide them to more junior politicians. LDP factions coalesced around those bosses who could best fuel the patronage machines. The sudden rise and long continuance of the Tanaka Kakuei faction exemplified this principle. Tanaka was a real-estate business wheeler and dealer who rose to power from the grassroots despite having only an elementary school education. He used government power to further his real estate and other businesses, and then used the profits to build his faction within the LDP and further extend his political power and profit.

10. In the original classical Japanese, *yorashimu beshi, shirashimu bekarazu*.

area (Chapter 4). The local bosses were supposed to distribute this to compensate disgruntled residents rather than to solve the problem. The occasional boss who rejected this social control role – for example, Katayama of Saeki or Inao Toru of Kozaki (a boss's son and status inheritor) – presented the machine with a particularly nettlesome problem.

The Prefectural Government maintained its own set of local bosses, often the same people as the LDP bosses, for similar purposes. They called them "good touches" (*atari no ii hito*) – "those who are easily controlled":

> The prefecture has relations with people who help put across their policies in the local area . . . those who can talk to others . . . people find it hard to resist approaches by friends.

Through these people, prefectural officials tried to keep local unions, youth groups, and other community organizations (and through them the whole community) politically cooperative. Because of social control by the LDP, the Prefectural Government, and businesses through their employees and by bribery, all the social organizations and many of the informal social networks of a hamlet or neighborhood could quickly become hostile to protest. A protest movement could most successfully continue when its leaders also had some degree of boss status themselves, as did Katayama and Inao. In that case, they could reject their traditional role as the bridge between outside elites and local residents. They could refuse to transmit patronage and status seduction, as long as they could resist those personal benefits themselves.

The Triple Control Machine

The preceding analysis shows that along with the LDP machines, other channels of social control also entered the local community. The Prefectural Government and big business enterprises had their means of exerting soft social control through personal contacts. Working together, these three channels of soft social control constituted a "Triple Control Machine" (Figure 6.1). The "Triple Control Machine" is not my invention. Locals acknowledged the existence of this machine, consisting of three channels of vertical social control. They identified the Triple Control Machine as the most salient feature of local politics. They explained, for instance, how the three elites (LDP, government officials, and business leaders) had jointly performed what, in a reference to baseball, locals called a "combination play" (*renkei purei*) on local protest movements.

The most concise description of the Triple Control Machine came from a local boss for an Oita LDP Diet representative. He had been arrested for passing out money to voters during one of his patron's campaigns. The full local

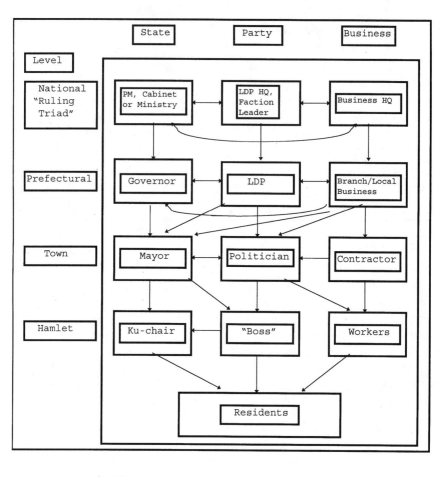

Figure 6.1: The Triple Control Machine

conservative political machine, he explained, operated through three types of local agents: (1) neighborhood officers within villages and towns (*ku* and *han* heads and chairs), (2) informal local political bosses who worked directly with LDP politicians, and (3) managers and workers for local branches of big companies. When necessary, the elites above these local agents coordinated their control efforts, thereby producing the Triple Control Machine. The operation and effects of these three channels have been already discussed in detail.

The three channels of the Triple Control Machine had their source in the prefectural Ruling Triad: the governor, the prefectural level LDP, and local branches of national big business. Their influence traveled down through local officials such as mayors, council legislators, and factory managers, to village bosses such as *ku* officials, former landlords, and factory foremen.

The Triple Control Machine used a mixture of sanctions and tactics. It delivered a mixture of rewards and costs – material (patronage and bribery), social institutional (status upgrading and persuasion through kinship and friendship networks) and cultural (the symbolic legitimacy of high office). And it delivered them by a mixture of open, closed, and propaganda tactics or faces of power. The machine operated continuously in the background of rural lives, setting an invisible framework for any exercise of political influence.

A fisherman noted that when someone worked with the machine, the machine served him well:

You go to the prefectural or Diet legislators and talk to them behind the scenes. Any group has to use this route. If you do, all of a sudden, your problem gets fixed up. Politicians have great power to make changes (Interview, Saganoseki, November 1979).

But this was a Faustian bargain. For solving personal problems, such as finding jobs or spouses, the machine could be of great help. But when someone's complaint touched on a key LDP policy, such as NIC Phase Two, the machine worked to muffle the complainer. The average rural Japanese resident was trapped at the bottom of a vast, hierarchical network of favors and obligations.

The Triple Control Machine worked by gnawing away (*nashikuzushi*) at the local support for the movement. It did so by sending local bosses, who were neighbors or relatives of the movement members, to talk to supporters and try to dissuade them from movement participation. In villages not yet mobilized against the project, the machine worked to prevent mobilization. In a few villages, it worked to mobilize a countermovement. With this dissuasion often went veiled threats, such as the withdrawal of money, advice, or parties formerly given by the boss (from the LDP machine) to the person, or inducements, such as the offering of secret payoffs from the same source. This tactic put any movement in a constant struggle to hold on to its leaders and members.

The difficulty of opposing the machine produced a political culture of acquiescence or defeatism, as expressed in the popular saying, "seek the support of the powerful" (*nagai mono ni makarero*). Only a person of very firm intentions could persist long against the subtle but insistent blandishments of the machine. The process of political conflict between elites and movements cannot be explained without reference to this "invisible" Triple Control Machine and its structural qualities.

Given the strength of the LDP machine, how could protest movements have emerged at all? One answer is that paternalism and personal patronage had weakened as a form of social control. The patronage system took root in poverty, which forced the poor to depend on the wealthy. Rising standards of living, new jobs that one did not get through a boss, more education, urbanization, and other changes had reduced the wealth gap in local communities. One villager commented:

Local bosses are not as strong as before because the differences of wealth are not as great as before. . . . Now, since people aren't as poor they don't follow bosses so readily, but even so, this system is still strong. . . .

In the past, those without independent wealth rarely attained office. But by the 1970s and 1980s, economic prosperity and political rights allowed new people and values to emerge, as one villager explained:

A young person. . . . could never have gotten elected as a town legislator under the old system unless their father was a boss; "by the light of the father (*oya no hikari*)" as we call it . . . Now, some people are . . . voting for . . . those with actual ability . . . Because of this, with the help of the (citizen's movement), . . . [a movement leader] . . . could get elected . . .

The patronage system had crumbled even more in the big cities like Tokyo. In those urban areas, LDP political bosses still played crucial and powerful roles (Bestor, 1989, p. 86). As in rural areas, these bosses operated powerful patronage systems, offering, for instance, overnight trips to hot springs resorts, an "incredible bargain" clearly subsidized by the LDP (Bestor, 1989, p. 93). Socialist or other opposition party candidates had no way to offer such patronage or compete on those terms.

Despite the continuing importance of bosses in urban areas, compared with the village situation, they had a weaker social infrastructure to work through. In the city, the social networks among community members were less encompassing and compelling. This made bosses less sure how to pull social strings. They were less sure of people's votes, even if they did give out patronage.

The Triple Control Machine resembled the U.S. political machines of Tammany Hall in New York or Mayor Daley in Chicago (Riordon, 1963; Eisenstadt & Roniger, 1984). Plunkitt of Tammany Hall, a famous New York machine boss in the early 1900s, captured the spirit of it when he said:

. . . the Tammany heads of departments looked after their friends, within the law, and gave them what opportunities they could to make honest graft (Riordon, 1963, p. 5).

Political machines such as these exist at times in many countries, but usually on a more local scale. U.S. political machines existed on a citywide basis and controlled their representatives to the Congress.[11] In contrast, the Japanese Triple Control Machine, while giving strong voice to prefectural and city conservative interests, was more controlled by national elite interests (Reed, 1986, p. 36). At least the LDP and big business legs of the Triple Control Machine served and integrated closely with national party and business interests. As an article in the Asahi newspaper put it:

> . . . a strong system of distribution of benefits has been established, covering everything from regional politics to corporate society under the domination of a conservative party (as cited in Christian Science Monitor, September 10, 1992, p. 4).

The machine was not always successful. Sometimes the threats of landfill, industry, pollution, and disruption outweighed the machine's positive inducements, resulting in the eruption of bitter challenges to elite hegemony. Protest movements sometimes caused great alterations in policy. But as several examples in Chapter 4 indicate, the machine managed to nip many nascent protest movements in the bud. Whenever grumbling and discontent surfaced in a village, the local bosses rushed to paper it over with yen, moral authority, and other inducements. Such was the fate of incipient movements in Ozai behind Landfills No. 6 and 7.

The activity of the Triple Control Machine may have been less traditional than part of a national response to protest. During the 1970s, the central government tried to augment its own legitimacy by claiming to approve of the wave of populist anti-pollution regulations and citizen participation schemes in local governments. The Ministry of Home Affairs (Jichisho) called the era the "Age of Regionalism" (*Chiho no Jidai*). Contrary to this claim, Japanese political scientist Furuki charged that behind the scenes, during that time, the central government did just the opposite. It intensified its efforts at local social control (Furuki, 1978, p. iv; Ishida, 1983, p. 16). Events in Oita may reflect this trend. Increasing control attempts by the Triple Control Machine over the Seki movements may have resulted, not just from the prefectural pro-growth elite's interests, but from the urgings of national government and elites toward stronger prefectural efforts to softly suppress protest movements.

Conclusions

When the Kozaki League and the Seki Union dissidents threatened elite growth goals, they startled a powerful patronage machine into reaction. This machine worked through channels controlled by the LDP, the Prefectural Government, and interested Tokyo-based businesses. These three channels each used forms

---

11. The southern Italian political machine is well known. For a variety of examples, see Eisenstadt & Roniger, 1984. For a similar Turkish example, see NYT, January 16, 1996.

of personal and institutional persuasion and manipulation. The Triple Control Machine reversed the representation that local democratic institutions had begun to give to anti-Landfill No. 8 views.

Even though the majority of Seki Township residents opposed No. 8, the mayor and the Town Council soon reneged on promised support for that stance. The machine also gnawed away at the movement. It mobilized conservative bosses in Seki, including the mayor, to persuade movement supporters to desist and leave the movement. This effort made the movements shrink in size and strength. Local conservative bosses accepted bribes and withdrew their support, taking their networks with them. Within the confines of Oita, these institutional and personal social control maneuvers boxed in the protest movement, seemingly heading it for decline and defeat.

The machines worked through a subtle combination of financial, status, and other incentives. Local bosses, highly knowledgeable about village social relations, tailored their mixtures of sanctions to the needs and weaknesses of each individual. Material bribery and patronage formed the skeleton of the influence structure, but they had to be fleshed out by adherence to status and face-saving customs.

Status seduction-type relations have some effect in all societies (Smith-Lovin, 1995, p. 140). But as a tool for macro-societal control, they seem to work better in Japan than in the United States or Europe. They have been recognized as a theoretical possibility in social movement studies (Oberschall, 1973). But empirical studies of U.S. or European protest movement do not report such forces affecting the mobilization process.

The relative importance of status seduction in Oita supports claims of a distinct Japanese emphasis on personal and vertical loyalties – a strong social institutional context.[12] While the basic reaction to the costs imposed by pollution may be described as material and agentic, the subsequent trajectory of resistance is more based on social institutional than on material or cultural structures. This explanation is congruent with arguments that the Japanese self-concept tends to be relatively weakly defined (Markus & Kitayama, 1991), that the typical Japanese person takes relatively more behavioral cues from the social situation than from internalized moral principles (Bachnik, 1989). These tendencies may also be found in other societies, as Riesman's "other-directed" personality type demonstrates. But these social institutional tendencies are better organized and reinforced in Japan.

An emphasis on vertical social relations should not obscure the role of mate-

---

12. As discussed in Chapter 1, citing such scholars as Nakane, 1970; Hamaguchi, 1985; Lebra, 1976; Bellah, 1957.

rial patronage. Personal monetary bribery and community public works brought many potential dissidents under machine control. The flow of money down the LDP pipe from the national center to the regional periphery often determined to which vertical relations, among the several available, individuals chose to give their loyalty. To operate its national social control pyramid, the LDP drained surplus profit from the corporate world and funneled it to the grassroots. With these incentives, the LDP bought voter loyalty, political stability and continued domination by the Ruling Triad (business/LDP/ministries). In other words, the LDP used the vertical social institutions as a vehicle to impose a vertical economic structuration upon national politics.

Ultimately, we must conclude, the ability of the LDP to drain surplus profit from the corporate world, and hence to maintain its dominance, depended on the continued expansion of the Japanese economy. The LDP's dependency upon these economic resources established the general structural dominance of the corporate world over the LDP. This structural dependency encouraged and demanded that the LDP support the rapid expansion of the Japanese economy. This relationship forced the LDP, in conjunction with MITI, business and conservative labor, to become parts of a massive Treadmill of Production. The resulting bureaucratic-industrial complex (or more specifically, economic ministry-business peak association-dominant party-conservative labor peak association complex) jointly accepted and pursued the goal of rapid economic growth. Therefore, this bureaucratic-industrial complex resisted grassroots pressures to slow down the pace of industrial growth. At the same time, though, cultural and institutional forces moderated this raw economic structural logic: conflicts among the ministries, the LDP's need to retain majority voter support, the cultural expectations of paternalism by government officials. In the end, these moderating forces, used as leverage by protest movements, forced a change in local growth policy.

7

The Governor gives in

Spreading ripples

The Prefectural Government and pro-growth elites tried to contain and muffle protest in Seki, but without success. Ripples of influence spread outward and upward from the grassroots Seki movements through the political hierarchy. Behind the scenes, the ripples lapped against Governor Kinoshita's decisions about what factories to invite to Landfill No. 8. The ripples also reached to the national ministries, eroding their support for Oita's Phase Two plans. Friction between local and national political opportunity structures tore holes in the web of elite dominance. At a certain point, the Governor crumbled and compromised, handing the Seki movements a decisive victory – a promise that Landfill No. 8 would not be built until Three Conditions were met: local citizen consensus, an end to factional fighting in the Fishing Union, and an environmental impact assessment. The granting of these conditions represented an important turning point in the path of Oita's GE dilemma.

What path, what sequence of moves and countermoves in changing contexts, led to this outcome? Back and forth, each side devised and applied new tactics and sanctions on the other in contrapuntal fashion (McAdam, 1983). This social dynamic unfolded step-by-step over time as a meso-level process among active organizations. Each step entered a new situation that influenced the following step. In the United States, typically, protest movements meet resistance from state agencies (allied with established interests) and generate countermovements (stirred up by established interests). Protest movements sometimes capture the state agency or force the creation of a new agency, in either case getting favorable policies. Their success sparks countermovement reaction, often leading to the loss of protest movement control over the state (Gale, 1986, p. 223; Zald & Useem, 1982; Mottl, 1980; Lo, 1982). Do Japanese movements follow a similar path? What institutional forces shaped the unfolding process (McAdam, 1982, p. 52)?

Aluminum Rashomon

In December 1970, Governor Kinoshita had made the surprising announcement that both Showa Aluminum and the Teikoku rayon complex could build on No. 8 (Chapter 5). Then on February 6, 1971, another unexpected shift took place. To the public's surprise and Kozaki's relief, the Showa Aluminum Company announced it was not coming to Oita after all. Plans were moving too slowly, the company said. It had decided to build the aluminum smelter in Venezuela. Critics called this the "export of pollution."

These sudden shifts in industrial suitors for No. 8 seemed inexplicable to the public. But behind the scenes, they followed a hidden logic. Governor Kinoshita had in fact orchestrated the entire sequence as a public performance. In his autobiography, he revealed the reasons. When Showa Denko had first put forward its bid to build an aluminum refinery in Oita in 1969, the Governor had been acutely aware of the company's bad reputation:

. . . suddenly, around that time, pollution became a big issue. The Showa Denko Company was being sued for pollution of the Agano River [and had been] . . . rejected by Hiroshima Prefecture. This was big news in the papers.

The governor felt personally that the aluminum smelter's pollution would not be so bad:

Experts told me that aluminum plants put out red mud pollution that looked horrible, but compared to the invisible pollution from chemical plants, was insignificant [in its harm].

But the governor also knew that bringing the aluminum refinery would have political repercussions. Already in early 1969, while No. 8 was still planned for across the Bay and the Kozaki movement had not yet erupted, the Governor had expressed his hesitancy to the company:

I frankly told the official at Showa Denko that 'the public thinks of your company as the grandfather of Japan's polluting industries.'

This (by United States standards) mild expression, a prefectural official explained, in Japan constituted a virtual refusal. As a result, Showa Aluminum "voluntarily" decided not to locate in Oita. As the Governor recounted it:

You might call it mental telepathy, but after a year, in the spring of 1970, Anzai Masao, president of Showa Denko, replied (personally to me) that they wanted to withdraw their plan for an aluminum plant on No. 8 (Kinoshita, 1973, p. 207).

None of this was public. Even LDP politicians did not know this backstage drama had occurred.

Because of the growing protest in Seki and the general concern nationwide, even the LDP and DSP had begun to express revulsion against the red sludge pollution of an aluminum refinery. In September 1970, Takeishi, head of the Oita Prefectural legislature, publicly appealed to the Governor to reject the aluminum refinery because of its pollution (OGN, September 7, 1970). At the same time, the president of one of the largest local construction companies counseled the Governor to refuse the plant for the same reason. He said the Governor was hard to convince, but eventually agreed. Little did they know that Showa Aluminum had already withdrawn its proposal.

This sequence of pressures and decisions is very curious. As noted, the Governor publicly announced the Showa Aluminum refinery's *acceptance* for No. 8 in December 1970. This was over six months *after* the company had privately notified the Governor of its decision to cancel the Oita aluminum refinery plan. Two months after that, in February 1971, Showa Aluminum publicly announced its decision to cancel its Oita plan. Clearly, the Governor orchestrated a public political performance in order to save face for Showa Aluminum – so the company could decline the prefecture's offer, not the reverse. This typifies how public officials manipulate public opinion by symbolic politics (Edelman, 1977). But it also expresses a particularly Japanese sensitivity to norms of face-saving.

The Governor's kindness to Showa Aluminum did not fully assuage its resentment against his original rebuff. An official of Showa Denko explained how his company framed the incident:

It was a fight between the Prefectural Government and the residents. . . . The prefecture refused the company because of the citizens' movement. The prefecture couldn't convince the movement . . . Governor Kinoshita needed full agreement from the residents.

The Governor had caved in to the citizens too easily, the official thought. The Showa Aluminum official did not deny the pollution. But he thought the public reaction extreme:

The environmental problems of aluminum refining were the biggest (obstacle). At that time, there was a lot of fluorine pollution from aluminum refining in Niigata, Ehime, and Chiba prefectures. There was worry about that in Oita. For a while, Japan got oversensitive . . .

Still, the company acknowledged, he said, that local protest and criticism might negate the company's efforts at polishing its environmental image in their Oita Phase One petrochemical plant:

If the residents' movement, because of its fear of fluorine pollution, had called Showa Denko a "pollution company," it would have tarnished the good image we had made on Landfill No. 2.

The company finally decided that the situation was intolerable. Public protest had made local governments too inhospitable to big, polluting refineries.

Since Showa Denko's image was worsening through the reputation of the aluminum refineries . . . (we went to Venezuela) . . . (Interview 417, 1979).

The Aluminum Rashomon vignette shone a powerful light into Japan's GE politics. It revealed, once again, their Rashomon-like quality – what an actor "sees" depends on his or her standpoint (Collins, 1991; Kaplan and Grewal, 1994; Smith, 1987). Observers framed an event differently, put a different gloss on it, depending on their interests and hopes. This exemplifies the dictum that "social space is plural, not singular, nor is social space stable" (White, 1992, p. 128). By any individual's frame, the concrete results fell short of hopes.

To the Kozaki activists, the Governor seemed dismissive of their fears. To the Showa Denko company, the Governor seemed overly influenced by the movement. The Governor tried to be fair to the protestors' fears without losing the public appearance of arbitrary authority (a useful political resource and, to his mind, a proper governor's attribute). In the end, this cost him some political legitimacy. No party ended up fully satisfied by the results, but no party went totally denied either – except perhaps the aluminum refinery.

Clashing expectations as well as clashing material interests drove the Aluminum Rashomon vignette. This "politics of perception" came about as a systemic, not individual, property. It arose in a multi-actor system with imperfect (or manipulated) communication. The politics of perception played an important role in shaping the further unfolding of Oita's GE dilemma.

The Aluminum Rashomon vignette typifies the politics of the era. Conservative administrations (as Kinoshita's had become in spirit) rejected any hint of being influenced by citizen protest, while partly responding to the complaints. Conservative chief executives sometimes fixed the worst pollution problems, as Kinoshita did by rejecting the aluminum smelter. But they did not want to publicly acknowledge the role of grassroots protest pressure in pushing them into those decisions. Acknowledgment would have reduced the administration's public image of smooth, uninterrupted control, an important political asset.

This grudging concession process resembled, at the prefectural level, the LDP's pattern of extending the party's domination by providing compensation to those hurt by rapid growth (Calder, 1988). Progressive administrations, in contrast, tried to seize the historical moment to build new democratic, participatory institutions and habits for the citizenry (Broadbent, 1988). In either case, these examples indicated a considerable autonomy of the state from total capitalist control, if and when threatened by sufficient electoral pressure.

Writ large, the Aluminum Rashomon vignette indicates that grassroots protest movements played a large role in forcing Japanese "dirty" plants to go abroad. Not only did they elect progressive administrations in places like Mishima/Numazu, which officially denied the dirty plants permission. They also forcibly shut down operations of some plants, and forced others to pay huge fines. The specter of that happening caused far-sighted conservative chief executives such as Kinoshita to anticipate such reactions in their own areas and preempt them. In addition, the publicity given pollution by the movements and the media gradually began to change the values of conservative elites such as Oita's Speaker of the Legislature and construction company owner. This multidimensional system of pressures made Japan less friendly to polluters. It led to an "export of pollution," as the refineries relocated overseas. This was the first of successive waves of domestic deindustrialization (Broadbent, 1989b).

Official rejection

In late 1971, despite the Prefectural Government's best efforts, the Regional Development Council turned down Oita's Phase Two plans. It refused to grant construction permission. World economic conditions and domestic resistance had changed, the council noted. Growing competition from other East Asian countries was putting domestic steel refining and shipbuilding into recession. Japanese refineries wanted to move abroad, closer to the sources of crude oil. The national government no longer saw much future for heavy industrial growth within Japan. The big landfills of Oita's Phase Two were predicated on the industrial needs of an era that had already passed.

Disappointed but undeterred, the Oita government officials determined to apply to the council for permission again. They wanted to build Phase Two, even if the national government and big business did not want to cooperate. They knew that time was not on their side. Every year that passed meant less favorable economic conditions for domestic heavy industrial growth, on which they had banked for their plan. If they wanted to succeed in building Phase Two, they would have to act quickly and secure solid official cooperation from Seki township.

Enter Governor Taki

Over the years of his tenure, Governor Kinoshita's political base had changed. In 1960, a conservative wing split off from the JSP and formed the Democratic Socialist party (DSP). The DSP, contrary to the JSP, advocated full cooperation with big business as the best way to help workers. Governor Kinoshita had similar thoughts (Chapter 2), so he aligned himself most closely with the DSP. In his 1963 election campaign, the Governor had received support from the JSP and DSP, with tacit support from the LDP and the business community as well. In his 1967 campaign, the LDP joined the JSP and DSP in making Kinoshita their candidate. Such joint candidates are not unusual in Japan, where candidates often try to downplay their party affiliation (as the many "undeclared" notations under party support in Table 6.2 testify).

In the fall of 1971, after four terms in office, Governor Kinoshita announced his coming retirement. He anointed his vice-governor, Taki, as his successor. By this time, given its continuing drive for NIC-style industrial growth, the dynasty had lost JSP support. Taki ran as a joint candidate of the DSP and the LDP and won the election (see Table 6.2). His new constituency was no longer the combined union one that Governor Kinoshita had begun with. Rather, it was in the business community and the conservative labor unions allied with them, such as those of the refineries in the NIC. The JSP never took a formal stance against the NIC Phase Two, but some unions within its solid voter base (teachers, local government, national railway, and postal) were strongly against it.

Taki then appointed Hiramatsu as the vice-governor. In Japan, vice-governors are appointed (by the governor), not elected. Hiramatsu, the same enterprising MITI bureaucrat who appeared earlier in this story, had helped plan Oita's NIC industrial complex (Chapter 2). He had also cooperated with Hashimoto to help start pollution legislation (Chapter 3). Hiramatsu wanted to take a direct hand in his favorite project, Oita Prefecture's NIC. In addition, Hiramatsu's placement gave MITI a direct "old-boy" connection to the Oita NIC complex, which had become an important node in the national economic system.

Central ministry bureaucrats usually left the ministry around age fifty-five. Their ministry sought good "retirement" positions for them. Getting a retired official appointed as vice-governor positioned him well to later win election as governor. Through such strategies, the central government established retired bureaucrats as governors in, at times, as high as 67 percent of all prefectures (Richardson & Flanagan, 1984, p. 270 fn.). This informal network helped integrate and coordinate the prefectural public policy-making process under central government guidance.

Once elected, in December 1971, Governor Taki quickly announced his intention to continue the NIC Phase Two plan. To strongly inform the new governor of their disapproval, the Kozaki League and the Seki Fishing Union movement jointly staged the sea and land protest that led to the belly-button confrontation (Chapter 1). This confrontation gave Governor Taki pause, but not for long.

In January 1972, the Prefectural Government publicly announced that by 1975, the oil refinery for the Teikoku Rayon complex would be in full production on Landfill No 8. In compliance with this program, the Seki Town Council produced the Saganoseki Long-Range Development Plan, with No. 8 playing a central role. The plan predicted the town would grow to a prosperous population of 30,000 as a result of the influx of workers from the plants who would come to No. 8. Mayor Furuta also reiterated his determination to seek a positive vote in support of No. 8 from the Seki Town Council.

In return, the Prefectural Government later announced that Seki Town would definitely receive $50 million of the promised $325 million in public works for the Phase Two project. This was to be used for building the roads, schools, and other infrastructure needed to handle the influx of workers. The prefecture's promise won support from Seki merchants and small contractors, who anticipated new customers and construction contracts.

To ensure smooth implementation, prefectural elites kept up an active campaign of pressure against the Seki protest movements. Without the threat of the aluminum refinery, the governor expected anti-No. 8 protests to subside. They did not.

The mayor's persuasion networks were not nearly as effective as prefectural officials had hoped. In February 1972, the Kozaki League circulated a petition against No. 8. As before, the vast majority of hamlet residents signed (918 signatures, 85 percent of registered voters). The League passed the petition around on the *ku*-heads' circulating board (*kairanban*), which usually only carried unremarkable notices like garbage collection times. The custom was for people to read the notice, sign their family name, and pass the board on to the next house. This was the first time the board had been used for mobilizing protest. Its use indicated the high degree of hamlet consensus against No. 8.

In June 1972, the Seki Townspeople's Association (formed by the Kozaki League and Fishing Union movement) carried out a petition against No. 8 through all of Seki Town. Reflecting the results of the prefecture's persuasion campaign, the number of signers declined from the earlier total of 12,300. Still, a total of 10,114 residents (63 percent of the registered voters) signed it (OGN, June 25, 1972). This public response made it very clear that the majority of Seki people opposed No. 8, despite Mayor Furuta and Governor Taki's efforts.

Widening the front

As a result of the continual rebuffs, the movement activists realized that petitions alone did no good. Even victory in local elections, they saw, had not made a difference. Mayor Furuta had betrayed them. The mayor and the Town Council danced like puppets (*ayatsuri ningyo*) and prefectural officials pulled the strings. Meanwhile, the Triple Control Machine reached right into Kozaki hamlet itself to dissuade movement members.

The activist youth felt betrayed by democracy more than by individuals. Local politicians had not represented the will of the people, as their high-school civics texts had said they should. The youth began to feel embittered and alienated from the formal political institutions. This feeling pushed them to consider more unorthodox tactics to get their point across. Their use of unruly tactics was not just a youthful emotional outburst, as some have asserted (Koschmann, 1978). It represented structurally-induced alienation from conventional politics. Continual rebuff also pushed the youth to overcome their habitual village parochialism and distrust of outsiders. They began to seek out allies around the prefecture. For resource-poor grassroots movements, appeal to third parties is one of the few ways they have to put pressure on elites (Lipsky, 1968; Gamson, 1990, p. 140).

Inao Toru and his wife had taken an intense interest in Kozaki's struggle against No. 8 since its inception. Inao Toru was the son of a Kozaki "boss" and had attended the prestigious Kyushu University. He had graduated and become a high-school teacher, as had his wife. They had taken teaching jobs in another prefecture on Kyushu, and had been working with the movement from that distance. In 1972, they quit their teaching jobs, moved back to Kozaki, and dedicated their lives to saving it from pollution and devastation. Inao Toru took an increasingly central leadership position in the Kozaki movement.

The Inaos' idealistic dedication and tactical experience, drawn from the student movement, greatly enhanced the protest capacities of the Seki movements. During his student days, Inao Toru had studied with liberal and Marxist professors, become conversant with the need for grassroots participation in democracy, and actively participated in the left-wing student movement. He had developed a thorough intellectual criticism of capitalism and of the authoritarian tendencies of the post-war Japanese state. He had also become very critical of the hierarchical tendencies of the Communist party. The student movements he joined were of the New Left variety. They emphasized grassroots organizing around popular causes. The most famous result of this approach has been the joint struggle of farmers and student activists against the Narita Airport (Apter & Sawa, 1984). But others applied the same approach elsewhere.

To counter the encroaching arms of elite control, the Kozaki leaders worked to widen the front. They sought out and strengthened allegiances with other movements and groups: Katayama in Saeki, Fujii in Misa, the Misa/Iejima movement, the Seki Fishing Union movement, the opposition (Sohyo) unions (JSP affiliated), the Communist party and others. Katayama, Inao, and other seasoned movement leaders counseled leaders of Misa and the Seki Fishing Union dissidents on the best protest tactics. Leaders from the various opposition groups met together with increasing frequency to map out broader strategies.[1]

---

1. Sohyo and JSP cooperation with Communist activists was particularly unusual. In most parts

Reviving the Misa/Iejima movement

Fujii's health survey had shown that Misa and Iejima had high rates of respiratory illness. But the residents felt they had no recourse but to suffer in silence. Grievances were present, but the victims lacked the will and hope to protest. Yet the Misa/Iejima people noticed the rising national furor over pollution and the earnestness of the new Environmental Agency.

Then Inao Toru and others from Seki and Saeki talked to Misa leaders about the dangers of Phase Two, and asked for their help in fighting it. The Kozaki activists found a friend and local leader in Hashimoto, a professional carver of festival masks and mannequins. Hashimoto was not employed by the local factories, so he had nothing to lose by protest. He was also an artist with a great sensitivity to natural beauty.

Hashimoto and other Misa/Iejima people knew that NIC Phase Two would put new refineries across the river from their hamlets. These would worsen their own pollution. They also saw that the timing was right – permission negotiations made the Prefectural Government vulnerable to protest.

In September 1972, the mask-carver Hashimoto took the lead. He passed a petition around Misa against the Phase Two Plan. Out of a total of 6,000 villagers (including children) in Misa, 3,000 adults signed it. The movement welled up so quickly that the conservative political machine could not smother it at first. Soon, however, a reaction erupted within Misa. Some villagers employed at Sumitomo and the other factories held important posts as village officials. At their employer's behest, they criticized the movement and dissuaded many people from joining it (Interview, Misa movement leader). Misa village officials called such efforts the work of "extremists and reds" (OGN, October 2, 1971). Despite the falseness of this charge, it made residents hesitant to express their protest against pollution.

Prefectural officials feared that official recognition of Misa pollution would quash the Phase Two plan. It would give the Environmental Agency (EA) the ammunition it needed to shoot down the plan. In its 1972 draft report on "The State of the New Industrial City" (intended for initial presentation to the Oita City Legislature), the Prefectural Government completely ignored Misa/Iejima pollution, baldly stating:

of Japan, they were competitors for the non-LDP vote. But in Oita, they overcame their differences and worked together to stop the NIC Phase Two plan. Yamagame, a Sohyo union leader, joked about sharing a jail cell with Yoshida, the lawyer and one-time JCP candidate (Interview data). They had been arrested together for earlier union activism, and were cooperating against the power-holding elite. What made Oita prefecture more conducive to such cooperation, perhaps, was the relative smallness of both Sohyo and JCP organizations.

At the present time, we don't see any conspicuous environmental pollution; we are at half the environmental standard for air pollution . . . and there is no influence on human health (Interview, Usuki, 1979).

The activists in Misa/Iejima took indignant exception to this conclusion. Five or six of them went in protest to Governor Taki. Hashimoto plopped his asthmatic infant on the Governor's desk. "Is not my child's asthma proof enough of pollution?," he queried the governor, accusing him of gross distortion of the facts. Air pollution from the surrounding factories was of course the most likely cause of his infant's asthma. This tactic proved surprisingly effective. It broke Governor Taki's resistance. He promised to do a thorough health survey of Misa.

The next day, when the prefecture presented its report to the Oita City legislature, the section that denied health damage had been blacked out. Shortly thereafter, the governor requested the Oita Doctors' Association to carry out a health survey in Misa and Iejima. The movement rejoiced in having gotten him to take the problem seriously. This was a tactical success for Oita's growing anti-Phase Two coalition.

Protest encampment

League leaders also reached out to potential supporters in Saganoseki town, especially among the fishing people. When Inao and others went to talk with them, at first they encountered a good deal of suspicion. One leader of the fishing people's protest group expressed their ambivalence:

We had a deeper and deeper . . . relationship with Inao . . . we realized that with just fishing people alone we'd never get a movement off the ground. Even though the reason the people in Kozaki opposed [Landfill No. 8] and the reason we opposed it were a little different, still we both opposed it.

Gradually, the fishing people overcame their suspicions toward the outsiders from Kozaki (five kilometers down the coast in the same township) and began to cooperate with the Kozaki movement.

So I started to think it would be all right to work with those kind of people (Kozaki), and worked on (our members) one at a time at first, (to convince them to cooperate with Kozaki) . . . (Interview, Saganoseki, 1980).

To the Western reader, this distrust might seem surprising, given the geographical closeness of the communities. The complement of strong hamlet solidarity, however, is the rejection of outsiders (Ishida, 1983). A common threat forced them to overcome this.

The Seki movements were upset with Mayor Furuta's intention to pass a resolution of support for No. 8 through the Town Council (Chapter 5). In late September 1972, the Seki movements presented their most recent anti-No. 8

petitions to the mayor and Town Council. They urged the politicians not to pass a resolution in favor of No. 8, hoping the weight of local opinion would persuade them (OGN, September 27, 1972).

To add punch to their point, the movement leaders hit on a new way to protest the upcoming Seki Council vote on No. 8. On October 12, 1972, the Kozaki protestors set up tents on the front steps of the Saganoseki town hall. Nishio and three or four other fishermen joined them. They sat there huddled in their tents, chatting and joking about the situation.

Suddenly, twenty or thirty fishermen from the village of Baba, next to Kozaki, surrounded the site and chased them out of their tents. This was the first unruly action by the Baba countermovement (Chapter 4). Nishio reacted with a flare of anger, but quickly cooled down and thought tactically. In his words:

. . . That got me mad, so I asked Sato, should we give them a fight? The young guys I brought along said, 'let's fight.' But I thought, 'if we fight here, it'll just look like a personal scuffle. Rather than that, let's show this scene to everyone.' So I dashed out an urgent message (to the other anti-No. 8 fisher people), 'emergency situation, assemble!'

Nishio's strategy to gather supporters worked:

At first, about ten people came to see the situation. When they saw our tent surrounded by the pro-8 faction, they said, 'hey, that's too brazen.' Before an hour passed, eighty men assembled. So, the tables were turned, and they (the pro-8 faction) were driven back.

This confrontation led to two tent camps on the steps of city hall – one against No. 8, one for it. Nishio commented:

Well, we set up two rows of tents in front of city hall. The tent flaps of the pro-landfill and the antis were flapping in the wind; this was certainly a legislative session rarely seen in this world (Nishio, 1978, pp. 13–17).

This conflict took place in a small, densely networked local society. The families from both sides had known each other for generations. Many people on both sides belonged to the Seki Fishing Union (which included Kozaki and Baba). This was literally a family feud. Outsiders, even people from Oita City, found it hard to understand. A local newspaper reporter's article captured the paradoxical flavor of the standoff:

. . . (on the steps of the Seki town hall) . . . the pro-8 and anti-8 groups were vehemently criticizing each other, close to coming to blows. Yet, right in the middle of all that, one anti-8 guy would call out in Oita dialect, 'hey, gimme a cigarette,' and a pro-8 guy would pass him a cigarette without a moment's hesitation. Then the first guy would say, 'just a cigarette's no good, how about a match?' So the second guy would light it. Then they'd start quarreling again. That was how they talked.

In their banter and quarreling, the two sides freely acknowledged the patronage and bribery that accompanied local politics. The newspaper article continued:

. . . when the mayor and anti-8 group were quarreling, someone suddenly said: 'Hey, mayor, during the election, didn't you come to my place and bring along an envelope with 1,000 yen in it? And didn't you ask for my vote?' The mayor answered, 'Hey, if you say that, it's an election law offense. Are you going to confess (your own crime in accepting the money)?' Just like that. Then they all laughed, and kept on talking.

This banter kept their disagreements at a civil and rather congenial level. Their ability to banter came from being members of the same community:

Whether they were the mayor, the pro-8 faction, or the anti-8 faction, they all played together when they were kids. Even when they quarreled, they had room for relaxation. You can't clearly tell which are enemies and which are friends (Fujii & Takaura, 1974, pp. 41–42).

Furthermore, with few exceptions, neither side saw the matter in larger national or ideological terms. They were trying to preserve their own immediate health and livelihood, not focus on an abstract concept such as "nature." The personal interests were important to them, of course. But they were not worth injuring another community member, emotionally or physically. If anyone did, he would have to live with the social echoes of that deed for generations.

When ideologically inspired outsiders joined the fray, however, the emotional tenor of the confrontation changed. The same article commented:

When you come upon some really hard, fierce debate, that's usually where non-Oitans, people from outside, are participating. In quarrels, those kind of people . . . give absolutely no chance for any breathing spaces. On this point, (genuinely local) citizens' movements really have a unique flavor . . .

Identity with the local community framed this local struggle. Deeply felt human relations wove the protagonists together, deeper than their disagreements estranged them. Nonetheless, the protestors did not sway the mayor. The sit-in continued for over a week, then dissolved without halting the upcoming legislative session.

Canned mayor

On November 1, 1972, at the opening session of the Seki Council, the mayor, not deterred by the sit-in on the front steps, asked for approval of the NIC Phase Two Plan and Landfill No. 8. The observers' gallery, filled with movement members, erupted in outraged and noisy protest. The cacophony drowned out the voices of the councilors, bringing the proceedings to a halt. The mayor appeared surprised.

On November 4, before the Council sessions resumed, the movement leaders presented a formal request to the mayor that he not ask the Council to approve No. 8. The mayor refused. The next day, to back up the mayor, Governor Taki addressed the prefectural legislature on the necessity of the Phase Two Plan for prefectural welfare.

On November 5, a crowd of irate protesters spilled into the mayor's office, shouting their objections. The crowd kept him "canned" (penned up), protestors said, in his office for hours. During intensive questioning by the protestors, the mayor accidentally let slip crucial information. The mayor said,

Actually, I wouldn't have done this sort of thing (submitting the pro-8 bill), but I was told by your Fishing Union president, "Anyhow, go ahead and do it first. If you go ahead with it, I'll take care of the union" (Fujii & Takaura, 1974, p. 44–48).

Unbeknown to the fishing people, Seki Fishing Union president Kawamura had prodded the mayor to support No. 8. This news shocked the fishermen and incensed them. It revealed secret politicking by their own president, contrary to the duty of his office. While canned in his office, the mayor never called the police. Finally, he bent to their demands and affixed his personal seal to a written promise never to submit a bill for approval of Landfill No. 8 to the Saganoseki Town Council. The movement members emerged jubilant from Town Hall.

A similar confrontation, but with a different outcome, took place in Oita City three days later on November 8. The Prefectural Government also needed Oita City legislative approval for the entire Phase Two plan (including No. 8), since Landfills Nos. 6 and 7 were within Oita City limits. LDP legislators made up the majority in the Oita City legislature, so the Prefectural Government was confident it could easily obtain that approval. On the day of vote, however, opposition (Sohyo) unions and twenty other protest groups, copying the Seki movement style, staged a sit-in in front of the legislature's doors. This was no coincidence. Inao and other Seki leaders had been in constant consultation with the prefectural Sohyo leaders to stimulate support.

Repeating the Baba countermovement tactic, the Prefectural Government used the LDP's local political bosses to mobilize a mass pro-Phase Two Plan rally at the same place (OGN, November 9, 1972). This counterdemonstration weakened public approval for the protest group. Still, in the end, Governor Taki had to call out the riot squad twice to remove the protestors, before the City legislature could vote to approve Phase Two (OGN, January 4, 1973).

Appeal to the Environmental Agency

Since local victory was so uncertain, movement leaders turned their eyes to outside politics. They realized they had a good national opportunity. By this time, the national wave of environmental movements had begun to create its own political openings (Chapter 3). Faced with such opposition, the national elites had fallen into dissension over the pollution issue. This provided the Seki movement with a strategic opening. The movements sent a small delegation to the newly founded Environmental Agency. It presented and discussed its grievances with apparently sympathetic officials. Shortly thereafter, the EA announced that it would not allow any more landfill within the Inland Sea (OGN, August 1972). The regulation did not apply to projects already underway, such as Oita's No. 8. But the decision gave the Seki activists the sense that the Environmental Agency might be a powerful new ally in Tokyo.

In December 1972, protesters from Kozaki and Saganoseki went again to Tokyo to appeal their case to the Environmental Agency. Escorted and introduced by Oita's Socialist party Diet Representative, they got the opportunity to express their grievances directly to EA Director General Miki. The Misa leaders told Miki about the existing severity of pollution from Phase One. Then the Seki people told him about the potential pollution from No. 8.

Miki had been appointed Director General of the EA a few weeks before, at his own insistence. He was actively campaigning for many environmental reforms. He promised the protestors from Oita that he would investigate their claims. Soon thereafter, the EA called Governor Taki and made an informal suggestion that he conduct an environmental assessment before making Phase Two.

Prefectural officials felt that under these circumstances, the EA would never approve Landfills No. 6 and 7. No. 6 was slated to hold a new oil refinery, just across the Oita River from Misa. If pollution were already present, that would only make it worse. In response, the Prefectural Government took issue with the Misa/Iejima image of pollution, and tried to reduce its legitimacy. The image had started with the survey by Fujii and his high-school students. Their findings of high rates of respiratory diseases had prompted concern, protest, and finally EA intervention. But Fujii's survey was by amateurs.

The prefectural officials hit on a good image-improving tactic. They commissioned Professor Ishinishi of Kyushu University, a well-respected authority, to carry out a proper health survey of Misa. Professor Ishinishi did so, and announced his findings in February 1973: Misa's residents did indeed suffer from high levels of respiratory illness. But the cause, he argued, was not industrial air pollution. Rather, their illness was due to their unsanitary lifestyle and the cracks in their old houses that let in the wind. The NIC factories were not at fault.

Some Misa/Iejima residents dutifully started patching up cracks in their houses. Movement leaders, however, accused the Prefectural Government of a cover-up. Officials, they charged, had falsely interpreted the survey results in order to hide Misa's real pollution problems. Prefectural officials made no reply. They assumed their case was proven. Authoritative public assurances, combined with soft social control, had quieted protest in the past. It might have worked for Misa/Iejima too, had not events conspired against them.

Union struggles

Seki Mayor Furuta's confession, while he was canned, that Union President Kawamura had pushed him to approve Landfill No. 8 shocked and angered many fishing folk. They felt deeply betrayed by their president's secret pro-8 politicking. Exposure of it made other events make more sense. Even though the Fishing Union had voted to oppose No. 8, President Kawamura had refused to join the big seaborne demonstration that led to the belly-button confrontation. Now they understood why.

For decades, the humble fishing folk had deferred to Kawamura's decisions. In the early post-war era, the Occupation had ordered the fishing union to be formed. The fishing folk had no education, and felt unqualified to administer the union. They elected a non-fisherman, Kawamura, to be its president. Some fishermen called him "Emperor Kawamura" because of his autocratic style. He was a close associate of Oita LDP Diet Representatives and bureaucrats.

Despite this history of control, many fishing folk wanted some say about No. 8 because it threatened their livelihood. The union divided mainly along livelihood lines. Fishing folk from Baba wanted No. 8 for the monetary compensation they would receive, but other fishers had no such incentive. Those who were part-timers had little to lose. They preferred to avoid trouble and go along with the president, as they always had. Most of the full-time fishers, who depended completely on their fishing income, joined Nishio's protest group (Interview).

Nishio and other leaders seized on the situation to try to "democratize" (*minshuka*) their union. They wanted to make it more truly representative of rank-and-file wishes. As a first tactic, they organized the fishermen into groups of thirty, and took them to talk with Kawamura. Each group tried to get him to support the union's vote against No. 8. But they concluded it was "like talking to a brick wall" (Nishio, 1978, pp. 13–17). Faced with this obstinate rejection, they finally decided they had to recall Kawamura, an unprecedented step.

Seki Fishing Union regulations stipulated that if over 20 percent of the members signed a recall petition, the union had to hold a general meeting to discuss and vote on the recall. These rules had been put in place by the Occupation and never used. Despite unfamiliarity with the procedure, the recall movement activists quickly amassed the signatures of over 30 percent of the union's

1,009 members (312 signatures). They took the recall petition to the union headquarters.

The fourteen members of the union board of directors, appointed under Kawamura, were very protective of his regime. They had good reason to be. The union law stipulated that recall of the president required recall of all fourteen directors as well. Totally ignoring their own bylaws, they rejected the recall petition, telling the organizers, "mind your own business."

Then the union officials went personally to the petition signers and got about one hundred of them to sign another statement canceling their original signature. The officials worked through social networks, getting local bosses to pressure the signers into reneging:

It seems they called people in to the president's house. Or else a local influential person (*kaoyaku*) with connections to that person went to them and said 'sign it' (Nishio, 1978, pp. 13–17).

The term "influential person" (*kaoyaku*) refers to a local boss in the LDP network. This comment indicates that the union leadership was cooperating with the LDP to strengthen its control over the rank and file membership of the union.

With the retraction of one hundred signers, the union officials rejected the recall petition because it did not have the requisite signatures. The movement decided to wait for an opportunity. On the day before the regular general meeting, they asked the Prefectural Government for redress of the union's illicit refusal of their petition.

As the formal guardian of law and order, the Prefectural Government felt compelled to express some public criticism of the union leaderships' violations of procedural law. However, at the same time, the Prefectural Government did not want the recall movement to succeed, because that would hamper its plans to build No. 8. Nishio recounts what happened:

. . . The prefecture replied (to our complaints and said), 'you're right (the cancellation is invalid)' and supported our position.

But the prefecture's verbal support had no effect on the union leadership:

[The union administration] said 'we absolutely won't open [a recall meeting].' We (the anti-8 group) replied 'open it according to regulation' about ten times. We put the prefecture into the middle of it and fought it out.

A strange drama ensued. Though repeatedly ordered to hold a recall meeting by the Prefectural Government, President Kawamura, with great bluster, refused to comply. As Nishio described the events:

Even though the prefecture sent him an 'administrative guidance' notification (*gyosei shido kankoku*) about three times, that president of ours is quite a big wheel and he wouldn't listen. He tried to stick it out. But finally, we kept on pushing until the prefecture had to put out an administrative order (*gyosei meirei*).

Even that did not faze the obstinate president.

Then the president [still resisted] and went so far as to say, 'You're going to try to order us? . . . We fishermen can ignore these administrative guidances and orders from the prefecture . . . We're going to show the whole country (that it's OK to ignore them) (Nishio, 1978, pp. 13–17).

President Kawamura argued that "administrative guidance" (*gyosei shido*) had no formal legal standing. Strictly speaking, he was right. As a bureaucratic tool of governance, ministries used administrative guidance as an informal way to organize and direct private sector investment, growth, and labor relations (Johnson, 1982; Yamanouchi, 1979). Skilled bureaucrats used it to persuade business and labor leaders (as the prefectural officer in the previous section noted, persuasion was the main job of government).

Eventually, after repeated guidance and complaint, President Kawamura agreed to a "general recall meeting," set for February 5, 1973. This looked like a victory for the protest movement and for democracy. But in the ambiguous world of Japanese politics, things are never what they seem. In fact, the public guidances issued by the Prefectural Government to President Kawamura had been nothing more than pretense (*tatemae*). All along, the Prefectural Government had intended to make sure that Kawamura would not lose his position. A prefectural official involved in the very events explained. From the beginning, he said, behind the scenes the Prefectural Government had manipulated the outcome so that the recall movement would not succeed:

(The Prefectural Government) set up the recall vote so that it wouldn't succeed . . . (The Prefectural Government) entered into the middle of the fight and succeeded in adjusting it to our liking (Interview, Oita, 1980).

Before the February 5 (1973) recall vote, the two sides engaged in a fierce competition for supporters and votes. President Kawamura's pro-No. 8 faction got help from the LDP and big businesses. It put great pressure on rank-and-file members of the union to stop supporting the recall movement. A fisherman involved in the anti-No. 8 group explained how this pressure system worked. The union president as well as town councilors, he said, received large bribes from the companies that wanted to locate on No. 8, which they used to persuade rank and file members to support No. 8. In addition, the fisherman explained, the union president worked closely with the top LDP politician in the area:

Kawamura worked as a political boss for LDP Diet Representative Murakawa, so the LDP helped him. He got money from the companies for the purpose of buying off votes [in the union recall election]. He got 3,000,000 yen ($30,000) from the companies that wanted to come [to Landfill No. 8], like the Showa Oil Company. The Town Councilors also got money from them (Interview, Saganoseki, 1979).

Another fisherman explained how the Prefectural Government and Tokyo big business worked in tandem to apply pressure on the rank-and-file fishing people:

. . . When the movement was active, the prefectural department heads . . . threatened to cut off our union pensions. And the companies did a lot of bribing. With a 10,000 or 30,000 yen (bribe) ($100 to $300) they changed a lot of people from opposing No. 8 to supporting it. Or they would give them drinks.

This fisherman explained that these pressures and bribes were especially effective because the fishing people had only a vague, uncertain idea of where their real interests lay:

There weren't so many (fishing people) that were that firmly against No. 8. They were just afraid that if No. 8 came, they wouldn't be able to fish anymore (Interview, Saganoseki, November 1979).

Helped by this vigorous pressure campaign from prefectural, business and LDP elites, the recall movement failed by a vote of 430 to 540.[2]

Discouraged by the defeat, Nishio and a few other leaders held a consolation party at a local temple. Nishio thought that "certain groups had given up completely" and the movement had lost most of its members. They expected only about 50 people at the party. But to their surprise, 400 showed up. Nishio commented:

. . . very willing people came forth. Out of 40 members in an area, 24 or 25 would come and say, 'no, we haven't quit [the movement] . . . we quit the village [instead]. We're joining up all over again . . . (Kino, 1978).

The fact that to persist, members felt they had to "quit the village," indicates the intensity of local social pressure they faced. The density and depth of social connections in hamlets and rural neighborhoods made them very vulnerable to pressure from kin, friends, and leaders. Quitting the village might not sound so difficult to an independently minded American. But the average Japanese far more deeply identified with and depended on the local community.

For some time, the Kozaki League leader Inao Toru had been trying to persuade Nishio to make his group into a formal organization with a name. At the consolation party, the fishing folk realized they still had a critical mass of dedicated protestors. Full of new enthusiasm, they realized the time had come. They created a formal protest organization with Nishio at its head, and called it the "Common Will Group" (*Doshikai*). Most of the fishing folk who stayed with

2. Similar pressures on unions are evident in the United States and other ACID countries (Gould, 1993; Weinberg, 1994; Brown & Mikkelsen, 1990).

the movement got their entire livelihood from fishing and were determined not to sacrifice it.

The EA visit

Oita activists kept up pressure on the EA. In March 1973, at their insistence, an Oita JSP Diet member petitioned EA Director General Miki to investigate potential pollution from Landfill No. 8. This time, Director Miki sent bureau chief Tomisaki with an official inspection group to Oita. When it arrived, the Oita JSP played official host, and the protest groups gave it an enthusiastic reception. Tomisaki complained that the anti-No. 8 group shepherded him around so closely that he could not talk to the other side. Pro-No. 8 fishing folk from Baba lay down in front of his bus; others shook it. But, he said, the anti-No. 8 group would not let him talk with them (Interview 416, 1979, Environmental Agency).

The anti-landfill fishermen took Tomisaki and company on a coastal inspection tour, with an accompanying flotilla of 150 boats. However, this almost turned into a sea battle. As the flotilla passed the hamlet of Baba, about 50 boats of the pro-landfill faction came out and bore down on them. Tomisaki told of his fright:

. . . they were going to fight at sea. I can't swim. They collided at sea. Then two Coast Guard ships came and stopped the fight just as it was beginning. Fishermen are very rough and emotional. They fight easily. They are always in the front lines (of residents' movements). Because damage to the water means the loss of their jobs, they lay their life on the line and fight (OGN, 1973).

As a result of Tomisaki's report to the EA, Director Miki announced that environmental problems existed in Oita. In the Diet, Oita's JSP Diet member asked Miki if he thought No. 8 should be built. Miki replied, "It should be done with caution," which conveyed a very negative nuance. In later statements, Miki explained that air pollution in Oita might already exceed the new, stricter standards for sulfur dioxide and nitrous oxides, the main air pollutants. Therefore, he said, before starting any new projects such as Landfill No. 8, the Prefectural Government should investigate the environmental impact of existing and projected facilities and also talk to residents and get their opinions (Interview 532, 1979, Environmental Agency).

Heartened by the EA visit and inspired by the Kozaki example, in the Spring of 1973 Nishio's Common Will Group started its own unruly tactics designed to prevent the Seki Union from voting in support of No. 8. It disrupted union meetings with a cacophony of loud objections. During that time, the Saganoseki Fishing Union set a national record for number of meetings canceled. The

Common Will Group also withheld dues payments to the union (Nishio, 1978). The amount of dues a member family paid depended upon how much fish they caught. Since the Group members were mostly full-time fishers, their dues-refusal meant a large revenue reduction for the union. This exerted great pressure on the union leadership against supporting No. 8. At the general union meeting of May 20, 1973, tensions peaked between the pro and anti-No. 8 factions. President Kawamura had proposed a vote on the No. 8 issue. The opposing factions started a fist fight, drawing blood from cuts and scrapes. The police entered the union hall and arrested several of the scufflers. The meeting ended without taking a vote.

Stunning victories

Cresting tensions

Governor Taki stated publicly that the expanding wave of protests against Land-fill No. 8 worried him, and the union bloodshed, though not life-threatening, shocked him. His personality and concerns did not make him comfortable with such chaos and harshness. So many confrontations had been piling up: the navel confrontation; use of the riot squad to clear protestors away from the Oita City legislature; pollution complaints from Misa; fighting in the Seki Fishing Union; the sit-in on the steps of the Seki Town Council; penning up the mayor; and the new involvement of the national government.

Local opposition to No. 8 was peaking just as the national pro-growth consensus was declining. This intersection of national and local pressures put the prefectural growth coalition in a bind. The governor felt increasingly desperate and confused. His weakening resolve precipitated a crucial turn of events.

Tensions peaked in late May 1973. That month, the Sumitomo Chemical factory, right next to Misa and Iejima, leaked a large amount of poisonous gas. This terrified the residents and angered protest leaders throughout the prefecture. They made the incident known to the EA. Shortly thereafter, Director Miki called Governor Taki and personally communicated his decision: the EA's formal request (*kankoku*) that Governor Taki conduct an environmental assessment and announce it publicly. Issuance of a formal request was unusual. It indicated a failure of administrative guidance. In his talk with Director Miki, the Governor privately indicated willingness to comply. But he made no public announcement to that effect (OGN, May 5, 1973).

The extent of EA involvement worried the Oita Prefecture officials. At the time, the new EA, although just an agency (not a full ministry), enjoyed strong support among the other ministries, agencies, and councils of government. In

1973, it had acquired a seat on the Harbor Advisory Council, joining the Ministry of Transportation and other related ministries. That made EA approval a prerequisite for all new harbor plans, including Oita's Phase Two plan.

An environmental impact assessment (EIA) represented uncharted political territory using imported ideas. Other than the Mishima-Numazu case (Chapter 3), Japan had no precedent for an EIA. In its advocacy of the idea, the EA had been strongly influenced by the U.S. National Environmental Protection Act of 1969 (NEPA). NEPA required an EIA with resident participation for all construction projects involving federal funds (Franck & Brownstone, 1992, p. 202).

A resolutely pro-growth and well-connected governor might have appealed to MITI to pressure the EA to change its decision. But Governor Taki, upset and confused by the growing tumult over No. 8, vacillated. His prior work as a prefectural welfare officer had given him a genuine concern about local health and social peace (Interview, Taki, 1980). He thought seriously about the advice of the EA. At the same time, he was a political realist. To gain reelection, he needed the support of the previous governor, the LDP, and business interests. He feared that conducting an assessment would slow down the NIC Phase Two project. For a while, the Prefectural Government made no public response. It continued working on its program of soft social control, but with only moderate success.

Frustrated with the governor's inaction, the Seki movements took further, even more radical, action. On May 23, a movement spokesperson suddenly announced the imminent departure of a group of seventy-four protestors to the Tokyo EA headquarters. This time, he said, they did not intend to merely discuss the matter. If the Phase Two plan, in particular No. 8, were not cancelled, they planned to make an angry scene, perhaps even riot and throw chairs through the windows of the EA. The group was to meet with EA Director Miki the next day at 9 am.

Granting Three Conditions

Early the next morning, Governor Taki hurriedly called his staff together. On the spot, he decided to make some concessions to the movement demands. Before 9 am, the governor publicly announced the suspension (*chudan*) of Landfill No. 8. The suspension, he promised, would continue until the government met Three Conditions: (1) local citizen consensus (*goi*) in support of No. 8; (2) "normalization" (*seijoka*) of relations within the Seki Fishing Union; (3) an EIA covering existing pollution from NIC Phase One and likely effects from Phase Two (OGN, May 24, 25, 1973). The Governor immediately called Director Miki to convey the news.

When the movement group arrived at 9 am at the EA, Director Miki told them:

This morning, I received an emergency telephone call from the governor of Oita. He told me . . . 'we want to cut No. 8 off from the Phase Two plan and think of it separately. Therefore, we suspend the current plan for No. 8' . . (Environmental Agency, 1972).

The Director added, "Your demand has been met! You can go home."

The news surprised and elated the protestors. The Three Conditions were more than they had hoped for. Relieved, they returned to Oita in a jubilant and victorious mood. Not that the Three Conditions totally satisfied them – they had demanded the total cancellation of No. 8, not just its suspension. But they saw the Three Conditions as a considerable victory, one that gave them new leverage toward their eventual goal.

Governor Taki's Three Conditions became the turning point in the Landfill No. 8 fight. Similarly structured turning points affect the trajectory of growth and environmental events throughout the ACID world. In this case, the Three-Conditions decision led to results that protected the Seki environment. As such, the social forces animating the decision bear directly on the causal questions of this book.

Why did Governor Taki decide on the Three Conditions? EIA alone would probably have satisfied the EA. Why add on two more conditions, especially such difficult ones? Trying to answer this question brings us into another Rashomon hall of mirrors.

Governor Taki explained his motives to me. First, he emphasized that the Three Conditions had not meant cancellation of No. 8:

. . . there was no change in my basic position . . . The EA did not tell me to quit. They just said, 'think carefully about it' . . .

Rather, he argued, the decision came out of his values:

I suspended No. 8 because I thought humanistically. The fishermen were all in an uproar, in a clash. The union was in a mess. Argument is OK, but not slugging each other . . . No matter how much progress you make, it's not progress if it comes to that . . . So I laid down (the Three Conditions).

In his view, the Governor acted out of revulsion against the social conflict that growth was causing. The governor's background in welfare services lends support to his claim. The Welfare Ministry had been the main voice of conscience about pollution health issues (Chapter 3). Perhaps the fortuitous shuffling of personalities that placed a "soft" Governor in power made the Three Conditions possible. On the other hand, contradicting himself, the Governor also said he made the decision because of the power of the EA:

The EA had power. It could stand in the way of the prefecture . . . So I suspended (No. 8) . . . If we couldn't fulfill the Three Conditions, we wouldn't have been able to convince the EA. Without that, we wouldn't have been able to go along with the LDP (and make No. 8) . . . (Interview 328, Oita, 1980).

Given EA opposition, the Governor said, he had no other real choice. A knowledgeable EA official concurred:

The EA was directing (the assessment procedure) . . . The Director of the Agency said, 'stop!', and do sufficient assessment . . . If [Oita] didn't, the EA could stop them at other levels, such as the Harbor Advisory Council (Interview 532, 1980).

At any rate, the decision, the EA official said, was not a response to pressure from the Seki movement.

In this light, the Three-Conditions concession looks like a rational response to the balance of power. That is how Governor Taki and the EA official remember it. Yet, other testimony indicates the intrusion of normative practices, as distinct from cultural values or the balance of coercive power.

A local newspaper reporter, famous for covering environmental issues in Oita, told me the "true story." A (former) top prefectural official, present at the morning meeting when the governor made the Three-Conditions decision, told him the real story while he lay on his death bed (Interview 328, 1980). The official said the Governor and top officials greatly feared the "demonstrative, unruly" behavior of the movement group. They thought the rioters might smash chairs and windows in the EA office.

Such unseemly behavior by Oitans, the official related, would bring great *shame* (*haji*) and consequent disfavor on the prefecture and the Governor. Usually, the official said, a major policy decision such as the suspension of No. 8 would proceed by elaborate informal discussions ("rootbinding," *nemawashi*) among prefectural officials, LDP politicians, and economic leaders. In this case, the fear of shame injected a note of panic that forced a snap decision in emergency session.

The threat by the Seki group to riot in the EA offices ran sharply contrary to the hierarchy of deference idealized by elites. An "effective" Governor, in the eyes of the central government, should be in charge of "his" citizens. For locals to bypass the Governor and complain directly to the national ministries was offensive enough. To smash windows and furniture would have been unthinkable and embarrassing to the Governor. It would have caused the Governor great loss of face and legitimacy among national government officials.

In the United States, if a group of home-state environmentalists went to Washington and rioted in the EPA offices, a Governor would not have felt a sense of shame, or any personal or governmental responsibility at all. Such an act might make the rioters look like lunatics and earn them jail sentences. But in

Japan, different norms wove into the construction of power. When the movement violated those norms, it produced some loosening of the bonds of power. In other words, its tactics accurately attacked a crucial binding sanction between two governmental elites, thereby weakening the internal cohesion of the state and gaining a temporary advantage.

To avoid a crisis of shame, the Governor's options were limited. He could not forcibly suppress the movement with the police. They were doing nothing illegal. "Soft" social control methods had not worked fully in Seki either. The EA's ability to stop permits (in other words, the political opportunity structure) necessitated some degree of compromise. Added to this, the shame panic (resulting from the cultural opportunity structure) pushed the Governor into making bigger concessions than necessary.

Aftermath

Governor Taki's suspension of Landfill No. 8 shocked Oita's LDP politicians and big business leaders. They had supported the Governor's 1971 election in the expectation that he, like Kinoshita, would steadfastly support Oita's drive for growth. The suspension of No. 8 delayed and even threatened lucrative construction contracts. Criticism mounted quickly. On May 25 and June 3, 1973, an LDP representative publicly blasted Governor Taki's "weakness" (*yowagoshi*) (OGN, May 25, 1973). A few days later, the LDP publicized a list of six criticisms: (1) The suspension of No. 8 was a strategic loss; (2) the Governor should have opened a special legislative session on the matter before deciding it; (3) the Prefectural Government should not decide such matters alone; (4) the Governor should have gone personally to calm down the local residents, but lacked the courage to do so; (5) the decision caused the people of the prefecture to lose faith in the Governor, (6) the prefecture's anti-pollution plans were poorly prepared (OGN, June 3, 1973).

For some time, the Governor appeared to stand his ground against the criticism. The day following the suspension decision, EA Director Miki announced demands for very strict control over potential pollution from Oita's Phase Two Plan. This enabled the Governor to rebut the LDP, arguing that the EA mandated the suspension and that compliance would improve the chances for later government approval of Oita's plans.

Nikko blockade

The Seki movements continued demonstrations demanding Landfill No. 8's total cancellation. On May 31, 1973, they staged a thirty-hour sit-in at the prefecture offices with 150 people. On June 11, 500 fishermen held a big anti-8 rally. On June 19, 700 people joined a protest meeting. Winning the Three Conditions had not weakened their resolve to totally eliminate No. 8.

In June 1973, Kawamura announced his retirement from the post of Fishing Union president. The Nishio group's recall had failed, but the suspension of No. 8 had made the president lose face among the pro-No. 8 fishermen. This added to the confidence of the movement.

During the month of June, the Prefectural Government announced the results of its environmental research on Saganoseki harbor. Effluents into Seki Harbor from the Nikko copper refinery, containing copper, cadmium, lead, and other heavy metals, had contaminated local shellfish and fish. They should not be eaten (Kino, 1978). The Japan Times reported:

> . . . [Oita] health officials said 8.71 ppm of cadmium, 164.9 ppm of copper, 208.5 ppm of zinc were detected from shellfish while 14.53 ppm of arsenic was detected from seaweed . . . All fishermen in the area took the day off Monday after fish dealers agreed . . . to stop buying their fish . . . (OGN, June 23, 1973)

Oita fish buyers immediately boycotted the catch of the Seki fishing people. The whole nation knew about the mercury-poisoned fish responsible for the Minamata disease. No one would want to buy fish from another contaminated area.

Overnight, the Seki fishing people (temporarily) lost their livelihood. This was exactly what they had feared from Landfill No 8. Enraged, the fishing people sought compensation from the Nikko refinery.

The Common Will Group, formed by Nishio to fight No. 8, was in fine fettle, and quickly took the lead. The group decided on a forceful, unruly tactic. It would blockade the entrance to the harbor with its small fishing boats, preventing the Nikko freighters from passing. Nikko depended on its freighters to bring in copper ore from Africa and ship out copper ingots to factories in Japan. The group would keep up the blockade until the company agreed to dredge up and remove its polluted sludge. The Japan Times Newspaper described the scene:

> . . . from 7:30 in the morning on the 24th (June 1973), the fishermen of the Common Will Group assembled about 160 fishing boats in the entrance to the . . . harbor which the copper refinery uses for shipping, roped off the entrance and made a sea blockade. After this, about 11:30, at the front and back entrances (of the refinery), about 400 people held a sit-in, requesting a mass group negotiation with chief manager Tsuzaki. Tsuzaki appeared a little after 5 pm. The fishermen made him bow to the ground (in apology), and with angry words demanded a total halt to plant operations (Japan Times, May 26, 1973).

Nikko could either call for police protection or negotiate. Worried by the level of public concern, it chose to negotiate. For the first time in response to protest, it stopped refinery operations. A few days later, Nikko agreed to clean up all the polluted sea-bed sludge at its own expense.

The slogan of the Common Will Group was "We don't need a cent. Just clean up our sea." The group made no compromises. Unlike some other fishing people's movements, the group's members refused to stop protesting if they got compensation payments. Instead of using the Prefectural Government as a bureaucratic intermediary, they went right to the company in a direct demand. These direct action tactics became famous nationwide as the "Saganoseki Method" (Asahi Newspaper, as quoted in Nishio, 1978, p. 5). The method's disregard for status, hierarchy, or proper form tore aside the intimidating veil of government and corporate authority. It revealed a weakened authority inside. This victory marked Nishio as a dangerous enemy of the pro-growth coalition.

Reaction

The pro-No. 8 fishermen in Baba, who wanted their compensation payments for No. 8, complained about the suspension too. On June 4, the Governor calmed them down by reaffirming his plans to build No. 8 eventually. The problem, he said, in an amazing show of sympathy for the protestors, was that an oil refinery would put out too much pollution, so they would have to get some other kind of industry (OGN, June 4, 1981). This statement, made so closely on the heels of the Governor's Three-Conditions decision, indicates that the protest movements had persuaded the governor to accept a new way of thinking. Evidently, Governor Taki took their objections much more seriously than he would earlier admit. Not only his preference for harmonious social relations, but also his genuine concern for welfare had convinced him of the merit of the protestors' point of view.

Also, the Governor continued to stress the need for social harmony. He told the mayor and business people of Saganoseki that No. 8 would remain suspended:

. . . until the pro and anti-[No. 8] factions have settled down and you have reached consensus as a town on how to handle the development problem (OGN, June 5, 1981).

To add to Governor Taki's worries, in August the Sumitomo factory exploded with an enormous blast that shook the neighborhood. Flames shot up and balls of ash as large as one meter in diameter fell on Iejima and Misa. The flames and soot solidified the horrified residents' doubts about pollution into a panicky desperation. In October 1973, the Usuki residents' movement won its court suit. This finally prevented the Osaka Cement Company from building a factory in Usuki Bay. The Oita Government had backed Osaka Cement, so loss of the suit made the Governor look all the weaker.

Despite his desire for harmony and welfare with another election approaching, Governor Taki had to win back LDP and business support if he wanted to win reelection. Given his support for No. 8 in principle, Taki could not expect much support from the JSP. To get central government permission for Phase Two, which would convince the LDP and business community of his good faith, Taki had to meet the Three Conditions. The prefectural elites began a joint campaign to do this as easily and quickly as possible. In the process, the original terms suffered an Orwellian twist. By the end, "consensus" no longer meant the majority of the residents' opinions or desires. "Normalization" no longer meant reconciliation and agreement within the Seki Fishing Union. And "assessment" no longer meant a thorough prediction of potential environmental damage.

Conclusions

Starting with vastly unequal resources, the actors in this drama attempted to influence each other in the hopes of having some long-range impact upon the policy outcomes. What types and pattern of these control pressures brought about the Three Conditions?

While this local struggle was ensuing, changing events at the national level changed its context and conditions, affecting both Governor Taki and the Seki movements. The national tide of environmental protest forced the Ruling Triad to set up an earnest Environmental Agency. News reports highly critical of pollution swayed the minds of even the governor and some top Oita politicians. In addition, national economic officials no longer favored growth centers such as the New Industrial Cities. Furthermore, a gradual erosion of popular trust in government officials had eroded the Governor's ability to rule by paternalist authority, even though the national government still expected it. The scales of decision over No. 8 and what industries should locate on it hung in such delicate balance that even a small shift in relative power could tip them.

Tactical move followed move within that changing context. The Triple Control Machine, operating through local bosses, penetrated the social practices and public political behavior of local people, dissuading some from movement participation. As a result, prefectural elites were better able to rule by non-decisions, making important decisions unchallenged, out of public sight (Bachrach & Baratz, 1970; Lukes, 1974; Crenson, 1971). This bolstered the power of the prefectural elites (Foucault, 1972, p. 131; Brulle, 1994, p. 100).

At the same time, Governor Kinoshita rejected the most blatant of the polluters, the aluminum smelter. He hoped this compromise, though publicly not acknowledged as such, would mollify the Seki movements. It did not. Their continued eruption added enough doubt that the Regional Council turned down Oita's first Phase Two application. Prefectural elections brought in milder Governor Taki, with his heartfelt concern for peace and welfare. This event further softened the stance of the Prefectural Government.

During this period, Inao Toru's masterful tactical guidance enhanced the power of the Seki movements. Mustering their sparse resources and allies, they responded skillfully to the gnawing inroads made by the Triple Control Machine. Movement initiatives attacked the pro-growth machine on all fronts: An asthmatic child tore away the prefecture's claim that no air pollution existed in Misa; Seki protestors camped on the steps of the Seki Town Hall, penned up the mayor, and made him promise not to support Landfill No. 8; bloody fistfights erupted in the Seki Fishing Union, challenging the dominance of its pro-growth president. These local actions, while effective, however, might not alone have halted the Governor's plans.

Serendipitous intervention by the EA tipped the scales. Help from a third party, the EA, proved crucial to movement success, as many theorists maintain (Burstein et al., 1995, p. 279; Lipsky, 1968, p. 1145; Jenkins, 1983). At that moment, the EA had the power to block approval of Oita's second Phase Two application. On investigating pollution in Oita, the EA requested an EIA before further landfill. The EA did not have the coercive power to directly force Oita Prefecture to comply. But its request implied that if it did not comply, the prefecture might not get its long-sought approval for Phase Two. Therefore, the request added to the pressures pushing the Governor toward complying.

Governor Taki ignored the EA's request for as long as he could. But when the Seki protestors threatened to riot in the EA's Tokyo headquarters, the Governor crumbled. A riot would have shamed the Governor and caused him to lose face. The threat of that provided the final pressure that forced him to comply with the EA's request, and to even go further.

Face, or status, is a crucial normative component of political relations in Japan (Pharr, 1990). As a social institutional structure, it helped constitute the dominant pattern of power. The central bureaucrats expected Taki to be in paternalistic control of "his" people. In that moral light, a riot would have labeled Governor Taki as incompetent. In effect, the movement performed a sudden skillful judo throw on this institutional form of power. It exercised a social agency made possible by the existing institutional pattern of power. Not only regulatory and fiscal control, but also a good dose of cultural symbolism and status relations, bound the Governor to the national ministries. By threatening the Governor with shame, given the other pressures already existing, the movement pushed the Governor into a panicked compromise. From the EA perspective, an EIA alone would have sufficed. In order to prevent a riot, though, the Governor overcompensated. He also granted the conditions of citizen consensus and union normalization, before Landfill No. 8 would be resumed.

Weber contends that ideal interests may, like railroad switchmen, sometimes shunt the juggernaut of political-economic interests onto new tracks of action

(Weber, 1946, p. 280; Griswold, 1994, p. 39). The granting of the Three Conditions represented such a switch onto new tracks for the growth of Oita's New Industrial City. The switching force, though, came, arguably, not from internalized ideals but from social institutional structures – expected normative practices. The social institutions presented a code of proper behavior that, like a language, provided a mode of mutual orientation. Like using a language, the use of such normative patterns for behavior is not a matter of belief. People just tend to follow normative rules for the ease they provide in coordinating collective action, whether of an elite or grassroots variety. Some scholars call norms "culture from the outside in" (Swidler, 1995). This concept of culture is the cornerstone of the new institutionalism in sociology (Powell & DiMaggio, 1991; Bourdieu, 1990). In the case of the Three Conditions, it was the potential violation of those norms – a form of social agency – that provided the final pressure upon the Governor (Sewell, 1992).

In other venues, movements imposed material, rather than social, costs upon an opponent and attained victory. Nishio led his tattered but still determined Common Will Group into a forceful blockade of the Nikko Copper refinery, shutting down its massive operations. Doing so extracted from its president a promise to dredge up the toxic sludge. In both cases, the sudden and unprecedented use of unruly tactics by movements provided a measure of success, as other research on social movements would predict (Gamson, 1990).

The use of unruly tactics came about, not as a form of irrationality, impatience (Smelser, 1963) or need for emotional expression (Koschmann, 1978). Rather, it was forced into existence by the persistent unresponsiveness of "normal channels," of the formal political institutions, to real problems. In effect, the Triple Control Machine had truncated the "normal" public space necessary to practice democratic styles of political change (Habermas, Burger, & Lawrence, 1989; Evans & Boyte, 1986). In fact, though, such public space was not normal in Japan – it was at that moment under contested construction.

The success of unruly protest was contingent both on shifts in the political opportunity structure and on unexplored channels of help it could provide, even if no sudden new opening occurred. The national wave of environmental protest, as described in Chapter 3, induced the dominant Ruling Triad to try to preempt the issue by granting new anti-pollution regulations and by establishing the EA. These shifts did not precede or stimulate the wave of environmental protest, but were produced by it. The exigencies of pollution pushed the movements into forms of resistance that tested the democratic potentials of the new Constitution. The dominant elites strove to control the new formal democratic institutions by reinventing the political patronage Triple Control Machine. But the movements used the new democratic institutions to elect progressive local governments that stood on their side. The resulting new political conditions then provided additional opportunities for later movements within the wave. The Oita movement exploited this opportunity by using the new EA to gain local policy advantages.

After Governor Taki granted the Three Conditions, what to both the Governor and the movements were "structural" forces reasserted themselves aggressively. The LDP and its business supporters launched into vituperative criticism of the Governor. The force of their resistance warped the implementation of the Three Conditions, as the following chapters show. The Governor had become dependent on the LDP for reelection. The LDP in turn favored national pro-growth business interests. The Governor was forced, in this way, to conform to the structural force of capital accumulation, the national Treadmill of Growth.

The policy outcomes, though, were the result of a plastic, historical process, not a static structure (Broadbent, 1989a; Broadbent, 1988). The plasticity of the power pattern allowed the governor to grant the Three Conditions, which in turn switched the tracks of Oita's NIC and response to its GE dilemma, despite structural resistance. The complexity of this process is not easily reducible to a single theorized factor, whether "value change," "class struggle," "encroaching bureaucratic state," "rationalization," "electoral competition," or "capital accumulation." The process and its outcomes were, in other words, multi-causal and path-dependent. At each step in the process, shifting mixtures of our nine factors (as noted in Table 10.1), operating on several levels, defined the immediate pressures between sets of actors. At longer intervals, the accumulated effects of these pressures led to new policy outcomes, which shifted the distribution of benefits and costs among actors. In both cases, changes in control relations and in outcomes generated new courses of action. Accordingly, the process is path-dependent – the detailed course of politics is not predictable from an overarching set of continuous structural conditions.

In broad outline, though, the sequencing and patterning of Oita's environmental conflict resembles those that have occurred in other ACID societies. In such industrial toxic pollution disasters as Love Canal, Three Mile Island, and the Michigan dioxin poisoning in the United States, and the Seveso case in Italy, protestors at first encountered official denial (Cable & Cable, 1995; Reich, 1991, p. 261). An analysis of twenty-five toxic waste cases found that the common trajectory of protest

was for victims to experience a nuisance, ask the government to investigate and solve the problem, receive inadequate and often incompetent government responses, and pressure for a more adequate government action . . . citizen activism is generally a response to government inactivity or failure (Finsterbusch, 1989, p. 65).

These conclusions from Western studies indicate that pollution politics, whether they occur in the West or in Japan, follow a similar process in all ACID societies. The broad similarity of pattern, despite great differences in Japanese and United States political institutions (Knoke et al., 1996), indicates that the basic causal processes must not lie in political elites or institutions. Following the same logic, the great differences in social and cultural structures among these ACID societies render those sources unlikely causes for this common process. Rather, the fundamental logic of producers treating nature as an externality, common to rationalized industrial production systems whether capitalist or socialist, seems a basic operating force here. Since both management and labor in producer institutions, whether capitalist or socialist, receive direct and vital economic benefits from using nature as a garbage can, they both support continued rapid industrial growth. This leads to a political-economic structure some theorists call the Treadmill of Production (Schnaiberg 1980; Schnaiberg and Gould 1994), which exerts a powerful political force supporting forms of industrial waste-disposal that disregard long-term environmental consequences. This common structure leads logically to common pattern of response to protest movements noted above.

Although equally under the sway of the Treadmill of Production, society-specific social and cultural factors among the ACID societies made for important variations in political process and outcomes. Outcome differences between the Oita and Japan cases on the one hand, and that typical of Western cases on the other – the ability of the protest movement to extract a convulsive over-compromise from the Governor, the rapidity of Japan's response to its GE dilemma – exemplify the results of such processual differences. These social and cultural differences were manifested in Japan in, for instance, the Triple Control Machine built on status seduction, the government's desire to appear as the paterfamilias of the prefectural "children," and the Governor's sensitivity to shame. In addition, among the movements, the environmentalist ideology so prevalent and deemed so necessary to mobilization in Western ACID societies was relatively weak in Oita. The Oita movements, to the contrary, were primarily motivated by health and livelihood concerns, not abstract moralistic ideologies. Likewise, the Triple Control Machine did not achieve its control over people by dominating their popular culture, preferences, and ideology (Lukes, 1986). Rather, the Triple Control Machine dominated society by its social institutional and material structural hegemony – by the transfer of patronage and status through a web of vertical social connections. This formed a structure of soft social control. Elite use of this structure, through the Triple Control Machine, indicated their *lack* of control over popular minds and hearts. If the pro-growth elites had not resorted to and reinvented this structure of social and material control, aggrieved residents would probably have generated a much stronger national wave of grassroots protest.

The next two chapters trace the politics of meeting the Three Conditions: "consensus" and "normalization" (Chapter 7), and "assessment" (Chapter 8). The political conflicts these conditions generated proceeded at the same time. Narrating all three together would produce a confusing jumble of events. To keep them coherent, I have not followed strict chronological order. The story of each condition starts after Governor Taki's 1973 Three-Conditions concession, and runs until it ends. Normalization, for instance, ends in 1980 (Chapter 7). I then jump back in time, to pick up the story of consensus soon after the 1973 concession, and run forward with it again. The story of assessment receives the same treatment.

8

Contested consensus

After winning battles over Landfill No. 8 and the cleanup of Seki harbor, the Seki movements were buoyed with enthusiasm. The movements wanted to delay fulfillment of the Three Conditions as long as possible, in order to keep No. 8 at bay. In contrast, their nemesis, the pro-growth business coalition, felt stymied and betrayed. The pro-growth group hated the Three Conditions, and wanted them fulfilled as soon as possible. Governor Taki was caught in the crossfire, bitterly criticized by each side. He was somewhat embarrassed by the extensiveness of his own concessions, and he depended on LDP support to win the next election (Table 6.2).

Implementing the Three Conditions immediately became Governor Taki's quandary and quagmire. In granting the Three Conditions, the Governor had surrendered much more, substantively, than his electoral backers thought necessary. The LDP, DSP, and business and industrial union groups complained bitterly. Once granted, however, proper political form and the watchful eye of the Environmental Agency demanded some kind of implementation. From that point on, the terms consensus, normalization, and assessment became political footballs, contested in definition and practice (Boulle, 1994; Grafstein, 1988).

In all ACID societies, policy implementation is fraught with pitfalls. Failed policies litter the political landscape. Sometimes policies are merely symbolic from the start, something which can be said of Japan's NIC law (Chapter 2), so their failure is no surprise. At other times, interest groups (within and outside the state) may twist the meaning of a policy and prevent its proper implementation (Pressman & Wildavsky, 1973). In particular, the decline of protest by watchdog groups may initiate a "natural cycle" of decay, of increasing regulatory ineffectiveness. On the other hand, continued popular support for a policy, coupled with regulatory agency activism, may enable regulatory strictness to continue as intended (Sabatier, 1975, pp. 303–304). In his attempts to implement the Three Conditions, Governor Taki was subject to these various factors and tendencies.

In order to reassure his LDP and business backers, Governor Taki had to show progress on the Phase Two plan, despite the Three Conditions. Accordingly, he decided to make Landfills No. 6 and 7 an accomplished fact, even without national government permission. The Regional Development Advisory Council had turned down Oita's first application for Phase Two permission; the second appeal was still pending. Despite the official uncertainty, the Governor secured promises from the Mitsubishi Corporation to buy No. 6, and from Mitsui Shipbuilding to buy No. 7, once they were built. Mitsui, the Governor argued, would build a shipyard on No. 7 that would provide skilled jobs for locals and would not pollute.

On the strength of these promises, the Oita government contracted with the Mitsui Real Estate Company to begin construction on landfills No. 6 and 7 (on June 1974 and November 1973, respectively). This gigantic construction company (in the same conglomerate [*keiretsu*] as the company that would buy No. 7) and its Oita subcontractors wanted to go ahead. The Oita government cleverly utilized national bureaucratic sectionalism to its own advantage. In December 1972 and May 1973, respectively, Oita secured permission from the Ministry of Transport and others to build the Landfills No. 6 and 7. Internal documents from the Environmental Agency note with seeming dismay that Oita Prefecture never consulted the EA about this permission (Interview 900, 1979). As long as Oita did not actually build polluting factories, apparently the EA could not stop the construction.

Along with starting construction on Landfills No. 6 and 7, the Oita government and pro-growth elites initiated a vigorous campaign to fulfill the Three Conditions as quickly as possible. The story of how the pro-growth forces captured and defined each condition starts soon after Governor Taki's announcement of the three, and proceeds until the condition is met. This chapter recounts the stories of conditions one and two, which, including aftershocks, run until 1976 and 1977, respectively. The next chapter recounts the story of condition three, followed by the story after the completion of the Three Conditions.

Achieving condition one: "consensus"

The meaning of "consensus"

As his first condition, Governor Taki had promised to wait for "consensus" in Seki, before starting up plans for Landfill No. 8 again. Consensus (*goi*) is a key term in Japanese culture, laden with powerful and evocative symbolism. In English, the term consensus means a "general agreement or concord" (Random

House, 1973). In Japanese, translated literally, the term *goi* has the same meaning – agreement (Katsumata, 1954). Both meanings signify an agreement of wills and goals. The concept serves as a much more central symbolic structure in Japanese politics, even if honored more in its breach than in reality.

An American governor or a French prefect would not have thought to seek "consensus" over a contentious issue. Their fractious democracies produce endless squabbling; the most one could hope for would be compromise – agreement on means, not ends. Japanese political scientists also recognize that democratic politics allow for the peaceful expression and settlement of differences (Aiba et al., 1987, p. 5). But to Governor Taki, steeped as he was in traditional Japanese political norms, consensus seemed the proper goal, or at least the proper public expression, of politics. Reference to this ideal, rather than one of recognizing differences, affected the political process and its outcome.

The Japanese cultural emphasis on *goi* (Lebra, 1976; Nakane, 1970) may be found in many venues. The term is closely associated with group harmony (*wa*), which also indicates a group concordance of purposes. Japanese groups, from informal ones to formal bureaucracies, use group concordance as an important justifying ideology. Corporations and bureaucracies stress the harmony of the group as one big family, and use forms of participatory decision-making (QC Circles, *ringisei*) to achieve consensus (Noda, 1975, p. 127; Rohlen, 1974). Prefectures, villages, and hamlets like to present the appearance of harmony to outsiders. In 1980, Prime Minister Suzuki Zenko publicly expressed his preference for "the politics of *wa*." As his immediate purpose, he was trying to prevent a split in the LDP. But his words had far deeper resonance: "On the basis of a spirit of *wa*, the responsive talents and harmony of the Japanese people, I want to forge the future of our country" (as cited in Aiba et al., 1987, p. 1). PM Suzuki defined the politics of *wa* as "the politics of talking together" (Aiba et al., 1987, p. 4). Throughout the post-war period, Japanese Prime Ministers made some variant of *wa* their basic theme (Aiba et al., 1987, p. 3).

However, critics within Japan attack the LDP's use of the ideal of *wa* as nothing more than a callous manipulation of traditional sincerely held values, as a means to avoid conflict and maintain order under LDP domination (Aiba et al., 1987, p. 4). Within this moral framework, once consensus is reached, dissent becomes immoral. Harmony as a social norm provided the moral basis, for instance, of the real estate company president's criticism of post-war populist movements (Chapter 4). Examined in detail, the process of reaching consensus in Japanese groups reveals less a free exchange of opinions than automatic adherence to the leader's goals, if not to his ways to achieve that goal. In prefectural politics, the power of these norms had declined, opening the door to continuing conflict. The meaning of "consensus" quickly became a very contested issue (Alford & Friedland, 1975).

The harsh Seki protest movements openly and defiantly broke with traditional norms of deference. They ignored the collective preferences (prefectural policies) as expressed by the leader (governor); they disrupted the public *wa*. The Governor deeply wanted to restore *wa,* and in so doing, restore his face as the prefecture's paterfamilias. As he set out to accomplish this, though, his means had to diverge increasingly from the new institutional strictures of law and democratic practice.

Town Council vote

In mid-October of 1974, the Saganoseki (Seki) Town Council continued its session unusually late into the evening. Members of the Kozaki Resistance League had been sitting in the observers' gallery all day long. They feared that the mayor might try again to introduce a pro-8 resolution. By evening, that seemed unlikely, so most of the League members had gone home. Suddenly, at 8 pm, Mayor Furuta introduced the feared resolution. He asked the Council to vote in support of Landfill No. 8. The two council members friendly to the League and opposed to No. 8, both affiliated with the JCP, attempted to raise objections. The Council chair abruptly cut them off and quashed any debate. The Council immediately voted in support of No. 8 (interview data, June 1979). As the newspaper described it: "The Council forced a decision in a brief time without questions or debate."

Governor Taki publicly expressed surprise at the Seki Council decision. He denied any prior consultation with the mayor over it. He reiterated his desire to meet the Three Conditions, including "perfect consensus of the Saganoseki people" (Interview data). One experienced prefectural official, however, thought that the Prefectural Government had been behind the vote. He said,

. . I imagine that the prefecture suggested to Mayor Furuta, to do that [submit the pro-No. 8 resolution].

Typically, the official explained, the Prefectural Government conveys its wishes to the mayor by "suggestion," not by direct order:

The prefecture doesn't order. It just gives a hint, such as, 'if there was a town legislative decision, it would be most convenient for us.' A mayor will always take up this kind of nuance quickly.

Sometimes, he added, such indirect guidance created confusing ambiguity. It was not a rigid or authoritarian command system. Vague communication like this was typical among Japanese elites, who term it *haragei* (belly-craft) or wordless communication (Lebra, 1976).

Mayor Furuta's legislative maneuvering incensed Kozaki League and the Seki Common Will Group members. They quickly convened a protest meeting of 300 people. The mayor, they complained, had already promised not to introduce a pro-No. 8 resolution. Furthermore, the protestors claimed, the legal irregularities of the resolution rendered it null and void. The mayor had introduced the resolution to the Council directly, without going through the appropriate committee. And the Council had not allowed a complete and proper debate of the resolution. These actions violated proper procedure stipulated by local government law.

Mayor Furuta disagreed. His promise, he said, had been made under duress, while canned in his office by protestors. The resolution was not improper or illegal, he contended, because it was "based on requests from many townspeople such as the town's economic groups and the Chamber of Commerce" (Interview, Furnta, 1980). This statement revealed his local backers.

The ensuing wrangle over the legality of the vote revealed a crucial aspect of the Japanese political context, Furuta, 1980: the lack of legal levers for ordinary people. If the mayor denied the illegality of the vote, where could ordinary people turn for support? First, movement leaders asked the Regional Affairs Department of the Prefectural Government about the matter. The official in charge, going strictly by the rules, declared the vote procedurally improper and in need of another vote:

> The pro (No. 8) decision did not follow the procedures required by the Local Autonomy Laws and therefore must be re-deliberated . . . (the decision) must be re-voted (OGN, 1974).

But in the same breath, using an odd logic, the official asserted that unless and until voted on again, the vote's contents stood:

> The contents [of the No. 8 resolution] are not illegal. Just the procedure is illegal . . . So the decision has official power. As long as it is not overturned by Council vote or court judgment, it is valid (OGN, 1974).

In other words, an illegal procedure could produce a binding decision. When the movement pointed out that it was the Prefectural Government's legal duty to enforce the revote, the prefectural official replied:

> (Prefectural administrative) guidance is usually done verbally. We won't send written guidance to the mayor and the council [on this matter].

Japanese bureaucracies are renowned for their administrative guidance of businesses and other organizations (Yamanouchi, 1979; Johnson, 1982). Some experts emphasize the consensual nature of bureaucratic guidance:

Administrative guidance is guidance, and therefore to follow it or not is up to the discretion of receiver (Yamanouchi, 1979, p. 6).

But the Oita case shows that administrative guidance had a much more compulsory quality. An Upper House Oita JSP Diet Representative explained that:

According to law, the prefecture and the cities, towns and villages are equal. But in fact the prefecture is the superior office and the latter the inferior. Ideas are transferred down the hierarchy, but don't come up from the bottom (Interview, 1978).

While lacking any legal justification, such guidance often takes on the force of law. Ignoring it can invite severe sanctions. Guidance from the Environmental Agency, for instance, had pushed Governor Taki toward an environmental assessment. Behind it stood the threat of another Phase Two application denial.

Behind the scenes, the prefectural government and associated elites exercised quite strong control over the mayor of Seki. One Seki mayor confessed this quite frankly:

In the planning process for the Phase Two plan (Nos. 6, 7 and 8 Landfills), the Prefectural Government decided the plans and told the town to follow along (Interview, 1978).

This vertical relationship appeared earlier as one leg of the informal triple control structure. In this case, however, the Prefectural Government found it politically useful to deny that informal reality. The official reverted to the literal (*tatemae*) meaning of "guidance." The Prefectural Government, he argued, could only suggest a revote, not force one. The official's response resembles the scene from the famous Kurozawa movie *Ikiru*, where the Tokyo bureaucracy shuffles a group of women petitioners from office to office in order to discourage them.

Still, the movements' public accusations of illegality made Mayor Furuta uneasy. He sought public support from Governor Taki. In response, the Governor publicly admitted that he had, after all, requested the mayor to submit the pro-No. 8 resolution. Stymied by both Governor and mayor, the Seki movements turned to Watanuki, the conservative head of the Seki Council. They complained about the procedural illegality of the vote. Watanuki rebuffed them with the cryptic words: "The decision is valid. If it is illegal, I will take responsibility." This was no help.

On November 2, the Oita Prefectural Government publicly accepted the pro-8 Seki Council vote, stating:

As long . . . as the mayor does not agree that the vote violates legislative regulations, the prefecture does not have the legal prerogative to make the Seki Council revote it . . . The mayor holds the final authority to decide whether a decision is illegal or not. The prefecture cannot . . . interfere in the town's internal politics (Prefectural document).

By presenting itself as legally hamstrung, the Oita government tried to provide a public rationale for not forcing a revote. An experienced reporter at the Oita newspaper considered this rationale nothing more than a public relations excuse. The prefecture did not force a revote, he said, not because of the lack of authority, but because it wanted the vote to stand:

This is the nasty side of the bureaucracy; if the result is good (for them) they recognize the means (if not, they don't).

That the ordinary people would accept such an excuse, the reporter said, was due to Japanese culture:

This happens because the Japanese tend to place great importance on social form.

By social form he meant proper procedure – social institutional structures. If the government could persuade people it was following the proper legal procedure, most people would not question the substance of a decision. Japanese officials wanted to maintain an image of propriety. The modern legal and rational state, vulnerable to the vote, depends on the maintenance of public legitimacy (Weber, 1978). In Japan, following proper form (the *tatemae* of accepted procedure) confers great legitimacy. If this is done, people more readily acquiesce to backstage, informal but real (*honne*) practices beneath it (Goffman, 1959). Under ordinary circumstances, people would not have pushed the issue to the point of causing public loss of face for the other party. When it came to pollution, however, the Seki movements felt little constrained by such niceties. On the contrary, unruly behavior had already brought them several successes. Breaking the polite facade, they realized, could be a useful tactic.

The Seki movements did not accept the prefecture's legal rationale. Movement leaders pointed out that, except for prefectural enforcement, the law had no other method for correcting illegal actions by local governments. The entire body of local autonomy law, they argued, depended on a hierarchy of authority. Not exercising prefectural authority would render the law empty and meaningless. Furthermore, since Mayor Furuta would not recognize the illegality of the pro-8 vote, his perception of truth was faulty (Kozaki movement document). This sort of hard, rational critique may sound familiar to Western ears. In Japan, though, it represented a form of innovative cultural agency. In practice, the government and courts hardly recognized the citizen's right to advance such a critique.

However, because of the EA's watchful presence, the Prefectural Government could not entirely ignore this critique (as it might have otherwise). The day after the Seki movements fielded this critique, the Oita government took a stronger stance. It informally guided the Seki mayor and Council head to consider a revote (OGN, 1974). Then on November 6, the Governor publicly called on the Seki Council to revote the issue. In another odd twist of logic, however, the governor added that the standing pro-8 Seki Council vote indicated "resident consensus" (OGN, 1974).

In this way, the Oita government, in response to grassroots criticism, adjusted its public stance to conform with the law. But at the same time, it still took no formal steps to enforce the law. By this subterfuge, the Oita government hoped the mayor would continue to reject the recommendation and let the Seki Council decision stand. This would constitute local consensus.

Frustrated by the Oita government's contradictory postures, the movement once again outflanked the prefectural elites. With the two supporting Seki Council members in tow, a delegation went to the Ministry of Home Affairs (MOHA) in Tokyo. MOHA had jurisdiction over the administration of local government. The delegation asked whether the prefecture's refusal to force a Seki revote was proper. A ministry official replied that it was not:

(The Seki Council decision) is in violation of Local Autonomy Law Article 176 paragraph 4. As a matter of course the Prefectural Government should direct (matters) so that law is upheld (OGN, 1974).

This paragraph of the Local Autonomy Law states,

When it is recognized that the elections or decisions of the legislature of a regular regional public entity overreach their proper limits or violate legal or legislative regulations, the head of that regular regional public entity must explain the reason and redeliberate the decision or hold another election (Hoshino, 1988, p. 156).

In other words, the law required the Seki mayor, as the prefecture claimed, to recognize the illegality and order another vote on No. 8 by the Seki Council. However, contrary to the prefecture's claim, subsequent paragraphs added that should the mayor not recognize such illegality, the prefecture should act. Paragraph 6 states that the Governor can nullify an illegal election or decision. The Oita Prefectural Government could not have been ignorant of this law, but it chose to ignore it.

The delegation returned to Seki with this news. On November 11, 1974, 120 movement supporters assembled in the Seki public hall to discuss the problem. The group wrote and distributed a pamphlet describing MOHA's comments, which rendered the actions of both the Seki Council and the Oita government improper. This new information made the prefecture's claim that the Seki vote indicated local consensus look ridiculous and not acceptable to the EA. Accordingly, the Prefectural Government gave in and requested a revote. This took a while to organize.

Attaining "consensus"

The prefecture's distorted presentation of its legal powers was not accidental. It was *tatemae* – an excuse to let the Seki Council vote stand. The Prefectural Government had both the informal influence as well as the legal authority to force a revote at any time. In its real intentions (*honne*), it did not want to. It had just used its informal influence to push the mayor to pass the pro-8 resolution. The lack of legal recourse and a compliant general public gave the prefectural officials the freedom to operate behind such *tatemae* excuses. In this situation of unaccountability, non-decisions became the norm of governance.

Furthermore, the prefectural officials saw little wrong with their behavior. On the contrary, they viewed the protestors as behaving selfishly, without concern for the welfare of the larger social body. To many of the officials, this justified the application of soft methods of social control. The Prefectural Government's social control strategy, one prefectural official explained, is to "try to strengthen the pro-group . . ."

The prefecture doesn't use force. It uses chances. It waits for a good opportunity to strike. The Japanese government is relaxed about oppositional movements (Interview, Oita).

Still, the Oita government wanted fairly quick results. Behind its placid veneer, the government worked hard to gain control over intermediary organizations (Town Council, *ku*-system, youth, and women's groups) that organized citizens' daily lives.

Why did the Seki Council play its part in this drama and pass the pro-No. 8 resolution? The obvious, common sense answer is because the majority of council members voted for it. Elected representatives of the people have the right and authority to decide on a range of public policy issues. The decision, in this light, followed the rules of representative democracy.

This answer would make the decision look unproblematic were it not for the demonstrated strength of local opposition to No. 8. Evidence presented earlier (Chapter 4) indicated that the vast majority of Seki residents opposed No. 8. Given this solid opposition, why did the Seki movements not "vote the rascals out?" Many other Japanese environmental movements did that (Chapter 3). For that matter, why did not the mayor and the Council fear losing the next election if they supported No. 8?

In a company town such as Seki, the Triple Control Machine (Chapter 6) exercised tight enough control over town politics that most of the Council members felt secure. The mayor, having won by a slim margin, was in a more precarious situation. But he too was closely tied to the Triple Control Machine, and had little incentive to resist it. Furthermore, the politicians knew that if they did support No. 8, the protest movement had little in the way of formal means to block or challenge that vote or to cast them out of office.

The legal system provided no footholds for grassroots groups. The vagueness of the laws gave the government maximum interpretive discretion. Japanese courts rarely recognized suits against the government (Upham, 1987). The Ministry of Local Autonomy, which controlled local government law, did not allow citizen referendums (Hasegawa, 1994). Civil laws gave the average citizen no power to sue an offending company (Upham, 1987). Therefore, the Town Council members felt they could vote in favor of No. 8 with electoral impunity.

The vagueness of Japanese laws enforced a generalized citizen *dis*empowerment. It provided citizens with little protection from government or corporate decisions or way to challenge them. In practice, law in other ACID societies also sometimes perversely shields the administration and special interests from public scrutiny (Bachrach & Baratz, 1970). But this practice in Japan seems much more systematic compared with the United States.

Lack of representation in the Seki Town Council forced the Kozaki Resistance League to seek other venues of influence. By themselves, the Kozaki League members felt weak and outnumbered. Rather than giving up, however, the League broke out of its hamlet parochialism. It reached out for allies, and tried to expand its support base into the whole prefecture. This is a typical defensive reaction by beleaguered social movements (Schwartz, 1976).

In 1975, the League joined a prefecture-wide umbrella organization, the Communication Council to Protect Oita's Nature. In 1976, with other groups the League formed a Prefectural Anti-Pollution Citizens Joint Struggle Council (*Kyoto Kaigi*). Other members included local opposition parties (JSP, JCP, CGP) and unions (of the Sohyo federation). The Joint Struggle Council planned social protests against a number of prefectural development projects, not all located in Kozaki village. It held several big meetings in Oita and Saganoseki with nationally known speakers. Through its participation in these associations, the Kozaki League accepted increasing support and advice from the Sohyo leader Yamagame and other union and JSP officials.

Still, the League was careful to protect its own autonomy and avoid being used for political advantage by parties. League leader Inao Toru rarely felt bound by collective tactical decisions by the Joint Struggle Council. If, in a confrontation with prefectural officials, he felt some other tactic was called for, he would spontaneously plunge ahead with it. This often dismayed his plan-bound collaborators.

The League's independence led to friction with other coalition members and disappointed outsiders who wanted to help. An Oitan working as a government official in Tokyo told how Inao Toru refused to give him any information about the movement. Inao, he claimed, criticized and rejected anyone not in direct active support of the movement. This, the Tokyo Oitan argued, had hampered the spread of support for the Kozaki movement in Oita Prefecture and in Tokyo. Despite this, he said, the movement continued strongly within Kozaki

because the members are fighting for their own profit, not for Japan or for Oita. They would only lose by having a factory complex come there (Interview 402, 1979).

Local JCP leaders also felt alienated from the Kozaki League. They opposed the League's unruly tactics of sit-ins or demonstrations. The JCP preferred that all protest take place through formal, legitimate channels, such as the courts. This counsel was in line with broader JCP political tactics at the time. It was trying to build an attractive image as a "lovable Communist party" that used only parliamentary means to effect political change.

Despite the expansion of movement alliances, local pressures had little effect. In May 1976, the Seki Council took a second vote on the pro-No. 8 resolution. This time, the resolution went through full debate, and faced vociferous protest from the observers' gallery. Once again, with a solid LDP majority, the Seki Council easily passed the resolution, this time without procedural irregularity. The Prefectural Government publicly announced that the Seki Council vote indicated the achievement of local "consensus." Now it had to finish the assessment in order to be free to build Landfill No. 8. The events recounted here indicate that the LDP and its affiliated prefectural administration used the morality of consensus to suppress political criticism.

A different path to consensus

Judging from the preceding events, one might conclude with some contemporary critical German sociologists (Dahrendorf, 1959; Habermas, 1987) that bureaucracy inevitably invades and controls local communities and suppresses dissent. Some Japanese sociologists, though, while recognizing this controlling aspect of bureaucracy, also recognize its potential beneficial administrative function (Funabashi, 1980). Certain political events in Oita demonstrate that government bureaucracy, even in "vertical" Japan, need not necessarily operate only in a control mode, but under certain circumstances, can also make decisions in a participatory and democratic fashion.

In 1975, two years after Governor Taki had agreed to the Three Conditions, the voters of Oita City elected a Socialist party candidate, Sato, as their new mayor (see Table 6.2). The city had been under an LDP mayor until then. Unlike most Socialist party candidates, Mayor Sato did not come from a union background. He had been a farmer and had led the agricultural cooperative

(Nokyo) in Oita Prefecture. This gave him strong support among the considerable number of farmers within the limits of Oita City. Given the close ties between Nokyo and the LDP, Sato's normal route to office would have been with the LDP. But, he related, the LDP already supported the incumbent mayor.

A pragmatic man, Sato entered the Socialist party and became a party leader. In this political gambit, he resembled Governor Kinoshita. JSP leadership gave Sato the support of the Sohyo unions in Oita City. This combination of support, from the farmers and from the Socialist party-affiliated unions, won him the election. The mayor had created his own local farmer-labor coalition, despite the fact that such a coalition did not exist at the national level. This class coalition strongly affected the latitude of his policies once in office.

But class and institutional support alone was not enough, the mayor confessed. In order to get elected, he said, he had to use his network of personal connections in traditional patron-client fashion. In other words, he distributed what patronage he could muster in return for votes. He created his own political machine, which operated against the LDP machine. The tactic embarrassed the mayor. His hope, he claimed, was to decrease the prevalence of machine politics and foster a proper democracy, where citizens voted on the basis of issues. His policies supported this claim.

By 1975, when Sato won office, the NIC had already walled much of Oita City from the sea. Mayor Sato generally supported the NIC project. Environmentally, he felt, its green belt was a great improvement over traditional factory towns such as those in North Kyushu, in which grimy refineries abutted residential areas. But the mayor opposed further use of city finances to build more roads, water mains, and other industrial infrastructure. He felt the city should turn to meeting social and residential needs, such as sewers and straightening neighborhood streets. Mayor Sato wanted to use Oita City's upcoming five-year development plan to set new priorities.

Japanese national policy required all towns, cities, and prefectures to draw up comprehensive development plans every five years. Usually, government bureaucrats created these entirely in-house, without public comment or participation. The making of Saganoseki township's five-year plan exemplified this bureau-centrism (Chapter 5). Oita's previous LDP mayor had made plans that way too. As one city official explained:

The 1971 [Oita City] plan was made by "experts" and bureaucrats based on assumptions of high economic growth.

The Prefectural Government's environmental assessment, he noted, had hardly modified this bureaucentric procedure. Furthermore, approval by a citizens' advisory council and the city legislature, the official explained, was "mere legitimatory formality" (*keishikiteki tatemae*). Even elected legislative politicians, he stressed, not to speak of the average citizen, had little voice in the planning process.

The wave of opposition, progressive mayors and governors elected in the late 1960s and early 1970s had challenged this situation (Chapter 3). Progressive local governments had experimented with a range of citizen participation methods that broke with traditional paternalistic bureaucentrism (Broadbent, 1988). They gave citizens' committees a strong hand in drawing up city and prefectural growth plans. The new forms broke with the traditional paternalism of Japanese local government (Steiner et al., 1980, pp. 138–52).

Inspired by this trend, Mayor Sato and his idealistic top staff incorporated a thorough system of citizen participation into their plan-making process. This system, Mayor Sato hoped, would foster more democratic habits among the people (Interview, 1979). At the same time, as a result of changing popular attitudes, Mayor Sato felt that such a move had become a political necessity. An Oita City official expressed this point of view:

. . . citizen participation is necessary to ensure the feasibility of the plan . . . In the future, if the bureaucracy just makes the plan as if the citizens did not exist, it will be hard to get citizen understanding and cooperation (Interview, 1977).

To provide avenues for citizen participation, Oita City officials set up thirty-five focus groups composed of citizens and chaired by citizen experts. These were asked to formulate the basic concerns of the five-year city plan. The resulting list of concerns went into a survey, distributed to city residents. The city government received back 2,400 completed survey forms. In addition, city officials held twelve open meetings in different parts of the city to discuss popular concerns. They then set up a number of citizen deliberative committees to draft the plan. The committees sought and encouraged public feedback. The idealism and thoroughness of the effort probably surpassed the best of U.S. participation efforts, as in the Model Cities program (Piven & Cloward, 1971).

The titles of the resulting city publications indicate the spirit of the effort: *The Oita of Tomorrow: Made by Everyone's Hands (Ashita no Oita o Minna no Te de)* quoted citizen opinions classified by issue and geographical area; *The Oita of Tomorrow: Made by Citizens (Shimin ga Kizuku Ashita no Oita)* reported the results of neighborhood opinion surveys on every conceivable welfare-related topic. For instance, the section on environmental sanitation reported citizen priorities on such diverse topics as "reduce cockroaches," "catch wild dogs," and "make a graveyard."

Through this system, the mayor tried to give average residents a stronger voice in the planning process. The process stirred up controversies and debates. Rather than fearing that public debate would break the appearance of *wa* (harmony) so treasured by conservatives, Mayor Sato relished the open debates. He crowed that

the only genuine debate over the NIC Phase Two has been in this plan, not in any other city or prefectural plans. [We had] pro and con debate about the New Industrial City and the Phase Two plan (Interview, 1980).

Just as the process differed from the prefectural one, so too did its conclusions. Rather than supporting continued rapid industrial growth, the draft plan concluded that city growth policies should give priority to social needs (sewage and education) and environmental protection. An independent NHK[1] survey done in 1978 confirmed that these conclusions accurately reflected public opinion (Table 9.1). The problem with this kind of participatory planning, the mayor said, was the time it took. It took over three years to produce the plan, whereas the old system had only taken four to six months. Yet, the mayor argued, this cost was minor, compared with the benefit: a more genuine democracy.

Numerous events recounted in this book have indicated the power of governors (and mayors) and the weakness of legislatures. Generalizing from this, the reader would have expected that once the plan was made, Mayor Sato should have easily rolled his completed plan through the Oita City legislature. However, this was not the case. The new social priorities enunciated by the Oita City plan raised the hackles of the LDP and its business backers. The LDP and the DSP, in a business-conservative union coalition, held the majority of seats in the Oita City legislature. This legislature had to pass the new five-year plan.

Following bureaucratic protocol, Mayor Sato had to approve the draft and send it to the city legislature for a vote. Before he could do that, though, the mayor related, leading conservative city-legislature politicians approached him in secret. They requested that he change the wording of the city development plan. They wanted words that would not give priority to social needs over industrial investment. Better yet, they wanted the plan to give priority to more industrial growth.

Mayor Sato refused their request. Unlike Governor Taki at a similar juncture (Chapters 6 and 7), Mayor Sato was not in need of LDP political support. He told the conservative politicians, "Since you control the legislature, change the plan's wording yourselves!" The conservative politicians had hoped to avoid blatantly gutting the popular plan, which might prove politically costly. But the mayor forced the conservatives to show their hand. In place of the draft plan's

---

1. NHK refers to Nihon Hoso Kaisha, the Japan Broadcasting System sponsored by the Japanese government.

statement of priority for social needs, the city legislature voted to put in the phrase, "try all means possible" to meet social needs. This wording no longer gave priority to investment in social needs. Instead, it boosted support for more NIC-style growth. As one city official noted:

The revised parts (of the plan) concerned the status of the New Industrial City. [These parts] . . . had occasioned great controversy in the participatory councils as well.

These revisions sorely disappointed Mayor Sato, his staff and many citizens. The plan no longer reflected the real citizen preferences. Now it served the interests of powerful business groups and their political partners. The city official noted:

This plan had been created through a long process of citizen participation. That it should be revised by the city legislature points to a problem in the relationship between citizen participation and legislative democracy.

The "problem" is the fact that the legislature, though elected by the people, refused to represent popular preferences on an important issue. On the contrary, the legislature erased those views and wrote in the views of a minority special interest group.

The sociologist Max Weber thought bureaucracies, as a result of their inherent efficiency, relentlessly expand their control over society. As they do so, they inevitably seek to rationalize – to make controlled, stable, and predictable – as much as possible about their societal context. As one part of their control project, bureaucracies try to hide their inner proceedings from outside view:

Bureaucratic administration . . . hides its knowledge and action from criticism . . . far beyond those areas where purely functional interests make for secrecy. The concept of 'official secret' is the specific invention of the bureaucracy, . . . [even though it] cannot be substantially justified beyond those specially qualified areas . . . Bureaucracy naturally welcomes a poorly informed and hence powerless parliament (Weber, 1946, pp. 233–234).

Bureaucracies, the thesis goes, relentlessly push to limit the choices of ordinary citizens. Bureaucracy puts the society into an iron cage of limited political roles and minimal political voice (Weber, 1958). Certain modern theorists, taking up this viewpoint, make the bureaucratic state's tendency to "invade" and "control" the everyday lives of citizens the primary stimulus to new social movements, including the environmental movement (Habermas, 1981).

However, the Oita City planning process shows that rather than inevitably imposing an iron cage on its citizenry, a bureaucracy can just as readily serve and facilitate democratic participation. Whether it does so or not depends in large part not on its inherent dynamics as a social institution, but on the motives and goals of its leadership. An administrative bureaucracy under the prefectural governor became a tool for social control; under Mayor Sato, it became a tool for citizen participation in policy-making.

Furthermore, the case of Mayor Sato in Oita City belies the thesis that institutional norms of vertical deference shape Japanese institutional relations. Mayor Sato was the peak authority figure within the city. As discussed earlier, chief executives traditionally decide on and submit the majority of bills to the legislature. But in this case, when the mayor's initiative was not to their liking, the legislators showed no hesitation in sabotaging his effort.

This example of Oita City's citizen participation planning indicates that neither an implacable bureaucracy nor a fixed sociocultural hierarchy determines the relationship between local state and local society. Rather, it is the class affiliation of the dominant parties that determines their interests and position (Broadbent, 1988). From that point, the power of their position provides the levers to defend those interests. In the Oita City case, the mayor and the legislature represented different class logics. The JSP mayor represented a farmer-worker class logic that welcomed broad citizen participation, even if the result modified the path to quickest industrial growth. On the other hand, the LDP and DSP dominated city legislature, because of its business-conservative union class-based interests, refused to ratify the results of the citizen participation process. This demonstrates that at the head of the bureaucracy and behind the cloak of cultural rhetoric stood naked economic interest, motivating the struggle if not defining its institutional expressions.

Condition two: "normalization"

The Baba split

As condition two, Governor Taki promised to normalize relations within the Seki Union. Friction between the pro- and anti-No. 8 factions had led to the blows and bloodshed. Beyond stopping the fighting, however, normalization had a deeper meaning. It was a way for the government to acquire construction rights it needed to build Landfill No. 8. The fishing folk of Baba and Kozaki hamlets held traditional rights to those shallow coastal waters.

The Seki Union, to which the Baba and Kozaki fishers also belonged, voted early against No. 8. In response, right after that vote, prefectural officials had started working with the Baba fishers to split them off from the Seki Union. In other words, the officials started to cultivate a countermovement. If the Baba fishers took their tiny sub-union out of the parent Seki Union, they would be able to decide on their own what to do with their waters. This would also remove the immediate reason for fisticuffs, their common presence in the Seki Fishing

Union. With prefectural support, the Baba fishing folk intensified their campaign to split off.

One conservative Baba boss described the tactics of their campaign:

. . . the movement for separation began in the Baba union and pulled in all the people in the Saganoseki union who would cooperate.

The Baba fishing people appealed to their friends and relatives in the Seki Union:

To get (the Saganoseki union members) . . . to allow the Baba union to separate, we used personal connections (*ningen kankei*) . . .

They begged their friends to understand and support their point of view. They needed the compensation payments to change over to a new livelihood (since fishing was no longer viable for them). Seki Union members who were not full-time fishers had less to lose personally, so they were more sympathetic. In addition, the Baba boss said, local elites gave them a lot of help:

. . . The LDP faction helped our Baba union to separate. It was because of the party faction that we could separate like this. So we have a lot of belief in Kawamura as a human being (Interview, Baba, March 1979).

President Kawamura and the local LDP bosses applied the same pressures they had used during the original No. 8 vote. This time, they had a better moral imperative – defense of the imploring Baba fishing folk. In the original vote, the conservatives had not been very successful. Seventy percent of the Seki Union members had voted against No. 8. For individual fishing folk, the individual logic had not changed. Filling in the Baba waters would still destroy the spawning grounds for their own catch in nearby waters. If acting alone, rationally, on those considerations, 70 percent would probably still have been against No. 8. They were not acting alone, however. They were embedded in social networks that persuaded them otherwise.

At the same time as the pro-No. 8 faction grew in strength, the anti-No. 8 faction declined. Since 1970, the Triple Control Machine had gnawed away at protest groups in Oita, smothering some. But in the Seki Union, despite its gnawing, Nishio and the Common Will Group had survived. More than that, as a result of their success in the Nikko blockade, they had acquired national fame as a fierce, uncompromising protest group. The Nikko blockade, however, marked the high tide of the Group's protest activities. After that, its activities dropped off sharply. When Union President Kawamura resigned in 1973, the Seki Fishing Union elected a new president, Kataura, who also pushed a pro-No. 8 policy. Oddly enough, the Common Will Group began to cooperate with Kataura. Something had happened to suddenly and severely weaken the protest forces within the Seki Fishing Union.

As a result of these factional and network shifts, on October 20, 1973, five months after No. 8's suspension, the Seki Union voted in favor of the Baba Union split. Shortly afterward, the newly independent Baba Union voted to relinquish its rights to the coastal waters. No fights broke out. The Prefectural Government announced that it had met condition two: normalization of the Seki Fishing Union. Factionalism had been quelled.

Submerged dissent

In Seki and Baba, though, turmoil and resistance still seethed beneath the surface. The actual fishers made up a larger proportion of the hamlet than in Kozaki, but still not the majority. Yet, in deciding the fate of the coast, only their voice counted. The other residents of the hamlet had no legal standing or rights in the issue. The Prefectural Government and the Baba Union ignored them. Despite their silence, other residents would pay the price of growth and get none of the direct compensation. Still, no protest erupted. On the surface, the whole hamlet seemed in perfect *wa* (concord) over the idea.

By chance, I became friends with a man married to a woman from Baba. They no longer lived in Baba and didn't know much about its internal politics. But his wife introduced me to her Baba relatives. They were secondary school teachers, aware of pollution consequences and currents of opposition. They told me that probably half the hamlet would oppose the landfill if it became imminent. "But," they added,

right now, we can't speak out . . . The fishermen are the oldest members of this community . . . The people who were here from the beginning have the strongest influence . . . my brothers are fishermen. Therefore, since the opponents are relatives and they are losing their livelihood [due to decline of catch], it's hard to deny them compensation (Interview, Baba, March, 1979).

Their words conveyed a benevolent concern for the fishing people's welfare. But in addition, they feared violent attack from the fishermen if they were to oppose No. 8 outright.

By their central position in the Baba union, the Baba bosses controlled not only the union, but the hamlet as well. Their control extended the Triple Control Machine deep into the hamlet. The bosses determined the decisions of the Baba Union, which bound all its members in support. The union, in turn, dominated the hamlet. Union members were the oldest families in the hamlet, and hence its main (*honke*) lineages. The teachers and other non-fishing residents were branch lineages, of lesser status. As one local informant put it,

. . . there is usually a "boss" within each extended family. He comes forth and summarizes everyone's opinions into one. This usually is done by the head of the main house (*honke*), over the branch-houses (*bunke*). It is hard to do something different from the leader, and they are generally older ones who are conservative . . .

This was a very typical traditional kinship hierarchy in Japan (Fukutake, 1989). It had profoundly anti-democratic implications, illustrated here. The main house patriarch represented the whole extended family, including both main and branch houses. This hierarchical structure of power dampened debate and criticism. The Occupation passed laws mandating equal inheritance and land to the tiller to weaken the material basis of this hierarchy, in order to sponsor democratic tendencies. The Occupation reforms had not extended to the fishing hamlet netlord (*amimoto*), though. The *amimoto* had retained their boats, nets, and hamlet main house status. The consequences may be seen in this example.

The traditional social structure, reinforced by threat and patronage, smothered dissent. In this case, the village bosses did not radicalize like Katayama or Inao Toru. On the contrary, they followed the usual path and coupled into the Triple Control Machine. This coupling infused further compliance incentives (material patronage) into the union and hamlet. The consequent muffling of dissent further normalized the Seki situation. In sum, this exercise of social control operated through a complex mixture of material and normative, not symbolic, exchanges, with normative social institutions playing the key structuring role. The social relations of compliance mobilization completely overpowered those that might have prompted protest mobilization (McAdam & Paulsen, 1993). In addition, the organizational context allowed for block recruitment into reactionary mobilization (Oberschall, 1973).

Union capitulation

In 1976, Mayor Furuta addressed a Seki Union meeting and asked for the members' support for No. 8. He hinted that the Prefectural Government would offer them financial compensation if they did. No disruptions broke out. Symbolic of this new posture, Union President Kataura commented that in the future, the Seki Union would "judge [No. 8] by the conditions," in other words by the amount of compensation (OGN, July 13, 1976). The Seki Union vote against No. 8 still stood, but its real stance had changed to conditional opposition, seeking for a better offer (as had other Oita movements, Chapter 4).

The deflation of Seki Union opposition enabled the Prefectural Government to take stronger steps on No. 8 landfill. In July 1976, Prefectural Government officials met with Mayor Furuta to discuss the amount of compensation payments to offer union members when No. 8 was built (Interview, Saganoseki, 1979). In September and October, the Seki legislature met and passed the

Saganoseki Long-Range Development Plan that included No. 8 Landfill. These steps made the landfill loom larger and closer in the popular mind. Women from the Kozaki League and some members of the Seki local government workers' union (*Jichiro*) conducted a small sit-in at the mayor's office to protest the new Seki Development Plan. But few, if any, fishermen participated.

Shortly thereafter, the Seki Union publicly asked the prefecture to financially compensate its members for the losses they would suffer as a result of No. 8 Landfill would damage their catch of the valuable tai fish by destroying some of its breeding grounds. This request indicated the Seki Union's capitulation to the No. 8 plan, and the total collapse of the Common Will Group as a protest organization. Just four years previously, the Common Will Group had won a major victory against the Nikko copper refinery. How could the Group have collapsed so completely as to offer no resistance at all? Movement leaders, union activists, and opposition party politicians puzzled over this question, but came to no clear answer. They had trusted in Nishio's fiery devotion to the cause. Something had put out that fire. It was strange.

The prefectural official who had handled the Baba case once again clarified the matter for me. Earlier, he explained, the Prefectural Government had "adjusted" the Kawamura recall election so that it would fail. At that time, the official explained, the Prefectural Government had also worked out an agreement with Nishio:

. . . this adjusting strategy was the occasion for getting friendly with the leader of the anti (No. 8) group (in the Seki Union). (We) became personally close and friendly. And (we) convinced him that we would make a Landfill No. 8 with no pollution.

"How did you convince him?," I asked. The official replied:

By offering an appropriate compensation payment to the Seki fishermen's union . . . At the time, we had prevailed upon the chief of the anti-group, but not all of the 200 followers would go along with their leader's change . . . (Interview, Saganoseki, November 1979).

In other words, the Prefectural Government had convinced Nishio to come around to its point of view through the offer of compensation payments and pollution protection. But these were not the only pressures on Nishio.

Nishio falls

The warrior

Despite superficial calm, the Nikko harbor pollution problem continued to bubble away under the surface. After the harbor blockade, the Nikko company had promised to remove 120,000 cubic meters of sludge from within the harbor and 450,000 cubic meters of it from outside the harbor.

Nishio complained that Nikko had greatly reduced the amount of dredging it planned to do outside the harbor. Nikko admitted that was so. The company justified the reduction by saying its research had shown that the sludge had not spread as far as thought. Nishio asked to see the research reports. Nikko refused. Nishio asked Seki Union president Kataura to find out why Nikko had reduced the dredging area. President Kataura also refused. This raised Nishio's suspicions – was Kataura secretly cooperating with Nikko?

Showing his old fighting spirit, Nishio called in Osaka University physics professor Dr. Kido to conduct an independent investigation of the polluting Nikko sludge. Nishio and Kita went out in a boat and took samples. Their results showed that the polluted sludge had spread as far as thought. Nikko had no objective basis for reducing the area of dredging. The results showed something even more shocking. Much of the 120,000 cubic meters of mud already removed by Nikko had not been from within the polluted sludge area. Instead, it seemed, Nikko had done the dredging to make a deeper channel for larger incoming ore freighters, which it needed anyhow (Kino, 1978).

Nishio took the results of his research to the Prefectural Government. After examining the results, the government official told him privately, "This appears to be boat-channel dredging" (OGN, October 28, 1978). Despite this confirmation, Nikko still refused to change its dredging procedures. Finally, on October 30, 1978, Nishio asked the prefecture to direct Nikko to dredge in the proper place.

Then the prefectural official told him something very shocking. "In November 1977," the official confessed, "the Seki Union agreed to let Nikko reduce the area of its dredging operations (Matsushita, 1978, p. 8). This news surprised and angered Nishio and his associates. They had not heard of this agreement. It had not been told to union members. Nishio asked the union directors. None of them had ever heard of such an agreement either.

On November 4, 1978, Nishio went into the union offices. He found the agreement in the files, concluded between union president Kataura and a Nikko representative and signed on November 22, 1977. The agreement had never been presented to the directors or the general meeting. It allowed for a reduction in sludge-removal area in return for 18 million yen (about $180,000) paid to the union.

This secret deal enraged Nishio. He printed up a notice with the contents of the agreement and tacked it up around Seki town. The notice ended with the caustic remark, "Nikko's policy of wining, womanizing, and bribing the people of Saganoseki has created this kind of union president" (Matsushita, 1978, p. 8).

In other words, Nishio charged that Nikko had bribed the union president. His anger mounted.

On November 6, 1978, the Seki Union Board of Directors met to discuss the issue. Nishio expected the board would cover up the problem and not punish the president. He decided to block this outcome by direct action. On the afternoon of November 6, Nishio took a taxi to the union offices and told the driver to wait outside. He climbed up the stairs to the board meeting room. He stormed into the directors' meeting and from a bag drew out a large curved samurai sword. Nishio slashed the right arm of President Kataura and cut it to the bone.

Nishio went down the stairs, got in the taxi, and went to the police station, where he surrendered himself. The police arrested Nishio. Fishing folk and neighbors circulated a petition justifying the attack. They collected 3,743 signatures and submitted it in his defense during the trial. Nishio was once again a hero, resurrected.

Nishio explained that he attacked Kataura because

> the president and the Nikko company made a secret, corrupt deal over the Nikko refinery's dredging operations in Saganoseki. I did it (the violence) to make him reflect (*hansei*) on his actions (Matsushita, 1978, p. 9).

The attack shocked the union board of directors. They canceled Kataura's agreement and negotiated a new agreement with Nikko that strengthened the dredging requirement. The board also forced president Kataura to resign, and brought back the old president, Kawamura.

People interpreted the attack in many different ways. In an article about the incident, Matsushita Ryuichi, the Nakatsu movement leader and author, pictured Nishio as a dedicated but hot-headed activist. He saw the attack on president Kataura as a continuation of Nishio's long and courageous fight against pollution. This was the popular opinion for a while.

However, the plot thickened. Nishio's case came to court. In the trial, a Nikko official, Sakamatsu, testified that his company had secretly given Nishio about 20 million yen ($200,000) over the past five years, starting in 1973. Reportedly, Nishio used most of this money for drinking and entertainment in the nightclubs and cabarets of Beppu, a town up the coast – exactly the "wining, womanizing, and bribing" he had mentioned in his poster.

Sakamoto testified that the Nikko company sometimes used this method to quiet down opposition leaders. Other evidence indicated the truth of his statement. An anonymous "former town legislator" passed out a broadside at election time entitled "Nikko's Abusiveness, Saganoseki's Shame" (*Nikko no Bogen, Seki no Chibu*) in the late 1970s that made similar accusations about Nikko's power in town politics. The copper refinery, the broadside complained, had given entertainment, drink, and gifts to almost everyone in the town hall, the Chamber of Commerce, the farmer's union, and "of course the legislators."

Such largesse might seem innocuous, a part of Japanese social custom.[2] But it served a political purpose. It generated a bond of loyalty and obligation to Nikko. At the same time, receiving such services left a union leader or a prefectural official vulnerable. If Nikko exposed him, it would damage his credibility. This would make him made all the more controllable.

Did Nikko really bribe Nishio? Or was the accusation just an attempt to tarnish Nishio's reputation? There are arguments on both sides. Nikko's testimony may be suspect, but Kozaki activists accepted it. It explained Nishio's puzzling drop in protest activity after 1973. Some Seki fishermen believed it too. One of the few remaining opponents of No. 8 in the Seki union related these suspicions:

> There were a lot of rumors about Nishio; that he was at the Bon Tsurumi and Bambi cabarets in Beppu and paid using the Nikko account. But no proof. This proof then all came out in the court case . . .

On the other hand, some fishing people and the Osaka physics professor refused to believe that Nishio would accept bribes. The accusation, they said, was a trick by the Nikko company. One of Nishio's supporting fishermen said:

> . . . Nikko made that testimony in order to break down Nishio's position, to gradually undercut him. But it's not true. He hardly drinks, and as for his home, he's very poor . . . He probably didn't take any dirty money . . . We know him well because we meet him all the time. When you become a leader, the company's attempts to cut you down get very strong . . . (Interview, Saganoseki, November, 1979).

But the same fisherman admitted that Nishio was no longer willing to lead the opposition, and that without him, a mass movement was impossible. "You need a good leader, and without Nishio, it won't occur . . ." (Interview, Saganoseki, November, 1979). By 1977, the fishermen's union became so "normalized," in fact, that both Nishio and Kataura, the attacker and the attacked, sat on the union's board of directors.

Nikko union officials provided a third, even more cynical interpretation of the reason Nishio had slashed president Kataura's arm. Nikko had paid bribe money to Nishio, they admitted. But not as a result of Nikko's initiative. Nikko had not done it to get rid of Nishio. On the contrary, they said, Nishio had used his position as anti-Nikko movement leader to extort the money from Nikko (Interview, Saganoseki, November, 1979). In either case, if Nishio had been getting

---

2. Japanese officials used the same terms to explain gifts to U.S. government officials.

bribes from Nikko, if he had sold out so completely, why would he risk it all by samurai heroics?

A member of the Kozaki movement explained the contorted logic behind Nishio's attack. Her explanation shocked me. Nishio had attacked Kataura with the sword, she said, not because Nishio was mad about Kataura's secret landfill agreement with Nikko. The real reason was that Nikko had stopped paying bribes to Nishio. The Nikko official who had been paying Nishio had been transferred to another part of Japan. The Nikko official who replaced him felt that since Nishio hadn't led any protests for four years, Nishio no longer posed a threat to Nikko. So why pay him off? Instead, the new Nikko official shifted the bribery to where he thought it would help the company more – to Kataura, the Seki Union president. Nishio's personal loss of the bribery and its seductive pleasures, the Kozaki movement member explained, not the secret sludge agreement, stirred his anger and revenge (Interview, Oita City, October 1979).

Why then, I asked, did Nishio call in the physics professor from Osaka and carry out a sludge pollution survey at his own expense? To me, it seemed that if Nishio had sold out, he would hardly continue this kind of activism. My question revealed my own naiveté. The movement member's answer shocked me again.

Because, she told me, this activism put Nishio back in the running as a real threat to Nikko. He carried out the survey to show them that he was still dangerous. He hoped, as a result, that Nikko would start paying him the bribes again. He used the naive physics professor to achieve this secret end. Later, I interviewed the professor in his Osaka office. He vehemently denied that Nishio would have used him in such a manner.

I interviewed a number of other people about Nishio's fall. Most of them believed that Nishio had accepted the bribery. The top leader of the Sohyo leftist unions in Oita, for instance, who had regularly cooperated with the Seki anti-No. 8 movements, thought that Nikko's court testimony was accurate:

Nikko's testimony in court about him is no doubt true . . . Nikko would have no reason to lie about that . . . because, by the time of the court case, Nishio was no longer a power they had to fear . . . What Nikko, what big industry and the bureaucracy fear, are mass movements, not individuals . . .

The labor leader agreed with the theory that Nishio had attacked Kataura because of the loss of the bribery, not because of the secret sludge agreement:

. . . the money (to Nishio) had been cut off. It was going to Kataura, the new president . . . So to build up his public image as a strong . . . enemy of Nikko, he conducted the survey and cut the arm of Kataura . . . (Interview, Oita City, 1980).

These Byzantine contortions of strategy once again reveal the mirrored maze of illusions that constitutes power. As in the tale of Rashomon, perceptions and beliefs floated and changed. Like expert fencers, the actors thrust and parried, feinted and dodged, each seeking an opening. Their goals were varied, and shifted over time. Perhaps none of them could pin down the whole reality.

The cut to union president Kataura's arm was severe, and took nineteen months to fully heal. On March 30, 1982, the Oita District Court sentenced Nishio, as the newspaper put it, to the "warm" (light) sentence of three years of hard labor with a stay of five years. The court statement recognized that Nishio's sword attack, while inexcusable, was not done simply out of personal anger, but under the rationale of defending the harbor (OGN March 31, 1982). However, said the newspaper article, the defense did not produce sufficient evidence to prove that Kataura had been bribed by Nikko or had cooperated in the reduction of the harbor dredging area. Therefore, while the court did not see the attack as motivated by a loss of patronage by Nishio, neither did the court make a judgment about the factual correctness of Nishio's stated rationale. This left the underlying reality ambiguous.

Broken icon

Whether the stories about Nishio's acceptance of bribes from Nikko were true or not, many people believed them. In these matters, perception counts. As the famous sociological dictum notes, "Situations that are defined as real are real in their consequences" (Thomas, 1966, p. 301). One fisherman related their feelings of betrayal:

. . . Now, there is a lot of reaction against Nishio. Everyone feels stabbed in the back. Everyone had helped him. He got rice from Kozaki and so forth.

The stories, the fisherman said, demoralized and embittered the small group who still adamantly opposed No. 8:

Many people were disappointed by Nishio and stopped doing the resistance. Nishio was sucked in by the company. So [the people] felt fooled and felt that the citizen's movement was foolish. They didn't get any money, so if their leader did, they felt like idiots. Nishio is a clever actor. He's good at fooling people (Interview, Saganoseki, November, 1979).

But, the fisherman concluded, this always happens to movement leaders. The elites always destroy them.

When you make a citizens' movement, the leaders are always seduced . . .

The severe impact of Nishio's fall demonstrates the relatively great importance of the trusted leader in Japanese social organization of all sorts, including protest movements. The leader's status is an essential element of what Nakane calls the vertical society (Nakane, 1970). The rare leader who can stand firm against the tide of seduction can hold the movement intact. When the leader crumbles, no new leader arises. The movement crumbles too. Other types of pressure on the movement – institutional manipulation, countermovements, loss of some members – did not damage the movement nearly as badly. But public corruption of the leader, even though he had already shown signs of decay, devastated the movement. That is why, as the fisher noted, leaders are the key target of the Triple Control Machine.

The stories about Nishio splintered the Seki Union into three factions: a small group clustered around Town Council legislator Hirano (JCP) that continued to oppose No. 8 and cooperated with the Kozaki League; a "conditional opposition" group clustered around Nishio that denied his corruption and worked to raise the amount of compensation from the Prefectural Government in return for supporting No. 8; and the original conservative faction that supported the returned union president Kawamura and gave more unconditional support for No. 8. This shifted the majority of union members into support for No. 8.

The pressures on Nishio and his Common Will Group indicate cooperation between the three elites at the top of the Triple Control structure: prefectural officials, LDP politicians, and business leaders. A top union leader, using a baseball metaphor, said this was an elite combination play on Nishio. Working together, the elites had tagged him out. Government officials are good at that, the union leader said:

One of the necessary abilities of a good bureaucrat is to be able to know a person (*hito o shiru koto*).

By that, he meant a good bureaucrat knows how to destroy the political effectiveness of an oppositional leader through soft social control. The elites know a leader's weaknesses and strike at them. They use this strategy, the union leader said, to destroy mass movements:

The purpose of removing a leader is not just to nullify or deactivate that one person; it is to create confusion and loss of heart among all the members of the movement . . . Leaders are subject to that . . .

The elite team had scored a number of times: foiling the recall of the union president, gnawing away at members of the Common Will Group, tagging Nishio out. That ended his role in the game. Ironically, Nishio may have been all too willing to cooperate in his own destruction as a leader, for a price. Soft social control returned the Seki Fishing Union to normality. The abnormality had been that certain fishermen had dared to stand up and demand basic rights: to a livelihood, a clean environment, and democratic union management. Normalization meant the restoration of elite paternalistic control, pushing ordinary members back down to the status of dependent, caged impotence.

Conclusions

The events recounted in this chapter show the highly politicized nature of the policy implementation process. Formal law plays a secondary and superficial role in this process. Informal connections pull the real strings of power. The consensus achieved in both the Seki Town Council and the Seki Fishing Union did not reflect a genuine concord of will. Prefectural elites produced a formal appearance of consensus by controlling the leadership of existing supposedly representative town institutions: the legislature and the union. They also spurred the mobilization of the Baba countermovement as a foil for the protest movements. When the Baba countermovement mobilized, its leaders, holding higher status within the hamlet, smothered other sources of potential dissent.

In addition, prefectural elites may have corrupted the leader of the protest movement within the Seki Fishing Union, leading to the early demise of protest. Not much research has been done on movement leadership, but I believe that the fall of a leader would have heavier consequences for movements in Japan than in the United States or Europe. In Japan, organizational form and member motivation focus strongly on a concrete personal leader, the removal of whom ushers in group chaos (Nakane, 1970). In the United States, organizational leadership is defined more as an abstract role. It can be filled with interchangeable persons, rather than a specific individual (Parsons, 1954). Furthermore, in the West, movement joiners are motivated to a great degree by internalized beliefs, values, ideologies, and identities (Tarrow, 1992, p. 187). In both the United States and Europe, personal loyalties and friendships play an important part in movement recruitment also (Friedman & McAdam, 1992). But such social relations, I submit, are even more central to mobilization in (at least rural) Japan. Given these differences, in the United States or Europe the corruption of a leader would have less devastating consequences for a movement. Individual members would more easily be able to regroup and continue. In Seki, though, the fall of Nishio caused the Common Will Group and organized resistance to disintegrate. In Kozaki, where Inao held firm, the movement continued.

These findings strongly support the critical view noted at the beginning of this chapter that the Prefectural Government and LDP played on the popular cultural ideal of consensus to prop up their tottering dominance. As the thesis of symbolic politics recognizes, such behavior is not at all unique to Japan (Edelman, 1977). Politicians regularly use the patriotic and popular symbols of their culture, ranging from the flag to dressing in working-class clothing, to attract popular support. The LDP and Prefectural Government also distributed large amounts of patronage to buy what support they could.

The cultural structural school argues that bureaucratic and LDP political dominance resulted from the traditional norms of deference encoded in Japanese culture (Pharr, 1990). The social institutional school, on the other hand, argues that government bureaucracy itself, by its very nature, tries to assert its dominance over the ordinary lives of residents and communities (Dahrendorf, 1959; Habermas, 1987). On the other hand, elite dominance could result from the imbalance of resources among social groups (Alford & Friedland, 1985, p. 260). As a result, some scholars argue, the political role of citizens in ACID societies is necessarily "participation without power" (Alford & Friedland, 1985, p. 260; Alford & Friedland, 1975).

The counterexample of Mayor Sato's success in making the city plan with full citizen participation demonstrated that neither culture nor bureaucracy posed insurmountable obstacles to a fuller democracy. Rather, the main causal force behind the manipulated consensus that appeared in Seki was the class-coalitional interests of the dominant political party in prefectural and town elected offices. However, these interests expressed themselves and struggled for dominance through normatively, institutionally defined "vocabularies" of collective action and organization (Zucker, 1991, p. 83). These norms took the form of status rankings built into chains of social control in the Triple Control Machine.

In Japan, the Triple Control Machine and the legal system, much more than a deferential political culture, hinder the formation of dissent. Under these conditions, a public appearance of consensus may cover a host of dissenting voices. Rather than indicating real concord arrived at through open discussion, "consensus" in this case meant the exclusion of contested meanings from the political arena (Brulle, 1994, p. 107; Schattschneider, 1975). Since this was accomplished by local Triple Control Machines, I refer to this means of social control as *social hegemony* rather than cultural hegemony (Lukes, 1974).

9

Pyrrhic victories

The new pollution regime

New regulations

While Oita's pro-growth coalition met the formal standards of conditions one and two fairly quickly, it had a harder time with condition three: environmental assessment. Oita's environmental pollution worsened in the early 1970s. The number of telemetering sites in Oita not meeting national sulfur dioxide standards of 0.020 ppm peaked in 1973 (four out of eighteen sites). Sulfur dioxide air pollution in Oita City reached its peak in 1974 (0.030 ppm at ground level). In January 1974, the Oita Doctors' Association announced that air pollution-related diseases in Oita had tripled or quadrupled, in some cases, over the past ten years. Under these circumstances, if an assessment found that a new project would contribute much pollution at all to the area, the public, the pro-growth elites worried, might deem it unacceptable.

To make matters worse for Oita's pro-growth coalition, in 1974, the national pollution regime got tougher. The Diet passed a set of tougher measures to reinforce the 1970 anti-pollution laws. The EA announced that all prefectures would have to meet standards of atmospheric sulfur dioxide concentration of 0.023 ppm or below (by March 1978). The EA increased its pressure on Oita and other prefectures to meet those limits. Targeting Oita, the EA stated publicly that the Oita government's "development first" attitude had prevented a solution to Misa/Iejima's pollution. This statement implied that Oita had not strictly implemented the new anti-pollution laws. Since the EA still held the ax of NIC Phase Two plan disapproval over the governor's head, this was a worrisome criticism. To build industrial plants on Landfills No. 6 and 7, prefectural officials thought, they would have to rid Oita of its polluted image.

In an attempt to reduce criticism, the Oita government installed electronic devices to measure atmospheric sulfur dioxide levels around the NIC area. It also reached new, tougher anti-pollution agreements with the local factories. The agreement with Sumitomo, for instance, directed the company to construct tall smokestacks that would disperse its smoke widely, rather than letting it fall on nearby Misa and Iejima. (The newer NIC factories had been constructed with tall smokestacks for just that purpose.)

Moving a village

These measures did not come quickly enough, though, to ease the brunt of pollution on the Misa/Iejima area. In early 1974, the Iejima people took an unprecedented step. Despite deep love for their ancestral village, they voted to move en masse to a safer, healthier location. They petitioned the Prefectural Government to subsidize a group village move (*shudan iten*). This petition put Governor Taki in a quandary. He did not want to ignore their plight. Neither did he want to admit that such severe pollution existed in Iejima that the village had to be moved. Moving the village to escape pollution would have forever framed Oita as a polluted prefecture.

EA scrutiny made the Misa/Iejima complaints inconvenient, however, and the Oita officials wanted to quiet them down. In September 1974, the Oita Prefectural and City Governments signed an agreement with the ku-heads of Iejima: The governments would buy up all the land and houses of the village. They would move the whole community to a inland site behind Oita City, which the government would provide. All this would be paid for with public funds.[1]

The agreement quieted protest in Iejima and allowed the Oita growth coalition to move ahead with its plans. The agreement amounted to a *de facto* admission of the severity of Iejima's pollution, but the government still refused to publicly acknowledge that. Rather, in its public pronouncements, the Prefectural Government attributed the agreement to "local unrest."

The Prefectural Government's offer to pay for the group move seemed generous, but it did not make financial sense. The finance department within the Prefectural Government suggested that the Governor instead use the new national environmental "polluter-pays" laws to force the polluting factories to pay for the move (see Chapter 5). If that had happened Sumitomo and other nearby polluting factories would have had to pay for moving Iejima and the other villages too.

Why did the Prefectural Government reject this public money-saving solution? A prefectural official involved in the issue explained the government's reasons. Quite frankly, he said, when Iejima first complained in 1973, prefec-

---

1. This information came from the Oita Prefectural publication, "The State of the NIC" as cited in Fujii & Takaura, 1974, p. 22.

tural officials believed them. They knew that pollution-induced illness existed in Iejima. The Governor, however, continued his public denials of the problem to save face for Sumitomo and the other polluting factories. He wanted to help the factories avoid both the stigma of the polluter label and the expense of paying for the village move.

Why, I asked, did the Governor want to serve business interests so much? "Because," the official replied,

. . . he has a sense of balance about actions necessary for his political survival; how to look best in any particular situation . . .

Why, I probed further, would applying the polluter-pays law to the factories have endangered the Governor's political survival? The official replied:

The companies around Iejima have connections with the Federation of Economic Organizations and can bring a lot of political pressure to bear . . . (Interview).

As a result, the official explained, the Governor decided the Prefectural Government should pay the moving cost out of public funds.

In other words, the investment priorities of Tokyo-based big business, given their potential for backup from the LDP when prodded by the corporatist peak association of all big business (the FEO), dictated the political choices of elected officials. Profit triumphed over public health. The big (and small) companies in Oita's NIC wanted to invest as little as possible in pollution control. The thinness of the "green belt" in front of the NIC area (except for that of the Showa plant) demonstrated that reluctance. Financing the group move of a polluted hamlet would set an even more expensive precedent – one with national implications.

Traced to its roots in this way, the Iejima group move issue revealed the power that big business exercised over the Prefectural Government. This power did not come about, as instrumentalists contend, because business representatives directly staffed the Prefectural Government (Miliband, 1969). Nor was it mainly because government wanted to preserve the tax revenues and jobs provided by business, as the structuralists argue (Poulantzas, 1973). Rather, big business power came about because of the thorough corporatist organization of big business as a class, and the electoral dominance of its associated party, the Liberal Democratic party. LDP control over national and local elections forced elected government leaders at all levels, on pain of losing the next election, to serve party goals. LDP control, in turn, depended largely on business campaign contributions. LDP dominance structured the political opportunities faced by the Governor: If Governor Taki did not serve the needs and interests of big business, the LDP could make sure he did not serve for another term.

Under the rationale that Iejima hamlet was going to be moved, the Prefectural Government rapidly built a giant elevated highway along its southern flank. This highway added the noise and fumes of cars and heavy trucks to the already polluted ambiance. Encroaching industrial urbanization began to dissolve Misa and Iejima as integral hamlets. For the people of Misa/Iejima, hopes for the fruits of progress, so vivid in the springtime of industrial growth, wilted and withered. Along with environmental decay, they mourned the decay of their community.[2]

Reducing pollution

In other regards, however, the EA's new regulatory regime brought good environmental results to Oita. Over the next few years, the new stricter enforcement regime caused considerable reduction in Oita's worst, most obvious air and water pollutants. Spurred by this new regime, the Prefectural Government required all the NIC refineries to change over to low-sulfur fuels. Following these directives, the NIC refineries gradually reduced the sulfur content of their fuels from 1.88 percent in 1970 to 0.82 percent in 1977. Though these fuels were more expensive, their use reduced the amount of sulfur dioxide and other air pollutants coming from the refineries. In addition, the 1973 increase in oil prices by OPEC brought on a recession in Japan that slowed down industrial activity generally. This reduced the total use of fuel, further reducing air pollution. By 1977, ground level sulfur dioxide air pollution in Oita City averaged 0.013 ppm, and all sixteen telemetering stations met the national standards.

Water pollution followed a similar course. Industries had been dumping chemical wastes into the rivers and bays. These wastes absorbed the oxygen in the water, leaving less available for aquatic life. They also provided nutrients for algae, which led to massive blooms of certain species of red algae, known as red tides, that killed off other forms of aquatic life. The number of red tides in Beppu Bay peaked in 1975 (twenty incidents) and then declined (1977 = three incidents).

The new laws dealt mainly with the most obvious and worst industrial sources of air and water pollution. Other air pollutants, such as nitrogen oxide, nitrogen dioxide, oxidants, and particulates, showed little change. Nitrogen oxide (or nitrogen dioxide) is very harmful to health and is a source of photochemical smog. It declined little because much of it came from car and truck exhaust, which was harder to control. Only a few heavy metals, although no doubt of latent danger, were covered by national standards.

2. Sociologists have stressed the importance of a stable community as an important contributor to the quality of life. See Erikson, 1976.

As the EA's measures improved environmental quality around the nation, however, they reduced citizen activism. People felt less threatened by environmental pollution, and so did not join protest movements. In addition, the 1973 recession caused people to worry more about the health of the national economy than about environmental and physical health. This change of popular motivations also reduced the number and intensity of environmental protest movements. The wave of pollution protest declined rapidly from its peak in the early 1970s (Figure 3.3). With the decline in popular pressure, the national and Prefectural Government anti-pollution regulatory regime, as predicted by decay theory (Sabatier, 1975, p. 303–304), went into parallel decline.

The national context

The wave ebbs

Opposition ebbed in the Seki Union along with the decline of the national wave of environmental protest in the mid-1970s. The wave of protest left only a faint high-water mark on the beach of national politics. Unlike their U.S. and European counterparts, the Japanese environmental movements had not been able to establish powerful national interest groups. With the decline in local movements, the numbers of progressive governors and mayors also went down rapidly (Figure 3.3). By the 1990s, despite the considerable successes of their grassroots movements, more Japanese than Americans, English or Germans ended up feeling that citizens' movements had little capacity to solve environmental problems. Furthermore, far fewer Japanese than other ACID citizens reported having joined environmental groups (Figure 9.1).

In the United States and Europe, in contrast to Japan, grassroots enthusiasm continued (Dunlap, 1992) and local environmental movements established national environmental interest groups of several types. Opposition from the state and other elites did not dampen the U.S. or European movements. "By threatening environmentalists' hard-won 'interest group' status," scholars argue, "the Reagan administration rekindled the movement's zeal and activism" (Dunlap & Mertig, 1992, p. 4). The U.S. movement gained support and membership and intensified its pressure on government, preventing the destruction of environmental laws. The Sierra Club, National Wildlife Federation, and other lobbying organizations built huge national memberships in the hundreds of thousands (combined total over three million members in 1990). Direct action groups also built huge memberships (Greenpeace USA alone claimed over two million members in 1990). These huge constituencies provided the organizations with the resources and clout needed to conduct effective lobbying and direct action

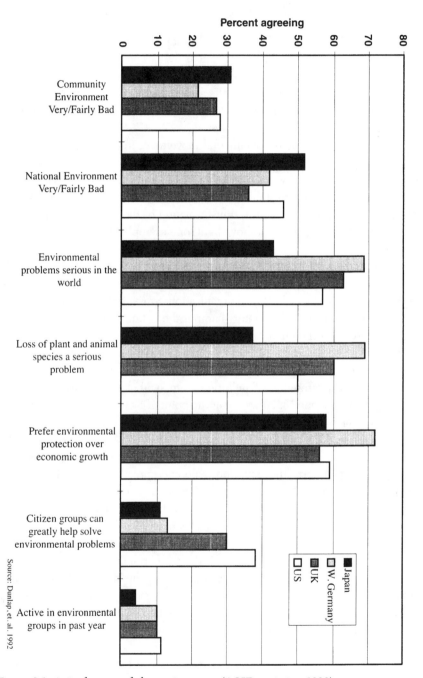

Figure 9.1: Attitudes toward the environment (ACID societies, 1992)

Source: Dunlap, et. al. 1992

(Mitchell et al., 1992). In Germany and other countries, too, the movement established its own political parties (such as the Greens).[3] These organizations became permanent fixtures of the national political scene. They carried out important research, aroused the public against bad legislation, stimulated new legislation, initiated suits against polluters, and became an important electoral bloc (Cable & Cable, 1995; Mitchell et al., 1992).

The national Japanese environmental movement, in contrast, declined to a low but constant level of sporadic local protests (see Figure 3.3) without much of a national political presence or effectiveness. Why did the Japanese environmental movements fail to establish a stronger permanent political presence? In the U.S., according to Szasz, the transformation of the toxic waste movement from NIMBYism to a national movement, one example of such establishment, depended on five factors: spread of publicity about environmental problems, issue formation and expansion (to encompass many types of toxic pollutants), the spread of a populist (anti-business) ideology, networking among activists, and the creation of formal national organization (Szasz, 1994: 69–83). Did a lack of one or more of these five factors hamper the national institutionalization of the Japanese environmental protest movement?

Pollution received plenty of publicity in Japan through the national news media, so that was not a significant difference. This publicity stimulated a widespread local reframing of pollution from symbol of progress to bane of illness (Chapters 4 and 5). However, at the point of factor two, issue expansion, the process slowed. The general spread of a movement depends in part on its ability to reframe local problems into national issues that grab the attention of a wide range of people (Snow & Benford, 1992). In Japan, some activists tried very hard to generalize the pollution issue and spread a popular ideology of environmentalism.[4] Likewise, among activists, an anti-business ideology was much in evidence (Chapter 5). However, the Japanese public, in light of the survey evidence of their degree of national concern cited above, never adopted environmentalism very earnestly. I do not have evidence on the spread of anti-business ideology at the national level, though certainly it was strong in left-union-affiliated families. As for factor four, during the 1960s and 1970s, Japanese activists energetically networked with others by attending regional or national environmental protest conferences (Chapter 5). In addition, several national magazines, such as *Ampo* or *Chiiki Toso* (Regional Struggles), circu-

---

3. A great deal of research and reporting has gone into the study of green politics. See Bahro, 1986; Capra & Spretnak, 1984; Lowe & Goyder, 1983; Ophuls, 1977; Paehlke, 1990; Porritt, 1985; Rensenbrink, 1992; Switzer, 1994; Tokar, 1992; Yearly, 1991.

4. Professor Ui Jun and his regular Jishu Koza forum on pollution at Tokyo University was at the forefront of this effort.

lated news about the movements. These efforts, as the above schema would predict, led to the founding of several national environmental groups that hoped and intended to mature into major political presences, like their U.S. cousins. However, this maturation did not occur. It was not that environmental groups were so new. Several national environmental groups had started even earlier in Japan. The largest, the Wild Bird Society (*Yacho no Kai,* est. 1934), which advocated nature conservancy, had about 47,000 members nationwide by 1990. The Nature Conservation Society (est. 1951) had about 25,000 members (Gordon, 1995). These were not large organizations by U.S. standards. These groups did not use the unruly tactics of protest and lawsuit, as the environmental movements of the 1960s and 1970s did. Environmental groups seeking deeper transformations and using more unruly tactics, as well as those concerned with international environmental causes – such as JATAN, the Japan Tropical Forest Action Network – found it impossible to attain even that limited size and presence. The few national-level environmental protest groups, whether of domestic or international origin, remained poor and powerless, unable to attract a sizable number of dues-paying members (Greenpeace Japan had 2,000 members, compared to Greenpeace USA with 2,300,000) (Gordon, 1995; Mitchell et al., 1992). All of the Japanese groups were tiny compared with U.S. national interest groups such as the National Wildlife Federation (975,000 members) or the National Audubon Society (600,000 members) (Mitchell et al., 1992).

Accordingly, even though the Japanese environmental movement went through all the stages identified by Szasz as necessary for establishing a national presence, they did not in any effective sense do so. Why? Was it due to material political-economic, social institutional, or cultural factors, or to some combination thereof? In the material dimension, the palpable environmental threat declined. Japan's pollution miracle – the rapid reduction of obvious and concentrated forms of air and water pollution – stole the thunder of many local antipollution movements. The environmental problems that continued or arose anew in the 1980s and 1990s – nuclear power plants and the rampant destruction of natural areas to make ski resorts and golf courses – generated their own forms of protest that attracted a small but vociferous national following. These problems did not, though, generate a national wave of protest. Nuclear power plants and ski/golf resorts were few in number and had less immediately obvious ill-effects on health and livelihood than the heavy industrial projects of the 1960s. Therefore, they did not call forth protest in many local communities around the country. The localized and hidden quality of the objective threat, confined to a smaller number of sites, spurred a continuing but low level of protest.

Szasz's factors emphasize attitudinal changes, which partake of the subjective world I label "culture." Cultural structures also may have contributed to the decline of the Japanese wave of pollution protest. If, as some scholars argue, Japan has a spectator rather than participant political culture (Chapter 1), this sort of culture might encourage local people to blindly defer to elites in matters of policy-making. The findings in this book tend to refute that argument. Uncritical deference may characterize some local people's attitudes on matters of national policy, but not nearly as much, it appears, on matters of local policy that affected residents directly. When Japanese pollution became local, appearing in people's own neighborhoods, large numbers became concerned. Their critical attitudes toward government policy show that people were not deferring policy matters entirely to the elite. When policy impinged on them, as pollution from often government-sponsored industrial projects did, they recognized the source of their problems and criticized it. Measurements of attitudes in 1992, for instance, show that, regarding the local environment, Japanese preferences closely resembled those of Americans and English – they all preferred better environmental protection over more economic growth (Figure 9.1). More Japanese than Americans, English, or Germans thought that the environment of their own local community was very or fairly bad (Figure 9.1). This difference no doubt partly reflected the objective reality of the situation. But it probably also reflected the localism of Japanese culture. These national survey findings parallel Mayor Sato's discoveries about the preferences of his electorate in Oita, when he used citizen participation to make the city plan (Chapter 7). The findings are also congruent with the results of a 1979 survey on environmental attitudes conducted by the NHK Oita Broadcasting Station (Table 9.1 below), which found that only 5.3 percent of the population wanted to "leave it to the experts." A study comparing Shizuoka City in Japan and Spokane in Washington state found that, while residents of both cities had much stronger support for preservationist, as opposed to developmentalist, policies, the Japanese city was much stronger in this regard than the U.S. one (Shizuoku 36 percent vs. 7 percent; Spokane 28 percent vs. 11 percent) (Pierce, Lovrich, Tsuruta & Abe, 1989, p. 132). Evidently, the preference for a clean and healthy local environment is very widespread, and perhaps virtually universal.[5] The subsequent Japanese movements exhibited a strong NIMBY (not-in-my-backyard) behavior toward pollution problems (Freudenberg & Steinsapir, 1992).

Once they solved their own community's pollution problem, though, most participants showed little interest in national pollution problems. Very few locals adopted pollution and the environment as an ideological cause awaiting

---

5. The Health of the Planet survey has revealed that even publics in developing countries, contrary to expectations based on ideas about their "hierarchy of needs," also often give priority to environmental protection over economic growth. See Dunlap, Gallup & Gallup, 1992.

national or global solution. Such a decline in interest is no doubt observable in all ACID societies. The question, though, is whether that decline was noticeably stronger in Japan, and if so, whether it contributed to the decline and weak residue of Japan's wave of environmental protest. Evidence suggests it was. Far fewer Japanese than Americans, English, or Germans saw world environmental problems as serious (Figure 9.1). If we assume that the respondents had roughly the same facts available (though this may not necessarily be so), their difference in perception (of the same situation) indicates the effect of culture telling people what realities to prioritize. The higher concern of Japanese for their own community, combined with a spectator political culture, could have contributed to the relatively high degree of NIMBYism (localism) in Japanese protest movements in the 1960s and 1970s. In other words, culture probably matters.

However, other information cautions us from attributing Japanese movement NIMBYism entirely to Japanese political culture. For one thing, NIMBYism itself was not at all unique to Japan. It typified many U.S. movements (Cable & Cable, 1995, p. 107). To some extent, it hampered the establishment of the environmental movement as a national interest group in all ACID societies. Despite similar tendencies to focus on parochial concerns though, in the United States and Europe, local leaders of originally NIMBY movements (such as Lois Gibbs, leader of the Love Canal movement) went on to establish national movements (such as the Citizens' Clearinghouse for toxic waste information) (Cable & Cable, 1995, p. 108).

By the 1970s, local Japanese attitudes gave environmental protection priority over economic growth and showed higher concern about their local *and* national environments (Figure 9.1). Lack of concern for international problems may have reduced public willingness to support internationalist environmental organizations. But the high public concern for the national environment, compared to other ACID societies, should have spurred support for national environmental organizations concerned about domestic problems (Figure 9.1). Why then did the new start-up national organizations in Japan in the 1960s and 1970s not experience a flood of new members? If not due to a lack of popular concern, the reluctance to join a "cause" movement may have stemmed from other cultural factors: a long history and self-protective habit among citizens of not raising one's individual voice against the government, the lack of a tradition of civic voluntarism (except as expected and demanded by local governance associations, as noted in Chapter 6), and a deep distrust of the integrity of such groups.

Looking beyond culture, though, we must consider the impact of social institutional and political-economic factors. The political opportunity structure – not noted among Szasz's analytical elements (perhaps because not present in the United States) – also hindered the Japanese national environmental movement. The Triple Control Machine had roots in the combined LDP-big business manipulation of national policy (Chapter 2). It found expression, though, through local vertical social hierarchies (Chapter 6). This machine constantly "gnawed away" at protest movements, thereby shrinking the organized local support national interest groups, further hampering their significant institutionalization. Previous chapters noted how soft social control – the Triple Control Machine – suppressed local movements in Oita. Such examples were repeated throughout Japan, contributing to the destruction of many protest movements. In other ACID societies, such pressures were much weaker if present at all.

Another version of soft social control worked at the national level. The government conducted a "backstage" campaign to weaken public interest groups. Among the elements of that campaign, the government released minimal information about pollution to the public (there is no U.S.-style Freedom of Information Act in Japan). It refused to grant tax-exempt status to public interest groups such as environmental organizations (thus limiting their donors). Furthermore, in order to incorporate and apply for tax-exempt status, a public interest group had to affiliate with a ministry. One condition of such affiliation was usually the employment of a retired government official on the organization's board of directors, usually as managing director. This was common practice in industrial associations (*gyokai*) for instance (Interview, 1990). This placement gave the retired official, and through him the ministry, a great deal of influence over the organization's operations. Furthermore, the EA and other ministries set up a large number of ersatz environmental "public interest groups," called "third sector" groups in Japan, sponsored by corporations and led by retired ministerial officials. These populated the public sphere, giving the illusion of vigorous grassroots representation where it did not in fact exist. Corporate philanthropies also behaved differently from their counterparts in the U.S. They largely confined their largesse to supporting these joint government-business groups.

I discovered these social-institutional and political-economic structural barriers when on research in Japan during the late 1980s. I spent some time working with Japanese and foreign environmentalists trying to set up a national environmental organization. As a form of action research (Thorne, 1988), this experience opened my eyes to the many structural barriers faced by Japanese NGOs. These themes deserve further research. Building on and reinforcing cultural barriers, the dominant elites used vertical institutions of social control as channels for social and material patronage to softly reduce and suppress dissent.

The Environmental Agency declines

With the decline in the political threat from grassroots movements and progressive local governments, the LDP felt less impelled to provide effective environmental protection. As a result, the LDP appointed more conservative cabinet ministers to environmental posts, and paid less heed to the policy recommendations of environmentally protective ministries and agencies. This led to a decline in the Environmental Agency's power. The LDP, big business, and the ministries started to head back to business as usual – fostering the economy.[6]

In 1977, the LDP appointed a new, more conservative cabinet minister (Director General) of the EA, conservative nationalist Ishihara Shintaro. He urged a weakening of the 1970 anti-pollution laws, which, he said, had been enacted during a "witch hunt against industrialists" (*Japan Times*, Oct. 23, 1977, as cited in Gresser et al., 1981, p. 423). As a result, the EA relaxed some pollution standards, allowing the legal limits for atmospheric NO_x levels to increase.

Both the LDP and the Reagan administrations appointed conservative agency leaders who attempted to stymie environmental protections and free businesses from their yoke (Landy et al., 1990, pp. 246–248). However, the Reagan administration faced a Democratic party-controlled House of Representatives, an array of powerful national environmental groups, and a public with a strong desire to defend the environment. These factors thwarted most of the administration's attempts to gut environmental regulations. The LDP faced no such formidable obstacles. As an agency rather than a ministry, the EA did not have the usual power of the entrenched Japanese ministerial bureaucracy. It did not have its own internal career lines, but borrowed officials from other ministries. It was quite vulnerable to LDP and MITI opposition.

The fate of the EA's repeated attempts to create an environmental impact assessment bill illustrated this new power alignment. In discussions among ministries, the EA repeatedly proposed that the EIA be made a national legal requirement, at least for government-related industrial projects. MITI repeatedly squelched the proposal. MITI thought an EIA requirement would give local citizens too much power to delay or deny the approval process. This would hamper MITI's freedom of industrial location planning.[7]

---

6. This again exemplifies the process of regulatory decay, as put forth by Sabatier, 1975, pp. 303–304.

7. A Japanese sociologist doing research on opposition to nuclear power in the U.S. was surprised at how the citizens of Sacramento were able to stop a government-sponsored nuclear plant with a referendum. He said this would never work in Japan. The central bureaucrats, in conjunction with a conservative local legislature, would reject any such motion (Hasegawa, unpublished).

Descriptions of this process have a Rashomon-like diversity. A knowledgeable reporter, who specialized in environmental matters for a major newspaper, described his view of how MITI squelched the EA's EIA proposal (Interview 516, 1979). When the EA showed its first two drafts to other ministries, MITI rejected them. MITI was under particular pressure from electric power companies to reject the EIA. MITI feared that local citizens would use the assessment requirements to slow down or stop generator plant construction. The EA knew that MITI, through its LDP connections, had the power to block any formal ratification, so it gave up at that stage.

For the third draft, the EA already knew it could not convince MITI, so it went directly to the LDP Pollution Countermeasures Committee. The members of this committee included a number of politicians who were genuinely concerned about environmental problems. The EA appealed for their support for the EIA bill. It looked as if the committee would approve the EIA proposal, but then it suddenly rejected the proposal. MITI had told the LDP Commerce and Industry Section, with which it had close connections, to pressure the LDP Environmental Section to reject the draft. In the reporter's view, MITI did not want to empower local governments and citizens to block state-led industrial growth.

An official of the EA, though, described the quashing process differently. Several times, he said, MITI and other ministries approved the EA's EIA bill. Once approved by the career bureaucrats who were the real heads of the ministries, the draft of the EIA bill went to the LDP Pollution Countermeasures Committee for approval. Several times, this committee too approved the EIA draft bill. But from that committee, the draft went to the central body of the LDP Policy Affairs Research Council, the policy-making core of the party (Richardson & Flanagan, 1984, p. 92). In that forum, the LDP economic policy committee repeatedly opposed the EIA bill, forcing its rejection. Once the draft was rejected by the LDP, MITI and the other economic ministries also rejected it.

In the first account, the rejection lay with MITI, a state ministry. In the second account, the rejection lay with the section within the LDP that represented business interests. Which version is correct has important implications for our model of Japanese politics. MITI's earlier action to reduce air pollution despite industry objections, and its attempt to reduce the number of NIC sites to two (both recounted in Chapter 4), indicate that the latter story is more likely the correct one. If so, evidently, not only the state but the LDP too is divided into internal factions that take opposing stances on policy issues. The crucial power of business over the state, in that case, conforms to neither the instrumentalist nor the structuralist class theories (Chapter 1), but to a party-mediated process. In this case, different policy-specialized groups (*zoku*) within the LDP take opposing stances on issues (Inoguchi & Iwai, 1987).

In this process, the negotiation process proceeded entirely by informal "back-stage" negotiation (*nemawashi*), not in public view. Operating strictly by the book, the EA could have taken its proposal to one of the opposition parties, and then watched it fail in the Diet. The EA would never do this, however, not only because it would not want to lose face, but also because the EA is staffed by officials from the full ministries – it follows a "gentlemen's agreement" to work things out privately. Open conflict would, officials think, reduce the public legitimacy of the government.

These non-decisions or agenda-control tactics prevented the EA from creating an EIA law. The LDP, its business backers, and the economic ministries conferred through informal networks, and decided privately which bills would see the light of day. Together, their relations wove a community of informal policymaking that constituted a Japanese-style corporatism. This pattern of non-decision corporatism allowed only a very weak voice, if any at all, to established labor and consumer groups, and even less to emergent movements.

As a political process, this pattern of policymaking differs sharply from the United States. Certainly, the United States has its share of "smoky back room" deals. But political disagreements foster more public debate, with uncertain outcomes. Both parties and individual members submit bills in Congress and vote on them in the glaring light of publicity. Representatives cross party lines to vote their convictions. Japan, by contrast, institutionalizes a government of non-decisions taken by the Ruling Triad (business-LDP-ministerial corporatism) as its typical and expected operating process.

Making the assessment

In the midst of this declining pollution regime, the events of Oita's Phase Two plans unfolded. In 1976, the national government ordered all NIC prefectures that wanted more funding to submit revised growth plans. The Oita prefectural officials prepared to submit their Phase Two plans. They felt it necessary to include plans for Landfill No. 8 in the plans. To leave No. 8 out might exclude it from future government permissions and aid. However, this posed a problem. Governor Taki had publicly promised not to revive No. 8 until meeting the Three Conditions. By 1976, the officials could only claim fulfillment of conditions one and two. They had hardly begun condition three, the environmental impact assessment (EIA). Trying to avoid trouble, the Prefectural Government buried mention of No. 8 in the appendix of the draft Phase Two plan (Interview, September 1980).

Citizens' movement activists secured a copy of the draft plan before it was submitted to the central government. They took strong exception to the mention of No. 8 in the appendix. Even mentioning No. 8 at this point, they argued, was of questionable legality. Members of the Joint Struggle Council met several times with Oita government officials to voice their complaints. The government made no retraction.

Rebuffed, the Joint Struggle Council sent representatives directly to the EA in Tokyo. The group demanded that the Prefectural Government finish the environmental assessment before it mentioned No. 8 in plans. At the same time, in the Diet, cooperative Oita JSP politicians questioned an EA official on this point. The EA official responded that No. 8 was still suspended, until the Oita government met all Three Conditions, and that the assessment was still unfinished. But the EA did not condemn the mention of No. 8 in the Phase Two plan.

Defining an assessment

At the same time, the Oita government continued its efforts to satisfy condition three. The EA demanded that Oita's EIA perform three tasks. It had to predict pollution from Phase Two, measure existing pollution from Phase One, and determine the effects of both upon community health. Even more annoyingly (to the growth elites), the EA asked the prefecture to allow local residents to participate in the assessment process. In addition, movement leaders wanted a movement-approved scientist to sit on the prefecture-picked board that would evaluate the assessment data. All this ran counter to the norm of government paternalism.

Furthermore, an impact assessment , depending on the results, could force the installation of expensive pollution control equipment or even the cancellation of industrial plans. Many parties had a stake in its outcome: politicians, enforcement agencies, businesses, victim groups, growth boosters, and environmental protection movements.

The EA also had a lot at stake here. It hoped to show other ministries that the scientific measurement of environmental impact could help resolve pollution conflicts. The agency hoped to make an impact assessment mandatory for all big projects.

Oita's pro-growth elites had met conditions one and two by manipulating the town government and the unions. Such soft social control would not work for condition three – the EA was peering too closely over Oita's shoulder. The Prefectural Government had to abide by a certain degree of objectivity.

Government approval of Phase Two

Governor Taki and his officials kept in constant contact with national ministries, businesses, and the LDP over growth and pollution issues. They realized that environmental concerns were cooling off among the national elites. Toward the end of 1976, the EA agreed that the prefecture had made good progress toward improving its environmental conditions. This tacit approval emboldened Governor Taki. He submitted the draft NIC Phase Two plan for approval, including the mention of Landfill No. 8 in the draft, to the Oita NIC Advisory Council. The Oita advisory council passed it and recommended submitting it to the central government. In late 1976, Governor Taki submitted the same NIC Phase Two Plan to the Regional Development Advisory Council, the point of entry for national government approval. Through its Diet representatives, the Oita government applied a great deal of political pressure on the council.

Although local opposition groups had extracted a promise from the EA to reject the plan because the EIA was not yet finished, the EA now had less voice in central policy issues. The EA's support from other Ruling Triad members had dramatically declined.

In March 1977, the Regional Development Advisory Council approved Oita's Phase Two Plan with Landfills No. 6, 7, and 8. The Council accepted Oita Government's argument that unruly grassroots opposition had slowed down the EIA, making approval of the plan more reasonable. The Council agreed that an on-paper assessment would suffice for the time being if, just before actual construction, the Oita government would arrange for actual on-site measurements. The EA did not block this decision. Soon after that, the Prime Minister put the final seal of government approval on Oita's Phase Two Plan.

Breaking a promise

Once the national government had approved NIC Phase Two including No. 8, the Prefectural Government felt less fearful of EA disapproval. Consequently, Oita officials also felt less impelled to keep their promise to move the hamlet of Iejima to a new, unpolluted location. Suddenly, in April 1977, the Prefectural Government publicly announced the cancellation of the Iejima group move plan. Land prices had gone up so much, the government claimed, it could no longer afford to pay for the new site. Furthermore, because of the recession, big companies no longer wanted to buy Iejima's old site, which would have paid for the new land. In addition, the Prefectural Government feared that if it moved

Iejima, it would also have to move the neighboring villages of Misa and Ona-kashima.

Cancellation of the group move angered and fired up the local movements. Leaders in Misa and Iejima worked with the Seki movements to devise a response. To show the falsity of the prefecture's claims that no pollution existed in Misa and Iejima, they decided to counter expertise with expertise. The movement asked Dr. Nagira of Okayama University, an expert in epidemiology whom they trusted, to conduct another survey of Misa's health problems. To counter the unsanitary lifestyle argument, Nagira compared respiratory illness rates in Misa/Iejima with rates in other less polluted but equally dilapidated sections of the city. The results showed that air pollution from the surrounding factories must have caused Misa's high incidence of respiratory diseases.

Movement leaders went to Kyushu University and confronted Dr. Ishinishi, who had conducted the earlier survey for the Prefectural Government. To their surprise, Dr. Ishinishi readily admitted that his survey procedures had serious flaws. He agreed to discuss the results in a public forum in Oita. The movement arranged for a public debate between Drs. Ishinishi and Nagira, the prefectural expert and the movement expert, on August 20, 1978, in Oita City.

Movement leaders invited the Prefectural Government to send an official observer to the debate. The Prefectural Government refused to attend the debate. It stated that no official was free that day. An official in the Prefectural Government's Pollution Countermeasures Bureau told me the real reason for the government's refusal. The Prefectural Government did not feel it was a "cool (*reisei*) debate by specialists," he said. Rather, it felt the debate would be a politicized and emotional scene controlled by the opposition movement (OGN, March 6, 1970).

At the debate, Dr. Ishinishi publicly conceded that his survey methodology was faulty. Moving closer to the movement position, he also agreed that air pollution could be a cause of Misa's ill health (Ministry of Justice, 1977, p. 1764). This strongly vindicated the movements' insistent claims that pollution had caused health problems in Misa/Iejima.

Dr. Ishinishi's retraction of his own survey results put the Prefectural Government in an awkward position. To maintain its claim of no serious pollution, the Prefectural Government had to refute its own expert. The government asserted that Dr. Ishinishi's retraction was not genuine. It had been the result, officials claimed, of emotional criticism from the movement, not reasoned discourse. But newspaper accounts of the debate do not support the prefecture's contention. The newspaper accounts of the debate state that Dr. Ishinishi attributed his retraction to the scientifically well-founded quality of Dr. Nagira's criticism.

Despite its public stance that no pollution existed, the Prefectural Government had been taking measures to reduce pollution, as noted here. These measures had their effect in Misa/Iejima as well. The Prefectural Government's new regulations and agreements had decreased sulfur dioxide air pollution and definitely improved the overall air quality in the area of Misa/Iejima. The leader of the Misa protest movement who had earlier plopped his coughing infant on the governor's desk told me that the child no longer suffered from respiratory illness (Interview 138, 1979).

However, many health-related issues still remained. Some movement activists charged that the NIC industries emitted their dirtiest, most polluting smoke at night, when no one could see it. My own experiences living near the factories in 1979 bore witness to their fears, and to the insidious nature of pollution illnesses (Chapter 4).

Iejima hamlet remained in the shadow of the towering chimneys and the rumbling overpass. From being a bucolic fishing village it had become a neglected lower-class neighborhood. In a final irony, the Prefectural Government offered to build the village a swimming pool as compensation for canceling the group move. From having access to Beppu Bay, the villagers were reduced to dickering over how big the swimming pool should be. In the eyes of many, Iejima had become a forlorn symbol of the fate of the natural village, and of nature itself, at the hands of a dubious form of progress.

Court suit

In 1977, the governor, satisfied that the protest movements could no longer put serious obstacles in his way, announced that he had finished talks with the protest movements. Frustrated that their leverage with the Environmental Agency had collapsed, and that negotiations had yielded no further compromises, Inao and other movement members took more direct, radical action. On December 22, 1977, the Oita NIC Advisory Council held a meeting. Protestors went to the place. Inao forced his way into the meeting and shouted his objections to the Phase Two plan. Officials ushered him out.

This direct action had severe repercussions. On January 6, 1978, some seventy policemen arrived in Kozaki. They surrounded Inao's house and arrested him on suspicion of "obstruction of a public function" (*komu jikko bogai*) and "illegal entry" (*kenzobutsu shinryu*). The police took Inao to the Oita central police station. A crowd of protesters soon gathered outside. The local court refused to recognize the police and the Governor's request that Inao be sentenced, and freed him after forty hours of confinement.

In an ironic counterpoint, movement leaders replied with legal tactics too. They had been thinking about it for some time. On January 10, 1978, movement lawyers filed suit against the Prefectural Government, over its revised Phase Two plan, in the Oita District Court. Up to that point, all pollution suits in Japan had been lodged after the fact – seeking compensation for damage already done. The suit by the Saganoseki citizens' movement was different – it tried to stop the pollution before it started, by preventing its industrial source from being built.

The movement contended that No. 8 was still in suspension, and that building it would cause unacceptable health damage to local residents. On its side, the Prefectural Government argued that a plan in the blueprint stage could not be subject to a suit. The 332 plaintiffs who signed the suit included a number of fishing folk, but not Nishio. Nishio's refusal to sign the suit cut off the last shreds of his cooperative relationship with Inao and the Kozaki League.

Whatever its chances of winning, the suit put the prefecture under extra pressure to finish the assessment. By 1978, the prefecture had not made much progress on it. In order to pressure the EA to force the Oita government into doing a better assessment with fuller citizen participation, the movement approached the Japan Socialist party for help. In March 1978, in a formal Diet interpolation, JSP Diet Representative Doi Takako (later to be Party Secretary [leader]) asked Kamimura, an EA official on the Special Council on Environmental Protection, about the status of Oita Prefecture's assessment. The EA official's response revealed no doubt about the legal status of Oita's approach to the assessment. Kamimura replied,

As you say, at the time of the suspension, assessment was one condition. The one being done now is not an assessment in that sense. Therefore, it has no direct relationship to No. 8.

He went on to say that lifting the suspension of No. 8 was only possible with the EA's approval, and that would require another, better, assessment. This reply heartened the Kozaki movement. But it upset the Oita LDP, DSP, and businessmen, who wanted the Prefectural Government to start building No. 8 as quickly as possible.

In March 1979, after unusually thorough hearings and research, the court convened to announce the verdict of the Seki suit against the Phase Two plan and Landfill No. 8. In its verdict, the court rejected the League suit. The suit, the court argued, had no appropriate legal basis. The prefecture's plan for Phase Two Landfill No. 8 was just a blueprint. Therefore, it did not violate Governor Taki's promise to defer Phase Two until after meeting the Three Conditions.

Despite rejecting the suit, however, the judge, in an unusually long commentary, fully recognized that the Kozaki residents' complaints had a basis:

When we consider the . . . actuality of pollution from the Phase One plan, the geographic susceptibility of Kozaki to pollution, the conspicuous tardiness of the responsible authorities in taking pollution prevention measures, and related to these, the vehement antagonism between the residents of that area and the administration, we must certainly acknowledge the misgivings held by the plaintiffs, the local residents . . .

Although the rejection disappointed League members, the acknowledgment heartened them. To them, the judge's comments constituted official legitimation of their fears. The comments, they thought, should make any concerned official want to stop the Landfill No. 8 plan.

Confrontation

Hoping to extract some political advantage from the judge's comments, movement activists called the Prefectural Government the next day and asked for an appointment with a planning official to talk about the verdict. The government refused.

Upset by this rebuff, a small group of movement activists – fifteen farmers, fishermen, senior citizens and young people, all native residents of Kozaki village – went in protest to the Prefectural Government building. At their invitation, I accompanied them. Waving copies of the judge's comments, the group crowded into the dark third floor hall in front of the planning offices. My tape recorder caught the ensuing encounter (abbreviated here):

Several prefectural officials came out of the planning office, somewhat dismayed. Inao Toru angrily accused them:

You probably have a lot to say about how you've received the court decision and how you're going to handle Landfill No. 8 from now on . . .

The officials replied that they had no appointment to speak with the protestors. Inao told his group:

Show the court statement to them. The Governor said he'd respect it.

While Inao was talking, two middle-aged women from Kozaki harshly criticized the officials: "Your attitude is too prideful"; "Who do you think you are? . . ." Inao added:

It's high time you listened to our opinions on Landfill No. 8 . . . If you read this (No. 8) verdict, you wouldn't be able to keep on forcing No. 8 like you have been. That's exactly what is written.

The official replied that although the judge's comments included passages sympathetic to the protestors, he had turned down the suit. Hence, the Prefectural Government had no legal obligation to stop plans for No. 8. Besides, the official contended, unswayed by the judge's criticism:

We're working to protect the environment as we go along.

A movement member interjected:

You say you'll work on it, but there's no real performance. It's lousy!

Seeing moral exhortation was going nowhere, Inao turned to pleading:

Well . . . we aren't saying meet today . . . You cut off the phone earlier, slam! So we've come to make an opportunity to talk about this. So even making it for next month is OK. Please do it.

Sensing the protestors' weak position, the official replied icily:

We don't do 'conversation (with the people) politics' (*taiwa kensei*) in this prefecture . . . We will follow the principle clause (of the judgment).

The official was referring to the citizen participation schemes of prefectures and municipalities under opposition parties, as in Oita City (Chapter 7).

Since the official would admit no legal responsibility, Inao turned to moral shaming:

Even in the case of the Minamata verdict . . . They all just abide by the principal clause. If they pay money, that's the end of it.

Inao then brought this moral argument to bear on the No. 8 case:

After [the principle clause], what's written in it? There, the judge takes up the reasons we're opposing you, all your lousy performance and jobs left undone, and he's added an extra punch to it all. Right? Now there is this document, so examine it carefully. Then we can talk about it.

The official dryly replied:

We can't promise you anything.

Departing, a woman in the protest group shouted at the official:

Don't you realize, you're the shame of Oita Prefecture!

In this confrontation, each side tried to justify its own stance and undercut the other. The official stuck to the narrow technical legal grounds on which he could win. The movement tried to broaden the debate to one of implicit moral responsibility. This time, however, unlike in the belly-button confrontation eight years earlier (December 1971; see Chapter 6), such moral exhortation gained the protestors no ground. By then, each side had developed its own entrenched rationale or ideology around the issue. Regarding Landfill No. 8 they lived in quite separate moral universes. As a result, the two sides simply talked past each other.

As the residents left the hall, I lagged behind, shocked by the anger and sharpness of the confrontation. Where was Japanese harmony, I wondered? A prefectural official called my name and beckoned me into the inner offices. The officials knew me well, since I had been interviewing them over the previous months. They had been very surprised to see me there, during the confrontation, and assumed it must have been a coincidence.

A top member of the planning staff, who had just confronted the protestors, was anxious to explain what had happened. The court had denied the movement suit, he said, because the administration's actions had not harmed anyone. They were just blueprints. They did not infringe on public rights or profits or create any actual pollution. In his comments, the judge had been unfair. He had only emphasized the bad aspects of the New Industrial City, not the many new pollution regulations the Prefectural Government had enacted. The official told me he wanted to create a consensus between the prefecture and the residents:

If there is consensus, there will be no suit . . . If there can be no agreement, it will lead to another suit.

His comments puzzled me. If he wanted a consensus with the residents, why had he refused to dialogue with this bunch of them? I asked how he would achieve that consensus. The official replied as if it were a purely technical matter. If the Prefectural Government carried out the promised environmental impact assessment, he said, it would be able to predict effects on the natural environment. Then the Prefectural Government would be able to judge whether planned pollution controls would be adequate or not. This information, he thought, would convince the Kozaki residents.

Playing devil's advocate, I pointed out that the residents already distrusted the Prefectural Government, so why should they believe the results of the government's assessment? The protest movement, I noted, had requested the right to appoint a scientist of its own choosing to the assessment committee. The Prefectural Government had rejected this request. If the goal was to achieve consensus with the movement, I asked, why not compromise with the citizens' movement on that point? The official expressed grave doubts:

As to whether No. 8 should be built or not – one must think of Saganoseki's future progress . . . will [the residents'] scientists do that? . . . Is there any guarantee that the residents will believe us even if we do allow their recommended scientist to participate?

To back up his reasoning, he cited a case from Tokyo:

Governor Minobe (of Tokyo) had the slogan, 'If even one person objects to us putting up a bridge, we won't put it up.' This is difficult in practice. There are always those who complain.

A small group of complainers will always exist, the official continued. At some point, he argued, the governor has to ignore them and make decisions for the general welfare:

Therefore, such matters have to be decided by a responsible politician . . . In Oita prefecture, the governor is that decision-maker . . . Even though some may protest to the bitter end, if the project will help everyone's welfare, he will decide to do it. That is, if push comes to shove.

However, he added, persuasion was the better way to get things done:

Right now, we're trying to get those opposed to No. 8 to change their minds. But there is a limit to our patience.

His comments implied that if necessary, the governor would eventually go ahead with No. 8, forcibly removing demonstrators if necessary.

What could account for the officials' rejection of dialogue with the Kozaki residents, while being in favor of persuasion? In the United States, people tend to think of dialogue as an opportunity for each side to try to persuade the other. Dialogue is a communicative act between (at least for that purpose) equals. But the Oita official did not relish that sort of egalitarian dialogue. To the official, persuasion did not require or even indicate dialogue. To the contrary, it meant presentation of information in formal venues, such as public meetings controlled by the state, or the mass media. The attainment of "consensus," likewise, did not refer to a meeting of minds, but rather another formal situation – the non-expression of protest. If protest quieted down after the Prefectural Government presented the results of its assessment, that would indicate the attainment of consensus. To the movement, however, "consensus" could only occur if the government took their objections into full account. Clearly, the officials and the protestors operated within very different normative frameworks, not only about pollution, but about the status of ordinary citizens in politics as well.

The difference between their frameworks was not purely the outcome of operating within two cultural and normative contexts, however. It also reflected their different placements in society. The officials operated within a government bureaucracy that served the chief executive. Bureaucracies have often been noted for their insensitive handling of citizen concerns, their blind pigeon-holing of individual situations, and numerous other faults (Dahrendorf, 1959; Funabashi, 1980; Habermas, 1981). Mayor Sato's example showed (Chapter 7) that bureaucracy itself need not be so insensitive. This indicates that it was the policy-intentions of the dominant elite, rather than any inherent problems with bureaucracy, that caused this divergence of viewpoints about dialogue and persuasion. The interplay of dominant (LDP) political party and business elites set the tone of prefectural bureaucratic behavior. The LDP, allied with national big business and prefectural medium- and small-sized business, continued to urge rapid expansion of the NIC project with Landfill No. 8. As a result, neither the Governor nor the bureaucracy could react favorably to citizen demands to the contrary, even if they felt sympathetic.

Molding the mass mind

The Prefectural Government, cooperating with other elements of the Triple Control Machine, had to work hard to "persuade" the Seki population of the continuing wisdom of its growth strategies. By the late 1970s, Landfills Nos. 6 and 7 stood fully or half-completed along the shores of Ozai, just to the west of Seki. Yet no industry rushed to locate there. Seki residents wondered increasingly, why bother to continue building landfill if no industry is interested in coming?

The ambiguity of future prospects for No. 8 put the local political machine in a difficult position. Local bosses and politicians, working at the behest of the prefectural LDP and governor, had shown strong support for No. 8. They had promised the town many benefits if it came. Now, were they to admit defeat? The way the political machine handled the situation revealed much about its character.

A top LDP Seki Council member described how he and his colleagues kept the Seki population mesmerized by dreams of progress. These politicians no longer believed the dreams themselves. When I interviewed him in 1979, this Seki Council member believed that the big Tokyo factories would never come to Landfill No. 8. Despite this, he and his colleagues continued to promote the idea that No. 8 would bring great benefits to the township:

. . . If we make it public [that the companies are not coming], the assessment will come to a halt . . . It is expedient (*toben*) to keep telling people that [the companies] are coming . . .

He had to do this, he said, so that the Prefectural Government could fulfill the third condition, environmental assessment. Otherwise, the central government would not approve the Phase Two plan. He explained:

[The prefecture has] to tell the legislature that those factories will come, or [the assessment] won't pass.

The council member further confided that by that time, he and many of his conservative colleagues no longer supported the plan for No. 8.

Basic industries (like refineries) only employ people with highly technical, highly trained skills. Our town has no such skilled workers, so we (Saganoseki legislators) dislike it . . . Now (in 1979) there are not so many strong supporters of growth left (among the elite) . . . If the proposed factories do not promise to employ many people, the legislators will not support it.

Surprisingly, this statement indicates that the conservative council members had essentially swung around to the protest movement's point of view. Despite that change of heart, this council member said, the LDP and DSP collaborated to maintain the appearance of support and delude the residents:

The regular citizens don't know that; they have only vague notions about what development will bring. The legislators' and the citizens' vision of development may be quite different . . . The citizens . . . think the Showa Oil refinery and the Teijin Rayon Co. will come to No. 8 and are just waiting until the economy improves . . .

The council member added that this kind of symbolic manipulation of the populace was fine, because it promoted social control:

I think it's OK for most people to have that aim for the time . . . Many people think the No. 8 project will stop Saganoseki's population decline . . . This is an easily understandable answer . . . To keep the people pacified, we decided to let them believe this . . . (Interview 314, 1979).

In other words, in order to support the smooth-ruling hegemony of the prefectural elite, the local conservative politicians continued to promote the Prefectural Government's growth plans, even though they personally no longer agreed with them.

These comments, by a knowledgeable Seki Council member, illuminate the extent to which the Triple Control Machine penetrated and controlled local politics. Local protestors sensed but could not fully explain this aspect or face of power. The machine used public debate as a smoke screen to cover the real (non-)decisions, made in private, that set the public agenda. It used public debate to control public opinion as much as possible (the third face of power). When that did not work, through its patronage networks, the machine used what I call the fourth face of power, social hegemony, to further dampen public reaction.

Public Opinion in Oita Prefecture

Expressions of public discontent put the Prefectural Government's claims to "consensus," except in the most formal sense, in doubt. For all the elites' attempts to exercise control over the popular mind, it was not very successful. Within Kozaki and Saganoseki, the high percentage of resident signatures on petitions against No. 8 clearly showed a high degree of popular resistance. This sentiment of resistance even pervaded the rest of the prefecture. In the fall of 1979, the NHK television station conducted a survey of public opinion on growth and the environment in Oita Prefecture (Table 9.1). Half of the 700 people surveyed lived within the NIC project area and half outside it. In the following discussion, I look at the responses of people living within the NIC area, who were most strongly affected by both its negative and its positive features. The results showed that the general Oita public was not very enthusiastic about the NIC project.

The majority of Oita residents felt that their living environment had changed quite a bit. When forced to choose, most people felt the changes had been more desirable than not desirable. They liked the availability of more stores, better services, and better transportation (water, sewage, paved roads, new houses) (Q. 1, 2, 3). This marked a vast improvement on their pre-war poverty, which they had happily left behind. However, about 20 percent felt that the changes had on balance been undesirable. In particular, this group mourned the loss of nature. Twenty-two percent disliked the increase in pollution (Q. 4).

When not forced to make a global choice between "increase" or "no increase," a large majority thought that pollution had increased (Q. 5). They noted especially a decline in river and water quality, but also noted noise and air pollution from cars and factories (Q. 6). The majority also thought that pollution was a serious worldwide problem (Q. 12).

As to further industrialization plans (NIC Phase Two was pending at the time), very few residents wanted to continue with NIC style industrialization (Q. 10). Most wanted the prefecture to switch to other forms of investment (Q. 11). The largest category (47 percent) preferred future investment in social infrastructure to help the environment, health, and children rather than building more roads, houses, and factories (Q. 11). The population split evenly on whether it thought the Prefectural and City Governments were really trying to reduce pollution, with about one-third harboring severe doubts that they were (Q. 7).

Related to that suspicion was the considerable interest in the protest movements (Q. 8) of well over half the respondents. The vast majority wanted residents' opinions fully considered hereafter before any big project (Q. 9). Only a tiny fraction trusted prefectural officials enough to want to leave planning to the experts (Q. 9). Only a few wanted to bring in industry as planned in Phase Two. Half called for extensive consultation with residents and research to prevent pollution (Q. 10). A quarter said that area residents should decide the fate of the project, and some wanted Phase Two cancelled outright (Q. 10). In sum, virtually no one trusted or believed the Prefectural Government's claim that it should make prefectural plans by its own technocratic expertise.

Table 9.1. *Attitudes toward the environment and social change (Oita, 1979)*

Question	Answer	In NIC	Out of NIC	Average
1. In your city (town, village) how much has the environment changed in the last ten years?	A great deal	29.1	20.1	25.1
	Quite a bit	52.7	58.3	55.1
	Can't say which	4.5	5.5	4.9
	Not much	11.2	12.9	11.9
	Not at all	0.0	0.9	0.4
	Don't know	2.5	2.3	2.4
2. Have the changes been desirable ones or not?	Desirable	53.8	71.8	61.5
	Not desirable	20.9	12.0	17.1
	Can't say	24.3	14.9	20.3
	Don't know	0.3	1.2	0.7
	Other	0.6	0.0	2.4
3. In what ways have the changes been desirable?	More shops, shopping convenient	53.9	46.7	50.3
	Better roads, sewage, water, homes	49.1	40.7	44.9
	More convenient transportation	46.1	53.3	49.7
4. In what ways have the changes been un-desirable?	Natural environment gotten worse	41.8	6.9	31.3
	Few places to work	13.4	37.9	20.8
	Goods and land prices gone up	35.8	31.0	34.4
	Traffic jams	26.9	17.2	23.9
	Too few parks and play places	22.4	6.9	17.7
	Pollution increased	22.4	3.4	16.7
5. Compared with ten years ago, is pollution in your home area worse or improved?	It's gotten worse	63.6	58.4	61.4
	It has improved	7.1	9.8	8.3
	Don't know	29.3	31.7	30.3
6. If answered "worse," what kind of pollu-tion is it? (choose 2)	Rivers and water quality	67.5	74.3	70.2
	Noise and vibration	42.2	35.7	39.5
	Automobile exhaust	40.6	27.5	35.2
	Air pollution by factories	30.5	11.1	22.6
7. Are the prefectural and city governments earnestly trying to re-duce pollution?	Earnest	9.9	7.0	8.7
	A little earnest	24.4	20.4	22.7
	Neutral	24.6	31.8	27.7
	Not very earnest	25.4	27.1	26.1
	Not at all earnest	7.5	7.4	7.4
8. How much attention do you pay to the movement against the NIC Phase Two plan?	Very much	15.2	8.3	12.3
	Quite a bit	39.5	28.3	34.7
	Not too much	35.7	39.1	37.2
	None at all	4.6	8.6	6.3

Table 9.1. *Continued*

Question	Answer	In NIC	Out of NIC	Average
9. From here on, with industrialization, how much should the opinions of the residents in the area be considered?	Fully include residents' opinions	81.1	76.2	79.0
	Better to consider their opinions	8.9	8.5	8.8
	Can't say either way	2.9	3.5	3.2
	Residents are amateurs, so don't consider their opinions heavily	0.0	1.8	0.7
	Leave it to the experts	5.3	4.9	5.1
10. What do you think should be done about the NIC Phase Two plan (Landfills No. 6, 7, and 8)?	Bring industry as planned	14.7	12.1	13.6
	Add residents' opinions, prevent pollution, investigate firms	47.1	42.5	45.2
	Change/cancel by residents' opinions	24.1	28.9	26.9
	Cancel the plan	8.1	2.1	5.6
11. Which should the prefecture stress – building roads home and factories or protecting nature & culture?	Both are important, but should stress protecting nature and culture	47.3	40.5	44.4
	Both are important, but should stress building roads, homes, factories	28.8	27.2	28.1
	Only stress building	12.9	17.7	15.0
	Only stress protecting nature	8.3	9.5	9.2
12. Some say, "If we keep on polluting, the earth will be unlivable." What do you think?	Fully agree	53.6	55.6	54.5
	Can't decide	24.9	21.8	23.6
	It's not that serious	16.2	16.0	16.1

Note: N = about 700
Source: NHK Oita Broadcasting Station.

The survey results show that claims of "consensus," in the sense of real agreement, as well as the Prefectural Government's claim that the protest movements represented only a small segment of public opinion, were not accurate. Even if people in Oita City did not feel personally threatened by pollution, they were much more sympathetic to the nature-protection goals of the Seki movement than to the growth goals of the Prefectural Government.

The strength of these opinions further showed up in the relatively strong showing the JSP made in the Oita City legislature elections, reflecting the greater concentration of both workers and pollution (see Table 6.2). In the prefectural legislature, however, the rural vote gave the LDP a much more comfortable majority, while the JSP consistently garnered less than 20 percent of the seats. The existence of a healthy cynicism among ordinary citizens toward Prefectural Government growth rationales shows the lack of elite control over the popular mind. In contrast, it provides further evidence that elite social control came from its successful exercise of social, rather than ideological, hegemony.

Decline of the Kozaki movement

Despite the constant barrage of social control measures, the Kozaki League stood its ground for many years and did not collapse. However, the intensity of hamlet support declined, and the leadership grew more radical. Inao, according to some hamlet residents and outside supporters, grew increasingly rigid, excluding those who did not fully agree him. This isolated the movement from some potential supporters, even within Kozaki, as well as more widely throughout the prefecture. One Kozaki resident confided:

The struggle has been long and we are getting tired. . . . If there is no leader, we can't do the movement. This is the special character of the Japanese. . . . Now, people are losing their enthusiasm and don't go out. They give in to political pressure. Not threats. You just become hesitant to make public protests that stand out (Interview 88, 1979).

In Seki town, the Seki Local Government Workers' Union had provided crucial support for Inao, helping to elect him to the Seki Town Council. Yet several union members, strong movement supporters, and participants criticized Inao:

He just has his own thoughts. He should try to persuade others a little more. He should go around to all the Kozaki people and convince them, if they are wavering. But instead, if someone wavers, the leader immediately makes them into an enemy.

They thought that Inao's behavior was bad for the movement:

The leader should try to make people into his allies. If someone does not immediately join hands with Inao, he pushes them away, thinking of them as pro-No. 8 . . . This is shrinking the movement.

They attributed Inao's behavior to his character and to his political style:

Inao's style is eccentric. A leader's heart has to be bigger. Inao does not give others a chance to think. He pushes them away . . . He does too much direct action. He's too much like a Trotskyite. . . . There is a lot of resistance building up to Inao . . . Then the movement gets smaller and even more extreme (Interview 89, 1979).

These union supporters mourned the loss of Professor Yuki Tsutomu, the original leader of the Kozaki movement, who died in 1975. He had been a great leader, they agreed, and had drawn large crowds of supporters. Yuki had been a university professor in the Japanese university that had been established in Manchuria. But now, they said, no great leader existed. "The leader's style is very important. We need a university professor in the movement, someone people can believe in."

Movement supporters in other Oita towns – in Oita City and Ozai – reported that they had been criticized severely by Inao for differences in tactics or opinions. Long-time supporters in Tokyo complained that Inao did not trust them, and would not give them good information about the Kozaki League's plans and tactics, limiting their ability to help. An Oita Prefectural Assembly politician from the Japan Communist party said that the JCP had been against Landfill No. 8 from the beginning, but the party disagreed with Inao's tactics. It's good to resist prefectural policies, he said. But Inao's "harsh tactics," he argued, such as taking over the microphone at the official assessment meeting and preventing the meeting from opening, only causes a loss of public support, not a gain.

It's better to get all the Kozaki people on your side by telling them why they must oppose No. 8. If over half the hamlet was against No. 8, the prefecture would not be able to build it. If the pro-No. 8 Seki Town Council members from Kozaki could not get elected, then the situation would change . . . A lot of prefectural people are uncertain about the NIC. It would be better to strengthen the opposition among the public, rather than just make a radical fight.

The JCP legislator said that by carrying on such radical tactics, Inao was playing right into the Governor's hands: "The Prefectural Government likes that, because the prefectural people will judge it badly." This judgment accords closely with that of foreign scholars, who saw the government as trying to goad protestor groups into radical tactics such as this, precisely to damage their public credibility (Pharr, 1990). The legislator further complained that Inao would not abide by collective tactics agreed on in the Joint Struggle Council (JSC): "The JCP is a member of the JSC, but the JSC is unable to control Inao's actions. Inao does not listen."

These criticisms do not seem entirely justified. Inao had been holding many discussion meetings in Kozaki for the entire hamlet, trying to strengthen opposition. He retained many admirers and supporters in Kozaki. But certainly he could be personally abrasive toward supporters who disagreed with him, and he did adhere to a harsher, more radical mode of protest tactics than older progressives liked.

Condition three completed.

In the spring of 1979, Governor Taki announced his decision to retire. Vice-governor Hiramatsu, the former MITI official who had introduced the concept of a refinery complex to Oita, ran for governor with LDP and DSP support (Table 6.2). By this time, the JSP had swung into public opposition to the NIC, and so withheld support or ran competing candidates (as did other opposition parties). Hiramatsu won the election and took office as governor in April 1979. With Hiramatsu's election, Oita completed its transformation from a JSP-controlled prefecture to an LDP-controlled prefecture. The new governor wanted to pursue NIC industrial growth, but also had a host of alternative routes to prefectural prosperity in mind.

To carry out the promised environmental impact assessment of the Oita NIC speedily and in a credible way, the Prefectural Government commissioned the Nomura Research Institute, a nationally known, prestigious private think tank, to conduct it. Nomura carried out its task with an air of technocratic expertise. It measured effluent gases from the existing factories and calculated their spread patterns in the prevailing winds. It estimated the same for the possible factories that might locate on the Phase Two landfills.

The movement objected strongly to these methods, citing the unreliability of government-produced data. It called for more citizen participation, citing the U.S. NEPA guidelines. The Prefectural Government rebuffed its requests. The Oita government had already agreed to present the first draft of the assessment for public comment. It had promised to take the comments into consideration. To the Oita government officials, this constituted an unprecedented degree of citizen participation.

In August 1979, a scientific team from the Nomura Research Institute went to the Kozaki coast for on-site data collection as part of the assessment procedure. The team wanted to raise weather balloons and measure wind velocity and direction, to see if Kozaki would in fact collect pollution from No. 8. Members of the residents' movement gathered around the scientists and prevented them from carrying out the measurements. The protestors said that since Nomura had not permitted resident participation in the research, they would not permit the research to proceed.

This disruption, unlike earlier ones such as the belly-button confrontation or the blockade of Seki harbor, had negative consequences for the movement. Disruption of what looked like a fair assessment process to observers weakened outside support for the protestors. After this disruption, the EA withdrew all support from the movement. It had to in order to preserve the legitimacy of the EIA process in its arguments with the economic ministries. The EA switched from criticizing the Nomura assessment to helping the Oita government finish it. Going further, the EA announced that Oita could separate its assessment into two parts. The first part would assess predicted pollution on paper, using calculations based on existing wind-flow data. The second part, involving actual on-site measurement of wind flow, could be done later when (and if) construction began.

This new approach allowed the Nomura Institute to eliminate the troublesome Kozaki on-site atmospheric measurements for the time being. Of course, this move also severely reduced the ability of the assessment to predict environmental damage, and rendered the whole exercise dubious. Even conservative politicians privately voiced cynicism about its validity. For instance, an LDP town legislator said:

Since the administration is doing [the assessment], of course it will produce an OK [to build No. 8] (OGN, July 28, 1970).

In November 1979, after prodding by a conservative Oita politician, LDP Diet leader Hata in Diet questioning asked the EA official if it were really the responsibility of the Oita governor, not the EA, to decide when the assessment was complete and the suspension of No. 8 landfill could be lifted. In a flat contradiction of its previous defense of the protest movement, the EA official replied, "You're right." Clearly, the political winds had shifted.

A conservative prefectural legislator explained to me how he had produced this shift of political wind. The legislator had gotten influential Diet representatives to talk to EA officials beforehand and convince them to change their stance (Interview 261, 1979). The earlier reply to Diet questioning by the EA, he explained, while seeming to favor the movement, had been so vague that its meaning could be bent. Ministerial officials questioned by progressive politicians in the Diet, he said, often make vague replies in order to avoid being held accountable later on.

In the same month, the Oita government presented the completed assessment draft to the prefectural legislature for comment. Then it put copies of it in the post office and other places for several weeks to allow public reading and comment. The draft assessment stated that no serious pollution would come from the Phase Two factories, so it was all right to proceed with their construction. Citizen participation consisted solely of the right to submit written suggestions.

Citizen comments had little effect. A comparison of the draft and final version shows that no major revisions occurred as a result of any comments written by citizens in this participation exercise. This procedure conceded no decision-making power to the public. It allowed the Oita government to retain complete control over the contents of the assessment. The government announced it would present its final version of the assessment to the public in an explanatory meeting on November 26, 1979.

A few days before that meeting, the Kozaki League distributed a mimeographed leaflet titled, "Let's smash the fake assessment!" It announced a "Big Meeting on Stopping the Assessment" for November 25. The pamphlet called for people to join a "prevention action" at the Prefectural Government's public announcement meeting on the assessment, to take place the day after the hamlet meetings. The pamphlet also included an open protest letter from the head of the prefectural Sohyo union federation, and several articles from magazines criticizing the assessment.

I attended the hamlet meeting on November 25. About fifty villagers had gathered, two-thirds of them older women dressed in rough work clothes. They were the typical farming and working housewives of the hamlet. Inao led the discussion, arguing that the Nomura assessment's "desktop" pollution data was

not a real survey, just a convenient excuse. From one to ten, it can't be believed . . . The residents had no way to ascertain whether the data was correct or not.

Therefore the assessment should not provide evidence about building Landfill No. 8. Furthermore, Inao argued, the only realistic industrial use of No. 8, if it were built, would be to hold big storage tanks for fuels. The Showa oil refinery and Teijin synthetic fiber plant originally planned for No. 8, Inao said, no longer had any economic rationale or possibility of coming to No. 8. As a result, he argued, contrary to the prefecture's claims, No. 8 would provide absolutely no local economic stimulus. He therefore concluded that No. 8 offered no benefits, only harm, for Kozaki and Seki.

On this basis, Inao argued that the Kozaki League, including the older women attending, should take desperate, determined action *("hisshi ni kodo shimasho")*. They should go to the prefectural offices, disrupt the meeting on the assessment, and try to stop it. That kind of radical tactic, he argued, was the only way to stop the approval process. Very little discussion or dissent followed. Inao seemed to sweep the attendees along with his charismatic leadership (from participant observational notes, November 25, 1979).

I attended the assessment explanatory meeting the next day. Twenty to thirty suited officials sat on a stage at the front of a large hall, ready to answer questions. Employees of Kyushu Oil Company and other big NIC factories, brought in by company buses, all still in their green work uniforms, filled the hall. The meeting was well-orchestrated to produce the appearance of public support for the assessment. But all did not go smoothly. The Seki League and the Joint Struggle Council had planned to shatter the seeming consensus. Inao and fifty or so villagers from Kozaki and some Sohyo-affiliated union members packed the front rows of seats. Their plan was to listen for a while, then get up as a group, walk out in protest, and have a rally outside.

A prefectural official started to explain that according to the results of the assessment, pollution from the Phase Two industries would not be severe. At that point, Inao, incensed by those statements, abandoned the plan. He jumped up on the stage, grabbed the microphone and started to argue with the speaking official. Police rushed in and gently but firmly ushered him out. The band of supporters stood up and trailed after him. They held a protest rally outside the hall, ignored by those inside.

In the meeting, prefectural officials continued to speak. With proper pollution controls, they said, the industries planned for the NIC Phase Two area could meet national pollution standards in air and water quality and avoid other forms of related "public nuisance" (*kogai*). Therefore it was safe to proceed with the NIC Phase Two growth plan.

After getting the document, the Kozaki movement and its allies subjected it to harsh criticism. Sympathetic scientists at Oita University analyzed the techniques the Nomura Institute had used to carry out its on-paper assessment and found a number of flaws. Nomura had not explored the effects of alternative industrial growth plans on the environment, nor had it examined the impact of different sorts of industry. Furthermore, the assessment relied on very uncertain assumptions about the amount of pollution output from smokestacks and other sources (Hearings on the Landfill No. 8 Suit, Oita Regional Court, May 15, 1978).

Nonetheless, the Oita government submitted the results of its EIA to the EA. In the spring of 1980, the EA approved Oita's assessment virtually as submitted, allowing prefectural officials to claim that they had met the third and final of Governor Taki's Three Conditions.

Outcome and aftermath

A *Pyrrhic victory*

In the eyes of the Prefectural Government, the approval of Phase Two brought its long Three Conditions detour back to the main highway of growth. By the late 1970s, national and Oita elites were once again unified in their willingness to give top priority to growth. Economic recession, some success in curbing the worst pollution, and a nationwide weakening of the environmental movement had left the field open once again. Approval of Phase Two gave the Oita government a free hand to pursue its vision of growth once again.

The Prefectural Government continued its ardent pursuit of heavy industrial growth. It proceeded with construction of Phase Two Landfills No. 6 and 7 and a port area. By October 1978, the construction companies had finished building Landfill No. 7 and the new harbor, and had completed two of Landfill No. 6's three components. The Oita government had to pay for the landfill construction out of public monies. But the Prefectural Government was confident it would quickly recoup this investment, because the Mitsubishi and Mitsui trading and shipbuilding companies had already contracted to buy Landfills No. 6 and 7, respectively, when they were completed.

However, national and prefectural elites had developed different ideas on what sorts of growth to pursue. During the 1970s, while the Prefectural Government was fighting the Seki movements and the Environmental Agency to proceed with the NIC Phase Two project, domestic political demands for growth as well as world economic conditions had shifted dramatically . Hinterland populations no longer demanded industrial growth so ardently; they no longer saw growth as a unqualified boon. As a result, the national LDP felt little pressure for industrial redistribution. In addition, global economic changes set a new context for Japanese domestic growth priorities. The collapse of the world currency system and the oil shock of 1973 had reduced the business expansionary drive. Further, the nature of the world market had shifted. Competition from Korea and Taiwan in textiles and shipbuilding had rendered new domestic plants unnecessary. The types of goods Japan could sell on the world market had shifted toward "knowledge-intensive" products such as computers. Following the "flying-geese" strategy of keeping at the head of product innovation, Japanese economic elites were trying to push the national economy in that direction (Kojima, 1977, p. 15). These products used less steel and oil and did not demand coastal refineries.

Accordingly, the national economic elites had little interest in promoting more NIC-style projects. Oita's Phase Two had received formal approval by dint of intense political pressure. But the two other legs of the Ruling Triad – big business and ministerial officials – no longer had much interest in bringing factories or refineries to Oita's NIC Phase Two project.

Given this new context, both Mitsubishi and Mitsui both felt unhappy with their agreements to pay for and build facilities on the Oita Landfills No. 6 and 7. Secretly, both companies wanted to renege on their contracts with Oita, but they each enjoyed different latitudes to do so. For decades, Mitsui had treated Oita as one of its "company-prefectures." When Hoshino of Mitsui Bussan and Governor Kinoshita had gone through common prefectural ties to make the Kyushu Oil Company, they had deepened that sense of long-term commitment. Mitsubishi, thinking ahead, had cleverly written an escape clause into its contract with Oita. Although the landfill was already half completed, Mitsubishi simply cancelled its plans to buy Landfill No. 6. Mitsubishi had no long-standing relationship with Oita Prefecture, so it felt little obligation to Oita.

The situation for Mitsui was quite different. Mitsui had signed a tight contract with Oita Prefecture to purchase Landfill No. 7. It had no contract escape clause. Bound by personal ties, Mitsui felt uneasy about cancelling the contract for No. 7. Besides their ties, Mitsui companies also had a deep economic involvement in Oita. They had done most of the construction of Oita's New Industrial City. Mitsui bought about one-third of the output of the Nikko copper refinery in Saganoseki, and about three-fifths of the oil from Oita's Kyushu Oil Company refinery. Prefectural officials appealed to Mitsui's sense of paternalism. According to a Mitsui official, one Oita vice-governor regularly urged the Mitsui leaders to make Oita City a "Mitsui town" (*kigyo joka machi*) (Interview 601, 1988). And, the Mitsui official added, this is how Mitsui regarded Oita City.[8] Even so, if Mitsui had not already paid for Landfill No. 7, one Mitsui official told me, after the oil shock and recession of 1973 the company might have withdrawn from the purchase despite the tight contract (Interview 485, 1978). In the end, Mitsui reluctantly bought the bulk of No. 7 landfill, though having little immediate use for it.

In July 1980, continuing the growth initiative, Governor Hiramatsu declared that the Oita government had met all Three Conditions: consensus, normalization, and assessment. He then lifted the suspension of Landfill No. 8 and said its construction could begin at any time. The Prefectural Government exulted in its victory over its opponents – the grassroots movements, the unions, and the leftist parties. The victory gave the Oita pro-growth elites a sense of public vindication over its critics.

The exultation was short-lived. Victory on the No. 8 issue turned out to be more symbol than substance. Eight years had passed since Governor Taki first agreed to the Three Conditions in 1972. In that time, the Japanese economy had changed profoundly. In addition to the problems in steel and shipbuilding, synthetic fiber plants had lost out in competition to Taiwan, Korea, and Hong Kong. The Teijin Company no longer wanted to build a synthetic fiber plant on Landfill No. 8. Because of the eight-year delay, the Oita Prefecture Government had lost its opportunity for heavy-industrial growth. This new economic situation had left the Oita government without an immediate rationale for building No. 8. Despite this, Governor Hiramatsu was determined to push ahead with No. 8:

---

8. The other, and more thoroughly Mitsui "company town" is, Ogawara (formerly named Miike), famous for its coal mines and post-war strikes and strike-breaking.

I will build Landfill No. 8, but there is no industry for it now. After 5 or 10 years, I will bring non-polluting industry, perhaps machinery, or computers, or the Asia Port [to No. 8]. The Seki population is decreasing, so they want to bring industry to Seki. It is the people's duty (Interview 806, 1981).

Meeting the Three Conditions had been important to prefectural officials. It preserved face and institutional legitimacy, secured national approval of the Phase Two plan, and paved the way for future industrial growth. These results meant little to the Baba fishers, who, at the Prefectural Government's behest, had campaigned in support of No. 8. The situation left the Baba fishers with their livelihood damaged by pollution and nearby landfill. Without No. 8, they got only a small proportion of the promised total compensation. They were bitter about the whole affair.

In strictly legal terms, the Governor and the growth coalition won the battle for No. 8. But in reality, the environmental coalition – the Kozaki Citizens' League, the Saganoseki Common Will Group of fishers and their supporters throughout the prefecture – had won the battle for the time being. The movement had delayed No. 8 so long that even the Prefectural Government, with Landfills Nos. 6 and 7 sitting empty, could no longer make a credible case for No. 8's construction. Japanese refineries had long since headed overseas.

However, the movement had not won the war. Movement leaders feared, accurately, that if the domestic economy improved, the Prefectural Government would renew its plan for No. 8. This fear kept the movement alive, watching and waiting, ready to spring into active protest again if necessary.

The rest of the New Industrial City had a variety of outcomes. Phase One, with its steel and oil refineries, kept up a vigorous level of production. Phase Two Landfills Nos. 6 and 7 moved slowly and provided very little local employment. The Oita government clung tenaciously to its Mitsui contract. It continued construction on both landfills, despite a lack of clarity about who or what would be located there. In the early 1980s, it finished No. 7 and parts A and B of No. 6, with part C remaining an outline in the water. The Oita government reasoned that Oita had one of the few really good harbors left in Japan with plenty of fresh water, cheap labor, and other attractive conditions. So, officials thought, some industry would certainly come in the future.

Meanwhile, Mitsui agonized over how to use No. 7. One plan was to build a golf course (Interview, 1980). But in 1980 the land had cost $480,000 per acre. Land at the Mitsui Shipyards in Chiba near Tokyo, a Mitsui official said, cost six to eight times that. That had made Oita attractive as a shipyard or other industrial site. A golf course would never have paid back such a massive investment, especially because with landfill surrounded on three sides by ocean and one by waterway, the water traps would have been terrible. In 1981, Mitsui constructed a hangar to build dirigibles and sheds to store steel. This employed 500 people. Nineteen smaller companies located on a small area of No. 7.

The prefecture sold the finished parts of No. 6 that Mitsubishi had abandoned (OGN, Jan. 27, 1981). Kyushu Electric bought fully half of the landfill to put up an electric power plant fueled by liquefied natural gas (LNG). This began operations in 1991, employing 122 people. Its associated Oita LNG Company bought a small piece of No. 6 for the unloading, storage, and transport of LNG. This began operations on 1990, employing 78 people. In addition, Kyushu Oil bought a small piece for oil tank storage connected with its refinery on Landfill No. 1, and the Showa Denko petrochemical refinery on No. 2 bought a small piece for related operations. As of 1996, neither of these had begun operations (Oita City Government, General Affairs Bureau, Planning Office, 1995).

The Prefectural Government proceeded to finish Part C of No. 6, and courted industrial suitors for it. On March 7, 1990, Showa Denko and the Japan Catalyst Company signed agreements with Oita Prefecture to build factories on Landfill No. 6C (OGN, March 7, 1990). Showa Denko had already built a second refinery on Landfill No. 2, which would bring its annual ethylene production to 730,000 tons, the largest site in Asia. It now planned to build a third ethylene refinery on Landfill No. 6C. Since market demand for ethylene was expanding, Showa Denko hoped to start operations in 1994. Japan Catalyst planned for a massive facility to produce ethylene glycol, acidified ethylene, acrylic acid esters, and other catalysts. It would invest about $800 million. The eventual output of the Japan Catalyst refinery would equal one-third of Japan's total output of these chemicals. It also hoped to start production in 1994. Showa Denko's investment in the new No. 6C facility would come to about $500 million, making its total investment in Oita facilities (including refineries on No. 2) about $2 billion. However, by 1995, these two refineries had not yet begun operations.

A 1990 editorial in the Oita Godo newspaper lauded the coming of the refineries to Landfill No. 6C as overcoming the pessimism of the critics:

These refineries will invest $1.3 billion and will hire 500 employees . . . In recent years, intellectuals have been saying 'from now on its the era of light, shallow, short and small [software], no doubt the era of heavy, thick, long and big [refineries] has ended.' . . . But an economically backward prefecture like Oita cannot deny the attractiveness of 'heavy, thick, long and big' . . .

After describing Oita as still backward, the editorial went on to praise the prospects for the No. 6C refinery project:

We can't expect much economic stimulus to the prefecture from software industries, which don't hire many people. They will not stop the outflow of young workers from the prefecture. Big basic materials refineries will give the young people a place to work, and their wages will revitalize the prefecture. Secondly, the big refineries will provide a lot of construction jobs. Also, if local companies work at it, they can learn skills and become sub-contractors for the new refineries. Finally, the new refineries will pay a large amount of taxes. Thinking about it this way, the merit of the new factories for Oita Prefecture is exactly the same as before [during NIC Phase One] (OGN, March 2, 1990).

The editorial poses exactly the same social problems, and paints exactly the same wondrous vision of the future benefits of industrial growth, that the paper and government had used to herald Phase One of the NIC in the early and mid-1960s. Given such wonderful effects, how could anyone be heartless enough to oppose the project?

The editorial shocked me. Had nothing changed? The Phase One refineries had not given many jobs to prefectural youth (Chapter 2). Why would new refineries do any better? The elites had held out the same promises in the 1960s, yet the promised jobs had only weakly materialized. Big companies such as New Japan Steel and Showa Denko had a lifetime employment policy. They had preferred to bring in their own workers from the closed plants in other parts of the country that the new refineries replaced (Chapter 2).

I thought that the tone of the editorial supported what some local critics had been saying all along – that the governmental bureaucracy dominated the people by dangling enticing visions of coming prosperity in front of them. Referring to the earlier phases of Oita's NIC growth, two Oitans – a newspaper reporter living in Oita and former employee of the Tokyo municipal government living in Tokyo – argued that the bureaucracy, not business, took the lead in this sort of manipulation:

The economic elites do not decide anything for themselves. Their leader is the bureaucracy [national government ministries]. . . . Since the Meiji Era, the bureaucracy has been nurturing industry to help the national economy . . .

Post-war democracy, these men argued, had forced the central bureaucracy to become less authoritarian, to change its tactics from the stick to the carrot:

Democracy led to treating each individual as important. With this, the bureaucracy couldn't so easily impose top-down policies. So, they use the bait [*esa*] of monetary profit. The country folk all compete for the money and approve of growth projects. But exactly who will profit is very vague . . .

These men used the seduction metaphor to describe national-prefectural government relations:

The national bureaucracy controls the hinterland folk by showing the bait and seducing them – for example, the New Industrial Cities plan. This is a skillful seduction. Then the prefecture grabs the bait, and has a very sweet dream. This made Governor Kinoshita a strong supporter of the NIC plan.

They added that the national bureaucracy exercised this control in the service of national economic growth goals:

During the total war [World War Two] the government had general power. [After the was] the New Comprehensive National Development Plan was modeled on the wartime controlled economy. It's not [now] fascist, but it decides the national goal and makes a general mobilization to win the economic war (Interview 144, 1979).

In 1990, the Oita newspaper editorial repeated the very same "bait," the same discredited claims, that it had used in 1965 – that refineries would provide local jobs and profits. Objectively, given the movement of Japanese refineries abroad, building refineries along Oita's shore in 1995 seemed even less likely to provide jobs for locals than it had in 1965. Probably the new refineries would once again cause an influx of skilled workers and managers from outside the prefecture. These new workers would contribute to the prefectural economy, as they had before. But local youth would still have to take menial jobs or migrate to the big cities.

From the standpoint of meeting national economic goals, though, Oita's New Industrial City Phase One was a great success. The highly modern steel mill and oil refineries replaced outdated refineries in other parts of Japan. As demand for their products changed, the older plants lost business, while Oita's remained at high levels of production. Between 1989 and 1994, the Oita New Japan Steel mill operated at an average of 88 percent of its total capacity, and provided 28 percent of the company's production (NJS itself produced 25 million tons, as much as Italy or Brazil, more than France or England, and about one-quarter of Japan's total steel production). During the same period, the Kyushu Oil refinery operated at 74 percent capacity, and the Showa Denko petrochemical plant at 88 percent. These plants drew their raw materials from all over the world. Most of the iron ore came from Australia and Brazil. Most of the crude oil came from the Middle East (United Arab Emirates 30 percent, Saudi Arabia 20 percent, Iran 15 percent), with some from China (13 percent), Indonesia (3 percent) and Mexico (1.6 percent). The plants supplied steel, fuel, and petrochemicals (the basis for plastics) to Japan's vast industrial system. This productivity kept a good percentage of Japan's citizens supplied with fuel for cars and heating and with the materials for consumer goods. It also provided the raw materials for Japan's production of export goods, the basis for the nation's competitive position in the world economy. From that national perspective, Oita's NIC complemented the national economy and made eminently good sense.

New directions

At the same time, the national slowdown in heavy industrial production, local protest against the pollution it produced, and the NIC's failure to stem the outward flow of Oita's youth propelled Governor Hiramatsu and his staff into creative thinking. With help from Tokyo think tanks such as Dentsu, they devised new "green" ways to bring about other kinds of economic growth. In 1990, Governor Hiramatsu said he was glad that Oita's heavy-industrial growth had been delayed and some of its coastal greenery preserved. He seemed to be obliquely thanking Oita's environmental movements. The creative efforts led to Oita's Technopolis, the "One-Village, One-Product movement," the drive to make an Asia port, and a number of other projects.

Oita Prefecture was designated as one of MITI's sites for the clustered construction of consumer electronics firms (Tatsuno, 1986). The Technopolis designation helped bring computer and electronics-related industries to Oita. However, unlike most Technopolises, Oita spread its new high-tech firms throughout the area of a historical peninsula (Kunisaki), interspersing the firms among rice-farming villages and ancient temples (Broadbent, 1989b). This allowed village people to work in the new firms, yet still live in their traditional homes and retain their traditional customs and village closeness. This kind of decentralized industrial growth represented a radical departure from the urban centralization associated with growth up to that time. It was made possible by creative thinking that took advantage of the new logistical transportation potentials of information-intensive industries. The products, such as cameras or integrated circuits, were light in weight and could be shipped by air. The new Oita international airport at the end of the Kunisaki peninsula, while a little removed from Oita City, was close to, and served the shipping needs of, these new plants very well.

The One-Village One-Product movement encouraged the manufacture and nationwide sale of traditional village specialty products such as wine, jam, shrimp, mushrooms, gourds, roses, bamboo ware, fish dishes, dried sardines, buckwheat liquor, charcoal, and special flavors of miso (a soybean paste used for soups and other foods) (Hiramatsu, 1983). The Oita government helped villages to mass-produce these items and deliver them in special trucks all over Japan, and held "Oita Fairs" in Tokyo and Osaka to promote sales. Other projects supported the fishing and other local industries. The actual economic benefit of these projects has been much debated. How many varieties of miso, one wag commented, can the country take? The Governor defended the project by saying that the purpose was "primarily a psychological one meant to encourage people to take pride in their own communities."

Through this encouragement, the Governor hoped to strengthen local village culture, preserving its distinct flavor. At the same time, he worked to open Oita to more contacts with the outside world. By pursuing these innovative projects, Governor Hiramatsu became Japan's most famous and popular governor. When a poll asked Japanese company presidents which prefectural governor they would most like to meet, by far the largest number (41 out of 230) chose Governor Hiramatsu. The governor of Tokyo, the runner up, received only 28 votes. The corporate presidents cited his "incredible farsightedness and vitality" (Takahashi, 1987). What corporate presidents like, of course, may be very different from what the average citizen likes – as events in this book have shown.

Social change in Oita

As a result of the many forms of societal and environmental change discussed in this book, the human community of Oita Prefecture went through a considerable transformation. By the 1980s, the prefecture had managed to stem the overall decline of its population. But oddly enough, this did not mean it had entirely solved the original problem of youth leaving to seek work in the big cities. As the editorial quoted earlier noted, this remained something of a problem. The percentage of high-school graduates seeking employment had declined, because so many more went on to post-secondary formal education (Figure 9.2). Of the high-school graduates who did seek immediate employment, the percentage finding work within the prefecture had improved. However, a large proportion still had to seek work outside the prefecture.

Of those who stayed in Oita, many had to leave the countryside and move to Oita City. There they usually found employment, not in the originally promised skilled industrial sector, but in the service industries. For the most part, they took jobs as store clerks, restaurant workers, barbers, and other service providers. Workers from other parts of the nation, already employed by the big companies, mostly moved in to fill the skilled industrial jobs. Between 1965 and 1990, the proportion of Oita City's labor force in the manufacturing sector stayed virtually unchanged, while the proportion in the service industries went up from 55 percent to 70 percent (Oita City Government, General Affairs Bureau, Planning Office, 1995).

As a result of this pattern, migration to Oita City peaked between 1969 and 1976, during and just after the NIC refineries' startup period. The population of Oita City as a percentage of the prefectural total went from 16.7 percent in 1960 to 33 percent in 1990 (see Figure 9.2).

As reflected in the survey results noted here, material conditions in Oita Prefecture and City improved greatly over the decades. Between 1965 and

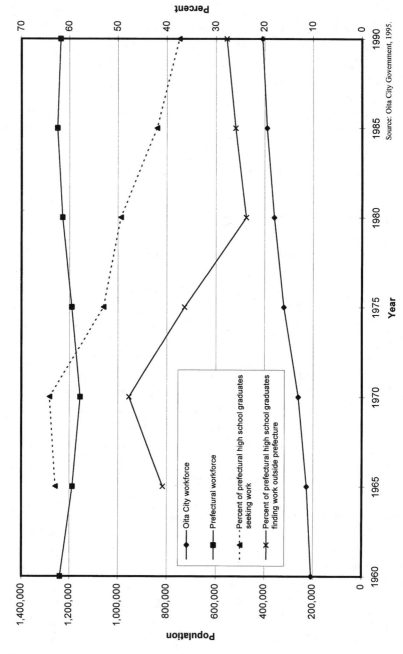

Figure 9.2: Changes in population and employment, Oita Prefecture, 1960–1990

Source: Oita City Government, 1995.

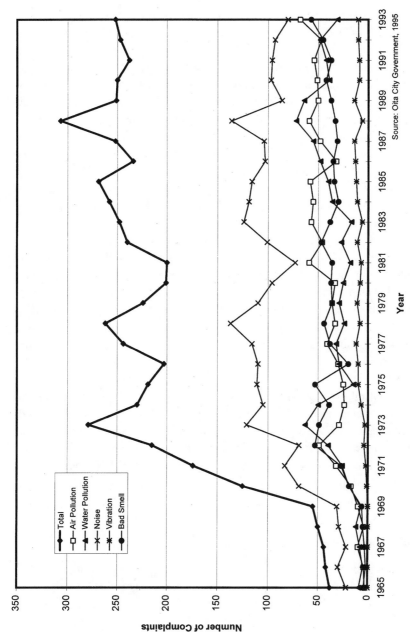

Figure 9.3: Pollution complaints to the Oita City government, 1965–1993, by type

1990, average prices in Oita City for goods quadrupled, but average wages rose by a multiple of twelve. In 1965, average wages in Oita City had been 88 percent of the national average, with Oita prefectural wages at 80 percent of Oita City's. By 1993, Oita City's average wages stood exactly even with the national average, with Oita prefectural wages at 83 percent of the city's. This improved economic stature, so hoped for by Oita's 1950s industrializers, had been more due to the central government policies of benefit redistribution through grants, the rise in prices for farmers' products, and the nationwide rise in real wages. These had supported a reduction in regional economic disparities, much more than the effects of the NIC program.

Along with its improving prosperity, however, Oita City had also become a city of permanent pollution complaint. The number of formal complaints to the city government about air, water, and other forms of pollution, as one might expect, climbed steadily through the 1960s and early 1970s, reaching a peak in 1973 (Figure 9.3). After that, given the new national anti-pollution regime and decline of the nationwide pollution protest movement, one would have expected that complaints would have declined precipitously. However, complaints stayed at a high level throughout the 1970s and 1980s, even surpassing the 1973 peak in 1988 (Oita City, 1995). At both peaks, people complained about noise more than anything. Air and water pollution and bad smells also rose and stayed at an active level.

These results agree with the results of the NHK survey noted earlier, in which a significant minority of NIC area residents complained about a worsening of their environment as a result of industrial pollution. The high steady level of complaints after 1973, despite the decline of protest movements, indicates that complaining was not a fad inspired by the media. After the media focus turned elsewhere, the complaints continued. This indicates that the complaints accurately reflected increased and steady levels of pollution, plus an increased willingness to complain.

Conclusions

The struggle between elites and movements over meeting condition three – environmental impact assessment – became increasingly evident and harsh in the prefectural community. Groups formerly without voice in politics, impelled by pollution and other problems, sought ways to make themselves heard. When the formal democratic institutions rebuffed them as minorities, they sought out other venues to voice their concerns.

In the process, the movements turned for the first time to the formal political levers given in the post-war political system. The formal legal and court system provided one such lever. The freedoms of public debate and of the press provided another. Citizen participation in making local government policy was a logical extension of the new democratic system.

These levers gave the citizen greater potential political influence, but few citizens had used them. In pre-Second World War times, these levers had not been so available. When pushed by necessity, movements discovered that these levers could help them appeal to other authorities and to mass publics for help. As Chapter 9 shows, using these levers, movements put the pro-growth elites on the defensive. Court suits and public debates forced the Oita elites to shift their tactics from soft social control, as it had been in the early stages of the movements, to control over how the public framed and interpreted pollution. In other words, given the new political institutional context, the diffusion of concern about pollution to third parties – mass publics and courts – forced the pro-growth elite to shift their social control tactics from social hegemony to ideological hegemony. In this attempt, though, the pro-growth elite was not very effective. The protest movement quickly fielded its own experts. "Truth" had become contestable.

The Prefectural Government stubbornly continued to defend its preferred interpretation of pollution in Misa/Iejima even after its own expert, Dr. Ishinishi, under criticism from movement experts, had abandoned that interpretation. The Prefectural Government also minimized the effect of citizen participation on the environmental impact assessment.

The Prefectural Government's resistance to citizen dialogue and participation can be interpreted from many angles: paternalistic ideology, prefectural costs sunk into Phase Two, national developmental state influence, capitalist class influence. All four forces were at work.

The officials seemed quite convinced of their rectitude in rejecting dialogue with oppositional citizens. The NIC Phase One had become an important hub within the national economy, supported by the national economic ministries. And the Governor's base of electoral support had definitely moved to the right, under the wing of big business, a sector of local business and the LDP. Paternalistic ideology was not the main driving force, as the planning procedure of Mayor Sato showed. Phase Two seemed to have little to recommend it. At that time, the prospects no longer looked good. The growth plans and citizen exclusion continued as a result of the synergy between the favorable place of Oita in MITI's long-range plans, the desire of the prefectural officials to recoup their lost investment in building Landfills No. 6 and 7, and demands from local construction companies.

Efforts by the Oita Prefectural Government to control and reduce local pollution proved very sensitive to the level of national pollution protest. Between 1970 and 1975, the cresting wave of national and international environmental protest put a lot of pressure on the national government. This filtered down to prefectural officials, who negotiated with NIC factories and refineries to install more effective anti-pollution equipment. As a result, some of the businesses installed tall smokestacks and started to burn low-sulfur fuel. Under this anti-pollution regime, Oita Prefecture also promised to move Iejima hamlet to a less polluted site.

After that, a number of forces weakened the national wave of pollution protest. Government and industries' success in reducing pollution, the rise in oil prices, and the resulting recession all dampened the ardor of protestors. The number of movement organizations and progressive local governments declined. As a result, protests posed less of a serious political challenge to the LDP. This gave the LDP less reason to let the EA actively push business to reduce pollution. The balance of power within the Ruling Triad shifted back toward the economic ministries and big business interests. This revived the growth-first regime, albeit this time with greater care to avoid the pollution excesses of the past.

As a result of this national shift, Oita Prefecture also backtracked on its own pollution regime. It fulfilled the letter of the Three Conditions, but not the spirit. It avoided using the new "polluter-pays law" to pay for the Iejima group move, and as a result it eventually had to renege on its promise to move Iejima.

That the national and local state should take a reverse course once the grassroots electoral threat had declined indicates that the State's conversion to an anti-pollution regime was pragmatic, not ideological. The state arrived at more effective pollution policies because of severe political challenges to the Ruling Triad, not because the environmentalists persuaded the elites to adopt new (environmental) goals or beliefs. However, once installed, the anti-pollution regime could not be entirely eliminated. Concerning certain key pollution sources such as power plant smokestacks and auto exhaust, the government continued to enforce high anti-pollution standards . Thus, the political struggles left an enduring policy legacy, if not a changed balance of power.

The Prefectural Government won the legal administrative battle over Landfill No. 8, but still could not build it. By delaying the decision, the movement had pushed the landfill project past its window of economic opportunity. In the new era of the world economy, Japanese companies no longer wanted to invest in the domestic hinterland. Big business and the national government no longer stood behind the prefecture's drive for growth. Delay was tantamount to defeat. Still, the Oita government continued vigorous efforts to bring industry to Landfills No. 6 and 7. If a suitable industrial company had wanted to locate on No. 8, the Oita government would have had no compunction in reviving the project.

Aside from bringing in Tokyo-based big business facilities, the Oita Prefectural Government also tried to generate innovative prescriptions for growth. This adds credence to the view that all along, the Prefectural Government's dedication to growth contained a good dose of concern for prefectural economic welfare. It was not driven by business-class interests alone. Among the new ventures, the One Village, One Product Movement, for instance, did not involve profits to medium or big business at all. The Technopolis project brought in new electronics industries, but these were not part of the older zaibatsu-style refineries that had come to the NIC landfills.

Prefectural officials saw these projects as ways to guide the community toward what they saw as greater collective welfare. Their continuing dedication to growth resulted from a mixture of ethical (if paternalistic) concern, technocratic officiousness, and business supporter push for growth. The officials saw industrialization as the best way to improve prefectural welfare with themselves as the best guides. Within this interpretive framework, protest movements seemed obstructionist and "selfish" at best, subversive at worst. The Oitan critics commented:

The Prefectural Government sees itself as taking the broad view, for the present and future profit of the mass of prefectural citizens. Therefore, if there are some victims, it can't be helped. In this light, opposition to prefectural growth policies is a stab-in-the-back. In their eyes, Inao is a traitor. To the prefectural officials, democracy is majority rule. The movement is small, so it should give in (Interview 144, 1979).

But the youth of the area had already reframed the position of the citizen. They believed that the individual had certain basic rights to life and health that should not be violated, even in the pursuit of the general good. In other words, the struggle between the growth coalition and the environment coalition overlapped with an intergenerational struggle between visions of proper social order: traditional hierarchical groupism versus a modern emphasis on individual rights and personal happiness. Post-war social change had weakened the ability of the state and elite to impose an overall integration (*matomari*) on the society through any means: coercive, economic, ideological, or social hegemonic.

Furthermore, objective NHK survey data shows that the prefectural citizens were not convinced by the government's claim to represent the *matomari*. On the whole, people distrusted the government's intentions, and did not want to leave growth planning to the experts. They wanted the citizens most affected by growth to be able to fully participate in the planning process, something the "radical" movement had been demanding all along. Elite manipulation of political institutions and pollution-related knowledge no longer sufficed, if it ever had, to sway the popular mind.

However, the relative lightness of pollution in the entire NIC area, coupled with persistent pressure against would-be activists by the Triple Control Machine, was sufficient to maintain LDP and pro-growth elite political domination at the prefectural level, and for the most part at the city and town levels. Through this mechanism, Oita continued to serve the national growth priorities of MITI, as well as provide profits for big business and local contractors and allow for innovative projects by a creative governor.

10

Power, Protest, and Political Change

What may we conclude now, having perused the foregoing stories and information, about the *how* and *why* of Japan's GE dilemma? What does that, in turn, tell us about the principles by which Japanese society operates? About the principles of politics and social movements more generally? About the GE dilemma in general? Have any lessons emerged that might prove helpful to the wider world, as it struggles to come to grips with intensifying environmental deterioration?

We can boil questions about the GE dilemma down to one main dimension of possibilities. Did the political conflicts around industrial growth directly reflect its realist, material effect – intensity of sulfur dioxide pollution in the air, prevalence of sickness, gain of profit and loss of livelihood, rearrangement of living patterns? Or were these conflicts also more or less influenced by interpretive, sociocultural factors – the manner in which our social roles and rules, and our collective, but subjective, values, beliefs and identities, interpret both natural and social events and channel our responses to them? This dimension of questioning stretches from realist through socially-constructed to culturally constructed sorts of explanations.

The preceding chapters have presented us with instances of all three sorts of behavior. We will want to disentangle the interactive skein of causation they brought about within the details of the case. But first, we should look once again at the bigger picture – Japan in comparison to other ACID societies – as we did in Chapter 1. This time, though, we can tailor the comparison more closely to these questions about the GE dilemma. The ACID societies responded at different rates to the pollution crisis of the 1960s (see Figure 10.1 and Figure 1.3). Did the relative rapidity of their response, in the above terms, reflect differences in their (realist, objective) natural intensity of pollution, or was it also affected by their social intensity of pollution – the numbers of people subjected to pollution and the way they construed it? If the latter is important, it will give important confirmation to some sort of socially or culturally constructed process at work.

Comparative ACID responses to the GE dilemma

So far, the analysis and theory in this book has focused on society. However, the point of environmental sociology is that social science must include pressures from nature too (Dunlap & Catton, 1994b). If the natural intensity of Japanese pollution – its parts per million in the air, for instance – was greater than in the other ACID societies, that fact, rather than Japanese culture or institutions, may have been responsible for its pollution miracle, not some social or cultural characteristic. On the other hand, if Japan had a moderate natural intensity, but a high social intensity of pollution, that would indicate the presence of social or cultural factors at work constructing its response.

The *natural intensity index* of pollution portrays the intensity of air pollution in the natural environment.[1] The *social intensity index* of pollution portrays its impact on the human community, based on the numbers of people affected by it.[2] The more people that experience a given level of air pollution in a certain area, the higher the social intensity of pollution. As Figure 10.1 shows, the social intensity index closely resembles the well-known IPAT index (column sets 2 and 4).[3]

If a society's reduction in air pollution parallels its rank on the natural intensity index, this indicates support for a realist theoretical position. On the other hand, if the society's reduction in air pollution parallels its rank on the social intensity index, this indicates that it is the numbers of people exposed, rather than the absolute level of exposure of the worst cases, that pushes a society into controlling air pollution. The latter outcome could be compatible with a realist

---

1. The index divides the total output of sulfur dioxide air pollution by the total area of the nation (using the figure for non-forested areas, which is only about 35 percent of the total for Japan, and higher percentages for the other ACID societies).
2. The social intensity of pollution index is arrived at by multiplying the annual tonnage of sulfur dioxide air pollution by the average population density (total population divided by total area of non-forested land).
3. Impact = Population size × Affluence × Technology in terms of pollution output. The IPAT formula, developed by Erlich and Holden (1992), has been implemented in comparative research. Dietz and Rosa, comparing 111 nations, found that pollution increased directly with population size, but at high levels of affluence, some countries stabilized or reduced their pollution emission (1994, cited in Harper, 1995, p. 248). The IPAT numbers in Figure 10.1 came from multiplying population density by GNP per square kilometer. I can ignore technology by assuming it to be of equal impact in all the ACID societies in 1970. The research presented here implies a criticism of the IPAT formula, incorporated in my affluence measure. To arrive at impact, we have to divide PAT by land area.

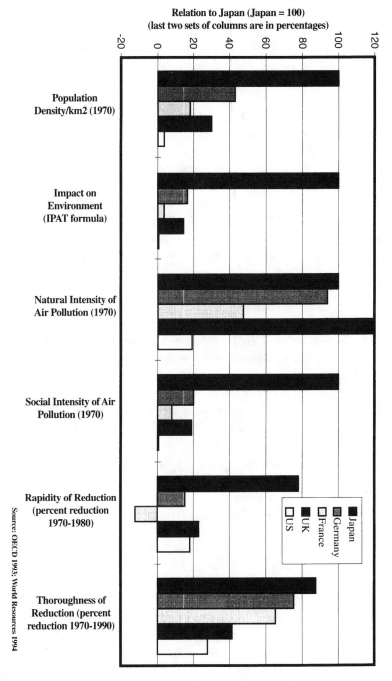

Source: OECD 1993; World Resources 1994

Figure 10.1: Natural and social intensity of pollution and societal response (ACID societies, 1970–1990)

explanation also, since more people might join interest groups or protest under that situation. But it also indicates that the social and cultural characteristics of that population may be important determinants of response. The values of the natural and social intensity indexes for five ACID societies appear in the third and fourth columns of Figure 10.1.

Surprisingly, not Japan, but the UK, had the highest *natural* intensity of pollution – its factories and power plants covered the UK's small island area with the thickest blanket of sulfur dioxide, as the famous fogs of London have long indicated. Japan and Germany tied for second place, with France having a much lower intensity because of its larger land area. The United States, given its massive land area, had the least natural intensity of pollution, despite having by far the greatest total output of pollution (Figure 1.4).

Japan, however, had by far the highest *social* intensity of pollution. Its very high population density and urban crowding of factories meant that the nation's air pollution settled on many people – the number of people suffering from its ill-effects far outnumbered those in the other ACID societies. The European ACID societies suffered only about one-fifth of Japan's social intensity of pollution, while the United States approached zero.

These two causal variables relate to two dependent variables, the rapidity and the thoroughness of air pollution reduction. The *rapidity* of a society's response to air pollution is indicated by its percentage of reduction in sulfur dioxide pollution tonnage from 1970 to 1980. The *thoroughness* of its response is indicated by its percentage reduction at the twenty-year mark (1990) (Figure 10.1). By the time twenty years had passed, I assumed, any policies started after 1970, even if implemented more slowly, would have had time to take effect.

By both measures, Japan far outperformed its competition (columns five and six in Figure 10.1). Within ten years, Japan had reduced its total sulfur dioxide tonnage by an amazing 78 percent. After twenty years, Japan had managed an 88 percent reduction. The other ACID countries showed varying degrees of success. At ten years, Germany, the UK, and the United States were in the same league (about 20 percent reduction), while France had even lost ground, and trailed badly (about a 10 percent increase). By twenty years, however, Germany and France had drawn close to Japan, while the UK and the United States trailed badly (although showing improvement).

Which pollution indicator, its natural intensity or its social intensity, is more predictive of the rapidity and thoroughness of a society's reduction in pollution? Figures 10.2 and 10.3 show the degree of change at the ten-year mark (in 1980) in the natural and social intensity of pollution of five ACID countries. Comparing these two figures for 1980 shows that the five societies were much more concerned about reducing their *social* intensities of pollution to roughly equal,

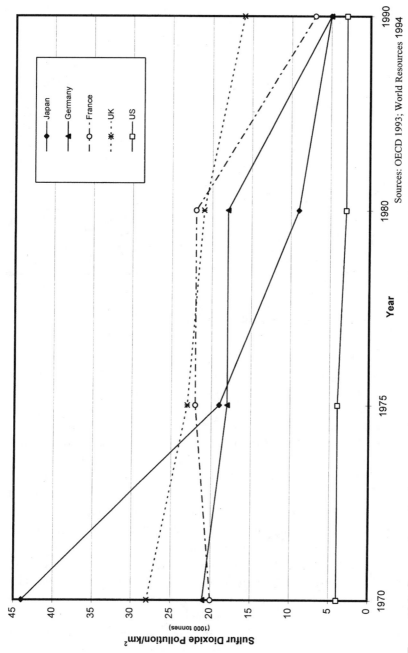

Figure 10.2: Comparative reduction in natural intensity of air pollution (ACID societies, 1970–1990)

Sources: OECD 1993; World Resources 1994

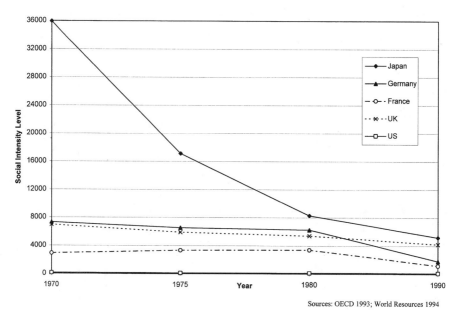

Sources: OECD 1993; World Resources 1994

Figure 10.3: Comparative reduction in social intensity of air pollution (ACID societies, 1970–1990)

fairly low levels, than they were about reducing their *natural* (absolute) levels of pollution. This finding indicates that the degree of social pressure on government is a much more important cause of their response—their degree of pollution control—than is the objective level of pollution.

By 1990, France, Japan, and Germany, despite having far denser populations than the United States, had all drawn close to the United States' low social intensity of pollution (Figure 10.3). Among the five societies, only the UK did not attain that standard. That may have been due to the age of its industrial plants, its declining financial ability to upgrade them, and its slowness to turn to nuclear power (due to strong public protest) (World Resources Institute, 1994). The fact that the UK started with and continued to have the highest natural density of pollution, yet was the slowest and least thorough in its response to that condition, indicates the weakness of the natural intensity of pollution as a direct stimulant of reform. Rather, a society's response is more strongly affected by its social intensity of pollution – the numbers of pollution victims.

In other words, a society's social intensity of pollution, not its natural intensity, was the better predictor of its rapidity of response to the problem. Social intensity was not a perfectly accurate predictor, though. Japan was first in social intensity and in rapidity of response. For Germany and the UK the relationship held well also. France, however, had a lower rank on response than its social intensity would have predicted, while the United States over-responded. This indicates that social intensity – the raw numbers of people polluted – alone is not a sufficient predictor. Besides social and natural intensity, variations in social institutions and patterns of power also play an important role in modulating a society's response to pollution.

In other words, the social intensity of pollution does not well predict the level of political pressure for regulation activism. Aside from natural and social intensity, another factor is affecting the political response – societal patterns of power and perception. Societies with higher social intensity, such as Germany and France in comparison with the U.S., have higher rates of protest (Kitschelt, 1995, p. 330). However, Japan, with the highest social intensity, had a much lower intensity of environmental protest than Germany or France. Environmental protest stayed local in Japan, whereas it produced huge national demonstrations in Germany and France.[4]

Germany's and France's initial slowness but eventual thoroughness in response to air pollution indicates greater state capacity than their Anglo-Saxon counterparts. The relatively strong bureaucratic centers in Japan and France, and the corporatism of Germany, fostered better coordination between state and society that made for a more effective response once pushed in that direction. The high social intensity of Japan's initial condition pushed it to respond more rapidly, but all three societies eventually responded quite thoroughly.

The United States and the United Kingdom, on the other hand, responded less rapidly and less thoroughly. The United States started with very low social and natural intensities of pollution. Despite less pressure to change, its pluralistic, relatively open political institutions and vocal populace pushed the country into moderate reductions in air pollution. This was progress more rapid and thorough than its social intensity alone would have predicted. The UK's slowness of response despite relatively high natural and social intensities reflects, perhaps, an ineffectual state, political gridlock, recession, and an aging industrial plant.

This comparison has shown that neither the natural nor the social intensities of pollution are perfect predictors of the rapidity and thoroughness of a society's response to the problem. Both contributed to the response, but their partial disjuncture with the response indicates the additional importance of the pat-

---

4. Kitschelt notes that "in France, between 1975 and 1977, approximately 175,000 people rallied against nuclear power in ten demonstrations. Determined police action against the demonstrators subsequently led to a decline in such mass events. In West Germany, the intransigence of political elites provoked demonstrations too, but a weak state did not act decisively to quell the unrest. From February 1975 to April 1979, approximately 280,000 people participated in seven demonstrations at nuclear sites" (1995, p. 330).

terns of power, social institutions and culture of the society. In its distribution of power, Japan's centralized state resembled France's most closely. In its tactics of dealing with protest, each state used both the carrot and the stick. Unlike the United States, Germany or the UK, both the Japanese and French states responded capably with preemptive projects to reduce air pollution, while at the same time actively attempting to quell protest. However, the French state used hard means of social control to quell the protests, while the Japanese state used soft social control. Let us now turn to the theoretical implications of the way Japan responded to its GE dilemma.

The how of Japan's response

The GE dilemma per se is a very abstract concept that begs for concrete examples and indicators. Chapter 1 identified five main policy shifts in Japan as appropriate examples that embodied the GE dilemma. The first two and the fifth policy shifts concerned the *causes* of the GE dilemma – decisions which encouraged "pollution as usual": 1) the New Industrial Cities (NIC) Law (Chapter 2), 2) the type of industry brought to Oita (Chapter 2), and finally, 5) Governor Hiramatsu's announcement of the fulfillment of the Three Conditions (Chapters 8 and 9). The third and fourth policy shifts contributed to *curing* the GE dilemma – by reducing pollution, and by slowing down the pace and reducing the extent of landfill and industrial growth: 3) the national Pollution Diet with its fourteen strict regulatory laws (Chapter 3), and at the prefectural level, 4) Governor Taki's granting of the Three Conditions (Chapters 4 through 7). In addition to these five main policy shifts, the chapters also considered related policy shifts made at lower levels of government. These included the confrontation between Oita City Mayor Sato and the LDP-dominated Oita City legislature over the city development plan, as well as the way Seki mayoral candidate Furuta and Kozaki ku-heads changed their stance on Landfill No. 8 once they assumed office. What patterns of power, what mechanisms of interaction, may we conclude determined these policy shifts? How do our conclusions reflect upon existing models of power for ACID societies?

As noted in Chapter 1, existing models of power include the pluralist, elite, class, corporatist, state-autonomy and party-centric (principal-agent) models developed in studies of the United States and European societies, as well as distinctive models of the East Asian state – the "network state" and the "bureaucratic paternalist" state. Which of these, if any, provide an accurate model of how Japanese politics works regarding substantive issues raised by the GE dilemma? Or, which of their elements should we retain and incorporate into a more accurate model that we build afresh?

The NIC Law

The original impetus for this national program "bubbled up" from grassroots demand. However, some of the Ruling Triad elites manipulated this demand to serve other ends. In this case, the more immediate interests of the dominant national political party and big business won out over the rational proposals of the state ministries. In order to curry political favor with those areas, the LDP agreed to designate fifteen NIC sites in hinterland areas. Due to their number, though, the central government would not provide these fifteen sites with grants-in-aid sufficient fulfill their designated purpose – attracting job-producing industries and slowing down the flow of population to the big cities. The "aid" turned out to be mainly permission to designated prefectures to sell bonds, so that they could finance the building of landfill and other industrial infrastructure as a speculative investment, at their own expense and risk.

In addition, due to political pressure from big business and with the assent of growth-advocate LDP, six special sites within the Pacific Coast Belt received the same forms of aid as the NIC sites, further diluting the social effects of the NIC program. The big conglomerates wanted to move the heavy shipping facilities outside the crowded central harbors of Tokyo and Osaka. This industrial redistribution fit well with the broader MITI/business goal of the most rapid capital accumulation, but did not address the original social concerns of local residents.

In this case, the LDP knowingly raised the number of NIC sites to an unreasonable number, in order to maintain its own dominance over the Diet by placating its rural voter base. Then it further tacked on the six more NIC-style sites in more crowded areas. Since the physical and societal effects of large-scale industrial plans do not become apparent for many years, NIC designation in itself cheered hinterland voters and retained their loyalty for the early 1960s, anyhow. This amounted to a successful exercise of symbolic politics, in which a party satisfies voters with symbol, not substance (Edelman, 1964; Edelman, 1977).

Since the LDP provided the crucial legislative component necessary to the continued collective dominance of national politics by the Ruling Triad, the other members (big business and state ministries) tolerated or acquiesced to its distortion of the NIC project. Government ministries advocating their respective rational plans proved the weakest member of the Triad.[5] Even MITI with

---

5. Scott attributes elite maltreatment of local demands to a process of hierarchical schematic representation – that the elites only see local demands as abstract numbers, not as human concerns (1995, p. 29). This is a Weberian style argument that depends on the rationalizing power of bureaucracy. However, the weakness of the government ministries in defining policy shows that this

its national economic rationalism, not to speak of the more social-welfare ori-
ented ministries, ended up with little say over these outcomes. This indicated
pattern of power had internal fractures among its member elites, but functioned
to deliver the main material benefits of growth – the accumulation of capital – to
centralized, large-scale corporations. Yet, it curtailed those benefits as necessary
in order to retain the collective dominance of the Ruling Triad as a whole over
the broader political system.

As a result of this pattern of power, far fewer benefits flowed to local, small
and medium businesses, as well as the general populations of hinterland and big
city areas. This kind of investment produced a rapid accumulation of profit and
capital for big business, but also produced a great deal of pollution and relatively
little social benefit. Even where an NIC site succeeded in attracting considerable industrial investment, it took the form of basic refining capacity, rather than
the hoped-for manufacturing plants. Hinterland health and lifestyle suffered.
The rush of population to the big cities continued, producing the urban debacle.
The unfortunate social outcomes are there for anyone to see – a crush of
population in the massive cities, and an increasingly abandoned countryside.
These outcomes are congruent with the expectations of "internal colonialism"
and "distorted development" – the latter advanced to account for the results of
Third World development (So, 1990).

The type of industry brought to Oita

The outcome of a policy, once implemented, often ends up quite different from
how it was envisioned in the original plan. This change represents an important
kind of policy shift, albeit an informal one (Pressman & Wildavsky, 1973).
Although the initial purpose of Oita's industrial growth plan was to bring jobs,
business contracts, and technical training to local residents, the actual outcomes
of the project failed to materialize much of those hopes. Investigation of how
this failure came about should provide additional evidence toward an accurate
model of Japanese politics.

As with the NIC policy, local demand stimulated the creation of Oita's industrial growth plan. At first, Governor Kinoshita's administration pursued a fairly
accurate representation of that demand, concentrating on bringing jobs and
business contracts to Oita. The Governor pumped the hometown loyalties of
influential Tokyo Oitans. Through these networks, he managed to bring an oil
refinery to Landfill No. 1 and start the ball rolling. However, these social
networks could at most bend, but could not overcome, the investment priorities

argument, though a piece of the puzzle, does not alone fully explain Japan's policy outputs in this
regard.

of big business and MITI. The realities of centralized power and resources, though – the investment capital of big business, the expertise and power of big construction companies, and the permissions necessary from central ministries – forced the mutation of Oita's growth plan. MITI and central business would only allow refineries, not job-providing manufacturing plants, to go to the hinterland. Accordingly, while the possession of good networks may have helped Oita attract refineries to itself rather than letting them go to some other hinterland site, networks could not *change* the priorities of the central elites. Ultimately, furthermore, even for Oita, the decisive factor in its "success" may have been not its networks but its geographical features: calm Beppu Bay, within the Inland Sea, with shallow, fillable coastal waters. As noted above, designation as a New Industrial City brought little external aid to Oita.

This pattern of growth did not help much with providing skilled industrial jobs for Oita's youth, although jobs in the service industry did increase. But it did greatly increase Oita's air and water pollution. Later, the investment of public funds in Phase Two landfills forced the Prefectural Government to continue seeking whatever buyers would come. This style of growth brought about Oita's own local version of the GE dilemma.

Accordingly, the macro-distribution among prefectures of networks as resources did little to influence the big picture, the industrial distribution map of Japan. Networks provided the necessary means of doing business for a prefecture. As in a "small world" experiment (Milgram, 1977), actors chose from among their social networks those that would place them in contact with their goal (in this case, central ministerial and industrial officials). Most, if not all, prefectures that sought industry, though, would have had available their own hometown clubs, and a sufficient variety of social networks to make the requisite contacts.[6] Therefore, networks were not a scarce resource.

These findings also support the model of highly centralized, business-dominated national growth policy. Additionally, they indicate a Prefectural Government caught between "a rock and a hard place" – local demands versus central resources and authority.

The Pollution Diet and pollution reduction

In the mid-1960s, local dissatisfaction with pollution finally erupted into a nationwide wave of grassroots anti-pollution NIMBY (localized) protests. MITI's efforts, informally pressuring companies to use low-sulfur fuel and tall smokestacks, had already begun to improve air quality. But the Ruling Triad did

6. Thus distinguishing them from individuals seeking jobs (Granovetter, 1973).

not want to make formal, legal policy concessions. Those might take arbitrary authority out of their hands and distribute it to local governments and citizens. At the beginning of the wave of protest, while protest was still weak, therefore, the government also responded with a weak measure – the mostly symbolic 1967 Basic Law on Pollution. This ineffective law did not mollify citizen anger, though, and the wave of protest continued to mount. Moreover, some of the movements succeeded in electing their allies, opposition-party affiliated candidates, to become mayors and governors. This new electoral wave threatened to affect even elections for the Diet, if the LDP did not address the pollution problem effectively.

In 1970, the protest cycle reached a peak. International criticism rained down on the government as well. Given the LDP's slowly declining hegemony in the Diet, these several challenges forced the LDP to produce a substantive improvement in the pollution situation. Under these circumstances, the Ruling Triad effectively shifted the weight it assigned to its two collective principles, giving temporary priority to *regime continuance* instead of *capital accumulation*. Using existing, but ignored, proposals by the Ministry of Health and Welfare, the LDP worked with the ministries to make up fourteen new pollution control laws and passed them in the 1970 Pollution Diet. These laws became the formal policy basis of Japan's "pollution miracle." Continued protest kept the new laws and the new Environmental Agency active and effective until the mid-1970s. When the national wave of environmental protest and the number of progressive local officials declined, though, so did the seriousness and effectiveness of the EA and the degree of enforcement of the new laws.

The Three Conditions

Governor Taki entered his office in 1971, at the peak of the national and local protest cycle. He had strong concerns about providing for local welfare, but had minimal political latitude. He was trapped between the two forces: local environmental protest and increasing pressure from local and central business and other elites to protect and foster Oita's refinery growth (which had become an important hub in the national economy). By 1973, the Pollution Diet and the new Environmental Agency had, in his mind, tipped the scales temporarily in favor of the local environmental movement. When the Seki movements executed their political "jui-jitsu" on him by threatening to riot in the EA's Tokyo headquarters offices, this additional pressure panicked Governor Taki with fear of shame, dishonor, stigma and possible loss of grants-in-aid from central bureaucrats.

Accordingly, the Governor offered to meet Three Conditions, instead of the one the EA had been demanding, before resuming activity on Landfill No. 8, if only the protestors would quiet down and return home. These Three Conditions were local citizen consensus over the issue of Landfill No. 8, an end to factional fighting in the Seki Fishing Union, and an environmental impact assessment. This tactic worked for its immediate purpose, but soon put the governor into the bad graces of the prefectural business community and LDP. Though the governor tried to backtrack by fulfilling only the letter, not the spirit, of the Three Conditions, as examined under the next policy shift, the process still ended the construction process until 1980. This represented a significant prefectural policy shift. In terms of the distribution of power, the Three Conditions incident shows that the broad course of policy, while largely determined by the Ruling Triad, is somewhat malleable in its local details by local actors.

The resolution of the Three Conditions

As Chapters 8 and 9 show, the prefectural elites applied methods of soft social control to quell the Seki protest movement, to meet the Three Conditions, and to present an inviting image to Tokyo businesses. To achieve "consensus," the LDP majority in the Seki Town legislature passed a vote in favor of No. 8 over the vociferous objections of a few legislators. Though this vote had elements of illegal process, was criticized by the Ministry of Home Affairs, and did not represent the preferences of the majority of people in the township, the Prefectural Government chose to recognize the vote as evidence of citizen consensus in favor of Landfill No. 8.

To "normalize" relations within the Seki Fishing Union, the Prefectural Government and associated elites worked with the union president to allow the Baba Fishing Union to split off. This gave the Baba Union the autonomy to sell its rights to the shallow waters proposed for Landfill No. 8, thus paving the way to its construction. After the Baba Union split off, the Seki Union had no jurisdiction over the matter any more. At the same time, the prefectural elites used soft social control to dissuade fishing people from supporting the opposition movement. The Nikko Copper Refinery also may have bribed the leader of the movement into quiescence. As a result, factional fighting in the Seki Union ended.

The Nomura Research Institute, given the opposition it encountered from Kozaki protestors, did a "desk-top" impact assessment using estimates of wind directions. In 1980, the results of this assessment, as expected, gave the green light to build Landfill No. 8.

In the mid-1970s, Hiramatsu, the MITI official who had been so involved in

Oita's growth plans, had been appointed as vice-governor. He put the legitimating stamp of a direct central government connection on Oita's industrial project. He also had greater freedom to operate, given the decline in local and national protest. In 1979, he ran as an LDP candidate for governor and won. In 1980, Governor Hiramatsu formally declared that the Three Conditions had been met, and that the prefecture could start building Landfill No. 8 at any time. He declared his intention to build the landfill when economic conditions permitted, despite any local protest that might erupt. During this period, creative environmental policy initiatives were possible only when a labor-farmer coalition dominated the elections, as happened with Mayor Sato of Oita City.

The Prefectural Government's method of meeting the Three Conditions illustrated its role as a proactive, policy-pursuing local political actor. By this time, the Prefectural Government had moved from its early ties to the Socialist party solidly out of that orbit and into the arms of the LDP. Its use of the Triple Control Machine to manufacture an appearance of consensus in Seki illustrated the weakness of civil society in Japan. When the state and associated dominant elites can so readily penetrate and largely control the arena of public discourse and assembly, democratic institutions lose much of their meaning. These incidents demonstrate the relatively arbitrary power that conservative local governments can exercise over "their" citizens in Japan.

Conclusions about models of power

How well do these findings support and meet the expectations of the various existing models of power put forth in Chapter 1?[7] If we contrast each model as an ideal type, stressing its basic postulates, we find varying degrees of support for each one.[8] They offer some degree of support for a pluralist model. Citizen preferences, expressed through protest movements and electoral threat, forced the Ruling Triad to compromise and clean up the most obvious and worst pollution. However, the pluralist model assumes that the formal political institutions will give greater, more immediate, voice in politics to public preferences. The patronage politics of the LDP, as examined in detail in Chapter 6 and elsewhere, tended rather to disempower the citizenry. The patronage machine truncated the public sphere and left popular participation with minimal influence over policy-making (Alford & Friedland, 1975).

7. Please refer to Chapter 1 for the bibliographic references for these political models.

8. Max Weber suggested the use of ideal types in social research. He defined the ideal type as a conception of how some form of social organization, such as bureaucracy, would work if it strictly and purely followed certain essential principles postulated by the researcher (Root, 1993, pp. 47–9; Weber, 1947, p. 110).

The findings offer more support to an elite model. The top actors in the major institutions, government, party and business – the Ruling Triad – were the dominant voices in policy formation. However, these three elites were not equal in power, as elite theory often assumes (Mills, 1956). When the interests of the three clashed, the ministries lost out. Clearly, in the long run, a state-autonomy view does not explain much here, even though major theorists of Japan (Johnson, 1982; Reed, 1986: 155) tend to support it. Rather, the party-business dyad held the greater power. The interests of party and business differed at times also, but they compromised according to an emergent principle of cooperation. When their joint regime was not threatened, capital accumulation reigned supreme, at least in the environmental policy domain. When strong public protest threatened the hegemony of the LDP, though, the business elite went along with some diminution in the rate of capital accumulation , as necessary to invest in pollution control equipment, placate the voters and save the regime.

Rather than an elite model, then, a class-dominant model may come closer to the realities of power. The findings show that big business interests got more of their demands met than any other interest group, thus providing considerable support for the class model. However, the class model too has its problems here. The class model tends to postulate a constant domination over politics by the capitalist class. Furthermore, class models imply sharply opposed differences (zero-sum games) in the economic interests of classes. The more resource-rich class – the capitalist class – dominates the state and its policies and uses that power to enforce its exploitation of the workers and the citizenry. This clash leads to open or covert class struggle (Chapter 1).

Given these assumptions, pure class models do not usually recognize that the capitalists may be disorganized, may lose in political battles, or may enter into alliances with the working class in the pursuit of common ends. Nor do they usually recognize that the political party allied with the capitalist class may mediate between different classes and interest groups, forcing compromise from all sides.

Yet, in this study, all those caveats were present. Business interests, though seemingly well-organized, sometimes lost out. Business and sections of labor cooperated to push forward the Treadmill of Production. And the LDP doled out patronage – the more personal or regulatory of it effectively portions of accumulated capital derived from the capitalist class – to voters in various forms: bribery, parties, services, pollution regulations. This patronage helped the LDP retain power. As a perhaps inadvertent result, then, responding to threats to its hegemony, the LDP moderated the negative impact of the regime of capital accumulation on public welfare.

Likewise, class struggle was not a given. Centrist, big company labor unions, such as in the NIC refineries and the Nikko copper refinery in Seki, gave solid, organized support to economic growth policies and disparaged concerns about pollution. Their position supports the corporatist model rather than the class-struggle model. At the same time, in Oita, the more left-wing unions associated with the Socialist party at first supported the program of rapid industrial growth, because they thought it would improve public welfare and increase the voting working class. This too speaks to an implicit cooperation, rather than conflict, between classes. However, once the true impact of the NIC on local public welfare became evident, the left-wing unions and the Socialist party turned against the NIC project and supported the protest movements. This appears to fit the class-struggle model, except for the fact that in Japan, the left-wing unions hardly drew from the industrial working class. The member unions mainly represented employees in government bureaucracies, such as the post office, the national railway, teachers, and local government clerical workers.

Moreover, big business did not dominate state policy formation through either of the most noted variations in the class model: instrumental (placing its own members into the state) or structural (by generating revenue for the state) means. Instead, big business dominated politics through its influence over the LDP, due to the importance of its political contributions, and through its presence on many government advisory committees. The highly organized and centralized nature of the Japanese capitalist class, evident in the unified front presented by big business in their investment priorities, more supports the corporatist model than the class model, with its assumptions of an anarchy of competition among capitalists.

The important role of the LDP does not justify assigning the LDP the role of principal with the ministries as its agents, though. Power relations within the Ruling Triad were not so fixed. They shifted according to external circumstances. Regarding environmental policy, the LDP couched its policies as much as possible in line with the vocal demands of its biggest financial backer – big business. Big business's profits were directly hurt by pollution controls, so it was an insistent voice in this policy domain. However, at times, the voices of the public or the ministries became so loud that the LDP and business had to listen.

How do the East Asian-specific models fare? The findings offer some support for the network state model, in that close personal ties were evident among the officials of various ministries and among them, the LDP and big business. Okimoto says that the network state is built on reciprocal relations between the ministries, the LDP and big business. But at the same time, he argues that the state must, and can, use its networks to persuade big business to go along with its national plans (Okimoto, 1989, pp. 145, 226). The state does so, he says, through its social networks – the "old boy" networks in which top ministerial retirees take up leading positions in the LDP and big business (Okimoto, 1989, p. 216).[9] Okimoto does not entertain the idea that the networks could flow in reverse – that business could control government or the party through the same networks.

Contrary to Okimoto's general argument, though, the events in this book show that the state, even MITI, often lost the intra-elite struggle over policy, even after exercising all its networks. The findings indicate that, within the Ruling Triad, the reciprocal networks transferred influence in both directions. They gradually wove a collective sense of what was possible and advisable, even if not in accord with what a given ministry wanted. The result may not have changed any basic interests, but it allowed for cooperation around a common plan. Accordingly, the state seems to have less guidance power than Okimoto would assign it. The findings do support the idea, though, that thinking of the ministries, the LDP and big business as separate "interest groups," in the Western sense may be quite misleading (Okimoto, 1989, p. 144). As pointed out in the next section, the dense social ties among these three spheres may make them more like a single interest group, clustered under a common umbrella of nationalism, rather than three competing groups.

If we go outside the Ruling Triad, the network state model quickly becomes less reciprocal, and the state attains greater informal power to persuade and guide – at least until it incites open revolt. Other interest groups in society, such as labor or social movements, have much weaker reciprocal ties to ministerial bureaucrats (Kabashima & Broadbent, 1986). Those ties they do have tend to remove their autonomy and subordinate them to ministerial priorities. The earnest petitions from hinterland local governments to ministries, for instance, did not produce much real support for industrial redistribution. The environmental movements that tried to establish themselves as national public interest groups ran into ministerial resistance. Those public interest groups that did get established as non-profits often had to accept a ministerial "old boy" retiree onto their board of directors and pay them. By this evidence, the network state operates in horizontal mode within the Ruling Triad, and in vertical mode outside it.

The paternalist bureaucratic inclusionary pluralism model also gets some support from the findings. Almost any group in society, it seems, could find a genuinely sympathetic ear somewhere in officialdom with concern for its problems and grievances. This paternalism was not dependent upon having a per-

---

9. Unlike patronage systems in many ACID societies, presumably, this "old boy" network inserts experts imbued with the national spirit into politics and business, rather than inserting opportunists into government bureaucracy. This should produce a greater collective dedication within the Ruling Triad to following rational policies good for the entire society.

sonal tie to an official, as in the network state model. For instance, in 1962, due to certain activist officers, the MHW succeeded in stimulating public concern over air pollution with the express purpose of putting pressure on other, more pro-growth ministries and the LDP (Chapter 3).[10] Certainly, too, the Seki movements found a receptive ear in the newly created national Environmental Agency. At the height of the wave of environmental protest in the early 1970s, the EA had considerable influence within the government. Therefore, Governor Taki felt compelled to comply with the EA's "guidance" that Oita undertake an environmental assessment of Landfill No. 8. The problem with the bureaucratic inclusionary model, though, is that the concerned ministry or agency may not have the power to affect policy outcomes. When national popular pressure declined, so did the influence of the EA within the government, and so did the standards and enforcement of pollution regulations. Accordingly, the bureaucratic inclusionary model does not offer pluralism's expectation of effective populist voice in and policy response from government.

In sum, if we synthesize the accurate parts of the different models and add in what the empirical data indicates, we find the interests of the three members of the Triad do indeed dominate the policy-making process. Among these three, the process ultimately delivered the main benefits of growth to centralized, large-scale corporations, rather than to local, small and medium businesses, hinterland or big city populations, or government ministries of various mandates advocating their respective rational plans. Accordingly, these findings indicate a model of power for Japan that could be called a "business-dominated, LDP-mediated and partly pluralized, and at the margins, ministerially rationalized and more pluralized within a strong vertical corporatist" political system. For shorthand, I will call this a "communitarian elite corporatist" (CEC) model of politics.

This model does not indicate a static or constant situation. It summarizes the results of interactions over several decades (Abbott, 1992; Aminzade, 1992). Many specific events in the system, such as Governor Taki's concession of the Three Conditions, occurred in largely unpredictable ways affected by complex mixtures of institutional contexts and actors' creative agency. These events set the conditions for new contentions and outcomes. In this sense, the unfolding system was path-dependent and partly random. Each step was contingent on what had sometimes unpredictably happened before. Therefore, the model is dynamic; it expects and accounts for shifts in the distribution of power. In order

---

10. Skocpol notes that state managers sometimes help insurgents against capital (1995). Block argues that state autonomy expands during times of internal class stuggle (1977), which the Pollution Diet outcome supports.

to determine its generality for Japan, we would have to investigate a number of other Japanese policy domains. In order to determine the model's cross-national generality, we would have to compare findings on Japan with findings on environmental policymaking in other ACID societies.

The CEC model and its features help explain some puzzles and refute some arguments. It shows, for instance, that the reason the government at first denied the severity of pollution was not "political gridlock" (Reich, 1991, p. 261). Nor was the reason for this denial that MITI's industrializing priorities dominated the triad (Johnson, 1982). Rather, the reason was that, without sufficient domestic political threat and challenge, the Ruling Triad stuck to its primary principle: capital accumulation. Its stubbornness in pursuing rapid economic growth at any cost did not indicate gridlock between opposed interests nor domination of the Triad by a single ministry, but simply a lack of sufficient domestic political challenge.

The CEC model also clarifies the changes in policy from the 1960s, from support for growth to environmental protection and then back to growth. Some scholars attribute this pattern of change to three different stages of government-business relations over environmental policy: collusive, adversarial, and cooperative (Pharr & Badaracio, 1986). The findings indicate two flaws in this three-stage scenario. Given the speed with which Japan reduced its air pollution, the middle stage could not have been truly adversarial. The United States tried adversarial regulation during the 1970s with indifferent success (Figure 1.4). The findings in this book indicate, rather, that Japan's pollution control took place, not by the adversarial and impersonal imposition of formal regulation, but with the informal cooperation – albeit grudging – of big business. Big business recognized the necessity of some pollution control in order to maintain LDP hegemony. Air pollution could not have been achieved so rapidly without business cooperation.

Second, the reason for the shift to effective pollution control, this book indicates, was not primarily international influence or the prevailing "climate of feeling" (Pharr & Badaracio, 1986). When national policies shifted back to support growth in the mid-1970s, international influence as well as many officials still supported pollution controls. Therefore, these factors were probably not determinative of the switch to pollution control policies in the first place. Rather, the findings indicate that key determinants of the Pollution Diet were the level of political threat posed by popular protest and a dominant elite community that enjoyed sufficient flexibility to shift national policies quickly.

Furthermore, this model clarifies the principles of LDP concession-making. Calder argues that the LDP follows a principle of crisis and compensation (Calder, 1988) – when there is a political crisis (a threat to LDP hegemony), give the challengers substantive compensation to quiet them down. To Calder, the NIC Law was one example of such *substantive* compensation, in this case hinterland prefectures. The findings of this book here do not refute that principle, but offer some refinement to it. In the policy shifts observed in this book, the LDP's behavior did not follow the binary, yes or no, granting of compensation suggested by Calder. Rather, the substantiveness of the compensation depended on the intensity of the political threat to the LDP regime. The threat to LDP national dominance posed by hinterland LDP Diet members and local governments demanding economic growth was weak. Accordingly, the compensation was also weak and largely symbolic. Similarly, the threat to the LDP regime posed by the wave of pollution protest in its early, weak stages elicited only symbolic compensation – the 1967 Basic Law. But when the wave of protest became stronger and elected a wave of progressive mayors and governors, the LDP granted substantive compensation in the 1970 Pollution Diet and subsequent legislation.

The model of Japanese environmental politics derived and presented here may accurately identify the distribution of power among the actors and the principles by which they operated. However, it does not tell us why – the deeper reasons for the existence of this model. To make an analogy, if we put together a balsa wood model airplane properly, it will glide and loop. That means the model correctly reproduces the essential qualities that allow a real airplane to fly. However, that does not mean we understand *why* it flies – the physics of flight. To understand why, we have to delve into the basic principles by which physical planar structures of certain composition interact with the fluid dynamics of air. Similarly, to understand the why of politics, we have to consider the constituent bonds that hold interested groups into hierarchical patterns of collective decision-making and policy implementation.

The why *of Japan's response to the GE dilemma*

An ontological framework

Why did the CEC model of power produce the observed response to the GE dilemma? Chapter 1 introduced three theoretical camps, each with many internal variations, that provided a host of different answers to this question. To simplify the analysis, we can array and compare the relevant theories along two fundamental dimensions (Table 10.1). On the horizontal dimension, the theories differ in their use of *realist, socially constructed,* or *culturally constructed* exchanges motivating collective action – respectively positing materialist, normative, and interpretive rewards and sanctions.[11] Along the vertical dimension, the theories differ in the degree to which they see *agency* or *structure* as the fundamental way in which social roles and actions are created – that is, actors' efforts to create their own behavioral patterns, or sets of roles imposed upon actors by preexisting higher-order patterns (Jepperson, 1991: 154). Between structure and agency, a "plastic" zone signifies the interaction between the two – the process of "structuration" (Giddens, 1983).[12] These two dimensions, horizontal and vertical, define the "ontological field" of theories of why political power is distributed unequally and hierarchically, in a phrase, of power structures (Table 10.1). Table 10.1 arrays the various power structure theories on this ontological field, according to their basic postulates. The same ontological field can also be used to array the potential types of exchanges between actors on the micro-level. An analytical thesis of this book is that these two ontological levels, macro-organizational and micro/meso exchange, imply each other (see Table A.1, Appendix 1).

Table 10.1 provides a shorthand way of comparing and synthesizing the theories in their essential postulates. If, for example, we argue that environmental conflicts and policy outcomes result from objective levels of pollution intensity, or the immediate profits and harm from it (including physical harm to health), that would be a structuralist, materialist, political-economic type of explanation (cell 1 of Table 10.1). On the other hand, if we explained such conflicts and outcomes as the result of different frames and interpretations that propelled the contending groups, that would be a cultural-structural type of explanation (cell 7). In this way, the framework heuristically clarifies the range of theoretical possibilities.

Table 10.1 is only a heuristic sketch of alternative possibilities, not a blueprint of reality. Nor does Table 10.1 encompass all the relevant theoretical dimensions. The cells have their formal and informal aspects, for instance. Actors exert influence through different tactics. Furthermore, their action unfolds through an historical, temporal process.[13] These additional aspects indicate the complexity of reality, and the advisability of not trying to reduce it to a single

---

11. This figure draws on those made by other scholars (Jepperson, 1991). However, it adds an additional category on each dimension and specifies the cell contents according to theories of collective action. On the vertical axis it adds the concept of "plasticity." This concept presents the central idea of structuration theory - that much action is neither purely structural nor purely agentic, but results from the interplay of structure and agency. In addition, the figure specifies the horizontal axis in terms of three categories of theory that roughly parallel and articulate it.

12. The concept of plastic as used here resembles "praxis," especially as defined by Harper: "the confluence of operating structure and purposely acting agents" (1996, p. 281). Sztompka defines this middle level as the "really real reality of the social world" (Sztompka, 1993, p. 217).

13. On the contextuality of action, see Foucault, 1980.

Table 10.1. *The formative dynamic of power structures: home domains of theoretical camps (with examples from theories of the GE dilemma)*

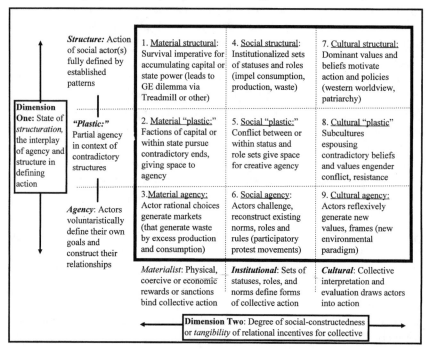

	Structure: Action of social actor(s) fully defined by established patterns	1. Material structural: Survival imperative for accumulating capital or state power (leads to GE dilemma via Treadmill or other)	4. Social structural: Institutionalized sets of statuses and roles (impel consumption, production, waste)	7. Cultural structural: Dominant values and beliefs motivate action and policies (western worldview, patriarchy)
Dimension One: State of *structuration,* the interplay of agency and structure in defining action	*"Plastic:"* Partial agency in context of contradictory structures	2. Material "plastic:" Factions of capital or within state pursue contradictory ends, giving space to agency	5. Social "plastic:" Conflict between or within status and role sets give space for creative agency	8. Cultural "plastic" Subcultures espousing contradictory beliefs and values engender conflict, resistance
	Agency: Actors voluntaristically define their own goals and construct their relationships	3. Material agency: Actor rational choices generate markets (that generate waste by excess production and consumption)	6. Social agency: Actors challenge, reconstruct existing norms, roles and rules (participatory protest movements)	9. Cultural agency: Actors reflexively generate new values, frames (new environmental paradigm)
		Materialist: Physical, coercive or economic rewards or sanctions bind collective action	*Institutional*: Sets of statuses, roles, and norms define forms of collective action	*Cultural*: Collective interpretation and evaluation draws actors into action

Dimension Two: Degree of social-constructedness or *tangibility* of relational incentives for collective

theoretical cell. Reality is more likely a complex amalgam of factors (Weber, 1947, pp. 110–2). What factors combined to produce the Japanese "communitarian elite corporatist" politics and its response to the GE dilemma? What explanatory cells in Table 10.1 should a good explanation draw upon?

First of all, as has already been argued, the CEC model did not act as a constant structure of power, always governing and channeling politics in the same way. To the contrary, the most powerful actors changed over time, if only to change the Triad's specific responses and not its operating principles. Accordingly, plastic and agentic levels entered in quite strongly. Secondly, while the basis of conflicts concerned the division of material benefits and costs – profits from industrial growth, damage to health or livelihood from pollution – social institutional and cultural factors intervened at times with appreciable effects on outcomes. The "navel" engagement and Governor Taki's Three Conditions provide ready examples. Already at this cursory level of consideration, therefore, it is clear that any explanation must draw from numerous cells in Table 10.1, and must vary the cells and their weights in explaining the several events and policy shifts.

Toward a synthetic explanation

Material realities seem to shape and drive interests very strongly in this study, so the structural material theory cell should be used as our initial ideal type. Against this, we can notice and measure variation caused by other factors (Weber, 1947, p. 92). The structural material cell assumes actors will respond rationally to the choices offered by the material structures they confront (Brustein, 1996; Hechter, 1983). Chapter 1 introduced two other popular hypotheses, though, concerning what drives Japanese politics and collective action, which do not make that assumption: the social institutional – Nakane's inverted V normative template for behavior – and the cultural structural – internalized and implicit categories and values of deference and loyalty – hypotheses.

Ordinarily, the observable behavioral results from these two factors might be the same – deference to elites. But under crisis situations, such as the GE dilemma, they might be carrying the "voice" of nature into politics in different ways. The introduction of environmentalism as a new ethical ideal and value, for instance, might be expected to produce greater structural changes under scenario 2 than under scenario 1 (because in scenario 2 behavior sprang from internalized categories and values).

These three perspectives touch upon the basic debates within environmental sociology about the relative importance of material interests, social norms and cultural categories, with their affiliated structures, in channeling a society's reaction to growing levels of pollution and ecological disruption (Chapter 1). How well do the three structuralist hypotheses – material, institutional and culturalist – explain the policy shifts presented in this book?

The shift in the basic thrust of state policy, from capital accumulation to regime stability and back again, fits well with theories that emphasize the dominance of business over the capitalist state, leading to its oscillation between the two goals of accumulation and legitimacy (O'Connor, 1973). The two principles of the Ruling Triad – capital accumulation and regime maintenance – perfectly parallel these posited goals. The public legitimacy of the Japanese state suffered because of its initial unwillingness to force business (by regulation or taxation) to invest in hinterland job creation and in pollution control. As a result of this reluctance, both the ministerial state and the dominant party lost public legitimacy and engendered a cycle of protest. Broadly speaking, then, the behavior of both state and party as actors fits the expectations of a material structuralist theory. In this picture, nature acquires voice in human politics only when it activates the material interests of claimant groups.

When we compare Japan's response to that of the other ACID societies, though, this theoretical explanation proves insufficient. Due to the similarity among the ACID political-economies, political-economic structural theory cannot readily explain the striking rapidity of Japan's response to air pollution, or the slowness of the United States' response. To explain that, we need to consider other aspects of the social intensity of pollution – social institutional and cultural structuralist factors such as horizontal and vertical networks and roles, and binding collective symbolism. Compared to other ACID societies, it seems, the density of horizontal social networks among the members of Japan's communitarian elite, and the collective ethnic nationalist identity which suffused them, allowed for effective informal coordination among the Triad members, at least during the 1960s and 1970s. A strong ethic of normative propriety imbued these inter-elite horizontal networks. Therefore, the Triad did not dissolve into a collection of rationalized and squabbling individual actors. Each member of the elite fought doggedly to promote their individual agenda, but did not identify their opponents as ideological enemies.

Rather, despite their differences, their common identity as "we Japanese" (*ware ware nihonjin*) in the same community of fate (*unmei kyodotai*) retained a basis for compromise. When the two overriding collective principles were endangered, they compromised judiciously and abided by their collective decision. As a result, the top elites in Japan were less subject to division into separate ideological camps, in which mutual antagonism would create systemic gridlock, than was the case, for example, in the United States or Italy (Reich, 1991). These findings support the implication of the social institutional structuralist cell (cell 4) in Table 10.1 that embedded networks facilitate decision-making within social organization. They also support the cultural structuralist cell (7), that collective identity has the same effect.

From 1955 until the early 1990s, this pattern of elite communitarianism held. When challenged by the wave of grassroots pollution protests and local victories by opposition parties, members of the triad responded with two tactics: preemptive policy compromise and soft social control. Their facility at enacting preemptive pollution control policies speaks to the effectiveness of the horizontal, relatively egalitarian networks among the members of the triad. The soft social control, however, reveals the presence of "inverted V" type vertical networks between elites and ordinary citizens. The triad made substantive policy compromise in order to preserve regime stability. When the electoral threat declined, however, the triad gradually reasserted capital accumulation as its central principle. This prevented the pollution regulation principles behind

Japan's "pollution miracle" from generalizing and making all production follow environmental principles, as happened in Germany (Hannigan, 1995, p. 184).

Accordingly, Nakane's inverted V social structure helps explain Japan's pollution politics. Elites attempted to use this vertical structure to impose social control over communities, not through overt coercive means, but through "social hegemony." Prefectural resistance to the central government shows that soft social control may have been as much a local initiative as a nationally coordinated one. The narrative gives evidence of considerable initiation of this social control by the prefectural elites, with clear success in damping down grassroots protest in Oita.

All three governors employed forms of soft social control. During their tenure, the Triple Control Machine worked in two ways: It stymied the efforts of local protest movements to achieve democratic representation through local political institutions, and it seduced local people away from association with the movement by offering personal incentives. These incentives included both material benefits (bribery of various sorts) and the social benefits of associating with higher-status persons. The latter attraction should not be discounted: In status-conscious Japan, this was an important perquisite, especially for the older generation.

At the same time, by continually proclaiming the virtues of industrial growth, prefectural elites also worked hard to establish ideological dominance over public values and preferences,. In this respect, though, they had much less success. As the pollution intensified and caused horrible human diseases, the mass media as well as movements and opposition unions and parties spread the news throughout Japan. Communities around the country took another look at their own state of pollution. As a result, the public rapidly reframed its general evaluation of growth from "good" to "bad" (Gamson, 1992).

This new master frame of industrial growth as "bad" resonated strongly (Snow & Benford, 1992, p. 141) with existing subcultures blaming politicians, the state, and big business for local troubles. These subcultures dated back to tales of resistance in the Tokugawa era a hundred years earlier. In the first half of the twentieth century, state repression of some unions, parties and movements had left a bitter taste. In addition, youth educated in the new, more democratic context were less enamored of the old values of self-sacrifice for the state. The combined effects of objective levels of pollution plus latent anti-elite subcultures gave many citizens sufficient justification for participation in protest activity.

"Environmentalism" as an ideology, however, was not a driving force in these movements. The Japanese anti-pollution movements were typical NIMBY efforts, concerned with removing threats to personal health and livelihood from local neighborhoods. With the exception of a few leaders, the participants were little motivated by commitment to a new environmentalist paradigm or set of values. Perhaps the prevalence of NIMBY attitudes was a realistic adaptation to what the residents thought they could achieve: at best a local improvement.

Vertical social hegemony existed on two levels, from central elites to peripheral elites and ordinary citizens, and from peripheral elites to local residents. On both levels, vertical social hegemony was a very important context for political struggles. At the local level, soft social control exercised by the Triple Control Machine shaped the course of environmental protest. The evidence suggests that soft social control was not merely an anomaly found in Oita, a rather conservative, rural prefecture. It played a crucial role in damping the outbreak (but not the feelings) of popular pollution protest at the local, hamlet, and neighborhood levels throughout Japan, and continues to operate today.

Through use of the Triple Control Machine, the Oita governors met the *letter* of Governor Taki's Three Conditions: consensus among the Seki residents, normalization of relations in the Fishing Union, and environmental assessment. But these results hardly resembled the *spirit* of the Three Conditions. Citizen consensus ended up meaning nothing more than a vote of approval by the town council. Normalization of the union entailed splitting it into two and destroying organized local opposition. Environmental assessment was conducted on paper only, without meaningful participation by citizens and without ways to ensure the accuracy of the results. In the process, these Three Conditions became in effect an "invisibility cloak," as many locals charged, hiding the reality of further industrial growth.

National soft social control made it hard for nascent environmental protest organizations to establish a national presence. The government did not grant tax-exempt status to public interest groups, including national-level environmental organizations. When public interest groups tried to incorporate, the government insisted that their boards of directors accept a ministerial retiree as managing director. Private philanthropies did not support public-sector initiatives as they do in the West. On the contrary, cooperative efforts between ministries and big business filled the public space with ersatz "third sector" environmental think tanks.

Vertical social hegemony was a two-edged sword, though. At times, vertical social control helped the protest movement. When the Seki protestors threatened to riot in the Tokyo offices of the Environmental Agency, for instance, they threatened to disrupt the patron-client bond between the national ministries and Governor Taki, which was based on the paternalistic expectation that if Taki was a good governor, he would control "his" citizens.

Also, in the Saeki and Seki movements, vertical networks enabled conscientious local bosses to lead their followers into the protest movement as a bloc. Multiplied many fold, local movements like these added up to an enormous national wave of environmental protest that forced a new national environmental regime into practice. This wave was not in response to a sudden opening in the national structure of political opportunities, as some theorists have claimed about cycles of protest in general. True, the wave of environmental protest was helped by veterans of earlier waves of labor and student protest. The entire cycle of post-Second World War protest, including all three waves, was only possible due to the new, liberalized political opportunity structure imposed on Japan by the Occupation. But these factors produced facilitating conditions, not the immediate stimulus to the wave of environmental protest.

The most immediate stimulus to protest came from the rising intensity of environmental pollution. Pollution set up the mobilization potential for the 1960s wave of environmental protest. High school teachers, who were middle-class in education terms but were also labor union members and had experience in the earlier waves of protest, as well as others of middle-class professional background like Katayama of Saeki, provided the initial intellectual and moral reframing of environmental pollution into something to be resisted. The new crop of high school graduates in the mid-1960s, instilled with a greater sense of democratic rights, readily picked up this new frame, carried it into activism, and spread it to the older generation, kindling their own latent values of resistance.

The sense of resistance and the new frames spread to other local communities, such as the Seki Fishing Union, giving even those who had strictly material or livelihood reasons to oppose industrial growth a larger rationale for activism. However, movement continuity depended upon having a leader who identified deeply with the new rights frame as a moral cause. Movement leaders protesting on the basis of material losses often succumbed to status seduction or material patronage, resulting in their loss of legitimacy and charisma, and the collapse of the movement.

Therefore, the events reported in this book do not support Nakane's argument that elites, once they establish their authority, can exercise it "without opposition." Opposition emerged, sometimes bursting right out of vertical LDP networks when local bosses worried about pollution led their "flocks" away with them. From that point on, an intense struggle between conservative bosses and protesting ones seethed beneath the surface of civil society. This form of protest mobilization, though, confirms in its own way the accuracy of Nakane's vertical network model. Successful protest mobilization required leadership by people who already held "boss" status in the community. Hamlet-level protest spread initially through high school teacher leaders and activist youth, as exemplified in agitation by the democratically educated youths of Kozaki. But to attract and hold a larger body of members, a movement required the assurance of traditional leadership (Chong, 1991).

Theories of power and protest

Looking at the qualities of bonds of collective action invites us to reconsider theories of power and protest formulated for the most part in the United States, European or Latin American societies. What sorts of ontologies, as denoted in Table 10.1, produced the observed forms of power and protest? What does this tell us about the adequacy of our theories? The findings suggest their relative applicability according to societal circumstances.

Many theories of power structures, as noted in Chapter 1, assume that policy outputs are determined by the distribution of material and coercive resources among the concerned actors (Table 10.1, cell 1). Numerous examples of this sort of power crop up in the study. For example, Governor Taki's decision to grant the Three Conditions reflected a split in the dominant elites – a sudden weakness in the national state. The national pollution crisis and wave of protest had forced the dominant national elites to set up the Environmental Agency, which immediately took an active role and demanded an EIA from the Governor. In further corroboration of this point of view, the main goals of the Ruling Triad remained focused on, and kept policy outputs in the service of, capital accumulation, to the extent such was compatible with regime maintenance.

At the same time, though, the outcomes in Oita did not depend *only* upon a clash of political-economic interests and structures. Elites with control over political-economic resources could not and did not control every move. Different factors moved the course of events in other directions. Panic over a feared loss of face, as well as personal moral doubts, for instance, led the Governor to grant Three Conditions instead of one to the Seki protest movement. This is not so unusual. Leaders often have to make important decisions quickly in uncertain, highly emotional situations. Under such circumstances, hunches and basic moral values rather than calculated rationality provide the guidelines for decisions (March & Simon, 1993).

These kind of factors affecting decisions made an enormous difference to the Prefectural Government's growth plans. If the governor had granted only one environmental assessment, the Prefectural Government could have accomplished it within two years, and work on Landfill No. 8 would have been resumed in 1974, not 1980. With earlier resumption, the Teijin Synthetic Fiber Company would still have wanted to build its plant on the landfill. With Nishio destroyed, the government would have overcome resistance by the Kozaki group – by arrest, if necessary. We must conclude that the two conditions added by Governor Taki delayed the resumption of No. 8 long enough to give the Seki movement a *de facto* victory. In this incident, Weber's "cultural switchman" came out of hiding, put shoulder to lever, and pushed a little. This was enough to change the tracks of history for Oita.

If we think of the switchman more broadly, as sociocultural forces, other examples come to mind. Throughout this book, horizontal and vertical social networks played important roles in the manifestation and realization of political-economic interests. In addition, Japanese culture supported the observed political process by its very emphasis on tangibility, localism, and practicality, and its anti-ideological quality.

Many sequences like these – not completely determined by structures, outcomes contingent upon shifting and unpredictable combinations of factors – occurred throughout the preceding narrative. Some of these outcomes were reversible, like Governor Taki's agreement to slow down growth after the "navel" engagement. Other outcomes were not reversible, like apparently the decision to postpone Landfill No. 8 until meeting the Three Conditions, even if only superficially. Given the state of the Japanese economy and the continuing presence of the Kozaki movement, No. 8 will probably never be built. In this fashion, even the centralized, corporatistic Japanese elite had to continually adjust to pressures that bubbled up from ordinary society.

As for theories of social movements, the immediate or recent acquisition of resources (McCarthy & Zald, 1977) did not seem crucial for generating protest. Japanese people had enjoyed rapidly increasing prosperity since the start of the Jimmu boom in the mid-1950s. Nor did a sudden opening of political opportunities (Tarrow, 1994) provide "the chance people had been waiting for." The LDP remained in power, as it had been since 1955. The post-war constitution provided many new democratic freedoms, but these were partly in abeyance. Nor did the membership of protest movements come primarily from a "postmaterial" new middle class that already enjoyed abundant material security (Offe, 1985b). Neither the leaders and participants nor the broad citizenry of the prefecture showed many signs of believing in the deferential norms of a spectator political culture. The majority of the local people were angry about the pollution and distrusted the elites. In most communities, the appearance of harmony (*wa*) regarding pollution issues was fictitious. An internalized political culture, therefore, did not constrain people from protest, and the elite did not exert an effective ideological hegemony over popular thinking.

Instead, the suddenly imposed costs of pollution started a chain of events that motivated working people in local communities to resist – as they had occasionally in crises dating back to Tokugawa times. By the 1960s, however, the political opportunity structure was less overtly repressive. Even while it blocked the use of formal political institutions to register protest, the new political structure imposed lower direct costs on those who mobilized. The state did not send out the police to beat them. This situation allowed local hamlet identities to solidify around the images of protest. The local protests then blossomed within the civic spaces created by the existing freedom from overt, coercive repression. The leaders were often high-school teachers or other professionals, who enjoyed both prestige and knowledge. Most of the participants, however, were ordinary working people and homemakers.

The findings suggest that both the mobilization and the later trajectory of social movements are not subject to a fixed general theory. Rather, they are exceedingly contingent upon the ontological quality of the structure of power, which they take shape within and against. The comparison of the mobilization of eight Oita movements illustrated that principle (Chapter 5). Once mobilized, furthermore, successful social movements adopted tactics that mirrored the structural weaknesses of the political opportunity structure. If forced to formal-ize this proposition with a name, perhaps "ontological contingency theory" would work.

In the Japanese case, the vertical networks of control and coordination be-tween national and prefectural officials were imbued with normative expecta-tions as much as material inducements. Some social movements struck at what unified this dominant state structure. Movements could only rarely impose an economic cost on the pro-growth elites, although that tactic worked when they could employ it (as in the Nikko Harbor blockade). In the Three Conditions case, instead, the movements leveraged the normative expectations binding the Governor and the national ministries. The Kozaki movement proved adept at this in many instances: when it threatened to riot in the Tokyo offices of the Environmental Agency, when it drew the Governor's attention to his possession of a belly-button, or when it used "harsh language" against its opponents. These tactics, though disruptive and to some seemingly "irrational," were not simply the "actions of the impatient," as early collective behavior theory would have assumed (Smelser, 1963). To the contrary, these outlandish actions were the considered tactics of a frustrated group who had observed for too long the failure of normal channels and proper politics.

When the prefectural elites tried to persuade the public there was no pollu-tion, the Seki movements sought out allies throughout the prefecture and began to engage in public debate with the conservative elites. They made common cause with the fragmented and weak progressive political machine, which con-sisted of opposition political parties and their supporting unions. They also engaged in public debate with prefectural officials and other elites over pollu-tion. Taking their arguments into the public arena, beyond the confines of the affected township, the Seki movements contested the "official truth." This act placed them squarely in the arena of prefectural politics and made them a threat to the legitimacy of the dominant elite. The public, on the whole, as revealed by surveys and by Oita Mayor Sato's participatory forums, tended to support the position of the movements and to distrust the official experts.

The parochialism of Japanese political culture, though, intensified the damping effect of structural barriers. This culture directed people's concerns toward NIMBY local and national pollution problems to the neglect of global pollution problems. It also discouraged joining voluntary groups outside personally known community and leadership circles. Japanese communities contain many social and political groups organized by elites, but Japan has little tradition or presence of grassroots civic voluntarism, whereby concerned people come together on the basis of personal convictions to serve general causes (such as feeding the starving). Such voluntarism is growing slowly in Japan, but it has not been strong enough to support locally based national environmental interest groups. These groups have been consistently unable to recruit enough donating members to fund a central staff, publications, and facilities.

Explaining the GE dilemma

If the GE dilemma arises because society ignores and abuses nature, the solution may require listening to nature. By what ontological channels, and specific varieties thereof, did the voice of nature enter into human politics, causing some amelioration of the damage being done? Most agency arose in the plastic zone, embedded within and struggling with existing political-economic, social institutional and cultural structures. The findings are ambiguous on the explanatory power of theories of cultural structuralism. Implicit categories (values) did not seem to justify the rampant exploitation of nature, nor did the amelioration of that problem depend upon elite or popular conversion to new environmentalist values. The traditional religions of Japan, Shintoism and Buddhism, taught respect, appreciation and even worship of the natural ecology, and did not celebrate mastery over it. In their rapid industrialization plans, though, as the book has shown, Japanese elites gave no evidence of respect for nature. Accordingly, a Weberian-style explanation of their behavior does not suffice. Likewise, the supposed traditional culture of vertical deference and domination did not seem strongly in evidence. Many people harbored feelings at odds with acquiescing to the authorities. The reason they did not express their opposition more frequently was not a matter of values or implicit categories, but a fear of punishment that might come for diverging from accepted norms. High school teacher Fujii, who dared to lead his students into a health survey of Misa/Iejima, for instance, found himself switched to the night shift in a non-academic school teaching high school dropouts – not a place from which he could launch such activities (Chapter 5).

The male dominance of elite and leadership posts, though, does support the ecofeminist cultural argument that male chauvinism incites the exploitation of nature. As we shall see, elites showed little sign of conversion to new environmentalist values at any point. Accordingly, the later pollution miracle the elites produced does not contradict the ecofeminist argument either. The crucial role of women, not men, as the foot soldiers of local movements lends further support to the ecofeminist argument (Chapter 5).

Most environmental movements in this study did not adopt an overtly environmentalist ideology. Some moral conviction was necessary to produce a steadfast protest leader, but only two leaders counted environmentalism in their ethical fibers. One, Inao Toru, enjoyed ancillary conditions that enabled the pursuit of those goals through a continued social movement. The other, Matsushita Ryuichi of Nakatsu, was unable to spread his ideology to enough local people to keep the movement going, in the absence of other strong incentives. The other successful leaders had other motivations, some ethical and some material, sufficient to keep them from seduction by the machine. The average resident mourned the loss of the coastal beaches enjoyed in times past.

At first most people thought that sacrifice was the necessary price of "progress." Eventually, however, many came to think the price was too high. Most people could not publicly articulate this feeling in civil society, the space of public discourse, due to strong norms against open, public criticism of leaders. Confucian norms reinforced the material patronage of the machine and rendered their voices inarticulate. Elite social hegemony placed most local command roles in the hands of conservative bosses who imposed their version of "harmony" on the community.

Most people, however, became increasingly disillusioned with the tradeoff – landfill and smokestacks (if built) in return for health damage, community disruption, and loss of beaches and traditional livelihood. They became increasingly distrustful of elites. The ubiquity of discontent observed in this book revealed that "Confucian" deference was barely skin deep. In short, industrial growth and pollution put people's internal feelings increasingly at odds with their expected norms of deferential behavior to elites and reluctance to express conflict.

Without the ferment of hot, widespread, involved debate in the local public sphere, though, the target of discontent stayed local, or at the most, national. Popular discontent never congealed into a national public environmentalist ideology that would bridge people's concerns for the local, the national and the international environment (as shown in Figure 10.1). A relatively weak sense of self, often without strong internal motivations, readily surrendered to vertical normative expectations.[14] Still, this particular form of tension between values and norms provided an important aspect of the mobilization potential and process in these communities and in Japan.

The logic of political-economic rationality governed the decisions of the Ruling Triad, but embedded social networks and collective ethnic-nationalist identity greatly helped its effective implementation. Through this logic, the dynamics of the entire system came to resemble the "Treadmill of Production" theory (Schnaiberg, 1980; Schnaiberg & Gould, 1994). Top business actors, with the support of the state and the corporate unions, extracted and processed a huge amount of raw materials from the global natural ecology (only a little of which came from Japan). They then sold the finished products in domestic and foreign markets with great success, extracting a huge flow of profits.

This inward flow of profit led to rapid capital accumulation. In the 1980s, Japanese banks quickly became the largest in the world. Organized labor in the manufacturing sector favored increasing the "speed" of the extractive treadmill so as to raise wages. The state and the dominant political parties regarded support of the treadmill as their main task. They designed the major social institutions, especially education and work, to support rapid growth as if it were a war. This thrust included overcoming the legacy of ascetic, "stingy" values, and encouraging a new consumerism (Fukutake, 1989; Oyama, 1990).

However, unlike the predictions of Treadmill theory, the Japanese state was not mainly concerned to implement the demands of big business, either through structural or instrumental pressures. To the contrary, many state ministries exhibited consistent autonomy in their policy formulations. It was not their lack of autonomy, but their lack of power over the Diet and business, that made them fail to impose their policy preferences.

The Ruling Triad "bureaucratic-industrial complex" largely excluded labor from political decision-making (Pempel & Tsunekawa, 1979) but rewarded it with good wage increases, thus buying labor's peace and support. The Ruling Triad system also managed to compromise judiciously with protest, granting actual "compensation" (for example, an anti-pollution policy) in portions as small as possible, and symbolic compensation otherwise. Through judicious

14. Hamaguchi argues that the Japanese sense of self is deeply embedded in social relations with particular people. He calls this "relationalism" (*kanjinshugi*) (Hamaguchi, 1985), a good example of what I have been calling social institutional behavior, and a good term to counterpoise against the Western insistence on individual possessive rationality.

compromise combined with soft social control, the Japanese political system minimized the ability of grassroots and opposition parties to slow its productive treadmill.

Consequently, Japan produced the most efficient version of the treadmill, extracting and processing raw materials faster than any other ACID society. This efficiency brought the Japanese state – the responsible nationalist officials in the central ministries – the central status in the white-dominated political-economic global system that they craved. With this position came power, security, and respect in a system by which Japan had long felt oppressed.

By the same token, the very efficiency of the Japanese treadmill caused it to produce great amounts of waste material. The Japanese treadmill of production did not wholly consume the raw materials it gathered so voraciously from Australia, Zambia, Saudi Arabia and other places around the globe. Fashioned into stereos and automobiles, the usable portions of these raw materials went back abroad and made Japan wealthy. The unusable parts, however – the rock tailings, the smoke from burned fuel, the acidic waste from copper ore, the heavy metals used as catalysts in refining processes – were concentrated heavily in Japan's limited air, soil, and water. Ironically, Japan became the world's waste bin. As a result, this crowded island country became a global focus of the GE dilemma.

In the long run, with its practices of patronage and its problematic social outcomes, the communitarian elite collectivist model has started to unravel. Cronyism between state, party, and big business in Japan intensified "structural corruption" (such as bribery in awarding government construction contracts and lax oversight of banking) and kept pollution control and other social welfare outputs at low levels. This corruption further eroded public confidence in the system, producing an enduring culture of cynicism toward the state and parties. In the 1990s, this cynicism led to the election of media personalities like the governors of Tokyo and other big cities, overturning the "sure" LDP candidates. It resulted in the loss of LDP control over the Diet and the party's fracture into two main conservative parties. As this is being written (in 1997), the future of the Japanese party system remains uncertain. It remains an open question as to whether the two main parties will continue separately, producing a more pluralistic and competitive democracy, or whether they will reunite, handing continued dominance to the Ruling Triad. If two major parties alternate in power, this should stimulate public debate over policy issues and weaken the Triple Control Machine. This would increase public scrutiny of politicians and produce a stronger democracy. However, current indications are that the LDP will resume control over the Diet and the Ruling Triad will continue as before.

Japan's GE dilemma has demonstrated the interaction between nature and society in one of its most blatant, aggressive expressions. Examination of this case has demonstrated that society in fact constructs its relationship with nature, but not entirely as it chooses. Among the ACID societies, Japan responded most rapidly and most effectively to the pollution debacle of the 1960s. From the perspective of the nature/society interaction, however, we noticed that the rapidity and thoroughness of Japan's response paralleled its rank in social density of pollution. Accordingly, the response of ACID societies to environmental limits must be viewed first of all as affected strongly by their *social intensity of pollution* – the severity and breadth of its harm to the human population. Over a certain threshold of social intensity, it seems, there is enough protest to force elites, over the course of two decades, to reduce the intensity to a similar level. The fact that the five ACID societies equalized their social intensity of pollution, not their natural intensity of pollution, bears striking witness to this conclusion.

Though broadly determined by the social intensity of pollution, however, social institutional and cultural factors also played a role. The coordination of Japan's dominant elites played a key role in both producing and partially resolving its GE dilemma. When the costs of rapid growth became so great that they threatened to overturn the political status quo (by electoral means), the Triad compromised and compensated the public with very strong pollution regulations. This discussion may seem to support a paternalistic, coordinated elite and weak democracy as the best solution to the GE dilemma, as some environmentalists seem to argue (Ophuls, 1977). As a result of this particular structural configuration, however, the Japanese pollution miracle left many important problems untouched.

Japanese big business reduced domestic pollution in part by moving its refineries to the countries where the raw materials were extracted, such as aluminum smelters in Indonesia and Brazil. Japanese aid helped build the Pasarl copper refinery in Leyte Island, the Philippines. The refinery severely polluted Izabel Bay (Mainichi Newspaper, April 20, 1986). Like France, Japan also embarked on the rapid construction of many nuclear reactors as the road to energy independence, despite considerable public protest (Hasegawa, 1996).

The Ruling Triad applied the lessons of soft social control learned during its struggle with pollution protest to muffle this new wave of anti-nuclear protest (Hasegawa, 1994). Nuclear power may bring greater energy independence, thus fulfilling the hopes of nationalistic elites, but it is also fraught with intense danger. One Chernobyl-type accident could cause incalculable havoc to this island nation. From that perspective, the more gradual, more uncertain response to the GE dilemma by a less bureaucratized, more pluralistic, even more gridlocked democracy, which gives a greater voice to a variety of movements and interest groups in civil society, may in the long run provide the safer and more effective path.

Without further study in other societies, the universality of any findings from this case study will remain hypothetical. But producing such hypotheses is one proper job of the case study. The fundamental hypothesis that I extract from this study, concerning the causes and cures of the GE dilemma in ACID societies, is that the path of effective local protest mobilization will differ greatly from society to society, depending upon the ontological qualities of the political opportunity structure. These ontological qualities include not only the political and economic interest groups, but the social institutions that define their proper roles in politics, and the implicit categories of understanding that motivate both elites and challengers.

In any case, the path to effective protest will depend upon the *creative agency* of advocates of change at both the local, mid-range and national levels, among both ordinary citizens and elites. Effective creative agency must act with cognizance and insight concerning the ontological qualities of the power structure it faces. Given its universal paucity of political and economic resources, though, it would best look for the implicit social institutional and cultural components of the defenders of the status quo. In a more individualistic and ideological society, for instance, both defenders of the status quo and advocates of change will be more driven by ideology, by culture rather than norms. In such a society, the reversal of paternalistic norms that Nishio accomplished in the "navel" engagement, for instance, would not work. One would have to invent a different form of agency, appropriate to the structure at hand. The elite might soon respond creatively too, with new forms of social control – just as the Triple Control Machine was partly a post-war invention. Accordingly, different dynamics of change would arise in different societal settings, each with its own ontological qualities and resultant trajectory. Such are the dynamic properties of societal reality.

Overall, then, to extend the findings of this study suggests a set of *tentative* broader hypotheses. A society's response to environmental degradation is not a direct reflection of the intensity of that degradation in the natural ecology. Nor is it a reflection of the amount of damage that pollution does to any individual person living within it. In each society, a scattering of people at all levels and in various professions will adopt a philosophy of environmentalism and try to defend the rights of nature. But, contrary to the social-constructionist viewpoint (Hannigan, 1995, p. 185), it seems futile to try to directly persuade elites of that viewpoint. Rather, environmentalists' ability to make an ACID society act according to environmentalist values – to pass policies that work – seems to depend upon their ability to link environmentalist values to pocketbook and health-related demands. Only then can environmentalists forge a voting constituency powerful enough to threaten pro-growth elites with political defeat, and thereby jog the elites into taking steps to repair environmental degradation, contrary to their immediate economic interests.

Appendix 1

Meso-networks and macro-structures

Vectors of pressure

One way to reduce the complexity of the political process is to think of its micro- or meso-level components – the relationships of influence between actors – as "vectors of pressure," a generic or formal term for an influence relationship.[1] This viewpoint decomposes the process of politics into multiple, generative, interacting series of dyadic influence relationships. Each influence relationship reflects its political, economic, social and cultural contexts. Applying the term vector simplifies and objectifies the influence relationship, allowing the conversion of qualitative information on it into categorical "data."[2]

To illustrate, in the "navel" engagement, Nishio and the protest group exerted a vector of pressure upon Governor Taki – a control vector. The immediate control the protestors exercised over the governor's immediate behavior had some, though not definitive, effect upon later policy outcomes – an impact vector. Each relationship therefore represents two types of pressure vectors.

1. I use the term pressure (for lack of a better term) here to indicate degrees of control over another actor or over an ultimate political outcome. On a spectrum, pressure runs from zero, through degrees of influence, and ends in power, which indicates total control over another actor in a relationship, or over an ultimate policy outcome perhaps many events later. I conceive of pressure operating between actors, in dyadic events. The "actors" range from individuals, through informal groups and formal organizations, to larger or looser collectivities that may respond or act collectively, such as mass publics. A key decision, one that redistributes collective benefits and costs, may result from a number of events happening either simultaneously or sequentially (Broadbent, 1989). My use of these terms differs from others' usage (Wrong, 1979). I draw the term "vector" from and use it in the sense of graph theory (Busacker & Saaty, 1965, pp. 205–14; Rorres & Anton, 1979, Ch. 4).

2. The transformation from complex and nuanced interpretations based on direct perception to a limited set of categories that capture and cut up that nuanced reality into discretely defined boxes – "variables" – represents the most contested divide within the social sciences. By being explicit about this point of transition, I am studying its nature and the debate around it. At the same time, I am setting the stage for a quantitative analytical version of the research in this book, to be published later, as a means of inquiry into that debate.

The vector from actor A to actor B represents direct inter-actor *control*. The vector from the dyadic relationship to the (usually much later) policy outcome of concern represents the ultimate *impact* of the relationship. Each control vector, exerting influence or power (total control) by one actor over another, can be composed of various, perhaps mixed, rewards, sanctions and tactical modes.[3] Each impact vector represents the gross quantity of influence that that particular combination of elements had upon a policy outcome at a certain time.

I do not mean the term vector to conjure up a billiard-ball image of politics as atomistic actors bouncing off each other. Vectors of pressure may travel as much along established, institutionalized pathways between actors as impact voluntaristically. The degree to which they do keep to established pathways is, in fact, a major theoretical question – the structure-agency debate.

From the vector viewpoint, the political process can be seen as a complex network of pressure vectors that unfolds over time.[4] This conceptual simplification reveals all the more the messiness of the process. The process is hard to follow because it is a partly orderly, partly chaotic mixture of overlapping contradictory structures and levels stirred by contradictory agencies. It is, in a word, a structuration process (Giddens, 1984), of a consistency resembling an "impacted, mineralized goo" (White, 1992, p. 127). Hence, the plastic category in Tables 10.1 (and A.1).

The unfolding political process occurs simultaneously at (at least) three societal levels: the interpersonal (the micro-level: relations between individuals occurring in the family, neighborhood or other organizational setting), the inter-organizational (the meso-level: influence and power among organizations occurring in the community and wider society), and the whole societal (the macro-level: broad social forces operating in the national and international society). These three levels are not distinct – they are simply levels of magnification of the same object. They interact constantly and affect each other, so must all be kept in mind as contexts for each other. The action in this study takes place mostly between organizations (or individuals representing them), at the meso-level.

For instance, in the navel engagement, Governor Taki was not acting as an individual – he was representing the prefectural government. Similarly, Nishio was not acting alone, but as part of a protest movement. Neither of them would

3. The factors at work in one social venue may differ from those in others, yet all may be responding to the same substantive problem – in this case, the GE dilemma. After empirically investigating the modes of pressure at work in the many venues, we can weight their relative contributions to the determination of policy events and outcomes.

4. Many theorists have had similar impressions. See Bourdieu, 1990; Broadbent, 1989a; Emirbayer & Goodwin, 1994; Giddens, 1984; Stark, 1994, p. 170.

have responded as they did, or even have been in the situation, if they had not been so organizationally situated.

Influence relations occur within a changing historical context, as well. If antinuclear power protestors had crowded into the office of the governor of a U.S. state, for instance, and their leader had challenged the governor with the belly button image, the tactic would not have worked so well. The image's implications of equality would not have shocked the U.S. governor because equality is the norm and basic value in the United States (however much breached in practice).

To give some examples illustrating the importance of these cross-level and temporal structurational processes, institutional changes in Japan had introduced a "structural potential" for protest (McAdam, 1982). The Allied Occupation had introduced a set of new democratic freedoms and teachings (Reischauer & Craig, 1978). Democratic education and the growth of unions had reframed paternalistic norms in a more egalitarian direction (Fukutake, 1989, p. 145). In the early 1970s, most people had not taken full advantage of these new institutional resources for popular democracy. Nishio's use of the belly-button image against Governor Taki resonated with these new institutional realities.

The meso-macro connection

As the vectors or influence relations intersect, they weave a social fabric. The nature of a fabric depends not only on its weave and pattern, but also on the quality of its thread. Cotton fabric is cooler, dacron doesn't wrinkle, wool is warmer but weaker. So too with the social and political "fabric" (Short, 1986). The mode of pressure determines the social fabric's shear tolerances – where it will rip and permit policies to change. Actors use many types of rewards, sanctions and tactics. Love, profit, health, nationalism, or coercion can convey influence and draw actors together into collective action (Broadbent 1989a). Open negotiation, manipulation of the agenda, or subtle persuasion constitute different tactics (Lukes, 1974). These qualities of the mode indicate the presence of different causal patterns. They indicate the theoretical *why* of the GE dilemma and its political manifestations in Japan.

Any vector of pressure between actors operates as an (at least implicit) exchange relationship supported by motivations valuing that exchange. The rewards and sanctions they exchange, as well as the supporting motivations, fall into the same three broad categories as the theories in Table 10.1: political-economic, social institutional and cultural, as presented in Table A.1. More detailed types of rewards and sanctions may be defined within each of the three categories (Broadbent, 1989a; Etzioni, 1975; French & Raven 1959; Weber,

Table A.1. *The home domains of power structure theories operationalized as micro/meso exchanges of (positive or negative) sanctions (benefits and costs) between social actors (individuals, organizations or collectivities) leading to their capacity to create collective action (exercising influence, dominating another actor through conflict, or entering into a collaborative relationship)*

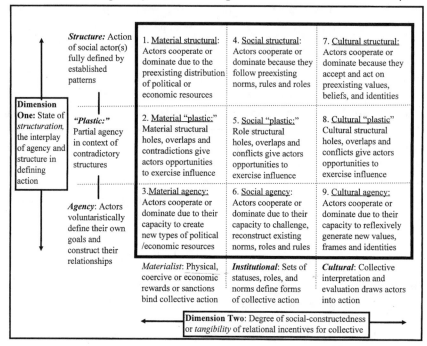

1978). Thinking of structures this way applies the logic of exchange theory (Homans, 1974) to the study of political process. But it does not import exchange theory's bias toward methodological individualism. As the top row of Table A.1, relationships leading to collective action may reflect structural arrangements as well as agentic ones. Furthermore, the table adds culture, with its collective identities, moralities and frames as a potentially important factor of collective action (while exchange theory focused more on material or social status exchange). This approach allows the researcher to "deconstruct" the typical structural and organizational elements of political studies – the state, classes, bureaucracies, mass publics, social movements – into their component and indicative micro and meso processes.

An emphasis on the causal power of internalized symbols, in the form of motivations and values, captivated social science for a long time (Parsons, 1951;

Almond & Verba, 1963). Weber distinguished "value-rational" behavior following internalized symbolic standards (Weber, 1978), from "goal-rational" utilitarian figuring of the best means to obtain an external (usually material) goal. The former recognizes the importance of culturally-defined variation in motives, while the latter tends to reduce motivation to the universal pursuit of material benefits (Weber, 1978). Some current research argues that values have little determining effect on behavior (Johnson, 1982). But at the same time, whole schools of research emphasize the importance of symbolic patterns such as identity, collective beliefs and cultural values. Norms, in contrast to symbolic values, are socially embedded, reinforced and constructed. They often stay in place without a deep value-commitment from the actors (Yamagishi, 1995, p. 326–328; Snow & Oliver, 1995, p. 586; Griswold, 1994, p. 53). Coercive sanctions concern the use of legal or illegal force and economic inducements that pertain to bodily existence (Etzioni, 1975). Exchanges of these sanctions undergird the institutionalized role patterns that express the pattern of power and the outcomes of politics. Actors for change confront these patterns, a situation which forces them, if they wish to achieve change, to strategize and produce counter-hegemonic tactics that attack the most vulnerable pressure vectors that bind the dominant system. This understanding of how change in the pattern of power occurs resembles that of Foucault, who advocated "analyzing power relations through the antagonism of strategies" (Foucault, 1983, p. 211).

Cultural influence, for instance, exists when actor A appeals to the internalized symbols (values, ideologies, identities) of actor B, such as loyalty, nationalism or the flag (Table A.1, cell 7). In social influence, A appeals to what is "proper and expected" between A and B (cell 4). In political-economic influence, A offers positive or negative extrinsic inducements, ranging from money to physical coercion. In each case, the causal force of the mode depends upon its effect net of the other exchanges present in the organic mixture. Each of these three types of rewards may be present in different structurational states, making nine modes of influence and power.

In other words, Table A.1 represents nine different *modes* of influence and power relations. These operationalize the axioms of macro-level theories as meso- and micro-level exchange modalities between actors that bind them into collective action. The table provides useful indicators for the presence of the theories that can be observed empirically in real influence and power relationships (Vogt, 1993, p. 159). On the vertical axis, Table A.1 represents the contribution of structure and agency to the production of collective action; on the horizontal axis, the rewards or sanctions that A and B exchange to create influence (a pressure vector). A given pressure vector may be a weighted amalgam of a number of these factors, or may be relatively single-factor homogeneous.

In addition to the factors represented in Table A.1, the researcher must also consider the *tactic* of collective action used by the actors. Actors draw upon and exchange rewards and sanctions in practices or "skilled performances" exercised through the use of often cleverly-designed tactics (Giddens, 1993, pp. 168–70). Tactics range from open, to closed, to manipulative. The types of tactics follow Lukes distinction between the three faces of power (Lukes, 1974). Not all exchanges are honest and open (the first tactic). Sometimes, one actor controls the topics of discussion, allowing only preferred options onto the table. In that case, the actor is exercising the second, agenda-setting tactic. In a third tactic, one actor shapes the preferences and values of the others, so that they actively desire the outcomes that A wants (Bachrach & Baratz, 1970; Crenson, 1971; Gaventa, 1995; Lukes, 1986). In the course of this research, I also noticed a fourth tactic, social hegemony, in which the bosses of a political machine personally persuade people to change their minds, dissuading them from protest. Given this diversity of tactics, we cannot assume free and independent, well-informed actors as the basis of politics. Actors are trapped within institutions and subject to manipulations that may lead them to judge their situation quite falsely.

To determine the relative importance of each type of reward or sanction and tactic in each pressure vector, the researcher must evaluate the qualitative data available for it. In the "navel" engagement, for instance, the governor had strong influence because of his control of political sanctions – the power to make binding decisions. He also had some symbolic and normative power resulting from the prestige of his office.[5] The protest movement, on the other hand, commanded no political sanctions. Governor Taki had solid backing from the Liberal Democratic Party and other political parties, so did not fear losing the next election due to disapproval from a small group of protestors. Rather, Nishio influenced the Governor more by symbolic and normative sanctions. Strong norms of deference had bound some villagers into acquiescence, and even froze some of those present into silence. Governor Taki expected those norms to let him play the role of "father figure" (*oyabun,* or paterfamilias) to his prefectural "children" (*kobun*). The phrase *kanson minpi* – "honor the officials and despise the people" – had described this relationship since feudal times.

Nishio's importation of an egalitarian image, the belly button, challenged that unequal, paternalistic relationship. By expressing his opposition through this image, Nishio both broke the norm against assertiveness and justified that breakage with a new moral value – equality and democracy. For a moment, this

---

5. In order to avoid reductionism, I have proposed a method of integrated structural analysis (Broadbent, 1989a).

act dissolved the old normative order and justified a new one, more amenable to open dialogue (Lamont, 1989).[6] The force of the belly button image pushed the Governor back into his chair and forced him to continue the discussion.

The Governor attempted to use his available sanctions to control the agenda of the meeting. He tried to confine the protestors to the presentation of a petition. By their countersanctions, though, the protestors succeeded in forcing a more open dialogue. In the belly button confrontation, economic sanctions did not play an important role on either side. Nor, obviously, had the Governor had much success in cowing the protestors into silence.

At the same time, more than deference had restrained people from protesting. The government had been insisting that more industrial growth would bring local jobs and prosperity. This left many people uncertain as to the justification for protest. Furthermore, protest consumed time, energy, and money, and raised the possibility of social criticism. The dominant political party, the LDP, had been pressuring people not to join movements. Many people preferred to wait, let others protest, and hope to enjoy the benefits of whatever gains they won as "free riders" (Jenkins, 1983). Despite these disincentives, protests occurred anyhow.

Conflicting political pressures impinged on Governor Taki. On the one hand, he genuinely sympathized with the protestors. On the other, he also had to attend to demands for more growth from national and local business, organized industrial labor, and the LDP. Furthermore, Taki had to contend with the national ministries, with their capricious infighting and bureaucratic deadlines. Leniency toward protest might invite a cutoff of government permissions and grants. Canceling the industrial growth plan would have caused great loss of face and further decay of the prefectural government's paternalistic authority.

Culturally, Governor Taki identified with traditional elitism and groupism. He thought the protestors, in their intense concern for their welfare, were behaving very selfishly and without regard for the welfare of the prefecture as a whole. He suspected that some radical ideology had pushed them into taking this irrational action. Taki's web of social relations, centered on prefectural business and political elites and Tokyo University classmates, reinforced his elitism. The prefectural "state," despite the reforms of the Occupation, still gave him greater local powers than a U.S. governor, but also subordinated him more to the national elites. The centralization of the Japanese economy made it

---

6. The concept of normative or symbolic appeals creating influence in encounters is not a new one to social movements. Mahatma Gandhi taught the use of "soul-power" (*satyagraha*) through such appeals to influence the British colonial administration. The Fellowship of Reconciliation and Martin Luther King brought that concept – in the form of "non-violent resistance" – into the civil rights movement.

imperative, if prefectural growth was to happen, that the governor, not local business, take the lead.

As noted above, each pressure vector between A and B also has some degree of impact over the ultimate outcome of a contended issue – the policy response. Accordingly, if we estimate that impact for each pressure vector, we may use the total pressure vectors to characterize the theoretical nature of the macro-pattern of power. Given the macro and meso/micro analogy in Tables 10.1 and A.1, we can say that the micro- and meso-level modes of power and influence working between all actors As and actor Bs operationalize the meta-theoretical assumptions of the diverse home domains of the macro-theories. The proportions of each type of pressure vector within the total impact upon a policy shift define the relative explanatory validity of each theory, thereby producing a new synthetic meta-theory of why the policy shift occurred. For instance, if the total set of pressure vectors causing a policy shift contained mostly the agentic use of cultural sanctions, this would indicate the validity of an explanation based on a cultural-agentic pattern of power (cell 9 in Table A.1 and Table 10.1).

To put this relationship in mathematical terms for preciseness, let V represent an A to B pressure vector, $\times$ the total number of vectors in the process, M_1 through M_9 the percentage presence of each of the nine types of relational influence modes within a given vector, and I the percentage of total impact on the ultimate political outcome held by a given vector. Then we can express the explanatory weight of a given mode W_{Mi} within the total set of vectors bearing upon an outcome as the formula: $W_{Mi} = (\Sigma_{iV1} \ldots M_{iVX})(\Sigma I_{V1} \ldots I_{VX})/X$. Given that the modes in Table A.1 operationalize the theories of the GE dilemma, W_{Mi} ipso facto also represents the relative explanatory weight of a given theoretical stance in a new synthetic meta-theory. The present study approaches the estimation of these parameters from this basic logic, albeit using qualitative data. I have coded my qualitative data into a form that can be analyzed quantitatively in the fashion just noted, and plan to carry out that analysis in the near future.

We might find that those influence relations with the most impact upon policy outcomes took their effectiveness mainly from the actors' use of mutually accepted cultural, moral principles and symbols. If so, we could call that a cultural structuralist-defined pattern of power (Table 10.1, cell 7). The Iranian Revolution under the Ayatollah Khomeini, where the mullahs in power attempted to structure the society around Islamic principles, might be an example. On the other hand, if collective actors followed existing norms defining their behavior, whether or not they individually believed in them, such forms of actions would define a social institutional structural pattern of power (Powell & DiMaggio, 1991). Of course, actors may use norms in a more calculating, utilitarian way, which would define, in distinction to the preceding, a social institutional *agentic* pattern of power (Swidler, 1986).

Alternately, power may arise from a more universal, rational, egocentric drive to acquire (or avoid) benefits and costs such as bullets, money, health, or votes (all of which imply material, physical sanctions). The market system would be a prototypical example of an political-economic agentic pattern of power. In contrast, domination by the capitalist class or by the state would exemplify two forms of political-economic structural patterns of power. In any case, it is crucial to look for the presence of theorized patterns of power within the pressure vectors between the actors that make up that pattern.

Appendix 2

Oita Prefecture and Japan National Growth and Environmental Key Events: 1955–1980

1955	National GNP equal to pre-war peak.
	Governor Kinoshita elected.
	Pulp plant locates in Tsurusaki.
	Fishing village of Nakajima opposes the pulp plant.
1957	OPG (Oita Prefectural Government) announces Oita Tsurusaki Seaside Industrial Area (OTSIA) including Landfills No. 6 and 7 in Tsurusaki, but with Landfill No. 8 across Beppu Bay.
1958	Misa/Iejima fishing village resistance to OTSIA.
1959	Construction started on Landfill No. 1 of NIC.
1961	Construction finished on Landfills No. 3 and 4.
	Tsurusaki Fishermen's Union holds a sit-in against the NIC.
	In the original OPG plans, the Second Phase of the NIC contained Landfills No. 6 and 7 along the Tsurusaki coast east of Oita City, but Landfill No. 8 was across Beppu Bay in Kitsuki.
1963	Oita designated as NIC.
1965	MITI tells OPG that the Second Phase landfill would have to be used for oil refineries, not high-employment machine industry.
1966	OPG decides on an oil refinery for No. 6 and a shipyard for No. 7.
	JCP legislator discovers high rates of pollution illness in Saganoseki.
1967	Several national pollution suits begin.
1968	First large anti-pollution movement in Japan launched in Osaka.
	Ministry of Construction designates Oita as one of the seventeen most polluted cities in Japan.
1969	OPG asks Mitsui Shipbuilding to construct a shipyard on No. 7.
	Full operation of the NJS blast furnace.
	Mitsui wants Landfill No. 7.

Showa Aluminum tells the government it wants to build a smelter on No. 8.

OPG unifies all Saganoseki fishing unions into one union.

Showa Oil and Sumitomo Chemical also want to build a refinery complex on the Second Phase landfill areas.

1970   Osaka Cement announces its intention of building a cement plant on landfill in Usuki Bay. Mobilization of the Usuki movement.

OPG makes the official announcement of the Second Phase plan with the surprise addition of Landfill No. 8 to be located in Saganoseki on the Kozaki/Baba coast.

First rumors of Showa Aluminum Refinery wanting to locate on No. 8.

Beginnings of Kozaki opposition movement.

Governor Kinoshita holds an "explanation meeting" in Kozaki.

Saganoseki Fishing Union votes against No. 8.

Eighty percent of Saganoseki voters sign a petition against No. 8, which is then presented to the Town Council.

The Pollution Diet passes a strict set of pollution laws.

1971   Showa Aluminum decides not to locate in Oita.

Mayor Furuta wins the Saganoseki election on an anti-No. 8 platform.

OPG has a second explanatory meeting and says Teijin Rayon and Showa Oil have been decided on for No. 8.

Usuki movement against Osaka Cement wins a court suit.

Saganoseki movement members make their first group trip to Tokyo to protest No. 8. They visit the Environmental Agency and companies planning to come.

New Governor Taki asks Mayor Furuta and the head of the legislature for cooperation.

Home "convincing" visits to Kozaki movement members are attempted by prefectural officials.

Mayor Furuta tells *ku*-heads to convince residents to support No. 8.

Kozaki movement makes linkage with other cooperative organizations in Oita Prefecture.

Big Saganoseki public meeting against No. 8.

Seabourne anti-No. 8 demonstration by Saganoseki Fishermen's Union with participation by seventeen groups. Nishio engages in "belly button dialogue."

1972   Mitsui Shipbuilding Co. signs the contract for No. 7 with OPG.
                   Seventy percent of Saganoseki voters sign a petition against No.
                       8.
                   OPG explains No. 8 to the Seki Town Council, and says it will put
                       9.6 billion yen into preparing the landfill.
                   OPG gets permission for Landfill No. 7 from the Ministry of
                       Construction.
                   The Environmental Agency says all landfill in the Inland Sea
                       (including Oita) should stop. OPG protests.
                   Two-thirds of the voters in Misa and Iejima sign a petition against
                       the Second Phase plan.
                   Oita Sohyo Union organization decides to stop the Second Phase
                       plans, and No. 8 in particular, by direct resistance.
                   Baba fishermen's union starts support campaign for No. 8.
                   Opposition leaders decide to make Misa pollution the crux of the
                       argument against proceeding with the Second Phase plans.
                   Saganoseki Mayor Furuta tries to pass a city plan, with approval
                       for No. 8 in it.
                   Leaders of the Kozaki and Seki movements stage a protest sit-in
                       in front of the town hall. Mayor Furuta leaks information
                       that union President Kawakami had tried to soften union
                       resistance.
                   Twenty-nine opposition groups decide to use demonstrations to
                       stop the Town Council from opening or passing the city
                       plan.
                   Mayor Furuta agrees not to try to pass a pro-No. 8 statement
                       again.
                   The Oita Doctors' Association announces an increase in the inci-
                       dence of asthma in the Misa area.
                   Fishermen start a recall movement against their union president.
                   Oita movement members meet with the Minister of the Environ-
                       ment (Mr. Miki), who promises to send an official to investi-
                       gate pollution in Oita.
1973   Union recall movement fails.
                   Opposition fishermen form "Common Purpose Group" and
                       disrupt all union meetings.
                   Kozaki and Seki movements use Misa asthma data to protest to
                       the Environmental Agency about the probable effects of
                       No. 8.

Environmental Agency officials visit OPG and discuss stopping No. 8 because of potential pollution.

The Environmental Agency expresses concern over Oita's pollution in the Diet committee handling the matter.

Governor Taki says he will go along with the Environmental Agency's decision on Oita pollution.

The Environmental Agency begins its Oita investigation.

Fighting between pro- and anti-No. 8 factions in the Seki union. Bloodshed and arrests result.

Seventy-four Kozaki and Seki movement representatives go to the Environmental Agency in Tokyo to petition against No. 8.

Governor Taki announces the "suspension" of the No. 8 landfill plan until three conditions are met: citizen consensus, settlement of the fishermen's union internal dispute, and completion of an environmental impact assessment.

Movements protest at the prefectural office buildings for total cancellation of No. 8.

The president of the Seki fishermen's union resigns.

The Oita LDP criticizes Governor Taki's suspension of the No. 8 plan.

OPG decides to go ahead with construction of Landfill No. 7.

OPG decides to buy up Iejima and move it.

The Usuki movement wins its high court suit to stop Osaka Cement. OPG gives up.

Ninety-five percent of the voters in Hoso sign a petition against Landfill No. 7.

Mitsui Real Estate gets a major contract for construction of Landfill No. 7.

1975   The Chamber of Commerce holds a meeting to support the Second Phase plan.

OPG changes its rationale for constructing No. 8 from providing employment to helping the town finances with taxes.

The Oita Chamber of Commerce backs the movements for No. 8 in Saganoseki, using citizens' movements.

Oita Council to Protect the Environment formed.

Oita environmental movement alliance formed.

Leader of the Kozaki movement elected to Saganoseki Town Council.

1976	OPG submits a new Second Phase plan, with plans for No. 8 attached.
	In response, the Kozaki movement initiates a suit against the OPG.
	Saganoseki Town Council passes a town plan with No. 8 in it. OPG calls this "citizen consensus."
	OPG commissions a professor do conduct pollution research. He concludes that no pollution exists in Misa and Iejima.
	The Kozaki movement holds its first formal meeting with other movements in the prefecture to request help in stopping No. 8.
	The "Joint Struggle Committee," a stronger prefecture-wide anti-No.8 organization, is formed.
	OPG forms its "No. 8 Problem Advisory Council."
	The leader of the Kozaki movement disrupts prefectural committee meetings on No. 8.
	Teijin Rayon cancels its offer to locate on No. 8.
1977	The Prime Minister approves OPG plans for the Second Phase of NIC.
	OPG says the Iejima move is not possible.
	The movement files suit against Landfill No. 8.
1978	OPG tries to carry out the environmental impact assessment in Kozai, but the movement prevents it with harassment tactics.
	The Environmental Agency tells OPG that it must also conduct an assessment of First Phase impact.
1979	The results of the assessment are announced. They permit the building of No. 8.
	Landfill No. 7 is finished.
	Suit against No. 8 is rejected.
1980	Governor Hiramatsu announces the fulfillment of the Three Conditions and ends the suspension of No. 8.

Appendix 3

Pollution legislation at prefectural and national levels, 1964–1985

Source: Oita Prefectural Government (Kankyo Gyosei Nenpyo)

Key to codes used in describing each legislative act

NL	Required by National Law and carried out by the national government
NLIP	Required by National Law but implemented by the Prefecture
PP	Policy created by Prefectural Government initiative and implemented by it
OPG	Oita Prefectural Government
OC	Oita City Government
MITI	Ministry of International Trade and Industry
MHW	Ministry of Health and Welfare
Memorandum	The Japanese word is *oboegaki,* a "memo" in legal terms
Agreement	The Japanese word is *kyotei,* legally binding

Year	Oita Prefecture	National government
1/64	Oita receives NIC designation(NL)	
5/65	NIC air pollution impact survey by MITI, OPG, and OC (NLIP, as required by NIC)	
9/65	NIC water water quality survey by MHW, OPG and OC (NLIP, as required by NIC)	
10/65	NIC air pollution impact survey by MHW, OPG and Oita City (NLIP, as required by NIC)	

11/65	OPG concludes the first pollution memorandum (*oboegaki*) with Kyushu Electric (PP)	
4/66	OPG establishes Pollution-Countermeasures Advisory Council (PP)	
6/66	NIC air pollution impact survey by MHW, OPG, and Oita City (NLIP, as required by NIC)	
8/67	Industrial pollution impact survey of sea near Oita, by MITI, OPG and OC (NLIP, as required by NIC)	Basic Law for Environmental Pollution Control (BLP)(NL)
5/68	OPG concludes pollution memorandum with Showa Denko (PP)	
6/68		Air Pollution Prevention Law (APPL) and Noise Control Law (NCL) (NL)
9/68	NIC air pollution diffusion impact survey by MHW, OPG and Oita City (NLIP, as required by NIC)	
12/68	OPG concludes pollution memorandum with Hachiman Chemical (PP)	
3/69	OPG concludes pollution memorandum with Kyushu Electric (PP)	
3/69	OPG concludes pollution memorandum with Kyushu Oil (PP)	
4/69	OPG promulgates Pollution Prevention Regulations (PP)	
8/69	Oita and Beppu Cities designated under Noise Control Law (NLIP)	
12/69	OPG concludes pollution memorandum with Fuji Steel (PP)	
12/69	Oita designated under Pollution Control Law (NLIP)	

2/70	OPG concludes pollution memorandum with Tsurusaki Pulp (PP)	
2/70	OPG implements requirements as designated under Pollution Control Law (NLIP)	
5/70	OPG concludes pollution memorandum with Nikko Saganoseki refinery (PP)	
6/70		Pollution Disputes Resolution Law (PDR)
9/70	OPG passes Pollution Disputes Resolution regulations (*jorei*) (NLIP, from PDR Law)	
12/70		The 64th Diet (the so-called Pollution Diet) passes and promulgates fourteen laws on pollution (14PL), including the Water Pollution Prevention Law
1/71	Prefectural Pollution Advisory Council begins work (NLIP, as required by PDR Law)	
5/71		Law for Special Consideration for Pollution Prevention in Nationally Funded Projects (SCL) (NL)
5/71		Regulation concerning authority to designate water and land area environmental standards (RADWL) (NL).
9/71	Oita area (Oita City and Saganoseki) required to prepare pollution prevention plan (NPIP, based on 1967 BL)	
10/71	OPG establishes pollution prevention regulations (PP)	
10/71	OC designated under Air Pollution Prevention Law (NLIP, based on 1970 14PL)	

12/71   Oita area (Oita City and
        Saganoseki) required to im-
        prove K levels (NLIP, based
        on 1970 14PL)

12/71   OPG Water Quality Advisory
        Council begins work (required
        by 14PL)

4/72   OPG designates water quality
        levels for Oita and Ono Rivers
        (PP, from RADWL)

12/72   Oita area Pollution Prevention
        Plan (first) approved (NLIP,
        required by 1967 BL and
        1971 SCL)

12/72   OPG establishes regulation for
        upstream water pollution
        (NLIP, required by 14PL)

10/73   Inland Sea Environmental Pro-
                                                tection Temporary Counter-
                                                measures Law (ISEP) (NL)

10/73   OPG successfully "directs"
        (*gyosei shido*) nine major
        firms to cut SO$_2$ output by 20
        percent (PP)

10/73   OPG makes revised pollution
        agreement (*kyotei*) with New
        Japan Steel (PP)

10/73   OPG pollution victims relief reg-
        ulations (*jorei*) (PP)

5/74   Because of revision of Water
        Pollution Prevention Law,
        Oita becomes a designated
        water quality city (NLIP)

6/74   OC finishes Matsubara green
        belt area (PP)

6/74   OPG makes revised pollution
        agreement with Kyushu Oil
        (PP)

7/74   OPG issues complete revision of
        upstream water pollution reg-
        ulations (NLIP, required by
        1973 ISEP)

12/74	OPG makes revised pollution agreement with eleven companies in the Showa Denko Group (PP)	
1/75	OPG makes revised pollution agreement with New Japan Steel Chemical (PP)	
2/76	OPG makes revised pollution agreement with Sumitomo Chemical	
6/76		Vibration Regulation Law (VRL)(NL)
9/76	Oita area K pollution standards partly revised because of changes in Air Pollution Prevention Law	Offensive Odor Law implementation (OOL)(NL)
1977	No major relevant pollution policy activity	
3/78	Oita and nine other cities designated under VRL	
3/78	Oita Area Pollution Prevention Plan (second) (NLIP, required by 1967 BLP)	
4/78	OPG SO$_2$ Overall Reduction Plan implemented (PP)	
6/78		Inland Sea Environmental Protection Temporary Countermeasures Law (ISEP) (NL). Partial revision with introduction of total volume regulation system
11/79	Presentation for public review of draft of "Environmental Impact Evaluation for Oita Area Industrial Growth Plan" (PP)	
3/80	Plan for reduction of total Chemical Oxygen Demand (COD) water pollutants (NLIP, from 1978 ISEP)	

4/80	Plan for reduction of phosphorous compounds (NLIP, from 1978 ISEP)
5/80	Overall volume standards determined for COD pollution (NLIP, from 1978 ISEP)
5/80	Public presentation of Oita Area Industrial Environmental Pollution Assessment (PP)
5/80	Oita City designated under Noxious Odor Prevention Law (1976 Law, NLIP)
10/80	OPG concludes pollution agreement with Mitsui Shipbuilding (PP)
7/81	OPG Plan for Inland Sea Environmental Preservation (NLIP, from 1978 ISEP)
3/83	Oita Area Pollution Prevention Plan (third) (NLIP, from 1967 BLP)
9/83	OPG revised pollution agreement with Kyushu Electric (PP)
12/83	OPG pollution agreement with Oita Chemical (Showa Denko Group)
3/85	Designation of Oita City and Saganoseki under Noise Pollution typology (NLIP, from 1968 NCL Law)
3/85	Designation of Saganoseki restrictions under Noise Control Law (NLIP, from 1968 NCL Law)
3/85	OPG memorandum with Nikko and Oita Nickel on pollution control (PP)

References

Abbott, A. (1992) "From Causes to Events: Notes on Narrative Positivism." *Sociological Methods and Research,* 20(40), May, 428–55. Newbury Park: Sage Publications.

Adachi, I. (1973) *Mura to Ningen No Hokai (The Collapse of the Village and People).* Tokyo: Sanichi Shobo.

Adam, B. (1993) "Post-Marxism and the New Social Movements." *Canadian Review of Sociology and Anthropology,* 30(3), 316–36.

Agar, M. (1983) "Ethnography and Cognition." In *Contemporary Field Research,* ed. R. M. Emerson, pp. 68–77. Prospect Heights: Waveland.

Aiba, J., Iyasu, T., & Takashima, S. (1987) *Nihon Seiji o Yomu (Understanding Japanese Politics).* Tokyo: Yuhikaku.

Alford, R. & Friedland, R. (1975) "Political participation and public policy." *Annual Review of Sociology,* 1, 429–74.

Alford, R. & Friedland, R. (1985) *Powers of Theory: Capitalism, the State, and Democracy.* New York: Cambridge University Press.

Almond, G. A. & Verba, S. (1963) *The Civic Culture: Political Attitudes and Democracy in Five Nations.* Princeton: Princeton University Press.

Amin, S. (1976) *Unequal Development: An Essay on the Social Formation of Unequal Capitalism.* New York: Monthly Review Press.

Aminzade, R. (1992) "Historical Sociology and Time." *Sociological Methods and Research,* 20(4), May, 456–80. Newbury Park: Sage Publications.

Appelbaum, R. & Henderson, J. (1992) *States and Development in the Asian Pacific Rim.* Newbury Park: Sage Publications.

Apter, D. & Sawa, K. (1984) *Against the State.* Cambridge: Harvard University Press.

Arrow, K. et al. (1995) "Economic Growth, Carrying Capacity, and the Environment," *Science, 268* (28 April), 520–1.

Bachnik, J. (1989) "Omote/Ura: Indexes and the Organization of Self and Society in Japan." In *Comparative Social Research,* ed. C. Calhoun, pp. 239–63. Greenwich: JAI Press.

Bachrach, P. & Baratz, M. (1970) *Power and Poverty.* New York: Oxford Unviersity Press.

Bahro, R. (1986) *Building the Green Movement.* Philadelphia: New Society Publishers.

Banfield, E. (1958) *The Moral Basis of a Backward Society.* Glencoe: Free Press.

Baran, P. (1957) *The Political Economy of Growth.* New York: Monthly Review Press.

Beardsley, R., Hall, J., & Ward, R. (1959) *Village Japan.* Chicago: University of Chicago Press.

Beck, U. (1992) *The Risk Society.* London: Sage.

Begley, S. & Takayama, H. (1989) "The World's Eco-Outlaw." *Newsweek,* May 1.

Bellah, R. (1957) *Tokugawa Religion. The Values of Pre-Industrial Japan.* Glencoe: Free Press.

Benedict, R. (1946) *The Chrysanthemum and the Sword.* New York: Houghton Mifflin.

Berger, B. (1995) *An Essay on Culture: Symbolic Structure and Social Structure.* Berkeley: University of California Press.

Bestor, T. C. (1989) *Neighborhood Tokyo.* Stanford: Stanford University Press.

Bix, H. (1986) *Peasant Protest in Japan, 1590–1884.* New Haven: Yale University Press.

Block, F. (1977) "The Ruling Class Does Not Rule: Notes on the Marxist Theory of the State." *Socialist Revolution,* 33 (May–June), 6–28.

Block, F. (1987) "The Ruling Class Does Not Rule: Notes on the Marxist Theory of State." In *Revising State Theory: Essays in Politics and Postindustrialism.* Philadelphia: Temple University Press.

Bourdieu, P. (1990) *The Logic of Practice.* Stanford: Stanford University Press.

Broadbent, J. (1975) *The Great Kamo Ikki: Peasant Revolt in Tokugawa Japan.* M.A. Diss. Cambridge, MA: Harvard University.

Broadbent, J. (1983) "Environmental Movements in Japan: Citizen Versus State Mobilization." Paper presented at the annual meeting of the American Sociological Association.

Broadbent, J. (1986) "The Ties that Bind: Social Fabric and the Mobilization of Environmental Movements in Japan." *International Journal of Mass Emergencies and Disasters,* 4, 227–53.

Broadbent, J. (1988) "State as Process: The Effect of Party and Class on Citizen Participation in Japanese Local Government." *Social Problems,* 35(2), 131–42.

Broadbent, J. (1989a) "Environmental Politics in Japan: An Integrated Structural Analysis." *Sociological Forum,* 4(2), 179–202.

Broadbent, J. (1989b) "The Technopolis Strategy vs. Deindustrialization: High-Tech Development Sites in Japan. Comparative Urban and Community Research, 2, 231–53." In *Pacific Rim Cities in the World Economy,* ed. M. P. Smith. New Brunswick: Transaction Publishers.

Broadbent, J. & Ishio, Y. (Forthcoming) "The 'Influence Broker' State: Social Networks and Political Organization in Japan." In *Networks and Markets: Pacific Rim Investigations,* ed. Mark Fruin. New York: Oxford University Press.

Brown, L. (1991) *Saving the Planet.* New York: Norton.

Brown, P. & Mikkelsen, E. (1990) *No Safe Place.* Berkeley: University of California Press.

Brulle, R. (1994) "Power, Discourse and Social Problems: Social Problems From a Rhetorical Perspective." *Perspectives on Social Problems,* 5, 95–121.

Brustein, W. (1996) *The Logic of Evil.* New Haven: Yale University Press.

Bullard, R., ed. (1993) *Confronting Environmental Racism.* Boston: South End Press.

Burawoy, M. (1985) *The Politics of Production.* London: Verso.

Burawoy, M., Burton, A., & Ferguson, A., eds. (1992) *Ethnography Unbound: Power and Resistance in the Modern Metropolis.* Berkeley: University of California Press.

Burstein, P., Einwhoner, R., & Hollander, J. (1995) "The Success of Social Movements: A Bargaining Perspective." In *The Politics of Social Protest,* ed. J. C. Jenkins & B. Klandermans, pp. 3–13. Minneapolis: University of Minnesota Press.

Busacker, R. G. & Saaty, T. L. (1965) *Finite Graphs and Networks.* New York: McGraw-Hill.

Buttel, F. (1987) "New Directions in Environmental Sociology." *Annual Review of Sociology,* 13, 465–88.

Cable, S. & Cable, C. (1995) *Environmental Problems, Grassroots Solution.* New York: St. Martin's Press.

Calder, K. E. (1988) *Crisis and Compensation: Public Policy and Political Stability in Japan.* Princeton: Princeton University Press.

Calhoun, C. (1995) "'New Social Movements' of the Early Nineteenth Century," In *Repertoires and Cycles of Collective Action,* ed. M. Traugott, pp. 173–215. Durham, N.C.: Duke University Press.

Campbell, J. (1984) "Policy Conflict and Its Resolution Within the Governmental System." In *Conflict in Japan,* ed. E. Krauss, T. Rohlen & P. Steinhoff, pp. 294–334.

Capra, F. & Spretnak, C. (1984) *Green Politics, The Global Promise.* New York: Dutton.

Cardoso, F. & Faletto, E. (1979) *Dependency and Development in Latin America.* Berkeley: University of California Press.

Catton, W. (1980) *Overshoot: The Ecological Basis of Revolutionary Change.* Urbana: University of Illinois Press.

Catton, W. & Dunlap, R. (1978) "Environmental Sociology: A New Paradigm." *The American Sociologist, 13* (February), 41–9.

Caves, R. & Uekusa, M. (1976) "Industrial Organization." In *Asia's New Giant,* ed. H. Patrick & H. Rosovsky. Washington, D.C.: Brookings Institution.

Chong, D. (1991) *Collective Action and the Civil Rights Movement.* Chicago: University of Chicago Press.

Clark, R. (1988) "Industrial Groups." In *Inside the Japanese System,* ed. Daniel Okimoto and Thomas Rohlen. Stanford: Stanford University Press.

Coase, R. (1988) *The Firm, the Market and the Law.* Chicago: University of Chicago Press.

Cohen, L., McCubbins, M., & Rosenbluth, F. (1995) "The Politics of Nuclear Power in Japan and the United States." In *Structure and Policy in Japan and the United States,* ed. P. Cowhey & M. McCubbins, pp. 177–202. Cambridge: Cambridge University Press.

Collins, P. H. (1991) *Black Feminist Thought: Knowledge, Consciousness and the Politics of Empowerment.* Ithaca: Cornell University Press.

Commoner, B. (1972) *The Closing Circle.* London: Jonathan Cape.

Commoner, B. (1990) *Making Peace with the Planet.* New York: Pantheon Books.

Cowhey, P. & McCubbins, M. (1995) *Structure and Policy in Japan and the United States.* Cambridge: Cambridge University Press.

Craiger, J. Philip, et al. (1996) "Modeling Organizational Behavior with Fuzzy Cognitive Maps." *International Journal of Computational Intelligence and Organizations, 1*(3), 120–33.

Crenson, M. (1970) *The un-Politics of Air Pollution: A Study of Non-Decision Making in the Cities.* Baltimore, MD: Johns Hopkins University Press.

Crozier, M. (1973) *The Stalled Society.* New York: Viking Press.

Crozier, M., Huntington, S., & Watanuki, J. (1975) *The Crisis of Democracy.* New York: New York University Press.

Cummings, W. (1980) *Education and Equality in Japan.* Princeton: Princeton University Press.

Curtis, G. (1971) *Election Campaigning, Japanese Style.* New York: Columbia University Press.

Dahl, R. (1961) *Who Governs? Democracy and Power in an American City.* New Haven: Yale University Press.

Dahrendorf, R. (1959) *Class and Class Conflict in Industrial Society.* Stanford: Stanford University Press.

Dale, P. N. (1986) *The Myth of Japanese Uniqueness.* New York: St. Martin's Press.

Dalton, R. J. (1995) "Strategies of Partisan Influence: West European Environmental Groups." In *The Politics of Social Protest,* ed. J. C. Jenkins & B. Klandermans, pp. 3–13. Minneapolis: University of Minnesota.

Dalton, R., Kuechler, M., & Burklin, W. (1990) "The Challenge of New Movements." In

Challenging the Political Order, ed. Russell Dalton and Manfred Kuechler. New York: Oxford University Press.

Daly, H. (1980) "Introduction to the Steady State Economy." In *Economics, Ecology, Ethics,* ed. Herman Daly. San Francisco: Freeman.

Daly, H. & Cobb, J. (1989) *For the Common Good.* Boston, MA: Beacon Press.

Davies, J. C. (1962) "Toward a Theory of Revolution." *American Sociological Review,* 27 (February), 5–19.

DeVall, B. & Sessions, G. (1985) "The Dominant Worldview and Its Critics." In *Deep Ecology.* Salt Lake City: Peregrine Smith Books.

DeVos, G. A. (1973) *Socialization for Achievement.* Berkeley: University of California Press.

Dietz, T. & Rosa, E. (1994) "Rethinking the Environmental Impacts of Population, Affluence and Technology." *Human Ecology Review,* 1, 277–300.

Doi, T. (1973) *The Anatomy of Dependence.* Tokyo and New York: Kodansha International.

Domhoff, G. W. (1995) "Who Rules America?" In *American Society and Politics,* ed. Theda Skocpol and John Campbell, pp. 32–47. New York: McGraw-Hill.

Dore, R. P. (1978) *Shinohata: A Portrait of a Japanese Village.* New York: Pantheon Books.

Dore, R. (1987) *Taking Japan Seriously: A Confucian Perspective on Leading Economic Issues.* Stanford: Stanford University Press.

Douglas, M. 1986. *How Institutions Think.* Syracuse, N.Y.: Syracuse University Press.

Douglas, M. & Wildavsky, A. (1982) *Risk and Culture: An Essay on the Selection of Technological and Environmental Dangers.* Berkeley: University of California Press.

Duke, B. C. (1973) *Japan's Militant Teachers: A History of the Left-Wing Teacher's Movement.* Honolulu: University Press of Hawaii.

Duncan, O. D. (1961) "From Social System to Ecosystem." *Sociological Inquiry,* 31, 140–9.

Dunlap, R. (1992) "Trends in Public Opinion Toward Environmental Issues: 1965–1990." In *American Environmentalism,* ed. Riley Dunlap and Angela Mertig, pp. 89–116. Philadelphia: Taylor and Francis.

Dunlap, R. & Catton, W. (1992) "Toward an Ecological Sociology: The Development, Current Status and Probable Future of Environmental Sociology." *Annals of the International Institute of Sociology,* 3, New Series, 264–84.

Dunlap, R. & Catton, W., Jr. (1994) Struggling with Human Exemptionalism: The Rise, Decline and Revitalization of Environmental Sociology. *The American Sociologist,* 25(1), 5–30.

Dunlap, R., Gallup, G. J. & Gallup, A. (1992) *The Health of the Planet Survey.* Princeton: The George H. Gallup International Institute.

Dunlap, R. & Mertig, A. (1992) "The Evolution of the U.S. Environment Movement from 1970 to 1990: An Overview." In *American Environmentalism,* ed. Riley Dunlap and Angela Mertig, pp. 1–10. Philadelphia: Taylor and Francis.

Edelman, M. (1964) *The Symbolic Uses of Politics.* Urbana: University of Illinois Press.

Edelman, M. (1977) *Politics as Symbolic Action.* New York: Academic Press.

Ehrlich, P. (1973) *The Population-Resource-Environment Crisis: With Special Reference to Japan.*

Ehrlich, P. & Ehrlich, A. (1990) "Why Isn't Everyone as Scared as We Are?" In *The Population Explosion,* pp. 13–23. New York: Simon and Schuster.

Eisenstadt, S. N. & Roniger, L. (1984) *Patrons, Clients and Friends.* Cambridge: Cambridge University Press.

Emirbayer, M. & Goodwin, J. (1994) "Network Analysis, Culture and the Problem of Agency." *American Journal of Sociology*, 99(6), 1411–54.

Environmental Agency of Japan (*Kankyocho*). (1972) "A Memo on Conversations with the Director General about the Oita NIC Phase Two Plan No. 8 Landfill Area Problem." Internal memorandum.

Environmental Agency of Japan (*Kankyocho*). (1982) *Environmental White Paper* (*Kankyo Hakusho*). Tokyo: Government of Japan.

Energii to Kogai Jyanaru (Journal of Energy and the Environment). Tokyo: Energii Jyanarusha.

Erikson, K. (1976) *Everything in Its Path: Destruction of Community in the Buffalo Creek Flood*. New York: Simon and Schuster.

Esping-Andersen, G. and R. Friendland. 1982. "Class Coalitions in the Making of West European Economies," pp. 1–52 in *Political Power and Social Theory*, ed. Maurice Zeitlin. Greenwich, CT: JAI Press, Inc.

Etzioni, A. (1968) *The Active Society*. New York: Free Press.

Etzioni, A. (1975) *A Comparative Analysis of Complex Organization*. New York: Free Press.

Evans, P. (1971) *Dependent Development*. Princeton: Princeton University Press.

Evans, P. (1995) *Embedded Autonomy: Stages and Industrial Transformation*. Princeton: Princeton University Press.

Evans, S. & Boyte, H. (1986) *Free Spaces: The Sources of Democratic Change in America*. New York: Harper and Row.

Eyerman, R. & Jamison, A. (1991) *Social Movements: A Cognitive Approach*. University Park: The Pennsylvania State University Press.

Ferree, M. M. (1992) "The Political Context of Rationality: Rational Choice Theory and Resource Mobilization." In *Frontiers in Social Movement Theory*, ed. A. D. Morris & C. McClurg Mueller, pp. 29–52. New Haven: Yale University Press.

Finsterbusch, K. (1989) "Community Responses to Exposures to Hazardous Wastes." In *Psychosocial Effects of Hazardous Toxic Waste Disposal on Communities*, ed. D. L. Peck. Springfield, IL.: Charles C. Thomas.

Fishman, M. (1978) "Crime Waves as Ideology." *Social Problems*, 25, 531–43.

Flanagan, S. (1978) "The Genesis of Variant Political Cultures: Contemporary Citizen Orientations in Japan, America, Britain and Italy." In *The Citizen and Politics: A Comparative Perspective*, ed. S. Verba & L. Pye, pp. 129–59. Stamford: Greylock Publications.

Fleischmann, A. & Feagin, J. (1987) "The Politics of Growth-Oriented Urban Alliances: Comparing Old Industrial and Sunbelt Cities." *Urban Affairs Quarterly*, 23, 207–302.

Foucault, M. (1972) *Power/Knowledge*. New York: Pantheon.

Foucault, M. (1980). "The Confession of the Flesh." In *Power/Knowledge: Selected Interviews and Other Writing*, ed. C. Gordon. New York: Pantheon.

Foucault, M. (1983) "The Subject and Power." In *M. Foucault: Beyond Structuralism and Hermeneutics*, ed. P. Rainbow & H. Dreyfus, pp. 208–26

Franck, I. & Brownstone, D. (1992) *The Green Encyclopedia*. New York: Prentice Hall.

French, J. & Raven, B. (1959) "The Bases of Social Power." In *Studies in Social Power*, ed. D. Cartwright. Ann Arbor: University of Michigan Press.

Freudenberg, N. & Steinsapir, C. (1992) "Not in Our Backyards: The Grassroots Environmental Movement." In *American Environmentalism*, ed. Riley Dunlap and Angela Mertig, pp. 27–38. Philadelphia: Taylor and Francis.

Friedland, R. and R. Alford. (1991) "Bringing Society Back In: Symbols, Practices, and Institutional Contradictions," pp. 232–63 in *The New Institutionalism in Organiza-*

tional Analysis, ed. Walter Powell and Paul DiMaggio. Chicago: University of Chicago Press.

Friedland, R., Piven, F., & Alford, R. R. (1977) "Political Conflict, Urban Structure, and the Fiscal Crisis. *International Journal of Urban and Regional Research,* 1, 447–71.

Friedman, D. & McAdam, D. (1992) "Collective Identity and Activism: Networks, Choices and the Life of a Social Movement." In *Frontiers in Social Movement Theory,* ed. A. D. Morris & C. McClurg Mueller, pp. 156–73. New Haven: Yale University Press.

Fujii, N. & Takaura, T. (1974) "Oita Shinsanto no Kogai (The Pollution of the Oita N.I.C.). Kogai Genron (Principles of Pollution)." Dai Nana Gakki (Seventh Quarter) (January 21). Tokyo: Aki Shobo.

Fukui, H. (1977) "Studies in Policymaking: A Review of the Literature." In *Policy-Making in Contemporary Japan,* ed. T. J. Pempel. Ithaca: Cornell University Press.

Fukui, H. (1992) "The Japanese State and Economic Development: A Profile of a Nationalist-Paternalist Capitalist State." In *States and Development in the Asian Pacific Rim, ed.* R. Appelbaum & J. Henderson, pp. 199–225. Newbury Park: Sage Publications.

Fukutake, T. (1989) *The Japanese Social Structure.* Tokyo: University of Tokyo Press.

Funabashi, H. (1980) "Kyodo Renkan no Ryogiesei–kei'ei shisutemu to shihai shisutemu (The Ambiguity of Coordination–Management System and Control System)." In *Gendai Shakai No Shakaigaku (The Sociology of Contemporary Society),* ed. Gendai Shakai Mondai Kenkyukai, pp. 209–31. Tokyo, Japan: Kawashima Shoten.

Funabashi, H. (1992) "Environmental Problems in Japanese Society." *International Journal of Japanese Sociology,* 1 (October).

Funabashi, H. (1995) "Kankyo Mondai e no Shakaigakuteki Shiza-Shakaiteki Jirema Ron to Shakaiteki Shisutemu Ron (Sociological Perspectives on Environmental Problems: The Theory of Social Dilemmas and the Theory of Social Control Systems)." *Kankyo Shakaigaku Kenkyu,* 1, 5–20.

Funabashi, H., Hasegawa, K., Hatanaka, M., & Kajita, T. (1988) *Kosoku Bunmei No Chiiki Mondai (Regional Problems of a High Speed Civilization).* Tokyo: Yuhikaku.

Furuki, T. (1978) *Chiho Seiji No Shakaigaku (The Sociology of Regional Politics).* Tokyo: University of Tokyo Press.

Gaard, G. (1993) *Ecofeminism, Women, Animals, Nature.* Philadelphia: Temple University Press.

Gale, R. P. (1986) "Social Movements and the State: The Environmental Movement, Countermovement and Governmental Agencies." *Sociological Perspectives,* 29, 202–40.

Gamson, W. A. (1988) "Political Discourse and Collective Action." In *International Social Movement Research,* ed. B. Klandermans, H. Kriesi, & S. Tarrow, pp. 219–44. Greenwich: JAI Press Inc.

Gamson, W. A. (1990). The Strategy of Social Protest, 2nd ed. Belmont, CA.: Wadsworth.

Gamson, W. A. (1992) "The Social Psychology of Collective Action." In *Frontiers in Social Movement Theory,* ed. A. D. Morris & C. McClurg Mueller, pp. 53–76. New Haven: Yale University Press.

Garon, S. (1987) *The State and Labor in Modern Japan.* Berkeley: University of California Press.

Gaventa, J. (1995) "Power and Participation." In *American Society and Politics,* ed. T. Skocpol & J. L. Campbell, pp. 14–27. New York: McGraw-Hill.

Gedicks, A. (1994) *The New Resource Wars.* Montreal: Black Rose Books.

Geertz, C. (1973) *The Interpretation of Cultures.* New York: Basic Books.

Gerlach, M. L. (1992) *Alliance Capitalism: The Social Organization of Japanese Business.* Berkeley: University of California Press.

Giddens, A. (1984) *The Constitution of Society.* Berkeley: University of California Press.

Giddens, A. (1993) *New Rules of the Sociological Method.* Stanford: Stanford University Press.

Giddens, A. (1994) "Industrialization, Ecology and Development of Life Politics." In *Ecology, Society and the Quality of Social Life,* ed. W. V. D'Antonio, M. Sasaki, & Y. Yonebayashi, pp. 1–10. New Brunswick: Transaction.

Glaser, B. & Strauss, A. L. (1967) *The Discovery of Grounded Theory: Strategies for Qualitative Research.* New York: Aldine.

Goffman, E. (1959) *The Presentation of Self in Everyday Life.* Garden City, N.Y.: Anchor.

Goldstone, J. (1980) "The Weakness of Organization: A New Look at Gamson's 'The Strategy of Social Protest.'" *American Journal of Sociology,* 85(5), 1043–60.

Goodman, R. (1979) *The Last Entrepreneurs: America's Regional Wars for Jobs and Dollars.* Boston: South End Press.

Gordon, R. (1995) *Conservation Directory.* Washington, D.C.: National Wildlife Federation.

Gore, A. (1993) *Earth in the Balance: Ecology and the Human Spirit.* Boston: Houghton Mifflin.

Gorz, A. (1980) "Labor and the Quality of Life." In *Ecology as Politics.* Boston: South End Press.

Gould, K. (1993) "Legitimacy and Growth in the Balance: The Role of the State in Environmental Remediation." *Industrial and Environmental Crisis Quarterly,* 8(3), 237–56.

Government of Japan. (nd) *Sangyo Richi Kogai Horei Soran (Compendium of Regional Location and Pollution Law and Regulations).* Tokyo: Government of Japan.

Grafstein, R. (1988). "A Realist Foundation for Essentially Contested Political Concepts." *The Western Political Quarterly* 41:9–28.

Granovetter, M. (1973) "The Strength of Weak Ties." *American Journal of Sociology,* 78, 1360–80.

Granovetter, M. (1985) "Economic Action, Social Structure, and Embeddedness." *American Journal of Sociology,* 91(3), November, 481–510.

Gresser, J., Fujikura, K., & Morishima, A. (1981) *Environmental Law in Japan.* Cambridge: MIT Press.

Griffin, L. J. (1992) "Temporality, Events, and Explanation in Historical Sociology." *Sociological Methods and Research,* 20(4), May, 403–27. Newbury Park: Sage Publications.

Griffith, J. (1990) "The Environmental Movement in Japan." *Whole Earth Review,* LXIX (Winter), 90–6.

Griswold, W. (1994) *Cultures and Societies in a Changing World.* Thousand Oaks: Pine Forge Press.

Haas, P. (1990) *Saving the Mediterranean: The Politics of International Environmental Cooperation.* New York: Columbia University Press.

Haas, P. (1992) "Obtaining international protection through epistemic consensus." In *Global Environmental Change and International Relations,* ed. I. H. Rowlands & M. Greene. Basingstoke: Macmillan.

Habermas, J. (1981) "New Social Movements," *Telos,* Fall, 33–7.

Habermas, J. (1987) *The Theory of Communicative Action. Vol. II. Lifeworld and System.* Boston: Beacon Press.

Habermas, J. (1989) *The Structural Transformation of the Public Sphere.* Cambridge: MIT Press.

Halliday, J. (1975) *The Political History of Japanese Capitalism.* New York: Pantheon Books.

Hamaguchi, E. (1985) "A Contextual Model of the Japanese: Toward a Methodological Innovation in Japanese Studies." *Journal of Japanese Studies*, 11(2), 289–321.

Hanayama, T. (1980) *Kankyoseisaku o Kangaeru (Thinking About Environmental Policy)*. Tokyo: Iwanami Shinsho.

Hannigan, J. A. (1995) *Environmental Sociology, A Social Constructivist Perspective*. New York: Routledge.

Hardin, G. (1980) "Second Thoughts on the Tragedy of the Commons." In *Economics, Ecology, Ethics,* ed. Herman Daly. San Francisco: Freeman.

Harper, C. L. (1996) *Environment and Society*. Upper Saddle River, NJ: Prentice-Hall.

Hasegawa, K. (1994) "A Comparative Study of Social Movements for a Post-Nuclear Energy Era in Japan and the United States." Paper presented at the World Congress of Sociology, Beilefeld, Germany, July 1994.

Hasegawa, K. (1996) *Datsu Genshiryoku Shakai No Sentaku (The Choice for a Post-Nuclear Society: The Age of New Energy Revolution)*. Tokyo: Shinetsu Sha.

Hasegawa, K. (unpublished) "A Comparative Study of Social Movements for a Post-Nuclear Energy Era in Japan and the United States." In *Social Movements in East Asia,* ed. J. Broadbent & V. Brockman (in review).

Hashimoto, M. (1988) *Shishi Kankyo Gyosei (Personal History: Environmental Administration)*. Tokyo: Asahi Shimbunsha.

Haupt, R. C. (1980) "The Power To Promote Growth: Business and the Making of Local Economic Development Policy." Unpublushed Ph.D. dissertation.

Hearings (1978) Hearings on the No. 8 Landfill Case. Oita Regional Court: May 15.

Hechter, M. (1975) *Internal Colonialism: The Celtic Fringe in British National Development, 1536–1966*. Berkeley: University of California Press.

Hechter, M. (1983) "Introduction." In *The Microfoundations of Macrosociology,* ed. M. Hechter, pp. 3–15. Philadelphia: Temple University Press.

Heclo, H. (1978) "Issue Networks and the Executive Establishment." In *The New American Political System,* ed. A. King. Washington, D.C.: American Enterprise Institute.

Heirich, M. (1968) *The Beginning: Berkeley, 1964*. New York: Columbia University Press.

Hiramatsu, M. (1983) *Technoporis e No Chosen (The Challenge of Technopolis)*. Tokyo: Nihon Keizai Shinbunsha.

Hirsch, F. (1976) *Social Limits to Growth*. Cambridge: Harvard University Press.

Hirschman, A. (1970) *Exit, Voice and Loyalty*. Cambridge, MA: Harvard University Press.

Hirschman, A. (1981) *Essays in Trespassing: Economics to Politics and Beyond*. Cambridge: Cambridge University Press.

Homans, G. (1974) *Social Behavior: Its Elementary Forms*. New York: Harcourt, Brace, Jovanovich.

Homer-Dixon, T. (1993) *Environmental Scarcity and Global Security*. New York, NY: Foreign Policy Association.

Hoshino, E. et al., eds. (1988) *Shoroppo (Public Law Statutes)*. Tokyo: Yuhikaku Books.

Huddle, H., Reich, M., & Stiskin, N. (1975) *Island of Dreams*. New York: Autumn Press.

Humphrey, C. & Buttel, F. (1980) *Environment, Energy, and Society*. Belmont: Wadsworth.

Hunter, A. (1995) "Local Knowledge and Local Power: Notes on the Ethnography of Local Community Elites." In *Studying Elites Using Qualitative Methods,* ed. R. Hertz & J. Imber, pp. 151–70. New York: Sage.

Hunter, F. (1953) *Community Power Structure*. Chapel Hill: University of North Carolina Press.

Iijima, N. (1979) "Pollution Japan Historical Chronology." Tokyo: *Asahi Evening News*.

Iijima, N. (1984) *Kankyo Mondai to Higaisha Undo (The Pollution Problem and the Victims' Movements).* Tokyo: Gakubunsha.

Iijima, N. (1994) *Kankyo Shakaigaku (Environmental Sociology).* Tokyo: Yuhikaku Books.

Iijima, S. (1990) "The Growth of Industrial Location Plans and Pollution Countermeasures." In *Tsusho Sangyo Shi (History of Trade and Industrial Policy), Vol. 11.,* ed. MITI. Tokyo: Japanese Government.

Ike, N. (1980) *A Theory of Japanese Democracy.* Boulder: Westview.

Inglehart, R. (1977) *The Silent Revolution.* Princeton: Princeton University Press.

Inkeles, A. (1974) *Becoming Modern.* Cambridge: Harvard University Press.

Inoguchi, T. (1983) *Gendai Nihon Seiji Keizai No Kozu (The Structure of Contemporary Japanese Political-Economy).* Tokyo: Toyo Keizai Shuppansha.

Inoguchi, T. and T. Iwai (1987) *"Zoku Giin" No Kenkyu (Research on "Tribal Lesiglators").* Tokyo: Nihon Keizai Shimbunsha.

Isard, W. (1975) *Introduction to Regional Science.* Englewood Cliffs: Prentice Hall.

Ishida, T. (1983) *Japanese Political Culture.* New Brunswick: Transaction.

Ishida, T. (1984) "Conflict and Its Accomodation: Omote-Ura and Uchi-Soto Approaches." In *Conflict in Japan,* ed. E. Krauss & P. S. Thomas Rohlen. Honolulu: University of Hawaii Press.

Ishida, T. & Krauss, E. eds. (1989) *Democracy in Japan.* Pittsburgh: University of Pittsburgh Press.

Ishimure, M. (1990) *Paradise in the Sea of Sorrow: Our Minamata Disease.* Kyoto: Yamaguchi.

Japanese Government. (nd) *Sangyo Richi Kogai Horei Soran (Compendium of Regional Location and Pollution Law and Regulations).* Tokyo: Japanese Government.

Jenkins, J. C. (1983) "Resource Mobilization Theory and the Study of Social Movements." *Annual Review of Sociology,* 9, 527–53.

Jenks, C. (1993). *Culture.* London: Routledge.

Jepperson, R. (1991) "Institutions, Institutional Effects and Institutionalism." In *The New Institutionalism in Organizational Analysis,* ed. W. Powell & P. DiMaggio, pp. 143–63. Chicago: University of Chicago.

Jessop, B. (1982) *The Capitalist State: Marxist Theories and Methods.* Oxford: M. Robertson.

Johnson, C. (1982) *MITI and the Japanese Miracle.* Stanford: Stanford University Press.

Kabashima, I. & Broadbent, J. (1986) "Referent Pluralism: Mass Media and Politics in Japan." *Journal of Japanese Studies,* 12(2), 329–61.

Kamishima, J. (1983) "Political Principles and Japanese Society." In *The Challenge of Japan's Internationalization.* Tokyo: Kodanshi.

Kano, M., Kinbara, S., & Matsunaga, S. (1977) *Minshu Undo to Shiso (People's Movements and Thought).* Tokyo: Yuhikaku Books.

Kaplan, D. & Dubro, A. (1986) *Yakuza: The Explosive World of Japan's Criminal Underworld,* Chs. 5 and 6. Addison-Wesley.

Kaplan, C. & Grewal, I. (1994) "Transnational Feminist Cultural Studies: Beyond Marxism/Poststructuralism/Feminism Debate." *Positions,* 2, 430–45.

Kato, S. (1989) "Kogai Taisaku Kihonho to sono seka (The World of the Basic Law against Pollution)." *Gesuido Kyokaishi,* 26(306), November, 2–9.

Katsumata, S. (1954) *Kenkyusha's New Japanese-English Dictionary.* Tokyo: Kenkyusha.

Kawana, H. (1987) *Dokyumento: Nihon No Kogai (Documents: Japan's Pollution).* Tokyo: Ryokufu Shuppan.

Kawana, H. (1988) *Dokyumento: Nihon No Kogai (Documents: Japan's Pollution).* Tokyo: Ryokufu Shuppan.

Kelley, D. (1976) *The Economic Superpowers and the Environment: The United States, the Soviet Union and Japan*, ed. D. Kelley. San Francisco: Freeman.

Kigasawa, M. (1978) "Ikki Keikaku wa Oita Ken no Keizai wo Kurushiku Shita (Phase One Hurt Oita's Economy), 1. *Adobansu Oita*, July–August, 28–32.

Kino, S. (1978) "Saganosekiko Osen Tsuiseki Chosa Hokohusho (Report on Investigation of Remaining Saganoseki Harbor Pollution)." In *Kane Wa Iran! Kirei Na Umi Ni Shite Modose! (We Don't Need Your Money! Make Our Sea Clean Again and Give It Back to Us)*, ed. Kino Shigeru. Osaka: Sakobe Kei Insatsu.

Kinoshita, K. (1973) *Chiji Juroku Nen (Sixteen Years as Governor)*, p. 207. Nishi Nihon Shimbunsha.

Kita Nihon Shimbun (Northern Japan Newspaper) (1984) *Maboroshi No Hanei, Shinsan Toshi Nijunen No Kessan (Illusory Prosperity, the Final Score on Twenty Years of the New Industrial Cities)*. Tokyo: Kita Nihon Shimbunsha.

Kitschelt, H. P. (1986) "Political Opportunity Structures and Political Protest: Anti-Nuclear Movements in Four Democracies." *British Journal of Political Science*, 16(1), 57–85.

Klandermans, B. (1991) "New Social Movements and Resource Mobilization: The European and the American Approach Revisited." In *Research in Social Movements: The State of the Art in Western Europe and the USA*, ed. D. Rucht, pp. 17–44. Boulder: Westview Press.

Klandermans, B. (1992) "The Social Construction of Protest and Multiorganizational Fields." In *Frontiers in Social Movement Theory*, ed. A. D. Morris & C. McClurg Mueller, pp. 77–103. New Haven: Yale University Press.

Klandermans, B. & Tarrow, S. (1988) "Mobilization Into Social Movements: Synthesizing European and American Approaches." In *International Social Movement Research*, Vol. 1, ed. B. Klandermans, H. Krisei, & S. Tarrow, pp. 1–38. Greenwich: JAI Press.

Klandermans, B. (1993) "A Theoretical Framework for Comparisons of Social Movement Participation." *Sociological Forum*, 8(3), 383–402.

Knoke, D. (1990) *Political Networks*. Cambridge: Cambridge University Press.

Knoke, D., Pappi, F., Broadbent, J., & Tsujinaka, Y. (1996) *Comparing Policy Networks: Labor Politics in the United States, Germany and Japan*. Cambridge: Cambridge University Press.

Kojima, K. (1977) *Japan and a New World Economic Order*. Boulder, CO: Westview Press.

Kokuseisha. (1988) *Nihon Kokusei Zue*. Tokyo: Kokuseisha.

Koschmann, V. (1978) *Authority and the Individual in Japan: Citizen Protest in Historical Perspective*. Tokyo: University of Tokyo Press.

Krauss, E. & Muramatsu, M. (1988) "Japanese Political Economy Today: The Patterned Pluralist Model." In *Inside the Japanese System*, ed. D. Okimoto & T. Rohlen, pp. 208–10. Stanford: Stanford University Press.

Kriesi, H., Koopmans, R., Duyvendak, J. W., & Guigni, M. (1995) *New Social Movements in Western Europe*. Minneapolis: University of Minnesota Press.

Kroll-Smith, S. & Laska, S. (1994) "The GEC Debate: Notes on Theorizing and Researching the Environment; or, Where is our Newton?" *Environment, Technology and Society*, 74 (Winter), 1–3.

Kumon, S. (1992) "Japan as a Network Society." In *The Political Economy of Japan, Volume 3: Cultural and Social Dynamics*, ed. S. Kumon & H. Rosovsky, pp. 109–41. Stanford: Stanford University Press.

Kyogoku, J. (1987) *The Political Dynamics of Japan*. Tokyo: University of Tokyo Press.

Laclau, E. & Mouffe, C. (1985) *Hegemony and Socialist Strategy: Towards a Radical Democratic Politics*. London: Verso.

Lamont, M. (1989) "The Power-Culture Link in a Comparative Perspective." In *Comparative Social Research*, ed. C. Calhoun, pp. 131–50. Greenwich: JAI Press.

Landy, M., Roberts, M., & Thomas, S. (1990) *The Environmental Protection Agency: Asking the Wrong Questions*. New York: Oxford University Press.

Lash, J., Gillman, K., & Sheridan, D. (1984) *A Season of Spoils*. New York: Pantheon Books.

Lebra, T. S. (1976) *Japanese Patterns of Behavior*. Honolulu: University of Hawaii Press.

Lewis, J. G. (1980) "Civic Protest in Mishima: Citizens' Movements and the Politics of the Environment in Contemporary Japan." In *Political Opposition and Local Politics in Japan*, ed. Kurt Steiner. Princeton: Princeton University Press.

Lijphart, A. (1971) "Comparative Politics and the Comparative Method." *American Political Science Review*, 65 (September), 682–93.

Lipsky, M. (1968) "Protest as a Political Resource." *American Political Science Review*, 62, 1144–58.

Lo, C. Y. (1982) "Countermovements and Conservative Movements in the Contemporary United States." *Annual Review of Sociology*, 8, 107–34.

Logan, J. & Molotch, H. (1987) *Urban Fortunes: The Political Economy of Place*. Berkeley: University of California Press.

Logan, R. & Nelkin, D. (1980) "Labor and Nuclear Power." *Environment*, 22(2), March 6–34.

Lowe, P. & Goyder, J. (1983) *Environmental Groups in Politics*. London: George Allen and Unwin.

Lukes, S. (1974) *Power: A Radical View*. London: Macmillan.

Lukes, S., ed. (1986) *Power*. Oxford: Blackwell.

MacNeill, J. (1990) "Strategies for Sustainable Economic Development." In *Managing Planet Earth: Readings from Scientific American*, ed. Scientific American. New York: W.H. Freeman and Company.

Mann, M. (1986) *The Sources of Social Power, Vol. 1*. Cambridge: Cambridge University Press.

March, J. & Simon, H. (1993) *Organizations*. Cambridge, MA: Blackwell.

Markus, H. & Kitayama, S. (1991) "Culture and the Self: Implications for Cognition, Emotion and Motivation." *Psychological Review*, 98(2), 224–53.

Marx, G. T. & Wood, J. L. (1975) "Strands of Theory and Research in Collective Behavior." *Annual Review of Sociology*, 1, 363–428.

Masaki, Y. et al. (1976) *Jumin Undo Shiron (Residents' Movements Self-Theory)*. Tokyo: Gakuyo Shobo.

Masumi, J. (1995) *Contemporary Politics in Japan*, trans. L. Carlile, p. 514. Berkeley: University of California Press.

Matsubara, H. (1971) *Kogai to Chiiki Shakai (Pollution and Regional Society)*. Tokyo: Nihon Keizai Shimbunsha.

Matsubara, H. (1977) "Chiiki Kaihatsu to Jumin (Regional Development and Citizens)." *Doboku Kogaku Taikei*, 20, 195–248.

Matsubara, H. & Nitagai, K. (1976) *Jumin Undo No Ronri (The Theory of Residents' Movements)*. Tokyo: Gakuyo Shobo.

Matsushita, Keiichi. (1980) "Decentralization and Political Culture: Whither Japan?" *Center News*, May, 7–11.

Matsushita, R. (1978) "Saganoseki de Okotta Koto (An Event that Occurred in Saganoseki)." In *Kane Wa Iran! Kirei Na Umi Ni Shite Modose! (We Don't Need Your Money! Make Our Sea Clean Again and Give It Back to Us)*, ed. Kino Shigeru. Osaka: Sakobe Kei Insatsu.

Matsushita, R. (1984) *Kazanashi No Onnatachi (The Women of Kazanashi)*. Tokyo: Shakai Shisosha.

McAdam, D. (1982) *Political Process and the Development of Black Insurgency.* Chicago: University of Chicago Press.

McAdam, D. (1983) "Tactical Innovation and the Pace of Insurgency." *American Sociological Review,* 48(6), 735–54.

McAdam, D. (1995) "Initiator" and "Spin-Off" Movements: Diffusion Processes in Protest Cycles. In *Repertoires and Cycles of Collective Action,* ed. M. Traugott, pp. 217–39. Durham: Duke University Press.

McAdam, D., McCarthy, J. D., & Zald, M. N. (1988) "Social Movements." In *Handbook of Sociology,* ed. N. J. Smelser, pp. 695–737. Newbury Park: Sage.

McAdam, D. & Paulsen, R. (1993) "Specifying the Relationship Between Social Ties and Activism." *American Sociology Review,* 99(3), 640–67.

McAdam, D., Tarrow, S. & Tilly, C. (1996) "To Map Contentious Politics." *Mobilization,* 1(1), March, 17–34.

McCarthy, J. D. & Zald, M. N. (1977) "Resource Mobilization and Social Movements: A Partial Theory." *American Journal of Sociology,* 82(6), 1212–41.

McCloskey, M. (1992) "Twenty Years of Change in the Environmental Movement: An Insider's View." In *American Environmentalism,* ed. Riley Dunlap and Angela Mertig, pp. 77–88. Philadelphia: Taylor and Francis.

McCormack, G. (1996) *The Emptiness of Japanese Affluence.* Armonk, N.Y.: M.E. Sharpe.

McKean, M. (1981) *Environmental Protest and Citizen Politics in Japan.* Berkeley: University of California Press.

McKean, M. (1993) "State Strength and the Public Interest." In *Political Dynamics in Contemporary Japan,* ed. G. Allinson & Y. Sone, pp. 72–104. Cornell: Cornell University Press.

Meadows, D. H. & Meadows, D. (1971) *Limits to Growth: A Report for the Club of Rome's Project on the Predicament of Mankind.* New York: Universe Books.

Melucci, A. (1995) "The Process of Collective Identity." In *Social Movements and Culture,* ed. H. Johnston & B. Klandermans, pp. 41–63. Minneapolis: University of Minnesota.

Merchant, C. (1990) "Ecofeminism and Feminist Theory." In *Reweaving the World,* ed. Irene Diamond and Gloria Ornstein. San Francisco: Sierra Club Books.

Merton, R. (1968) "Patterns of Influence: Local and Cosmopolitan Influentials." In *Social Theory and Social Structure,* ed. R. Merton, pp. 441–74. New York: Free Press.

Messick, D. M. and Brewer, M. B. (1983) "Solving Social Dilemmas: A Review." In *Review of personality and social psychology,* ed. Wheeler, L. and Shaver, P. Beverly Hills, CA: Sage.

Mies, M. & Shiva, V. (1993). *Ecofeminism.* Halifax, N.S.: Fernwood Publications.

Milbrath, L. W. (1989) *Envisioning a Sustainable Society.* Albany: State University of New York Press.

Milgram, S. (1977) *The Individual in a Social World: Essays and Experiments.* Reading: Addison-Wesley.

Miliband, R. (1969) *The State in Capitalist Society.* London: Weidenfeld and Nicolson.

Miller, A. (1989) "Report on Reports." *Environment,* July/August.

Mills, C. W. (1956) *The Power Elite.* New York: Oxford University Press.

Ministry of Justice. (1977). "Shin Sagyo Toshi Kensetsu Sokushin Ho (New Industrial Cities Construction Promotion Law)." In *Kokudo Roppo (Land Use Laws),* p. 1764. Tokyo: Ministry of Justice.

Mitchell, R. C. (1979) "National Environmental Lobbies and the Apparent Illogic of Collective Action." In *Collective Decision Making: Applications from Public Choice Theory,* ed. C. S. Russel, pp. 57–85. Baltimore: Johns Hopkins University Press.

Mitchell, R., Mertig, A., & Dunlap, R. (1992) "Twenty Years of Environmental Mobilization: Trends Among National Environmental Organizations." In *American Environmentalism*, ed. R. Dunlap & A. Mertig, pp. 11–26. Philadelphia: Taylor and Francis.

Miyamoto, K. (1970) *Kogai to Jumin Undo (Pollution and Residents' Movements)*. Tokyo: Jichitai Kenkyusha.

Miyamoto, K. (1973) *Chiiki Kaihatsu Wa Kore de Yoi Ka* (Is Regional Development Ok as It Is?) Tokyo: Iwanami Shotem.

Miyamoto, K. (1978) "Sengo Chiiki Kaihatsu no Shiteki Kyokun to Kadai (The Historical Lessons of Postwar Regional Growth)." In *Enerugi to Kogai Soran*, ed. Enerugi Jyanarusha. Tokyo: Enerugi Jyanarusha.

Miyamoto, K. and H. Shoji. 1972. *Osorubeki Kogai (Fearful Pollution)*. Tokyo: Iwanami Shinsho.

Moe, T. (1984) "The New Economics of Organizations." *American Journal of Political Science, 28*(4), November, 739–77.

Molotch, H. (1975) "The City as a Growth Machine." *American Journal of Sociology, 82*(2), 309–32.

Molotch, H. & Vicari, S. (1988) "Three Ways to Build: The Development Process in the United States, Japan, and Italy." *Urban Affairs Quarterly*, XXIV (December), 188–214.

Morris, A. D. (1984) *The Origins of the Civil Rights Movement: Black Communities Organizing for Change*. New York: Free Press.

Morris, A. D. (1992) "Political Consciousness and Collective Action." In *Frontiers in Social Movement Theory*, ed. A. D. Morris & C. McClurg Mueller, pp. 351–73. New Haven: Yale University Press.

Mottl, T. L. (1980) "The Analysis of Countermovements." *Socal Problems, 27*(5), 620–35.

Mouer, R. & Sugimoto, Y. (1979) "Nakane Chie Setsu e no Hohoronteki Gimon (Methodological Questions about the Nakane Chie Thesis)." *Gendai No Me, 20*(7), 124–35.

Mouer, R. & Sugimoto, Y. (1986) *Images of Japanese Society: A Study in the Social Construction of Reality*. London: KPI Ltd.

Muramatsu, M. (1986) "Center-Local Political Relations in Japan." *Journal of Japanese Studies, 12* (Summer), 303–27.

Muramatsu, M. & Krauss, E. (1988) "The Japanese Political Economy Today: The Patterned Pluralist Model." In *The Political Economy of Japan, Vol. 1*, ed. K. Yamamura & Y. Yasuba. Stanford: Stanford University Press.

Nakamura, H. (1978) "Shinkoshi Chosa no Saikento." In *Chomei No Kenkyu Jisseki o Yu Suru Shotoshi No Tsuisekiteki Jissho Kenkyu*, ed. Tokyo Toshi Shakai Gakkai. Tokyo.

Nakane, C. (1970) *Japanese Society*. Berkeley: University of California Press.

Narumi, M. (nd) *Chiho Bunken no Shiso (On the Regional Dispersion of Authority)*. Tokyo: publisher unclear.

Nash, R. (1989) *The Rights of Nature*. Madison: University of Wisconsin Press.

National Land Agency (Kokudocho). (nd) *Shin Sangyo Toshi no Kuiki oyobi Kensetsu Kihon Hoshin (Basic Policies for the Area and Construction of the New Industrial Cities)* Tokyo: Kokudocho.

National Land Agency (Kokudocho). (1961) Zenkoku Sogo Kaihatsu Keikaku (First National Comprehensive Development Plan). Tokyo: Kokudocho.

National Land Agency of Japan (official English translation by Jeffrey Broadbent). (1979) *Sanzenso: The Third Comprehensive National Development Plan*. Tokyo: National Land Agency.

Nelson, L. (1990) "The Place of Women in Polluted Places." In *Reweaving the World*, ed. I. Diamond & G. Ornstein, pp. 173–88. San Francisco: Sierra Club Books.

Nishimura, H. (1989) *How to Conquer Air Pollution, A Japanese Experience.* Amsterdam: Elsevier.

Nishio, M. (1978) "Seki no Gyoshi no Tatakai (The Struggle of the Seki Fishing Folk)." In *Kane Wa Iran! Kirei Na Umi Ni Shite Modose! (We Don't Need Your Money! Make Our Sea Clean Again and Give It Back to Us)*, ed. Kino Shigeru. Osaka: Sakobe Kei Insatsu.

Noda, K. (1975) "Big Business Organization." In *Modern Japanese Organization and Decision-Making*, ed. E. Vogel, pp. 115–45. Berkeley: University of California Press.

Nomura (Sogo Kenkyujo) Nomura Research Institute. (1979) *Oita Shinsango Toshi Kenetsu Koka Sokutei Chosa (Oita New Industrial City Construction Effect Measurement Survey).* Kamakura: Nomura Soken.

Oberschall, A. (1973) *Social Conflict and Social Movements.* Englewood Cliffs: Prentice Hall.

Oberschall, A. (1978) "Theories of Social Conflict." *Annual Review of Sociology,* 4, 291–315.

O'Connor, J. (1973) *The Fiscal Crisis of othe State.* New York: St. Martin's Press.

OECD (Organization of Economic Cooperation and Development). (1977). *Environmental Policies in Japan.* Paris: OECD Publications.

OECD (Organization of Economic Cooperation and Development). (1982) *OECD National Accounts Data.* Paris: OECD.

OECD (Organization of Economic Cooperation and Development). (1993) *OECD Environmental Data Compendium 1993.* Paris: OECD.

OECD (Organization of Economic Cooperation and Development). (1985) *OECD National Accounts Data.* Paris: OECD.

OECD (Organization of Economic Cooperation and Development). (nd) *Environmental Performance Reviews.* Paris: OECD.

Offe, C. (1984) *Contradictions of the Welfare State.* Cambridge, MA: MIT Press.

Offe, C. (1985a) *Disorganized Capitalism.* Cambridge: MIT Press.

Offe, C. (1985b) "New Social Movements: Challenging the Boundaries of Institutional Politics." *Social Research,* 52(4), Winter, 817–67.

Oita City Government, General Affairs Bureau, Planning Office. (1995) '95 *Oita Shi Ni Okeru Shin Sangyo Toshi Kensetsu No Jokyo (The Situation of the Construction of the Oita City New Industrial City in 1995).* Oita, Japan: Oita City.

Oita Prefectural Government. (1983) *Flowing Prosperously–Thirty Years of the Oita Seaside Industrial Area.* Oita: Oita Prefectural Government.

Okimoto, D. (1989) *Between MITI and the Market: Japanese Industrial Policy for High Technology.* Stanford: Stanford University Press.

Okimoto, D. & Rohlen, T., eds. (1988) *Inside the Japanese System*, ed. D. Okimoto & T. Rohlen. Stanford: Stanford University Press.

Okuda. (1978) "Ikki Keikaku wa Oita Ken no Zaikei o Kurushiku Shita (Phase One Hurt Oita Prefecture's Finances)." *Adobansu Oita,* May.

Oliver, P. (1993) "Formal Models of Collective Action." In *Annual Review of Sociology,* Palo Alto: Annual Reviews.

Olson, M. (1975) *The Logic of Collective Action.* Cambridge: Harvard University Press.

Ophuls, W. (1977). *Ecology and the Politics of Scarcity.* San Francisco: W.H. Freeman.

Ostrom, E. (1990). *Governing the Commons, The Evolution of Institutions for Collective Action.* New York: Cambridge University Press.

Oyama, N. (1990) "Some Recent Trends in Japanese Values: Beyond the Individual-Collective Dimension." *International Sociology,* 5(4), 443–59.

Paehlke, R. (1990) *Environmentalism and the Future of Progressive Politics.* New Haven: Yale University Press.

Parsons, T. (1951) *The Social System.* New York: Free Press.

Parsons, T. (1954) *Essays in Sociological Theory.* New York: Free Press.

Parsons, T. (1960) "The Distribution of Power in American Society." In *Structure and Process in Modern Societies,* ed. T. Parsons. New York: Free Press.

Pempel, T. & Tsunekawa, K. (1979) "Corporatism Without Labor? The Japanese Anomaly." In *Trend Toward Corporatist Intermediation,* ed. S. A. Philippe, Gerhard Lehmbruch, pp. 231–70. Beverly Hills: Sage Publications.

Pharr, S. (1990) *Losing Face.* Berkeley: University of California Pres.

Pharr, S. & Badaracio, J. (1986) "Coping with Crisis: Environmental Regulation." In *America Versus Japan,* ed. T. McCraw. Boston: Harvard Businss School Press.

Pierce, J., Lovrich, N., Tsuruta, T. & Abe, T. (1989) *Public Knowledge and Environmental Politics in Japan and the United States.* Boulder, CO: Westview Press.

Pinard, M. (1971) *The Rise of a Third Party.* Englewood Cliffs: Prentice-Hall.

Piven, F. F. & Cloward, R. (1971) *Regulating the Poor.* New York: Pantheon Books.

Piven, F. F. & Cloward, R. A. (1977) *Poor People's Movements: Why They Succeed, How They Fail.* New York: Vintage Books.

Pollack, A. (1977) "Japan's Road to Bankruptcy is Paved With Public Works." *New York Times,* March 1.

Pollner, M. & Emerson, R. (1983) "The Dynamics of Inclusion and Distance in Fieldwork Relations." In *Contemporary Field Research,* ed. R. M. Emerson, pp. 235–52. Prospect Heights: Waveland.

Polsby, N. (1995) "How to Study Community Power: The Pluralist Alternative." In *American Society and Politics,* ed. T. Skocpol & J. Campbell, pp. 9–14. New York: McGraw-Hill.

Popkin, S. (1979) *The Rational Peasant.* Berkeley: University of California Press.

Porritt, J. (1985) *Seeing Green The Politics of Ecology Explained.* Oxford: Blackwells.

Poulantzas, N. (1973) *Political Power and Social Classes.* London: New Left Books.

Powell, W. & DiMaggio, P. (1991) "Introduction." In *The New Institutionalism in Organizational Analysis,* ed. W. Powell, Paul DiMaggio, pp. 1–40. Chicago: University of Chicago Press.

Pressman, J. & Wildavsky, A. (1973) *Implementation.* Berkeley: University of California Press.

Prigogine, I. & Stengers, I. (1984). *Order Out of Chaos: Man's New Dialogue with Nature.* New York: Bantam.

Pye, L. (1985) *Asian Power and Politics.* Cambridge: Harvard University Press.

Quirk, P. (1995) "Deregulation and the Politics of Ideas in Congress." In *American Society and Politics,* ed. T. Skocpol & J. Campbell, pp. 118–28. New York: McGraw-Hill.

Ragin, C. & Becker, H. (1992) *What is a Case?* Cambridge: Cambridge University Press.

Ramseyer, M. & Rosenbluth, F. (1993) *Japan's Political Marketplace.* Cambridge: Harvard University Press.

Random House. (1973) *Random House Dictionary of the English Language.* New York: Random House.

Reed, S. (1981) "Environmental Politics: Some Reflections based on the Japanese Case." *Comparative Politics XIII.*

Reed, S. (1986) *Japanese Prefectures and Policy-Making.* Pittsburgh: University of Pittsburgh.

Reed, S. (1993) *Making Common Sense of Japan.* Pittsburgh: University of Pittsburgh Press.

Reich, M. (1984) "Mobilizing for Environmental Policy in Italy and Japan." *Comparative Politics,* XVI (July), 379–402.

Reich, M. (1991) *Toxic Politics.* Ithaca: Cornell University Press.

Reischauer, E. O. & Craig, A. M. (1978) *Japan's Tradition and Transformation*. Boston: Houghton Mifflin.

Rensenbrink, J. (1992) *The Greens and the Politics of Transformation*. San Pedro: R. and E. Miles.

Richardson, B. & Flanagan, S. (1984) *Politics in Japan*. Boston: Little, Brown.

Riesman, D. (1950) *The Lonely Crowd*. New Haven: Yale University Press.

Riordan, T. (1963) *Plunkitt of Tammany Hall*. New York: Dutton.

Rohlen, T. (1974) *For Harmony and Strength*. Berkeley: University of California.

Root, M. (1993) *Philosophy of Social Science*. Oxford: Blackwells.

Rorres, C. & Anton, H. (1979) *Applications of Linear Algebra*. New York: Wiley.

Rostow, W. W. (1960) *The Stages of Economic Growth: A Non-Communist Manifesto*. New York: Columbia University Press.

Roussopoulos, D. (1993) *Political Ecology*. Montreal: Black Rose Books.

Rucht, D. (1990). The Strategies and Action Repertoires of New Movements. In *Challenging the Political Order: New Social and Political Movements in Western Democracies*, ed. R. Dalton & M. Kuechler, pp. 156–75. Cambridge, England: Polity Press.

Sabatier, P. (1975) "Social Movements and Regulatory Agencies: Toward a More Adequate – and Less Pessimistic – Theory of 'Clientele Capture.'" *Policy Sciences*, 6, 301–42.

Samuels, R. (1983) *The Politics of Regional Policy in Japan*. Princeton: Princeton University Press.

Samuels, R. (1987) *The Business of the Japanese State*. Ithaca: Cornell University Press.

Sayer, A. (1993) *Methods in Social Science*. London: Routledge.

Schattschneider, E. (1975) *The Semi-Sovereign People*. New York: Holt, Rinehart and Winston.

Schmitter, P. (1981) Interest Intermediation and Regime Governability in Contemporary Western Europe and North America. In *Organizing Interests in Western Europe*, ed. S. Berger, pp. 285–327. Cambridge: Cambridge University Press.

Schnaiberg, A. (1980) *The Environment, from Surplus to Scarcity*. New York: Oxford University Press.

Schnaiberg, A. & Gould, K. A. (1994) *Environment and Society, The Enduring Conflict*. New York: St. Martin's Press.

Schuman, H. (1995) "Attitudes, Beliefs, and Behavior." In *Sociological Perspectives on Social Psychology*, ed. K. Cook, G. Fine, & J. House, pp. 68–69. Boston: Allyn & Bacon.

Schwartz, M. (1976) *Radical Protest and Social Structure: The Southern Farmers; Alliance and Cotton Tenancy, 1880–1890*. New York: Academic Press.

Scott, J. (1976) *The Moral Economy of the Peasant*. New Haven: Yale University Press.

Scott, J. (1985) *Weapons of the Weak*. New Haven: Yale University Press.

Scott, J. (1995) The Role of Theory in Comparative Politics. *World Politics*, 48 (October), 1–49.

Sewell, W. J., Jr. (1992) "A Theory of Structure: Duality, Agency, and Transformation." *American Journal of Sociology*, 98, 1–29.

Shiva, V. (1990) Development as a new project of western patriarchy. In *Reweaving the World*, ed. I. Diamond & G. Ornstein, pp. 189–200. San Francisco: Sierra Club Books.

Short, J. Jr., (ed.). (1986) *The Social Fabric: Dimensions and Issues*. Beverly Hills, CA: Sage Publications.

Shukan Daiyamondo. (1975) "Shinsantoshi-Kotokuchiiki Junen no Kozai (New Industrial Cities and Special Development Areas – The Accomplishments of Ten Years)." *Shukan Daiyamondo*, Oct. 30.

Skocpol, T. (1985) "Bringing the State Back In: Strategies of Analysis in Current Research." In *Bringing the State Back In*, ed. P. Evans, T. Skocpol, & D. Reuschmeyer. New York: Cambridge University Press.

Skocpol, T. (1995) "Political Response to Capitalist Crisis: Neo-Marxist Theories of the State and the Case of the New Deal." In *American Society and Politics*, ed. T. Skocpol & J. L. Campbell, pp. 48–73. New York: McGraw-Hill.

Skocpol, T. & Campbell, J. L. (1995) *American Society and Politics*. New York: McGraw-Hill.

Smelser, N. (1963) *The Theory of Collective Behavior*. New York: Free Press.

Smith, D. (1987) *The Everyday World as Problematic: A Feminist Sociology*. Boston: Northeastern University Press.

Smith, M. P. (1984) *Cities in Transformation*. Beverly Hills: Sage Publications.

Smith, R. J. (1983) *Japanese Society: Tradition, Self and the Social Order*. Cambridge: Cambridge University Press.

Smith, W. (1973) *Confucianism in Modern Japan*. Tokyo: Hokuseido Press.

Smith, Z. (1992) *The Environmental Policy Paradox*. Englewood Cliffs: Prentice Hall.

Smith-Lovin, L. (1995) "The Sociology of Affect and Behavior." In *Sociological Perspectives on Social Psychology*. Boston: Allyn & Bacon.

Snow, D. A. & Benford, R. D. (1992) "Master Frames and Cycles of Protest." In *Frontiers in Social Movement Theory*, ed. A. D. Morris & C. McClurg Mueller, pp. 133–55. New Haven: Yale University Press.

Snow, D. A. & Oliver, P. (1995) "Social Movements and Collective Behavior, Social Psychological Dimensions and Considerations." In *Sociological Perspectives on Social Psychology*, ed. K. Cook, G. Fine & J. House, pp. 517–99. Boston: Allyn & Bacon.

Snow, D. A., Rochford, E. B., Jr., Worden, S. K., & Benford, R. D. (1986) "Frame Alignment Processes, Micromobilization, and Movement Participation." *American Sociological Review*, 51 (August), 646–81.

Snow, D. A., Zurcher, L. A., & Ekland-Olson, S. (1980) "Social Networks and Social Movements: A Microstructural Approach to Differential Recruitment." *American Sociological Review*, 45(5), 787–801.

So, A. (1990) *Social Change and Development*. Newbury Park: Sage Publications.

So, A. & Chiu, S. (1995) *East Asia and the World Economy*. Thousand Oaks: Sage Publications.

Stark, D. (1994) "Path Dependence and Privatization Strategies in East Central Europe." In *Comparative National Development: Society and Economy in the New Global Order*, ed. A. D. Kincaid & A. Portes, pp. 169–98. Chapel Hill: University of North Carolina Press.

Steger, M. & Witt S. (1988) Gender Differences in Environmental Orientations: A Comparison of Publics and Activists in Canada and the U.S. *Western Political Quarterly*.

Steiner, K., Krauss, E., & Flanagan, S., eds. (1980) *Political Opposition and Local Politics in Japan*. Princeton: Princeton University Press.

Steinhoff, P. (1992) "Death by Defeatism and Other Fables: The Social Dynamics of the Rengo Sekigun Purge." In *Japanese Social Organization*, ed. T. S. Lebra, pp. 195–224. Honolulu: University of Hawaii Press.

Steinmo, S., Thelen, K., & Longstreth, F. (1992) *Structuring Politics: Historical Institutionalism in Comparative Analysis*. Cambridge: Cambridge University Press.

Stern, P. C. (1993) A Second Environmental Science: Human-Environment Interactions. *Science*, 260 (June 25), p. 1897.

Suzuki, D. (1973) *Zen and Japanese Culture*. Princeton: Princeton University Press.

Swidler, A. (1986) "Culture in Action: Symbols and Strategies." *American Sociological Review*, 51, 273–86.

Swidler, A. (1995) "Cultural Power and Social Movements." In *Social Movements and Culture*, ed. H. Johnston & B. Klandermans. Minneapolis: University of Minnesota.

Switzer, J. (1994) *Environmental Politics: Domestic and Global Dimensions.* New York: St. Martin's Press.

Szasz, T. (1994) *Ecopopulism.* Minneapolis: University of Minnesota Press.

Sztompka, Piotr. 1993. *The Sociology of Social Change.* Oxford: Blackwells.

Takahashi, F. (1987) "Governor Hiramatsu Morihiko's 'One Village One Product' Campaign." *Japan Quarterly*, 34(1), Jan–Mar, 19–23.

Tarrow, S. (1983) *Struggling to Reform: Social Movements and Policy Change During Cycles of Protest.* Center for International Studies: Cornell University.

Tarrow, S. (1988) "National Politics and Collective Action: Recent Theory and Research in Western Europe and the United States." *Annual Review of Sociology*, 14, 421–40.

Tarrow, S. (1989). *Democracy and Disorder: Protest and Politics in Italy 1965–1975.* New York: Oxford University Press.

Tarrow, S. (1991) *Struggle, Politics and Reform: Collective Action, Social Movements, and Cycles of Protest.* Ithaca: Cornell Studies in International Affairs, Western Societies Papers.

Tarrow, S. (1992) "Mentalities, Political Cultures, and Collective Action Frames: Constructing Meanings through Action." In *Frontiers in Social Movement Theory*, ed. A. D. Morris & C. McClurg Mueller, pp. 174–202. New Haven: Yale University Press.

Tarrow, S. (1994) *Power in Movement.* Cambridge: Cambridge University Press.

Tatsuno, S. (1986) *The Technopolis Strategy.* Englewood Cliffs: Prentice Hall.

Taylor, D. E. (1989) Blacks and the Environment: Towards an Explanation of the Concern and the Action Gap Between Blacks and Whites. *Environment and Behavior*, 21(2) 175–205.

Tekunoporisu to Chiiki Kaihatsu (Technopolis and Regional Growth) (1985). Ed. Nihon Kagakusha Kaigi. Tokyo: Otsuki Shoten.

Teune, H. (1988) *Growth.* Newbury Park: Sage Publications.

Thayer, N. (1969) *How the Conservatives Rule Japan.* Princeton: Princeton University Press.

Thomas, W. I. (1966) "The Relation of Research to the Social Process." In *W. I. Thomas on Social Organization and Social Personality*, ed. Morris Janowitz. Chicago: University of Chicago Press.

Thorne, B. (1988) "Political Activist as Participant Observer: Conflicts of Committment in a Study of the Draft Resistance Movement of the 1960s." In *Contemporary Field Research*, ed. R. Emerson, pp. 216–34. Prospect Heights: Waveland.

Thurston, D. R. (1973) *Teachers and Politics in Japan.* Princeton: Princeton University Press.

Tilly, C. (1978) *From Mobilization to Revolution.* Reading, MA: Addison Wesley.

Tilly, C. (1984) *Big Structures, Large Processes, Huge Comparisons.* New York: Russell Sage Foundation.

Tokar, B. (1992) *The Green Alternative, Creating an Ecological Future.* San Pedro: R. and E. Miles.

Traugott, M. (1995) *Repertoires and Cycles of Collective Action.* Durham, N.C.: Duke University Press.

Tsujinaka, Y. (1993) "Rengo and its Osmotic Networks." In *Political Dynamics in Contemporary Japan*, ed. Gary Allinson and Yasunori Stone. Ithaca: Cornell University Press.

Tsuru, S. and H. Weidner (eds.). (1989) *Environmental Policy in Japan.* Berlin: Edition Sigma Rainer Bohn Verlag.

Tsurumi, K. (1977) "Social Price of Pollution in Japan and the Role of Folk Beliefs." *Research Paper Series* A-30. Tokyo: Sophia University.

Tuma, N. (1992) "Social Dynamics." In *Encyclopedia of Sociology,* ed. E. Borgatta & M. Borgatta, pp. 1823–30. New York: Macmillan.

Uchino, T. (1983) *Japan's Postwar Economy.* Tokyo: Kodansha International.

Uchiyama, T. (1978) "Evaluating Ten Years of Pollution and Environmental Administration." In *Energii to Kogai Soran (Energy and Pollution Compendium),* ed. editorial staff, pp. 265–76. Tokyo: Energy and Pollution Company.

Ui, J. (1979) *Kogai Jumin Undo (Pollution Residents' Movements).* Tokyo: Oki Shobo.

Ui, Jun (ed.). (1992) *Industrial Pollution in Japan.* Tokyo: United Nations University Press.

Ui, J. (nd) "Pollution: The Basic Theory of Kogai." In *Postwar Japan 1945 to the Present,* ed. J. Livingston et al., pp. 573–5. New York: Pantheon Books.

Upham, F. (1987) "Environmental Tragedy and Response." In *Law and Social Change in Postwar Japan,* pp. 28–77. Cambridge: Harvard University Press.

van Wolferen, K. (1989) *The Enigma of Japanese Power.* New York: Knopf.

Veblen, T. (1992) *The Theory of the Leisure Class.* New Brunswick: Transaction Publishers.

Vig, N. & Kraft, M. (1990) "Environmental Policies in the 1990s United States." *Congressional Quarterly.*

Vogel, E. (1979) *Japan as Number One.* Cambridge: Harvard University Press.

Vogt, W. P. (1993) *Dictionary of Statistics and Methodology.* Newbury Park: Sage Publications

Wallerstein, I. (1983) *The Capitalist World-Economy.* Cambridge: Cambridge University Press.

Walsh, E. J. (1981) "Resource Mobilization and Citizen Protest in Communities Around Three Mile Island." *Social Problems,* 29(1), 1–21.

Walton, J. (1992) "Making the Theoretical Case." In *What is a Case? Exploring the Foundation of Social Inquiry,* ed. C. A. Ragin, Howard S. Becker, pp. 121–37. Cambridge: Cambridge University Press.

Warner, W. L. (1963) *Yankee City.* New Haven: Yale University Press.

Warren, K. J. (1990) "The power and the promise of ecological feminism." *Environmental Ethics, 12* (Summer), 125–46

Watanabe, S. (1975) *Oita Ken No Rekishi (The History of Oita Prefecture).* Tokyo: Yamakawa Publishers.

Weber, M. (1946) *From Max Weber: Essays in Sociology,* ed. H. Gerth & C. W. Mills. New York: Oxford University Press.

Weber, M. (1947) *The Theory of Social and Economic Organization,* ed. T. Parsons. New York: Oxford University Press.

Weber, M. (1958) *The Protestant Ethic and the Spirit of Capitalism.* New York: Scribners.

Weber, M. (1968) *On Charisma and Institution Building,* ed. S. Eisenstadt. Chicago: University of Chicago Press.

Weber, M. (1978) *Economy and Society, Vols 1 & 2,* ed. Guenther Roth and Claus Wittich. Berkeley: University of California Press.

Weinberg, A. (1994) "Environmental Sociology and the Environmental Movement: Toward a Theory of Pragmatic Relationships of Critical Inquiry." *American Sociologist,* 25(1), 31–57.

Weir, M. (1992) "Ideas and the Politics of Bounded Innovation." In *Structuring Politics: Historical Institutionalism in Comparative Analysis,* ed. S. Steinmo, K. Thelen, & F. Longstreth, pp. 188–216. Cambridge University Press.

White, H. C. (1992) *Identity and Control.* Princeton: Princeton University Press.

White, L. J. (1967) "The Historical Roots of Our Ecological Crisis." *Science,* 155 (March 10), 1203–7.

Williamson, O. (1975) *Markets and Hierarchies.* New York: Free Press.

World Commission on Environment and Development. (1987) *Our Common Future.* New York: Oxford University Press.

World Resources Institute. (1994) *World Resources 1994–1995: A Guide to the Global Environment.* New York: Oxford University Press.

Wrong, D. (1979) *Power: Its Forms, Bases and Uses.* New York: Harper Colophon Books.

Yamagishi, T. (1995) "Social Dilemmas." In *Sociological Perspectives on Social Psychology,* ed. K. Cook, G. Fine & J. House, pp. 311–35. Boston: Allyn & Bacon.

Yamanouchi, K. (1979) *Gyosei Shido (Administrative Guidance).* Tokyo: Kobundo Hogaku Sensho.

Yanaga, C. (1968) *Big Business in Japanese Politics.* New Haven: Yale University Press.

Yearly, S. (1991) *The Green Case.* New York: Harper Collins Academic

Zald, M. (1991) "The Continuing Vitality of Resource Mobilization Theory: Response to Herbert Kitschelt's Critique," pp. 348–54 in *Research in Social Movements: The State of the Art in Western Europe and the USA,* ed. Dieter Rucht. Boulder, CO: Westview Press.

Zald, M. & Useem, B. (1982) "Movement and Countermovement: Loosely-Coupled Conflict." Paper presented at annual meeting of American Sociological Association.

Zukin, S. (1985) "The Regional Challenge to French Industrial Policy." *International Journal of Urban and Regional Research,* 9(3).

Index

Abe Genshi, 43
administrative guidance (*gyosei shido*), 238, 241, 258–9
Advance Oita (magazine), 81
advanced capitalist industrialized democratic (ACID) societies: and avoidance of pollution problems, 103n; and environmental conflict, 11–12, 251–2, 286–8, 291; GDP in, 13; industrial density, 17; politics of, 6–7; and pollution politics, 19; power of special interests in, 209; regional growth plans in, 95; response to GE dilemma, 332–8, 354
Advisory Commission on Pollution, 115, 116
advisory council, 216
Advisory Council on Regional Industrial Development, 63, 69n
Age of Regionalism (*Chiho no Jidai*), 219
agency, 7n, 9, 30–1, 88, 89, 128, 178, 351, 361, 366
agenda-control tactics, 29, 295
Agricultural Chemical Control Law, 123
Air and Water Pollution Prevention Laws, 123, 383
Air Pollution Control Law (1968), 118
alienation, 229
aluminum refineries, 154, 223, 226
Ampo (magazine), 288
Ando Toyoroku, 55, 57
Anzai Masao, 223
Association of Small and Medium Businesses (ASMB), 80
asthma, 12, 103, 106–7, 119, 140, 142, 162, 231
Ayabe Kentaro, 56–7

Baba, 3, 34, 139, 156, 178, 232, 236, 247–8
Baba (Fishing) Union, 171–5, 198–9, 269–72, 343. *See also* Saganoseki Fishing Union
balance of power, 328
Basic Law on Environmental Pollution (1967),

36, 84, 108, 342; and business, 118, 121–2; harmony clause, 120–1; revision of, 114, 120–2; symbolic nature of, 128, 132
belly-craft (*haragei*), 199, 258
Beppu Bay, 1, 34, 70, 84
bonds, 58, 68, 339
boss(es), 143–6, 169, 172–4, 179–80, 192–6, 214–5, 217–8
bribery, 191, 194, 196, 212–3, 221, 238–9, 275, 277, 355
bronchitis, 142, 152
Buddhism, 27, 142, 169, 361
bureaucentrism, 265–6
bureaucracy, 264, 268–9, 279, 304–5, 320–1, 363; arrogance of, 28; and divergent local/elite interests, 93–4; effect on citizen initiatives, 74; and pollution control, 20
bureaucratic paternalist state model, 20, 338
business, 82, 94; and anti-pollution measures, 21, 108, 365; and Basic Law, 118, 121–2; and industrialization, 86–7, 341; and labor, 201–5; and LDP, 91, 305, 346; and ministries, 113–4; and MITI, 63–4; and NIC, 79–80, 81; power over Prefectural Government, 284; and state policy, 22; structural bias favoring, 96; threat to productivity of, 128. *See also* Ruling Triad; Triple Control Machine
business-corporatism, 26
Buzen, 149

Cabinet Ministers' Pollution Countermeasures Conference, 121, 123
cadmium poisioning, 103, 119
Calder, K. E., 85–6, 132, 349–50
campaign contributions, 91
capital accumulation: and Governor Taki, 251; as goal of Ruling Triad, 103, 113, 128, 342, 349, 353–5; and local networks, 95; and NIC Law, 86; rate of, 345, 363
Central Pollution Countermeasures Headquarters, 120–1